GLOBAL STRATEGIC MANAGEMENT

GLOBAL STRATEGIC MANAGEMENT

NEETA BAPORIKAR
MBA, LL.B (Spl), PhD (Mgt).
Accredited Management Teacher (AIMA)
Diploma Training & Dev (ISTD)
PhD-Guide, Faculty of Management, University of Pune
Professor (Management),
International Institute of Information Technology (I^2IT)
P-14, Pune Infotech Park, Hinjawadi, Pune-411 057
INDIA

Himalaya Publishing House

MUMBAI • NEW DELHI • NAGPUR • BENGALURU • HYDERABAD • CHENNAI • PUNE
LUCKNOW • AHMEDABAD • ERNAKULAM • BHUBANESWAR • INDORE • KOLKATA

First Edition : 2008
Reprint : 2011

Published by : Mrs. Meena Pandey
for **HIMALAYA PUBLISHING HOUSE PVT. LTD.,**
"Ramdoot", Dr. Bhalerao Marg, Girgaon, **Mumbai - 400 004.**
Phones: 2386 01 70/2386 38 63, Fax: 022-2387 71 78
Email: himpub@vsnl.com
Website: www.himpub.com

Branch Offices:

New Delhi : "Pooja Apartments", 4-B, Murari Lal Street, Ansari Road, Darya Ganj, **New Delhi - 110 002.**
Phone: 23270392, 23278631 Fax: 011-23256286

Nagpur : Kundanlal Chandak Industrial Estate, Ghat Road, **Nagpur - 440 018.**
Phone: 2738731, 3296733 Telefax : 0712-2721215

Bengaluru : No. 16/1 (Old 12/1), 1st Floor, Next to Hotel Highlands, Madhava Nagar, Race Course Road, **Bengaluru - 560 001.**
Phone : 22281541, 22385461, Telefax: 080-22286611

Hyderabad : No. 3-4-184, Lingampally, Besides Raghavendra Swamy Matham, Kachiguda, **Hyderabad - 500 027.**
Phone: 040-27560041, 27550139, Mobile:- 09848130433 Telefax: 040-27560041

Chennai : No. 85/50, Bazullah Road, T. Nagar, **Chennai - 600 017.**
Phone: 044-28344020, 32463737, 42124860

Pune : No. 527, "Laksha" Apartment, First Floor, Mehunpura, Shaniwarpeth, (Near Prabhat Theatre), **Pune - 411 030.**
Phone: 020-24496323/24496333/32326733

Lucknow : Jai Baba Bhawan, Near Manas Complex, Church Road, Aliganj, **Lucknow - 226 024.** Phone: 0522-2339329, 9305302158, 9415349385

Ahmedabad : No. 114, "SHAIL", 1st Floor, Opp. Madhu Sudan House, C.G.Road, Navrang Pura, **Ahmedabad – 380 009.**
Phone: 079-26560126, Mobiles: 09327324149,09314679413

Ernakulam : No. 39/104 A, Lakshmi Apartment, Karikkamuri Cross Rd., Ernakulam, **Cochin – 682011**, Kerala. Phone: 0484-2378012, 2378016, Mob.: 09344199799

Bhubaneswar : 5 Station Square, **Bhubaneswar (Orissa) - 751 001.**
Mobile: 9861046007, E-mail:- orissa@himpub.com

Indore : Kesardeep Avenue Extension, 73, Narayan Bagh.Flat No. 302, IIIrd Floor, Near Humpty Dumpty School, Narayan Bagh, **Indore (M.P.) 452 007** Mobile: 09301386468

Kolkata : 108/4, Beliaghata, Main Road, Near ID Hospital, Opp. SBI Bank **Kolkata - 700 010.** Mobile: 09910440956, E-mail:- nkmitra@himpub.com

Printed by : A to Z Printers, New Delhi

DEDÍCATED TO MY GUIDE

1937 - 2008

Dr. P S Palande, IAS (Retd),
Ex-Director, National Insurance Academy,
PUNE

Preface

What can be said about the new, globalized, borderless economy facing managers today and in the future that has not already been said before - perhaps only this "uncertainty". When I first conceived the need for a global strategic management text, businesses were operating from a premise of unlimited world economic growth and opportunity. Then with the implosion of Eastern Europe, the economic crisis in Southeast Asia, the bursting of the dot-com bubble and 9/11 happening, that left the world never the same. The result of these defining events have been a roller-coaster ride for international managers around the world. Nearly at the end of the first decade of this century, the premise has changed from unlimited growth to uncertainty and caution, but importantly, the premise of opportunity in global business remains unchanged. The uncertain economy and increasing geopolitical complexity simply levels the playing field for managers around the world. How managers respond, how they manage and turn the increasing threats into opportunities becomes vital to success in today's environment.

Now, more than ever, all students must recognize that they will have the qualifier "international" in front of whatever their chosen career field. The whole world is now connected electronically and psychologically; it is hard to imagine any business or non-business organization that is not directly affected by globalization. The challenge in the uncertain global economy is to learn and effectively practice global strategic and international management. Nothing can be taken for granted and international managers no longer have the luxury of burying their inadequacies and mistakes in a robust world economy. Those with the knowledge and skills to apply the contents of this text on international management will be taking a big step toward gaining a competitive advantage in today's uncertain, unprecedented environment. Consequent upon the restructuring of organizations, management curricula by many universities and autonomous courses are not far behind. Many new subjects on thrust areas have recently been introduced. One such broad area is Globalization which comprises of global marketing, global strategies, global HRM and global management. Strategic management has been strongly influenced by the global strategies in recent times. In the aftermath of globalization and the opening up of the markets, students of management are badly in need of a suitable text book covering all these aspects incorporating the latest developments in the field.

Realizing the imperative need to bring out a suitable book on "Global Strategic Management" tailored to meet the specific requirements of students of many universities, a modest attempt has been made to present this edition in the hands of the academic community. The specialty of this volume is that all the matter is presented in a simple and lucid manner, not compromising on the quality of the subject matter. All the latest developments have been covered and above all, it is student friendly. Whereas other texts stress one of these, I feel that balance and the resulting synergy are needed for a true global management text and course. Hence, I have adopted a balanced approach to this edition of Global Strategic Management.

Global Strategic Management is designed as a core textbook for those students studying strategy or international business. It offers an insight into the impact of globalization on business organizations and how managers can deal with this. It is also suitable as a supplementary text for any Strategic Management or International Business courses. This brand new text is the first to offer a truly global, as opposed to multinational, perspective on strategy. It covers both traditional strategic management topics and new topics, thereby; it combines a strategic and managerial approach to global issues covering future trends, including e-business, cultural issues, corporate social responsibility and new technologies.

Global Strategic Management gives the student a thorough understanding of the wide range of theories and research available in this field. It also provides a comprehensive overview of the subject area using chapter introductions, key points, summaries, key terms, discussion questions, suggested reading and mini-examples to illustrate and guide the student to facilitate better learning. It also includes cases of successful global companies, case questions and a student area with links to websites of interest.

Key Features

- Comprehensive coverage of the subject - this text will serve as the single core text for almost any international and global strategy course.
- Provides both mini - and full-length cases that give opportunities for students to analyze global strategic issues in real business situations and emerging markets.
- Does not rely on students having already taken a strategic management module, so ideal for students with a wide range of previous experience.

Contents

For the convenience of the taught and teach, this book consists of thirteen broad chapters:

1. **Global Economy** - The Road to Global Economy - International Management - Impact of Regional Developments on Internationalizations- International Investment and Trade -The Economic Status and Issues of the Major Regions.

2. **Globalization and World Developments** – Globalization, Global Development and Trends, Cultural Awareness and Implications, Cross Cultural Management, Global Strategic Skills, Culture and Cross Cultural Research Findings, The Global Manager and Management Perspective to Globalization.

3. **Managing Global Environment** - Managing a Global Environment, Trading Blocs, Workforce Diversity, The Global Managers Role, Technological Environment, E-business and Telecommunications, Outsourcing and Off-shoring and Business Ethics and Corporate Social Responsibility.

4. **Cultural Context of Global Management** - Cultural Context of Global Management, Meaning and Dimensions of Culture, Understanding the Role of Culture, Culture and Its Effect on Organization, Managing across Cultures, Organizational Cultures and Diversity, Communicating Across Cultures and Cross Cultural Negotiation and Decision Making.

5. **International Strategic Management** - International Strategic Mânagement, Strategic Planning, Formulating Strategy, International Functional Strategies, Managing Political Risk and Negotiation, Organizational Structure and Decision Making and Control systems.

6. **Implementation of Strategy** - Strategy Implementation, Management of Change, Organizational Culture and Strategy Implementation, Leadership and Strategy implementation.

7. **Leadership and Group Behaviour** – Leadership, Models of Leadership, Process of Leadership and Group Behaviour.

8. **Motivation** - Motivation Across Cultures, Theories of Motivation, Implications for Managers, Culture Effect on Motivation and Motivation Strategies.

9. **Strategic Human Resource Management** - Strategic Human Resource Management - Recent Developments - Human Capital Management (HCM) - Talent Management - The New SHRM Imperative - Benchmarking for SHRM - SHRM in Different Cultures.

10. **Developing Global Management Cadre** - Developing a Global Management Cadre - Women in International Management.

11. **Challenges of Global Management** - Challenges in Global Management, The World Wide Learning Challenge, and Knowledge Management, Managing Across Boundaries, Transnational Corporations, Multinational Corporations and Indian Multinationals.

12. **Innovation and Global Organizations** - The Foundation For Innovation - Is Your Groundwork In Place? -

Cultivating the Habit of Innovation - Managing For Innovation - The Only Sustainable Advantage - Innovation through Global Collaboration: A New Source of Competitive Advantage.

13. Global Strategic Management in a New World - The Trajectory to Global Maturity, Critical Issues Blocking the Passage Ahead and Strategy Based on a New Global Perspective.

14. Case Studies – World Wide Cases – Corporate Cases.

Each chapter is complete in itself and well linked with the next for comprehensive understanding of the subject matter. The whole subject matter owes its consummation to various experts and distinguished personalities who have expressed their views on this subject matter in different books, journals, magazines and papers.

I would like to acknowledge those who have helped to make this book a reality. Special thanks go to our growing number of colleagues throughout the world who have given many ideas and inspired to think internationally. Closer to home, I would like to give special recognition to management scholars who have had a direct influence on me. Among them notably are Late Dr. P.S. Palande, Retired IAS Officer and Ex-Director, National Insurance Academy, Pune and Prof. Ishwar Dayal, Founder Director, Indian Institute of Management (Lucknow). They are true "Global-Academic," and I appreciate their stimulation, advice, and support. I would also like to thank my other colleagues for their support and help from time to time.

Mr. Anuj Pandey and Mr. Niraj Pandey, my publishers, deserve special thanks for their whole hearted commitment and dedication in bringing out this book. In particular, I would like to thank Mr. Surendra, Ms. Nimisha and the team members at the Himalaya Publishing House, for their whole hearted co-operation and outstanding contributions to development and publication of this book. It is my pleasure to acknowledge the support of my spouse Jayant and daughter Neha. I greatly appreciate the love and support provided by my family.

Last but not the least, my students at all times, has been a source of inspiration for undertaking writing as a professional hobby. I am greatly indebted to them and all my well wishers. Critical comments and constructive suggestions for the improvement of the book are most welcome and will be highly appreciated.

Neeta Baporikar
neetajb@rediffmail.com

6/76 Ballaji Park,
Subhash Nagar,
Pune 411015.

Contents

Detailed Contents

1 Global Economy

• The Road to Global Economy • International Management • Impact of Regional Developments on Internationalizations • The 21st-Century Competitive Landscape • International Investment and Trade • The Economic Status and Issues of the Major Regions

The worldwide proliferation of mobile phones and Web accounts by itself will not bring about a more vibrant global economy. What are also needed are dramatic changes in core institutions that will translate technology into faster productivity growth. That means financial markets better able to fund innovation, more flexibility in corporations and labour markets, a faster pace of deregulation, and increased Competition.

The Road to Global Economy

Here's what countries must do to get a high-productivity, low-inflation economy:

- **Boost Investment Spending** on information technology as a share of GDP
- **Restructure Corporations** to cut costs, improve flexibility, and make better use of technology
- **Open Financial Markets** to direct capital to the best uses
- **Develop Venture Capital and IPO** markets to aid innovative companies
- **Encourage an Entrepreneurial Culture** and make it easier to start new businesses
- **Increase the Pace of Deregulation** especially in telecom and labour markets
- **Adjust Monetary Policy** to the realities of the New Economy by waiting for inflation to appear before raising interest rates.

The process of shifting to a fast-growth track is still in its early stages in most of the world. Europe is at least two or three years behind the United States with Asia lagging even farther behind. While there are pockets of entrepreneurial vigor in places such as Finland, it has turned out to be an enormous challenge to reshape cultures to allow more risk-taking in Europe and Asia, where caution is a virtue.

Moreover, investment in risky innovation—a linchpin of the new economy—depends on open global markets, since national markets do not provide a big enough payoff for taking big risks. But as shown by the demonstrations against the World Trade Organization in Seattle, there are groups in every country who feel threatened by free trade. A widespread backlash against globalization could remove a key underpinning of the new economy.

Open Access

The global economy is not a zero-sum game. Faster growth in the rest of the world would have a big payoff for the United States as well. Commodity prices might rise at first, but so would exports, bringing down the swelling trade deficits and creating manufacturing jobs at home. U.S. companies would start to see overseas profits accelerate.

And then there's the innovation factor. For corporations, the most important justification for spending big bucks on information technology is that it supports restructuring and cost-cutting. But from a global perspective, a critical benefit of the information revolution is that for the first time it makes data available worldwide. Historically it has taken years, if not decades, for even the most important technological and business innovations to spread across national borders.

But that's changing. Now, an engineer in China, say, can log on to the Internet and have immediate access to the treasure trove of data on U.S. Websites. More important, engineers in developing countries can communicate much more quickly with counterparts in other countries and learn what works and what doesn't. The gains from faster transmission of innovation can add up to 1% to global growth rates, according to research by economists Jonathan Eaton and Samuel S. Kortum of Boston University. That's an enormous potential boost.

But new technology has to be nourished within a larger framework of institutional changes. For one thing, openness of domestic markets to foreign trade is vital for turning innovations into real improvements in output. Without competition from overseas, companies make changes slowly and reluctantly.

International Management

International management is the process of applying management concepts and techniques in a multinational environment. Today, more firms than ever are earning some of their revenue from international operations. Many of these companies are multinational corporations (MNCs, for short).

An **MNC** is a firm that has operations in more than one country, international sales, and a nationality mix of managers and owners. One example is BP Amoco PLC, the giant British petroleum firm that recently committed $2 billion in a joint venture with PetroChina, which owns most of China's gas reserves and the infrastructure to transport and deliver the product. Another is Dell Computer which now has three manufacturing plants in Ireland, passing Intel as the country's largest foreign employer. A third is the Solectron Corporation of Milpitas, California, known worldwide for its high quality manufacturing processes, which bought Japanese-based auto electronics plant from the Sony Corporation. A fourth is IBM whose Global Services division has helped the company to provide quality service to clients in more countries than any industry rival. A fifth is General Electric which has operations in every major market worldwide including China where its businesses run the gamut from medical-imaging equipment to plastics to insurance. And in the automobile industry, every major manufacturer has multinational operations. In the last five years in Latin America alone, Ford built a car plant in Brazil, Volkswagen retooled its Mexico facilities to launch the New Beetle, and Daimler Chrysler built a new plant to produce engines in Brazil. General Motors has not only been actively investing in Latin America, but is making pickup trucks and sport utility vehicles in China and Buicks in Shanghai and recently agreed to spend $99 million on a joint venture with Russian auto maker Avtovaz to sell cars in emerging markets worldwide. In recent years, GM has also paid $125 million to buy the remaining 50 percent of Saab, laid out $2.4 billion for a 20 percent stake in Fiat, $1.3 billion for 20 percent of Fuji Heavy Industries, and $653 million to double its 10 percent position in Suzuki Motor.

These companies are not alone. In recent years such well-known American MNCs as Avon Products, Chevron, Citicorp, Coca-Cola, Colgate Palmolive, DuPont, Exxon, Eastman Kodak, Gillette, Hewlett-Packard, McDonald's, Mobil, Motorola, Ralston Purina, Texaco, the 3M Company, and Xerox have all earned more annual revenue in the international arena than they have stateside. As a result, increasingly firms are finding that they must develop international management expertise. Managers from today's MNCs must learn to work effectively with those from many different countries. Moreover, as this decade unfolds, more and more small and medium-sized businesses will find that they are being affected by the trend toward internationalization. Many of these companies will be doing business abroad and those who do not will find themselves doing business with MNCs operating locally. In either event, these growing businesses will need to be concerned with international management if only to improve their ability to interact and work well with MNCs that they are supplying and/or are supplying them on a local basis.

Increasing Internationalization

International business is not a new phenomenon; however, the volume of international trade has increased dramatically over the last decade. Today, every nation and an increasing number of companies buy and sell goods in the international marketplace. A number of developments in regions around the world have helped to fuel this activity.

The 21st-Century Competitive Landscape

The fundamental nature of competition in many of the world's industries is changing. The pace of this change is relentless and is increasing. Even determining the boundaries of an industry has become challenging. Consider, for example, how advances in interactive computer networks and telecommunications have blurred the boundaries of the entertainment industry. Today, networks such as ABC, CBS, Fox, NBC, and HBO compete not only among themselves, but also with AT&T, Microsoft, Sony, and others. Partnerships among firms in different segments of the entertainment industry further blur industry boundaries. For example, MSNBC is co-owned by NBC (which itself is owned by General Electric) and Microsoft. With full-motion video and sound rapidly making their way to mobile devices, cellular telephones are also competitors for customers' entertainment expenditures. Wireless companies, for example, are partnering with the music industry to introduce music-playing capabilities into mobile phones. Entertainment giant Walt Disney Company is selling wireless-phone plans to children. That Disney videos can be streamed through phones is yet another example of the difficulty of determining industry boundaries.

Other characteristics of the 21st-century competitive landscape are noteworthy as well. Conventional sources of competitive advantage such as economies of scale and huge advertising budgets are not as effective as they once were. Moreover, the traditional managerial mind-set is unlikely to lead a firm to strategic competitiveness. Managers must adopt a new mind-set that values flexibility, speed, innovation, integration, and the challenges that evolve from constantly changing conditions. The conditions of the competitive landscape result in a perilous business world, one where the investments required to compete on a global scale are enormous and the consequences of failure are severe. Developing and implementing strategy remains an important element of success in this environment. It allows for strategic actions to be planned and to emerge when the environmental conditions are appropriate. It also helps to co-ordinate the strategies developed by business units in which the responsibility to compete in specific markets is decentralized.

Hypercompetition is a term often used to capture the realities of the 21st-century competitive landscape. Under conditions of hypercompetition, "assumptions of market stability are replaced by notions of inherent instability and change." Hypercompetition results from the dynamics of strategic maneuvering among global and innovative combatants. It is a condition of rapidly escalating competition based on price-quality positioning, competition to create new know-how and establish first-mover advantage, and competition to protect or invade established product or geographic markets. In a hypercompetitive market, firms often aggressively challenge their competitors in the hopes of improving their competitive position and ultimately their performance. Several factors create hypercompetitive environments and influence the nature of the 21st-century competitive landscape. The two primary drivers are the emergence of a global economy and technology, specifically rapid technological change.

The Global Economy

A **global economy** is one in which goods, services, people, skills, and ideas move freely across geographic borders. Relatively unfettered by artificial constraints, such as tariffs, the global economy significantly expands and complicates a firm's competitive environment. Interesting opportunities and challenges are associated with the emergence of the global economy. For example, Europe, instead of the United States, is now the world's largest single market, with 700 million potential customers. The European Union and the other Western European countries also have a gross domestic product that is over 35 percent higher than the GDP of the United States. China's economy is now larger than Canada's, causing an analyst to suggest, "It's hard to talk meaningfully about the world economy any more without China being included." One indicator of the rapid rise in the capabilities of China's economy is the fact that from roughly 1986 to 2005, China lifted "some 400 million of its 1.3 billion people out of grinding \$1-a-day poverty."

India, the world's largest democracy, has an economy that also is growing rapidly and now ranks as the worlds fourth largest. By 2050, the United States, China, India, Japan, Britain, France, Germany, and South Korea are expected to be the world's largest economies. Russia and Italy are two economies projected to decline in size and influence between 2005 and 2050. The statistics detailing the nature of the global economy reflect the realities of a hypercompetitive business environment and challenge individual firms to think seriously about the markets in which they will compete. Consider the case of General Electric (GE). GE is moving boldly into China and other emerging markets. Although headquartered in the United States, GE expects that as much as 60 percent of its revenue growth between 2005 and 2015 will be generated by competing in rapidly developing economies (e.g., China and India). The decision to count on revenue growth in developing countries instead of in developed countries such as the United States and European nations seems quite reasonable in the global economy. In fact, according to an analyst, what GE is doing is not by choice but by necessity: "Developing countries are where the fastest growth is occurring and more sustainable growth." Based on its analyses of world markets and their potential, GE estimates that by 2024, China will be the world's largest consumer of electricity and will be the world's largest consumer and consumer-finance market (business areas in which GE competes). GE is making strategic decisions today such as investing significantly in China and India in order to improve its competitive position in what the firm believes are becoming vital sources of revenue and profitability.

Similarly, FedEx estimates that in no more than 10 years, the firm will generate the bulk of its revenue growth from business activities outside the United States, not from its domestic operations. Brazil and India are two markets in which the firm is now making significant investments in anticipation of revenue growth possibilities.

The March of Globalization

Globalization is the increasing economic interdependence among countries and their organizations as reflected in the flow of goods and services, financial capital, and knowledge across country borders. Globalization is a product of a larger number of firms competing against one another in an increasing number of global economies. In globalized markets and industries, financial capital might be obtained in one national market and used to buy raw materials in another one. Manufacturing equipment bought from a third national market can then be used to produce products that are sold in yet a fourth market. Thus, globalization increases the range of opportunities for companies competing in the 21st-century competitive landscape.

Wal-Mart, for instance, is trying to achieve boundaryless retailing with global pricing, sourcing, and logistics. Through boundaryless retailing, the firm seeks to make the movement of goods and the use of pricing strategies as seamless among all of its international operations as historically has been the case among its domestic stores. The firm is pursuing this type of retailing on an evolutionary basis. For example, most of Wal-Mart's original international investments were in Canada and Mexico, because it was easier for the firm to rehearse or apply its global practices in countries that are geographically close to its home base, the United States. Based on what it has learned, the firm has now expanded into Europe, South America, and Asia. Today, Wal-Mart is the world's largest retailer (with over 3,600 total units). Internationally, Wal-Mart now employs over 3,30,000 people in its more than 1,500 international units.

Globalization makes it increasingly difficult to think of firms headquartered in various economies throughout the world as domestic-only companies. Consider the following facts about three U.S. based organizations: On an annual basis, Wal-Mart continues to increase the percent of its total revenue that is coming from its international operations. Approximately 47 percent of operating income in 2004 was generated by McDonald's international operations. And as we just explained, GE expects more than 60 percent of its growth in sales revenue in the foreseeable future to come from operations in emerging markets. The challenge to companies experiencing globalization to the degree of these three firms is to understand the need for culturally sensitive decisions when using the strategic management process and to anticipate ever-increasing complexity in their operations as goods, services, people, and so forth move freely across geographic borders and throughout different economic markets.

Globalization also affects the design, production, distribution, and servicing of goods and services. In many instances, for example, globalization results in higher-quality goods and services. Global competitor Toyota Motor Company provides an example of how this happens. Because Toyota initially emphasized product reliability and superior customer service, the company's products are in high demand across the globe. Because of the demand for its products, Toyota's competitive actions have forced its global competitors to make reliability and service improvements in their operations. Indeed, almost any car or truck purchased today from virtually any manufacturer is of higher quality and is supported by better service than was the case before Toyota began successfully competing throughout the global economy.

Overall, it is important for firms to understand that globalization has led to higher levels of performance standards in many competitive dimensions, including those of quality, cost, productivity, product introduction time, and operational efficiency. In addition to firms competing in the global economy, these standards affect firms competing on a domestic-only basis. The reason for this is that customers will purchase from a global competitor rather than a domestic firm when the global company's good or service is superior. Because workers now flow rather freely among global economies, and because employees are a key source of competitive advantage, firms must understand that increasingly, "the best people will come from . . . anywhere." Overall, firms must learn how to deal with the reality that in the 21st-century competitive landscape, only companies capable of meeting, if not exceeding; global standards typically have the capability to earn above-average returns. As we have explained, globalization creates opportunities (such as those being pursued by Toyota, Wal-Mart, McDonald's and GE, among many other firms). However, globalization is not risk free. Collectively, the risks of participating outside of a firm's domestic country in the global economy are labelled a "liability of foreignness."

One risk of entering the global market is that typically a fair amount of time is required for firms to learn how to compete in markets that are new to them. A firm's performance can suffer until this knowledge is either developed locally or transferred from the home market to the newly established global location. Additionally, a firm's performance may suffer with substantial amounts of globalization. In this instance, firms may over diversify internationally beyond their ability to manage these diversified operations. The result of over diversification can have strong negative effects on a firm's overall performance. Thus, entry into international markets, even for firms with substantial experience in the global economy such as Toyota, McDonald's, and GE, requires proper use of the strategic management process. In this regard, firms should choose to enter more international markets only when there is a viable opportunity for them to do so and when they have the competitive advantages required to be successful in those markets.

It is also important to note that while global markets are attractive strategic options for some companies, they are not the only source of strategic competitiveness. In fact, for most companies, even for those capable of competing successfully in global markets, it is critical to remain committed to and strategically competitive in the domestic market. And, domestic markets can be testing grounds for possibly entering an international market at some point in the future. For example, some banks operating in Texas recently recognized the attractiveness of Latinos as a distinct customer group. Woodforest National Bank has focused on attracting Latino customers. One reason this group is attractive is that fewer than 50 percent of Latinos living in Texas have bank accounts. To attract Latinos, banks took actions such as redesigning their interiors to resemble haciendas, reduced fees on money transfers to Mexico, and started sponsoring community events that are important to the target population. If these efforts prove successful, at some point these banks may, assuming that regulations permit such actions, use the skills gained locally as the foundation for entering an international market such as Mexico.

Technology and Technological Changes

There are three categories of trends and conditions—technology diffusion and disruptive technologies, the information age, and increasing knowledge intensity —through which technology is significantly altering the nature of competition and contributing to unstable competitive environments as a result of doing so.

Technology Diffusion and Disruptive Technologies

The rate of technology diffusion — the speed at which new technologies become available and is used—has increased substantially over the last 15 to 20 years.

Consider the following rates of technology diffusion:

It took the telephone 35 years to get into 25 percent of all homes in the United States. It took TV 26 years. It took radio 22 years. It took PCs 16 years. It took the Internet 7 years.

Perpetual innovation is a term used to describe how rapidly and consistently new, information-intensive technologies replace older ones. The shorter product life cycles resulting from these rapid diffusions of new technologies place a competitive premium on being able to quickly introduce new, innovative goods and services into the marketplace.

In fact, when products become somewhat indistinguishable because of the widespread and rapid diffusion of technologies, speed to market with innovative products may be the primary source of competitive advantage Indeed, some argue that increasingly, the global economy is driven by or revolves around constant innovations. Not surprisingly, such innovations must be derived from an understanding of global standards and global expectations in terms of product functionality. Another indicator of rapid technology diffusion is that it now may take only 12 to 18 months for firms to gather information about their competitors' research and development and product decisions. In the global economy, competitors can sometimes imitate a firm's successful competitive actions within a few days. Once a source of competitive advantage the protection firms previously possessed, through their patents has been stifled by the current rate of technological diffusion. Today, patents may be an effective way of protecting proprietary technology in a small number of industries such as pharmaceuticals. Indeed, many firms competing in the electronics industry often do not apply for patents to prevent competitors from gaining access to the technological knowledge included in the patent application.

Disruptive technologies — technologies that destroy the value of an existing technology and create new markets — surface frequently in today's competitive markets. Think of the new markets created by the technologies underlying the development of products such as iPods, PDAs, WiFi, and the browser. Products such as these are thought by some to represent radical or breakthrough innovations. A disruptive or radical technology can create what is essentially a new industry or can harm industry incumbents. Some incumbents, though, are able to adapt based on their superior resources, experience, and ability to gain access to the new technology through multiple sources (e.g., alliances, acquisitions, and ongoing internal basic research). When a disruptive technology creates a new industry, competitors follow. Example: Amazon.com's launching created a new industry by making use of a disruptive technology we know as the Internet. In addition to making innovative use of the Internet to create Amazon.com, Jeff Bezos also uses core competence in technology to study information about its customers. These efforts result in opportunities to understand individual customers' needs and then target goods and services to satisfy those needs. Clearly, Amazon understands the importance of information and knowledge as competitive weapons for use in the 21st-century competitive landscape.

The Information Age

Dramatic changes in information technology have occurred in recent years. Personal computers, cellular phones, artificial intelligence, virtual reality, and massive databases (e.g., Lexis/Nexis) are a few examples of how information is used differently as a result of technological developments. An important outcome of these changes is that the ability to effectively and efficiently access and use information has become an important source of competitive advantage in virtually all industries. Both the pace of change in information technology and its diffusion will continue to increase. For instance, the number of personal computers in use in the United States is expected to reach 278 million by 2010. The declining costs of information technologies and the increased accessibility to them are also evident in the 21st-century competitive landscape. The global proliferation of relatively inexpensive computing power and its linkage on a global scale via computer networks combine to increase the speed and diffusion of information technologies. Thus, the competitive potential of information technologies is now available to companies of all sizes throughout the world, not only to large firms in Europe, Japan, and North America.

Internet is another technological innovation contributing to hypercompetition. Available to an increasing number of people throughout the world, the Internet provides an infrastructure that allows the delivery of information to computers in any location. Access to significant quantities of relatively inexpensive information yields strategic opportunities for a number of companies in global markets. Virtually all retailers, such as Abercrombie & Fitch, Gap, and Benetton, use the Internet to provide abundant shopping privileges to customers in multiple locations. As a distribution channel, the Internet's popularity is growing in the United States. In mid-2005, for example, over 3 percent of all retail sales (excluding car dealers and gas stations) were accounted for by the Internet. The exploding use of the Internet in China (94 million users in mid-2005, second only to the United States) is creating opportunities for U.S. Internet companies (Google, Yahoo!, and eBay). In fact, the huge potential for these firms caused an analyst to suggest that Internet companies without a major stake in China would experience less growth and a greater possibility of poor long-term performance as a result.

Increasing Knowledge Intensity

Knowledge (information, intelligence, and expertise) is the basis of technology and its application. In the 21st-century competitive landscape, knowledge is a critical organizational resource and is increasingly a valuable source of competitive advantage. Indeed, starting in the 1980s, the basis of competition began shifting from hard assets to intangible resources. For example, "Wal-Mart transformed retailing through its proprietary approach to supply chain management and its information-rich relationships with customers and suppliers." Relationships are an example of an intangible resource. Knowledge is gained through experience, observation, and inference and is an intangible resource. The value of intangible resources, including knowledge, is growing as a proportion of total shareholder value. The probability of achieving strategic competitiveness in the 21st-century competitive landscape is enhanced for the firm that realizes that its survival depends on the ability to capture intelligence, transform it into usable knowledge, and diffuse it rapidly throughout the company. Therefore, firms must develop (e.g., through training programs) and acquire (e.g., by hiring educated and experienced employees) knowledge, integrate it into the organization to create capabilities, and then apply it to gain a competitive advantage. In addition, firms must build routines that facilitate the diffusion of local knowledge throughout the organization for use everywhere it has value. Firms are better able to do these things when they have strategic flexibility.

Strategic flexibility is a set of capabilities used to respond to various demands and opportunities existing in a dynamic and uncertain competitive environment. Thus, strategic flexibility involves coping with uncertainty and its accompanying risks. Firms should try to develop strategic flexibility in all areas of their operations. However, those working within firms to develop strategic flexibility should understand that this is not an easy task, largely because of inertia that can build up over time. To be strategically flexible on a continuing basis and to gain the competitive benefits of such flexibility, a firm has to develop the capacity to learn. In the words of John Browne, CEO of British Petroleum: "In order to generate extraordinary value for shareholders, a company has to learn better than its competitors and apply that knowledge throughout its businesses faster and more widely than they do." Continuous learning provides the firm with new and up-to-date sets of skills, which allow it to adapt to its environment as it encounters changes. Firms capable of rapidly and broadly applying what they have learned have strategic flexibility and the resulting capacity to change in ways that will increase the probability of being able to successfully deal with uncertain, hypercompetitive environments. As discussed in the Strategic Focus, some firms must change dramatically to remain competitive or to again become competitive.

Will the changes being sought at Kodak and Albertsons lead to improved firm performance? Time will provide the answer to this question. What is known is that being prepared to consistently engage in change improves the likelihood of a firm achieving above-average returns across time.

Organizational Change: Be Ready, Because It Can't Be Avoided!

In the 21st-century competitive landscape, some argue that competition is about change— being able to change effectively, quickly, and in ways competitors will find difficult to imitate. Through change, organizations have opportunities to grow and to learn. In a continuous cycle, new learning resulting from one change is the foundation for a new cycle of growth and future change. Without change and the resulting learning that pushes this continuous, reinforcing cycle, the likelihood of organizational decline and eventual death greatly increases. Being able to rapidly and successfully change is increasingly an irreplaceable dimension of being able to earn above-average returns in the global economy. Inspite of its importance, change is difficult, for individuals and organizations. If we think of individuals, it may surprise us to learn that roughly 90 percent of heart-bypass patients do not change their lifestyles—even at the risk of dying. The difficulty individuals experience trying to change their behaviour suggests the challenge of achieving change in an organization, which, after all, is a collection of what are often change-resistance people!

The March of Globalization

Foreign direct investments (FDI) and international trade patterns demonstrate globalization's rapid spread across many of the world's economies. For example, both FDI and international trade have been growing at a faster rate than the U.S. economy as a whole for some time. And there are other patterns of importance. Significant investment in developing countries such as India and China has shifted investment from well established economies to emerging economies over the last 10–15 years. Looking at these patterns can be very informative with respect to understanding how global business patterns are changing.

Managers in the 21st century must be aware of these patterns if they are to successfully lead their firms. In particular, strategic managers who have responsibility for establishing the firm's vision and making certain that the firm pursues its mission must have a broad awareness of the shifting trends in global business practices and the different nature of different nations' economics.

Impact of Regional Developments on Internationalizations

Although the status and issues facing major regions of the global economy are given detailed attention in the last part of this chapter, several important developments have had a direct impact on internationalization and should be noted. Obviously, the horrific consequences of terrorism and its threat around the world have made a permanent mark on how and where international business is conducted. However, some of the more routine, but still important developments have been:

1. The United States, Canada, and Mexico make up the **North American Free Trade Agreement (NAFTA)**. NAFTA is a free trade agreement between the United States, Canada, and Mexico which has in essence removed all barriers to trade and created a huge North American market. Although not occurring as fast as once assumed, this market eventually will be expanded to include Latin American countries as well. Chile will probably join NAFTA in the near future, and others, such as Argentina and Brazil, are likely to follow. The result may be a giant "American Market" that would parallel similar developments in Europe and Asia. In the early 1990s an "Alliance of the Americas" was proposed. During the first six months of his presidency, President Bush has echoed this basic idea. He

wants to win negotiating authority with the Congress to build a free trade area from Alaska to Argentina. His goal, as well as that of other leaders in the Western hemisphere, is to create the world's largest free trade zone, encompassing over 800 million people, by January 2005.

2. **The European Union (EU)** is now well on its way to creating a unified market that many have described as the United States of Europe. This group consists of 15 nations including Austria, Belgium, Denmark, Finland, France, Germany, Great Britain, Greece, Holland, Ireland, Italy, Luxembourg, Portugal, Spain, and Sweden. Not only have most trade barriers between the members been removed, but the group has adopted a unified currency called the "euro." As a result of this agreement, it will now be possible for customers to compare prices between countries because everything can be done in a uniform currency. In other words, business done in the EU will be in euros. Even though long standing cultural differences remain, the EU is better integrated as a single market than either NAFTA or the allied Asian countries. Additionally, other nations such as Turkey have applied for membership. In the near future, the former communist bloc countries of Central and Eastern Europe undoubtedly also will become part of the EU. For example, Poland, Hungary, and the Czech Republic are already making progress toward membership, and others such as Albania, Romania, Slovakia, Lithuania, Latvia, Estonia, and Bulgaria have the goal to become members. Once East and West join together, the result will be a giant economic market that no major MNC can afford to ignore.

3. Although Japan has experienced economic problems for about 10 years, it continues to be the primary economic force in the Pacific Rim. Japan recently has invested relatively more in its own backyard of Asia than in any other part of the world. Japanese MNCs want to take advantage of the underdeveloped and huge Asian markets. At the same time, China is proving to be a major economic force (some experts forecast that China eventually will be the biggest economy in the world). Although all of the economies in Asia are now feeling the impact of the economic uncertainty similar to the rest of the world, the Four Tigers (Hong Kong, Taiwan, South Korea, and Singapore) have been doing relatively well and the Southeast Asia countries of Malaysia, Thailand, Indonesia, and even Vietnam should bounce back to become major export-driven economies. As in other parts of the world, an economic bloc called ASEAN (Association of Southeast Asian Nations) made up of Indonesia, Malaysia, the Philipines, Singapore, Brunei, Thailand, and in recent years Cambodia, Myanmar, and Vietnam, promotes exports to other countries.

4. Central and Eastern Europe, Russia, and the other republics of the former Soviet Union currently are still trying to make the transition to market economies. Although the Czech Republic, Slovenia, Poland, and Hungary have a start, but remaining problems, the others (the Balkan countries, Russia, and the other republics of the former Soviet Union) still have a long way to go. However, all are a target for MNCs looking for expansion opportunities. For example, after the fall of the Berlin Wall in 1989, Coca-Cola quickly began to sever its relations with most of the state-run bottling companies in the former communist bloc countries. The soft drink giant began investing heavily to import own manufacturing, distribution, and marketing techniques. To date, Coca-Cola has pumped billions into Central and Eastern Europe—and this investment is beginning to pay off. Its business in Central and Eastern Europe has been expanding at twice the rate of its other foreign operations.

5. Economic activity in Latin America continues to be up and down. Despite the continuing political and economic setbacks these countries periodically experience, economic growth and exports continue in Brazil, Chile, Venezuela, and Mexico. Additionally, while outside MNCs continually target this geographic area, there also is a great deal of cross-border investments between Latin American countries. Regional trade agreements are helping in this cross-border process, including NAFTA which ties the Mexican economy more closely to the U.S. than Latin America. Within South America there is Mercosur, a common market created by Argentina, Brazil, Paraguay, and Uruguay, and the Andean Common Market, a sub-regional free trade compact that is designed to promote economic and social integration and co-operation between Bolivia, Colombia, Ecuador, Peru, and Venezuela.

6. There also is recent economic progress among less developed nations. A good example is India, which for years has had a love-hate relationship with multinational businesses. The Indian government has been known for its slow moving bureaucracy and this has been a major stumbling block in attracting foreign capital. In recent years, however, there has been a dramatic turnaround in government policy, and a growing number of multinationals recently have been attracted to India. Much of this spurt has resulted from the current Indian government's willingness to reduce the bureaucratic red tape that accompanies the necessary approvals to move forward with investments.

These are specific, geographic examples of emerging internationalism. Equally important to this new climate of globalization, however, are the recent developments in both international investment and trade.

International Investment and Trade

Approximately 80 percent of all international investments come from developed countries. For example, foreign direct investment (FDI), the term used to indicate the amount invested in another country, in the United States currently stands at almost $1 trillion, while U.S. FDI is $1.1 trillion.

The largest investors in the United States in recent years have been Great Britain, Japan, the Netherlands, Germany, and Canada. Conversely, the major stake for U.S. investors has been the EU, followed by Canada, and then Japan. Tables 1-1 and 1-2 provide additional information on FDI in the United States and by U.S. investors.

As nations become more affluent, they begin looking for countries with economic growth potential where they can invest funds. Over the last two decades, for example, Japanese MNCs have invested not only in their Asian neighbors, but in both the United States and the EU. European MNCs, meanwhile, have made large financial commitments in Japan, and more recently in China, because they see Asia as having continued growth potential. American multinationals have followed a similar approach in regard both to Europe and Asia. For example, GE Capital has gone to Asia to acquire a majority stake in a charge-card issuer, boost to 100 percent its ownership of an auto financing business, purchase a 49 percent stake in a consumer finance company, and enter Japan's insurance market with a $575 million investment in a joint venture with Toho Mutual Life Insurance. Other U.S. MNCs such as Merrill Lynch acquired 33 branches of the Japanese Yamaichi Securities firm, Coca-Cola bought a 50 percent interest in a Thai bottler, and Microsoft recently purchased 60 percent of Titus Communications, Japan's second-largest cable operator. In addition, U.S. auto firms hold substantial ownership positions in the Japanese car industry. For example, General Motors owns 49 percent of Isuzu and 10 percent of Suzuki and Ford holds a 33.4 percent equity position in Mazda. In addition to these types of investments, international trade had increased substantially over the last two decades. For example, in 1983 the United States exported slightly over $200 billion of goods and services and imported $269 billion of goods and services. At the end of the century U.S. exports were in the range of $700 billion annually and imports were over $1 trillion. In other words, during this period, the United States more than tripled its trade with the rest of the world.

EU trade has also increased sharply. This is particularly true for exports and imports between EU members both of which are now in excess of $2 trillion annually. Japan, despite its ongoing economic problems, has also seen continual increases in its annual exports and imports. In the early 1980s, exports and imports were around $440 billion and $335 billion respectively; by the end of the century imports and exports were in the neighbourhood of $450 and $325 billion respectively with a large amount of this positive trade balance accounted for by its sales to the United States.

When international trade statistics for all countries are examined, what is particularly interesting about these data is that the *percentage* of world trade that is accounted for by the three major trading blocs—the United States, the EU, and Japan—has remained fairly consistent. Over the last two decades this group's share of world exports and imports has remained in the range of 55–59 percent. Simply stated, this triad accounts for most of the world's international trade, and the United States is the major economic power among the three. U.S. sells over $450 billion of goods and services to its

TABLE 1.1. Foreign Direct Investment in US (in millions of dollars) 1998–1999

	1988	*1999*
All Countries	793,748	986,668
Canada	74,143	79,716
Europe	528,601	685,845
South and Central America	9,819	10,606
Other Western Hemisphere	18,034	33,984
Africa	882	1,545
Middle East	6,346	7,087
Asia and Pacific	155,943	167,884

TABLE 1.2. Foreign Direct Investment by the US (*in millions of dollars*) 1998–1999

	1988	*1999*
All Countries	1,104,012	1,132,622
Canada	101,871	111,707
Europe	528,113	581,791
South and Central America	74,254	74,839
Other Western Hemisphere	68,459	77,569
Africa	14,241	15,062
Middle East	10,632	11,137
Asia and Pacific	155,364	185,912

Source: Bureau of Economic Analysis: U.S. Department of Commerce, 2001.

top 10 trading partners and, in turn, buys over $730 billion of goods and services from them. And in the future, the amount of international trade by all countries will continue to rise, making an understanding of international management even more important than it has been in the past.

Finally, it is important to note that foreign investment and trade do not rely exclusively on MNCs exporting or setting up operations locally. In some cases, it is far easier to buy a domestic firm. Beer companies, for example, are finding that customers like local products, so rather than trying to sell them an imported beer, the MNC will invest in or buy a local brewery. Moreover, the name of the local company may remain the same, so that many local residents are unaware that the firm has changed hands.

To illustrate this point, answer the following questions about well-known products sold, and then check your answers:

1. Where is the parent company of Braun household appliances (electric shavers, coffee makers, etc.) located?
   a. Switzerland *b.* Germany *c.* the United States *d.* Japan
2. The BIC pen company is
   a. Japanese *b.* British *c.* U.S.-based *d.* French
3. The company that owns Häagen-Dazs ice cream is in
   a. Germany *b.* the U.S. *c.* Sweden *d.* Japan
4. RCA television sets are produced by a company based in
   a. France *b.* the United States *c.* Malaysia *d.* Taiwan
5. The firm that owns Green Giant vegetables is
   a. U.S.-based *b.* Canadian *c.* British *d.* Italian
6. The owners of Godiva chocolate are
   a. U.S.-based *b.* Swiss *c.* Dutch *d.* Swedish

7. The company that produces Vaseline is
   a. French *b.* Anglo-Dutch *c.* German *d.* U.S.-based
8. Wrangler jeans are made by a company that is
   a. Japanese *b.* Taiwanese *c.* British *d.* U.S.-based
9. The company that owns Holiday Inn is headquartered in
   a. Saudi Arabia *b.* France *c.* the United States *d.* Britain
10. Tropicana orange juice is owned by a company that is headquartered in
    a. Mexico *b.* Canada *c.* the United States *d.* Japan

This quiz helps to illustrate how transnational today's MNCs have become. This trend is not restricted to firms in North America, Europe, or Asia. An emerging global community is becoming increasingly interdependent economically. Although there may be a true, totally integrated global market in the near future, at present regionalization, as represented by North America, Europe, Asia, and the less developed countries, is most descriptive of the world economy.

The Economic Status and Issues of the Major Regions

International investment and trade are more likely to occur between nations in close geographic proximity; for example, in North America, Mexico and Canada are two of the United States' largest trading partners. However, there also is a growing trend toward expanding these horizons and doing business with nations thousands of miles away. For example, Japan is a major trading partner of the United States, and China does more business with the United States than with most other nations. The following sections examine trends that are occurring in each major region of the world and the impact of these developments on international management.

North America

As noted earlier, North America constitutes one of the three largest trading blocs in the world. The combined purchasing power of the United States, Canada, and Mexico is close to $11 trillion. In 1989, the United States and Canada officially had a free trade agreement, and in 1994, Mexico officially joined, thereby creating the North American Free Trade Agreement (NAFTA). A number of economic developments have occurred because of this agreement, and all are designed to remove trade barriers and promote commerce between these three countries. Some of the more important include: (1) the elimination of tariffs as well as import and export quotas; (2) the opening of government procurement markets to companies in the other two nations; (3) an increase in the opportunity to make investments in each others' country; (4) an increase in the ease of travel between countries; and (5) the removal of restrictions on agricultural products, auto parts, and energy goods.

The NAFTA provisions will take place over time. For example, in the case of Mexico, quotas on Mexican products in the textile and apparel sectors were phased out over time with customs duties on all textile and apparel products completely eliminated by the year 2004. Similarly, in 2001 outside investors were allowed to own no more than 51 percent of auto and truck companies but in 2004 these limitations are totally eliminated. Steps such as these are helping to create a unified trading bloc. Even though there will be more integration both globally and regionally, effective international management still requires knowledge of individual countries.

United States

U.S. MNCs have holdings throughout the world. In Europe, General Motors and Ford command dominant market positions, and they are finally beginning to make inroads in Asia as well. U.S. MNCs also do extremely well in the European computer market and are a major force in this industry throughout the Pacific Rim. Telecommunications is another high-tech area where the United States has a large international market share. U.S. firms compete with each other in the international arena as well. For example, AT&T now finds itself getting international competition from the U.S. "Baby Bells" (the regional firms that used to be part of AT&T). These firms are becoming more interested in expanding their market coverage and meeting the growing worldwide demand for higher-quality telephone services.

U.S. consumer-goods companies also are finding overseas markets to be very attractive. For example, Coca-Cola has a soft drink plant and distribution operation in Moscow and has a huge presence throughout Eastern Europe. Toys "R" US has expanded in Germany and Japan, and it is gaining market share in both locales. U.S. airline companies, such as Delta, United, and American, also are expanding into Europe. At the same time, foreign MNCs are finding the United States to be a lucrative market for expansion. BMW has set up operations in South Carolina, and Mercedes produces a lower-priced car ($20,000 range) in Alabama designed to help it gain U.S. market share. Other examples of outside investment in the United States include SmithKline Beecham PLC of Britain, which paid almost $3 billion to acquire the over-the-counter drug business of Sterling Winthrop, Inc., an Eastman Kodak unit. Hoechst AG of Germany paid over $7 billion for Marion Merrell Dow, Inc., a Dow Chemical subsidiary. France Telecom and Deutsche Telecom combined to pay over $4 billion for a 20 percent stake in the Sprint Corporation.

Even though Japanese firms are going to Asia more than in the past, they now are turning to the United States to find suppliers who can help increase the quality of their products while keeping down costs. For example, Toyota, Isuzu, and Suzuki all are buying antilock brake systems from General Motors. IBM is selling computers to Mitsubishi Electric, and Sun Microsystems Inc. is selling workstations to Japanese firms. Understanding these developments in the United States contributes to the field of international management.

Canada

Canada is the United States' largest trading partner, a position it has held for many years. The United States also has considerable foreign direct investment in Canada, more than in any other country except the United Kingdom. This helps to explain why most of the largest foreign-owned companies in Canada are totally, or heavily, U.S.-owned. The legal and business environment in Canada is similar to that in the United States, and this similarity helps to promote trade between the two countries. Geography, language, and culture also help, as does NAFTA, which will assist Canadian firms in becoming more competitive worldwide. They will have to be able to go head-to-head with their U.S. and Mexican competitors as trade barriers are removed. This should result in greater efficiency and market prowess on the part of the Canadian firms, which must compete successfully or go out of business.

In recent years, Canadian firms have begun investing heavily in the United States. For example, Canadian Pacific has purchased the Delaware & Hudson Railway, and Bombardier, Inc., has bought the Learjet Corporation of Wichita, Kansas. Meanwhile, Bronfman, Inc., best known for its Canadian whiskeys, sold its large stake in Du Pont for $1.4 billion (less than market value) to buy 80 percent of MCA (now called Universal) and purchased Polygram, the largest music company in the world.15 Canadian firms also do business in many other countries, including Mexico, Great Britain, Germany, and Japan, where they find ready markets for Canada's vast natural resources, including lumber, natural gas, crude petroleum, and agri-products.

At the same time, Canada is becoming a target for increased international investment, especially by firms from the United States. American, Delta, and Northwest airlines all have expanded their Canadian routes. DaimlerChrysler, Ford, and General Motors all have plants in Canada, and so do other major U.S. MNCs, including IBM, Kodak, and Xerox. Again, a major reason for this outside investment is to tap Canada's vast natural resources, which offer a potential bonanza to enterprising firms. Another reason is the growing population and increasing purchasing power of the country. Still another is the chance to take advantage of the opportunities provided under the NAFTA provisions.

Mexico

By the early 1990s, Mexico had recovered from its economic problems of the previous decade and become the strongest economy in Latin America. In 1994, Mexico became part of NAFTA, and it appeared to be on the verge of becoming the major economic power in Latin America. The country's economic optimism proved to be short-lived, however. By late 1994, the value of the peso collapsed, and the economy took a nosedive.

By early 1995, the United States, the International Monetary Fund, and the Bank for International Settlements were teaming up to create a $50 billion assistance package. At the same time, the government of Mexico was instituting a number of important economic changes, which included cutting the federal budget (thus holding down the country's spiraling deficit), instituting wage and price controls to limit growing inflation, and privatizing more state-held businesses to raise money and stimulate economic growth. These moves helped to bring the Mexican economy back on its course, and the loans were paid back before they were due.

In 2000 the 71-year hold of the Institutional Revolutionary Party on the presidency of the country came to an end and many investors believe that under the new administration of Vicente Fox the government will be more pro-business than ever. Economic growth in 2001 was in the range of 3 percent16 and the country is now producing almost 2 million light vehicles annually.17 In addition, Mexico now has a highly competitive textile industry that has replaced China as the major exporter of garments to the U.S.18 However, like the U.S. and other countries of the world, Mexico's economy faces an uncertain future.

In the mean time, Mexico has built a very strong **maquiladora industry**. Derived from the Spanish word for the fee that a miller collected for processing grain that now represents the arrangement created by the Mexican government that permits the flow of materials and products in and out of Mexico with only the value added being taxed.

Long before NAFTA, this was an arrangement by the Mexican government that permitted foreign manufacturers to send materials to their Mexican-based plants, process or assemble the products, and then ship them back out of Mexico with only the value added being taxed. Ford Motor, for example, took advantage of this opportunity and annually exports engines from its Chihuahua plant to the United States. General Motors assembles car radios in its Matamoros plant for shipment north. Hundreds of other large firms have followed suit, taking advantage of the low-cost, but quality conscious, Mexican workforce.

U.S. labour unions argue that this arrangement has cost many jobs in the United States, but the U.S. Department of Labour reports that *maquiladora* operations actually support jobs by helping U.S. firms maintain their international competitiveness. For example, Packard Electric has noted that without *maquiladora* operations, it would have closed its Warren, Ohio, plant and moved everything to Southeast Asia. Because of NAFTA, Mexican businesses are finding themselves able to take advantage of the U.S. market by replacing goods that were previously purchased from Asia.

Mexican firms are now able to produce products at highly competitive prices thanks to lower cost labor and proximity to the American market. Location has helped hold down transportation costs and allows for fast delivery. As a result, Hewlett-Packard has increased imports of copier products from Mexican manufacturers; and IBM is pushing its Asian suppliers to set up joint ventures in Mexico, so that its own costs and inventories can be reduced.

Overseas auto producers are also turning their attention to this market location opportunity. Volkswagen, Nissan, and DaimlerChrysler have production facilities in Mexico. As a result, when coupled with the American auto firms that have operations there, almost 1 million cars and trucks for the U.S. market are now being made in Mexico. Mexican firms are also expanding their worldwide operations. A retail group controlled by billionaire Carlos Slim Helu recently bought CompUSA, the largest chain of personal computer stores in the United States. Grupo Industrial Bimbo SA, a large food company that provides all of the buns for McDonald's units in Mexico, Peru, Colombia, and Venezuela, has built a factory in the Czech Republic to manufacture candy for the local market. Mexican firms, taking advantage of a new arrangement which the government has negotiated with the EU, can now export goods into the European community without having to pay a tariff. So Volkswagen of Mexico, as long as the Mexican content of the cars is in the prescribed 45–60 percent range, can export cars to the EU and save the 7 percent duty it used to pay.

Today Mexican companies employ approximately 70,000 workers in more than two dozen countries and generate almost $8 billion in revenues. n addition, the country's trade with both the EU and Asia is on the rise which is important to Mexico because it wants to reduce its over reliance on the U.S. market.

South America

Over the years, countries in South America have had difficult economic problems. They have accumulated heavy foreign debt obligations and experienced severe inflation. Although most have tried to implement economic reforms, reducing their debt, the last few years have again seen a downturn in the economy. Brazil is a case in point. From 1992 to 1995, the country's GDP rose by 5 percent annually, and inflation, which was running as high as 50 percent in some months, had dropped to 5 percent by mid-1998. Most important, Brazil attracted outside investors. Examples include Compaq Computer, which opened a factory capable of producing 400,000 personal computers annually. Anheuser-Busch spent $105 million on a brewery to market Budweiser to Brazilians, and General Electric constructed $9 billion worth of coal fired power electricity plants in the southern part of the country. At the same time, many other well-known companies have set up operations in Brazil, including Arby's, J.C. Penney, Kentucky Fried Chicken, McDonald's, and Wal-Mart. All of this international business activity should spell success. However, by the turn of the century, Brazil was experiencing difficulties in the volatile world economy and its future is uncertain. Chile has been an economic success story in South America. Annual average growth of GDP in 1997 was 8.1 percent, which was higher than that for any other country in South America except Argentina. In addition, Chile's export volume increased dramatically and the amount of foreign direct investment was on the rise. However, in the last couple of years the economy has weakened, GDP has declined, and its future is uncertain. For example, beginning in 1995, 90 percent of trade among Mercosur members was duty free. Also, members of the Andean Pact formed a customs union by adopting common external tariffs and eliminating most duties between the members. Currently, negotiations are under way for merging Mercosur and the Andean Pact into a South American Free Trade Association. Because of such developments, inter-country trade is increasing sharply. At the same time, South American countries are increasingly looking to do business with the United States.28 In fact, a survey of businesspeople from Argentina, Brazil, Chile, Colombia, and Venezuela found that the U.S. market, on average, was more important for them than any other. Some of these countries, however, also are looking outside of the Americas for growth opportunities. Mercosur has begun talks with the EU to create free trade between the two blocs, and Chile has joined the Asia-Pacific Economic Co-operation group. These developments help to illustrate the economic dynamism of South America and, especially in light of Asia's recent economic problems, explain why so many multinationals are interested in doing business within this part of the world.

Europe

Although often in the past overshadowed because of Asia's spectacular growth, major economic developments have occurred in Europe over the past decade. One interesting development has been the privatization of traditionally nationalized industries. Another has been the full emergence of the EU as an operational economic union, and yet another close economic linkage established between the EU and newly emerging Central and Eastern European countries. Including the former communist bloc, today Greater Europe is a trading area of about 550 million, mostly middle-class consumers in at least 25 countries.

The EU The ultimate objective of the EU is to eliminate all trade barriers among member countries (like between the states in the United States). This economic community eventually will have common custom duties as well as unified industrial and commercial policies regarding countries outside the union. Another goal that has finally largely become a reality is a single currency and a regional central bank. Such developments will allow companies based in EU nations that are able to manufacture high-quality, low-cost goods to ship them anywhere within the EU without paying duties or being subjected to quotas. This helps to explain why many North American and Pacific Rim firms have established operations in Europe; however, all these outside firms are finding their success tempered by the necessity to address local cultural differences.

As a result of differing local tastes, EU-based firms follow the international strategy adage, "plan globally, act locally." Although, this strategy also applies to other parts of the world and will be covered in subsequent chapters, it must be given special consideration if unity in Europe is to become a reality. For example, EU appliance makers will add a self cleaning option to those ovens for the French market, but leave this option out of units for the German market, where food generally is cooked at lower temperatures. Another interesting strategy is to draw heavily on a network of factories in the EU that can produce both components and finished goods. For example, the Philips television factory in Brugge, Belgium, uses tubes that are supplied from a factory in Germany, transistors that come from France, plastics that are produced in Italy, and electronic components that come from another factory in Belgium.

The most common way that foreign MNCs have gained a foothold in the EU is by using two strategy approaches: acquisitions and alliances. Also, co-operative research and development (R&D) programs are becoming increasingly common as firms team up to share expenses. Siemens and Philips have used this approach to develop computer chips, and IBM has a number of agreements with European firms for developing advanced computer technology. EU-based firms also are able to obtain financial assistance through the **European Research Cooperation Agency (Eureka)**, an EU agency that funds projects in a number of fields with the objective of making Europe more productive and competitive in the world market. Eureka, funds projects in the fields of energy, medical technology, biotechnology, communications, information technology, transportation, new materials, robotics, production automation, lasers, and the environment.

The objective of Eureka is to make Europe more productive and competitive in the world market. In the years ahead, the EU will continue to be a major focal point for international investment; U.S. firms in particular have been buying businesses in the EU, joining in strategic alliances with EU firms, and exporting into the European market.

The challenge for the future of the EU is to absorb their Eastern neighbours, the former communist bloc countries. This could result in a giant, single European market. In fact, a unified Europe could become the largest economic market in terms of purchasing power in the world. Such a development is not lost on Asian and U.S. firms, which are working to gain a stronger foothold in Eastern European countries as well as the existing EU. In recent years, foreign governments have been very active in helping to stimulate and develop the market economies of Central and Eastern Europe to enhance their economic growth as well as world peace.

Central and Eastern Europe

In December 1989, the Berlin Wall came down, and 2 years later, on December 8, 1991, the Soviet Union ceased to exist. Each of the individual republics that made up the U.S.S.R. in turn declared its independence. The Russian Republic has the most population, territory, and influence, but others, such as Ukraine, also are industrialized and potentially can be important in the global economy.

Of the ideas promoted by former Soviet president Mikhail Gorbachev, *glasnost* (openness) has been achieved, but *perestroika* (economic and political restructuring) is still having major problems.

Of most importance to the study of international management are the Russian economic reforms, the dismantling of Russian price controls (allowing supply and demand to determine prices), and privatization (converting the old communist-style public enterprises to private ownership). Clearly, Russia still has tremendous problems. In fact, by the turn of the century, once-mighty Russia's economy was not nearly as strong as those of its once-dominated neighbours, the Czech Republic,

Hungary, and Poland. Even with rapid economic progress, closing the gap with their Western European neighbors will take many more years.

A brief overview of the historical developments in Russia is shown in Table 1.3.

TABLE 1.3. The Three Eras of the Soviet Union

Traditional Russian Society (Pre-1917)
Centralization of authority and responsibility
Collective action
Dual ethical standards (honesty in personal relationships, deception in business relationships)
Feelings ranging from helplessness (only a religious savior will deliver people from their plight) to bravado (belief in one's ability to outsmart others).
Red Executive Managers (1917–1987)
Centralized leadership
Communist domination
Party service
Rise of collective enterprises
Dual ethical standards (honesty in personal conduct with employees, dishonesty in business dealings)
Use of informal influence to obtain favours
Feelings of helplessness due to producing inferior products and bravado in operating some of the world's largest organizations.
Market-Oriented (1987–present)
Sharing of power with numerous stakeholders in state enterprises
Responsibility for private enterprise success
Effective delegation of responsibility to employees
Use of informal influence to obtain favours
Bipolar extremes of cynicism in problem solving
Use of over promising to both clients and business partners
A high degree of achievement motivation regarding quality service and products but social contempt for success.

Source: Adapted from Sheila Puffer, "Understanding the Bear: A Portrait of Russian Business Leaders," Academy of Management Executive.

One of the ways that Russia is attempting to get its economy going is by removing many administered prices and subsidies and letting free market forces take over. The problem with this strategy is that it results in very high inflation (demand is much greater than supply). Hyperinflation is very hard on the people, and for political expediency, this slows down price reforms.

On the positive side, many efforts are under way to help stimulate the Russian economy. Russia has been given membership in the International Monetary Fund (IMF), which has pledged development loans to help the country make the transition to a free market economy, and also put together a loan package to help keep the economy from collapsing.

In addition, the Group of Seven (the United States, Germany, France, England, Canada, Japan, and Italy) has pledged billions for humanitarian and other types of assistance. So, while the Russian economy likely will have a number of years of painfully slow economic recovery and many current problems, most economic experts predict that if the Russians can hold things together politically and maintain social order, things should get better in the long run. Besides freeing up prices, the other major development that is needed for Russia to transform into a market economy is privatization. Russian enterprises no longer are fully subsidized, and they no longer can automatically sell all their output to the state. Enterprises are increasingly becoming more self-sustaining and are operating in more of a market-based environment. Privatization has taken a number of different forms, including turning a large number of state-run businesses over to the workers and managers, letting them set up a board of directors and run the operation. In addition, an increasing number of public enterprises issued stock, and both employees and outside investors purchased ownership. Shareholders not only get equity but also a vote in how the company is run. Although these economic reforms are being implemented slowly, there are significant problems in Russia associated with growing crime of all kinds as well as political uncertainty. Many foreign investors feel that the risk is still too high.

Russia is such a large market, however, and has so much potential for the future; many MNCs feel they must get involved. For example, DaimlerChrysler of Germany has a contract for a $140 million plant to build buses. The Carroll Group of Britain is constructing a $250 million hotel-trade center. Alcatel, the giant French telecommunications company, has a $2.8 billion contract to supply advanced digital telephone equipment switches. McDonald's opened a restaurant in Moscow about 10 years ago and now operates more than 50 restaurants throughout the country. Overall, however, Russia still has a long way to go in becoming like its Western neighbours. The *Economist* Intelligence Unit (EIU) has reported that Russia was one of the least successful countries in Central and Eastern Europe in making the transition to a market economy, and it also was ranked as one of the most politically risky countries in the world. Former communist countries that have become most visible in the international arena include the Czech Republic, Hungary, and Poland. All three initially were battered by inflation, unemployment, and slow economic growth during their transition efforts. All three made significant progress, and they have been successful in attracting Western capital.

Although recently they have been experiencing economic problems, they have been able to attract outside investors, including:

(1) Volkswagen taking a $6.6 billion stake in the Skoda Auto Works;
(2) Japan's Fravalex purchasing the glass manufacturer Sklo-Union Teplice for $1 billion;
(3) Linde of Germany investing $106 million in Technoplyn, a natural gas company;
(4) US West and Bell Atlantic entering into an $80 million telecommunications joint venture with the Czech government to produce telephone switches;
(5) Swedish furniture maker Ikea investing $60 million in a furniture production plant in Trnava; and
(6) Siemens of Germany investing $35 million for an interest in Electromagnetica, a medical equipment company, and $15 million in Tesla Karin, a telecommunications firm.

There also has been a movement toward teaching Western-style business courses, as well as MBA programs in all the Central European countries. In Hungary, state-owned hotels have been privatized, and Western firms, attracted by the low cost of highly skilled, professional labour, have been entering into joint ventures with local companies. MNCs also have been making direct investments, as in the case of General Electric's purchase of Tungsram, the giant Hungarian electric company. Another example is Britain's Telfos Holdings, which paid $19 million for 51 percent of Ganz, a Hungarian locomotive and rolling stock manufacturer. Still others include Suzuki's investment of $110 million in a partnership arrangement to produce cars with local manufacturer Autokonzern, Ford Motor's construction of a new $80 million car component plant, and Italy's Ilwa $25 million purchase of the Salgotarjau Iron Works. Poland had a head start on the other former communist bloc countries. General political elections were held in June 1989, and the first non-communist government was established, well before the fall of the Berlin Wall. In 1990, the Communist Polish United Workers Party dissolved, and Lech Walesa was elected President. Earlier than its neighbours, Poland instituted radical economic reforms (characterized as the so-called "shock therapy").

Although the relatively swift transition to a market economy has been very difficult for the Polish people, with very high inflation initially, continuing unemployment, and the decline of public services, Poland's economy has done relatively well. However, political instability and risk, large external debts, a still-deteriorating infrastructure, and only modest education levels have led to continuing economic problems.

Although Russia, the Czech Republic, Hungary, and Poland are the largest and receive the most media coverage, the other former communist countries also are struggling to right their economic ships. A small but particularly interesting example is Albania. Ruled ruthlessly by the Stalinist-style dictator Enver Hoxha for over four decades following World War II, Albania was the last, but most devastated, Eastern European country to abandon communism and institute radical economic reforms. At the beginning of the 1990s, Albania started from zero. Industrial output initially fell over 60 percent, and inflation reached 40 percent monthly. Today, Albania still struggles but is slowly making progress. The key for Albania and the other Eastern European countries is to maintain the social order, establish the rule of law, rebuild the collapsed infrastructure, and get factories and other value-added, job-producing firms up and running. Foreign investment must be forthcoming for these countries to join the global economy. A key challenge for Albania and the other "have-not" Eastern European countries will be to make themselves less risky and more attractive for international business.

Asia

Despite the severe economic downturn starting in 1997, Asia in general has bounced back and promises to continue being one of the major players in the world economy. Because there are far too many nations to allow for comprehensive coverage here, the following provides insights into the economic status and international management challenges of selected Asian countries.

Japan

During the 1970s and 1980s, Japan's economic success had been without precedent. The country had a huge positive trade balance, the yen was strong, and in manufacturing and consumer goods the Japanese became recognized as a world leader. Analysts ascribe Japan's phenomenal success to a number of factors. Some areas that have received a lot of attention are the Japanese cultural values supporting a strong work ethic and group/team effort, consensus decision making, the motivational effects of guaranteed lifetime employment, and the overall commitment that Japanese workers have to their organizations. However, as seen in "International Management in Action: Separating Myths from Reality," at least some of these assumptions about the Japanese workforce have turned out to be more myth than reality and some of the former strengths have become weaknesses in the new economy. For example, consensus decision making turns out to be too time-consuming in the speed-based new economy. Some of the early success of the Japanese economy can be attributed to the **Ministry of International Trade and Industry (MITI)**. This is a governmental agency that identifies and ranks national commercial pursuits and guides the distribution of national resources to meet these goals. In recent years, MITI has given primary attention to the so called ABCD industries: automation, biotechnology, computers, and data processing. Another major reason for Japanese success was the use of **Keiretsus.**

Keiretsus is an organizational arrangement in Japan in which a large group of vertically integrated companies bound together by cross-ownership, interlocking directorates, and social ties provide goods and services to end users. This Japanese term stands for the large, vertically integrated corporations whose holdings provide much of the assistance needed in providing goods and services to end users. Being able to draw from the resources of the other parts of the keiretsu, a Japanese MNC often can get things done more quickly and profitably than its international competitors.

Over the years, Japanese multinationals have invested billions of dollars abroad. In both the United States and the EU, Japanese auto firms have built new assembly plants. Japanese MNCs have made controversial acquisitions as well, including such well-known U.S. landmarks as Rockefeller Center, the Pebble Beach golf course, and Columbia Pictures. Beginning in the 1990s, however, there was a marked slowdown in overseas investment, and Japan's international holdings declined. This decline was mostly attributable to the slowing of the Japanese economy; however, poor management decisions also played an important role. For example, in the case of Rockefeller Center, Mitsubishi found that it was unable to generate sufficient revenue to pay the huge interest on its mortgage. As a result, it sought protection under American bankruptcy laws, causing a furor among the investors who held the mortgage and demanded the company dip into its corporate coffers and make the payments. Now for over 10 years, the Japanese economy has endured a serious recession. The government has had great difficulty correcting the situation. During the 1980s many major Japanese banks made large loans to local businesses. Some of these loans were backed up with real estate, while others were based on projected revenues. In the early 1990s when the Japanese real estate market collapsed, these loans were no longer fully collateralized and the borrowers, in most cases, could not afford to pay the debt. At the same time, the economy began slowing up and many businesses found that with reduced profits they could not meet their loan obligations to the banks. By the turn of the century the situation was so bad that most of the major banks had billions of dollars in uncollectible loans on their books and lacked the financial resources to make additional loans that could help turn around the economy. At the same time, the government began insisting that the banks write off their bad loans and straighten out their portfolios. Coupled with these problems, international competition increased and small and medium-sized Japanese firms found themselves scurrying to stay afloat and corporate bankruptcies have reached record levels. Yet, despite these setbacks, Japan remains a formidable international competitor (the second largest economy behind the U.S.) and is well poised in all three major economic regions: the Pacific Rim, North America, and Europe.

Japan also has been the target of foreign investment. Automakers such as BMW and Mercedes annually dominate foreign auto sales in the Japanese market. Meanwhile, Ford and General Motors, among others, are working on building market share in the Japanese auto market. IBM, Coca-Cola, Dow, McDonald's, and Toys "R" US also do well in Japan, collectively accounting for annual sales of over $150 billion. Moreover, the future likely will see even greater progress. Other MNCs, particularly those from the EU and newly industrialized Pacific Rim countries, are targeting the Japanese market as well. Given that Japan relies heavily on exporting to sustain its economic growth, the years ahead should prove to be interesting as international managers from around the world continue to compete against the down but not out Japan, Inc.

China

During the 1980s, China's average annual real economic growth was about 10 percent. From 1990 to 1995 GDP maintained this spectacular rate of growth and by the turn of the century, despite a severe economic downturn in the late nineties by its Asian neighbours, the awakened giant China reported an annual GDP growth of 8 percent. This continuing growth in tough times shows that its economy is healthy and growing stronger. At the same time, however, some international economists believe that China may overstate its growth rate and that it is really closer to 6 percent. Others contend that even if the country has been growing at a healthy rate, China will be unable to maintain it and, in fact, the Asian Development Bank recently forecasted the country's growth rate for the early years of the new century at 6 to 6.5 percent. The ruling communist government has set 8 percent as a target which is needed to handle the continual influx of workers from the countryside.

Despite being caught up in the economic problems facing all of Asia, China continues to attract foreign investment. Among others, Motorola has put $120 million into facilities producing semiconductors and mobile phones; General Motors has a $100 million investment in a truck assembly plant, and Procter & Gamble has invested $10 million in a joint-venture factory to produce laundry and personal care products. Additionally, the country's exports remain high with the U.S., Japan, and the EU importing billions of dollars of goods from China every year. At the same time, however, China remains a major political risk for investors. The one country, two systems (communism and capitalism) is a delicate balance to maintain and foreign businesses are often caught in the middle.

Most MNCs find it very difficult to do business in and with China and have yet to make a profit. Many of them have also found that product pirating is still common, and while the government has promised to prosecute companies that engage in this illegal and unethical practice, much remains to be done about it. Perhaps even more disconcerting for MNCs is that contractual agreements often prove to be worthless. For example, McDonald's received a long-run lease on property in Beijing and built a large restaurant there; since then the government has told the company that it must move because the entire area is to be razed and turned into a huge office and retail complex. This is not an isolated incident. Outside chemical producers have found themselves facing $10,000-per-product "registration fees," and U.S. law firms operating in Shanghai were forced to close until the government granted them new licenses. German and Japanese banks have found that collecting loans from the government can be extremely difficult as well. In addition, some securities firms have learnt that Chinese clients sometimes refuse to pay for trades that turn out to be losers, and there is no government protection for such actions. Simply put, China remains a complicated and high risk venture. Even so, MNCs know that China with its 1.3 billion people will be a major world market and that they must have a presence there.

The Four Tigers In addition to Japan and China, there are four other widely recognized economic powerhouses in Asia. Note that the traditionally used term "newly industrialized countries" (NICs) is not used, because they are not really new anymore. South Korea, Hong Kong, Singapore, and Taiwan have arrived as major economic powers and probably now should be referred to more accurately as the "Four Tigers." The GDP of all four had grown rapidly up until the problems starting in the Southeast Asian countries of Thailand, Indonesia, and Malaysia in 1997 began to affect them also.

In South Korea, the major cônglomerates, called **chaebols,** are the very large, family-held Korean conglomerates that have considerable political and economic power. These include such internationally known firms as Samsung, Daewoo, Hyundai, and the LG Group.

Many key managers in these huge firms have attended universities in the West, where in addition to their academic programs; they learned the culture, customs, and language. Now they are able to use this information to help formulate competitive international strategies for their firms. This will be very helpful for South Korea, which among the Four Tigers was hardest hit by the 1997 Southeast Asian economic crisis. Its GDP declined in the late 1990s and the value of its currency dropped almost 50 percent against the dollar. This led the government to announce plans for investigating the ethical and even illegal practices of the chaebols, privatizing a wide range of industries, and withdrawing some of the restrictions on overall foreign ownership. Since then, things have started improving. GDP increased by more than 7 percent at the turn of the century and new company formations reached an all-time high. Additionally, auto exports rose sharply with Hyundai and Daewoo, in particular, dramatically increasing their U.S. market share. Bordering southeast China and now part of the PRC (People's Republic of China), Hong Kong has been the headquarters for some of the most successful multinational operations in Asia.

Hong Kong has had some economic problems like its neighbors but has bounced back. Although it can rely heavily on southeast China for manufacturing, there is still uncertainty about the future and the role that the Chinese government intends to play in local governance. Although the transition has gone smoothly so far, there is the risk that the business climate could radically change. However, the former British colony should continue to play a strong international role in the Pacific Rim.

Singapore is a major success story. It has been hurt least by the economic downturn because of its solid foundation. A major problem Singapore now faces is how to continue expanding this economic foundation in the face of increasing international competition. To date, however, Singapore has emerged as an urban planner's ideal model and the leader and financial centre of Southeast Asia. As shown in Table 1.2, Singapore continues to be near the top of the list of the world's most competitive nations.

The fourth Tiger, Taiwan, has progressed from a labour-intensive economy to one that is dominated by more technologically sophisticated industries, including banking, electricity generation, petroleum refining, and computers. Although its economy has also been hit by the downturn in Asia, like the other Tigers, it has bounced back and remains a major economic power in the Pacific Rim. China considers Taiwan to be a breakaway province and this continues to be a real threat not only to geopolitics but also contributes to risk in doing business there. However, Taiwan's government continues to work out its relationship with the mainland to at least maintain the *status quo.*

TABLE 1.4. The World's Most Competitive Nations

Country	*Rank*
United States	1
Singapore	2
Finland	3
Netherlands	4
Switzerland	5
Luxembourg	6
Ireland	7
Germany	8
Sweden	9
Iceland	10
Canada	11
Denmark	12
Australia	13
Hong Kong	14
United Kingdom	15

Source: World Competitiveness Scoreboard, 2000.

Each of the Four Tigers has been the target of foreign MNCs. For example, IBM and Hewlett-Packard, determined to build their local shares of the computer market, have invested in laboratories and factories within these countries. Motorola has followed the same strategy in enlarging its telecommunications market. Other major MNCs in "Tiger Country" range from the Japanese (Matsushita, Nissan, and Sharp) to the Europeans (Volkswagen, Philips, and Nestlé). As a result, the amount of trade and investment occurring between the Four Tigers and the rest of the world continues to expand.

Southeast Asian Countries

Besides Singapore, other countries of Southeast Asia also should be recognized. Although not yet having the economic prowess of the Four Tigers and suffering economic problems starting in 1997, Thailand, Malaysia, Indonesia (sometimes called the "Baby Tigers"), and now Vietnam have economically developed along the lines of the Four Tigers. All have a relatively large population base, inexpensive labor, and, unlike the Four Tigers, they do have considerable natural resources. These countries were also known to have social stability, but in the aftermath of the economic crisis there has been considerable turmoil in this part of the world, especially the fourth largest populated country in the world, Indonesia. Nevertheless, as Japan and the Four Tigers have begun to level off and mature, these export-driven Southeast Asian countries remain attractive to outside investors. MNCs from Japan, the Four Tigers, North America, and the EU all want to have a presence in these countries.

Less Developed Countries

In contrast to the fully developed countries of North America, Europe, and Asia are the less developed countries (LDCs) around the world. An LDC typically is characterized by two or more of the following: low GDP, slow (or negative) GDP growth per capita, high unemployment, high international debt, a large population, and a workforce that is either unskilled or semiskilled. In some cases, such as in the Middle East, there also is considerable government intervention in economic affairs. In recent years, some of these LDCs have shown improvement, but they still have a long way to go to fully compete in the world market place. Here, the focus is on representative LDCs and regions.

India

With a population of about 1 billion and growing, India has traditionally had more than its share of political and economic problems. Per-capita GDP remains low, but there is still a large middle- and upper-class market for goods and services. Although India's economic growth does not compare with that of countries such as China, there has been a steady growth in recent years. The government continues its attempt to attract investors and further stimulate economic growth.

For a number of reasons, India is attractive to multinationals, and especially to U.S. and British firms. Many Indian people speak English and are very well educated and are known for advanced information technology expertise. Also, the Indian government is providing funds for economic development. For example, India is expanding its telecommunication systems and increasing the number of phone lines five-fold, a market that AT&T is vigorously pursuing. Many frustrations remain in doing business in India, but there is little question that the country will receive increased attention in the years ahead.

Middle East and Central Asia

Israel, the Arab countries, Iran, Turkey, and the Central Asian countries of the former Soviet Union are considered by the World Bank to be LDCs. Because of their oil, however, some people would consider these countries to be economically rich. Recently, this region has been in the world news because of the aftermath of the September 11, 2001 terrorism attack on the U.S. However, these countries continue to try to balance the geopolitical, religious forces with economic viability. For example, Israel has been hard hit by inflation, and although the GDP per capita is well over $18,000, there are balance-of-payment problems. Economic problems continue to plague all the countries in the region. Despite the tragedies and economic problems, the Middle East countries continue to be active in the international business arena, and students of international management should have a working knowledge of these countries' customs, culture, and management practices.

The Arab and Central Asian countries rely almost exclusively on oil production. The price of oil greatly fluctuates and the Organization of Petroleum Exporting Countries (OPEC) has trouble holding together its cartel. In recent years the price has been relatively high and world demand is likely to keep it there. Most industrial nations rely, at least to some degree, on imported oil and Arab countries have invested billions of dollars in U.S. property and businesses. Many people around the world, including those in the West, work for Arab employers. For example, the bankrupt United Press International was purchased by the Middle East Broadcasting Centre, a London-based MNC owned by the Saudis.

Africa

Even though they have considerable natural resources, on the whole African nations remain very poor and undeveloped, and international trade is not a major source of income. Although African countries do business with developed countries, it is on a limited scale. One major problem of doing business in the African continent is the overwhelming diversity of about 750 million people divided into 3,000 tribes that speak 1,000 languages and dialects. Also, there is political instability in many countries with the associated risks, especially as far as direct foreign investment is concerned.

In recent years, Africa, especially sub-Saharan Africa, has had a number of severe problems. In addition to tragic tribal wars, there has been the spread of terrible diseases such as AIDS and Ebola. Other big problems include poverty, starvation, illiteracy, corruption, social breakdown, vanishing resources, overcrowded cities, drought, and homeless refugees. There is still hope in the future for Africa despite this bleak situation, however, because African countries remain virtually untapped. Not only are there considerable natural resources, but the diversity can also be used to advantage. For example, many African people are familiar with the European cultures and languages of the former colonial powers (e.g., English, French, Dutch, and Portuguese), which can serve them well in international business. Also, the spirit of these emerging countries has not been broken. There are continuing efforts to stimulate economic growth. Examples of what can be done include Togo, which has sold off many of its state-owned operations and leased a steel-rolling mill to a U.S. investor, and Guinea, which has sold off some of its state-owned enterprises and cut its civil service force by 30 percent. A special case is South Africa, where apartheid, the former white government's policies of racial segregation and oppression, has been dismantled and the healing process is progressing. Long-jailed former black president Nelson Mandela is recognized as a world leader. These significant developments have led to an increasing number of the world's MNCs returning to South Africa; however, there continue to be both social and economic problems which, despite Mandela's and his successors' best efforts, signal uncertain times for the years ahead.

❆ ❆ ❆

2 Globalization and World Developments

• Globalization • Global Development and Trends • Cultural Awareness and Implications • Cross Cultural Management • Global Strategic Skills • Culture and Cross Cultural Research Findings • The Global Manager • Management Perspective to Globalization

The global economy has arrived. In the United States, dramatically increasing numbers of not only large corporations but medium and small firms going international, and a growing percentage of overall revenue coming from overseas markets. The same is true throughout Europe, Asia, and the rest of the world. In addition, globalization is presenting challenges for governments, corporations, and communities around the world. As a result, international management, the process of applying management concepts and techniques in a multinational environment, is rapidly gaining importance.

Although there has been considerable historical evolution, the overriding focus of this chapter is to examine the process of globalization and developments of the last few years. The end of the cold war and the onset of the Information Age have created a new world and true global competition. These developments both create and influence the opportunities, challenges, and problems that managers in the international arena will face during the years ahead.

International trade and investment have been increasing dramatically over the years. Major multinational corporations (MNCs) have holdings throughout the world, from North America to Europe to the Pacific Rim to Africa. Some of these holdings are a result of direct investment; others are partnership arrangements with local firms. Small firms also are finding that they must seek out international markets to survive in the future. The internationalization of nearly all business has arrived.

International economic activity is most pronounced in the triad of North America, Europe, and the Pacific Rim. In North America, the United States, Canada, and Mexico have the North American Free Trade Agreement (NAFTA) that is turning the region into one giant market. In South America, there is an increasing amount of inter-country trade, sparked by Mercosur and the Andean Pact nations. Additionally, others such as Chile have been projected to may be part of NAFTA. In Europe, the 15 countries of the European Union (EU) form a major economic power, and the former communist countries to the east are seeking membership in the EU. The Central European countries of the Czech Republic, Poland, and Hungary already are becoming trading partners, and if Russia and the other Eastern European countries make progress in their transformation efforts, then Greater Europe will be an even more formidable market in the future. Although having economic problems and uncertainty like the rest of the world, Asia is another major regional power, as shown not only by Japan but also the economies of China and the Four Tigers (Singapore, South Korea, Hong Kong, and Taiwan). Other areas of the world, including India, the Middle East and Central Asia, and Africa, continue to have complex problems, but still hold economic promise for the future.

Globalization

Globalization is the increasing interconnection of people and places as a result of advances in transport, communication, and information technologies that causes political, economic, and cultural convergence. Globalization is viewed as a century's long process, tracking the expansion of human population and the growth of civilization that has accelerated dramatically in the past 50 years. Early forms of globalization existed during the Roman Empire, the Parthian empire, and the Han Dynasty, when the Silk Road started in China, reached the boundaries of the Parthian empire, and continued onwards towards Rome. The Islamic Golden Age is also an example, when Muslim traders and explorers established an early global economy across the Old World resulting in a globalization of crops, trade, knowledge and technology; and later during the Mughal Empire, when there was greater integration along the Silk Road. Global integration continued through the expansion of European trade, as in the 16th and 17th centuries, when the Portuguese and Spanish Empires reached to all corners of the world after expanding to the Americas.

Globalization became a business phenomenon in the 17th century when the Dutch East India Company, which is often described as the first multinational corporation, was established. Because of the high risks involved with international trade, the Dutch East India Company became the first company in the world to share risk and enable joint ownership through the issuing of shares: an important driver for globalization.

Liberalization in the 19th century is sometimes called "The First Era of Globalization", a period characterized by rapid growth in international trade and investment, between the European imperial powers, their colonies, and, later, the United States. It was in this period that areas of sub-Saharan Africa and the Island Pacific were incorporated into the world system. The "First Era of Globalization" began to break down at the beginning with the First World War, and later collapsed during the gold standard crisis in the late 1920s and early 1930s

Policy Factors

Global development policy is a task for the whole government and not merely a development assistance issue. All policy areas have a common overall objective for global development policy: to contribute to equitable and sustainable global development. Where development is concerned there are no simple solutions. A number of factors have emerged that are mutually reinforcing and represent the values that will permeate country's global development policy. These are:

- Respect for human rights
- Democracy and good governance
- Gender equality
- Economic growth
- Social development and welfare.

The rights perspective highlights the central importance of human rights as expressed in the United Nations Universal Declaration of Human Rights and subsequent declarations including the Convention of the Rights of the Child and the Convention on the elimination of All Forms of discrimination against women. Human rights regulate the relationship between the state and the individual. It is the responsibility of the state to ensure that individuals can enjoy their rights and those rights are respected. These rights and conventions provide a normative basis for what constitutes a dignified life and include civil and political rights as well as economic, social and cultural rights.

Gender equality is a cross-cutting policy task and also a key Millennium Development Goal. Despite all the progress that has been made, when it comes to promoting gender equality and empowering women, the achievements of development policy to date are far from satisfactory.

The global economy has been especially strong in recent years. World-wide per capita income is growing as rapidly as ever before. Incorporating recently available projections for 2007, global gross domestic product (GDP) per capita has increased in the last five years (2003-2007) at an annual average rate of 2.3 percent. This compares with 1.2 per cent from

1990 to 2002 and with 1.4 percent from 1981 to 1989. Sustained global growth rates of this magnitude are unprecedented since the immediate post-WW II era and part of the 1960s.

Developing countries are now playing a major role as drivers of global growth. High income countries were responsible for 85 percent of the global cumulative growth in GDP from 1960 to 1973, 78 percent from 1973 to 2001, but only 63 percent from 2001 to 2005. If GDP is measured at purchasing power parities (PPPs) developing countries are now by far the largest contributors to global growth. Also reflecting the increasing weight of developing countries, when global GDP is measured at PPPs global per capita growth registers about 3 percent a year since the beginning of this century. And since the developing economies that are expanding rapidly are very large, such as China and India, if we weight per capita GDP growth by population, global growth has been even more impressive – it goes up to values above 4.5 percent a year, with GDP in PPP.

Developing countries are propelling global growth and capturing, as whole, increasing shares of global income. But how widely shared across developing countries have been the benefits from global economic growth?

One group of developing countries, representing a huge share of world population, has been at the forefront of global growth. Their economies are growing faster than those of developed countries. They are also starting to catch up with the wealthiest nations in terms of human development. Millions of their citizens are being lifted out of poverty every year, with life expectancy, child mortality and literacy converging on first-world levels. These countries are accessing global markets for goods, capital, and technology; they are trading more and more with each other as well as with rich countries. The share of global trade captured by developing countries – primarily due to these well performing developing countries – is now 37 percent, compared with 29 percent in 1996.

However, another group of developing countries – greater in number, if smaller in population – is being left behind. These countries are today farther away economically from the richest countries than ever before. Cross-country inequalities in mean income, which have grown relentlessly over the last two hundred years, continue to widen. The ratio of PPP GDP per capita in the 10 richest countries to PPP GDP per capita in the 10 poorest increased from about 21 in 1960 to 34 in 1990, and increased further to 47 in 2001 and to 50 in 2005. With GDP expressed in market exchange rates, the ratios are much higher. Some countries have also seen a sharp drop in life expectancy, in most (but not all) cases as a result of HIV/AIDS.

Social Welfare Policy can be defined as a clearly articulated statement of the government describing a course of action/s to be implemented in order to achieve set goals and objectives as far as social welfare is concerned. The aim of the Government of the British Virgin Islands is to build a socially cohesive, a thriving community through integrated social and economic policies which seek to strengthen community relations, minimize social tensions, strengthen families, and eradicate poverty. The long term objectives of the government is to establish a policy and institutional framework which will promote the rights of poorer and more vulnerable members of society, enhance their livelihood opportunities and increase their access to social services. Therefore, the Government needs to formulate community development and social welfare policy guidelines particularly as regards issues affecting children, juveniles, the elderly, the disabled, the poor families and gender. The government provides a wide range of services for the less fortunate and senior members of the society. These include, social security benefits, home care for the aged, children with special problems, as well as help for women affected by domestic abuse, rehabilitation facilities and programmes, a learning centre for children with the special needs and free and subsidised health care. The free and subsidized health care is supposed to cover a number of groups that are exempted from charges. These include persons aged 65 years and over, school children, the mentally ill, the indigent, prisoners; public sector health workers etc. In the absence of a national health insurance scheme, the Social Security Board (SSB) plays a significant role in financing health care in the territory. Under the social security scheme to which contributions are mandatory, all employees over the age of 15 are covered for a range of health related benefits. The SSB also allocates a portion of its income to improvements in public health services on an ad hoc basis. While the welfare system has been expanding in recent years, its efficiency and effectiveness are hampered by the absence of clear policies and inadequacy of the database. Therefore, to provide better services we need to develop clear policies in respect of procedures, rules, benefit payments etc. Also we need to strengthen and improve the database. In addition the quantity and quality of human resources need to be improved.

The annual report of World Bank, **Global Development Finance 2007**, released today says that sustaining recent high growth in South Asia will require continued economic reform, expansion of infrastructure capacity, and further reduction of security threats. The report predicts that these efforts will also contribute to higher capital inflows, which have been spurred by progress in these areas in recent years.

Revamping tax collection systems to reduce evasion and improve tax collection to help finance the extensive government agendas is also important.

Increased political instability represents another main risk. Heightened security concerns could hurt investor sentiment and undermine foreign capital inflows, which have contributed to the region's record four-year expansion.

The continued easing of political tensions between the governments of India and Pakistan bodes well for continued progress toward improved relations.

Gross Domestic Product (GDP)

GDP in South Asia expanded a robust 8.6 percent in 2006, reflecting generally expansionary policy conditions. Growth was down slightly from 2005 due primarily to a deceleration of growth in Pakistan.

In **Afghanistan**, GDP growth is expected to accelerate over the forecast horizon, initially due to an anticipated recovery from drought in the agricultural sector, and over the forecast horizon due to the simulative impact 135 of donor-led construction projects.

In **Bhutan**, growth is expected to remain robust, rising by a projected 17 percent in 2007—a sharp acceleration from the estimated 5.5 percent in 2006.

- This is driven primarily by the effects of the Tala hydropower project (the plant is expected to begin operating at full capacity in mid-2007), and to a lesser extent by the expanding tourism industry.
- Growth in Bhutan is expected to decelerate to 10 percent in 2008 and 5 percent in 2009 as impacts of the hydropower project unwind.

In **India**, GDP increased by 9.2 % although signs of slowing appeared at the end of the year. India's restrictive policy conditions are expected to lead to deceleration in investment growth and weaker private consumption and government spending, contributing to a slowdown in GDP growth to 7.8 percent and 7.5 in 2008 and 2009, respectively.

In the **Maldives**, an expansion of GDP growth is expected to be supported by the ongoing reconstruction effort following the devastating December 2004 tsunami.

Growth is projected to strengthen in **Nepal** due to improved political conditions and cessation of fighting.

Pakistan's GDP increased by 6.6 percent in 2006 significantly down from the 7.8 percent growth rate recorded the previous year.

Sri Lanka is projected to hover close to 6.0 percent during 2007–09, down from 7.4 percent in 2006, due to disruptive effects of civil war.

Capital Inflows

Net capital inflows to South Asia increased to $40.1 billion (3.6 percent of GDP) in 2006, up from $28.3 billion (2.8 percent of GDP) in 2005.

Strong capital inflows were largely due to a $12 billion expansion in net private debt flows, while net equity inflows to the region increased only slightly, as a $3 billion increase in FDI was partly offset by a decline in portfolio equity flows.

At $22.9 billion in 2006, net equity inflows nonetheless account for the bulk (60 percent) of net private inflows to the region. Much of the FDI inflows into India were concentrated in the service sector (telecommunications in particular) in response to liberalization policies designed to attract FDI, such as easing ownership restrictions.

FDI outflows from India are also on the rise due to increasing cross-border M&A purchases by Indian companies, mainly in high-income economies. Since 2004, FDI flows from India to the United Kingdom exceeded flows from the United Kingdom to India. The Indian multinational Tata acquired the Dutch steel company Corus for more than $10 billion in early 2007.

FDI inflows to Pakistan increased from $2.2 billion in 2005 to $3.5 billion in 2006 with much of investment in the oil and gas and financial sectors, along with installments made on a major telecom privatization deal in 2005.

Inflation

Rapid growth and the relatively expansionary stance of fiscal and monetary policies in the region have provoked a rise in inflation.

Higher oil prices in the first half of 2006 and strong domestic demand contributed to deterioration in the region's current account balance, despite strong exports and remittances inflows.

Global Development and Trends

Globalization offers extensive opportunities for truly worldwide development but it is not progressing evenly. Some countries are becoming integrated into the global economy more quickly than others. Countries that have been able to integrate are seeing faster growth and reduced poverty. Outward-oriented policies brought dynamism and greater prosperity to much of East Asia, transforming it from one of the poorest areas of the world 40 years ago. And as living standards rose, it became possible to make progress on democracy and economic issues such as the environment and work standards.

The crises in the emerging markets in the 1990s have made it quite evident that the opportunities of globalization do not come without risks—risks arising from volatile capital movements and the risks of social, economic, and environmental degradation created by poverty. This is not a reason to reverse direction, but for all concerned—in developing countries, in the advanced countries, and of course investors—to embrace policy changes to build strong economies and a stronger world financial system that will produce more rapid growth and ensure that poverty is reduced. Markets promote efficiency through competition and the division of labour—the specialization that allows people and economies to focus on what they do best. Global markets offer greater opportunity for people to tap into more and larger markets around the world. It means that they can have access to more capital flows, technology, cheaper imports, and larger export markets. But markets do not necessarily ensure that the benefits of increased efficiency are shared by all. Countries must be prepared to embrace the policies needed, and in the case of the poorest countries may need the support of the international community as they do so.

20th Century Income Trends

The story of the 20th century was of remarkable average income growth, but it is also quite obvious that the progress was not evenly dispersed. The gaps between rich and poor countries, and rich and poor people within countries, have grown. The richest quarter of the world's population saw its per capita GDP increase nearly six-fold during the century, while the poorest quarter experienced less than a three-fold increase. Income inequality has clearly increased. But, as noted below, per capita GDP does not tell the whole story.

The 20th century saw unparalleled economic growth, with global per capita GDP increasing almost five-fold. But this growth was not steady—the strongest expansion came during the second half of the century, a period of rapid trade expansion accompanied by trade—and typically somewhat later, financial—liberalization.

Consider four aspects of globalization:

- Trade
- Capital movements
- Movement of people
- Spread of knowledge (and technology)

As globalization has progressed, living conditions (particularly when measured by broader indicators of well-being) have improved significantly in virtually all countries. However, the strongest gains have been made by the advanced countries and only some of the developing countries.

That the income gap between high-income and low-income countries has grown wider is a matter for concern. And the number of the world's citizens in abject poverty is deeply disturbing. But it is wrong to jump to the conclusion that globalization has caused the divergence, or that nothing can be done to improve the situation. To the contrary: low-income countries have not been able to integrate with the global economy as quickly as others, partly because of their chosen policies and partly because of factors outside their control. No country, least of all the poorest, can afford to remain isolated from the world economy. Every country should seek to reduce poverty. The international community should endeavor—by strengthening the international financial system, through trade, and through aid — to help the poorest countries integrate into the world economy, grow more rapidly and reduce poverty. That is the way to ensure all people in all countries have access to the benefits of globalization

Cultural Awareness and Implications

In today's global workplace, business is constantly changing. Companies acquire, merge or partner with other firms to promote business internationally. The workplace has become increasingly diverse; employees are expected to relocate often to destination halfway around the world. Therefore cultural awareness is imperative in our global environment.

Cultural Awareness is the key to a successful international relocation and cross-cultural orientation. Employees deal with a variety of relocation and intercultural challenges as they transition to their new home and workplace.

Important issues include dealing with an unfamiliar language, the lack of cultural awareness, limited knowledge of new business protocol and the complexities of finding suitable housing.

So basically, Cultural Awareness is the foundation of communication and it involves the ability of standing back from us and becoming aware of our cultural values, beliefs and perceptions.

Four Levels of Cultural Awareness:

1. First level uses information about the 'other' culture to create superficial stereotype.
2. Second level based on an expanded knowledge of 'other' culture that focuses on its differences, the subsequent difficulties it presents.
3. The third level accepts the 'other' culture at an intellectual level and uses it as frame of reference for understanding.
4. In the fourth level, empathy of the 'other' culture is achieved through direct experience.

Implications

Global identity promotes working for the good of the whole, with its emphasis on universal human rights. At its best, it inspires co-ordination and co-operation among the people of all nations to improve the quality of life for all.

Yet people who see themselves as 'world citizens' may not fully appreciate or respect national differences.

Well intentional internationalists may over-generate or generalize a practice that has proved useful in their own country and take an appropriate "one-size fits all" approach that is actually based on ethnocentric assumptions. Less well-intentioned internationalists may take an imperialist view of the world as a field of operations for oneself and one's country, often with scant regard for the aspirations of people who interests are not in harmony with one's own.

Global development promotes cooperation across national boundaries with similarly identified others, through trade, political ties or mutual aid.

Global development thus, helps in improving efficiency and making market more optimized by taking advantage of the opportunities of the global environment.

Cross-Cultural Management

Culture is derived from the Latin word "cultura" stemming from "colere", meaning "to cultivate". Generally, culture refers to patterns of human activity and the symbolic structures that give such activities significance and importance. Different definitions of "culture" reflect different theoretical bases for understanding, or criteria for evaluating, human activity.

Culture is manifested in music, literature, painting and sculpture, theater and film and other things.

1. Although some people identify culture in terms of consumption and consumer goods (as in high culture, low culture, folk culture, or popular culture).

2. Anthropologists understand "culture" to refer not only to consumption goods, but to the general processes which produce such goods and give them meaning, and to the social relationships and practices in which such objects and processes become embedded. For them, culture thus includes technology, art, science, as well as moral systems.

Anthropologists most commonly use the term "culture" to refer to the universal human capacity to classify codify and communicate their experiences symbolically. This capacity has long been taken as a defining feature of the humans. However, primatologists have identified aspects of culture among humankind's closest relatives in the animal kingdom.

3. As a rule, archaeologists focus on material culture (the material remains of human activity), whereas social anthropologists focus on social interactions, statuses and institutions, and cultural anthropologists focus on norms and values. This division of labor reflects the different conditions under which different anthropologists have worked, and the practical need to focus research. It does not necessarily reflect a theory of culture that conceptually distinguishes between the material, the social, and the normative, nor does it reflect three competing theories of culture.

To understand the importance of culture in the context of new technologies, it is important to examine current definitions thereof. Most of these definitions are too narrow. First, sociologists and media theorists have focused on mass media aspects of popular culture. Some have even claimed that technology in itself is value-free. As a result debates have often been limited to whether (or not) technology plays a role in culture. Second, the institutions in which culture is shown, such as museums, galleries and theatres remain the products of highly specialized, nationalistic definitions of culture.

"*Culture is not just something we consume, but something we participate in. One by one, family by family, we signal what is important by what we respect, what we support and what we are grateful for.*"

Cross-Cultural Communication Strategies

The key to effective cross-cultural communication is knowledge. First, it is essential that people understand the potential problems of cross-cultural communication, and makes a conscious effort to overcome these problems. Second, it is important to assume that one's efforts will not always be successful, and adjust one's behaviour appropriately.

For example, one should always assume that there is a significant possibility that cultural differences are causing communication problems, and be willing to be patient and forgiving, rather than hostile and aggressive, if problems develop. One should respond slowly and carefully in cross-cultural exchanges, not jumping to the conclusion that you know what is being thought and said.

William Ury's suggestion for heated conflicts is to stop, listen, and think, or as he puts it "go to the balcony" when the situation gets tense. By this, he means withdraw from the situation, step back, and reflect on what is going on before you act. This helps in cross cultural communication as well. When things seem to be going badly, stop or slow down and think. What could be going on here? Is it possible I misinterpreted what they said, or they misinterpreted me? Often misinterpretation is the source of the problem. Active listening can sometimes be used to check this out–by repeating what one thinks he or she heard, one can confirm that one understands the communication accurately. If words are used differently between languages or cultural groups, however, even active listening can overlook misunderstandings.

In short we can make some observations on culture:

- Set of commonly held values.
- A way of life of a group of people includes knowledge, belief, art, morals, law, customs and habits.
- Everything that people have, think and do as members of their society.
- An integrated system of learned behaviour patterns that is characteristic of the members of any given society.

Cross Cultural Myths:

- Myth One: We really are all the same
- Myth Two: I just need to be myself and everything will be okay
- Myth Three: I have to adopt the practices of the other culture to succeed (Adapt rather than adopt).

Culture of the United States Towards their Work

In United States occupation is one of the prime factors of social class and is closely linked to an individual's identity. The average work week in the US for those employed full-time was 42.9 hours long with 30% of the population working more than 40 hours a week? It should be noted, however, that many of those in the top two earning quintiles often worked more than 50 a week. The Average American worker earned $16.64 an hour in the first two quarters of 2006. Overall Americans worked more than their counterparts in other developed post-industrial nations. While the average worker in Denmark enjoyed 30 days of vacation annually, the average American only had 16 annual vacation days. In 2000, the average American worked 1,978 hours per year, 500 hours more than the average German, yet 100 hours less than the average Czech. Overall the US labour force was the most productive in the world (overall, not by hour worked), largely due to its workers working more than those in any other post-industrial country (excluding South Korea). Americans generally hold working and being productive in high regard and being busy as well as working extensively may also serve as the means to obtain esteem.

US Values & Possible Alternatives

- Beliefs - control *versus* destiny
- Change - action *versus* accept
- Attitude - practical versus dreams, aspirations
- Approach/work ethic - hard work *versus* luck
- Promises - keep *versus* perhaps
- Time - depends on priorities
- Obligation -company or family
- Employment - short term *versus* lifelong
- Meritocracy - best person.

Stereotypical American (as seen by people of other countries):

- Inconsiderate of other people's cultures
- Ignorant of other countries
- Violent, aggressive
- Always in a hurry
- Outgoing, friendly
- Informal
- Loud, rude
- Hard working
- Arrogant, proud
- Innovative
- Extravagant, wasteful,
- Confident they have all the answers.

Language

There is a need to understand language because:

1. There is a close relationship between language and culture
2. Language is a precondition to success in international business
3. Languages help in understanding culture
4. Second language is first step to learning third and fourth language
5. Learning other languages helps us appreciate our own language (and culture).

High Context Versus Low Context Cultures

Low context cultures: task oriented, communication is specific, elaborate, and direct. (Swiss, German, American, British)

High context cultures: based on relationships, rely on communication that is: indirect, nonverbal, and the context. (Japanese, Chinese, Arab)

Negotiations

"A process between two or more parties aimed at reaching a mutually acceptable agreement"

Goal - to bring about a win-win situation where all parties benefit.

Process - preparation, relationship building, and exchange of task related information.

Effective Strategies for International Negotiators

1. Concentrate on long term relationships
2. Focus on interest behind the positions
3. Avoid reliance on cultural generalizations

4. Be sensitive to timing
5. Remain flexible
6. Prepare carefully
7. Learn to listen
8. Be patient

"Management is a form of work that involves co-ordinating an organization's resources - human and capital – to accomplish organizational goals."

In general terms, there are two approaches to management:

The Industrial Organization Approach: This approach is based on economic theory which deals with issues like competitive rivalry, resource allocation, economies of scale. This approach to management assumes rationality, self-interested behaviour, profit maximization.

The **Sociological Approach:** This approach deals primarily with human interactions. It assumes rationality, satisfying behaviour, profit sub-optimality.

Management theories can also be divided into two sets. One is the set that concentrates mainly on efficiency and another is the set that concentrates mainly on effectiveness. Efficiency is about doing things the right way. It involves eliminating waste and optimizing processes. Effectiveness is about doing the right things.

A good management style is a blend of both efficiency and effectiveness. There is no point in acting efficiently if what you are doing will not have the desired effect.

Management techniques can be viewed as either bottom-up, top-down, or collaborative processes.

In **India**, largely the top down approach is popular. In the top-down approach, the management makes the decisions, which the employees have no choice but to accept. On the other hand, in the bottom-up approach, employees submit proposals to their managers who, in turn, funnel the best ideas further up the organization. However, the bottom up approach is not a very popular approach in India, as most of the Indian businesses are family run businesses.

Roles of a Manager

Interpersonal - leader, figurehead

Informational - monitor, represent

Decisional - allocate resources, negotiate, problem solving

Management Skills

Conceptual skills - decision making, planning, organizing

Human relations skills - understand people, motivating, collaborating

Technical skills - able to get a particular job done.

What is International Management?

"Process of developing strategies, designing and operating systems, and working with people around the world to ensure sustained competitive advantage"

What are the variables affecting the management function?

National variables - economic system, political system

Socio-cultural variables - religion, education, language

Cultural variables - values, norms, beliefs

Attitudes - work, time, individualism, materialism

Response - motivation, productivity, ethics, commitment.

Global Strategic Skills

During the last half of the twentieth century, many barriers to international trade fell and a wave of firms began pursuing global strategies to gain a competitive advantage. However, some industries benefit more from globalization than do others, and some nations have a comparative advantage over other nations in certain industries. To create a successful global strategy, managers first must understand the nature of global industries and the dynamics of global competition.

A global industry can be defined as:

- An industry in which firms must compete in all world markets of that product in order to survive.
- An industry in which a firm's competitive advantage depends on economies of scale and economies of scope gained across markets.

Despite nearly two decades of corporate globalization efforts, many organizations still struggle to find managers who are comfortable and effective in the increasingly global economy. Most suffer from a lack of cultural awareness when dealing with employees and partner overseas and from a lack of experience managing increasingly complex processes over long distances.

Global leaders and managers have to develop two sets of skills, strategic hard skills and leadership behaviour. This combination of hard and soft skills is often very difficult to find in one person. That is why teams should be formed around every major strategic initiative, and a balance should be struck between right-brained inspirational leaders and left-brained analytic leaders. The key is to always have respect, and always value differences, how ever opposed opinions could be, remembering there is never one right solution.

Strategic Hard Skills will always include:

- Understanding the needs of customers that want to benefit from the Global Market, and those that would benefit, but don't know or understand.
- Understanding how competitors, whether traditional rivals, newly formed companies, or emerging substitutes, can challenge your organization.
- Understand how to review current strategic activities, looking for opportunities and threats and comparing these with inside the organization's strengths and weaknesses.
- Understanding how to review new potential markets that can be developed profitably, how to engage with them, and go to market in them.
- Understand alternative sources of tangible and intangible supply and how to adapt the organization's supply chain to capitalize on value added identified.
- Understand how to build a global organization and the global communications structures and strategic pathways of knowledge flow that goes with that.

Leadership Behavioural Skills must include:

1. Intellectual capital:

- A knowledge of a range of appropriate and relevant global industries, normally gained by research and reading.
- To have global value networks, to understand different social, political, economic, and technological environments and the working of people from diverse cultures.
- Understanding how to build a global organization, remembering the rule of 'unswerving flexibility' as there is never one right answer, and the answer will change as more is known and understood.
- Being able to cope with cognitive complexity, as a one size fits all model can never work.
- Being open to cultural intelligence, and understanding the nuances of cultural and custom differences that exist even within parts of a country or region.

2. **Psychological capital:**

- A strong psychological profile that will value difference, welcome change, accept team think, be curious, be open, give and accept leadership, and build an empowered learning organization
- Display a positive attitude to cultural diversity, and without prejudice, value all differences
- Be transparent in all strategic endeavours with all of the team that comprise the global workforce and network.
- Is passionate about the execution of the strategy and capable of generating excitement around the journey to the completion of the vision.
- Will be cosmopolitan and be comfortable in a range of societies.

3. **Social capital:**

- Have the ability to connect to and work with people from other parts of the world.
- Have the skill to generate positive energy in people from other parts of the world, lead them and excite them.
- Have the ability to build mutually trusting relationships with people from other parts of the world.

Strategy is always open to interpretation and opinion, largely around cost, risk and speed of market entry or development. The logical skills and the process that all organizations must do to gain sufficient information and forecasts to enable them to embark upon a global strategy are highlighted here.

Strategy Formulation and Implementation in all Organizations

Strategy occurs at three levels:

1. Corporate Strategy: Deals with surviving and thriving; sets overall long term objectives; determines the scope of the business portfolio; manages the overall finances and often shareholder expectations; considers organizational competences and is co-ordinated amongst business streams. Resources are frequently allocated as a result of portfolio choice, and so the decisions about global strategy often reside here. The decisions tend to be around which business streams, in which region, and at what rate of return.

Only at this level can all-embracing global strategy be decided. It is an important to observe that nearly all organizations are not truly global. Because of their history or their aspirations, most organizations will be cautious about geographic entry strategies that fundamentally change their business model. Selectivity appears to be the rule.

2. Business Strategy: Is co-ordinated amongst functions and tends to have a one-or two-year time horizon. Business strategy is based on the goals and objectives given by corporate, and will be related to market and product development, growth and profit objectives. Go-to-market strategies are built at this level and joint business plans with partners are created. Much time is spent considering the development of competitive advantage by considering business chain elements, upstream and down stream. Marketing, distribution, and systems plans and policies are created and implemented at this level.

The outcome of the many business strategies (with separate missions and visions, building from the corporate strategic statements) would be a series of key actions and critical issues, that would be specific and measurable and time bound that could be then acted upon at functional level.

3. Functional Strategy: At this level, leadership is so important, from top down and bottom up. Functional strategy has much to do with co-ordinating amongst functions. Pricing strategies, promotion campaigns, and production and delivery schedules means there has to be much integration and balancing between functions to achieve a common goal.

Global strategy should start with corporate, but frequently, in reality, it starts with business strategy. Business level is very driven by expansionist targets and goals, and so by attempting to service the ever expanding needs of a key customer, individual business units can travel to far distant foreign lands with that customer, with nodding acquiescence from corporate, as long as the unit is 'beating the budget.' Functional strategy in all regions and countries and verticals within these countries, is actually the way in which global strategy is translated locally. So for global strategy to work, you do need local presence and local understanding. This of course means that all organizations must be "Glocal."

Culture and Cross Cultural Research Findings

Culture is the set of values, customs and beliefs that people have in common with other members of a social unit. The word **"Culture" derived from the** Latin word "*cultura*" stemming from "*colere" means* 'to cultivate," generally refers to patterns of human activity which have been cultivated over a period of time and gained acceptance.

Cross-culture means dealing with or comparing two or more cultures. Understanding organizational culture is vital in seeking new ways for changing organizations in a time of global economy, however organization culture doesn't exist in vacuum; it is always embedded with national culture. Managing international business means handling both national and organization culture differences at the same time. Organization cultures should be distinguished from national cultures.

National cultures distinguish similar people, institutions and organizations in different countries.

Organizational cultures distinguish different organizations within the same country or countries.

Research is the systematic process of collecting and analyzing information to increase our understanding of the phenomenon under study.

Understanding Cultural Differences

The world of today is drastically different from that of twenty, or even ten, years ago. The influence of multinational corporations, the technological revolution, the "Information Superhighway", and the movement of the private and public sectors towards globalization, sets the scene.

New laws, agreements and regional partnerships - from NAFTA to GATT to the EUROPEAN UNION or ASEAN — have contributed to make this massive change not only possible but also achievable.

This development demands a completely new approach to business or to any type of international relations and calls for a re-evaluation of strategies, of expansion and the use of **human resources.**

Because when it comes right down to making the deal, *it's people who make the difference.* It's the people in your company who have to make the contacts, make the commitments, and follow through on them. It's people who have to learn to understand and work with each other, whether it happens in person, over the phone, through the fax or by e-mail. And its people who have to make sure these new business relationships are built on a sound basis of understanding and mutual respect.

This is necessary because **globalization** could be a two-edge sword. The opposite site of immense potential markets is the challenge of understanding or *misunderstanding* an entirely new cultural milieu.

No matter whom you are or where you live, no matter what nation or culture you come from, you will need to recognize one very important truth when you do business with colleagues in other countries. Other people — although they may dress like you, speak your language, or even work for the same company - are not "just like you".

You'll do business with people that have very different histories, languages, and ways of doing business. They will have a different sense of time, and a different sense of humour. They will have different ways of negotiating, and different perceptions of when a deal has truly been made. They will also have different expectations of what it means to follow through on commitments and agreements. In a word, they will have different cultures.

Are you a sales manager setting up new distribution channels, a service representative working with overseas colleagues to set up new systems, a manager helping to run an overseas subsidiary or open a new manufacturing plant? Whoever you are, whatever you are doing, if you are interacting with people from other cultures, you need to know something about them

In one survey entitled what is the biggest barrier in doing business in the world market, cultural differences ranked first in all eight items including "law, price competition, information, language, delivery, foreign currency, time differences, and cultural differences.

A separate research project into organizational culture differences, conducted by IRIC across 20 organizational units in Denmark and the Netherlands in the 1980s, identified six independent dimensions of practices:

- Process-oriented *versus* results-oriented,
- Job-oriented *versus* employee-oriented,
- Professional *versus* parochial,
- Open systems *versus* closed systems,
- Tightly *versus* loosely controlled,
- Pragmatic *versus* normative.

The position of an organization on these dimensions is partly determined by the business or industry the organization is in. Scores on the dimensions are also related to a number of other 'hard' characteristics of the organizations. These lead to conclusions about how organization cultures can be and cannot be managed.

Cross-Cultural Similarities and Differences

For those who work in international business, it is sometimes amazing how different people in other cultures behave. We tend to have a human instinct that 'deep inside' all people are the same — but they are not. Therefore, if we go into another country and make decisions based on how we operate in our own home country the chances are we'll make some very bad decisions.

Also facing a completely new culture gives rise to what is known as culture shock.

It is not possible to do business the same way in every global location. Procedures and strategies that work well at home cannot be adopted overseas without modification.

One example of cultural differences in business is between the Middle Eastern countries and the Western countries, especially the United States.

When negotiating in Western countries, the objective is to work toward a target of mutual understanding and agreement and 'shake-hands' when that agreement is reached — a cultural signal of the end of negotiations and the start of 'working together'.

In Middle Eastern countries, much negotiation takes place leading into the 'agreement', signified by shaking hands. However, the deal is not complete in the Middle Eastern culture. In fact, it is a cultural sign that 'serious' negotiations are just beginning.

Imagine the problems this creates when each party in a negotiation is operating under diametrically opposed 'rules and conventions.'

This is just one example why it is critical to understand other cultures you may be doing business with - whether on a vacation in a foreign country, or negotiating a multi-million dollar deal for your company.

Some similarities have been found between cultures of countries. E.g., Russia and U.S. They have certain similarities regarding:

- Traditional management

- Communication
- Human Resources
- Networking activities

But there are far more differences than similarities *e.g.* there are differences in wages, compensation, pay equity, maternity leave, importance of criteria used in evaluation of employees etc.

Geert Hofstede Cultural Dimensions

According to Prof. Geert Hofstede - Emeritus Professor at Maastricht University, *"Culture is more often a source of conflict than of synergy. Cultural differences are a nuisance at best and often a disaster."*

Hofstede demonstrated that there are national and regional cultural groupings that affect the behavior of societies and organizations, and that are very persistent across time.

He conducted perhaps the most comprehensive study of how values in the workplace are influenced by culture. Geert Hofstede analyzed a large data base of employee values scores collected by IBM between 1967 and 1973 covering more than 70 countries. Now the scores are listed for 74 countries and regions, partly based on replications and extensions of the IBM study on different international populations.

From the results, Hofstede developed a model that identifies five dimensions to assist in differentiating cultures:

- Power Distance Index – PDI
- Individualism – IDV
- Masculinity – MAS
- Uncertainty Avoidance – UAI
- Long Term Orientation – LTO

Power Distance Index (PDI) that is the extent to which the less powerful members of organizations and institutions (like the family) accept and expect that power is distributed unequally. This represents inequality (more *versus* less), but defined from below, not from above. It suggests that a society's level of inequality is endorsed by the followers as much as by the leaders. Power and inequality, of course, are extremely fundamental facts of any society and anybody with some international experience will be aware that 'all societies are unequal, but some are more unequal than others'.

Individualism (IDV) on the one side *versus* its opposite, collectivism, that is the degree to which individuals are integrated into groups. On the individualist side we find societies in which the ties between individuals are loose: everyone is expected to look after him/herself and his/her immediate family. On the collectivist side, we find societies in which people from birth onwards are integrated into strong, cohesive in-groups, often extended families (with uncles, aunts and grandparents) which continue protecting them in exchange for unquestioning loyalty. The word 'collectivism' in this sense has no political meaning: it refers to the group, not to the state. Again, the issue addressed by this dimension is an extremely fundamental one, regarding all societies in the world.

Masculinity (MAS) *versus* its opposite, femininity refers to the distribution of roles between the genders which is another fundamental issue for any society to which a range of solutions are found.

The IBM studies revealed that:

- Women's values differ less among societies than men's values;
- Men's values from one country to another contain a dimension from very assertive and competitive and maximally different from women's values on the one side, to modest and caring and similar to women's values on the other.

The assertive pole has been called 'masculine' and the modest, caring pole 'feminine'. The women in feminine countries have the same modest, caring values as the men; in the masculine countries they are somewhat assertive and competitive, but not as much as the men, so that these countries show a gap between men's values and women's values.

Uncertainty Avoidance Index (UAI) deals with a society's tolerance for uncertainty and ambiguity; it ultimately refers to man's search for Truth. It indicates to what extent a culture programs its members to feel either uncomfortable or comfortable in unstructured situations. Unstructured situations are novel, unknown, surprising, and different from usual. Uncertainty avoiding cultures try to minimize the possibility of such situations by strict laws and rules, safety and security measures, and on the philosophical and religious level by a belief in absolute Truth; 'there can only be one Truth and we have it'. People in uncertainty avoiding countries are also more emotional, and motivated by inner nervous energy. The opposite type, uncertainty accepting cultures, are more tolerant of opinions different from what they are used to; they try to have as few rules as possible, and on the philosophical and religious level they are relativist and allow many currents to flow side by side. People within these cultures are more phlegmatic and contemplative, and not expected by their environment to express emotions.

Long-Term Orientation (LTO) *versus* short-term orientation: this fifth dimension was found in a study among students in 23 countries around the world, using a questionnaire designed by Chinese scholars It can be said to deal with Virtue regardless of Truth. Values associated with long term orientation are thrift and perseverance; values associated with short term orientation are respect for tradition, fulfilling social obligations, and protecting one's 'face'. Both, the positively and the negatively rated values of this dimension are found in the teachings of Confucius, the most influential Chinese philosopher who lived around 500 B.C.; however, the dimension also applies to countries without a Confucian heritage.

Geert Hofstede gathered extensive data on the world's cultures and impressions of that data are generated into charts and graphs that help to better understand the many sublet implications contained in his raw data.

Cultural Dimensions Scores for India Compared with World Average

Figure 2.1

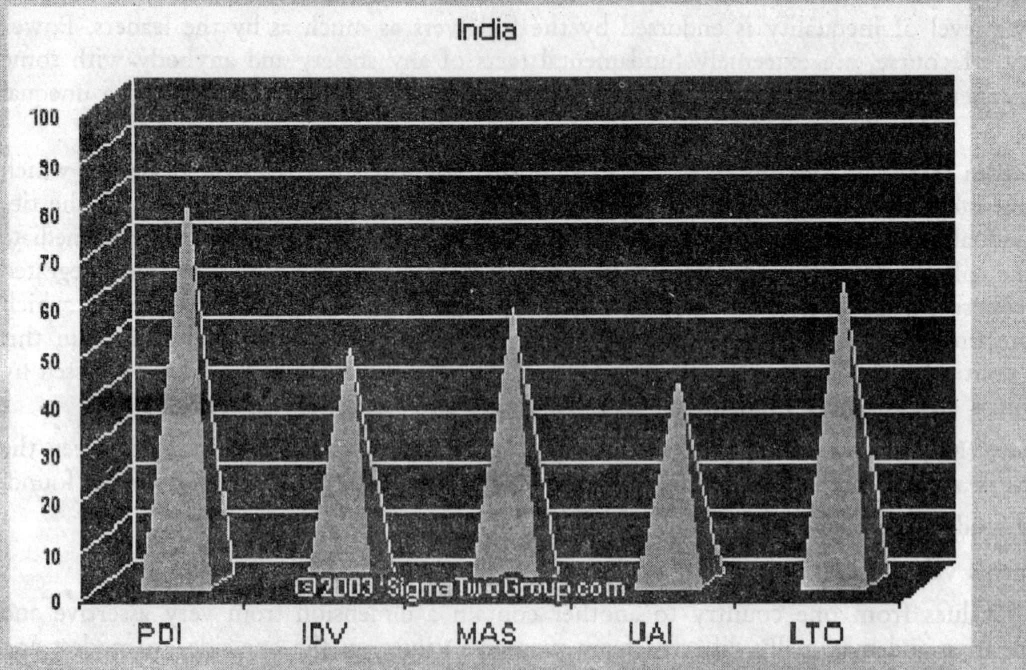

Source: **http://www.geert-hofstede.com/hofstede_india.shtml**

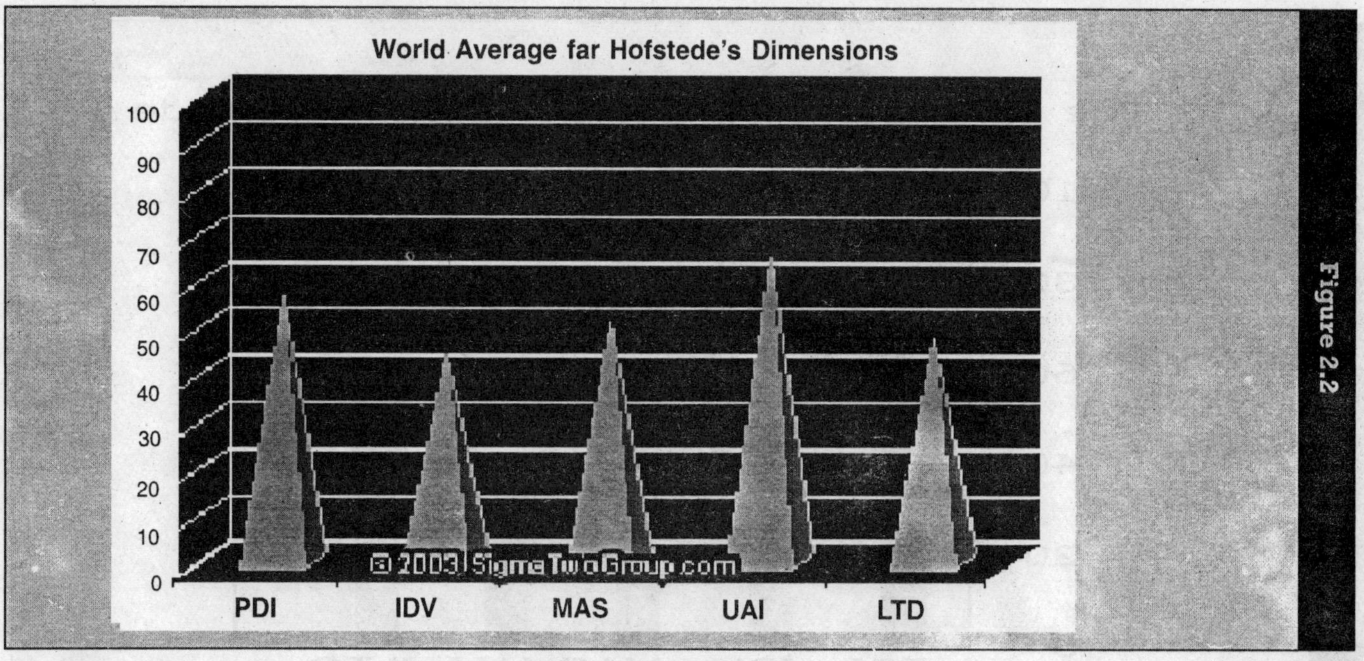

Source: http://www.geert-hofstede.com/hofstede_india.shtml

India has Power Distance (PD) as the highest Hofstede dimension for the culture, with a ranking of 77 compared to a world average of 56.5. This Power Distance score for India indicates a high level of inequality of power and wealth within the society. This condition is not necessarily subverted upon the population, but rather accepted by the population as a cultural norm.

India's Long Term Orientation (LTO) dimension rank is 61, with the world average at 48. A higher LTO score can be indicative of a culture that is perseverant and parsimonious.

India has Masculinity as the third highest ranking Hofstede dimension at 56, with the world average just slightly lower at 51. The higher the country ranks in this dimension, the greater the gap between values of men and women. It may also generate a more competitive and assertive female population, although still less than the male population.

India's lowest ranking dimension is Uncertainty Avoidance (UA) at 40, compared to the world average of 65. On the lower end of this ranking, the culture may be more open to unstructured ideas and situations. The population may have fewer rules and regulations with which to attempt control of every unknown and unexpected event or situation, as is the case in high Uncertainty Avoidance countries.

Comparison between India and United States

Fons Trompenaars' Research

Fons Trompenaars (1993) has studied cultural diversity in business and developed a model of culture that represents seven dimensions. Trompenaar's research in particular was based on extensive studies that explored cultural difficulties and misunderstandings that can arise when working in business across cultures in various parts of the world, even when those involved are working for the same company.

Fons Trompenaars' 7 Dimensions

- Universalism *versus* particularism (What is more important, rules or relationships?)
- Individualism *versus* collectivism (Do we function in a group or as individuals?)
- Neutral *versus* affective (Do we display our emotions?)
- Specific *versus* diffuse (Is responsibility specifically assigned or diffusely accepted?)

Figure 2.3

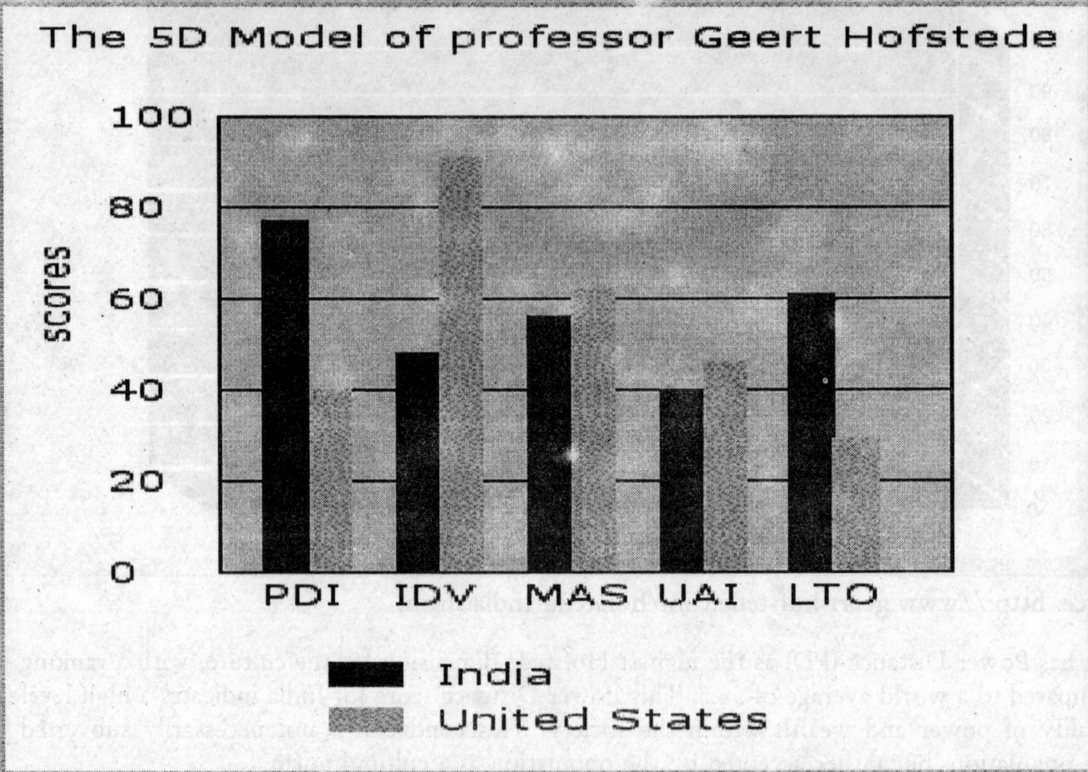

Source:www.geert-hofstede.com/hofstede_dimensions.php?culture1=42&culture2=95

- Achieved status *versus* ascribed status **(Do we have to prove ourselves to receive status or is it given to us?)**
- Time orientation **(Do we do things one at a time or several things at once?)**
- — Oriented toward the past, present, or future
- — Sequential time *versus* synchronic time
- Internal *versus* external orientation **(Do we control our environment or are we controlled by it?)**.

Other Research Findings

One Nation, Many Cultures

A Cross-Cultural Study of the Relationship between Personal Cultural Values and Commitment in the Workplace to In-Role Performance and Organizational Citizenship Behaviour was carried out by Prof. Aaron Cohen from University of Haifa, Israel. This study examines the relationship between commitment forms (organizational commitment, occupational commitment, job involvement, work involvement, and group commitment), personal cultural values (individualism—collectivism, power distance, uncertainty avoidance, and masculinity— femininity), and in-role performance and organizational citizenship behaviours (OCB). Five groups of Israeli teachers who were assumed to represent different cultural groups (secular Jews, orthodox Jews, kibbutz teachers, Druze, and Arabs) were examined. The findings showed substantial differences among the five groups in the four cultural values. Both membership in a cultural group, measured as a dummy variable, and cultural values were associated with OCB and in-role performance in addition to the effect of multiple commitments. The results also showed that organizational commitment and group commitment were related to forms of OCB more than to the other commitment foci.

A study on Work Group Collectivism and the Centrality of Work a Multinational Investigation was carried out by Keith Hattrup, M.A., Ph.D. San Diego State University. This study examined relationships at the individual level of analysis between work group collectivism and work centrality and pride in work, and the moderating effects of nations on these relationships. Participants from Ecuador, Germany, India, Mexico, and the United States completed questionnaire measures of the constructs of interest. Multiple-groups confirmatory factor analyses were performed to evaluate and control for psychometric non-equivalence in the measurement of latent constructs, prior to multiple-groups structural equation modelling analyses of the relationships between work group collectivism and work centrality and pride in work. Results showed positive relationships between collectivism and work centrality and work pride in each country, and non-significant differences between countries in these relationships. Tests of mean differences at the nation level of analysis also showed somewhat higher work centrality and pride in work among countries that scored higher in work group collectivism.

In these days of international trade and management of human personnel across national boundaries, it is more important than ever to investigate organizational dynamics on a cross cultural level. The research findings can be used for global expansion of the company. Also the research findings can be used as a strategic tool for mergers and acquisitions.

The Global Manager

"After one look at this planet any visitor from outer space would say, "I want to see the manager."
William S. Burroughs

To be successful, global companies need to develop unique set of capabilities which allows them to:

- Take advantage of resources available to it on world-wide basis — regardless of where these resources are located. These resources may be company owned or may belong to other independent firms.
- Enter any country it chooses and sell products in any country based on business opportunities. These companies are constantly in the lookout for new opportunities and are not limited by geographic/national boundaries.

As companies continue to expand globally they need managers who understand global business, operate effectively across cultural boundaries and balance strategic integration with adaptation to local markets. The opportunities the company pursues, and how it deals with the many challenges of a global business approach, depends critically on how good its managers are at interpreting and responding to the dynamic and diverse challenges facing the organization.

The ability to accept and deal with diversity and differences is not that someone is born with. And yet, it is the defining attribute of successful managers. Apart from the real need for people with a healthy attitude and skills when it comes to dealing with a diverse cross-section of people from varied backgrounds, those with attributes defining them as global leaders will, as a rule, be more tolerant and less exacting in their demands.

Globalization is the increasing interconnection of people and places as a result of advances in transport, communication, and information technologies that causes political, economic, and cultural converge? Globalization refers to a set of processes leading to the integration of :

- Economic
- Cultural
- Political
- Social

In general, the term "globalization" describes the phenomenon that transforms local markets, policies and systems into international markets, policies and systems. In business, the need for globalization becomes apparent when a company wants to penetrate a foreign market. To do this, the companies first develop new products or services or adapt existing products and services to their new customers. They then need to adapt these products and services to the cultural and linguistic differences of their customers. So, in information and communications technology, globalization refers to two processes. The first is the internationalization and the second is the localization of software and Internet applications.(http://www.cidif.org)

Globalization and its Four Dimensions

Value Form of Labour

- Labour as a social force creates value.
- This further creates surplus value.
- Globalization of labour leads to a specific form of social life.

Globalization of Capital

The social universe involved in the generation of capital:

- Political economy.
- Financial economy.
- Real economy.

M & A of Local & Global SBUs

- Explores the relationship between the local and the global.
- Re-organization/Disappearance of nations.

Cultural Phenomenon

Cross fertilization & increasing hybridization of cultural forms. A few years back, global leaders were defined as an extraordinary class of people functioning at higher niches of organization. Today, the middle manager level leaders are fast taking up the role and spreading the trend.

Then, who is a global manager?

Figure 2.4

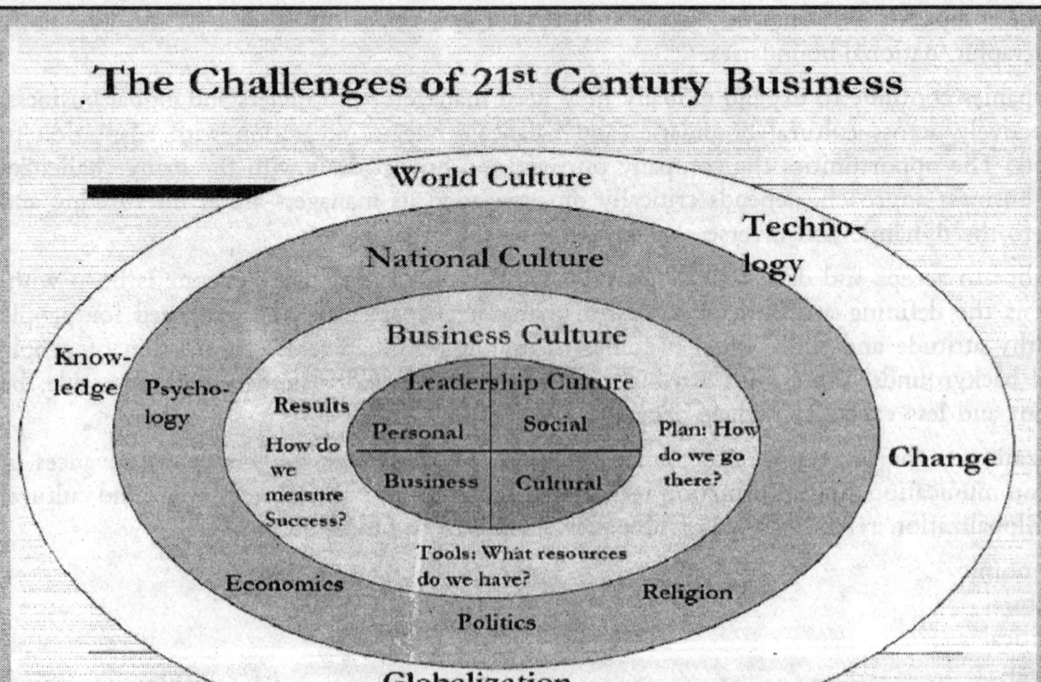

What does he do?

How does he do it differently?

Globalization has various aspects which affect the world in several different ways such as:

Industrial - emergence of worldwide production markets and broader access to a range of foreign products for consumers and companies.

Financial - emergence of worldwide financial markets and better access to external financing for corporate, national and sub national borrowers.

Economic - realization of a global common market, based on the freedom of exchange of goods and capital.

Globalization, when considered in a sociological context, has increased economic inequality throughout the world and within the United States.

Shift from manufacturing to service work: The low cost of off-shore workers have enticed corporations to more production to foreign countries. The laid off unskilled workers are forced move into the service sector where wages and benefits are low, but turnover is high. This has contributed to the widening economic gap between skilled and unskilled workers.

The rise of contingent work: As globalization causes more and more jobs to be shipped overseas, and the middle class declines, there is less need for corporations to hire full time employees. Companies are less inclined to offer benefits, or reduce benefits, to part time workers. Most companies don't offer any benefits at all. Such benefits include health insurance, bonuses, vacation time, shares in the company, and pensions. Even though most of the middle class workers still have their jobs, the reality is that their buying power has decreased due to decreased benefits. Job security is also a major issue with contingent work.

Political - political globalization is the creation of a world government which regulates the relationships among nations and guarantees the rights arising from social and economic globalization.

Informational - increase in information flows between geographically remote locations.

Cultural - growth of cross-cultural contacts; advent of new categories of consciousness and identities such as Globalism - which embodies cultural diffusion, the desire to consume and enjoy foreign products and ideas, adopt new technology and practices, and participate in a "world culture".

Social - the achievement of free circulation by people of all nations.

Greater international cultural exchange: Spreading of multiculturalism, and better individual access to cultural diversity However, the imported culture can easily supplant the local culture, causing reduction in diversity through hybridization or even assimilation. The most prominent form of this is Westernization, but Sensitization of cultures has taken place over most of Asia for many centuries.

Technical: Development of a global telecommunications infrastructure and greater trans border data flow, using such technologies as the Internet, communication satellites, submarine fiber optic cable, and wireless telephones. Increase in the number of standards applied globally; e.g., copyright laws, patents and world trade agreements. "Today, 90 percent of the information collected by companies is about what's going on inside the business. That's changing...In the future; companies will require essentially new information about the outside world: customers, markets, technologies, competitors, and national cultures." - Robert Rosen

"Tomorrow's business challenges are less technical than they are cultural. Culture must be managed just like any other business phenomenon." as Peter Drucker warns.

The Indian companies are looking at globalization for various reasons, such as:

- Latent demand abroad

Figure 2.5

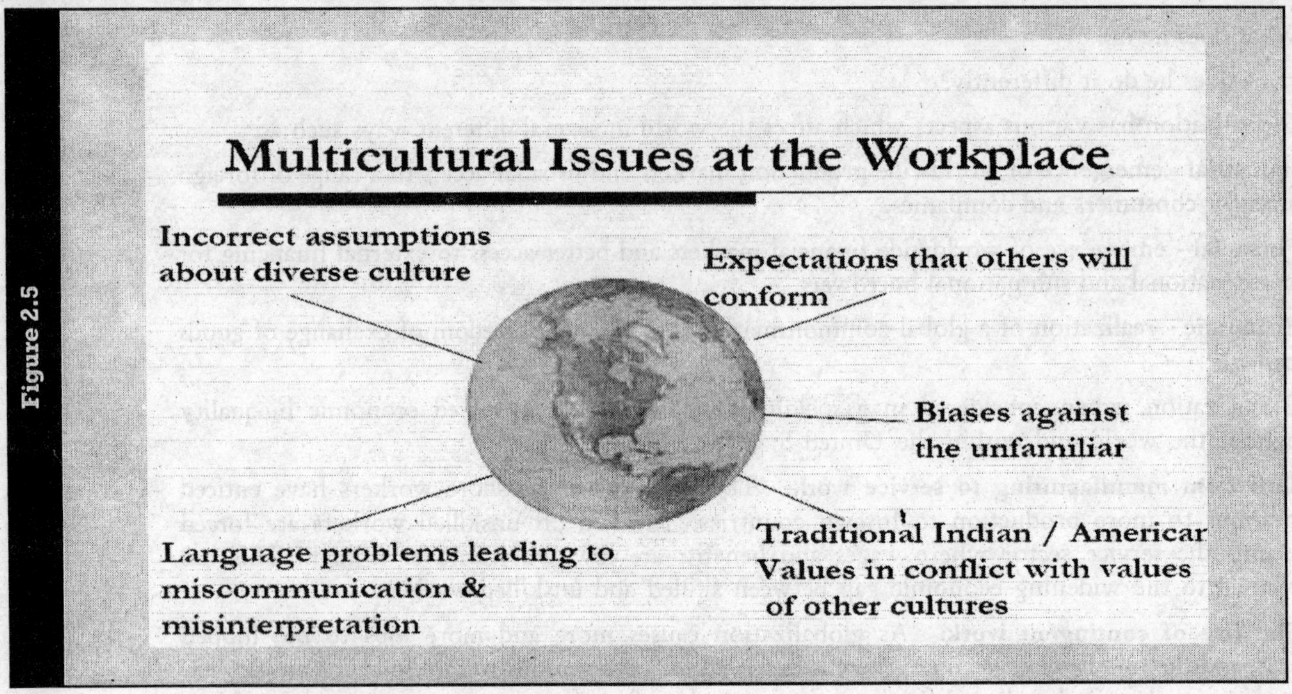

- Intense competition in local market
- Stagnation in local market.
- Lower cost of capital and revenues in Forex
- Deregulation and technological advantages
- Better facilities abroad.
- Human resource (Talent pool)
- Higher profits.

Most of the companies were startups and yet global companies:

- Aarohi Communications,
- Sonoa Systems,
- EFI, Tavant,
- RelQ,
- Open-Silicon.

These companies are called "Born Global" companies. (Born Global companies are those companies which have operations in multiple companies within one/two years of their existence). To be successful these companies need Global Managers. The top management and senior management in these companies need to have a special management skills'. Successful managers need to have global vision.

To be successful, global companies need to develop unique set of capabilities which allows them to take advantage of resources available to it on world-wide basis — regardless of where these resources are located. These resources may be company owned or may belong to other independent firms. For example, company having the ability to use (third party) factories in Taiwan, Israel, China & Korea.

Enter any country it chooses and sell products in any country based on business opportunities. These companies are constantly in the lookout for new opportunities and are not limited by geographic/national boundaries. Having customers in USA, Canada, Israel, Portugal — and is/was negotiating with firms in Thailand, India, Korea, France, Ireland and Japan.

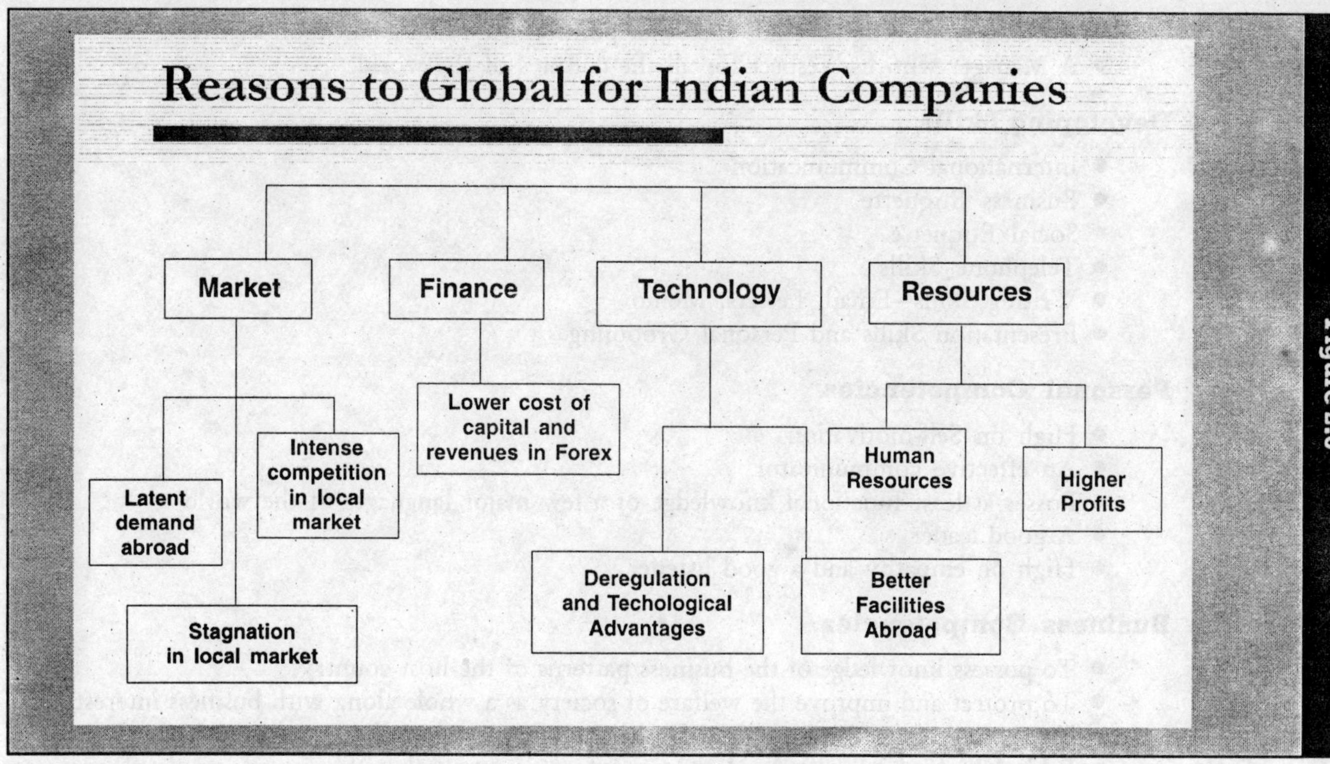

Figure 2.6

To succeed in a global market place, managers need to have a global vision and a complementing strategy which enables managers to develop a global vision which helps in breaking down existing geographic and competitive boundaries.

The manager's global vision is shaped by several factors. One of the biggest driving factors is having a global mindset — i.e., ability to look at the global markets as a whole. This can be summarized by the slogan "Think Local Act Global".

Global managers' work with the assumption that global markets are best served by adaptation to local conditions - and has local initiatives in different markets around the world. Diversity — ethnic, consumer, geographic, and economic diversity is looked as sources of opportunity. Global strategy focuses on optimal global sourcing, selling standard products and the ability to react globally to competitors' moves.

Managers have to retrain their thinking process to become global managers. This is a difficult task as their thoughts are often crafted by 'traditional' practices: Home country practices, ethnocentric views, preference to local/home country candidates/process/procedures etc. These 'traditional' thoughts have to be replaced by global thinking. A global manager's thought process is characterized by:

- Multicultural approach to reflect global operations
- Shift of focus on "soft tools" — Vision, process and people to achieve objectives
- Collaboration with a network of vendors, partners and customers
- Recruitment from global talent pool - to get best set of people
- Global transfer of human resources - global learning/training process
- Creating a learning organization
- Focus on big picture - respond rapidly to global business environment changes.

Profile of a Global Manager

- A Manager with all the Soft Skills in place
- A Manager who understands the ethics that govern business

- A Manager who understands the other point of view and is not ethnocentric
- A Manager who has respect for all the cultures of the world.

Developing Skills

- International Communication
- Business Etiquette
- Social Etiquette
- Telephone Skills
- Writing Skills—Email, Letters, Memo
- Presentation Skills and Personal Grooming.

Personal Competencies

- High on Self-motivation
- An effective communicator
- Posses at least functional knowledge of a few major languages of the world
- A good leader
- High on empathy and a good listener.

Business Competencies

- To possess knowledge of the business patterns of the host country
- To protect and improve the welfare of society as a whole along with business interest
- To apply ethics of business (social values, consumer protection, environmental concerns)
- Ethical leadership must stand the test of environmental performance and development of corporate social performance.

Socio- Cultural Competencies

- To understand the social patterns of the host country
- To understand the implicit and explicit social behaviour
- To respect people's religious sentiments
- To know the historical, political, and geographical background of the country.

In a global economy, high tech companies need to go successfully global. Such companies can then maximize the sales potential from existing customers and attract new customers without stepping into new product ranges, focus on innovation and offer improved and new products, services and reshape the industry through a network of partnerships. For a strong global performance, the organization needs a group of global managers. Only then the global strategies can be implemented successfully, thus making the company successful.

New global companies develop a global mindset from scratch. The primary motivations in these companies are either 'growth hungry' or "deliver the best for the lowest price'. Depending on their primary motivation the companies develop a global strategy — which has to be successfully implemented by global managers.

As companies continue to expand globally, they need managers who understand global business, operate effectively across cultural boundaries and balance strategic integration with adaptation to local markets. The opportunities the company pursues, and how it deals with the many challenges of a global business approach, depends critically on how good its managers are at interpreting and responding to the dynamic and diverse challenges facing the organization.

Then, who is a global manager? What does he do? How does he do it differently? What skills they have. Let's find out.

Penchant for discovery and learning: The global manager is someone who is ready to learn. A person who clings to preconceived notions and stereotypes will run into communication troubles sooner or later.

Has a global perspective: The global manager can broaden his or her focus from local conditions to a global business perspective. He is capable of comparing and evaluating the required parameters when it comes to dealing with certain business issues in an alien cultural environment.

Cultural adaptability: The global manager is someone who recognizes the potential of cultural synergies. This is what brings adaptability. This also brings in an understanding and respect for cultural sensitivities. He realizes that differences are perceived on both the sides.

Cross- cultural collaboration: The global manager can function as effectively in a multicultural environment. Collaboration involves treating all the team members equally to get the maximum contribution from all.

Realistic expectations: The global manager knows that one could mess up in setting up expectations from employees belonging to a different cultural background. He understands that handling in-group differences is more important to increase the performance levels.

Developing Skills of Global Managers

One problem is that many companies still believe the best way to help managers develop a global mind-set is to put them in positions in other countries.

But that hasn't been very effective, primarily because companies station people abroad and then forget about them. If anything, advancement is even more difficult for the expatriate when he returns to headquarters, having missed out on opportunities to network with top management. Also, many people have reasons for not wanting to hop from location to location.

Where on the one hand a global manager will not shun an overseas assignment, there, one need not necessarily leave one's country to get the skill set. With fruits of globalization now spreading to services, there are enough opportunities around to develop the skills. The global manager exhibits traits that are positive in them and have a healthy undertone. He is open-minded and welcomes newness. He is someone who understands that 'an obstinate man does not hold opinions; they hold him'.

Successful global managers need to have global vision. The manager's global vision is shaped by several factors. One of the biggest driving factors is having a global mindset - i.e., ability to look at the global markets as a whole. **Mindset** is a fixed mental attitude or disposition that predetermines a person's responses to and interpretations of situations.

Things help in development of global managers

- Focus on big picture and changes in corporation's global business environment
- Strong confidence in vision and organizational process
- High value of multi-cultural teams
- Diversity seen as a source of opportunities
- Constantly challenging own experiences and assumptions
- Always open to change.

Driving Forces Behind the Global mindset

There are four influences on the manager:

Leadership View of the World

One of the leading forces is the leadership view of the world. This is often driven by the CEO. A visionary leader can drive the global strategy — but he also shapes the managers' view and his actions. Often times, top leaders in global companies have worked in many countries.

Administrative Heritage

Administration style of the company can either be centralized or decentralized. In a global company, administration is often highly centralized. All decisions on use of tangible and intangible assets are centrally controlled. Local business units do not have control over local assets.

Organizational Structure

Manager's mindset is also influenced by the organization structure. Global companies are structured around products and functional roles. Global companies are not structured according to regional offices.

Industry forces

No firm can work in isolation. It has to deal with vendors, suppliers, customers and competitors. The needs to achieve economies of scale and scope have forced vendors and customers to globalize.

While the environment of business has become global and more complex, the organization as one knows it has remained static and hierarchal. To succeed, corporations must develop strategies and management approaches from the perspective of people and culture allows us to understand the influence of national and ethnic cultures on organizational functioning.

As we investigate the influence of cultural diversity on multinational and global firms, it becomes clear that national differences are important but that their relative impact depends on the stage of development of the firm, industry and world economy.

The importance of world business has created a demand for managers sophisticated in global management and skilled at working with people from other countries. Cross cultural management explains the behaviour of people in organizations around the world and shows people how to work in organizations with employee and client populations from many different cultures. cross cultural management describes organizational behaviour across countries and cultures; and perhaps most important seeks to understand and improve the interaction of co-workers, managers, executives, clients, suppliers and alliance partners from countries and cultures around the world. Cross cultural management thus expands the scope of domestic management to encompass international and multicultural dynamics. Rather than global management being a subset of traditional domestic management approaches, single-culture/domestic management is now recognized as a limited subset of global cross- cultural management.

To successfully manage the geographical dispersion and multiculturalism of multinational organizations, managers must develop a global mindset. In fact, it is the mindsets of key managers that shape business strategy and ultimately determine the success of the firm. Similarly, using their highly developed cognitive complexity, managers with global mindsets simultaneously consider the multiple complex multicultural situations facing the firm, and consistently make appropriate trade-offs and decisions among competing multinational options.

Both domestically and globally, the multicultural workforce has become a reality. The impact of multiculturalism, however, varies significantly with the type of competitive environment and firm's overall strategy. By the time firms adapt global strategies, the impact of cultural diversity becomes extremely important. Global firms must understand cultural dynamics to formulate their business strategies, to locate production facilities and suppliers world-wide, and to design and market culturally appropriate products and services, all while managing cross-cultural interaction throughout the organization, from the most senior executive committees to the shop floor. As more firms more from domestic, multi-domestic, and multinational strategies to operating as truly global companies and alliances, the importance and impact of cultural diversity increase markedly. In global firms, the impact of cultural diversity, which once was merely "nice to understand", becomes imperative for survival, let alone success.

Similar to the increasing importance of cultural diversity, the location of its impact varies with changes in the firm's competitive business environment and strategy. In multi-domestic firms, which focus primarily on exporting and producing abroad, to the lowest cultural diversity strongly affects relationships external to the firm, especially those with potential buyers and workers in other countries. only expatriates have a high need for developing cultural sensitivity strongly affects the internal organizational culture, many more employees and managers need cross-cultural management skills.

Global firms must continually manage cultural diversity both within the company and between the company and its external environment. To work effectively, everyone from the CEO level worker must use cross-cultural skills. This progression from cultures relative lack of importance, with respect to the firms' external environment as well as its internal organizational culture, underlies the general recognition that executives and managers must know how to work effectively in multi national and multi cultural teams if they wish to succeed. We manage people who differ from us by leading, motivating, communicating, decision making, planning and organizing.

The potential for superior productivity of culturally diverse teams is high; they possess the breadth of resources, insights, perspective, and experiences that facilitate the creation of new and better ideas. Regrettably, culturally diverse teams rarely achieve their full potential. Process losses due to mistrust, misunderstanding, miscommunication, stress and a lack of cohesion often negate the potential benefits of diversity to the team. Only if diversity is well managed, can multicultural teams hope to achieve full potential.

The last part of the global managers personalities are his effective communicating skills and presentation skills. Communication is the process of producing results through people. A manager spends 30% of his time is speaking, 45% of his time listening, 9% writing and 16% reading. Language, values, attitudes, and other cultural traits change very slowly. Therefore, communicating inter-culturally calls for recognition of the cultural elements that cause people to view things differently and thus create barriers to communication. For multinational and transnational corporations, global managers are important for building global cadre for implementing their global strategies.

Management Perspective to Globalization

Management globalization don't only mean only able to develop global strategies .it is also to be able to implement global policies at the local level, respecting local specificity. Globalization in this century is about awareness of the technologies and how they are adapted around the world, it also calls for the ability to differentiate products from competition that can originate anywhere in the world.

As many firms are going to globalize, there is a slight probability that the competitive advantage will be achieved at a global level. That is the capability to succeed in local operations that will give the advantage. To be successful at the local level, all the functions of management should be seen global. We know that management functions include-

- Planning
- Organizing
- Staffing
- Leading
- Controlling.

If these basic functions are not done properly, no organization can stand and the objectives cannot be meeting to be globally competitive.

Planning is a very important function as it promotes the accomplishment of enterprise objectives, which are clear, attainable, verifiable and logically precedes all managerial functions. So it's the major activity. It is done differently in different countries, for e.g., Japan considers long term and collective decision making strategy is different. A tool widely known as TOWS analysis is used for the competitive advantage analysis which is a useful tool to know about the internal and external environment.

Organization is to aid in making objectives meaningful and contribute to organization efficiency. An organization is efficient if it is structured to aid the accomplishment of enterprise objective with a minimum cost. The steps in organizing include formulating objective and supporting policies and plans to achieve the ends, identifying and classifying activities, grouping these activities, delegating authority and coordinating authority as well as information relationships. Since managership depends to great extent on the quality of leadership of those in managerial positions, it follows from the principles of leadership facilitation that the organization structure should do its part in creating a situation in which a manager can most effectively lead. In this senses organizing is a technique of promoting leadership staffing is the next important function of the management, as without no human recourse an organization work. The basic objective of staffing is to ensure that organizational roles are filled by qualified personals who are and willing to occupy them. The clearer the definition of the organizational roles and their human resource requirements, and the better the techniques of manager appraisal and training employed, the higher manager quality.

Effective staffing includes job satisfaction, managerial appraisal and open competition. Change is an important activity when taken into consideration. The forces for change may come from the external enjoyment, from within the organization or from the individual themselves. There are various ways to respond to these forces. One approach is to simply to react to a crisis, another approach is to deliberately plan a change. Errors in selection can lead to actualization of Peters Principle, which states that managers tend to be promoted to the level of their incompetence. Although the advice of several people should be sought, the selection decision should generally rest with the immediate superior of the candidate for the position.

Leadership is the art process of influencing people so that they will strive willingly and enthusiastically toward the achievement of group goals. Leadership basically includes power, a fundamental understanding of people, and the ability to inspire followers to apply their full capabilities, the leaders' style and the development of a conductive organizational climate. Since people tend to follow those who offer them a means of satisfying their personal goals , the more managers understand what motivates their subordinates and the more they reflect this understanding in their actions, the more effective they are likely to be as leaders.

Leadership involves a variety of styles, ranging from one that is highly boss centred to one that is highly subordinate centred. The appropriate leadership style depends on the leader, the followers and this situation. Controlling the measurement and correction of performance in order to make sure that enterprise objectives and the plans devised to attain them are being accomplished control techniques and system, are essentially the same for controlling cash, office procedures, product, quality and everything else.

The basic controlling process wherever it is found and whatever being controlled involves three steps: establishing standards, measuring performance against these standards and correcting variations from standards and plans.

❆ ❆ ❆

3 Managing Global Environment

• Managing Global Environment • Trading Blocs • Workforce Diversity • The Global Managers Role • Technological Environment • E-business and Telecommunications • Outsourcing and Off shoring • Business Ethics and Corporate Social Responsibility

Today's political environment presents a myriad of challenges for MNCs. China is going through a transition as the old guard passes from the scene. The political situation in Europe also continues to change. Russia is facing economic problems and social upheaval, and the rest of Central and Eastern Europe has had varying degrees of success with their newfound freedom and continue to struggle with their past.

The current legal and regulatory environment is both complex and confusing. There are many different laws and regulations to which MNCs doing business internationally must conform, and each nation is unique. Also, MNCs must abide by the laws of their own country. For example, U.S. MNCs must obey the rules set down by the Foreign Corrupt Practices Act. MNCs doing business in Japan and the EU face a wide range of bureaucratic rules and regulations that often are both time-wasting and inefficient.

The technological environment is changing quickly and is having a major impact on international business. This will continue in the future. For example, money transfers and exchanges are changing dramatically.

Also, areas such as telecommunications offer developing countries new opportunities to leapfrog into the twenty-first century. New markets are being created high-tech MNCs that are eager to provide telecommunications service. Technological developments also impact on both the nature and the structure of employment, shifting the industrial structure toward a more high-tech, knowledge-based economy. MNCs who understand and take advantage of this high-tech environment should prosper, but they also must keep up or ahead, to survive the highly competitive years ahead.

Managing a Global Environment - Assessing the Environment

Global management is the process of developing strategies, designing and operating systems, and working with people around the world to ensure sustained competitive advantage. The term Globalism refers to global competition characterized by networks that bind countries, institutions, and people in an interdependent global economy.

Global Indicators

- International Trade Figures
- Foreign Direct Investment Figures
- Regional Economic/Trade Unions
- Workforce Diversity
- Information Technology.

Volume of International Trade

In 1990, volume of international trade in goods and services surpassed $4 trillion and in 2001, international trade in goods and services reached $7.6 trillion. One-fourth of everything grown or produced in the world is now exported. Quadrupling of world exports in 31 years demonstrates that the opportunity to increase sales by exporting is a viable growth strategy.

FDI Explosive Growth

- Foreign Direct Investment
- World stock of FDI rose from $519 billion in 1980 to $5.976 trillion in 2000
- An eleven fold increase in just 20 years
- The United States, the nation with the highest sales of companies in 1999, was replaced by the United Kingdom as the largest acquirer of foreign companies.

Foreign Direct Investment in the United States

- Foreign direct investment in the United States rose rapidly from
- $185 billion in 1985 to $1,321 billion in 2001
- Over 80 percent of the total stock was owned by firms or individuals from just seven nations United Kingdom, Japan, Netherlands, Germany, France, Switzerland, and Canada.

Number of International Companies

- In 2000,only 20 nations had gross domestic products (GDPs) greater than the total annual sales of Wal-Mart
- Also in 2000, the total amount of money spent in Wal-Mart world-wide was greater than the sum of the GDPs of the Czech Republic, Algeria, Peru, and Pakistan.

Global Trends and Forces

External or Uncontrollable Forces

- Competitive
- Economic/ Financial
- Socioeconomic
- Legal
- Political
- Socio cultural
- Labour
- Technological
- Political risks are any governmental action or politically motivated event that could adversely affect the long-run profitability or value of a firm.

Terrorism Risk

- Terrorism is "the use, or threat of use, of anxiety-inducing — violence for ideological or political purposes" (Micklous).
- The increasing incidence of terrorism around the world concerns MNCs.

Typical Political Risk Events

- Expropriation of corporate assets without prompt and adequate compensation.
- Forced sale of equity to host-country nationals, usually at or below depreciated book value.
- Discriminatory treatment against foreign firms in the application of regulations or laws.
- Barriers to repatriation of funds (profits or equity).
- Loss of technology or other intellectual property (such as patents, trademarks, or trade names).
- Interference in managerial decision making.
- Dishonesty by government officials, including canceling or altering contractual agreements, extortion demands, and so forth.

Managing Political Risk (Taoka and Beeman's suggestions)

- Equity sharing
- Participative management
- Localization of the operation
- Development assistance.

Economic Risk

The economic risk incurred by a foreign corporation usually falls into one of two main categories, its subsidiary (or other investment) in a specific country may become unprofitable:

- If the government abruptly changes its domestic monetary or fiscal policies or
- If the government decides to modify its foreign-investment policies.

Some Means that Managers Might Use to Maintain Dependency

- Input control
- Market control
- Position control
- Staged contribution strategies.

The Legal Environment

- A host country's legal system may be derived from common law, civil law, or Muslim law, and is a reflection of the country's culture, religion, and traditions.
- Under common law, past court decisions act as precedents to the interpretation of the law and to common custom.
- Civil law is based on a comprehensive set of laws organized into a code. Interpretation of these laws is based on reference to codes and statutes.
- Islamic law combines, in varying degrees, civil, common, and indigenous law. It is followed in approximately 27 countries.

The Technological Environment

- Techno globalism is the phenomenon in which rapid developments in information and communication technologies (ICTs) are propelling globalization and *viçe-versa.*
- An MNC's major concern is the appropriability of technology – that is, the ability of the innovating firm to profit from its own technology protecting it from competitors.

Global E-Business

- E-business is "the integration of systems, processes, organizations, value chains and entire markets using Internet-based and related technologies and concepts."
- E-commerce refers directly to the marketing and sales process.
- The Internet and e-business provide a number of uses and advantages in global business.

Trading Blocs

Trade blocs are intergovernmental associations that manage and promote trade activities for specific regions of the world.

Trade bloc activities have political as well as economic implications. For example, the European Union, the world's largest trading bloc, has "harbored political ambitions extending far beyond the free trading arrangements sought by other multi usage regional economic organizations."

Some well-known trading blocs include the EU(European Union), NAFTA(North American Free Trade Agreement), MERCOSUR(Mercado Comun del Cono Sur) also known as Southern Common Markets(SCCM), and ASEAN(Association of Southeast Asian Nations).

Trade blocs are desirable because they compliment globalize trade. Others view regionalism as a threat to free trade because trade blocs advocate and install protectionist policies that shield bloc members from the effects of free trade.

A trade bloc is a large free trade area formed by one or more tax, tariff and trade agreements. Typically trade pacts that define such a bloc specify formal adjudication bodies, e.g., NAFTA trade panels.

Since the de mise of most of the world's empires, a number of international-generally regionally based-economics blocs have been developed to promote trade between member states.

Several blocs also have stated or implicit political goals-notably the EU. Varieties of economic blocs include free trade areas, custom unions and single markets.

A trade bloc is established through a trade pact covering different issues of the economic integration.

Trade blocs have reasons to protect the trade interests of their region:

1. To establish some form of regional control regarding trade that fulfills the interests of nations within that region.
2. To establish tariffs that protects intra-regional trade from "outside" forces.
3. To promote economic and technical cooperation among developing countries.

Although the notion that the world is fragmenting into trade blocs is popular, what must be remembered is that there is no clear definition of what a trade bloc is. The efficacy of trade blocs "depends upon the definition of a trade bloc" which must also include an assessment of current political conditions of the region.

Regional Trading Blocs

- The Triad
- Western Europe
- Asia
- North America
- Other Regions
- Central and Eastern Europe
- China
- Less Developed Countries (LDCs).

The European Union (EU)

- 12 of the 15 member states of the European Community have adopted a common currency and monetary policy.
- The Euro is now a legally tradable currency.
- The EU is the largest and most integrated common market in the world with 376 million consumers.
- The creation of EU has not eliminated national pride. Most people in W. Europe still think of themselves first as British, French, Danish or Italian, and are wary of giving up too much power to centralized institutions, or of giving up their national culture.

Global Managers and the E.U.

- Global managers face two major tasks with respect to the E.U.
- How firms outside of Europe can deal with a market giving preference to insiders
- How to deal effectively with multiple sets of national cultures, traditions, and customs within Europe.

North America

- The North American Free Trade Agreement (NAFTA) between the United States, Canada and Mexico has created a single market of 360 million consumers.
- The "one America" trading bloc has the potential for expansion in South America as trade liberalization among the Latin American countries progresses.

- *Maquiladoras* are U.S. manufacturing facilities that have operated just south of the Mexican-American border since the 1960s under special tax concessions.
- Joint ventures between Mexican and American companies are common. Examples include the one between Wal-Mart and Cifra, which in 2001 was Mexico's biggest chain.

Asia

- Japan and the Four Tigers – Singapore, Hong Kong, Taiwan, and South Korea – provide most of the capital and expertise for Asia's developing countries.
- In the 1980s and early 1990s, much of Asia's economic power and competitive edge was attributed to Japan's *keiretsu* and S.Korea's *chaebol.*
- Recent economic woes have slowed growth in the region.

Other Regions

- The Central and Eastern European bloc, where communism proved unworkable and crumbled, has created a new market of 430 million people.
- Impediments to business growth here are the lack of capitalist structure and systems to reproduce Western management practices easily.
- China has enjoyed recent success as an export powerhouse.
- Its GDP growth rate, though slowing, was the fastest in the world for several consecutive years.
- The economic situation and the often unacceptable level of government intervention discourage foreign investment in less developed countries (LDCs).
- Assessing the risk-return trade-offs and keeping up with political developments in the LDCs are two of the many demands on international managers.

Measures to restrain global competition:

- Import quotas i.e., limiting the amount of imports into the country so that domestic consumers buy products made by their countries in their region.
- Custom delays i.e., establishing bureaucratic formalities that slow down the ability for the imported product from abroad to enter the domestic market.
- Boycotts and technical barriers.
- Bribes and voluntary restraints.

Workforce Diversity

Workforce diversity is vital to ensure success in today's knowledge economy. Firms that want fresh ideas, strong growth, a positive company image, fewer discrimination lawsuits, and an enhanced ability to hire qualified workers should be aggressive about workforce diversity.

A recent study demonstrated that firms with senior leader teams consisting of multi-cultural and female members had higher growth rate than firms with teams consisting of only white males.

These findings strongly suggest that firms that seek to employ personnel with specialized abilities should ensure that their organizations are open-minded and tolerant of all groups. Firms that desire to grow by attracting customers from the country's numeric ethnic groups like, firms that hire a significant number of Chinese-American accountants should find it easier to attract Chinese clients than firms that don't employ any Asian-Americans.

Diversity helps firms when they compete in foreign markets. Like, what a firm learns about marketing to Hispanics in the US will be helpful if it decides to expand its business into Latin America. Some of the huge markets that's opening up to the US are in China and India, with over 2 billion people. Firms which don't practice workforce diversity are at a big disadvantage of competing globally.

It is extremely important for firms to understand that workforce diversity works. It helps create a work environment in which female and minority employees and customers feel welcome. Workforce diversity is vital for firms that desire to thrive in the future. Discrimination is costly not only on the individual level, but also on the corporate level and even on a national level. The world labour force is undergoing considerable change as a result of the increasing movement across borders of workers at all skill levels; the rising average age of employees; and the addition of great numbers of women to the workforce (particularly in developing countries), many with higher levels of education.

Managing Diversity

- Diversity as a core issue – Diversity issues are typically addressed through ad hoc programs funded on soft money, the focus groups argued. Diversity initiatives typically disappear when grants end or new priorities emerge so success is more likely when new initiatives become part of Extension's core budget.
- Support system to reduce isolation – Extension must look more holistically at the needs of employees. Both formal support systems and informal networks should be encouraged. More attention to helping newly-hired staff settle into the community would help culturally diverse staff: "We orient people to Extension," one person stated, "but not to the community."
- Content of programs – Some suggested that Extension's programs reflect its old audiences rather than society's current problems and priorities. Until it more directly addresses issues of urban poverty, economic development, job creation, and social disorganization, Extension is unlikely to recruit and retain strong minority candidates.
- Multicultural communication and organizational development skills – Several people suggested that Extension develop its expertise in multicultural communication and organizational development. The land-grant connection provides a research base upon which to build leadership in organizational change and multicultural effectiveness.
- Relocation of Extension offices – Extension offices are seldom chosen on the basis of accessibility to multicultural audiences. They are often based in county complexes, in affluent business districts, or even outside of town far from public transportation. Relocation, the focus groups suggested, may be required.
- "Growing" a diverse staff – Extension increasingly expect its agents to hold graduate degrees. Entry level requirements, the focus groups argued, limit the pool of minority applicants. If Extension hired strong candidates without such degrees but provided opportunities to earn the requisite credentials, staff diversity would increase.
- Flexible work place – In keeping with the literature, the focus groups suggested that a more flexible work place would increase diversity. The literature shows that job-sharing, part-time work (with benefits), flexible scheduling, accommodating work at home (through E-mail and fax), greater use of consultants, more liberal parental leave policies, child care, career breaks, and sabbaticals would broaden the diversity of the work force.
- Mentoring – Mentoring is a well-documented success. The focus groups suggested that mentoring must be built into the job descriptions of senior staff.
- Learning styles and Extension methods – While cultural differences in learning and communication styles have been clearly established by research, these lessons have seldom been applied to Extension programs. More work must be done, the focus groups argued, to develop appropriate instructional methods that reflect the learning styles of diverse audiences.
- Testing educational materials. The focus groups questioned the appropriateness of some Extension materials. Many were developed by affluent, white university professors for poor and culturally diverse audiences. Participatory curriculum development and more testing of materials are needed.
- Celebrating good practice – Although Extension has many examples of effective practice, the focus groups suggested, many multicultural programs are poorly documented. Extension must identify effective multicultural programs, analyze why they work, and share the lessons learned through conferences, consultations, case studies, in-house publications, and the professional literature.

- Language competence — The focus groups identified the lack of language skills in multicultural environments as a significant barrier to building a multicultural organization. More bilingual staff and increased learning opportunities for current staff are also needed for Extension to become more inclusive.

Diversity means difference, and people's differences can be many and varied:

- Race
- Culture
- National origin
- Region
- Gender
- Sexual Orientation
- Age
- Marital Status
- Politics
- Religion
- Ethnicity
- Disability
- Socio-economic differences
- Family structure
- Health
- Values
- And more.

Making Diversity Happen - A Checklist

Do you know what diversity means for your organization?

1. Yes/No
2. Need to ask [name of person] for more information
3. Need to persuade [name of person] to do this
4. What I need to do
5. By when?

Do you know what the benefits of diversity are?

1. Yes/No
2. Need to ask [name of person] for more information
3. Need to persuade [name of person] to do this
4. What I need to do
5. By when?

Can you think of any other benefits for your organization?

1. Yes/No
2. Need to ask [name of person] for more information
3. Need to persuade [name of person] to do this
4. What I need to do
5. By when?

Does diversity mean your mission statement has to change?

1. Yes/No
2. Need to ask [name of person] for more information
3. Need to persuade [name of person] to do this
4. What I need to do
5. By when?

Do you need to change any of your existing equality/ diversity policies, strategies and action plans?

1. Yes/No
2. Need to ask [name of person] for more information
3. Need to persuade [name of person] to do this
4. What I need to do
5. By when?

The planned change-corporate diversity strategy serves as the motivation for the learning of new behaviors and attitudes. Hence, once the planned change-corporate diversity strategy is articulated, the move through the eight steps of the managing diversity process should be instituted to assist individuals and organizations in culturally reengineering and moving to the desired state of managing diversity. The eight sequential steps of the managing diversity process include: exposure; experience; knowledge; understanding; appreciate; respect; modify attitudes and behaviour and healthy interaction.

The Global Managers Role - Managing a Global Environment

Environmental analysis is defined as the process by which strategists monitor the economic, governmental/legal, market/competitive, supplier/technological, geographic, and social settings to determine opportunities and threats to their firm.

Environmental diagnosis consists of managerial decisions made by analyzing the significance of data (opportunity and threats) of the environmental analysis.

Environmental analysis ensures organizational success in following ways:

1. It helps firms to adjust environmental change at right time.
2. It tries to improve organizational performance by making management aware of issue that arises in the firm's environment by having a direct impact on planning.
3. It helps strategists to focus on alternatives that will achieve predetermined goals.

The Environment of the Global Manager

Political Environment

- Form of government
- Political stability
- Foreign policy
- State companies
- Role of military
- Level of terrorism
- Restrictions on imports/exports.

Many political factors influence how managers formulate and implement strategic decisions. Due to socialist leaning of some of the ministers, Coca Cola and IBM had to move out of the India in the late 70s. A deep seated fear of multinational made the political leaders to shut the door on giant multinational companies for a painfully long time. Entry barriers, protectionist policies, high tariffs, anti-nationalist slogans, bad publicity have had a cumulative effect in creating closed economic model where people had to wait for years to buy a Bajaj scooter or Fait car in India. When things are turned from bad to worse, the situation was sought to be remedied through a bold liberalization program in the early 90s. Apart from a willingness to bend the rules and get long with the times, political stability is also essential for economic growth. After the Babari Masjid demolition in 1992, economic reforms again took a back seat and the Prime Minister, P.V. Narasimha Rao, could not carry on the bold liberalization program further. Subsidies were never cut as planned at that time, public sector units could not be put on sale, Industrial Dispute Act remained intact, Urban Land Ceiling Act could not be amended (it happened finally in 1999), a National Renewal Fund could not be set up.

Certain changes in government policies such as industrial policy, fiscal policy, tariff policy etc., may have profound impact on business. Some policy developments create opportunities as well as threats. In other words, a development which brightens the prospect of some enterprises may pose a threat to some others. For example, the industrial policy liberalizations in India have opened up enormous new opportunities and threats. They have provided a lot of opportunities to a large number of enterprises to diversify and make their product mix better. But they have also given rise to serious threat to many existing firms by way of increasing competition; many sellers markets have given way to buyers markets. Even products which were seldom advertised have come to be promoted very heavily. The battle for the market has provided a splendid opportunity for the advertising industry.

Economic Environment

- Economic system
- Stage of development
- Economic stability
- GNP
- International financial standing
- Monetary/fiscal policies
- Foreign investment.

The economic condition of a country for example, the nature of economy, the stage of development of economy, economic resources, the level of income, the distribution of income and assets, etc. are among the very important determinants of business strategy.

Consumption patterns are usually governed by relative affluence of market segments. Therefore while carrying out strategic planning exercises, the firm must focus attention on economic trends in the segment that affect its industry. Low interest rates on personal savings, for example, could compel individuals to move towards equity and bonds markets, leading to a boom for the capital market activity and mutual fund industry. At the national and international level, the firm must look into the general availability of credit, the level of disposable income and propensity of people to spend.

Major factors of Global Economy:

- Market opportunities
- Policy towards private enterprise & competition
- Policy towards foreign investment
- Foreign trade & exchange controls
- Taxes
- Financing
- The labour market
- Infrastructure.

Global Challenges Ahead

- To raise the productive capacity and incomes of the fifth of the world population who remain in the grip of absolute poverty.
- Large amounts of internationally mobile capital combined with domestic policy imbalances and volatile exchange rate expectations can generate serious international financial crises.
- Success in promoting economic growth and international trade may lead to increasing pressure on finite global resources and the environment.

Legal Environment

- Legal system
- Prevailing international laws
- Protectionist laws

- Tax laws
- Role of contracts
- Protection for proprietary property.

The legal framework/regulatory environment is decided by political party in power. The government, therefore, may legislate on matter like wage fixation, managerial remuneration, safety and health at work, location of plants, entry of multinationals, price control, import-export policy, licensing policy etc. In a centrally planned and controlled economy like India, it is the government that lays down the rules of the industry has to scrupulously adhere to the rule book. Lobbing, political donations, public awareness campaigns still help in bending the policy stipulations a bit but, by and large, the levers of control are held by the ministers and bureaucrats only. During the license-permit-raj that prevailed till the late 80s, CEO's of the most companies of India were expected to know the domestic market, know the government, make short term plans, be able to handle diversified companies. The family-owned businesses preferred fixers, yes-man, collaborators and people with right connections with government officials.

Following are the important legal environmental factors which affected the organization:

- Licensing policies
- Quota restrictions
- Import duties
- Forex regulations
- Restrictions on corporate financing.

A sort of love-hate relationship between corporate heads and bureaucrats prevailed for a frustratingly long time. The liberalization measures, macroeconomic reforms and structural adjustments brought about in the early 90s have altered the economic scenario quite dramatically.

Obviously companies that want to do business globally must pay attention to the above factors closely and learn to adopt themselves to the laws of the land. The rules of the competition, trademark rights, price controls, product quality laws and a number of other legal issues in individual countries may be of special importance to global companies such as Coca-Cola, Pepsi, Unilever, IBM and McDonald's etc.

Regulatory Environment

Regulatory environment consists of the laws and regulations that federal, state and local governments develop in order to exert control over business practices.

Regulatory environment is that part of the firm's external marketing environment on which legal and political forces act to change regulations which affect the marketing effort; regulation changes can pose threats or present opportunities.

Regulatory environment shows how labour laws are affected, what is industrial policy, taxation etc. and some of regulatory environment is given below.

- Industrial Policy
- Foreign Exchange Controls
- Trade Policy
- Intellectual Property Rights
- Labour Laws
- Capital market regulation
- Taxation.

Industrial Policy

The Industrial Policy Resolution of 1956 and the Statement on Industrial Policy of 1991, provide the basic framework for the overall industrial policy of the Government in regard to the manufacturing industries. In the initial stages of the country's development, growth of industry was regulated through the granting of industrial licences and other industrial approvals. The Industries (Development and Regulation) Act, 1951 was the principal legislation providing the legal basis for industrial licencing. The industrial policy announced on 24th July, 1991 substantially dispensed with industrial licensing, announced measures facilitating foreign investment and technology transfers, and threw open the areas hitherto reserved for the public sector.

Areas where an industrial license is required

The requirement of obtaining an industrial license for manufacturing activity is limited to:

- Industries reserved for the pubic sector.
- 16 industries of strategic, social or environmental concern.
- Industries reserved for the small scale sector.

Foreign Exchange Controls

India's foreign exchange control regime is governed by the Foreign Exchange Regulation Act, (FERA), 1973. Comprehensive amendments to FERA, especially with respect to foreign investment have been undertaken in order to give effect to the liberalizations announced in the economic policies. FERA provisions that imposed restrictions on locally incorporated companies with foreign equity holding in excess of 40 per cent (known as "FERA companies") have been removed. Such companies are now permitted to operate in India without any special restrictions, effectively placing them on par with wholly Indian owned companies.

Although the Indian *foreign exchange market* is not yet fully developed, a variety of instruments have been introduced in the recent past. The dollar rupee forward market is very active, and firms have access to cross-currency options.

Trade Policy

Trade Policy Reforms have been one of the major planks of the new economic policies initiated from July 1991 onwards. Changes in trade policies have included a significant scaling down of tariff barriers, and a partial dismantling of the system of import and export licences and simplification of procedures.

The new trade policy is spelt out in the Export Import (EXIM) policy, which is valid for the period 1992 to 1997; *amendments* to this policy were announced on 31st March 1995.

Intellectual Property Rights

The concept of Intellectual Property established soundly at all levels: statutory, administrative and judicial. The four main aspects of India's Intellectual Property Rights regime are:

Copyrights: India's copyrights law, laid down in the Indian Copyright Act, 1957, fully reflects the Berne convention on Copyright, to which India is a party. It has been amended periodically to keep pace with changing requirements. The most recent amendment was in 1994, which ushered in comprehensive changes and brought the Copyright law in line with the new developments in satellite broadcasting, computer software and digital technology. Indian Copyright law is now on par with the most modern laws in the field.

Trade Marks: India affords full protection to Trade Marks under the Trade Marks and Merchandise Act. Service Marks are not specifically included in the Trade Marks and Merchandise Act. However, they have been protected in judicial decisions by the Courts. Government has introduced a Bill in Parliament seeking to amend the earlier Trade Marks and Merchandise Act and provide for statutory protection of Service Marks.

Patents: Under the Patent Act, 1970, India recognizes product patents under a 14 year period of protection for patents. However, it provides an exception in three areas: food, chemicals and pharmaceuticals, where it recognises only a process patent for a period of 7 years.

Industrial Designs: Industrial Designs are governed by the Designs Act of 1911. The registration of a design confers on the registered proprietor the right to take action against third parties who apply the registered design without license or consent. The duration of protection afforded to a design registered under the Act is five years initially, with renewals for two further periods of five years each.

Labour Laws

India is a member of the International Labour Organization and complies with conventions which it has ratified. It has enacted comprehensive legislation to provide a good working environment for labour and protect their interests. The government continuously reviews various labour laws in line with changing circumstances. The following are the key labour laws:

- Industrial relations are regulated by the Industrial Disputes Act,1947 which provides for just and equitable settlement of disputes through negotiations, conciliation, arbitration or adjudication.
- The Factories Act, 1948, regulates working conditions in factories. The Act prescribes minimum standards for working conditions and facilities related to manufacturing processes, handling and storage of materials, discharge of effluents, fire precautions, working hours and health facilities etc.
- The Minimum Wages Act 1948 empowers the appropriate Governments to fix and revise the minimum wages and allowances payable to workers and also to regulate the conditions of work such as hours of work, overtime, etc. for workers in the notified employment under their respective jurisdiction.
- The Payment of Bonus Act, 1965, requires payment of bonus to certain categories of workers whose wages do not exceed Rs.2,500 per month. The Act ensures payment of minimum bonus of 8.33 per cent per year, with maximum bonus not to exceed 20 per cent of salary or wage earned during the accounting year.
- The Payment of Gratuity Act 1972 requires the employer to pay gratuity to certain categories of workers on termination of service. This Act applies to all workers without any wage limit.
- The Employees' Provident Fund Act 1952 applies to workers whose wages do not exceed Rs.3,500 per month in some industries and establishments. The employer and the employee are required to make matching contributions of 8.33 per cent to 10 per cent of the employee's salary to the fund.
- The Employees' State Insurance Act 1948 covers sickness, maternity and employment related injuries. The Act applies to workers whose wages do not exceed Rs.3,000 per month.
- In addition to the above Acts, several states have enacted Shops and Establishment Acts which regulate working hours, prescribe minimum standards of working conditions and provide for overtime and leave salary payments to workers in certain categories of shops and other establishments.

Taxation

India has a well developed tax structure with the authority to levy taxes divided between the Union Government and the State Governments. The Union Government levies direct taxes such as personal income tax and corporate tax, and indirect taxes like custom duties, excise duties and central sales tax. The states are empowered to levy state sales tax apart from various other local taxes like entry tax, octroi etc.

In 1991, the government set up a special committee, the Raja Chelliah Committee on Tax Reforms, to review the country's tax system. Its mandate was to make recommendations to maekthe tax system more elastic and broad based, and to suggest means required for simplifying existing laws and regulations to facilitate better enforcement and compliance. The recommendations made by this committee envisaged simplified procedures and a rationalized rate structure. The government has implemented a large number of recommendations such as:

- drastic reduction in customs and excise duties
- lowering of corporate tax rates
- removing distinction between widely held and closely held companies
- extending MODVAT to more industries
- simplifying income tax return filing procedures
- levying taxes on services like insurance, stock brokering and telephones.

Trade Regulation:

Trade within a state is regulated exclusively by the states themselves. As with any commercial activity, intrastate and interstate trade is often times indistinguishable.

Federal agencies that help in trade regulation include the *Department of Commerce (DOC) (http://www.doc.gov)* and the *International Trade Administration (ITA) (http://www.ita.doc.gov/)*.

The DOC is an agency of the executive branch that promotes international trade, economic growth, and technological advancement. The ITA is a branch of the DOC that works to improve the international trade position of the United States.

There are different Trade associations like

- NAFTA (national American Free Trade Association)
- ASEAN (Association of Southeast Asian Nations)
- GATT (General Agreement on Tariffs and Trade)
- EU (European Union)

Commercial Law:

Commercial law governs the brands areas of business, commerce and consumer transactions.

Specific laws have developed in a number of commercial fields like banking, bankruptcy, contracts, mortgages etc.

Investment

When people think about globalization, they often first think of the increasing volume of trade in goods and services. Trade flows are indeed one of the most visible aspects of globalization. But many analysts argue that international investment is a much more powerful force in propelling the world toward closer economic integration. Investment often alters entire methods of production through transfers of know-how, technology, and management techniques, and thereby initiates much more significant change than the simple trading of goods.

Over the past ten years, foreign investment has grown at a significantly more rapid pace than either international trade or world economic production generally. From 1980 to 2000, while the volume of goods traded has increased significantly, foreign investment has grown even faster (See figure below).

This investment has been a powerful catalyst for economic growth.

The tremendous growth in levels of foreign direct investment is a recent phenomenon and is one of the most powerful effects—and causes—of globalization. In 1982, the global total of Foreign Direct Investment (FDI) flows was $57 billion. By the year 2000, that number had grown to $1.271 billion—nearly 20 times the level two decades earlier.

But as with many of the other aspects of globalization, foreign investment is raising many new questions about economic, cultural, and political relationships around the world. Flows of investment and the rules which govern or fail to govern it can have profound impacts upon such diverse issues as economic developme, environmental protection, labour standards, and economic stability.

Figure 3.1

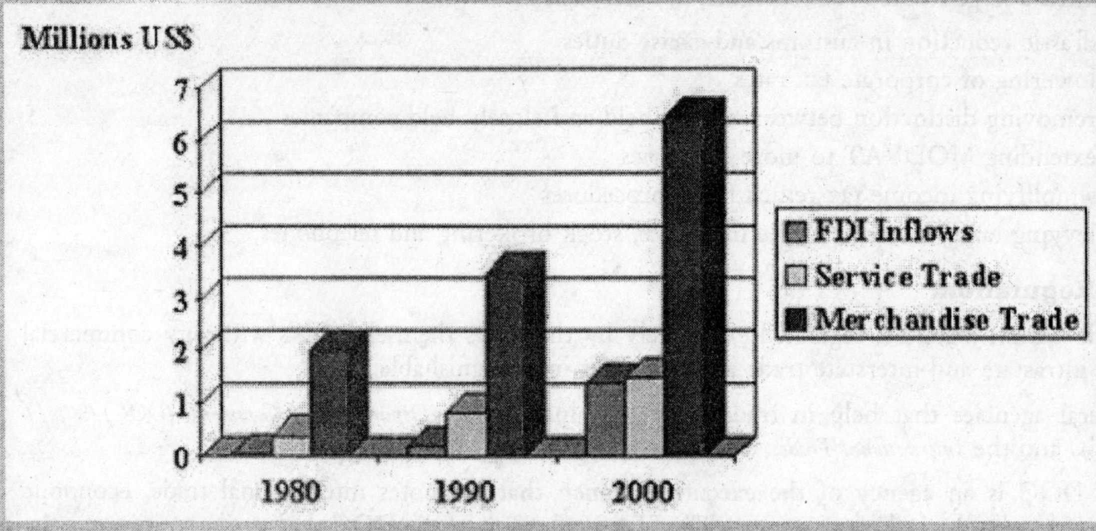

Different Kinds of Foreign Investment

International investment or capital flows fall into four principal categories:

1. **Commercial loans:** These primarily take the form of loans by banks to foreign businesses or governments.
2. **Official flows:** This category refers generally to the forms of development assistance given by developed countries to developing ones.
3. **Foreign direct investment (FDI):** This category refers to international investment in which the investor obtains a lasting interest in an enterprise in another country.
   - Most concretely, it may take the form of buying or constructing a factory in a foreign country or adding improvements to such a facility, in the form of property, plants, or equipment.
   - FDI is calculated to include all kinds of capital contributions, such as the purchases of stocks, as well as the reinvestment of earnings by a wholly owned company incorporated abroad (subsidiary), and the lending of funds to a foreign subsidiary or branch. The reinvestment of earnings and transfer of assets between a parent company and its subsidiary often constitutes a significant part of FDI calculations.
   - According to the United Nations Conference on Trade and Development (UNCTAD), the global expansion of FDI is currently being driven by over 60,000 transnational corporations with more than 8,00,000 foreign affiliates.
4. **Foreign Portfolio Investment (FPI):** Foreign Portfolio Investment is a category of investment instruments that are easily traded, less permanent, and do not represent a controlling stake in an enterprise.
5. These include investments via equity instruments (Stocks) or Debts (bonds) of a foreign enterprise that does not represent a long-term investment. Investments in FPI that are made for less than one year are distinguished as short-term portfolio flows.

Technological Environment

- Level of technology
- Availability of local technical skills
- Technical requirements of country
- Appropriability

- Transfer of technology
- Infrastructure
- Environmental protection.

Technological factors represent major opportunities and threats that must be taken into account while formulating strategies. Technological breakthroughs can dramatically influence the organizations products, services markets, supplies, distributors, competitors, customers, manufacturing processes, marketing practices and competitive position. Technological advancement can open up new markets, result in proliferation of new and improved products, change relative cost position in an industry and render existing products and services absolute. Technological changes can reduce or eliminate cost barriers between businesses, create shorter production run, create shortages in technical skills and result in changing values and expectations of customers and employees.

Technological advancements can create new competitive advantages that are more powerful than existing ones. Recent technological advances, as we well know, in computers, lasers, robotics, satellite networks, fiber optics, biometrics, cloning and other related area have paved the way for significant operational improvements. Manufactures, banks, retailer, for example, have used advances in computer technology to carry out their traditional tasks at lower cost and higher level of customer satisfaction. Consider a case of old economy giant, Ford Motor Company, which is morphing into a new economy animal using web based technologies to the best advantage. Thanks to the internet, the old days of being able to concentrate only on the nuts and bolts of the business seem to be over. The winners are going to be companies that move closer and connect well with customers. Technological driver is one of the principal drivers of competition. It plays a vital role in industry structural change as well as in creating new industries.

Technology and Industry Structure

Technology is an important determinant of overall industry structure, if the technology employed in value activity becomes wide spread. Technological change that is diffused can potentially affect each of the 5 forces.

1. **Technology and Entry Barriers:** Technological change is powerful determinant of entry barrier. it can raise or lower the economic of scale in nearly any value activity, by quickening the pace of production introduction or raising investment required for a new model.

2. **Technology and Buyer Power:** Technology can shift the bargaining relationship between an industry and its buyers. The role of technology in different and switching cost is instrumental in determining buyers' power. Technological change also influences the ease of backward integration by the buyer, a key buyer power lever.

3. **Technology and Supplier Power:** Technology can eliminate the need to purchase from powerful supplier group or can force an industry to purchase from a new supplier. Technological changes also allow a number of substitute input to be used in a firms product, creating bargaining leverage against suppliers.

4. **Technology and Substitution:** Substitute and technology is a function of relative value to price of competing product and the switching costs associated with changing between them. Technological change creates entirely new product or product uses that substitute for other.

5. **Technology and Rivalry:** Technology can alter the nature and basis of rivalry among existing competitive several ways. It can dramatically alter the cost structure and hence affect pricing decision.

Technological Change and Industry Boundaries

Technological change widens industry boundaries in number of ways. It can reduce transactions and logistics cost, thereby enlarging the geographic scope of market. Technological change that reduces the cost of responding to national market difference can help in "Globalization of industries". It can also help in enhancing the product performance, thereby bringing new customer into a market.

Technological Strategy

Technology strategy is a firm's approach to the development and use of technology. Because of technology change to influence industry structure and competitive advantage, a firm's technology strategy becomes an essential ingredient in its overall competitive strategy. Innovation is one of the principal ways of attacking well entrenched competitor.

Technology strategy must address three broad issues:

1. What technology to develop?
2. Whether to seek technological leadership in these technologies?
3. The role of technology licensing.

Sustainability of Technological Lead: Technological leadership favored lead can be sustaining because:

a. Competitor can't duplicate the technology.
b. The firm innovate as fast as or faster then competitor.

The second condition is important because technology often fuses, requiring a technological leader to remain a moving target. The sustainability of technological lead is a function of various factors.

1. The Source of Technological Change: THE sustainability of a technological lead depends heavily on whether technology is being developed inside or being coming from outside it.
2. Relative Technology Skill: A firm with unique technological skill *vis-a-vis* competitor is more likely to sustain its technological lead.

Technological Evolution

Since technological change has such a powerful role in competition, forecasting the path of technological evolution is extremely important to allow a firm to anticipate technological change and thereby improve its position. Most of research on how technology evolves in an industry has grown out of the product life cycle concept. According to the life cycle model ,technological change early in the life cycle is focused on the product innovation, while the manufacturing process remain flexible. As an industry matures, product design begin to change more slowly .

Process innovation takes over from product innovation as a primary form of technological activity, with the aim of reducing the cost of increasing standard product. Finally, all innovation slow down in later maturity and decline as investment in the various technological in the industry reach the point of diminishing returns.

E-Business

The e-business strategic management process illustrated is based on the traditional model of strategic management. It is a systematic process consisting of four interrelated steps as shown in the figure on next page.

Every organization should experience this process, and described below is how organizations should approach each stage of the process.

Step 1: Analyze the company's external and internal environments

In the traditional strategic planning model, managers identify their company's strengths and weaknesses, as well as the obstacles and opportunities in their business environment. They are then ready to make strategic decisions that seek to balance their company's competencies with the business opportunities around them. This step is equally crucial for e-business planning.

The main barriers to e-business adoption

A wait-and-see attitude and skepticism on the part of clients and partners can put up barriers that

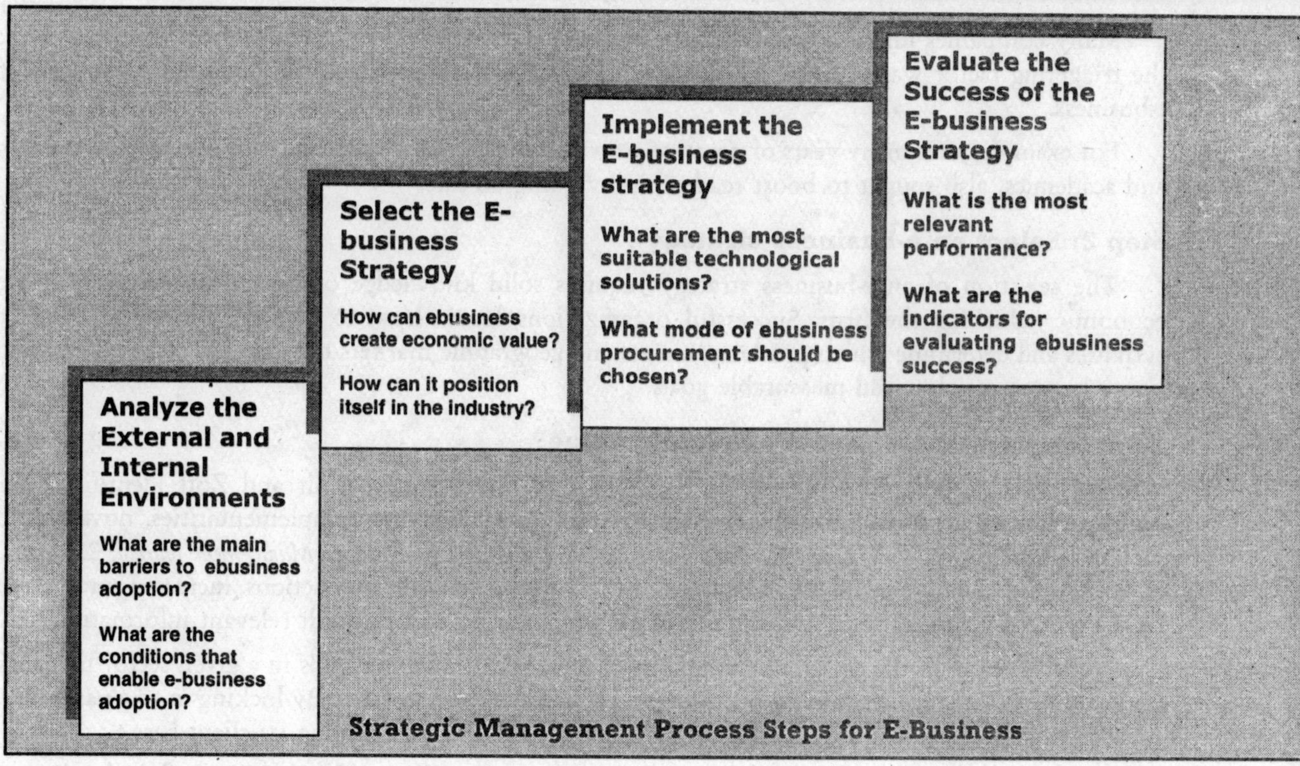

Figure 3.2 Strategic Management Process Steps for E-Business

discourage e-business solutions. In other cases, the nature of the company's product can make it more difficult to introduce e-business.

Consider the example of Moules Industriels, a Sherbrooke, Que., firm that manufactures rubber and plastic moulds-a customized product that is generally unsuitable for Web-based sales because transactions cannot occur without prior personal contact. Moules Industries can, however, use the Web to foster initial client contact, and when an agreement is reached with a client, the Internet can make further contact easier during the prototype development phase.

However, it is found from various studies that by far the most important obstacle to e-business adoption among was lack of financial resources. The size of the investment and the long and sometimes uncertain payback period frequently cause organizations to postpone investing in ebusiness.

For example, 20 per cent of Polar Plastic's customers wanted the Montreal-based plastic-ware manufacturer to adopt an electronic data interchange (EDI) system, which was too costly, given the company's small client base. Polar Plastic knew that it would be very difficult to pay off the $30,000 cost of the system over the short term. Instead, the company opted for EDI Gateway, a technological solution offered by an external supplier that processes customer orders and lets Polar Plastic transmit information to its clients' EDI systems. Through this intermediary company, Polar could receive and transmit information by fax to clients like McDonald's Restaurants. Until recently, the cost of contracting this particular EDI solution through an intermediary was a few hundred dollars per month.

What conditions enable e-business adoption?

When developing their e-business strategic plan, managers must take into account the number and nature of external factors that are compatible with the adoption of e-business. Depending on the industry, government financing may be an incentive for adopting e-business. Other proven incentives are the time spent with SMEs to understand their needs and the investments in technological infrastructure made by the leaders of sector-based associations like the QICG (Quebec Institute of Graphic Communications) and the funding and technological expertise of partners such as government agencies and large corporations.

Many companies know how to identify and take advantage of such arrangements. In our study, the triggering factor was usually the initiative of managers who realized the potential advantages of e-business.

For example, after many years of negative growth, *Revue Gestion*, a magazine for business practitioners and academics, also sought to boost readership by going on-line.

Step 2: Select an e-business strategy

The selection of an e-business strategy requires solid knowledge of how e-business can create economic value for the firm. Successful organizations know how to identify the scope of their activities and determine which products, clients and geographic markets they should target. They also know how to set clear and measurable goals.

How can e-business create economic value?

The ultimate goal of any strategic decision is to create value. Amit and Zott identified four opportunities to create value with the help of ebusiness: efficiency, complementarities, novelty and lock-in. (R. Amit and C. Zott, "Value Creation in E-Business", *Strategic Management Journal*, 22, 2001, p.493-520.) Efficiency is mainly derived from lower costs due to faster transactions, increased automation of the company's operations, and the ease with which clients can research relevant information.

Novelty refers to the design and adoption of new operational methods in a given sector that link up new or existing participants, or introduces new products and services. By locking in to a particular, reliable technological solution, a company gains approval and trust among its client base.

Complementarities are mainly concerned with the bundling of resources and technological capabilities, as well as the bundling of products and services, of various partners in one electronic network. the principal value driver was efficiency for the firm and the customer. Using ebusiness allowed SMEs to reduce costs and find new clients, as was the case with Montreal's Auberge de La Fontaine, whose Web presence boosted the inn's revenues by 30 per cent.

Step 3: Implement the e-business strategy

After defining the targeted client base and geographic markets for new or traditional products, managers should plan the implementation of their e-business and decide what type of technological solution and supply chain to adopt.

What mode of e-business procurement should be chosen?

The procurement model that a company selects needs to complement the strategic importance of the project and the in-house availability of resources to develop such solutions (See V. Roy and B.A. Aubert, "Valeur stratégique, compétences clés et développement technologique", *Gestion*, Vol. 28, No.1, 2003, p.28-35).

There are four different procurement models:

- Partnership
- Preservation
- Outsourcing
- Recovery.

Businesses that enter into partnerships generally seek a partner (consultant or service provider) who can supply the expertise they lack to develop the new information system. However, most prefer to hire freelance programmers, because a partnership arrangement with a consulting firm is often expensive and time-consuming.

In the preservation model of procurement, the ebusiness system is developed entirely in-house. This model is usually adopted by businesses that have the internal skills to carry out the e-business project on their own. In addition, firms that select this model generally place a high strategic value on the project.

When the strategic value and expertise of in-house resources are low, outsourcing is a logical solution.

In the recovery procurement model, there are two approaches that can be followed: The first is to share development costs among several companies because of the obvious economic benefits. The second approach is to market the application developed by the company, and Revue Gestion is a good example. In order to recover part of its investment to develop a Web site, *Revue Gestion* offered Web hosting to other journals that were not close competitors.

Step 4: Evaluate the success of the e-business strategy

After acquiring a sound understanding of how to create economic value with e-business and determining the firm's desired positioning, managers must finalize objectives relating to sales growth, cost reduction and profitability. They must also select the indicators that will enable them to assess the success of the e-business solution-scorecards showing financial, client, internal process and learning and growth indicators can be vital tools.

Indicators for evaluating e-business success

Overall, the businesses use number of unsophisticated indicators for evaluating the success of e-business. They place importance on the profitability of transactions, and measure performance by analyzing additional sales volume and the savings realized by using e-business.

Standard Performance Indicators

1. *Financial indicators*

- Lower average cost per subscription
- Increased revenue per subscription
- Higher number of subscriptions
- Payback period for technological investments.

2. *Internal processes indicators*

- Number of service denials
- Performance of search tools
- Graphic quality of articles
- Variety of download formats
- Ease of maintaining Web site
- Average time to prepare an issue
- Decreased workload for managing and handling subscriptions
- Download speed.

3. *Customer indicators*

- Higher number of subscriptions
- Variety of articles
- Quality of articles
- Number of queries per user
- Number of downloads per user
- Number of complaints.

4. *Learning and growth indicators*

- % of budget devoted to ICT
- Number of site updates
- Number and type of Web site functionalities compared with competitors
- Average age of technology infrastructure.

Example: *Revue Gestion* established a set of indicators to assess the performance of its e-business project prior to implementing e-business. Many of these indicators are automatically captured on *Revue Gestion's* Web site. *Revue Gestion's* on-line presence has increased the company's revenues by over 25 per cent. This improvement is largely due to the introduction of corporate on-line subscriptions for businesses and associations, which increased subscription rates from 2,500 to more than 30,000 in one year. At the same time, handling, marketing and printing costs declined, saving the journal an estimated $194,000. Auberge de la Fontaine's Web site expanded the company's client base by 15 per cent. In 2003, 24 per cent of the company's clients discovered the hotel through the Internet-49 per cent were American, 42 per cent Canadian, and 3 per cent French. Moreover, 52 per cent of the hotel's clients entered the site directly through its e-mail address, aubergedelafontaine.com; nine per cent through the bonjourquebec.com reservation portal; and the remainder through approximately 50 out of the 300 sites on which the hotel is registered.

Telecommunication

The liberalization of telecommunications markets abolished the state monopolies and opened up markets to competition. All telecommunications markets were placed under sector-specific regulation and the supervision of a national regulatory authority; for instance, in Germany by the Regulierungsbehörde für Telekommunikation und Post (RegTP – the Regulatory Authority for Post and Telecommunications). Right from the beginning it was clear that competition will not come overnight. As regulators abstained from imposing structural remedies (as, e.g., the 1984 AT&T breakup into a long-distance operator and seven regional Bell operating companies in the US), price and access regulations have become important regulatory instruments to ensure the development of competition at various levels. Similar to the "ladder of investment" idea of Martin Cave and Ingo Vogelsang, [1] it was assumed that ex ante regulation of the former monopoly would be necessary to kick-start competition – first at the service and later on at the infrastructure level. Accordingly, access regulation to the network of the former monopoly operator has been a primary concern. Moreover, the intention was to create effective competitive structures within telecommunications markets, and with this, to review the possibility of removing specific telecommunication markets from *ex ante* regulation and placing those markets under the supervision of general competition law.

The question how to phase out regulatory supervision has gained new momentum with the implementation of the new regulatory framework in the EU. The new regulatory framework takes account of the rapid pace of technological progress by providing a uniform legal framework that covers the convergence of telecommunications, media and information technologies Moreover, it aims at bringing the regulation of electronic markets into line with the principles of competition law.

A critical aspect of the new framework is that telecommunications markets are no longer lumped together under the supervision of the regulatory authority. Rather, specified criteria have first to be applied to define markets, which may become candidates for ex ante regulation in a further procedural step.

In the first stage, the list of markets is defined on relevant product and service markets. It requires selecting those markets which cannot be expected to generate effective competition and are, therefore candidates for same sort of sector-specific regulation. Precisely, recommendations regarding the definition of markets susceptible to ex ante regulation, as follows: "In identifying markets in accordance with competition law principles, recourse should be had to the following three criteria. The first criterion is the presence of high and non-transitory entry barriers whether of structural, legal or regulatory nature. However, given the dynamic character and functioning of electronic communications markets, possibilities to overcome barriers within a relevant time horizon have also to be taken into consideration when carrying out a prospective analysis to identify the relevant markets for possible ex ante regulation. Therefore, the second criterion admits only those markets the structure of which does not tend towards effective competition within the relevant time horizon. The application of this criterion involves examining the state of competition behind the barriers of entry. The third criterion is that application of competition law alone would not adequately address the market failure(s) concerned."

Thus the three criteria, all of which have to be satisfied so that a certain market should be included in the list are:

1. There must be "high and non-transitory" structural or legal barriers to entry.
2. There must be no tendency towards effective competition within a certain time horizon.
3. The market failure cannot be addressed with competition law alone.

It is noteworthy that this takes into account the dynamic character of markets and requires an assessment of their tendency towards competition. Other retail markets and wholesale markets that should be subjected to market analysis by the national regulatory authorities also need to be taken into account. Those markets not explicitly included in the list will not be subjected to any market analysis and will therefore not come under sector-specific regulation (unless particular circumstances justify regulation by national authorities).

After having defined the relevant product and service markets, the second step is to examine the competitive intensity in those markets. If effective competition is absent, then the national regulatory authority must put firms with substantial market power under sector-specific regulation.

An important issue determining the effectiveness of the new legal framework is the adjustment of the list of relevant markets over time and the associated problem of how new markets should be treated.

The concept of "new and emerging markets" introduced by the new regulatory framework explicitly recognizes the need to guarantee "first-mover" advantages so as to protect innovation incentives, and hence, the development of new infrastructures. While this approach intends to rule out any *ex ante* regulation for new markets, there is still ample scope for discretion. Moreover, the new regulatory framework leaves many questions unanswered which are important for making it operational and effective. In particular:

1. What is a new and emerging market and how can it be distinguished from more mature markets?
2. What degree of "first-mover" advantage is desirable in terms of efficient investment in infrastructure and innovation?
3. How should the development of new markets towards effective competition be assessed and reviewed?

To answer these questions, it is necessary to keep in mind that new markets pose different regulatory challenges when compared with existing networks and infrastructures. Whereas, in the latter case, infrastructure investments have already been made, this is typically not the case with new markets. The Regulatory framework has barely considered the concept of new markets or new infrastructures, which thereby, highlights the interdependencies between regulation and private investment incentives as an issue; the key for understanding the regulation of new markets is, therefore, the difference between static and dynamic market power.

Saying that the last decades have been a period of unparalleled technological and regulatory change in the telecommunications environment is not new. The truth is the tendency towards deregulation and the introduction of competition is now visible. Inevitably, extra competition has effects on firm profitability. In this sense, it is important to capture the "*underlying behavioural predilections of firms*" and to observe their responses, in order to better guide policymakers. It is known that many policies are characterized by ambiguous policy preferences, incomplete understanding of causal relationships, distributed knowledge and limited time for action. Policymakers lack the necessary information to make certain decisions, and even though the information may be available, computational or cognitive limitations may prevent them from pursuing their objectives.

Until the early 1990 years mobile phones were expensive and technically not very matured products. As a consequence they were mainly used by business customers who mostly needed the possibility of mobile communications. This situation changed after the implementation of GSM digital technology, because mobile phones became mass products, demand increased and prices declined significantly (Hausman, 2002; Gruber, 2005). Since 2000 the number of mobile subscriptions exceeds the number of exchange line telephone subscriptions much more than in the year 2000 and the trend still continues.

The markets for exchange and mobile telecommunications are subjects of regulatory obligations, (Lacont and Tirole, 2000), but the amount of regulation in these two markets is quite different. After the liberalization of telecommunications markets world over the former state owned telecommunications companies (the incumbents) were (partially) privatized and new competitors were enabled to enter the market. Because these new competitors needed (and until now still need) the incumbent's infrastructure (Cave and Prosperetti, 2001), markets for exchange line telecommunications are regulated quite heavily. In contrast mobile communications markets were more competitive until their beginning, compared with their exchange line counterparts (Haucap, 2003). As a result regulation in these markets is less restrictive. But today the demand on exchange and mobile markets raises a new question: Are exchange and mobile phones substitutes?

If these products were substitutes, different regulatory arrangements would be hard to justify. While there is some casual evidence that exchange line and mobile telephony are converging and becoming closer substitutes, the number of econometric studies has been rather limited. Some first evidence that exchange-mobile substitution is increasing has been provided by Yoon and Song (2003). However, there is virtually no econometric study of exchange-mobile substitution in India.

The delineation of electronic communications markets provided for in the current regulatory framework may be no longer adequate if exchange and mobile telephony markets are converging. Additionally, if markets converge new regulatory questions arise.

How should a company be treated that exhibits significant market power in exchange line telecommunications but not in mobile communications? But there is still a lack of detailed empirical studies examining this substitution. Regarding to regulation of telecommunications markets exchange mobile substitutability has a wide ranging impact. Most mobile telecommunications markets in India, are not very strongly regulated, an observation which holds for most parts of the world. Exceptions are issues like mobile number portability, mobile termination rates, and international roaming.

In contrast exchange line telecommunications markets are subjects of considerable regulatory obligations. These differences were quite reasonable when mobile communications services were very expensive and only available for a small group of customers. Today continuously falling prices and the growing substitution between exchange and mobile services raises the question if two different regulatory regimes for exchange and mobile markets are an appropriate solution. Consider the verification of significant market power. If exchange and mobile services are substitutes, it is not sufficient that a telecommunications company has significant market power (or a main share of the market) in the market for exchange line services, because customers use mobile services as substitutes to the company's exchange line services and are not constrained to exchange line telephony. As a result it would be impossible to gain rents as a consequence of significant market power in exchange or mobile markets only. When the evolution of usage patterns suggests that mobile telecommunications services constrain exchange line companies market power, regulatory obligations on exchange telephony markets have to be reconsiderd (Rodini, Ward and Woroch, 2003).

In conjunction with these developments the suitability of the definition of markets in the current regulatory framework has to be reconsidered for future telecommunications regulation. But there are other aspects besides the convergence of exchange and mobile networks, which will affect the development of telecommunications markets fundamentally. One of these aspects is the market success of Voice Telephony over Internet Protocol (VoIP) (Majumdar, Vogelsang and Cave, 2005). If VoIP becomes the industry standard for voice telephony, services of classical exchange and mobile networks could be substituted by VoIP and different forms of networks will converge. An interesting subject for future research is the impact of increasing availability as well as quality and security of VoIP on the numbers of exchange and mobile subscriptions. But in India as well as in other countries, the availability of appropriate data is always problematical.

In transition or developing countries the situation is quite different as a result of the poor exchange line infrastructure and the corresponding low growth rates. Growth rates of mobile communications are much higher, than growth rates of exchange networks in these countries. As a consequence we will observe other forms of network convergence than in developed countries. The future development and regulation of telecommunications, its impact on strategic planning in global markets will remain an important field of research, particularly because of technological change which will be a key aspect for exchange mobile substitution and the meaning of telecommunications for economic growth and development (Munnell, 1992; Seth, 1992; Röller and Waverman, 2001).

Outsourcing and Off shoring

Off shoring is the practice by which companies outsource processes, chiefly IT-based services, across large distances to other parts of the world, often low-wage countries. It is a technical term from financial economics, in which offshore centres are used to describe tax havens attracting foreign investment with low rates of taxation and strict banking secrecy. But regulatory differences play only a very minor part in off shoring, the main aim being to exploit wage cost differentials in the services sector. As a rule the activities involved are simple ones, such as data entry and processing, call centre and support services (help desks) or processes entailing the standardized treatment of insurance claims. But even more demanding tasks such as application development and maintenance or the analysis of computer scans from Europe by Indian radiologists come under the heading of off shoring.

The key characteristic of off shoring is that the services are rendered abroad. Normally, the provider and client are located on different continents: India, as the major provider, and the United States, as the biggest taker, determine this mental image. But there are also many exceptions to the rule. Co-operation between partners on the same continent is termed near shoring. From a Central European perspective the East European EU accession countries and Russia, and in some cases Spain and Portugal are countries of destination for near shoring. Many people are confused by the terms off shoring and outsourcing. In a nutshell, outsourcing is hiring another company to do some of your work. Off shoring is moving some of your work to another country with cheaper labour. The two ideas often overlap – for example, when outsourcing work to a supplier located offshore – but they aren't the same. In the early days of off shoring, most companies chose to outsource because it was fast and easy. But according to recent research, more and more companies are electing to retain control and ownership by establishing their own wholly owned offshore subsidiaries. In addition, more of the benefits fall to the bottom-line.

> For example, offshore business process outsourcing is the exporting of work from the United States to areas of the world where there is lower labor cost or tax savings. In this type of arrangement, the foreign-based firm provides services for a U.S.-based company that could also be, or usually has been, provided in the U.S. onshore outsourcing keeps the business process that is being outsourced in the U.S. and utilizes a partner to supply U.S. based labour and expertise for the completion of the work.

Things are even more confusing in the United States where some off shoring proponents have attempted to divert public criticism by substituting terms like global sourcing, inter-sourcing, blended sourcing and right sourcing. But beneath the smart word-smiting, it's still off shoring.

In most companies, important processes such as customer relationship management (CRM—customer service, pricing, billing, etc.), finance and accounting (F&A—accounts payable, accounts receivable, etc.), and supply chain management (SCM—shipping, warehousing, purchasing) are deeply dependent upon the IT systems that enable them. Yet few companies see managing an IT infrastructure as a core competence. Whatever the importance of IT infrastructure in enabling these and other essential processes, IT itself is for most firms a hygiene factor: critical to the successful operation of the business but not a distinguishing element of their value chains. Because they consider IT to be "non-core," many firms are looking to outsource the IT component of significant processes, and frequently the processes themselves. For example, applications maintenance outsourcing (AMO) is an increasingly popular way for firms to cope with the escalating demands of managing the tens of millions of lines of code in the CRM software that drives many call centres.

Regardless of whether a company selects an offshore or onshore relationship the reasons are typically the same:

- Reduce and control operating costs
- Improve company focus on its core competencies and strategic imperatives
- Access to world-class capabilities and best of breed technology
- Re-allocate internal resources to higher-value purposes
- Address the issue of limited internal resources
- Accelerate re-engineering/transformation efforts
- Manage more effectively a difficult or problematic function.

Off shoring was initially driven by economic pressure and the need to cut costs, but today most executives in financial services say they are committed to the practice and expect it to continue regardless of the economic environment. The off shoring trend is gaining momentum to a point where the vast majority of financial institutions have or are evaluating the implications for their business – whether they want to or not – to understand potential future strategic options. Firms with offshore operations are also finding they can afford to hire workers that are more highly skilled than their domestic counterparts – and still save money – delivering an appealing combination of higher quality and lower cost. This means that international financial institutions need to dramatically refashion their business and operational models. However, the balance of staff is likely to remain in onshore locations. As expected, off shoring is encountering a significant backlash from labour groups, the public, the media and government – but most executives don't expect it will have much impact on the growth of off shoring in the long-term. Companies are continuing to expand their off shoring capabilities from IT operations to multiple functions, including a wide range of back-office and customer-facing functions. Off shoring offers compelling benefits, but only for companies that do it right.

> Example: Five years ago, if you were an Indian engineer, the dream was to come to America. A fortune could be made very quickly. Indeed many engineers did come. Now, according to a recent *Business Week* article on the globalization of the work force, you can live like a king in India. Being paid with American dollars, an engineer can earn 20 times the average yearly income.

Execution and rigorous governance are the keys to success. An institution's first attempt at off shoring generally requires four to five months of planning, followed by a three- to six-month deployment. Average payback time is one to two years a figure that is expected to shrink even further as firms build offshore experience and capabilities. For financial services institutions, India remains the dominant off shoring location and continues to extend its lead over rival countries – despite some challenges over labor turn-over and costs. In the early days, outsourcing was the preferred approach to off shoring, but the captive model has recently pulled into a virtual tie, with more and more companies electing to retain control and ownership through a wholly owned offshore subsidiary. That's a clear sign off shoring has been accepted as a core element of the global business model for financial services.

The impact of off shoring varies widely for financial institutions of different sizes with larger firms driving change across the financial services industry and using off shoring to open up an increasing competitive advantage over their smaller rivals. By estimate, as many as 80 percent of the world's largest financial institutions (i.e., those with market capitalization exceeding $10 billion) are already working offshore – with less than 20 percent keeping everything at home. For smaller companies, the numbers are split 50:50 between those offshore and those staying home. That disparity creates a significant cost advantage for the larger institutions – and the gap is likely to get wider.

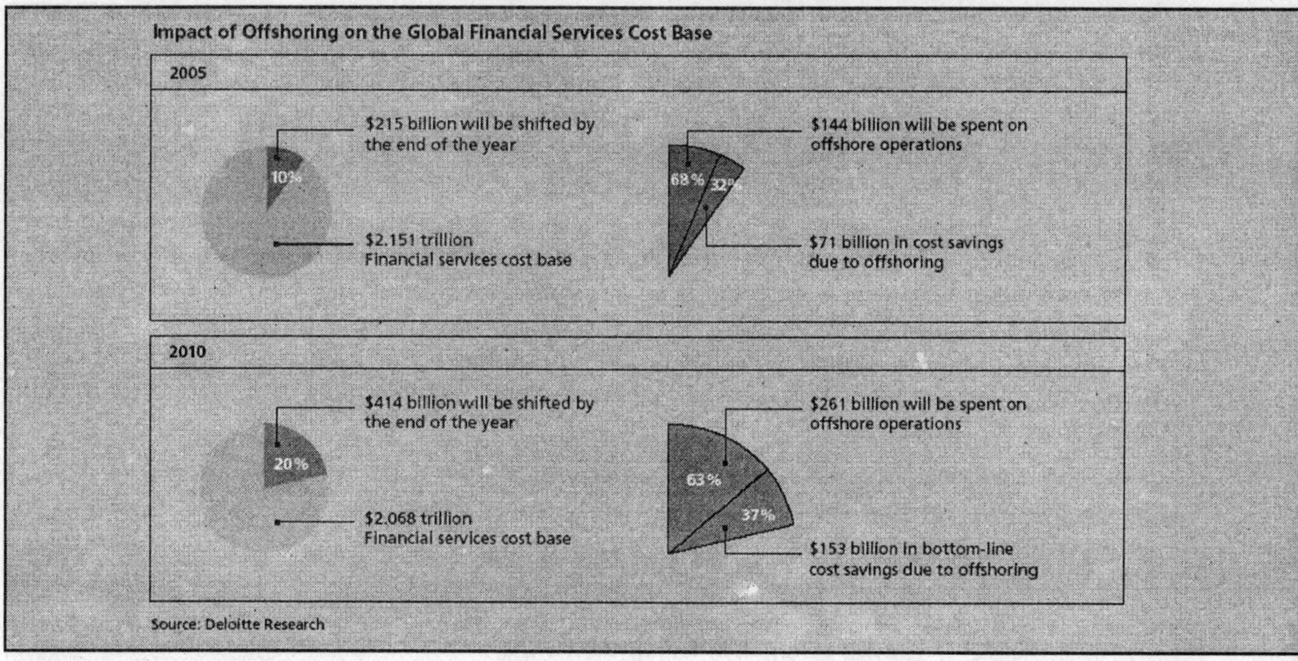

Figure 3.3

Value Chain Dynamics

Value Chain Dynamics begins by asking what you should outsource and what you should keep in-house. Conventional wisdom says to hang on to anything that is core and outsource the rest—functions typically derided as "back office" or "infrastructure." Yet many successful companies do not follow these rules, and those that have are now trying to undo some of those same long-term deals.

Making the right outsourcing decisions requires answering three questions:

1. What to outsource?
2. Whom to outsource it to?
3. How to structure the outsourcing deal?

WHAT
Deciding what to outsource is the most important question when thinking about outsourcing. Get this one right, and you're on your way to creating a competitive advantage that competitors will find hard to beat. Get it wrong, and you'll undermine even your best efforts in every other aspect of your business.
WHO
Every outsourcing decision has two value chains that need to be analyzed: yours and your outsourcing vendors. Once you've concluded that your value chain doesn't need to include a given process, you need to determine that your vendors has all and only the necessary complementary value chain elements to deliver the performance you need and can respond appropriately as your needs change.
HOW
How to structure a deal is a function of how and how quickly the basis of competition in your industry will change. Long-term deals only make sense if what you're outsourcing is very unlikely to figure in your ability to perform against the basis of competition in your industry now or in the future. A flexible approach to outsourcing is critical if a firm is to be able to reconfigure its value chain and deliver the kind of sustained performance that result in consistent shareholder value creation.

Getting the right answers to these questions can transform your outsourcing initiatives into what you have always thought they should be: powerful components of your firm's overall competitive strategy. Outsource correctly, and you can position your company to spring strategic surprises that will defeat your competitors and delight your investors. Get it wrong, and prepare for declining market share, decreasing margins, and a falling stock price. How do you get the answer right? Use an approach we call "Value Chain Dynamics."

One of the reasons focusing on the core can lead to such problems is that it encourages navel gazing: you end up basing outsourcing decisions on what you think you are good at, instead of what you should be good at. So we recommend beginning by identifying your firm's competitive requirements as defined by the markets you serve. Then, use outsourcing to configure your value chain and that of your outsourcing vendor in order to optimize your competitive position. In other words, core competence thinking can be too "inside out," when competitive success can require looking from the "outside in."

In short, applying Value Chain Dynamics is critical to making the right outsourcing decisions. It is an essential tool for enabling your organization to compete effectively today and tomorrow.

4 Cs of Off shoring

Figure 3.4

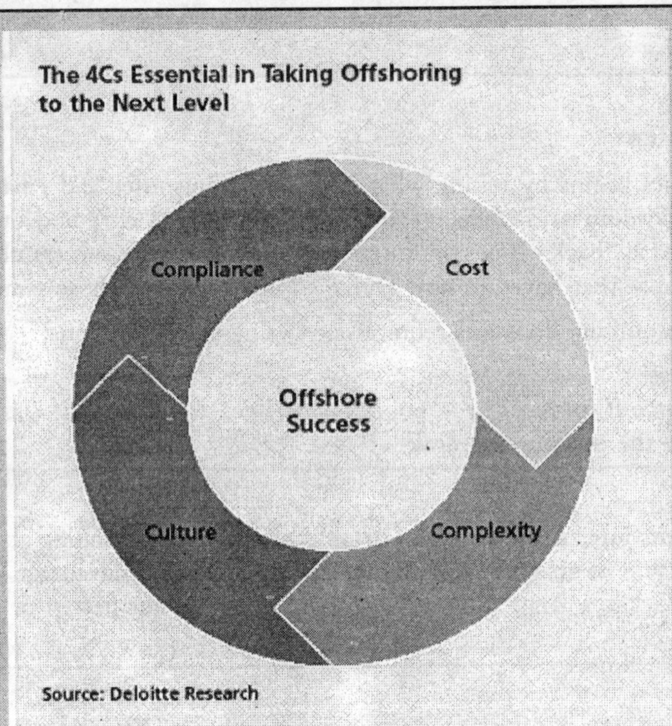

Complexity	*Compliance*
• Scale or fail? The principle challenge facing organization going forward is enhancing operational efficiency. • Building a business model to enable this transition and the part to be played by off shoring can be central. • The survey shows that it's not possible to stand still – the big challenge ahead will be to scale, focus or fail?	• Building global ethics: A key way to improve moral and ethics is a longer-term program of management activities. • The integration of offshore and operation. • Finding a balance between short-term investor demands and long term strategic development is imperative.

Cost	*Culture*
• Recycling savings: The bottom line impact can only be sustained if saving is recycled back into existing offshore operation. • Finding a balance between short-term investor demands and long term strategic development is imperative.	• Tour of duty : A truly global operating model requires more top managerial spending years setting up and operation offshore unit to embed ethics and establish the management framework.

Off shoring as a process of creative destruction

From a macroeconomic perspective, off shoring as a business model makes production by the domestic services sector. In the course of what is termed "creative destruction", such process innovations enable companies to make do with fewer staff.

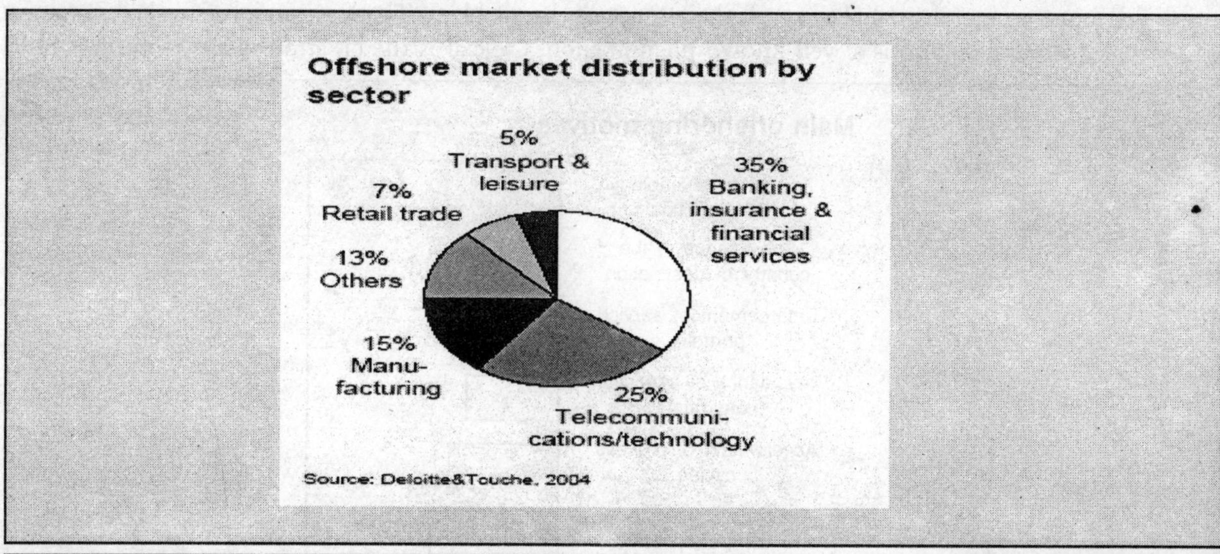

Figure 3.5

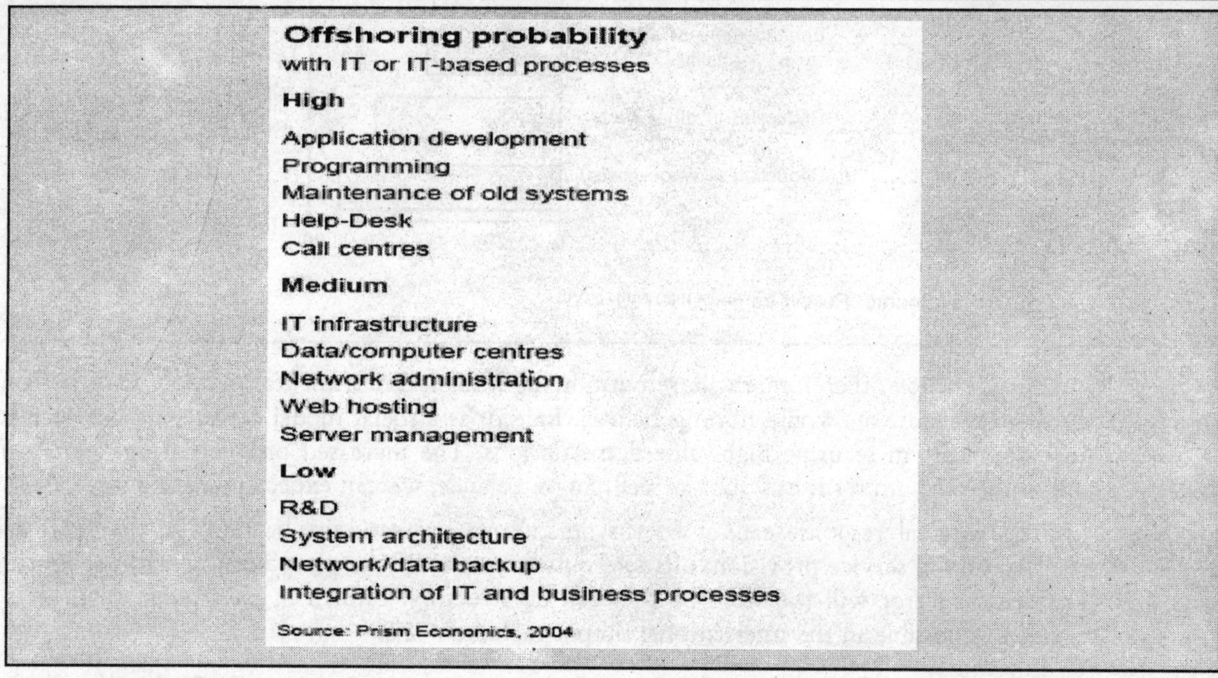

Figure 3.6

Productivity increases assuming the same output, boosting the owners' profits. This, in turn, attracts new providers onto the scene, before competition intensifies and margins contract again. On the demand side, the fact that services are provided at lower prices raises clients' purchasing power.

Lower production costs reduce the prices of the goods and services produced for the established clientele. What is more, smaller businesses not previously able to afford software solutions for their in-house processes can also be gained as customers. Aggregate demand is stimulated, growth generated, and jobs created at other companies.

And indeed, it is estimated that between 1995 and 2002, the United States would have grown 0.3 percentage points a year less if companies had passed up the possibility of IT offshore outsourcing.

Off shoring is part of the solution, not the problem

The off shoring debate will continue to rage for some time to. Yet concerns geared strictly to the outsourcing of workplaces miss the essence of the problem. That certain jobs are shed in the course of structural change is a well known phenomenon. Crucial is the creation of new jobs in parallel.

Figure 3.7

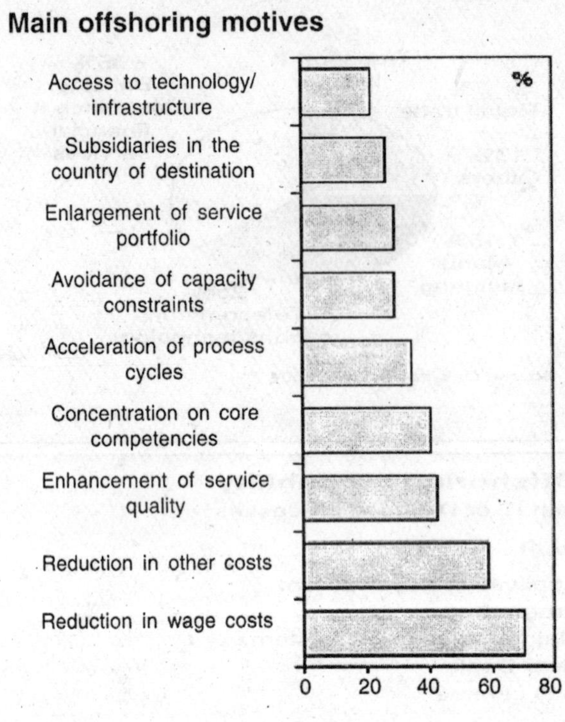

Source: Roland Berger, UNCTAD, 2004

On the whole, therefore, offshore outsourcing is far less detrimental to folk and fatherland than the new-style patriots would have us believe. Indeed, as a social model off shoring can even play an important part in securing high-value domestic jobs. The increased productivity generates growth, and in the medium term new jobs as well. So on balance, we can expect positive effects.

The political response cannot be the erection of protectionist barriers. In the process of the globalization of service provision, offshore outsourcing will take place with or without protagonists. The critical factor will therefore be to speed up structural reform in an attempt to field as many winners as possible in the international output rachides.

No cheap-jack: Costs are not the only argument in favour of off shoring

However, costs are not the only reason for western companies to outsource processes to other countries. As in earlier periods of globalization, they are driven by a variety of considerations.

Essentially, these can be summarized into four motivation groups. But since more than one motive may be relevant simultaneously, the expected effects cannot always be assigned categorically to one single cause.

1. Cost-based outsourcing plays the most prominent part, not only in the public perception. With IT off shoring, the low wage costs in the emerging markets in particular, but also in the East European EU accession countries, are attractive enough to make it worthwhile off shoring processes even when the increased monitoring and initiation costs caused by the distances involved are taken into account. The hourly rate for a software developer with significantly lower costs of just EUR 14 in China. In the Czech Republic and India labour costs, at EUR 8 and 7 an hour respectively, are half less again.

Typically, offshore labour costs make up only 15% to 50% of the total costs of a project, against 75% in the home country. But added to this are off shoring-related management and operating costs such as vendor management. All in all, the estimated cost savings work out at between 20% and 65%, although 20% to 30% is the realistic and typical figure.

2. If the necessary skilled staff cannot be found in the home country, production may be shifted for procurement motives to countries that possess the required specialists in abundance. Human capital is the scarce "resource" in a knowledge society. Computer specialists and skilled engineering staff are in particularly strong demand. The currently just over 5,000 IT graduates in Germany and the 25,000 in the USA that enter the labour market each year contrast with 120,000 in India and as many as 250,000 in China.

The quality of the skilled staff evidently also plays a crucial part, and not just their mere availability. However, it is extremely difficult to compare international qualifications – indeed, this causes problems even at the national level. More meaningful than the theoretical training acquired by university graduates are internationally recognized standards that objectively measure and assess process quality in companies (Capability Maturity Model (CMM), ISO 9000 or Six Sigma certificates) and hence the effective use of specialists. The emerging markets, foremost among them India, have caught up enormously in this regard.

3. One of the oldest rationales behind a commitment abroad is to tap new markets. As a rule, a company's activities abroad are built up as a complement to its domestic engagement. Particularly in the case of near-end-user products, it is a good idea to use staff locally to take advantage of local knowledge of markets, requirements and tastes. Populous, dynamic growth regions like India, the Philippines or China hold out substantial sales potential for manufacturers of mobile telephones through to business software. To exploit this, a local presence is necessary.

Some governments in the new markets even make it mandatory for foreign companies to build up local production facilities before they are allowed to sell their products there.

4. Finally, locational quality acts on the motivation to shift production facilities or services. A business-friendly institutional framework with liberal rules on labour dismissal, and subsidies and tax breaks can exert a pull effect on foreign companies. Restricted business scope, too much regulation or an excessively high tax load in the home country can act as push factors, driving production processes abroad.

How would you say outsourcing affects globalization?

You can't separate outsourcing and globalization anymore — they are directly connected and reinforce each other.

For example, American companies are the leaders in providing outsourcing services globally. Companies like IBM, EDS, Solectron (manufacturing) and Aramark (food and facilities) have extensive global operations providing outsourcing services to others. At the same time, American companies are outsourcing to global providers, such as Siemens, Capgemini and Flextronics (manufacturing). Then there's the entire offshoring dimension. Whether folks like it or not, it's now a global job market for many types of work.

All of this is enabled by the global information infrastructure built during the 1990s and finally secured when we sailed through Y2K with barely a hiccup. The result is the rapid movement toward a network of companies and internal operations, running every hour of the day somewhere, all connected in real time by IT, and all staffed by highly trained professionals working in every corner of the globe.

India: The mother country of offshore outsourcing

India is the most prominent offshore location in the IT sector. Depending on the statistical source, its share of global offshore outsourcing business is estimated at 70 – 90%. Its service portfolio focuses on application development, taking over the entire IT infrastructure or individual business support services (business process outsourcing), and call centre services.

As India's major trading partner, North America accounts for the lion's share – two thirds – of the subcontinent's software and IT-based services exports. Of particular note is the high quality of India's software and BPO industry: the most companies in the world with CMM Level 5 certification were to be found 2002 in India.10 In this reference model Level 5 denotes the highest stage of maturity of a software supplier's development processes.

India's IT export boom can trace its beginnings back to the mid-1980s, when Texas Instruments opened a branch in Bangalore to focus on development, followed a year later by Motorola. Mainly American and West European multinationals from the electronics industry followed suit in the period to the middle of the 1990s; but it was not until the second half of the 1990s that big software houses such as Microsoft, SAP or Adobe opened development centres in India.

In a parallel development, the number of Indian companies to which American principals in particular contracted out programming assignments has soared to more than 3,000. Meanwhile, India's exports of software and services total more than USD 12 bn. If it succeeds in maintaining the momentum of latter years, they will be brushing the USD 38 bn mark by 2008. This trend has been encouraged, first, by India's greater opening since 1991 to foreign investment and co-operation agreements. Second, the national industry association NASSCOM's commitment has successfully promoted its members.

India has long outgrown the status of a strictly IT discount provider. Its major players operate in a league of their own, building themselves a huge international reputation on the strength of their service quality. Indeed, they have now begun outsourcing work to even lower-priced countries such as China or the Philippines. They are also expanding into Western Europe, buying up small local firms.

Business Ethics and Corporate Social Responsibility

Business Ethics is a form of art, and applied ethics examines ethical rules and principles within a commercial context, the various model or ethical problems that can arise in business setting and any special duties or obligations that apply to persons who are engaged in commerce.

Business ethics can be both a normative and a descriptive discipline, as a corporate practice and a career specialization, the field is primarily normative but in the academia, descriptive approaches are also taken. The range and the quality of business ethical issues reflect the degree to which business is perceived to be at odds with non-economic social value. Historically, interest in business ethics accelerated dramatically during the 1980s and 1990s, both within major corporations and within academia. For example, today most major corporate websites lay emphasis on commitment to promoting non-economic social values and even other values under a variety of headings. Business ethics is also commonly refered as "Professional Ethics" and can be broadly classified under:

1. Ethics of accounting information:

- Creative accounting, earnings management, misleading financial analysis.
- Inside trading, securities fraud.
- Executive compensation.

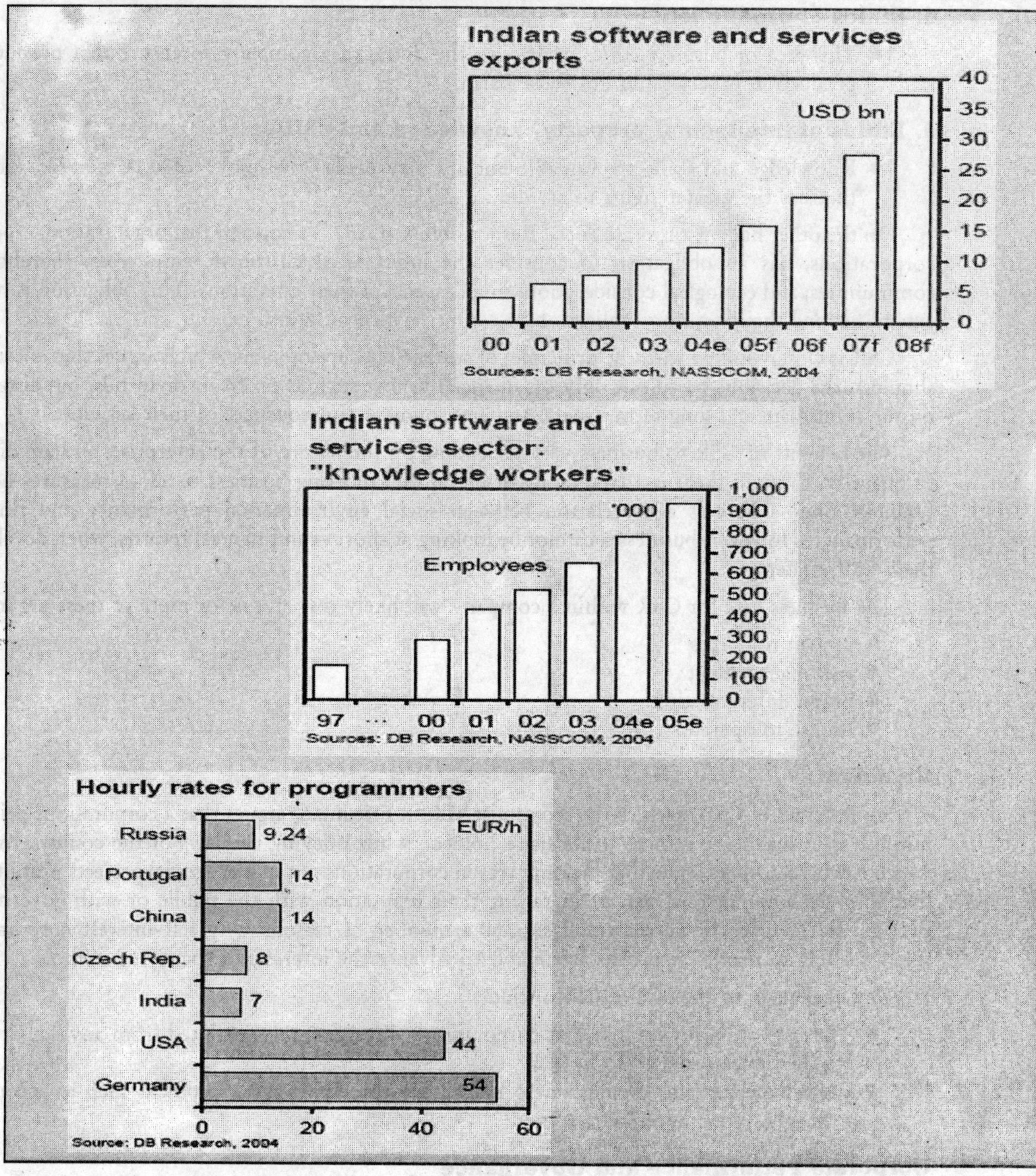

Figure 3.8

2. Ethics of human resource management:

- It covers that ethical issue arising around the employer –employee relationship, such as the rights and duties owed between employer and employee.

3. Ethics of sales and marketing:

- Marketing which goes beyond the mere provision of information about a product may seek to manipulate values and behavior .to some extent society regards this as acceptable.

4. Ethics of production:

- This area of business ethics deals with the duties of a company to ensure that product and production processes do not cause harm.

5. Ethics of intellectual property, knowledge and skills:

- Knowledge and skills are valuable but are they easily "own able" objects, nor is it obvious that has the greater rights to an idea.

On the other hand, Corporate Social Responsibility (CSR) is a concept that organization, especially corporations, has an obligation to consider the interests of customer, employees, shareholders, communities, and ecological considerations in all aspects of their operations. This obligation is seen to extend beyond their statutory obligation to comply with legislation.

CSR is closely linked with the principles of sustainable development, which argues that enterprises should make decisions based not only on financial factors such as profit or dividends, but also based on the immediate and long term - social and environment consequences of their activities.

The benefits of CSR to business vary depending on the nature of the enterprise, and are difficult to quantify, through there is a large body of literature exhorting business to adopt measures beyond financial ones. There is a correlation between social environmental performance and financial performance. However, businesses cannot be looking at short –run financial returns, when developing their CSR strategy.

The business case for CSR within a company will likely rest on one or more of these arguments.

- human resources
- risk management
- brand differentiation
- license to operate.

Criticism

Some critics of CSR, such as the economist Milton Friedman, argues that a corporations principle purpose is to maximize returns to its share holders, while obeying the laws of the countries within which it works. Others argue that the only reason corporations put in place social projects is utilitarian, that they see a commercial benefit in raising their reputation with the public or with government. Proponents of CSR, however would suggest a number of reasons why self–interest corporations, solely seeking to maximize profits are unable to advance the interests of society as a whole.

Key challenges to the idea of CSR include:

- The rule of corporate low that corporation's directors are prohibited from any activity that would reduce profits.
- Others mechanisms established to mange the principal –agent problem such as accounting oversight, stock option etc.

Corporate Performance and Governance

- The causes of persistently poor company performance include poor management, a high cost structure, inadequate differentiation, extensive diversification, structural shifts in demand, the emergence of powerful new competitors, and organization inertia.
- Instituting a successful turnaround strategy requires new leadership, a change of strategy, and a change in organization.
- Stakeholders are individuals or groups that have an interest, claim, or stake in the company, in what it does, and in how well it performs.
- Stakeholders are in an exchange relationship with the company. They supply the organization with important resources (or contributions) and in exchange expect its interests to be satisfied (by inducements).

- A company cannot always satisfy the claims of all stakeholders. The goals of different groups may conflict. The company must identify the most important stakeholders and give highest priority to pursuing strategies that satisfy their needs.
- A company's stockholders are its legal owners and the providers of risk capital, a major source of the capital resources that allow a company to operate its business. As such, they have a unique role among stakeholder groups.
- Maximizing long-run ROIC is the route to maximizing returns to stockholders, and it is also consistent with satisfying the claims of several other key stakeholder groups.
- Although maximizing long-run ROIC is the best way to satisfy the claims of several key stakeholder groups, a company has the obligation to do so within the limits set by the law and in a manner consistent with societal expectations.
- An agency relationship is held to arise whenever one party delegates decision-making authority or control over resources to another.
- The essence of the agency problem is that the interests of principals and agents are not always the same, and some agents may take advantage of information asymmetries to maximize their own interests at the expense of principals.
- A number of governance mechanisms serve to limit the agency problem. These include the board of directors, stock-based compensation schemes, and the threat of a takeover.
- Many strategic decisions have an ethical dimension. Any action by a company inevitably has an impact on the welfare of its stakeholders.
- The purpose of business ethics is not so much to teach the difference between right and wrong, but to give people the tools for dealing with moral complexity-for identifying and thinking through the moral implications of strategic decisions.

Ethical issues such as setting vision, senior manager's remuneration, implementing strategic change, changes in organization ownership and global strategic operation question the management to what extent such decisions are proper. In such a scenario, managers make use of ethical decision model, to make a right decision and while taking decisions an organization should know the principles that enable an ethical approach to take strategic decisions.

❄ ❄ ❄

4 Cultural Context of Global Management

• Cultural Context of Global Management • Meaning and dimensions of culture • Understanding the role of culture • Culture and its effect on organization • Managing across cultures • Organizational cultures and diversity • Communicating across cultures • Cross cultural negotiation and decision making

A culture is the unique pattern of shared assumptions, values, and norms that shape the socialization, symbols, language, narratives, and practices of a group of people. This elements form the base of a culture but they can't be observed directly. They can only be inferred from culture's more visible elements — its socialization activities, symbols, language, narratives, and practices.

Assumptions are the underlying thoughts and feelings that are taken for granted and believed to be true. Values are basic beliefs about a condition that has considerable importance and meaning to individuals and stable over time. Socialization is a systematic process by which new members are brought in to a culture and taught the norms for behaviour. A symbol is anything visible that can be used to represent an abstract shared value or something having special meaning.

Language is shared system of vocal sounds, written signs, and used to convey special meanings among members. Narratives are the unique stories, sages, legends, and myths in a culture. Shared practices include taboos and rites and ceremonies.

Cultural elements and their relationships create pattern that is distinct to an organization, just as a personality is unique to an individual. As with a classification of individuals that share common characteristics, several general organizational cultures can be described. Cultures develop in both large and small groups of people. An organization's culture is influenced by larger societal and industry cultures.

Types of Organizational Cultures

The different types of organizational cultures of global management are given below:

- Entrepreneurial Culture
- Bureaucratic Culture
- Market Culture
- Clan Culture.

Figure 4.1

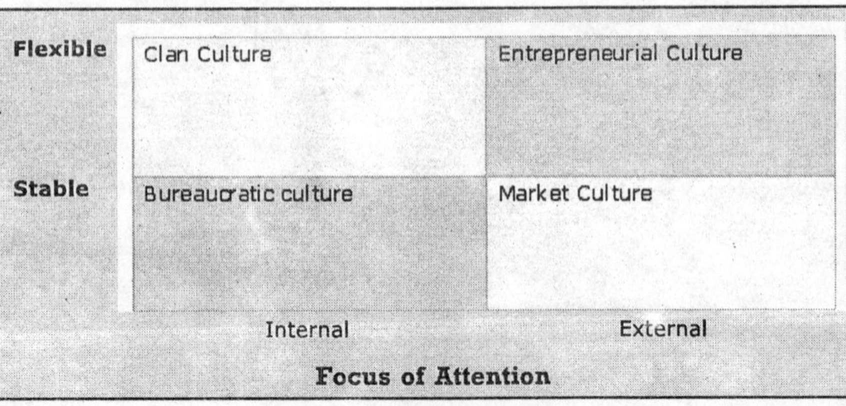

In the given figure, the vertical axis reflects the relative formal control orientation, ranging from internal functioning to external functioning. The four quadrants represent four pure types of organizational culture. Different cultures may be appropriate under different conditions, with no type of culture being ideal for every situation.

In a bureaucratic culture, the behaviour of employees is governed by formal rules and standard operating procedures, and coordination is achieved through hierarchical reporting relationship. The focus of attention is on the internal operations of the organization. The cultures are often found in organizations that produce standardized goods and services. They are particularly common in local, state, and federal governments. Governments create rules in their efforts to ensure that all citizens are treated the same, regardless of their backgrounds, wealth, or status. These same values often are reflected in the cultures of global management.

In clan culture the control over behaviour is more subtle. Here members share feelings of pride in membership. They have a strong sense of identification and recognize their need to work together.

In entrepreneurial culture, the external focus and flexibility create an environment that encourages risk taking, dynamism, and creativity. There is a commitment to experimentation, innovation, and being on the leading edge. This culture doesn't just quickly react to changes in the environment; it creates change. This culture suits a new company's start-up phase. It also fits well with the demands faced by the employees who are seeking to create and develop new products with in the environment of a larger company.

In a market culture, the values and norms reflect the importance of achieving measurable and demanding goals, especially those that are financial and market based. Hard driving competitiveness and a profits orientation prevail throughout the organization. A market culture doesn't exert much informal social pressure on an organization's members. Managers in one department are expected to co-operate with managers in other departments only to the extent necessary to achieve their performance goal.

Cultural Synergy

Cultural synergy is an approach followed by managers in the various cultural context of diversity in globally. Cultural synergistic organizations create new forms of management and organization that transcend the distinct culture of their members. This approach recognizes both the similarities and differences among the cultural that compose a global organization and suggest that we neither ignore nor minimize cultural diversity, but rather view it as a resource in designing and developing organizational systems. From a synergistic perspective, cultural diversity is a key resource in all global learning organizations.

Cultural synergy is an approach, not the approach; it is the one of five options that highly effective global managers use regularly. The synergistic problem solving is not a quick fix. It's a systematic process for increasing the options open to executives, managers, and employees working in increasingly global business environments. The synergy approach works equally effective for competing successfully in multicultural domestic environments.

The various steps in creating cultural synergy are given below:

- Describing the situation
- Interpreting the cultures
- Increasing cultural creativity and finally creating cultural synergy.

In global management, organizational culture has the potential to enhance organizational performance, individual satisfaction, the sense of certainty about how problems are to be handled, and other aspects of work life. However, if the organizational culture gets out of step with the changing expectation of external stake holders, it can be hinder effectiveness. The need to determine which attributes of an organization's culture should be preserved and which should be modified is constant.

Culture (from the Latin cultura stemming from colere, meaning "to cultivate"), generally refers to patterns of human activity and the symbolic structures that give such activity significance. Different definitions of "culture" reflect different theoretical bases for understanding, or criteria for evaluating human activity.

'Total inherited ideas, beliefs, values, attitudes, norms of behaviour, which constitute the shared bases of social action' and 'the total range and ideas and activities of a group of people with shared traditions which are transmitted and reinforced by members of a group' (Chambers Dictionary).

Most general, the term culture denotes whole product of an individual, group or society of intelligent beings. It includes technology, art, science, as well as moral systems and the characteristic behaviours and habits of the selected intelligent entities. In particular, it has specific more detailed meanings in different domains of human activities.

It is noticed that different human societies have different cultures, and the personal culture of one individual can be different than another one.

Culture has four social dimensions, which can lead to development

Culture is a living thing, consisting of elements inherited from the past, outside influences, which have been embraced and new elements invented locally. Culture has an important role to play in society.

Culture first of all provides self-esteem - Self-esteem, whether it be personal or collective, is an essential precondition if culture is to flourish. Without a minimum consciousness of his or her values or abilities, without a quiet confidence in his or her own resources and means, the individual remains static and muted, both metaphorical, and occasionally in the literal sense. Paolo Freire has analyzed this culture of silence, which is a characteristic of societies, which have grown dependent and inarticulate. This silence, this apathy, is a specific result of the loss of a sense of society's self-esteem. If it is told incessantly that it is backward, ignorant, incapable, uncompetitive, lazy, marginal, and underdeveloped and outdated, the population finally internalizes this message and behaves in conformity with this negative image. Affirming its value and potential opens a society to creativity and action.

Culture is a selective mechanism for all kinds of external influences-The ability to select outside influences, to make a choice, is extremely important. Every community must be able to make a free choice between what it considers to be useful and beneficial and what it considers to be superfluous and harmful. This is equally true of the cultural elements inherited from the past. The past heritage is ambiguous; it may be harmful. It is for this reason that the inhabitants of isolated villages often have only one concern – to jettison a culture, which they associate with a past filled with isolation, discomfort, deprivation and humiliation. They aspire to greater material welfare. Who can blame them for this?

The ability to stand up to cultural imperialism or the harmful elements of the past, the ability to select, is determined by culture. It is culture, which contains these values and determines the priorities; it is also culture, which directs the choices in accordance with these priorities.

Culture inspires strategies for resistance by creating a counterweight-Resistance to everything, which is imposed from outside and which is considered to be damaging and unacceptable, is an essential element for harmonious development of every community. After selecting everything, which can be usefully adopted and earmarking the harmful elements for rejection, a strategy of resistance has to be organized. If this is not done, power politics mean that a society will rapidly be overrun by unwanted elements, and finally will passively or unconsciously accept them.

So resistance is to be advised. It should not condemn a region to remaining a fruitlessly isolated community or an outdated backwater – a dream for the city-dweller, but unacceptable to the rural population. Once more, only a strong, confident culture can assess the advantages and the disadvantages, can weigh up the benefits of an immediate financial profit against long-term consistency and a lifestyle open to the outside world. This is a difficult choice; in the final analysis, no magic formula or expert opinion can act as substitute for the judgement of those involved; but if they want to be capable of judging and acting according to this value judgement, they must have a living cultural identity. Culture is primarily a force, which provides direction.

Development must have a direction-making sense of what one does is of primary importance. Development must have a direction. In every process of social change, economic shift and general development, we must be able to keep to the same course if we do not want to be swept away be different events and pressures. In several European languages, the word sense means both deep significance and direction.

Culture is, after all, the vitality, which provides sense-This is exactly what this means; on the one hand attaching appropriate importance to the values which make us do what is sensible – that is, full of good sense, and on the other hand, orientation towards the future, progress in a given direction. The faculty of providing direction for what one undertakes is unique to man. This faculty presupposes some kind of self-esteem and the capacity for selection and resistance as mentioned above, but it is far more than this. It is closely allied to life and the joy of living. Culture is, after all, the vitality, which provides sense. In this regard its symbolic dimension (values, spirituality, etc) plays a crucial role. This search for sense is not only an individual activity. It is also collective and encroaches on the political: co-existing, social relationships, which in this time of fragmentation and change are often of a new kind, or need to be re-established.

When Ricardo Petrella, a senior European Commission civil servant stressed in the October 1993 edition of the magazine Economie et Humanisme the necessity of providing direction for our societies, he wrote that it fundamentally concerns cultural development. According to him, "To a certain extent it means passing from an object culture (building more houses, infrastructure, roads, machinery, ferrying and transporting more passengers, goods, capital, etc.), which has been given priority over the last 30 to 40 years to a subject culture (developing links for co-existing, the search for quality of life …..)"

This subject/object culture distinction has to be looked at individually for each intervention. This is why the methodology behind the intervention is at least as important as the intervention itself; it is this on which the real cultural nature of the intervention depends: the capacity to make it catch fire under the ashes of passiveness and resignation, the glowing embers.

Geert Hofstede conducted perhaps the most comprehensive study of how values in the workplace are influenced by culture. He analyzed a large data base of employee values scores collected by IBM between 1967 and 1973 covering more than 70 countries, from which he first used the 40 largest only and afterwards extended the analysis to 50 countries and 3 regions. Subsequent studies validating the earlier results have included commercial airline pilots and students in 23 countries, civil service managers in 14 counties, 'up-market' consumers in 15 countries and 'elites' in 19 countries.

From the initial results, and later additions, Hofstede developed a model that identifies four primary Dimensions to assist in differentiating cultures: Power Distance - PDI, Individualism - IDV, Masculinity - MAS, and Uncertainty Avoidance - UAI. Latter, he added a fifth Dimension after conducting an additional international study with a survey instrument developed with Chinese employees and managers. That Dimension, based on Confucian dynamism, is Long-Term Orientation - LTO and was applied to 23 countries. These five Hofstede Dimensions can also be found to correlate with other country, cultural, and religious paradigms.

India has Power Distance (PDI) as the highest Hofstede Dimension for the culture, with a ranking of 77 compared to a world average of 56.5. This Power Distance score for India indicates a high level of inequality of power and wealth within the society. This condition is not necessarily subverted upon the population, but rather accepted by the population as a cultural norm.

India's Long Term Orientation (LTO) Dimension rank is 61, with the world average at 48. A higher LTO score can be indicative of a culture that is perseverant and parsimonious.

Figure 4.2

Geert Hofstede™ Cultural Dimensions: India-Case Study

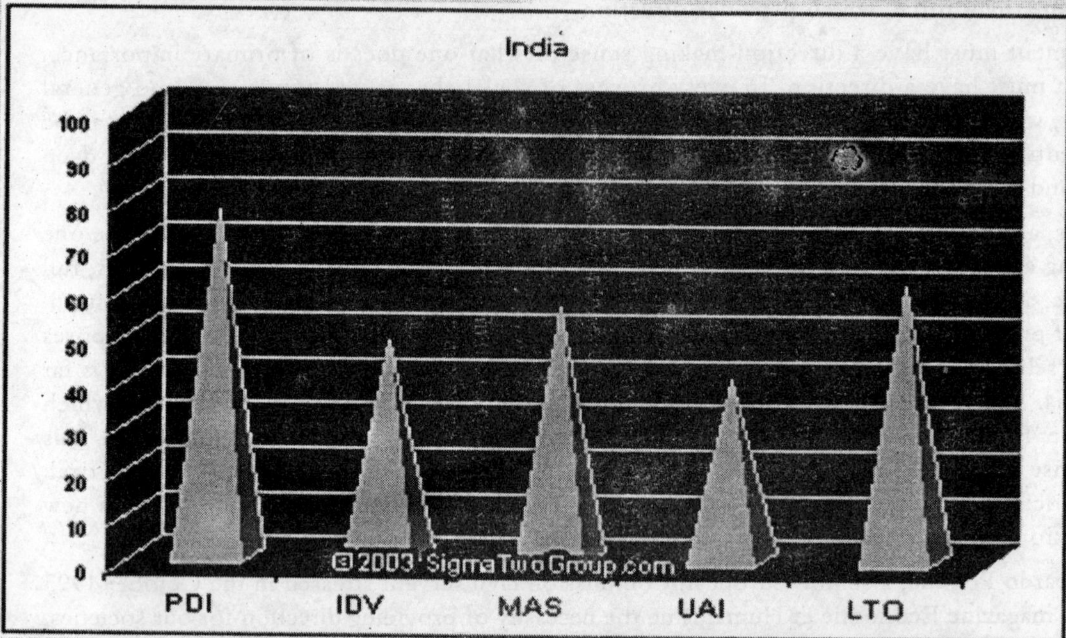

*** Description for each of Hofstede's Dimensions listed below**

Figure 4.3

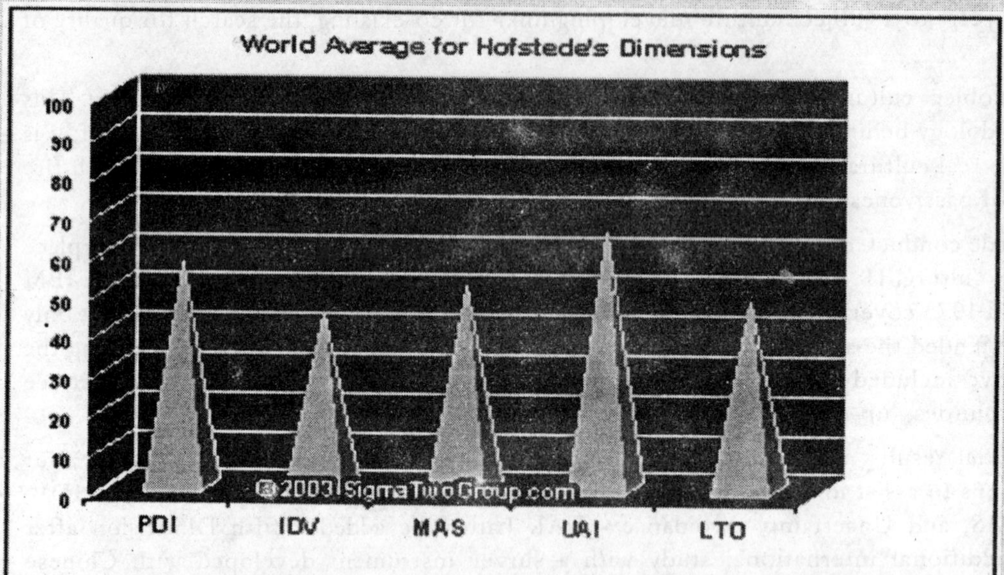

*** Average Hofstede Dimensions of all counties surveyed**

India has Masculinity as the third highest ranking Hofstede Dimension at 56, with the world average just slightly lower at 51. The higher the country ranks in this Dimension, the greater the gap between values of men and women. It may also generate a more competitive and assertive female population, although still less than the male population.

India's lowest ranking Dimension is Uncertainty Avoidance (UAI) at 40, compared to the world average of 65. On the lower end of this ranking, the culture may be more open to unstructured ideas and situations. The population may have fewer rules and regulations with which to attempt control of every unknown and unexpected event or situation, as is the case in high Uncertainty Avoidance countries.

Power Distance Index (PDI) that is the extent to which the less powerful members of organizations and institutions (like the family) accept and expect that power is distributed unequally. This represents inequality (more *versus* less), but defined from below, not from above. It suggests that a society's level of inequality is endorsed by the followers as much as by the leaders. Power and inequality, of course, are extremely fundamental facts of any society and anybody with some international experience will be aware that 'all societies are unequal, but some are more unequal than others'.

Individualism (IDV) on the one side versus its opposite, collectivism, that is the degree to which individuals are integrated into groups. On the individualist side we find societies in which the ties between individuals are loose: everyone is expected to look after him/herself and his/her immediate family. On the collectivist side, we find societies in which people from birth onwards are integrated into strong, cohesive in-groups, often extended families (with uncles, aunts and grandparents) which continue protecting them in exchange for unquestioning loyalty. The word 'collectivism' in this sense has no political meaning: it refers to the group, not to the state. Again, the issue addressed by this dimension is an extremely fundamental one, regarding all societies in the world.

Masculinity (MAS) *versus* its opposite, femininity, refers to the distribution of roles between the genders which is another fundamental issue for any society to which a range of solutions are found. The IBM studies revealed that (*a*) women's values differ less among societies than men's values; (*b*) men's values from one country to another contain a dimension from very assertive and competitive and maximally different from women's values on the one side, to modest and caring and similar to women's values on the other. The assertive pole has been called 'masculine' and the modest, caring pole 'feminine'. The women in feminine countries have the same modest, caring values as the men; in the masculine countries they are somewhat assertive and competitive, but not as much as the men, so that these countries show a gap between men's values and women's values.

Uncertainty Avoidance Index (UAI) deals with a society's tolerance for uncertainty and ambiguity; it ultimately refers to man's search for Truth. It indicates to what extent a culture programs its members to feel either uncomfortable or comfortable in unstructured situations. Unstructured situations are novel, unknown, surprising, and different from usual. Uncertainty avoiding cultures try to minimize the possibility of such situations by strict laws and rules, safety and security measures, and on the philosophical and religious level by a belief in absolute Truth; 'there can only be one Truth and we have it'. People in uncertainty avoiding countries are also more emotional, and motivated by inner nervous energy. The opposite type, uncertainty accepting cultures, are more tolerant of opinions different from what they are used to; they try to have as few rules as possible, and on the philosophical and religious level they are relativist and allow many currents to flow side by side. People within these cultures are more phlegmatic and contemplative, and not expected by their environment to express emotions.

Long-Term Orientation (LTO) versus short-term orientation: this fifth dimension was found in a study among students in 23 countries around the world, using a questionnaire designed by Chinese scholars It can be said to deal with Virtue regardless of Truth. Values associated with Long Term Orientation are thrift and perseverance; values associated with Short Term Orientation are respect for tradition, fulfilling social obligations, and protecting one's 'face'. Both the positively and the negatively rated values of this dimension are found in the teachings of Confucius, the most influential Chinese philosopher who lived around 500 B.C.; however, the dimension also applies to countries without a Confucian heritage.

Understanding the role of culture

With the globalization of markets, a good understanding of cultural differences is an integrated part of success in global strategic management. Culture has been recognized to have a general influence on behaviour, consumption, in addition to serving as one of the key determinants of manner and approach in which company and individual do business to respond to international strategies.

Organization Culture - Exercises

Review Questions

1. Describe institutionalization and its relationship to organizational culture.
2. Define the common characteristics making up organizational culture.
3. Contrast strong and weak cultures.
4. Identify the functional and dysfunctional effects of organizational culture on people and the organization.
5. Explain the factors determining an organization's culture.
6. List the factors that maintain an organization's culture.
7. Clarify how culture is transmitted to employees.
8. Outline the various socialization alternatives available to management.

Review Statements

State the below mentioned as True or False:

1. One of the important changes in the viewing of organizations that has taken place since the 1980s is the realization that organizations have personalities, just like people.
   • True • False
2. In an organization, the degree to which management focuses on outcomes, rather than techniques and processes used to achieve the outcomes, is the organization's outcome orientation.
   • True • False
3. An organization's subculture expresses the core values of the majority of the organization's members, excluding senior management.
   • True • False
4. A strong corporate culture has a number of benefits for a firm, including the reduction of employee turnover, and an internal climate of high behavioural control.
   • True • False
5. The boundary-defining role of organizational culture serves as the control mechanism that guides and shapes employee attitude. It is the "sense-making" function.
   • True • False
6. When an organization has a strong culture that organizational culture can act as a barrier to diversity within the organization.
   • True • False
7. The primary cause of many of the failed mergers and acquisitions of the 1990's was conflicting organizational culture.
   • True • False
8. The primary shaper of an organization's culture is the business environment in which the organization operates.
   • True • False
9. The actions of top management have little influence on an organization's culture, due to the extensive nature of subcultures within any given organization.
   • True • False
10. An individual going through socialization in an organization confronts the dichotomy between his/her expectations and those of the organization in the encounter stage.
    • True • False
11. Joan is a new employee of We 'R Smarter. In her socialization process she is separated from the current work situation and her role in the organization is clearly defined by the orientation process she goes through. Joan's experience shows that this company has a highly informal and collective socialization process.
    • True • False

12. Tomas' Shoes is a manufacturer of an exclusive line of men's shoes. All new employees who successfully complete their probationary period receive two pairs of shoes of their choice in an elaborate ceremony, to emphasize the quality and commitment expected by the company. This act is an example of the use of stories to teach employees the company's culture.
    • True • False
13. When Mary was promoted to VP, she was moved from her cubicle to a corner office on the tenth floor overlooking a park with a lake. This is an example of a ritual reinforcing her company's organizational culture.
    • True • False
14. An organizational culture that is low on sociability and low on solidarity exemplifies a fragmented culture.
    • True • False
15. Nancy's company's culture is one in which both friendship and performances are valued. People feel that they belong but there is a ruthless drive for goal achievement. Her company's culture is an example of a communal culture.
    • True • False

Multiple Choice Questions

1. If the failures of Mitsubishi Corporation could be summarized into one primary cause, that cause would be:
   a. Poor pricing strategies and a weak marketing effort.
   b. A failure in the new employee selection process and their socialization.
   c. An inability to change their corporate culture to match the competitive environment.
   d. The failure of management to convey the change message to rank and file employees in a way the employees would believe it.
2. When an organization becomes its own entity, it takes on a life of its own, apart from its founders or any prominent members, and then we say the firm has experienced:
   a. A fragmented culture b. Institutionalization
   c. Socialization d. Alienation
3. An organization's culture is defined by several primary characteristics. That characteristic demonstrated by activities that emphasize maintaining the status quo *versus* growing exemplifies which primary characteristic?
   a. Attention to detail b. Outcome orientation
   c. People orientation d. Stability
4. __________ focuses on how employees perceive their organization's culture, not whether they like it or not.
   a. Organizational culture b. Job satisfaction
   c. Socialization d. Core values
5. Tanya is looking for a job. She has two interviews next week, both with companies she would like to work for. If Tanya wanted to assess or "read" each company's culture while on-site for her interview, she should:
   a. Note with whom she interviews and who the company lets her meet.
   b. She should pay attention to material symbols in the headquarters.
   c. Ask questions of the people with whom she meets.
   d. Do all of these things.
6. Which of the following is true regarding organizational culture?
   a. Companies with strong dominant cultures do not tend to have subcultures.
   b. A firm's core values are not accepted or expressed by its subcultures, which leads to organizational conflict.
   c. Subcultures retain the firm's core values but modify them to reflect the separate unit's issues.
   d. Subcultures tend to form only in fragmented or mercenary organizational cultures.

7. A strong corporate culture can serve as a substitute for__________ in terms of company structure.
   a. Technology   b. Formalization
   c. National culture   d. Vertical communication
8. Which of the following is true about organizational culture today?
   a. It is declining in importance due to the increasing use of technology and matrix organizational structure.
   b. It is increasing in importance due to flatter structures, wider spans of control, and empowering of employees.
   c. It is neither increasing nor decreasing in importance, it is simply studied more.
   d. It is relatively unimportant in mechanistic organizations but critically important in organic ones.
9. In the opening case about the decline of Mitsubishi Motors, we see that the firm's organizational culture was a liability in terms of it being a barrier to:
   a. Diversity   b. Merger and acquisition
   c. Change   d. None of these
10. An organization's culture is created by:
    a. The hiring and keeping of employees who fit in.
    b. Indoctrinating and socializing new employees to think in a particular way.
    c. The role model set by the founders' own behaviour.
    d. All of these.
11. The __________ is one key way a company maintains its culture through the identification and hiring of individuals who have the knowledge, skills, and abilities to be successful.
    a. Role model of top management   b. Selection process
    c. Metamorphosis   d. Reward and compensation system
12. When a firm uses role models to train and encourage new employees, places the employee directly into his/her job, and does not move the employee on to the next stage of orientation until "he/she is ready," the firm's socialization options may be described as:
    a. Formal, individualistic, and random   b. Serial, informal, and variable
    c. Fixed, collective, and investiture   d. None of the above
13. At a highly aggressive financial services firm, managers talk about "drop dead" dates, their shop "blowing up," and "let us succeed or let none of us come back." This behaviour is an example of the use of __________ to express company culture.
    a. Material symbols   b. Rituals
    c. Stories   d. Language
14. Similar to contingency management theory, organizational personality can be framed in terms of social and task orientation. A firm that views employees as family members and friends, shares information openly, but tolerates poor performance and political cliques, has a __________ type of organizational culture.
    a. Networked   b. Mercenary
    c. Fragmented   d. Communal

Case Analysis

1. Metropolitan Hospital

Metropolitan hospital was built two years ago and currently has a work force of 235 people. The hospital is small, but because it is new, it is extremely efficient. The board has voted to increase its capacity from 60 to 190 beds. By this time next year, the hospital will be over three times as large as it is now in terms of both beds and personnel. The administrator, Clara Hawkins feels that the major problem with this proposed increase is that the hospital will lose its efficiency. "I want to hire people who are just like our current team of personnel – hardworking, dedicated, talented, and able to interact well with patients. If we triple the number of employees, I don't see how it will be possible to maintain our quality patient care. We are going to lose our family atmosphere. We will be inundated with mediocrity and we'll end up being like every other institution in the local area – large and uncaring!"

The chairman of the board is also concerned about the effect of hiring such a large number of employees. However, he believes that Clara is overreacting. "It can't be that hard to find people who are like our current staff. There must be a lot of people out there who are just as good. What you need to do is develop a plan of action that will allow you to carefully screen those who will fit into your current organizational culture and those who will not. It's not going to be as difficult as you believe. Trust me everything will work out just fine."

As a result of chairman's comments, Clara has decided that the most effective way of dealing with the situation is to develop a plan of action. She intends to meet with her administrative group and determine the best way of screening incoming candidates and then helping those who are hired to become socialized in terms of the hospital's culture. Clara has called a meeting for the day after tomorrow. At that time she intends to discus her ideas, get suggestions from her people, and then formulate a plan of action. "We've come too far to lose it all now," she told her administrative staff assistant. "If we keep our wits about us, I think we can continue to keep Metropolitan as the showcase hospital in this region."

Discuss how Clara can ensure that those who are hired come to accept the core cultural values of the hospital? What steps would you recommend?

2. A Culture of Endurance - Lead Story: The Plain Dealer, December 31, 2001

"Men wanted for hazardous journey - Small wages, bitter cold, long months of complete darkness, constant danger, and safe return doubtful. In case of success honour and recognition,"

Ernest Shackleton

Quite an invitation, don't you think? Yet with exactly those words, the explorer Ernest Shackleton attracted 27 other adventurers to sail with him to Antarctica in 1914. A recent documentary film entitled "The Endurance: Shackleton's Legendary Antarctic Expedition" is a chronicle of the truly harrowing adventures the crew experienced.

The expedition faced extraordinary obstacles from Mother Nature. Their ship was locked in place by ice for months, then crushed, then they had to row across more than 200 miles of open sea to one island, then a small group had to row across more than 800 miles of open sea to another island for rescue, and then climb and then descend a steep mountain range to reach a remote whaling station. Yet in more than two years of travel and hardship in the most extreme weather conditions, not a single man was lost.

All of the evidence points to the leadership qualities of Shackleton himself, and especially to the culture of tenacity and vigor that he promoted among his crew. In the last few years, a book by Caroline Alexander and an exhibit at the American Museum of Natural History have exposed Shackleton to new generations. In late 2001, the documentary movie was issued commercially.

The opening image of the documentary seems out of place—it is not Castle Rock, or New Line, or Miramax, or any other well-known film company whose logo appears ... instead, it is Morgan Stanley, the Wall Street investment bank that the audience sees on the first screen. This unorthodox pairing of Hollywood and Wall Street comes from a desire on the part of Morgan Stanley to align the firm's culture with the values of staying power and mutual support exhibited by the crew of the Endurance. In late 2001, a culture of endurance became especially meaningful to Morgan Stanley; 3,700 of its employees worked in the World Trade Center, unfortunately six of them perished on September 11.

Quite understandably, the firm regards the amount of survivors as a miracle. For so many companies who were directly affected by the World Trade Center's destruction, regrouping and reorganizing have been agonizing tasks, involving memorials for lost co-workers and serious problems caused by the loss of organizational knowledge and memory. Morgan Stanley funded the film, produced by independent film company Cowboy Pictures, and has used it to build up morale within the company.

Talking it over and thinking it through!

Morgan Stanley sees the experience of Shackleton's crew as a metaphor for mutual support and survival under difficult circumstances. Can this apply equally well to other companies?

What are some ways that a company like Morgan Stanley can disseminate to their employees the values of shared sacrifice and *esprit de corps* that are exemplified by the film?

Corporate culture is (in part) a matter of what leaders pay attention to and the models that they set for behavior. It appears that Morgan Stanley's leaders are trying to model themselves after Shackleton, and to encourage managers in the firm to do the same. In your opinion, are these uses of the film likely to be sustainable for a long time?

Thinking about the future!

This story brings up a number of interesting possibilities, relating to corporate culture and to the involvement of industry in the production of culture. One of the issues that this illustrates is how firms try to instill values that are if not unique, then at least identifiable with a particular company. To that end, Morgan Stanley has not only screened the film for employees, but also for its clients.

Somewhat surprisingly, some of its competitors (Goldman Sachs and Deutsche Bank) have also planned to present it to their employees. Perhaps, they feel that the spiritual lessons of the movie create more value than is lost by showing a competitor's product.

Another implication of this story is the branding of a theatrical release by a company from another industry. Will Marlboro, Pepsi, Kraft, Miller Brewing, Microsoft Windows XP, and Kodak may be the next company to present movies? One wonders what effect this would have on the art of the cinema!

Sharing the news!

In a group, discuss other movies that you have seen together and consider what they might tell you about corporate culture and organizational behavior. For example, in Apollo 13, Jim Lovell (played by Tom Hanks) exhibited courageous leadership and imagination in bringing his crew safely back to Earth. Even in Chak de, Shah Rukh Khan has displayed what cultural harmony is for team spirit which leads to victory. Can you think of other, more recent films that serve as models of how business managers and workers can succeed?

Managing across cultures

The ability to read an organization's culture can be a valuable skill. For instance, if you're looking for a job, you'll want to choose an employer whose culture is compatible with your values and in which you'll feel comfortable. If you can accurately assess a potential employer's culture before you make your job decision, you may be able to save yourself a lot of grief and reduce and reduce the likelihood of making a poor choice. Similarly, you'll undoubtedly have business transactions with numerous organizations during your professional career, such as selling a product or service, negotiating a contract, arranging a joint work project, or merely seeking out who controls certain decisions in an organization. The ability to assess another organization's culture can be a definite plus in successfully performing those pursuits.

One can be more effective at reading an organization's culture if you use the following behaviors. For the sake of simplicity, we're going to look at this skill from the perspective of a job applicant. We'll assume that you're interviewing for a job, although these skills are general to many situations. Here's a list of things one can do to help learn about an organization's culture.

Do background work

Get the names of former employees from friends or acquaintances, and talk with them. Also talk with members of professional trade associations to which the organization's employees belong and executive recruiters who deal with the organization. Look for clues in stories told in annual reports and other organizational literature; and check out the organization's Web sites for evidence of high turnover or recent management shake-ups.

Observe the physical surroundings

Pay attention to signs, posters, pictures, photos, style of dress, length of hair, degree of openness between offices, and office furnishings and arrangements.

Make note about those with whom you met from the organization the way they liked to be addressed. Also note the characteristics and the style of the people met from the organization and their interaction style whether they were formal, casual, serious, jovial, open and reticent about providing information.

Look at the organization's human resources manual and understand the company's formal rules and regulations printed there. If so, how detailed are they and what do they cover?

Ask questions of the people with whom you meet and try to know:

The most valid and reliable information tends to come from asking the same questions of many people (to see how closely their responses align). Questions that will give insights into organizational processes and practices might include the background of the founders and that of current senior managers. Try to know these managers' functional specialties and whether they are promoted from within or hired from outside. Any formal orientation program, the organization has to integrate its new employees. The structure adopted for their formal employee training programs.

Interacting with the boss, how does he define his or her job success? Many more aspects can be found out but what is mentioned above is adequate enough to understand the organization culture well for the employee and conduct himself well in the organization.

Organizational culture

The culture of an organization is an mixture of the values and beliefs of the people in an organization. It can be felt in the implicit rules and expectations of behaviour in an organization where, even though the rules are not formally written down employees know what is expected of them. It is usually set by management whose decisions on policy usually set up the culture of the organization. The organizational culture usually has values and beliefs that support the organizational goals.

Values and Beliefs which support Organizational Goals

The culture of the organization, if it is positive and helpful can help to motivate staff or at least prevent them from becoming dissatisfied. At I.B.M. the attitude of management to their employees is an attraction to prospective staff and would probably help maintain the staff that they have. If the climate does not satisfy the needs of staff, then it will probably become a demotivator, that is, that it would cause dissatisfaction and so people would become less inclined to want to work towards the organizational goals.

Things in an organization which contribute to the culture or climate are :

- the organizational structure of reporting and relationships
- company policy
- personnel practices
- work flow and work loads
- job design
- management and supervisory styles.

Factors affect the organizational culture on an individual or personal level are:

- levels of trust
- risk taking
- stress
- fears and anxieties
- social interaction
- factions and politics.

The pivotal point and the starting point for the identification of organizational culture and company development is the corporate history.

Traditional approaches to corporate diversification are inadequate for understanding ... it requires changes in existing organizational culture and power

Organizational culture is a system of shared values (what is important). Most appropriate in organizations pursuing unrelated diversification strategies.

One of the most intriguing but difficult concepts that leaders and managers have to grapple with is organizational culture. Yet an understanding of this phenomenon is vital, partly because one cannot understand how an organization works if one neglects its culture, and partly because the whole concept of the culture of the organization has become central to the management of change.

The approach taken in OPUS is that while it may not be possible to change the organizational culture per se it is possible to influence the culture indirectly. The key to this approach lies in an understanding of how organizational culture develops. In simple terms we can say that the members of all organizations develop a construct of their organization. This is frequently referred to as 'The bosses'; 'They'; 'The Governors'; or, 'Them up there'. These are not references to any particular senior manager(s) but a construct that fits their perceived view of the organization. From this construct, they develop a shared view about the forms of behaviour they should adopt which they feel are appropriate to that construct. This results in 'the way things are done around here', or put another way, the organizational culture.

However, to actually get to the point where we can begin to influence the organizational culture we need to identify what influences the members' view of their organization. Several factors may be influential, but we can say that the most influential are likely to be the official structures, strategies, policies, management styles and decisions, especially those of senior managers.

Everyone, including senior managers both influence and are influenced by the organizational culture. But, if we want to change organizational culture we need to start at the top and ensure that official structures, strategies, policies, management styles and decisions all reflect the sort of culture desired. It is imperative that the most senior managers are able to provide the leadership necessary to bring about change. All sorts of initiatives can be taken, but without leadership, little may actually change.

Cultures are held to generate powerful norms of belief and conduct with which members are expected to comply, and these norms help to distinguish members of one culture from another. The term 'cultures' is used here to refer to the multiple interacting cultural spheres that may influence individual and organizational relationships at any one

Understanding the Culture of Your Workplace

Many hard-working, no-nonsense managers and supervisors think the word "culture" is something remote and alien to what they do for a living. To them, culture is highbrow art and music, or a glob of micro plasma that medical researchers study through a microscope in a sterile laboratory somewhere. They don't think of culture as any part of a supervisor's daily life on the job. They're missing an important point.

The truth is that supervisory personnel encounter culture every day — the culture of the workplace (their factory, shop or office). This culture is more important to productivity than wages, benefits or working conditions. More than almost anything else, the culture determines the success or failure of the organization. It's something every supervisor needs to understand and work with.

What is it?

Every group or organization (e.g., family, clan, brotherhood, scout troop, street gang, bridge club, corporation, labour union, staff, team or crew) has its own unique culture. The culture is simply the "personality" of the group.

The culture is the unwritten code of conduct (My dictionary calls it the "socially transmitted behavior patterns.") made up of the mores, core values, cherished beliefs, priorities, traditions and informal rules and roles of the organization. The culture defines what's important, what's expected, what's accepted, what's preferred, what's tolerated, what's rewarded, what's punished and what taboo within the group is. If you want to know who has the real power, how things really get done and what it takes to go along and get along in the organization, you won't find the answers in the office rules, union contract, official policy manual or employee handbook. The only way to learn these things is to understand the culture of the organization. If you are to succeed as a supervisor, you can't afford not to.

Why Is culture so important?

Workplace cultures are interactive. They are shaped by the workers who make up the culture; and, in turn, those workers are shaped by the culture in which they work. There is no question that behavior is heavily influenced by the culture of the group. That's why no supervisor or manager can be effective without understanding how the culture in their workplace actually operates.

Unfortunately, some managers spend their entire career completely unaware of how things really work in their section, division or department. They come to the job every day without a clue about what's going on around them. It is almost as if they lived and worked in some parallel universe, rather than in the real world of the workplace.

Of course, supervisors who are not in tune with the culture of the organization quickly become irrelevant. They don't lead the employees who work under them. Their workers merely tolerate them; and, then, pretty junks do things their own way. You don't want that to happen to your career. If you don't have a handle on the culturally-embedded behaviours, biases and beliefs of your employees, you are deprived of a powerful tool for motivating and managing them. As it turns out, how people in the organization feel about the organization, themselves, their job and their future is largely the result of the culture in the workplace.

It is the culture on the job that determines how people interact, how they treat each other, how they communicate and what they communicate, how open and honest they will be, how hard they work, how loyal they will be and how much they will put up with.

Likewise, it is the culture that often attracts people to the organization or drives them away. In many cases, workers don't leave jobs because of low-pay or work loads. They leave because of the culture.

Wow! Obviously, culture is a huge deal for workers — and for supervisors. It should be no surprise, then, that managers or supervisors ignore the culture of the workplace at their peril. Look around at the organizations of workplaces you know best. Some are closed, rigid, inflexible and oppressive. Others are open, empowering, flexible and upbeat. What makes the difference? Often, it is the supervisor or manager in charge.

Role of the supervisor

More than anyone else, from the top to the bottom of the organization, supervisors and middle managers can shape and mold the culture of the workplace. Of course, supervisors can't mandate or dictate a particular culture; but they can nudge, cajole, convince and lead by example. Effective supervisors establish a tone and set the agenda for the organization. By reminding people, at all levels, of the group's mission, defining lofty goals, articulating expectations, raising standards and rewarding preferred performance, the leader can dramatically influence workers' beliefs and behaviours.

The most lasting impact leaders can have on the work environment is by living their values ("walk the talk") and modelling desired attitudes and actions.

Employees in all businesses and industries respond to authentic, principle-driven leadership. If the supervisor consistently sets an example of trust, respect, civility, honesty and integrity, these values will eventually catch on with others. Supervisors can actually create the kind of culture they want in their workplace. It's not easy. It takes times and hard work; but it is possible.

Noted writer, Robert Townsend, may describe the leader's influence best: If people are coming to work excited, if they are making mistakes freely and fearlessly, if they are having fun, if they are concentrating on doing things, rather than preparing reports and going to meetings — then somewhere you have a leader.

Its obvious managers can have subtle influences on the way workers think and perform. But can a supervisor really change an existing, well-established culture? You bet. It happens every day. In his best seller, Authentic Leadership, Bill George uses the classic example of Marilyn Nelson, CEO of the Carlson Companies. Shortly after taking over the company, Nelson invited a group of MBA students to evaluate and give her feedback on the culture within the giant hospitality and travel corporation. Upon completion of their study, Nelson asked for their findings. With some reluctance, one of the students finally responded, "We hear from employees that Carlson is a sweatshop that doesn't care."

Shocked and disappointed, Nelson immediately began to apply her considerable talent, passion, energy and motivational skills to transform the corporate culture. Over time, Carlson Companies was changed from a hard-nosed, growth-driven, unfeeling organization to a "culture of caring" widely recognized as one of the nation's best places to work. Not so incidentally, profits also improved in the process. If Nelson can turn around the culture of a large company like Carlson, you can do it in your factory, shop or office. But how?

How to improve the culture of the workplace

Cultures are organic. They are constantly growing, morphing, reforming, adjusting and adapting, sometimes, without the people in them even realizing it. Cultures in every workplace are continuously being shaped and sculpted by a myriad of forces and influences. Organizations can learn. When they do, their internal environment is altered. In short, cultures can change and supervisors can change them. It's something you can do too.

Workers in all fields and industries relate and respond most to their immediate supervisor, rather than to some remote corporate headquarters. That's why, as a manager, you can create an improved workplace culture in your area of responsibility.

In addition to modeling the beliefs and actions you value, following are ten specific ways to make the culture in your workplace better, stronger, healthier, more humane and more productive:

- Concentrate on building positive relationships. People work better together when they know and respect each other as individual human beings.
- Practice open communication. It makes employees feel valued and involved. When you override gossip with hard facts and accurate information, you build trust in the process.
- Watch your language. The words you choose can shape the way people in the organization think and feel about the organization. If you use militaristic metaphors, you can expect a war-like organization.
- Be inclusive. When everyone is involved in the planning and dreaming, as well as the hard work, you multiply talent.
- Practice the Golden Rule. It still works. If you only have one rule in your organization, this

should be it. When followed, the Golden Rule eliminates self-defeating rivalries, petty politics and wasteful turf battles.

- Strive to be a "servant leader." If you remove obstacles and give workers what they need to do their best work, everyone benefits.
- Use "Founders' Tales" to remind all employees of the original vision of the organization and what it was intended to stand for. The founding heroes can still inspire current workers to do and be their best.
- Grant everyone in the organization permission to have fun on the job. When people are having fun, they work better, faster, harder and longer.
- Institutionalize ethical behaviour. Formally include honesty, respect and integrity in the organization's mission statement, goals and objectives and strategic planning documents. When this happens, workers become convinced that you mean it.
- Hire people who espouse the values you want for your workforce.
- Using the strategies above or whatever else works, effective supervisors strive to align the everyday culture of the workplace with the overall goals of the organization. When that happens, look outward - big things are about to happen. Culture is a powerful determinant of long-lasting success. Individuals come and go, but organizations preserve knowledge, behaviours, mental maps, norms and values over time and translate those cultural expectations to newcomers. It is the culture that keeps the organization going beyond the tenure of any single supervisor manager.

The best leaders strive to create a culture that empowers individual self-actualization and promotes optimum, creative collaboration at the same time. If you build that kind of workplace, they (workers) will come. They will stay. They will produce. And you will have made your workplace better. That's what good supervisors do. You don't want to do any less.

Differences in Cultures

Increasingly, managers must deal with multiple ethnic groups with very different cultures. Thanks to globalization, you are likely to work with Japanese, French, Chinese, German and all sorts of other nationalities. It is important to recognize that people from different cultures have are different in a variety of ways, including

- different ways of looking at things
- different ways of dressing
- different ways of expressing personality/goodness

In an ideal world ...
• the policemen would be English • the car mechanics would be German • the cooks would be French • the innkeepers would be Swiss, • and the lovers would be Italian
In a living hell ...
• the policemen would be German • the car mechanics would be French • the cooks would be English • the innkeepers would be Italian • and the lovers would be Swiss

These differences can cause problems interpreting what the other person is doing. Some simple examples:

- In the US, a firm, short handshake indicates self-confidence and (heterosexual) masculinity. A limp handshake by a man can be interpreted (usually wrongly) as a sign of homosexuality or wimpiness. But in most parts of Africa, a limp handshake is the correct way to do it. Furthermore, it is common in Africa for the handshake to last several minutes, while in the US a handshake that is even a few seconds too long is interpreted as familiarity, warmth and possibly sexual attraction.

- In Britain, men do not look at women on the streets. The French do. Recently, a French public figure mentioned in a speech that the Brits are all gay – the evidence was their lack of overt interest in women.

Some dimensions along which cultures vary.

High Context *vs.* Low Context

A low context culture is one in which things are fully (though concisely) spelled out. Things are made explicit, and there is considerable dependence on what is actually said or written. A high context culture is one in which the communicators assume a great deal of commonality of knowledge and views, so that less is spelled out explicitly and much more is implicit or communicated in indirect ways. In a low context culture, more responsibility is placed on the listener to keep up their knowledge base and remain plugged into informal networks.

Low context cultures include Anglos, Germanics and Scandinavians. High context cultures include Japanese, Arabs and French.

Implications

- Interactions between high and low context peoples can be problematic.
  - Japanese can find Westerners to be offensively blunt. Westerners can find Japanese to be secretive, devious and bafflingly unforthcoming with information.
  - French can feel that Germans insult their intelligence by explaining the obvious, while Germans can feel that French managers provide no direction.
- Low context cultures are vulnerable to communication breakdowns when they assume more shared understanding than there really is. This is especially true in an age of diversity. Low context cultures are not known for their ability to tolerate or understand diversity, and tend to be more insular.

Monochronic *vs.* Polychronic

Monochronic cultures like to do just one thing at a time. They value a certain orderliness and sense of there being an appropriate time and place for everything. They do not value interruptions. Polychronic cultures like to do multiple things at the same time. A manager's office in a polychronic culture typically has an open door, a ringing phone and a meeting all going on at the same time.

Polychronic cultures include the French and the Americans. The Germans tend to be monochronic.

Implications

- Interactions between types can be problematic. German businessman cannot understand why the person he is meeting is so interruptible by phone calls and people stopping by. Is it meant to insult him? When do they get down to business?
- Similarly, the American employee of a German company is disturbed by all the closed doors – it seems cold and unfriendly.

Future vs. Present vs. Past Orientation

Past-oriented societies are concerned with traditional values and ways of doing things. They tend to be conservative in management and slow to change those things that are tied to the past. Past-oriented societies include China, Britain, Japan and most Spanish-speaking Latin American countries.

Present-oriented societies include the rest of the Spanish-speaking Latin American countries. They see the past as passed and the future as uncertain. They prefer short-term benefits.

Future-oriented societies have a great deal of optimism about the future. They think they understand it and can shape it through their actions. They view management as a matter of planning, doing and controlling (as opposed to going with the flow, letting things happen). The United States and increasingly, Brazil, are examples of future-oriented societies.

Quantity of Time

In some cultures, time is seen as being a limited resource which is constantly being used up. It's like having a bathtub full of water which can never be replaced, and which is running down the drain. You have to use it as it runs down the drain or it's wasted. In other cultures, time is more plentiful, if not infinite. In old agricultural societies, time was often seen as circular, renewing itself each year.

Implications

- In societies where time is limited, punctuality becomes a virtue. It is insulting to waste someone's time, and the ability to do that and get away with it is an indication of superiority/status. Time is money. In cultures where time is plentiful, like India or Latin American, there is no problem with making people wait all day, and then tell them to come back the next day.
- Time-plentiful cultures tend to rely on trust to do business. Time-limited cultures don't have time to develop trust and so create other mechanisms to replace trust (such as strong rule-by-law).

Power Distance

The extent to which people accept differences in power and allow this to shape many aspects of life. Is the boss always right because he is the boss, or only when he gets it right?

Implications

- In high power distance countries (most agrarian countries), bypassing a superior is insubordination. In low power distance countries (US, northern Europeans, Israel), bypassing is not usually a big deal.
- In the US, superiors and subordinates often interact socially as equals. An outsider watching a party of professors and graduate students typically cannot tell them apart.

Individualism *vs.* Collectivism

In individualist cultures, individual uniqueness, self-determination is valued. A person is all the more admirable if they are a "self-made man" or "makes up their own mind" or show initiative or work well independently. Collectivist cultures expect people to identify with and work well in groups which protect them in exchange for loyalty and compliance.

Paradoxically, individualist cultures tend to believe that there are universal values that should be shared by all, while collectivist cultures tend to accept that different groups have different values.

Many of the Asian cultures are collectivist, while Anglo cultures tend to be individualist.

Implications

- A market research firm conducted a survey of tourist agencies around the world. The questionnaires came back from most countries in less than a month. But the agencies in the Asian countries took months to do it. After many telexes, it was finally done. The reason was that, for example, American tourist agencies assigned the work to one person, while the Filipinos delegated the work to the entire department, which took longer. The researchers also noticed that the telexes from the Philipines always came from a different person.

Problems Caused by Cultural Differences

- You greet your Austrian client. This is the sixth time you have met over the last 4 months. He calls you Herr Smith. You think of him as a standoffish sort of guy who doesn't want to get really friendly. That might be true in America, where calling someone Mr. Smith after the

6th meeting would probably mean something — it is *marked* usage of language — like "we're not hitting it off". But in Austria, it is normal.

- A Canadian conducting business in Kuwait is surprised when his meeting with a high-ranking official is not held in a closed office and is constantly interrupted. He starts wondering if the official is as important as he had been led to believe, and he starts to doubt how seriously his business is being taken.
- A British boss asked a new, young American employee if he would like to have an early lunch at 11 am each day. The employee said 'Yeah, that would be great!' The boss immediately said "With that kind of attitude, you may as well forget about lunch!" The employee and the boss were both baffled by what went wrong. [In England, saying "yeah" in that context is seen as rude and disrespectful.]
- A Japanese businessman wants to tell his Norwegian client that he is uninterested in a particular sale. So he says "That will be very difficult." The Norwegian eagerly asks how he can help. The Japanese is mystified. To him, saying that something is difficult is a polite way of saying "No way in hell!". Dave Barry tells the story of being on a trip to Japan and working with a Japanese airline clerk on taking a flight from one city to another. On being asked about it, the clerk said "Perhaps you would prefer to take the train." So he said "No, I want to fly." So she said "There are many other ways to go." He said "yes, but I think it would be best to fly." She said "It would very difficult". Eventually, it came out that there were no flights between those cities.

Three basic kinds of problems: interpreting others comments and actions, predicting behavior, and conflicting behavior.

Some Perceptions of Americans

Europe and especially England. "Americans are stupid and unsubtle. And they are fat and bad dressers."

Finland. "Americans always want to say your name: 'That's a nice tie, Mikko. Hi Mikko, how are you Mikko.'

Indian. "Americans are always in a hurry. Just watch the way they walk down the street."

Kenyan. "Americans are distant. They are not really close to other people — even other Americans."

Turkey. "Once we were out in a rural area in the middle of nowhere and saw an American come to a stop sign. Though he could see in both directions for miles, and there was no traffic, he still stopped!"

Colombia. "In the United States, they think that life is only work."

Indonesia. "In the United States everything has to be talked about and analyzed. Even the littlest thing has to be 'Why, why why?'."

Ethiopia. "The American is very explicit. He wants a 'yes' or 'no'. If someone tries to speak figuratively, the American is confused."

Iran. "The first time my American professor told me 'I don't know, I will have to look it up', I was shocked. I asked myself 'Why is he teaching me?'"

Try this experiment:

Start by reading this:

FINISHED FILES ARE THE RESULT OF YEARS OF SCIENTIFIC STUDY COMBINED WITH THE EXPERIENCE OF YEARS

Now, quickly count the number of "F"s in that sentence. On average, Anglos find fewer F's than do others. Why?

Gender Diversity in the Workplace

In the past, all women in the workplace were automatically assigned to temporary or part-time or low responsibility jobs because it was understood that their first priority was taking care of their families. Unmarried women were likely to quit as soon as they married (often to an up-and-coming executive in the company), and married women were likely to quit as soon as they became pregnant. Women with children were understood to care more about the children than about work. In addition, there was a widespread belief that women were not as capable as men, either physically or mentally or emotionally.

Today, women are not generally seen as inferior to men (in fact, it is common to hear that men are inferior to women). And there are women who want to put work first and family second. Most women in the workforce do not see it as temporary — something to do until they "catch a man" — nor as "extra" income.

Organizations have been slowly adjusting to these changes, learning to treat women as the equals of men and not as a pool of potential dates. Both discriminating against female employees (in terms of hiring and advancement) and treating them in a sexual manner (sexual harassment) are now against the law.

However, since there remain some women in the workforce who do place family first, Felice Schwartz has suggested creating a "Mommy Track" which would allow them to have more flexible and shorter hours and lesser responsibility in exchange for lower pay and limited career growth. In other words, recognize the wider diversity of needs of employees today and set up systems to accommodate them all.

Feminists worry that creating a Mommy Track effectively licenses corporations to discriminate against women. They feel that women (and presumably men!) should be allowed to have flexible work arrangements and remain on the fast track.

Some people regard issues of treatment of various employee groups, such as those based on gender, race, and sexual orientation as primarily an issue of moral fairness. Women should be given the same career opportunities as men; homosexual couples should be given the same health insurance benefits as heterosexual couples. American society and culture has changed considerably on these issues over the last 150 years (when women were not allowed to vote and slavery was still practiced), and organizations are asked to not only follow suit but lead the way. However, many managers would counter that organizations are not supposed to change American society. They are supposed to manufacture goods and provide services for money. Their responsibilities are to their stockholders, not women's groups. It might be morally desirable for corporations to give all their profits to the poor, but it would not be responsible action.

Others see the issues primarily in strategic terms. Organizations compete for human resources and as the workforce becomes more heterogeneous, organizations will have to serve the diverse needs of this workforce or they will lose them to their competitors. Organizations that discriminate against women are forced to select workers from a smaller pool, reducing their ability to find top performers. At the same time, some managers would point out that increased diversity can cause management problems. For example, having more women has meant more problems with sexual harassment (even if it's the men's *fault*). Increased diversity brings with it the need for more flexibility, which makes management more complicated (e.g., scheduling, compensation plans, interpersonal communication).

Communicating Across Cultures

Communication allows people to exchange thoughts by one of several methods. There are auditory means, such as speaking or singing, and physical means, such as sign language, touch, or eye contact.

Purposes of Communication

Communication is a process by which information is exchanged between or among individuals through a common system of symbols, signs, and behaviour. As a process, communication has synonyms such as expressing feelings, conversing, speaking, corresponding, writing, listening and exchanging. People communicate to satisfy needs in both their work and non-work lives. People want to be heard, to be appreciated and to be wanted. They also want to accomplish tasks and to achieve goals. Obviously, then, a major purpose of communication is to help people feel good about themselves and about their friends, groups, and organizations. For true communication, there must be a transmitting of thoughts, ideas and feelings from one mind to another. If love may be called the heart of happy family living, then communication could be called its lifeblood.

Definition

Cross-cultural communication (also frequently referred to as intercultural communication) is a field of study that looks at how people from differing *cultural* backgrounds endeavour to communicate.

Cross-culture communication core is to establish and understand how people from different cultures communicate with each other. Its charge is to also produce some guidelines with which people from different cultures can better communicate with each other.

For example, how does a person from China communicate with a person from America? Furthermore, what underlying mental constructs appear from both parties that allows for constructive communication?

Cross cultural communication is the combination of many other fields. These fields include anthropology, cultural studies, psychology and communication. The field has also moved both toward the treatment of interethnic relations, and toward the study of communication strategies used by co-cultural populations, i.e., communication strategies used to deal with majority or mainstream populations.

The main theories for cross-cultural communication are based on the work done looking at value differences (or Cultural dimensions) among cultures, especially the works of Edward T. Hall, Geert Hofstede, Harry C. Triandis, Fons Trompenaars and more recently Shalom Schwartz. Clifford Geertz was also a major contributor to this field. The first Ph.D. in intercultural communication was awarded to William J. Starosta (Indiana University, 1973).

These theories have been applied to a variety of different communication theories and settings, including general business and management (Fons Trompenaars and Charles Hampden-Turner) and marketing (Marieke de Mooij, Stephan Dahl). There have also been several successful educational projects which concentrate on the practical applications of these theories in cross-cultural situations. Notably, the European-funded research project media-net-works which illustrates ways in which virtual communities can be established to achieve an understanding of how people from different cultures communicate with each other.

These theories have also been criticized mainly by management scholars (e.g., Holden, Nigel) for being based on the culture concept derived from 19th century cultural anthropology and emphasizing on culture-as-difference and culture-as-essence. Another criticism has been the uncritical way Hofstede's dimensions are served up in textbooks as facts. There is a move to focus on 'cross-cultural interdependence' instead of the traditional views of comparative differences and similarities between cultures and cross-cultural management is seen as a form of knowledge management.

Cultural anthropology is one of four fields of anthropology (the holistic study of humanity) as it developed in the United States. It is the branch of anthropology that has developed and promoted "culture" as a meaningful scientific concept; it is also the branch of anthropology that studies cultural variation among humans.

The anthropological concept of "culture" reflects in part a reaction against earlier Western discourses based on an opposition between "culture" and "nature", according to which some human beings lived in a "state of nature". Anthropologists argue that culture is "human nature," and that all people have a capacity to classify experiences, encode classifications symbolically, and teach such abstractions to others. Humans acquire culture through learning (the processes of enculturation and socialization), people living in different places or different circumstances may develop different cultures. Anthropologists have also pointed out that through culture people can adapt to their environment in non-genetic ways, so people living in different environments will often have different cultures. Much of anthropological theory has originated in an appreciation of and interest in the tension between the local (particular cultures) and the global (a universal human nature, or the web of connections between people in distinct places/circumstances).

Parallel with the rise of cultural anthropology in the United States, social anthropology, in which "sociality" is the central concept and which focuses on the study of social statuses and roles, groups, institutions, and the relations among them, developed as an academic discipline in Great Britain. Some anthropologists have drawn on both traditions and identify themselves as socio-cultural anthropologists

Cross-Cultural Interaction Limitations

A primary source of misunderstanding among cultures is the differences in values and priorities. Some of the most common lie in the way dissimilar cultures perceive, time, thought patterns, personal space, material possessions, family roles and relationships, language, religion, personal achievement, competitiveness and individuality, social behavior, and other interrelated environmental and subjective issues. Another important source of miscommunication and misunderstanding is in the perceptions of the leaders, managers, and communicators about the persons with whom they are dealing. For example, if people presume their values and habits are superior and more sophisticated than those of other cultures, this attitude will be reflected in the way they communicate. Some of the factors that affect intercultural relationships are outlined below.

Promotion of cross-cultural understanding

When individuals have had only very limited or no contact at all with a particular culture, they commonly hold stereotypical, or broad behavioural generalizations, about that culture and its members. In the absence of direct experience stereotypes provide a set of usually negative and inaccurate guidelines that indicate what can be expected when encountering members of that culture. Commonly held stereotypes include the beliefs that the English are arrogant and aloof, that the Scottish are dour and cheap and that Americans are loud, aggressive and wealthy. In times of impending or actual warfare, governments frequently evoke exceptionally crude stereotypes that demonize and depersonalize the enemy, or 'other', thereby making it easier for the public, or 'us', to hate and kill 'them' Such attitudes, for example, were deliberately cultivated by the Australian government towards the Japanese people during World War II, while the 'White Australia' immigration policy, which prevailed until the 1970s, was based in large part on imaginary fears of being overwhelmed by the 'faceless hordes' of Asia.

Advocates of tourism contend that direct contacts between tourists and residents can serve to dispel such stereotypes and allow the members of each group to perceive one another as individuals and, potentially, as friends. People who travel extensively are often characterized as more broad-minded, tolerant and cosmopolitan than people who maintain limited contact with the world at large (Mcintosh, Goeldner & Ritchie 1995). Hence, tourism is seen as a potent force for cross-cultural understanding because huge numbers of people come into contact with members of other cultures both at home and abroad. In Australia direct contacts with Japanese and other Asian tourists have undoubtedly contributed to the erosion of stereotypes held by some Australians, while the same effect has also occurred through the exposure of outbound Australians to Asia and other overseas destinations. In addition, the government now actively encourages such positive attitudes because of the economic benefits that are associated with the inbound Asian tourist market.

Dell Computer Corporation

When Dell Inc., moved into Asia, people told them that their Western concept wouldn't work there. "But rather than tailoring the strategy to fit the culture, we said, "We think our direct model will work cross-culturally. And we're willing to take the risk," writes Michael Dell1, Chairman and CEO of the Dell Computer Corporation.

"To be sure we do some localization," he continues. You obviously can't sell English-language computers in China. And from a cultural perspective, customers in other countries are different. We learned, for example, that some Germans aren't comfortable telephoning in a response to an advertisement; they find it too forward. They will, however, respond to an ad that features a fax number. They'll send in a fax, asking for more information, and will provide their name and phone number so that a Dell representative can call them. The conversation that ensues is almost exactly the same as that which would have occurred if the German customer had made the call himself. It was a slight modification that allowed us to adapt to cultural differences without altering our business strategies."

Cross Cultural Negotiation and Decision Making

Negotiation is the process by which at least two partners with different needs and view-points try to reach agreement on matters of mutual interest. A negotiation becomes cross-cultural when the parties involved belong to different cultures and therefore do not share the same ways of thinking, feeling and behaving.

All global negotiations are cross-cultural. Negotiating effectively cross-culturally is one of the important global business skills. Business people should consider negotiating when any of the following conditions exists:

- Their power position is low relative to that of their counterpart.
- The trust level is high.
- Sufficient time is available to explore each party's multiple needs, resources and options.
- Commitment is important to ensure all parties carry out the agreement.

The success of a negotiation depends on the three areas-individual characteristics, situational contingencies and strategic and tactical processes. Negotiators bring into contact unfamiliar and potentially conflicting set of categories, rules, plans and behaviors. The negotiator cannot take common knowledge and practices for granted. The qualities possessed by a negotiator, for successful negotiations depends on the culture involved.

A synergistic approach may be used to negotiate cross culturally. The stages of negotiating globally are the following:

- Preparation (cross cultural training, define interests)
- Relationship building (separate people from problem, adjust to their style)
- Information exchange (exchange task and participant related information, clarify interests)
- Inventing options for mutual gain appropriate to both parties.

Because people from different cultures perceives, interpret and evaluate the world differently, accurately communicating needs and interests in a way that people understand becomes more challenging. In such a case win-win solutions or mutually beneficial solutions in which both parties gain becomes possible. For instance, based on their different perspectives, a seller from one culture may no longer want to keep a particular business, whereas a buyer from another culture may find the same business an especially attractive prospect.

Russians generally do not expect to develop a continuing relationship with their counterpart and therefore see little need for relationship building. By contrast, Arabs generally want to build long relationships with their counterpart. Therefore, they are ready to make concessions throughout the negotiation process and almost always reciprocate their counterpart's concessions. Russians make few, if any concessions and view their counterpart's concession as signs of weakness.

Situations also have an effect on the success of negotiation. Effective negotiators recognize and manage the impact of each situational factor taking into consideration both, their own and their opponents' cultural perspective. Location, physical arrangements, participants, time limits, status differences are to be determined effectively by the negotiator for successful negotiation.

Countries vary in the emphasis placed on each phase and the style used to approach it. Effective negotiators can approach each stage of the negotiation through principled strategies such as:

Separating people from problem and thus building interpersonal relationships.

- Focusing on the interests and not on positions.
- Inventing options for mutual gain.
- Using objective decision criteria to reach an agreement and make appropriate concessions.

Cross Cultural Differences in Decision Making

In a world as complex as ours, each of us is shaped by many factors, and culture is one of the powerful forces that acts on us. Anthropologists Kevin Avruch and Peter Black explain the importance of culture this way: ...One's own culture provides the "lens" through which we view the world; the "logic"... by which we order it; the "grammar" ... by which it makes sense.

In other words, culture is central to what we see, how we make sense of what we see, and how we express ourselves.

As people from different cultural groups take on the exciting challenge of working together, cultural values sometimes conflict. We can misunderstand each other, and react in ways that can hinder what are otherwise promising partnerships. Oftentimes, we aren't aware that culture is acting upon us. Sometimes, we are not even aware that we have cultural values or assumptions that are different from others'.

The roles individuals play in decision-making vary widely from culture to culture. For example, in the U.S., decisions are frequently delegated — that is, an official assigns responsibility for a particular matter to a subordinate. In many Southern European and Latin American countries, there is a strong value placed on holding decision-making responsibilities oneself. When decisions are made by groups of people, majority rule is a common approach in the U.S., in Japan consensus is the preferred mode. Be aware that individuals' expectations about their own roles in shaping a decision may be influenced by their cultural frame of reference.

Today, more than ever, North Americans - as well as people in or from the East - have a greater chance to interact with people from different cultures. During their interactions, people from individualistic cultures tend to value personal goals over group goals, personal concerns over group concerns, and personal rights and needs over collective responsibilities and obligations. In contrast, people from collectivistic cultures tend to value group goals over personal goals, group concerns over personal concerns, and collective needs over personal needs. Because of these different value systems in societies, people of different cultural origin are likely to reveal different attitudes and styles of decision making in negotiation, bargaining processes, and problem solving in various social settings.

Japanese, Chinese, and Korean - that are more skilled than Americans at collective decision making. This opinion appears to be particularly pertinent because people from collectivistic cultures, such as Japanese and Korean prefer group decision by consensus with emphasis on co-operation, harmony, and interdependence in social life.

On the other hand, people from individualistic cultures prefer decision by majority vote when making decisions, and the values of a certain culture motivate its members to behave co-operatively or competitively. Because people's behaviour is shaped by - and adjusted to - the particular culture in which they live and mature, cultural values might influence people to exhibit different behavioral patterns, including decision-making styles. These cultural characteristics might be important elements in understanding different decision-making styles presented by people from different cultures.

Among many cultural factors, the individualism ("I" culture) - collectivism ("we" culture) dimension might be the most important influential factor to be considered when studying cultural differences, including decision-making styles. Traditionally, individualism has been identified as the habit or principle of being independent and self-reliant: self-centred feeling or conduct; egoism or "a situation in which people are supposed to look after themselves and their immediate family only." This is a common cultural pattern found in North America, including Canada, and most northern and western European countries. Collectivism, in contrast, represents the cultural values, attitudes, and patterns of people in Asia, Africa, Latin America, and the Pacific. The term has been used to refer to the general pattern that pertains to societies in which people from birth onwards are integrated into strong, cohesive in groups, which throughout people's lifetime continue to protect them in exchange for unquestioning loyalty. This characteristic involves the need to maintain group harmony above the partisan interests of subgroups and individuals.

This collectivism-individualism dimension is a very important component to consider when one examines differences in the decision-making styles of people from different cultures. People in different cultures, however, are not born with fixed cultural traits. People's "behaviour is shaped by the beliefs, attitudes, and values they acquire growing up in a particular culture".

In terms of child development, people in the West emphasize the importance of individual autonomy and the development of an independent, self controlled, self - directed and self-reliant who will eventually become a self-contained adult with a high degree of independence. Bringing up an independent and self-reliant child, however, is not a major concern for Asian parents, especially for Japanese and Korean parents much greater importance is placed on establishing interdependent, co-operative, and harmonious relations between the child and other members of the family, group, and society.

As companies in the East prosper and become more global, North American and European enterprises stretch out to foreign countries as well. In addition, government officials from many countries interact with others for the benefit of their own countries. These phenomena lead managers, executives, and government officials from differing cultures to be involved frequently in negotiations with foreign clients and officials. Interactions with people from other cultures do not generate much confidence in many of us because often we do not know what to expect nor how to negotiate for meaning. Therefore, understanding cultural differences, in terms of different decision making and problem-solving styles employed by people from various cultures, is very important and well worth investigating in modern business and social relationships.

❄ ❄ ❄

5 International Strategic Management

• International Strategic Management • Strategic planning • Formulating strategy • International functional strategies • Managing Political risk and negotiation • Organizational structure • Decision Making and Control Systems.

International Strategic Management

International Strategic Management (ISM) is an ongoing management planning process aimed at developing strategies to allow an organization to expand abroad and compete internationally. Strategic planning is used in the process of developing a particular international strategy.

Strategy is a long term plan of action designed to achieve a particular goal(An objective or goal is a personal or organizational desired end point in development. It is usually endeavoured to be reached in finite time by setting deadlines), most often "winning". Strategy is differentiated from tactics (A tactic is a conceptual action used to implement a specific strategy to achieve a specific objective, to advance toward a specific goal. A tactic is implemented as one or more tasks.) Or immediate actions with resources at hand by its nature of being extensively premeditated, and often practically rehearsed. Strategies are used to make the problem or problems easier to solve, and also for you to understand it more.

Strategic planning is an organization's process of defining its strategy, or direction, and making decisions on allocating its resources to pursue this strategy, including its capital and people. Various business analysis techniques can be used in strategic planning, including SWOT analysis and PEST analysis.

The outcome is normally a strategic plan which is used as guidance to define functional and divisional plans, including Technology, Marketing, etc.

Strategic Planning is the formal consideration of an organization's future course. All strategic planning deals with at least one of three key questions:

1. "What do we do?"
2. "For whom do we do it?"
3. "How do we excel?"

In many organizations, this is viewed as a process for determining where an organization is going over the next year or more -typically 3 to 5 years, although some extend their vision to 20 years.

In order to determine where it is going, the organization needs to know exactly where it stands, then determines where it wants to go and how it will get there. The resulting document is called the "strategic plan".

It is also true that strategic planning may be a tool for effectively plotting the direction of a company; however, strategic planning itself cannot foretell exactly how the market will evolve and what issues will surface in the coming days in order to plan your organizational strategy. Therefore, strategic innovation and tinkering with the 'strategic plan' have to be a cornerstone strategy for an organization to survive the turbulent business climate.

Vision, mission and values

Vision: Defines where the organization wants to be in the future. It reflects the optimistic view of the organization's future.

Mission: Defines where the organization is going now, basically describing the purpose, why this organization exists.

Values: Main values protected by the organization during the progression, reflecting the organization's culture and priorities.

Strategic planning saves time, every minute spent in planning saves ten minutes in execution.

The purpose of individual strategic planning is for you to increase your return on energy, the return on the mental, emotional, physical and spiritual capital you have invested in your life and career.

An organization must be able to determine what products or services they intend to sell, where and how the organization will make these products or services, where they will sell them, and how the organization will acquire the necessary resources for these tasks. Even more importantly, an organization must have a strategy on how it expects to outperform its competitors.

Complexity in developing an international strategy

When an organization moves from being a domestic entity to an international organization it must consider the possible broad complexities that accompany such a decision. In a domestic country, an organization must only consider one national government, a single currency and accounting system, one political and legal system, and usually a similar culture. Entering into one or more foreign countries can involve multiple governments, currencies, accounting systems, legal systems, and a large variety of languages and cultures. This can create numerous barriers to entry for an organization looking to expand internationally.

In foreign countries, there are the possibility of:

- local languages required in many situations.
- very diverse cultures, both between countries and sometimes even within countries.
- often volatile politics.
- varied economic systems.
- scarcity of skilled labor, with possible costs in training labour or redesigning procedures.
- poorly-developed financial markets and government-controlled capital flows, in some of the countries.
- limited advertising, subjected to lots of restrictions.
- possible low literacy rates, not to mention the possibility of making mistakes in the language when advertising.
- currency exchange fluctuations.
- inadequate or limited communication
- mandatory worker participation in management in some countries.

Types of International strategies

Two sets of factors impinge upon a firm's decision to adopt international strategies extent of cost pressure and the extent of pressures for local responsiveness. Cost pressure denotes the demand on a firm to minimize its unit costs. Pressure for local responsiveness makes a firm tailor its strategies to respond to national-level differences in terms of variable like customer preferences and tastes, government policies, or business practices. Often these two factors are contradictory: minimizing unit costs may not be possible when products and services have to be differentiated across countries. According to Bartlett and Ghoshal, there are four types of international strategies.

1. Global strategy

2. Transnational strategy
3. International strategy
4. Multi-domestic strategy.

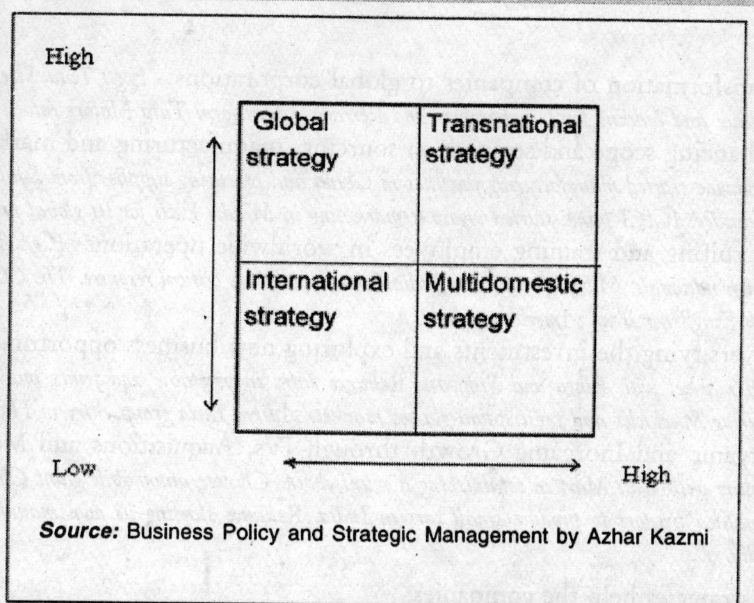

Source: Business Policy and Strategic Management by Azhar Kazmi

Figure 5.1

Global strategy

Firms adopt a global strategy when rely on low cost approach based on reaping the benefits of experience-curve effects and location economics and offering standardized products and services across different countries.

Transnational strategy

Firms adopt a transnational strategy when they adopt a combined approach of low-cost and high local responsiveness simultaneously for their products and services. Dealing with these two often contradictory objectives is a difficult proposition and calls for a creative approach to managing the production and marketing of product and services.

International strategy

Firms adopt a international strategy when they create value by transferring product and services to foreign markets where these products and services are not available. This is a simple strategy in the sense that an international firm, maintaining a tight control over its overseas operation, offers standardized products and services in different countries with little or no differentiation. Example Coca-Cola, IBM, Kellogg.

Multidomestic strategy

Firms adopt a multidomestic strategy when they try to achieve a high level of local responsiveness by matching their products and services offerings to the national conditions operating in the countries they operate in. In this case, the multidomestic firm attempts to extensively customize their products and services according to the local conditions operating in the different countries.

National Strategies

Free trade agreements

Free trade agreements line NATO, ASEAN and WTO have smoothened the cross border trade

E.g.: more than 30% of utility and fancy products sold in US are.

New protective measures and non-tariff barriers

Encouraging foreign investments being supportive to national industries.

Business Strategies

- Transformation of companies to global corporations - *E.g.: Tata Steel acquiring Corus for its global presence and bidding for Lamborghini and Ferrari to transform Tata Motors into a global corporation.*
- Enhancing scope and strength in sourcing, manufacturing and marketing - *E.g.: Most companies worldwide started manufacturing facilities in China and procuring supplies from South East Asian countries for cost advantage. ICICI bank started vigorous marketing in Middle East for its global presence.*
- Recruiting and training employees in worldwide operations- *E.g.: 8% of the Infosys employees are foreign nationals. Microsoft considers Indian employees as its critical resource. The COO of Air Deccan till it merged with Kingfisher is an American.*
- Diversifying the investments and exploring new business opportunities - *E.g.: ITC entering retail food market with Bingo and Sunfeast, Reliance entry in vegetable and fruits market with Reliance Fresh. Titan entering Spectacles and prescription glasses market. Aditya Birla group entry in Hospitals and Health ventures.*
- Organic and Inorganic Growth through JVs, Acquisitions and Mergers - *Bharti Group's joint venture with Wal Mart in establishing a retail chain. Chinese automobile giant Chery planning for a time up with Sonalika tractors to produce small cars in India. Reliance starting its own manufacturing of CDMA mobiles in India.*

These strategies help the companies:

- to grow in the competitive market
- to reduce the entry barriers
- to increase efficiency and optimizing the market.

Strategic Planning

Strategic planning is an organization's process of defining its strategy, or direction, and making decisions on allocating its resources to pursue this strategy, including its capital and people. Various business analysis techniques can be used in strategic planning, including SWOT analysis.

Strategic planning determines where an organization is going over the next year or more and how it's going to get there. Typically, the process is organization-wide, or focused on a major function such as a division, department or other major function.

Strategic planning determines where an organization is going over the next year or more, how it's going to get there and how it'll know if it got there or not. The focus of a strategic plan is usually on the entire organization, while the focus of a business plan is usually on a particular product, service or program.

There are a variety of perspectives, models and approaches used in strategic planning. The way that a strategic plan is developed depends on the nature of the organization's leadership, culture of the organization, complexity of the organization's environment, size of the organization, expertise of planners, etc. For example, there are a variety of strategic planning models, including goals-based, issues-based, organic, scenario (some would assert that scenario planning is more a technique than model), etc. Goals-based planning is probably the most common and starts with focus on the organization's mission (and vision and/or values), goals to work toward the mission, strategies to achieve the goals, and action planning (who will do what and by when). Issues-based strategic planning often starts by examining issues facing the organization, strategies to address those issues, and action plans. Organic strategic planning might start by articulating the organization's vision and values and then action plans to achieve the vision while adhering to those values.

The major activities in strategic planning activities that it includes are:

1. Strategic Analysis:

- It includes conducting some sort of scan, or review, of the organization's environment (for example, of the political, social, economic and technical environment).
- Planners carefully consider various driving forces in the environment, for example, increasing competition, changing demographics, etc.
- Planners also look at the various strengths, weaknesses; opportunities and threats (*SWOT*) regarding the organization.

2. Setting Strategic Direction:

- Planners carefully come to conclusions about what the organization must do as a result of the major issues and opportunities facing the organization.
- These conclusions include what overall accomplishments (or *strategic goals)* the organization should achieve, and the overall methods (or *strategies*) to achieve the accomplishments.
- This includes identifying the organization's
  — Vision
  — Mission
  — Values statements.

Vision

Vision statements are usually a compelling description of how the organization will or should operate at some point in the future and of how customers or clients are benefiting from the organization's products and services.

Mission

Mission statements are brief written descriptions of the purpose of the organization.

Mission statements vary in nature from very brief to quite comprehensive, and including having a specific purpose statement that is part of the overall mission statement.

Values

Value statements list the overall priorities in how the organization will operate.

Action Planning

- *Action planning* is carefully position out how the strategic goals will be accomplished. Action planning often includes specifying *objectives*, or specific results, with each strategic goal.
- *Action planning* also includes specifying *responsibilities* and *time-lines* with each objective, or who needs to do what and by when.
- It's common to develop an *annual plan* (*management plan*), which includes the strategic goals, strategies, objectives, responsibilities and timelines that should be done in the coming year. Often, organizations will develop plans for each major function, division department, etc., and call these *work plans.*

Strategic Plan Checklist

A good strategic plan should be

- FEASIBLE - Does the organization have the resources to carry out the plan?
- MEASURABLE - Are the goals specific enough that you will know when you have achieved them?
- TIME-SPECIFIC - Is the plan translated into comprehensible time-lines and time-specific work plans with clear deadlines?
- FLEXIBLE - Have you scheduled regular review sessions for assessment and revision?
- INSPIRING - Does the plan give people a sense of something worth working for? Is it bold and imaginative?

Strategic Planning Process in Indian Corporate

In today's highly competitive business environment, budget-oriented planning or forecast-based planning methods are insufficient for a large corporation to survive and prosper. The firm must engage in strategic planning that clearly defines objectives and assesses both the internal and external situation to formulate strategy, implement the strategy, evaluate the progress, and make adjustments as necessary to stay on track.

The Strategic Planning Process

Step 1: Information Gathering and Analysis

- External Assessment
- Market Assessment
- Internal Assessment

External Assessment

Purpose of step: To identify and assess changes and trends in the world around the organization likely to have a significant impact on it over the next 5-10 years. We look at political, economic, technological, social, lifestyle, demographic, competitive, and philanthropic trends. We then determine which changes are opportunities for us (for example, opportunities to grow) and which could be threats to us in some way (trends that can keep us from being successful). Finally, we identify implications for selected changes and trends — ways the organization might respond to the opportunities and threats we identify. (Saying that something is an implication does not require the organization to adopt that course of action.)

Market Assessment

Purpose of step: To identify and assess changes in the needs and perceptions of the organization's markets and constituencies. For most non-profits, these include clients or consumers of services, funders, donors, volunteers, paid staff, board members, collaborators, and competitors. The market assessment attempts to answer the following questions:

1. Who are the organization's key markets and constituents?
2. What are the needs, perceptions, and service expectations of each market?
3. What are the emerging market trends?
4. What are the implications for the organization — how should the organization respond to these changes and trends in its markets?

Internal Assessment

Purpose of step: To assess internal structure, process and operations of the organization and based on this assessment, to pinpoint strengths and weaknesses. Areas examined include organizational personnel (paid and volunteer), fundraising, physical facilities, equipment, use of technology, location, financial condition, management, board governance, special programs/products and services, markets, market position, etc.

Step 2: Identification of Critical Issues and Choices Facing the Organization

Purpose of step: To identify critical strategic issues facing the organization. Critical issues are fundamental policy or program concerns that define the most important situations and choices an organization faces now and in the future. Critical issues can reflect long-standing problems in the organization, the community served or recent events that are anticipated to have a significant impact on the organization and/or community served. Critical issues can also reflect major shifts in thinking that challenge "business as usual". The selection of issues is important because it determines range of decisions the organization's leaders will consider in the future. In some instances, an organization is already aware of the critical issues that the strategic planning process must help it address. In most situations, the planning process participants discern critical strategic issues as they work on the external, market and internal assessments.

In developing the actual wording of the critical issue statements, it's helpful to reflect on the following: The external changes and trends having the greatest positive and/or negative impact on the organization . . . Major changes and trends in the needs, perceptions and service expectations of our markets and constituencies . . . Internal strengths and weaknesses of the organization that will seem to have an impact on our future success . . .

Step 3: Development of a Strategic Vision Statement that Sets Future Direction

Purpose of step: To develop a strategic vision statement. The vision statement describes what we want the organization to look like in ideal terms in the future - the results we will be achieving and characteristics the organization will need to possess in order to achieve those results. The strategic vision statement provides direction and inspiration for organizational goal setting. Through the vision statement, the organization attempts to respond to the challenges and issues expressed in the form of critical issues.

Step 4: Mission Statement Review/Revision

Purpose of step: To develop an organizational mission statement. The mission statement is a broad description of what we do, with/for whom we do it, our distinctive competence, and WHY we do it (our ultimate end). If a mission statement already exists, the focus of this step is on reviewing it in light of the emerging vision statement and if necessary revising the language. Here are some questions that can aid in the review of an already-existing mission statement:

Questions for a Critical Review of an Existing Mission

1. Is the mission statement clear and on target in today's operating environment?
2. Do you have any specific questions or concerns with respect to the mission statement?
3. Does the mission statement duplicate the mission of any other organization? If so, what should we do about it?
4. Considering the answers to these questions, how, if at all, should the mission statement be changed?

Step 5: Development of Strategic Goals

Purpose of step: To develop strategic goal statements consistent with the vision statement. Strategic goals are broad statements of what the organization hopes to achieve in the next 3 years. Goals focus on outcomes or results and are qualitative in nature.

Step 6: Formulation of Strategies for Each Goal

Purpose of step: To develop strategies for each goal. Strategies are statements of major approach or method for attaining goals and resolving specific issues. Ideas for strategy emerge from the earlier internal, external and market assessments, — especially the strengths and weaknesses identified in the internal assessment as well as the implications statements developed as part of the market and external assessments. A strategy is judged potentially effective if it does one or more of the following:

1. Exploits environmental opportunities
2. Defends against environmental threats
3. Leverages organizational competencies.

Step 7: Preparation for Operational Planning Based On the Annual Objectives

Purpose of step: To develop annual objectives consistent with the goals and strategies of the strategic plan. Objectives are specific, concrete, measurable statements of what will be done to achieve a goal generally within a one-year time frame. Objectives include what will be accomplished, by when and by whom. Strictly speaking annual objectives are not part of the Strategic Plan of an agency. Objectives are the core of the agency's Annual Operational Plan that is based on the strategic plan itself.

Formulating Strategy

It is useful to consider strategy formulation as part of a strategic management process that comprises three phases: diagnosis, formulation, and implementation. Strategic management is an ongoing process to develop and revise future-oriented strategies that allow an organization to achieve its objectives, considering its capabilities, constraints, and the environment in which it operates.

Diagnosis includes:

- Performing a situation analysis (analysis of the internal environment of the organization), including identification and evaluation of current mission, strategic objectives, strategies, and results, plus major strengths and weaknesses;
- Analyzing the organization's external environment, including major opportunities and threats;
- Identifying the major critical issues, which are a small set, typically two to five, of major problems, threats, weaknesses, and/or opportunities that require particularly high priority attention by management?

What is Formulating Strategy?

It the second phase in the strategic management process, produces a clear set of recommendations, with supporting justification, that revise as necessary the mission and objectives of the organization, and supply the strategies for accomplishing them. In formulation, we are trying to modify the current objectives and strategies in ways to make the organization more successful. This includes trying to create "sustainable" competitive advantages, although most competitive advantages are eroded steadily by the efforts of competitors. *"Selecting and Implementing the Best Suited Strategy is called as Formulating Strategy".* It is the process of determining appropriate courses of action for achieving organizational objectives and thereby accomplishing organizational purpose.

A good recommendation should be: effective in solving the stated problem(s), practical (can be implemented in this situation, with the resources available), feasible within a reasonable time frame, cost-effective, not overly disruptive, and acceptable to key "stakeholders" in the organization. It is

Figure 5.2

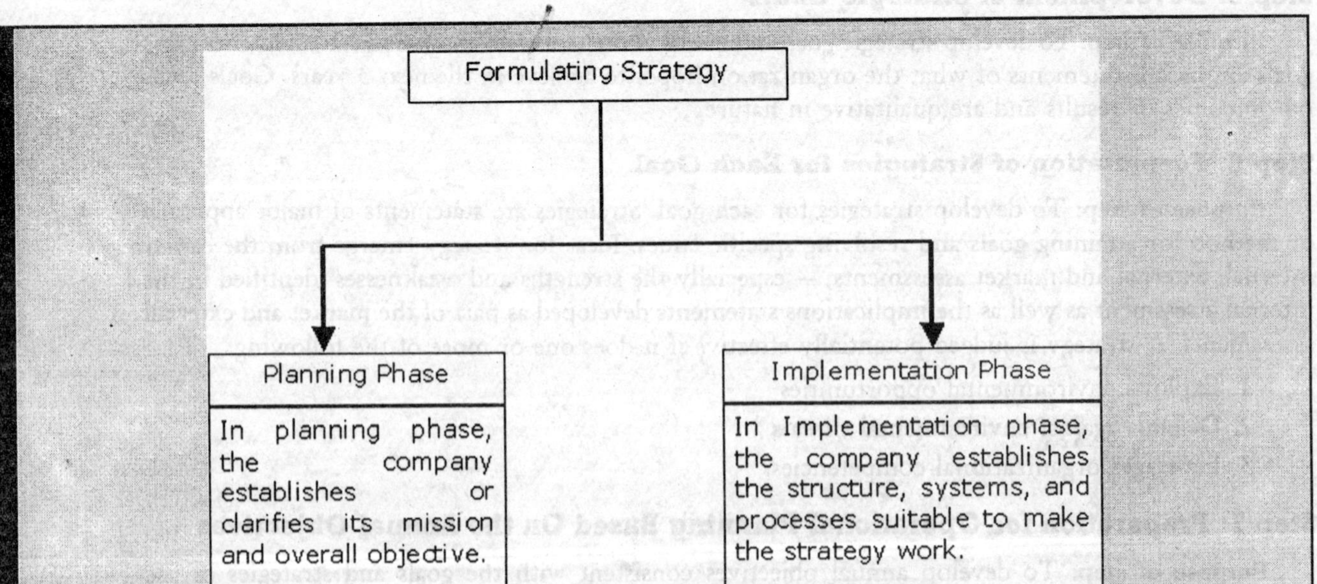

important to consider "fits" between resources plus competencies with opportunities, and also fits between risks and expectations.

In organizations, and in the practice of strategic management, strategies must be implemented to achieve the intended results. The most wonderful strategy in the history of the world is useless if not implemented successfully. This third and final stage in the strategic management process involves developing an implementation plan and then doing whatever it takes to make the new strategy operational and effective in achieving the organization's objectives.

Aspects of Strategy Formulation

The following are the three aspects or levels of strategy formulation, each with a different focus; need to be dealt with in the formulation phase of strategic management. The three sets of recommendations must be internally consistent and fit together in a mutually supportive manner that forms an integrated hierarchy of strategy, in the order given.

Corporate Level Strategy

In this aspect of strategy, we are concerned with broad decisions about the total organization's scope and direction. Basically, we consider what changes should be made in our growth objective and strategy for achieving it, the lines of business we are in, and how these lines of business fit together.

The three components of corporate level strategy:

- Growth or directional strategy (what should be our growth objective, ranging from retrenchment through stability to varying degrees of growth and how do we accomplish this),
- Portfolio strategy (what should be our portfolio of lines of business, which implicitly requires reconsidering how much concentration or diversification we should have),
- Parenting strategy (how we allocate resources and manage capabilities and activities across the portfolio.)

It involves four kinds of initiatives:

- Making the necessary moves to establish positions in different businesses and achieve an appropriate amount and kind of diversification. A key part of corporate strategy is making decisions on how many, what types, and which specific lines of business the company should be in. This may involve deciding to increase or decrease the amount and breadth of diversification. It may involve closing out some LOB's (lines of business), adding others, and/or changing emphasis among LOB's.
- Initiating actions to boost the combined performance of the businesses the company has diversified into: This may involve vigorously pursuing rapid-growth strategies in the most promising LOB's, keeping the other core businesses healthy, initiating turnaround efforts in weak-performing LOB's with promise, and dropping LOB's that are no longer attractive or don't fit into the corporation's overall plans. It also may involve supplying financial, managerial, and other resources, or acquiring and/or merging other companies with an existing LOB.
- Pursuing ways to capture valuable cross-business strategic fits and turn them into competitive advantages, especially transferring and sharing related technology, procurement leverage, operating facilities, distribution channels, and/or customers.
- Establishing investment priorities and moving more corporate resources into the most attractive LOB's.

It is useful to organize the corporate level strategy considerations and initiatives into a framework with the three main strategy components: growth, portfolio and parenting.

Strategic Formulation Process

Strategy formulation is both a skill and a process that leaders use to focus their organizations on where they need to go.

There are four primary steps in this process:

- Reviewing the current key objectives and strategies of the organization, which usually would have been identified and evaluated as part of the diagnosis
- Identifying a rich range of strategic alternatives to address the three levels of strategy formulation outlined below, including but not limited to dealing with the critical issues
- Doing a balanced evaluation of advantages and disadvantages of the alternatives relative to their feasibility plus expected effects on the issues and contributions to the success of the organization
- Deciding on the alternatives that should be implemented or recommended.

Mission and Objective

Mission of an organization is its overall function it performs in society. Objectives flow from mission and guide the formulation of strategy. Each strategy will have a set of objectives, which define the metric, planned outcome that will support strategies.

Environmental Analysis

Gathering information and forecasting relevant trends, competitive actions and circumstances that will affect operations in a geographic area. It includes:

- Political instability
- Currency instability
- Nationalism
- International competition
- Environmental scanning.

Figure 5.3

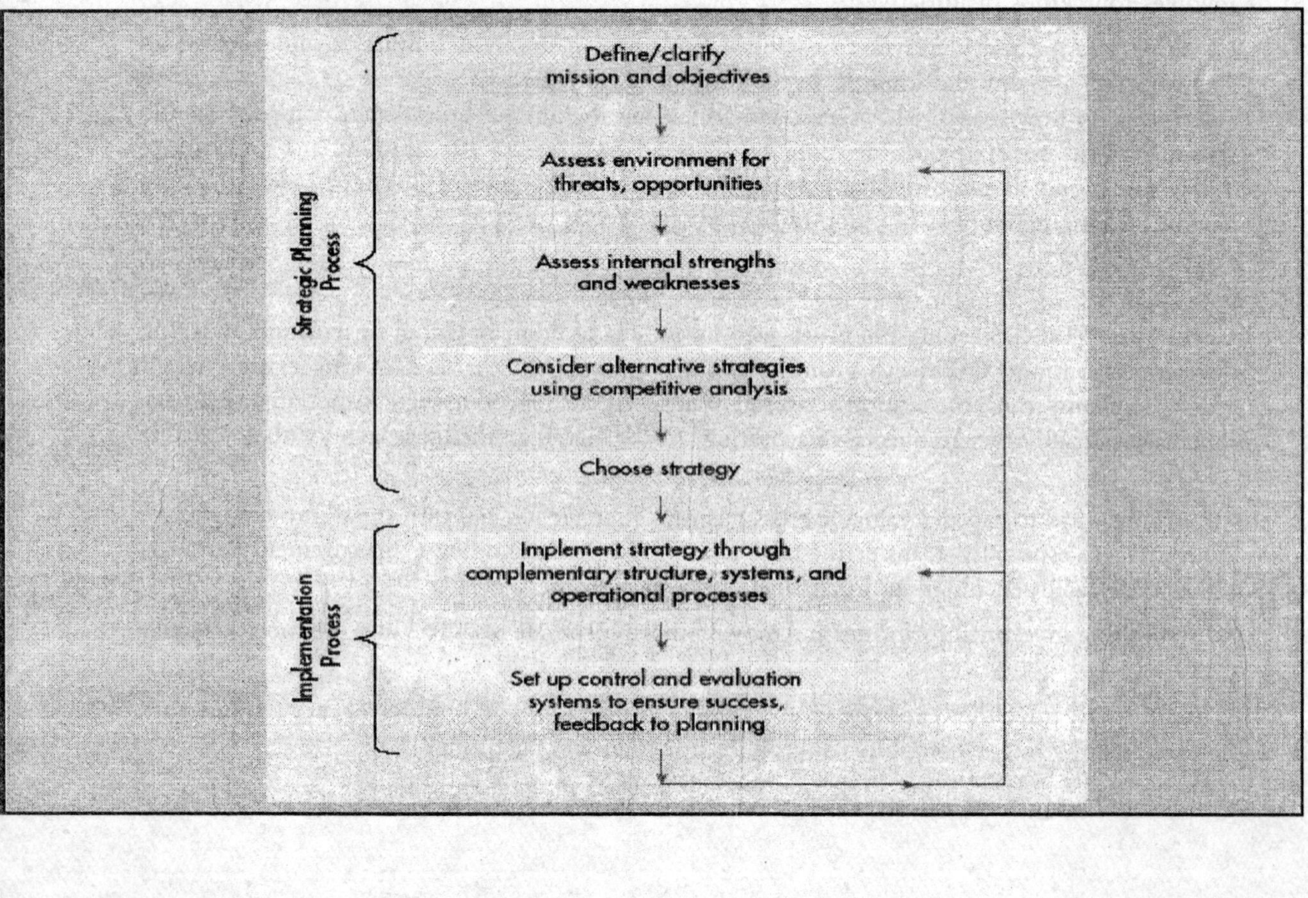

Internal Analysis

Internal analysis determines which areas of the organization's operations represent strengths or weaknesses compared to competitors, so that the organization may use that information to its strategic advantage. Strengths and weaknesses of the organization's financial and managerial expertise need to be understood for effective management. It focuses on the company's resources and operations. The functional capabilities are evaluated to determine the key success factors.

Competitive Analysis

Assess the organization's capabilities and key success factors compared to those of its competitors. Enables strategic planners to determine where the organization has distinctive competencies that will give it an advantage. Most companies develop strategies around key strengths or core competencies. This stage is often called a SWOT (Strengths, Weaknesses, Opportunities, and Threats) analysis.

Global/International Strategic Alternatives

Global strategic alternatives determine the overall approach to the global marketplace. Entry strategy alternatives determine what specific entry strategy is appropriate for each country the firm plans to operate in.

Reasons for Failure of Strategy Formulation

There are mainly two reasons for failure of strategy formulation:

- Strategic objectives are not clearly defined
- Management systems tied only to budgets.

As a result, key processes and initiatives could remain strategically aimless.

Tools used in Formulating Strategies

The tools that are used in formulating strategies are:

Critical question analysis: In this several questions are considered such as What is the main idea of strategy?, List the support for the point, What evidence does the strategy maker's provide to back up his or her support?, List the ideas the strategy maker's attributes to people with the opposite viewpoint., Is the support reasonable and valid? Evaluate each point; Label each statement as fact or opinion.

SWOT analysis: It is a strategic planning tool used to evaluate the Strengths, Weaknesses, Opportunities, and Threats involved in a project or in a business venture. It involves specifying the objective of the business venture or project and identifying the internal and external factors that are favorable and unfavorable to achieving that objective.

Business portfolio analysis: Business portfolio analysis is an enterprise strategy development tool based primarily on the market share of your business and the growth of market in which your business exists.

Porter's model for industry analysis: He argues that a business needs to make two fundamental decisions in establishing its competitive advantage: (*a*) Whether to compete primarily on price (he says "cost," which is necessary to sustain competitive prices, but price is what the customer responds to) or to compete through providing some distinctive points of differentiation that justify higher prices, and (*b*) How broad a market target it will aim at (its competitive scope). These two choices define the four generic competitive strategies, which he argues cover the fundamental range of choices. These are as follows:

- Differentiation Focus
- Price (Cost) Focus
- Differentiation
- Overall Price (Cost) Leadership.

Resource based model: Resource based model of firms is based on the concept of economic rent and the view of the company as a collection of capabilities. This view of strategy has a coherence and integrative role that places it well ahead of other mechanisms of strategic decision making.

These five strategy development tools are related but distinct. These are the tool or combination of tools that are used in the organizations and business environment for formulation of strategies.

International Functional Strategies

Competitive Strategy

It is often called Business Level Strategy. This involves deciding how the company will compete within each line of business (LOB) or strategic business unit (SBU).

In this second aspect of a company's strategy, the focus is on how to compete successfully in each of the lines of business the company has chosen to engage in. The central thrust is how to build and improve the company's competitive position for each of its lines of business. A company has competitive advantage whenever it can attract customers and defend against competitive forces better than its rivals. Companies want to develop competitive advantages that have some sustainability (although the typical term "sustainable competitive advantage" is usually only true dynamically, as a firm works to continue it). Successful competitive strategies usually involve building uniquely strong or distinctive competencies in one or several areas crucial to success and using them to maintain a competitive edge over rivals. Some examples of distinctive competencies are superior technology and/or product features, better manufacturing technology and skills, superior sales and distribution capabilities, and better customer service and convenience.

"Competitive strategy is about being different. It means deliberately choosing to perform activities differently or to perform different activities than rivals to deliver a unique mix of value. (Michael E. Porter)."

Functional Strategy

These more localized and shorter-horizon strategies deal with how each functional area and unit will carry out its functional activities to be effective and maximize resource productivity.

Functional strategies are relatively short-term activities that each functional area within a company will carry out to implement the broader, longer-term corporate level and business level strategies. Each functional area has a number of strategy choices that interact with and must be consistent with the overall company strategies.

Three basic characteristics distinguish functional strategies from corporate level and business level strategies: shorter time horizon, greater specificity, and primary involvement of operating managers.

A few examples follow of functional strategy topics for the major functional areas of marketing, finance, production/operations, research and development, and human resources management. Each area needs to deal with sourcing strategy, i.e., what should be done in-house and what should be outsourced?

Operations management strategies: Operations management, involves a number of strategic decisions such as make or but; if buy, from where to buy; to go for partnering or not; in which country and place to locate the manufacturing or other facilities; logical factors and so on.

4 C's of manufacturing: The success of a manufacturing strategy depends on four key factors – compatibility, configuration, co-ordination, and control.

Compatibility: Degree of consistency between the foreign investment decision and the company's competitive strategy. Company strategies that managers must consider are:

1. Efficiency/cost – reduce manufacturing cost.
2. Dependability – degree of trust in a company's product and its delivery and price promises.

3. Quality – performance, reliability, service quality, speed of delivery, and maintenance quality of the products.
4. Flexibility – ability of the production process to make different kinds of products and to adjust the volume of output.
5. Innovation – ability to develop new products and ideas.

Cost minimization strategies often prompt companies to opt for offshore manufacturing locations like developing countries for outsourcing.

Manufacturing configuration refers to the strategy of centralization or dispersion of manufacturing facilities. Three broad categories of manufacturing configuration, *viz;* centralized facility, regional facilities, and multi domestic facilities. The choice of the configuration strategy is influenced by several factors such as scale economies, nature of technology and skill requirements.

Locations Strategy

Location of production facilities may be influenced by a number of factors.

Nature of organization: The organizational model is a major determinant of the location.

E.g. In a multinational company, the subsidiaries do most of the production for their respective markets. In an International company and global company, there is a tendency to centralize core production activities in the home country.

Cost: with other factors like political, organizational model and strategic orientation, the overall cost of operations is important in location decision making.

- Scale economies: where there is large scale economies in production, production tend to concentrate in one or very limited number of locations.
- Nature of assembly operations: If there is large economies of scale in production of companies and if the assembly operations are labour intensive, they should be carried out in the countries where labour is very cheap.
- Taxes and Transport cost: Import duty structure also influences the location of production phases. If import duty is high on finished goods, they should be assembled in foreign market.
- Exchange rate variations: It may influence the import versus manufacturing decisions.
- Nature of product: Perishables, weight losing or weight gaining characteristics during production process etc influence the location decision.

Make or Buy: The make or buy decisions are influenced by a number of factors:

- Organizational technologies environment: Out source components design or re-design the component parts in house.
- Make to print: Buying companies provides the product technology to the suppliers who required process technology.

Marketing Management Strategies: The marketing strategy is influenced by the SBU strategy which in turn is formulated with in broad framework of corporate mission, objectives and strategy.

The crux of the marketing strategy is the marketing mix strategy, i.e., the strategic decisions in respect of product, price, promotion and place.

Marketing SWOT analysis and choice of product-market set: SWOT analysis with a marketing perspective is to be done to determine the product-market portfolio of the SBU. This determines whether the SBU should continue with all its existing product-market folios or to drop any of it, and whether it should start any new product market folios.

Market Development and Marketing Mix Strategy: It is the strategy to develop existing and new markets for the product. Both market development strategy and marketing mix strategy go hand in hand.

Implementation and Evaluation: The strategy often employed in respect of weak cash cows is to harvest i.e., to increase the short term cash flows regardless of the long term effects. In case of strong cash cows some reinvestment may be required to keep them in good stead for harvesting for long.

Human resource management strategies: It involves ascertaining the corporate strategy of the company and assessing the corresponding human resource needs; determining the recruitment, staffing and organizational strategy, recruiting, inducting, training & developing and motivating the personnel; putting in place the performance appraisal and compensation plan and industrial relations strategy and the effective management of these.

It is important the people recruited fit into the organizational culture and the demand of the diverse environments in which organization functions.

Factors Affecting HRM

Labour market characteristics: The skill levels, the demand and supply conditions and the behavior characteristics of the labour very widely between and within countries. In the past, developing countries was considered as pool of unskilled labour. However, today it's not the same this changing trend is causing shift of the location in business activities. E.g. Hard disk drive manufacturers are reported to be shifting the production base from Singapore to Malaysia and China.

Cultural factors: Cultural differences cause a great challenge to HRM. The behavioral attitude of workers, the social environment, values, beliefs, outlooks etc., are important factors, which affect industrial relations, loyalty, productivity, etc. cultural factors are very relevant in interpersonal behavior also. E.g., in some countries it is common to address the boss Mr. so, and so but in India this may not be welcome.

Regulatory environment: A firm operating in different countries is confronted with different environments with respect to government policies and regulations regarding labour.

Attitude towards employment: In some countries hire and fire is common, whereas in other ideal norms has been lifetime employment.

Conditions and employment: The system of rewards, promotions, incentives and motivation, system of labour welfare and social security etc., vary significantly between countries.

Staffing Policy

There are three types of staffing policies in international business.

Ethnocentric Approach: In this staffing policy, all key management positions in the company are filled by the parent country national.

Polycentric Approach: A company with a polycentric staffing policy recruits host country nationals to manage subsidiaries while the key positions at the corporate headquarters are occupied by the parent country nationals. E.g., multinational corporations.

Geocentric Approach: Geocentric staffing policy connotes seeking the best people from anywhere in the world for managing the organization. e.g., Global and translational corporations.

Staffing Policy Determinants

The Cultural Dimension: The foreign subsidiary top executives to communicate directly with corporate head quarters, MNC's from some countries e.g., Japan may need to depend more on home-country nationals because relatively few foreigners are fluent in mother-tongue of home country.

Subsidiary Characteristics: When the MNC establishes a new subsidiary a new subsidiary or plant, it is likely to ensure that someone already very familiar with corporate culture heads the operation.

Parent Company Characteristics: Here EPRG (ethnocentric, polycentric, geocentric, regiocentric) profile, will influence staffing policy.

Host Country Characteristics: The social environment, government policies, host country human resource characteristics, government policies etc., also may influence the staffing policy.

Cost. Its important consideration because of significant variations between nation's salary levels.

Financial Management Strategies: The objective financial strategy is to improve the firm competitive advantage through a low cost of funds and a flexible ability to raise capital to support a business strategy and to maximize the financial value of the firm.

It encompasses such areas as capital structure, sources and cost of funds, fund flow and cash flow management etc. Financing through long-term debt can help a corporation to use financial leverage to boost earnings per share, thus raising stock price and overall value of the company.

Major Decisions Pertaining to Financial Strategy

Capital Structure: It is concerned with the optimum debt equity ratio, i.e., the optimum mix of equity capital and debt capital. The decision is influenced by the factors like interest payment burden, raise of excessive borrowing and the company's objective of maximization of owners' wealth.

Sources of Finance: Broadly, there are two sources of funds, *viz.,* external sources and internal sources.

- The external sources include equity capital, preference capital, debenture capital, public deposits, and loans from banks.
- The internal sources of finance includes reserves of the company for long term purposes and bank balances and cash in hands with the company for short-term purposes.

Dividend Policy: Dividends to shareholders is an important part of company's financial strategy. Fast-growing companies do not declare dividends in the initial stages. They use profits in rapid growth.

Dividend policy is influenced by factors such as shareholders' preference to current dividend income against capital gains, the reinvestment opportunities and financial needs of the company, need for stability of dividend distribution.

Managing Political Risk and Negotiation

In the years since the end of the Cold War, the United States has struggled to improve its international debt situation and enter more fully into the international economic competition for which it has long been the foremost advocate. Investment opportunities and markets throughout the developing world have drawn increasing attention in the U.S. The term "developing" has even evolved-from being strictly a reference to what is lacking (as in "underdeveloped") to being more a reference to opportunity than to needs. The outcome of the Vietnam War and consequences of the Iranian revolution and its aftermath, however, have made foreign investors and Americans in particular cautious about investments and other business relationships in what are often seen as uncharted waters. Medium and small size firms in particular, who must also be a part of any successful global economy, have been very tentative while lacking the information about the nature and development of the nations in which their hope for business development now lies.

Investors have begun to move slowly into the regions of new opportunity, while trying to keep a close eye on the political situations in these states, wary of processes that seem alien and events that seem unpredictable. But how does an investor "keep a close eye" on a political situation? What elements of the very complex and unfamiliar political situation require attention and assessment before the new investor risks personnel and critical amounts of capital? An analytical structure is needed to sort among the multitude of factors that contribute to the puzzles and riddles that often seem the best characterizations of politics and society in the new world of business opportunity. Such structures are provided for observers in the field referred to as 'political risk analysis.'

In providing **political** risk analysis, the elements of that phrase require attention. In this field we are examining political as distinct from economic risk. Political means having to do with:

- the governance system of a country (political structure);
- the nature of particular governors (authority);
- the response of the population to the government (legitimacy); and
- the nature of the society being governed (culture, social phenomena).

When politics is the subject, one is dealing with the behaviour of people who run the government, with laws, rules, and guidelines they establish, with the reactions of the governed to that behaviour and the rules, and with the ability of the political system (the government and the governed) to respond to demands and events in its domestic and international environments. These characteristics of society are tightly linked with business operations and corporate success.

Over the last thirty years, the nature of the relationship between the business world and the political and social worlds in which those businesses must operate has changed dramatically. In the 1960s and 1970s, much of the developing world was undergoing radical change, shifting from systems of colonial governance and control to independent and often innovative systems of governance. In the turmoil and uncertainty of the times, many took on an authoritarian character. Today, the last of the post-colonial dictators are falling and the world is increasingly governed by principles of what is known as 'political economy.'

Nationalization and expropriation became the greatest fears of foreign owners in the developing world during this era. Alliances with political parties or major personages and, eventually, political risk insurance became the means for protecting foreign owned businesses from the ravages of decolonialization. In the 1980s, after the colonialism issue had faded into the shadow of the destruction of the Soviet and Communist empires, other elements of the relationship between politics and business have become more evident. Current forms of government involvement in business processes are more subtle but the impact of politics on business operations has, if anything, become even more potent.

The impact of politics on business operations has almost always been seen in the negative.

- expropriation,
- inconvertibility of profits,
- war damage,
- damage from civil strife, and
- breach of contract for political reasons.

These have been the consequences of political interference that have been insured by agencies such as the U.S. government's Overseas Private Investment Corporation (OPIC) and the Multilateral Investment Guarantee Agency (MIGA) of the World Bank. Obviously, there is a positive side to the relationship as well. The presence of a stable and structured legal system, for example, provides a set of expectations that foreign corporations find familiar and protective. But the startling challenge of expropriations and nationalizations in the 1950s and 1960s has left the field of political-business analysis focused on the side we now refer to as "risk."

Many forms of loss are covered by political risk insurance that may be obtained from public insurance companies like OPIC or MIGA or from private insurers like the American International Group (AIG) or Johnson & Higgins. But much of the harm that can be done is not coverable or is not covered by choice. In some instances, risk can be "managed" if it is anticipated. A major form of harm to international investors occurs through corruption, an affliction in the business world that is social in its origin but often politically condoned. For any firm, corruption costs are a direct loss. Particularly for American companies, which are under the jurisdiction of the Foreign Corrupt Practices Act, involvement in corruption can mean fines and prison terms in addition to the illegal payments made. In some societies bribes or "gifts" are expected at many levels of the transaction and can amount to as much as 3% of total costs. When the profit margin is hardly more than that, the costs to corruption may make the total difference as to whether the investment succeeds or not. In any case, it is not insurable.

Kidnapping for ransom by guerrilla or other political groups is another means by which the investor may lose money because of a political risk. If a manager or a family member is kidnapped, the cost of regaining that person may be in the millions of dollars. Other sources of loss in the political sector exist as well. The AIG list of political causes of contract repudiation is instructive. They include unilateral termination of a contract by a government, payment defaults, license cancellations, embargoes, war or civil war, default on an arbitration award, and government acts, laws, decrees, or regulations that result in breach or alteration of an agreement.

There are other politics-based losses that are commonly encountered. Property is confiscated in a manner that doesn't amount to expropriation. Investment property is damaged in politically motivated strikes. The government may interfere in the terms of a contract, such as in dictating ethnic quotas in hiring or forced procurement decisions. Limits may be placed on remittances by foreign nationals employed by the investor in the host country. There may be discriminatory taxation. The absence or loss of copyright protection is a particular problem. The potential for government or societal interference in business operations where harm could be done extends well beyond this list.

The ultimate concern in political risk analysis is that there will eventually be a loss or harm done to a business operating in a foreign environment, the source of which lies in political or social characteristics or phenomena. The investor's interest in political risk lies in forecasting that risk, so that it can be managed or avoided. Working backwards from the loss or harm, the analyst—whether corporate or academic—tries to anticipate the loss by envisioning the circumstances under which losses might occur. Those circumstances in turn are anticipated in an examination of societal attributes.

The Analysis of Risk

The attributes to be examined fall into two categories. One is **trends**; the other is current but compared **characteristics**. In the case of trends, the matter is relatively simple, although perhaps somewhat deceptive. If there is a record of expropriation, the new investor obviously needs to be concerned. If the current government of a host country has previously nationalized foreign industry, potential investors obviously need to pay attention to the possibility that they, too, could be nationalized. Similarly, a history of civil strife and especially the occurrence of ongoing wars indicate a high likelihood that direct damage could occur to the investment or that contracts could be repudiated under war circumstances.

The second approach is to examine current societal attributes and the circumstances under which losses have occurred before, either in that same country or others like it. If high levels of ethnic tension are often followed by open ethnic conflict, for example, that civil strife could result in damage to businesses or in forced abandonment of the investment, as happened in 1994 in Algeria. Many of the forecasting methods, such as that presented by *The Economist* in 1986, rely on this approach.

In an article entitled "Countries in Trouble," *The Economist* provided sixteen variables which described current political, social, and economic circumstances wherein investors would face risks of the types of losses discussed above. A selected set of variables was chosen as representative in each of the three areas and they were weighted to result in a potential accumulation of 100 "risk" points for any of the fifty countries they analyzed. *The Economist* used proximity to a trouble spot or super power, extent of authoritarianism, degree of legitimacy of the government, staleness of the regime, involvement of the military, and extent of current war or civil strife as predictors of future harm to the foreign business. As social circumstances portending trouble, it chose rapid and concentrated urbanization, extent of corruption, degree of Islamic fundamentalism, and level of ethnic tension as critical predictors. Each, it was argued, foretold problems for the investor. Among these ten variables, only war was likely to cause direct losses. The other variables are simply precursors to war or other forms of damage.

In designing a model, the relationships between abstract concepts, such as authoritarianism, and acts of damage to the investor need to be grounded in social science knowledge and research. A variety of approaches have been put forth by corporate analysts and by political risk organizations in their efforts to describe the circumstances of incipient loss. Larger corporations such as oil companies or banks may have "in-house" advisory groups to examine the context in which the investment will occur. They may have their own models that encompass selected sets of variables and relationships among them that they have determined are appropriate forecasting tools for the types of decisions they will make with regard to investment. Chase Manhattan Bank, for example, has included the basis of political stability, social cohesiveness, corruption, and external factors such as war and vulnerability to fanaticism in its model. These firms, and especially smaller firms, may rely wholly or in part on political risk advisory services such as Political Risk Services, a division of International Business Communications, or the Business Environment Risk Intelligence (BERI) Index. The choice of the system of analysis can affect the investment decision dramatically.

The Nature of "Risk"

In examining the models underlying various risk analyses, it is critical that the concept of "risk" be clearly understood. The term risk implies a probabilistic assessment. That is, political risk analysis does **not** result in a prediction. It has as its product a **forecast**. The difference is that there are elements to the analytical process that prevent the projection of specific events. The projection is that given a history, **usually** or **"there is a high probability that"** history will repeat itself. Or given a set of circumstances, an outcome has a high probability of following.

A number of elements of the analytical method and model prevent precise prediction. One is the model itself. Modellers select different variables as representative of the situations that they believe will precede investor harm. Social systems are notably complex and some representative approximations of societal attributes are utilized in any model. The projection of outcomes from the situation becomes probabilistic because (*a*) a complex set of circumstances is necessarily simplified and abbreviated in any model, and (*b*) the selection of representative variables and their relationships may not be the optimal one.

A second and related element is the complexity of social phenomena. Even with the best of models, variables that are not included will still have **some** effect on the situation and will eliminate the possibility of perfect prediction. There is always the possibility, and perhaps high probability, that some unforeseen event outside the scope of the analysis will affect the government processes that result in losses. For example, a heavy rainstorm up river could result in flooding that, in turn, causes great damage to crops that is followed by food riots that bring the downfall of a democratic government and the installation of an authoritarian one that imposes strict controls on foreign business that deal in food products. While the probability of such events is low, they do occur and would not likely be included in even a good political risk model.

Another element that prevents prediction is partial information. Even if an optimal model is employed, the information that is incorporated as the basis of the assessment and forecast is inevitably incomplete and sometimes inaccurate. Whether there are direct observations of such phenomena as "press freedom," or media reports or authoritative testimony, there is no perfect descriptions of such circumstances that can be introduced into the analysis.[3] Variations in the data introduce some margin of error in the projection. This is unavoidable in social science analysis.

Human intervention also prevents prediction. Just as the person who is predicted to die in an automobile accident can stay away from automobiles for the rest of her life and thereby avoid the prediction circumstance, political risk analysis is provided with the specific intention that investors will somehow prevent the forecast from coming true. Unfortunately, many investors still don't pay attention to political risk forecast—as OPIC payments to its insured clients will show—or many proceed to take the risks because the opportunity is far greater than the risk. Many forecasted losses therefore do occur, but not all. The ones that are avoided result in a differentiation between forecast and outcome. Thus, the forecast appears as a probability that is less than one hundred percent.

Many host country governments have argued that political risk forecasts are inaccurate because "ethnic tension" didn't turn into "civil strife" and subsequently war damage, for which an investor had been insured. This by no means is an indication that the risk was not there. It may have been avoided probabilistically, or it may have been manage—by the investor or the host government—such that the potential harm was avoided or eliminated.

Managing Political Risk

After receiving a risk assessment, investors presumably take some action as a result. They may proceed with the investment and ignore the risks or simply count them as risks as they do with economic risk. They may try to modify the arrangements or circumstances of their investment. For example, if one part of a country has civil strife and another does not, they may choose to operate in the less dangerous part of the country and leave the other, until the situation changes. The investors may choose to go to an entirely different country. Some investors are now leaving China, for example, and choosing Vietnam instead, to avoid social problems they have encountered.

Another approach to managing political risk is to negotiate a better deal with the host country government. If there is a high level of government interference in personnel decisions, for example, prior to the investment the investor can seek (and often obtain) a variation in convertibility limits or in tax levels in exchange for accommodating the government on the personnel issues. This can only be done, however, if the investor knows the social environment of the personnel issue and its implications for business operations. The risk assessment can be turned directly into an asset.

In some circumstances, the risk can be managed by direct action. In the case of kidnapping possibilities, for example, some firms have hired bodyguards or taken other protective measures to prevent situations from arising where a kidnapping could take place. Such measures entail some cost, of course, but would presumably be commensurate with minimizing the cost or harm to the investor.

Investors can develop alliances within the host country and even within the government that can elevate their position and help avoid the risk circumstance. This may be risky in itself if the faction or government they have aligned themselves with falls into disfavour. But it does constitute one method of active management of risk.

Perhaps the most common form of risk management is to obtain political risk insurance. Political risk insurance, as indicated above, is available in the public and private sectors and is widely held by international investors and businesses. That OPIC insurance was originally provided under the auspices of the U.S. Agency for International Development (AID) is an indication of the argument that risk should not lead to limitations on investment. Risk analysis offers advice to the investor on how to manage risk in a world full of political and social danger but also full of extraordinary opportunity, especially in the 1990s. OPIC's level premium rates for all countries covered are an indication that international investment is being encouraged, despite the difficulties to be faced, not discouraged. The prudent investor isn't avoiding risk but is simply taking advantage of available knowledge to deal with societies in the same manner that he would deal with economic or financial uncertainties. Political risk analysis and political risk management are therefore intricately and intimately intertwined.

A variety of successful political and country risk forecasting systems are available. These should be useful both to the experienced foreign investor and to the new investor seeking to determine how unfamiliar political systems and societies should be approached.

Organizational Structure

Definitions

- Responsibilities, authorities and relations organized in such a way as to enable the organization to perform its functions.
- The structure and/or hierarchy of an organization and how its component parts work together to achieve common goals.
- Lines of authority and responsibility.
- Organizational structure is the way in which the interrelated groups of an organization are constructed. From a managerial point of view the main concerns are ensuring effective communication and co-ordination.

Organizational structure formally determines the hierarchy within an organization. In other words, who reports to whom? Some companies refer to this as the organizational chart. Types of organizational structure include: **functional structure, divisional structure**, and **matrix structure**. Divisional structure is further broken down into three sub-types: product structure, market structure, and geographic structure.

Functional Structure

The functional structure groups' employees together based upon the functions of specific jobs within the organization. I used to work for a division of an internet service provider (ISP). The organizational structure at that division was functional. The organizational chart was as follows:

Vice President

— Sales Department (sales function)
— Customer Service Department (customer service function)
— Engineering Department (engineering function)
— Accounting Department (accounting function)
— Administration Department (administration function).

Divisional Structure

The divisional structure is broken down into three areas: product, market and geographic.

Product Structure

Product structure groups employees together based upon specific products produced by the company. An example of this would be a company that produces three distinct products, "product a", "product b", and "product c". This company would have a separate division for each product.

Market Structure

Market structure groups employees together based upon specific markets in which the company sells. When I worked at the ISP, we also used a form of market structure. We sold internet access to individual consumers and business customers. So the sales and customer service departments were organized using market structure. Consumer sales and consumer customer service worked together, and corporate sales and corporate customer service worked together.

Geographic Structure

Geographic structure groups employees together based upon specific geographic location. This is often used by large companies that operate in many areas throughout the United States or in both the U.S. and overseas.

Matrix Structure

Matrix structure groups employees by both function and product. This structure can combine the best of both separate structures. An example would be a company that produces two products, "product a" and "product b". Using the matrix structure, this company would organize functions within the company as follows: "product a" sales department, "product a" customer service department, "product a" accounting, "product b" sales department, "product b" customer service department, "product b" accounting department. Matrix structure is the most complex of the different organizational structures.

Conclusion

Finding the organizational structure that works best for a particular company is very important. Using the wrong structure can result in poor communication, poor product development, poor customer service, and a myriad of other business problems. Any of these things can be detrimental to a company and could result in lost revenue or even complete failure of the company.

Functional Organizations

Reduces duplication of activities
Encourages technical expertise
Creates narrow perspectives
Difficult to co-ordinate.

Divisional Organizations

Improves decision making
Fixes accountability for performance
Increases co-ordination of functions
Hard to allocate corporate staff support
Loses some economies of scale
Fosters rivalry among divisions.

Matrix Structures

Reinforces & broadens technical excellence
Facilitates efficient use of resources
Balances conflicting objectives of the organization
Increases power conflicts
Increases confusion & stress for 2-boss employees
Impedes decision making.

Lateral Relations

Dotted-line supervision
Liaison roles
Temporary task forces
Permanent teams
Integrating managers

Organizational Theory: Determinants of Structure

The objective here is to understand why organizations have the structure that they do. By "structure" I mean things like degree and type of horizontal differentiation, vertical differentiation, mechanisms of coordination and control, formalization, and centralization of power. According to Taylor, Fayol, Weber and other classical theorists, there is a single best way for organization to be structured. Yet organizations vary considerably on structural attributes. The objective of much research has been to understand what determines these variations. Is it random or systematic? Are some organizations simply less perfect than others, or are different designs better for different situations?

Contingency Theory

In contrast to the classical scholars, most theorists today believe that there is no one best way to organize. What is important is that there be a fit between the organization's structure, its size, its technology, and the requirements of its environment. This perspective is known as "contingency theory" and contrasts with the perspective of classical theorists like Weber, Taylor, Fayol, etc., who thought that there probably was one way to run organizations that was the best.

Size

This refers to capacity, number of personnel, outputs (customers, sales), and resources (wealth).

Blau's studies show that differentiation (# of levels, departments, job titles) increases with size, but at a decreasing rate. In contrast, the % of the organization that is involved in administrative overhead declines with size, leading to economies of scale.

Increasing size is also related to increase structuring of organizations activities but decreased concentration of power.

Managerial practices, such as flexibility in personnel assignments, extent of delegation of authority, and emphasis on results rather than procedures, are related to the size of the unit managed.

Technology/Task

Consider check processing at a bank. This activity is usually performed by a business unit that is highly formalized, has a great deal of specialization and division of labor, and high centralization of decision-making. In contrast, the creative section of an ad agency is usually not formalized at all, the division of labour is often blurry, and it is highly decentralized.

It appears that certain activities naturally "go with" certain structures. Joan Woodward found that by knowing an organization's primary system of production, you could predict their structure:

Unit production/small batch. Companies that make one-of-a-kind custom products or small quantities of products (e.g., ship building, aircraft manufacture, furniture maker, tailors, printers of engraved wedding invitation, surgical teams).

- In these companies, typically, people's skills and knowledge is more important than the machines used.
- Relatively expensive to operate: work process is unpredictable, hard to pre-program or automate.
- Flat organization (few levels of hierarchy).
- CEO has low span of control (direct reports).
- Relatively low percentage of managers.
- Organic structure.

Mass production/large batch. Companies that sell huge volumes of identical products (e.g., cars, razor blades, aluminum cans, toasters). Make heavy use of automation and assembly lines. **Typically,**

- Bigger than small batch
- Taller hierarchies
- Bottom level is huge (supervisor span of control is 48)
- Relatively greater number of managers (because hierarchy is so tall)
- Mechanistic, bureaucratic structure
- Relatively cheap to operate.

Continuous Production. Primarily companies that refine liquids and powders (e.g., chemical companies, oil refineries, bakeries, dairies, distilleries/breweries, electric power plants). Machines do everything; humans just monitor the machines and plan changes.

- These organizations are tall and thin or even inverted pyramid: almost nobody at the bottom
- At the very top there is an organic structure
- Lower levels more mechanistic, but because machines do everything, there is not much paper work, low level supervision, etc.

Chick Perrow '67 looked at how the frequency and type of exceptions that occurred during production affected structure. Two types of exceptions: (*a*) can be solved via orderly, analytic search process (like mechanic fixing car), (*b*) no analytic framework, rely on intuition, guesswork (like advertising, film-making, fusion research).

It turns out that bottom left organizations (analyzable and few exceptions) tend to be highly centralized and formalized — in short, bureaucracies. Bureaucracies are the best possible organizational form when the task is well-understood, and how to best execute it can be specified in advance.

At the other extreme, the top right organizations (unanalyzable and many exceptions) are not

	Few Exceptions	*Many Exceptions*
Un-analyzable	pottery, specialty glass, motel room artwork; plumbing; computer technical support (craftwork)routine work, but when problems crop up, it is hard to figure what to do	film making; aerospace; (non-routine research)tasks that no one really knows how to do: work on intuition, implicit knowledge
Analyzable	routine, like screws; (routine manufacturing)the few problems that occur are usually easy to understand	custom machinery, building dams; (engineering production)the application of well-known principles and technologies to lots of new and different situations

well handled by bureaucracies. There are so many exceptions and new situations that having a set of formal procedures which specify how to handle every situation is out of the question. Organizations in this box tend to be highly decentralized and use informal means of co-ordination and control. The reasons have to do with human bounded rationality. (Bounded rationality refers to the fact that since humans have limited brain capacity, we cannot always find the absolute optimal solution to a given problem – we only have the time and capacity to consider a few possible solutions, and choose the best among those. But we can't consider all possible solutions.) Really complex systems are difficult to pre-plan: there are too many contingencies. We simply can't figure it all out. Need to allow for real-time, flexible adjustment.

Environment

Adaptation

Organizations actively adapt to their environments. For example, organizations facing complex, highly uncertain environments typically differentiate so that each organizational unit is facing a smaller, more certain problem. for example, if Japanese tastes in cars are quite different from American tastes, it is really hard to make a single car that appeals to both markets. It is easier to create two separate business units, one that makes cars for the Japanese market, and the other that makes cars for the US market.

Natural Selection

Organizations whose structures are not fitted to the environment (which includes other organizations, communities, customers, governments, etc.) will not perform well and will fail. Most new organizations fail within the first few years.

If the environment is stable, this selection process will lead to most organizations being well-adapted to the environment, not because they all changed themselves, but because those that were not well-adapted will have died off.

Dependence

The economy is a giant network of organizations linked by buying and selling relationships. Every company has suppliers (inputs) and customers (outputs). Every company is dependent on both their suppliers and their customers for resources and money. To the extent that a company needs it's suppliers less than they need it, the company has power. That is, power is a function of asymmetric mutual dependence. Dependence is itself a function of the availability of alternative supply. A depends on B to the extent that there are few alternatives to B that are available to A. Dependence is also a function of how much A needs what B has got. If the Post It's company starts to play hardball with you, and there are no good alternatives, it's still not a big deal because Post It's are just not that important.

Organizations that have power over others are able to impose elements of structure on them. For example, GM is famous for imposing accounting systems, cost controls and manufacturing techniques on their suppliers.

Figure 5.4

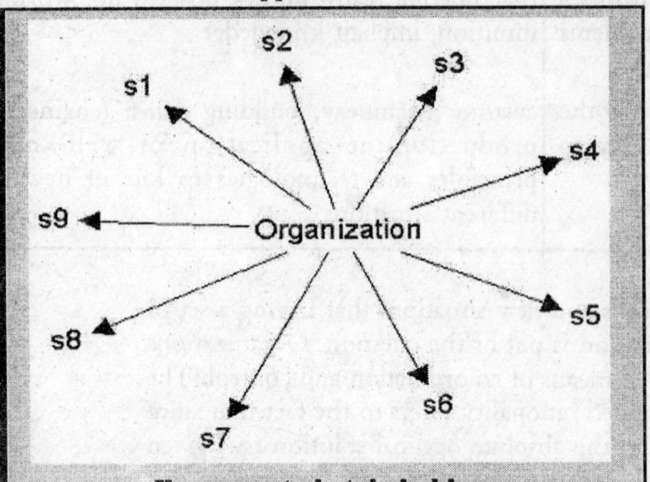

Unconnected stakeholders.

Figure 5.5

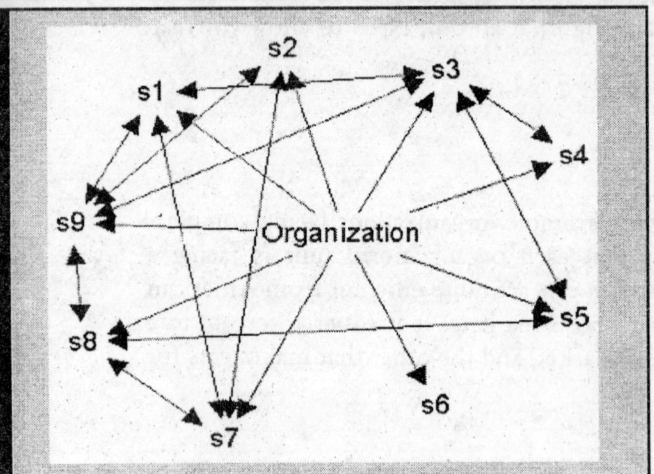

Well-connected stakeholders.

The sets of entities in an organization's environment that play a role in the organization's health and performance, or which are affected by the organization, are called stakeholders. Stakeholders have interests in what the organization does, and may or may not have the power to influence the organization to protect their interests. Stakeholders are varied and their interests may coincide on some issues and not others. Therefore, you find stakeholders both co-operating with each other in alliances, and competing with each other.

When stakeholders are unconnected to each other (as in Figure 5.4), the organization usually has an easier time of playing the different parties off one another. For example, it can represent its goals and needs differently to each stakeholder, without fear of being found out. Or, such competitive stakeholders into outbidding each other (e.g., a university can tell one alumnus that another alumnus is about to give a huge donation). Furthermore, when the stakeholders are unconnected, they cannot co-ordinate their efforts, and so have trouble controlling the organization.

In contrast, when the stakeholders are well-connected (as in Figure 5.5), the organization cannot represent itself differently to each one, or it will be found out. Furthermore, if the bonds among the stakeholders are closer than the bonds with the organization, the stakeholders may side with each other against the organization, and won't act in ways that negatively affect other stakeholders.

Institutionalization

Under conditions of uncertainty, organizations imitate others that appear to be successful. In other words, if nobody really knows what makes a movie successful, and then somebody has a blockbuster hit, everybody else copies the movie, and the organizational structure that produced the movie, hoping that they will get the same results. This can cause whole industries to adopt similar structural features.

One reason why this happens is the fear of litigation or simply blame. If several well-known, successful companies start adopting some new management style — say, self-governing teams — and you don't because you know its not appropriate for your company, and then things start to go wrong for your company, people will say 'see? you should have adopted self-governing teams. we told you so'. So to avoid that, if the top companies in a field all adopt some new style, then all the others do, to avoid being blamed.

In addition, diffusion of ideas due to personnel transfer and professional school training can create uniformity as well.

21st Century Organizational Trends

There are five key organizational trends that you should be aware of.

Globalization

- Increasingly globalized sales, manufacturing, research, management
- Movement from direct exports to having sales offices in different countries to having manufacturing to all functions spread across the globe
- Increasingly globalized labour market
- Due to:
  - — reduced cost and improved quality of international transportation and communication
  - — search for unsaturated markets
  - — exploit regional cost and expertise differences.

Diversity

- Workforce getting more heterogeneous sexually, racially, culturally, individually, etc.
- Source of both innovation and conflict/communication problems
- Need to cope with different styles of interaction, dress, presentation, physical appearance
- Due to:
  - — changing demographics
  - — globalization of the labour market.

Flexible

- Organizational systems and processes and people that can respond differently to different situations
- Fewer detailed rules and procedures
- Greater autonomy, encouragement for initiative
- Customizable employment relationships: telecommuting, job sharing, mommy tracks, pay for skills
- Lifetime employability, not lifetime employment
- Due to:
  - — differentiated customer needs — filling them exactly is source of competitive advantage
  - — increasing diversity in workplace
  - — increased pace of change in technology and markets.

Flat

- Fewer levels of management,
- Workers empowered to make decisions
- Fewer differences in responsibility (not in pay) across levels
- Due to:
  - — need for speed, which makes it helpful to empower employees to make decisions, which means fewer managers are needed
  - — changes in information technology mean less need for the communication and control functions of middle managers
  - — globalization means intensified competition, which increases the need to cut costs.

Networked

- Direct communication across unit & firm boundaries, ignoring chain of command
- Cross-unit team structures
- Outsourcing & downsizing
- Strategic alliances with competitors and others
  - — Now have firms that are your competitors, customers and collaborators all at the same time.
- Close co-ordination among firms (e.g., JIT systems) and information sharing (open computer systems)

- Across the board contact with customers, not just official boundary spanners
- Customization
- Decentralization
- Due to:
  - — new information technologies, especially groupware, client-server, distributed computing
  - — fast changing customer needs and competitor offerings
  - — more complicated products require better integration of manufacturing, design, and marketing functions.

Here is a diagram linking up all the concepts above.

Figure 5.6

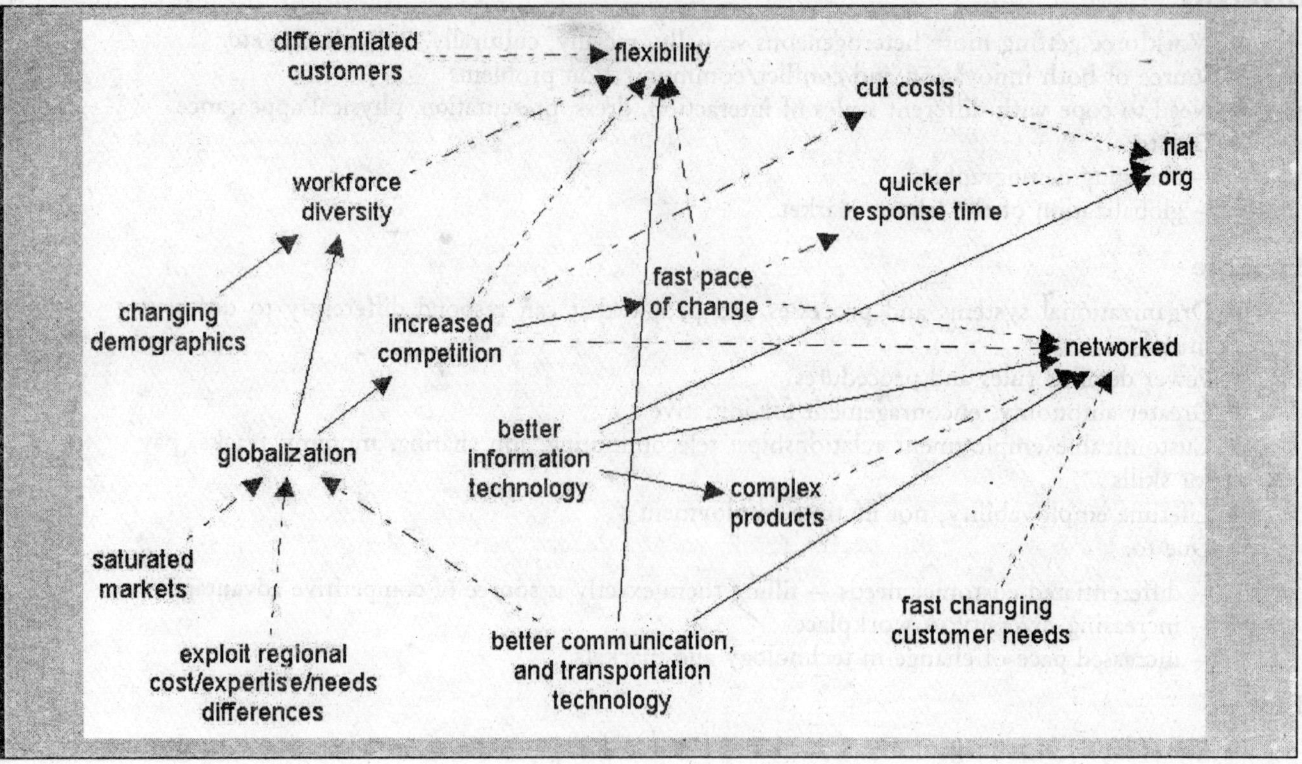

The dashed arrows with blue heads mean "creates the need for", while the solid arrows with black heads mean "causes" or "enables".

Selecting an Organizational Structure for Your Business

A business is established with the objective of making a profit. The business may be raising something to sell: sugar beets, livestock, wheat or Christmas trees. The business may be the performance of a service: altering clothes, housekeeping or painting. Or the business may be manufacturing or making something: fishing waders, coats or wedding gowns.

Regardless of the product or service provided, every business owner needs to decide what form of business organization is most appropriate.

- the sole proprietorship;
- the partnership, which may be a general partnership, a limited liability partnership or a limited partnership;
- the corporation, which for tax purposes may be a C or a S corporation; or
- the limited liability company.

The purpose here is to explain some of the features of each business type.

Sole Proprietorship

A common form of business ownership is the sole proprietorship. Because it is the least complicated form of business ownership and is the easiest to set up and to terminate, it is understandable why the majority of businesses nationwide (85 percent) are of this type.

A business with a sole proprietorship is owned and controlled by one person; the owner is the business. The funds for the business come from the owner's personal funds such as savings and/or investments, loans from lending agencies, and sometimes loans or gifts of monies from friends or family members.

All the owner's personal assets can be used to satisfy debts and taxes owed by the sole proprietorship. Personal assets also may be tapped to pay any legal damages resulting from lawsuits filed against the business, subject to certain statutory exemptions. This means all the owner's assets — land, home, vehicles, checking and savings accounts, and investments — is subject to claims by creditors for satisfaction of business loans, contracts and legal judgements. For these reasons, liability insurance for business activities is an important risk management tool for the sole proprietor, just as it is for other business owners.

A sole proprietorship files a income tax form, report income or losses from the business as part of the owner's personal income tax return. The sole proprietor pays social security taxes on his or her "before tax" net income, and is allowed an income tax deduction equal to one half of the self-employment taxes paid.

Retirement plans available to sole proprietorships include simplified employee plans (SEP) and savings incentive match plans for employees (SIMPLE).

A sole proprietorship has serious limitations from the perspective of estate planning and inter-generational transfers. First, business continuity is linked to the life of the proprietor. When the proprietor dies, so does the business. Second, the proprietor's wealth consists of business assets—equipment and land that are titled in the proprietor's name only.

Most proprietorship do not transfer either the title to or the control of business assets until retirement or death. Because assets in a sole proprietorship may be subject to probate, federal estate taxes and Montana inheritance and estate taxes, this situation provides limited opportunity for minimizing "death" costs.

Families with a goal to continue the business into the next generation often consider other business forms such as a partnership, a corporation or limited liability company.

Partnership

A partnership is a voluntary association of two or more people for the purpose of operating a business. Each person contributes money, property, labour or skills, and shares in the business profits and losses. To protect others from using the partnership name, the partners must register the business name as an assumed business name with the Montana Secretary of State.

A ***general partnership*** is similar to a sole proprietorship with respect to taxes and liability. Each general partner has unlimited personal liability for all debts and obligations of the partnership and acts of the partners, even if he or she is not directly involved in a particular debt or decision.

Although a partnership is not a taxable entity, total income must be reported on IRS Form 1065, which provides information on partnership income or losses for the year. Partners must also report their share of the partnership income — gains, losses, deductions or credits — on their respective individual tax returns. Even if the partnership income is reinvested in the business rather than distributed to the partners, it must be reported on each partner's individual tax return. The social security tax for partners is similar to that for sole proprietors. Keogh and SEP retirement plans are available to partnerships.

A partnership can be formed with an oral or written agreement. A written agreement is recommended to help avoid misunderstandings among the partners. Attorneys recommend that, at a minimum, the following should be included:

- Names and addresses of the partners and the name of the partnership
- Purpose of the partnership
- Duration, events resulting in termination of the partnership and the rights and obligations of the partners on termination of the partnership; how partnership assets are to be divided when the partnership is terminated
- Who is contributing what resources (cash, personal property, real estate, labour and services) and how they will be contributed (outright to partnership, on a use-only basis or rental)
- How profits and losses will be calculated and shared
- How decisions are to be made
- Any limitations on the activities of the partners
- How to add new partners and how to buy out partners
- How to resolve disagreements among the partners (dispute resolution by a third party).

There are three kinds of partnerships recognized — general, registered and unregistered.

In a ***general partnership***, two or more people contribute assets to the partnership, and these general partners share the management, profits and losses. The general partners manage the business and are personally liable for all partnership debts and liabilities and acts of any of the partners.

At the death or withdrawal of one of the general partners, the partnership may be subject to dissolution. If a partner dies, that partner's interest is subject to probate, federal estate taxes and Montana inheritance taxes. The partnership agreement may include provisions for business continuity by requiring the partnership or the surviving partners to purchase the interest of the deceased partner. Buy-sell agreements among the partners or between the partnership and a partner can also be used to provide a market for the interests of a deceased or withdrawing partner.

As of 1995, a general partnership may achieve many of the same limited liability benefits that corporations and limited liability companies enjoy simply by registering the partnership with the Montana Secretary of State and including the words ***limited liability partnership*** or "llp" in the business name.

By registering as a ***limited liability partnership***, a partner limits his or her liability except for the partner's own negligence or the negligence of someone under the partner's direct supervision.

The ***limited partnership*** is a way for the general partner(s) to acquire additional capital without giving up management control. It must include at least one general partner and one or more limited partners. A certificate of limited partnership must be filed with the Montana Secretary of State. Limited partners take no active role in the management of the business, and their liability is limited to the extent of their partnership investment.

Limited partnerships can allocate a percentage of gross receipts to the general partners as a "cost" for management and use such costs as a deductible expense in computing profits and losses for the limited partnership. Profits or losses are then typically allocated to limited partners based on their percentage of ownership.

Corporation

A corporation has a legal and tax identity separate from its owners, who are called *shareholders*. Law requires that a corporation be chartered by the state and that articles of incorporation be filed with the Secretary of State. The articles of incorporation should include the name of the corporation, purpose of the corporation, names and addresses of incorporators, location of the registered office, name of registered agent, duration of the corporation, amount and kinds of capital stock that may be issued at the beginning, and description of the voting rights of shareholders. Articles of incorporation and by-laws should be prepared by legal counsel who is familiar with Montana corporate law.

Once formed, law requires that a corporation file an annual report with the Secretary of State. It should list names and addresses of directors and officers and the number of shares issued. In addition, annual meetings of directors and shareholders must be held with written minutes reflecting important transactions or decisions. Corporations must file tax returns.

The primary advantage of the corporation is its "limited liability." While the corporation is fully liable for all its business obligations, individual shareholders are liable only to the extent of their investment. In practice, however, owners of small closely held corporations (family members, for example) are often required to personally guarantee the debts of their corporation.

While the corporation offers shareholders some protection from liability claims, it is not a substitute for a comprehensive business and personal liability insurance program.

For income tax purposes, business owners must choose whether the corporation is a C or a S corporation. C corporations pay taxes on income. Shareholders do not report any portion of corporate income or losses on their individual returns, but when income is passed on to the shareholders as salary or dividends, it is taxable income for them.

C corporations are eligible for a wide variety of retirement and benefit plans, as well as these fringe benefits: $50,000 group term life insurance; disability insurance and medical expense reimbursement plans; certain types of deferred compensation plans and employee stock ownership plans.

A corporation with 75 or fewer employees may make a special election to be taxed as an S corporation. Though an S corporation must file a income tax return, income is allocated to the shareholders and is taxed at their personal state and federal rates, similar to a partnership.

Shareholders who own two percent or less of stock also are entitled to the fringe benefits available to C corporation employees. The shareholders of a S or C corporation elect a board of directors that is responsible for the overall direction and management of the corporation. Directors elect officers who are responsible for day-to-day operations. A shareholder can be a director and officer.

A corporation facilitates estate planning, as it is easier for an owner to give or bequeath shares of corporate stock to heirs than it is to give or bequeath title to equipment, buildings or an interest in land. However, it is usually difficult to liquidate a C corporation or, usually to a lesser degree, a S corporation without adverse tax consequences.

Limited Liability Company

In 1993 the Montana legislature joined 35 other states in authorizing a limited liability company (LLC). As of 1996, 47 states have adopted limited liability company laws. When properly formed and maintained, the LLC provides the benefits of limited liability protection, operational flexibility and pass-through taxation without the restrictions applied to S corporations and limited liability partnerships.

However, pass-through taxation may not be available to a one-member LLC. The IRS is in the process of issuing final regulations on pass-through treatment. Contact your tax professional for the latest developments.

In Montana, one or more people may form an LLC by signing and filing articles of organization with the Secretary of State. The articles of organization must include:

- Name of the limited liability company.
- Latest date on which the limited liability company is to dissolve.
- Address of its principal place of business in Montana and, if different, its registered office and the name and address of its resident agent at the registered office in Montana
- Statement of whether the limited liability company is to be managed by a manager or by its members.
- Names and street addresses of managers if managed by managers and of the initial members if managed by members.

The LLC may wish to create an operating agreement, which is an internal document governing an LLC's operations and respective rights and obligations of its members. While not required in Montana, an operating agreement is advisable as the state has default provisions that apply unless provided otherwise.

The owners of an LLC are called ***members*** and have both economic and management rights (including voting rights) and may constitute the management of an LLC. A manager is a person or entity charged with management responsibility for an LLC. The manager may or may not be a member.

A limited liability company is required to deliver an annual report of its business activities to the Secretary of State between January 1 and April 15. Because limited liability company laws differ from state to state, extreme care is needed in drafting legal documents that meet the requirements of Montana law.

Prioritize Objectives

Before deciding on a business organizational form, prioritize objectives for your business and decide what issues of business arrangements are most important to you:

- Decision making/management organization
- Liability for personal injury and product liability
- Taxation issues, including the tax treatment of profits/losses and the deductibility of employee benefits such as health insurance, group term life insurance, and retirement plans
- Ease of making inter-generational transfers while owners are alive
- Desire for the business to continue after the death of the current owner.

When starting a business, or when changing from one organizational structure to another, it's appropriate that owners consider advantages and disadvantages of each structure in meeting business, personal and family goals. The best structure for one type of business may not be best for another. The best structure for a new business may not be suitable as the business expands.

After you have listed your objectives, discuss your specific situation with tax and legal professionals. Their recommendations will depend in part on how the characteristics of each type of business organization apply to your specific situation, preferences and objectives.

Here some, but by no means all, of the general concepts and facts about sole proprietorships, partnerships, corporations and limited liability companies. It is not designed to make you an expert in the various forms of business arrangements, but rather to provide you with background information to better prepare you for discussions with professionals.

Decision Making and Control System for Strategic Planning

Decision Making in Strategic Planning is based on Portfolio Model (BCG Matrix, GE Matrix), Ansoff Matrix and SWOT Analysis etc. These models help for better decision making in strategic planning.

E.g. A manager want to analyze:

- which product has maximum market growth rate.
- which product has maximum relative market shares.
- which product has both relative market share and growth rate.
- which product does not have both relative market shares and growth rate.

So according to these analysis — managers can take better decision and can prepare a good Strategic Planning that.

- which product will retain
- on which product company can invest more money
- which product will be considered later
- to which product company has to remove from the market or has to stop investing.

These all analysis is done by **BCG Matrix**. BCG Matrix works on SBU (Strategic Business Unit). So in BCG matrix, by these 2 parameters

- Relative Market Shares.
- Market Growth Rate.

We position our product in matrix and having positioned our product. We take a better decision and can make a better strategic planning.

In BCG Matrix, there may be some condition

- High Relative market shares, Low Growth Rate = "Cash Cow"
- High Relative Market Shares, High Growth Rate =-Star [*]
- Low Relative Market Shares, High Growth Rate = ?
- Low Relative Market Shares, Low Growth Rate = Dog

This is the 1 example of Decision Making for Strategic Planning. There can be more procedure for making better decision making by "GE Matrix, Ansoff Matrix & SWOT Analysis etc."

These all are tools, which helps us for taking better decision.

Control System for Strategic Planning

Control System for strategic planning is designed to support managers in evaluating the organization's progress regarding its strategy and when discrepancies exist, taking corrective action.

Most strategic control systems include "Budget" to monitor and control major financial expenditures. The dual responsibilities of the control system are efficiency and flexibility.

❄ ❄ ❄

6 Implementation of Strategy

• Strategy Implementation • Management of Change • Organizational Culture and Strategy Implementation • Leadership and Strategy Implementation.

New techniques, changing contexts, novel managerial perspectives and aspirations have all resulted in evolution and occasionally revolution in the design of strategic planning systems. It is widely known that the fate of many strategic plans is to be entombed in an impressively produced document that is promptly shelved and periodically displayed to visitors who need to be impressed by the managerial acumen of the organization, but otherwise serves little or no useful purpose.

Strategic planning has gone through enormous changes since its emergence and acceptance almost three decades ago. New techniques, changing contexts, novel managerial perspectives and aspirations have all resulted in evolution and occasionally revolution in the design of strategic planning systems. However, the challenge of effective implementation has always been and still remains a difficult hurdle faced by many organizations.

Two recent studies, one by the International Benchmarking Clearing-house, a service of the American Productivity & Quality Center (APQC) and another by the Asian Benchmarking Clearing-House, a unit of the Hong Kong Productivity Council, examined the issue of "turning strategy into action." I served as "subject matter expert" for both of these studies. APQC's state- of-the-art benchmarking methodology was used in both studies to identify and understand "best practices" in strategy implementation. These parallel studies employed the same methodology and employed almost identical data gathering instruments. Together they gathered information on 26 companies, seven of which were systematically identified as employing best practices in the area of strategy implementation. The findings of both studies, one focusing primarily on U.S. based companies and the other looking at Hong Kong organizations came up with very similar guidelines for ensuring that strategic plans are effectively implemented.

The findings of the studies suggested that implementation guidelines apply to the following four areas:

1. Linking Strategy to Performance: In order for an organization to meet its financial and performance goals, the actions of all groups, departments, functional levels, and individuals must support strategic plans. This area relates to the various approaches that leading organizations use to bring about consistency between organizational strategy and managerial decisions and actions throughout the organization. It also includes the strategic control processes that check the continued relevance and validity of the current plans.

2. Communication and Incentives: To ensure success in strategy implementation, the process must engage and involve employees at all levels of the organization. This area focuses on ways of effectively communicating with and motivating all employees to accept and support implementation strategies and initiatives.

3. Organizational Structure: A key enabler for effective strategy implementation is the ability to align organizational structure with strategic goals and objectives. The structure and strategy of the organization must be complementary. This area looks at the various methods by which companies manage their organizational structures to support strategy implementation.

4. Tools and Techniques: This area relates to the trends in management techniques that are employed to effect the transition from strategy to action.

Strategy implementation skills are not easily mastered, unfortunately. In fact, virtually all managers find implementation the most difficult aspect of their jobs - more difficult than strategic analysis or strategy formulation. U.S. managers spend more than $10 billion annually on strategic analysis and strategy formulation. Managers themselves report that less than half the plans resulting from these efforts are ever implemented. Outside observers put the success rate even lower: less than 10%.

Strategies that are not implemented constitute little more than academic exercises. The ability to implement strategies is one of the most valuable of all managerial skills. Manager's intent on implementing strategy must:

1. Master systems thinking to be able to co-ordinate a broad range of interconnected efforts aimed at transforming intentions into action, and
2. Take care of the factors impeding strategy implementation.

Organizations effective at strategy implementation successfully manage six strategy supporting factors:

1. Action Planning
2. Organization Structure
3. Human Resources
4. The Annual Business Plan
5. Monitoring and Control
6. Linkage.

Action Planning

First, organizations successful at strategy implementation develop detailed action plans — chronological lists of action steps (tactics) which add the necessary detail to strategies and assign responsibility to a specific individual for accomplishing each of those action steps. Also, they set a due date and estimate the resources required to accomplish each of their action steps. Thus, they translate their broad strategy statement into a number of specific work assignments.

Organizational Structure

Next, successful implementers give thought to their organizational structure... and ask if their intended strategy is appropriate for that current structure. And they ask a deeper question as well — "Is the organizational structure appropriate to the intended strategy?"

Example: A company was experiencing problems implementing its strategy calling for the development of two new products.

The reason the firm had been unable to develop those products was simple — they had never organized to do so. Lacking the necessary commitment for new product development, management didn't establish an R&D group. Rather, it assigned its manufacturing engineering group the job of new product development — and hired two junior engineers for the task. Since the primary function of the manufacturing engineering group was to keep the factory humming, those engineers kept getting pulled off their "new product" projects — into the role of the manufacturing support. Result — no new products.

Human Resource Factors

Organizations successful at implementation consider the human resource factor in making strategies happen. Further, they realize that the human resource issue is really a two part story. First, consideration of human resources requires that management think about the organization's communication needs. That they articulate the strategies so that those charged with developing the corresponding action steps fully understand the strategy their tactics are to implement.

Second, managers successful at implementation are aware of the effects each new strategy will have on their human resource needs. They ask themselves the questions — "How much change does this strategy call for?" And, "How quickly must we provide for that change?" And, "What are the human resource implications of our answers to those two questions?"

In answering these questions, they'll decide whether to allow time for employees to grow through experience, to introduce training, or to hire new employees.

The Annual Business Plan

Organizations successful at implementation are aware of their need to fund their intended strategies. And they begin to think about that necessary financial commitment early in the planning process. First, they "ballpark" the financial requirements when they first develop their strategy and later when developing their action plans, they "firm up" that commitment. As a client of ours explains, they "dollarize" their strategy. That way, they link their strategic plan to their annual business plan (and their budget). And they eliminate the "surprises" they would otherwise receive at budgeting time.

Monitoring & Control

Monitoring and controlling the plan includes a periodic look to see if you're on course — and it also includes a list of options to get back on course if you should veer off. Those options (listed in order of increasing seriousness) include changing the schedule, changing the action steps, changing the strategy or (as a last resort) changing the objective.

Linkage - Foundation for Everything Else

Many organizations put together the above five supports for implementing strategy. They develop action plans, consider organizational structure, take a close look at their human resource needs, fund their strategies through their annual business plan, and develop a plan to monitor and control the accomplishment of their strategies and tactics and yet they still fail to successfully implement those strategies and tactics. The reason, most often, is they lack linkage. Linkage is simply the tying together of all the activities of the organization to make sure that all of the organizational resources are "rowing in the same direction."

It isn't enough to manage one, two or a few strategy supporting factors. To successfully implement your strategies, you've go to manage them all and make sure you link them together.

Strategies require "linkage" both vertically and horizontally. Vertical linkages establish co-ordination and support between corporate, divisional and departmental plans. For example, a divisional strategy calling for development of a new product should be driven by a corporate objective — growth, perhaps — and on knowledge of available resources — capital resources available from corporate as well as human and technological resources in the R&D department.

Linkages which are horizontal — across departments, across regional offices, across manufacturing plants or divisions — require co-ordination and co-operation to get the organizational units "all playing in harmony." For example, a strategy calling for introduction of a new product requires the combined efforts of — and thus co-ordination and co-operation among — the R&D, the marketing, and the manufacturing departments.

Strategy Implementation

Despite the experience of many organizations, it is possible to turn strategies and plans into individual actions, necessary to produce a great business performance, but it's not easy. Many companies repeatedly fail to truly motivate their people to work with enthusiasm, all together, towards the corporate aims. Most companies and organizations know their businesses, and the strategies required for success. However, many corporations — especially large ones — struggle to translate the theory into action plans that will enable the strategy to be successfully implemented and sustained. Most companies have strategies, but according to recent studies, between 70% and 90% of organizations that have formulated strategies fail to execute them. The message is clear – "effective strategy realization is the key for achieving strategic success".

Strategy realization essential elements:

- motivational leadership — concentrates on achieving sustained performance through personal growth, values-based leadership and planning that recognises human dynamics.
- turning strategy into action — entails a phased approach, linking identified performance factors with strategic initiatives and projects designed to develop and optimize departmental and individual activities.
- performance management — involving the construction of organizational processes and capabilities necessary to achieve performance through people delivering results.

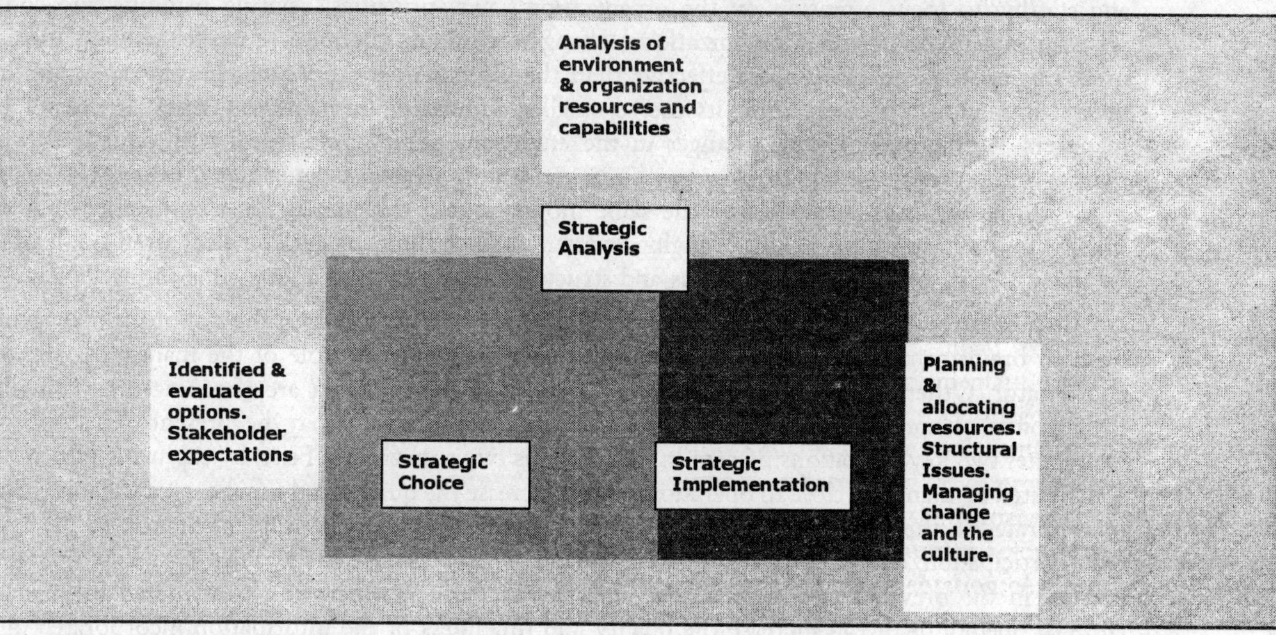

Figure 6.1

Here are some leading edge methods for effective strategic corporate implementation.

Approaches to Strategy Implementation

Commander Approach: The manager will determine the "best" strategy either alone or with the help of a group of experts. Once the desired strategy is formulated, the manager passes it along to subordinates who are instructed to execute the strategy. In this scenario, the manager does not take an active role in implementing the strategy, but rather uses explicit or implied power to see that the strategy is implemented. There are three conditions that must be met in order for the new strategy to be implemented. First, the manager must have enough power to command the implementation of the strategy. It should be recognized that implementation under this approach is resisted if the new strategy threatens the position of employees. Second, accurate and timely information regarding the strategy must be available, and the environment in which the company operates should be reasonably stable. If the environment is changing so that information becomes dated before it can be assimilated, effective implementation under the approach is unlikely. Finally, the manager formulating the strategy should be insulated from personal biases and political influences that might affect the outcome of the strategy.

One drawback to this approach is that it can reduce employee motivation and employees who feel that they have no say in strategy formulation are unlikely to be very innovative. However, the approach can work in smaller companies within stable industries.

Advocates of this approach say that managers who utilize it can gain a valuable perspective from the company and the approach allows these managers to focus their energies on strategy formulation. Second, young managers in particular seem to prefer this approach since it allows them to focus on the quantitative, objective aspects of a situation rather than on the qualitative, subjective elements of behavioural interactions. Many young managers are better trained to deal with the objective rather than the subjective. Finally, such an approach may make some ambitious managers feel powerful, in that their thinking and decision making affects the activities of the workforce (people).

The Organizational Change Approach: It focuses on how to get an organization to implement a strategy. Managers who implement this approach assume that a good strategy has been formulated and view their task as getting the company moving toward new goals. The tools used to accomplish this approach are largely behavioural and include such things as changing the organizational structure and staffing to focus attention on the organization's new priorities, revising planning and control systems, and invoking other organizational change techniques. Because these behavioural tools are used, this approach is often more effective than the Commander Approach. However, it does have several limitations that may limit its use to smaller companies in stable industries. It doesn't help managers stay abreast of rapid changes in the environment. It doesn't deal with situations where politics and personal agendas discourage objectivity among strategists and since it imposes strategy in a top down fashion, it is subject to the same motivational problems as the Commander approach. Finally, it can backfire in rapidly changing industries, since the manager sacrifices strategic flexibility by manipulating organizational systems and structures that may take a long time to implement.

Collaborative Approach: The manager in charge of the strategy calls in the rest of the management team to brainstorm strategy formulation and implementation. The role of the manager is that of a coordinator. Other members of the organization's management team are encouraged to contribute their points of view in order to extract whatever group wisdom may be present. This approach overcomes two key limitations present in the previous two approaches. First, by capturing information contributed by managers close to operations, it can increase the quality and timeliness of the information incorporated in the strategy. Also, it improves the chances of efficient implementation to the degree that participation enhances strategy commitment. This approach overcomes two key limitations present in the previous two approaches. First, by capturing information contributed by managers close to operations, it can increase the quality and timeliness of the information incorporated in the strategy. Also, it improves the chances of efficient implementation to the degree that participation enhances strategy commitment. However, it may result in a poorer strategy since the strategy is negotiated among managers with different points of view and possibly different goals. This may reduce the chances of management's ability to formulate and implement the "best" strategy. Furthermore, it is not really collective decision making from an organizational viewpoint, since management retains centralized control over the strategy. This can lead to political problems within the organization that may impede rapid and efficient strategy formulation and implementation.

Cultural Approach: This approach enlarges the Collaborative Approach by including lower levels of the company. It partially breaks down the barriers between management and workers since each member for the organization can be involved to some degree in both the formulation and implementation of the strategy. It seems to work best in organizations that have sufficient resources to absorb the cost of building and maintaining a supportive value system. Often these are high-growth firms in high-technology industries.

It has the advantage of more enthusiastic implementation of strategies by all members of the company. Limitations include: (1) It seems to only work in organizations composed primarily of informed, intelligent people; (2) It consumes enormous amounts of time; (3) It can promote such a strong sense of organizational identity that it becomes a handicap (for example, bringing in managers from outside the organization can be difficult because they aren't accepted by the other members of the organization since they didn't "grow up" with the organization); (4) It can promote a strong organizational culture to an extent that change and innovation becomes difficult.

Cursive Approach: This approach address strategy formulation and implementation simultaneously (cursive means "increasing" or "growing"). The manager does not focus on performing the formulation and implementation tasks himself, but encourages subordinates to develop, champion, and implement sound strategies on their own. This approach is a "bottom-up" approach rather than a "top-down" approach since it moves upward from the workforce to management. Second, the strategy becomes the sum of all the individual proposals that are "successfully" proposed throughout the planning period. Third, the manager in charge of the strategy shapes the employees' notions of what are acceptable strategies and acts as a judge evaluating the proposals rather than a master strategist.

Advantages to this approach include:

1. It encourages middle managers to formulate several effective strategies and gives them the opportunity to carry out the implementation phase. This autonomy increases their motivation to make the strategy succeed.
2. Strategies developed by those closest to the firm's operational and marketing functions are more likely to be operationally sound more effectively implemented.

Limitations include:

1. Resources are available for individuals to develop good ideas.
2. Tolerance is extended in the cases where failure occurs despite a worthy effort having been made.

Management Systems Perspective

Finally, another commonality observed in effective organizations was a remarkably similar perspective on addressing the total "management system." Strategic planning and implementation was not seen as an independent exercise, but as part of a system of processes that constitute the management function in an organization. Consequently, the design of the planning system and the implementation process was not designed in isolation but as part of a mutually supportive, integrated set of processes such as the capital budgeting process, human resources development process and the management information and control process. The range of staff functions (finance, quality, human resources, management information, controller, etc.) involved in the development and implementation of plans attest to the integrated approach adopted by these organizations.

It is possible to map the elements of their concept of the "management system" onto the 7-S model promoted by McKinsey (the management-consulting firm). However, a more parsimonious, equally effective, and much more comprehensible and manageable 4-S model may be more useful here. The 4-S model employs only four components with six interconnections, while the 7-S model utilizes seven components with 21 interconnections. The 4-S model employed by the partner organizations is diagrammed in the chart above. The model and its elements capture and illuminate the logic of the various practices described above as key guidelines for effective implementation of strategic plans.

Balanced Scorecard Approach to Strategy Implementation

It is a strategic management system that forces managers to focus on the important performance metrics that drive success. It balances a financial perspective with customer, internal process, and learning & growth perspectives.

The system consists of four processes:

1. Translating the vision into operational goals;
2. Communicate the vision and link it to individual performance;

3. Business planning;
4. Feedback and learning and adjusting the strategy accordingly.

A Comprehensive View of Business Performance

The **scorecard** seeks to measure a business from the following perspectives:

Financial perspective - measures reflecting financial performance, for example number of debtors, cash flow or return on investment. The financial performance of an organization is fundamental to its success. Even non-profit organizations must make the books balance. Financial figures suffer from two major drawbacks:

— They are historical. Whilst they tell us what has happened to the organization they may not tell us what is currently happening, or be a good indicator of future performance.

— It is common for the current market value of an organization to exceed the market value of its assets. Tobin's-q measures the ratio of the value of a company's assets to its market value. The excess value can be thought of as intangible assets. These figures are not measured by normal financial reporting.

Customer perspective - measures having a direct impact on customers, for example time taken to process a phone call, results of customer surveys, number of complaints or competitive rankings.

Business process perspective - measures reflecting the performance of key business processes, for example the time spent prospecting, number of units that required rework or process cost.

Learning and growth perspective - measures describing the company's learning curve — for example, number of employee suggestions or total hours spent on staff training.

The specific measures within each of the perspectives will be chosen to reflect the drivers of the particular business. The method can facilitate the separation of strategic policymaking from the implementation, so that organizational goals can be broken into task oriented objectives which can be managed by front-line staff. It can also help detect correlation between activities. For example, we might find that the internal business objective of implementing a new telephone system can help the customer objective of reducing response time to telephone calls, leading to increased sales from repeat business. In many senses, the objectives chosen are leading indicators of future performance. Effort we make today is reflected in the future profits of the company. In this way, current expenditure can be viewed as investment in the future of the company.

Public Sector Balanced Scorecard

Originally introduced as a tool intended for commercial organizations (which are focused on financial performance), the Balanced Scorecard has found considerable support and is widely used in the public sector. It is particularly popular as a public sector performance management tool in the USA, UK, Australia and Scandinavia.

Purpose of the Balanced Scorecard

Kaplan and Norton found that companies are using the scorecard to:

- Clarify and update strategy
- Communicate strategy throughout the company
- Align unit and individual goals with strategy
- Link strategic objectives to long term targets and annual budgets
- Identify and align strategic initiatives
- Conduct periodic performance reviews to learn about and improve strategy.

Evolution of the Balanced Scorecard

The first **balanced scorecard** was created in 1987 and introduced in 1989 in the Sloan Management Review and developed through the work of Arthur M. Schneiderman during his tenure at Analog

Devices Incorporated 1986-1992. The CEO of ADI, Ray State described it explaining Arthur M. Schneiderman's half-life Method for goal setting and his 7-Steps of Process Management integrated model of process and control improvement as the foundational elements of the balanced scorecard. Schneider man, in his historical reporting (http://www.schneiderman.com/) reported that Kaplan, Shank and Hendrickson had extensive interviewing of ADI to begin their current version of the balanced scorecard model.

In 1997, Kurtz man found that 64% of the companies questioned were measuring performance from a number of perspectives in a similar way to the balanced scorecard. It is difficult to interpret the impressive survey based adoption statistics for the Balanced Scorecard; however, without being clear on how the term was both defined and understood by those participating in the survey. In practice, it appears, there are wide variations in understanding between organizations. In 2002, Cob bold and Lawrie developed a classification of balanced scorecard designs based upon intended method of use within an organization. They describe how a balanced scorecard can be used to support two distinct management activities, management control and strategic control, and assert that due to differences in the performance dâta requirements of these applications, planned use should influence the type of balanced scorecard design adopted. They also describe characteristics of balanced scorecards appropriate for each purpose, and suggest a framework to help select between them.

Later that year the same authors reviewed the evolution of the Balanced Scorecard as a strategic management tool, recognizing three distinct generations of balanced scorecard design. In their paper, they relate the empirically driven developments in balanced scorecard thinking with literature concerning strategic management within organizations. Cob Bold and Lawrie argue that over the dozen years that have passed since its introduction significant changes have been made to the physical design, application and the design processes used to implement the tool within organizations. This Balanced Scorecard evolution can largely be attributed to empirical evidence of changes driven primarily by weaknesses in earlier design processes, rather than in the architecture of the original idea they write. They conclude that it is these changes, in what they refer to as the 3rd Generation Balanced Scorecard that have enhanced the utility of balanced scorecard as a strategic management tool.

Components of Strategy Implementation Phase

There are three components of the strategy implementation phase:

1. Operationalizing the strategy
2. Institutionalizing the Strategy
3. Evaluation and control.

Operationalizing the strategy

While executives have learned many lessons about planning and strategy in recent times the majority of all transformational strategy still falls short of its objectives. It seems that there are still many lessons yet to be learned about 'how' to operationalize it successfully. Strategy is usually clearly articulated within the board room - yet outside the room, strategy becomes more difficult to communicate, especially to those at the "coal face". For example, in the Australian finance industry, research shows only 20% of middle managers and 5% of junior managers fully understand their company's strategy.

1. Can companies operationalize strategy successfully when their managers do not understand where the company is going or what the company's priorities are in a way that makes sense to them?

Here's why getting clarity on these issues is crucial: when they lack strategic direction and leadership, managers gravitate towards solving the operational problems directly in front of them, whether those problems relate to strategy or not. Before long, company 'life' becomes about never ending fire-fighting, trying to get on top of problems the strategy was conceived to address. Over time, managers build silos, protect their patch and play politics; all things that increase organizational drag, pulling performance down. Operationalizing strategy means engaging people in doing the critical things at the right time. When staff sees strategy as disconnected from operational reality, they return to their desks and carry on as before using the "unwritten rules of the game".

2. The average company has a gap between strategy and operational reality that must be closed before strategy can be operationalized.

Institutionalizing the strategy

An experienced, trustworthy facilitator is needed to take the strategic aspirations of the board room and enable honest 'who, what, why and how' conversations about the critical business realities facing the company, with teams who will work together to achieve turnaround based on the following truths:

1. Execution without sound strategy leads people to confuse activity for progress.
2. As there is rarely a plan B, unsuccessful operationalization of strategy leads to the business losing its way (and sometimes, its existence).
3. Team members who are stuck in problem mode rarely see obstacles as challenges to be overcome.

Evaluation and control

The basic premise of strategic management is that the chosen strategy will achieve the organization's mission and objectives. A firm's successive strategies are greatly affected by its past history and often take shape through experimentation and *ad hoc* refinement of current plans, a process James Quinn has termed **"logical incrementalism"**. Therefore, the reexamination of past assumptions, the comparison of actual results with earlier hypotheses has become common features of strategic management.

An organization's effectiveness is in major part a measure of the effectiveness of its master strategy. Selection of the appropriate basis for assessing organizational effectiveness presents a challenging problem for managers and researchers.

There are no generally accepted conceptualizations prescribing the best criteria. Different organizational situations — pertaining to the performance of the organization's structure, the performance of the organization's human resources, and the impact of the organization's activities require different criteria.

J. Barton Cunningham, after reviewing the relevant literature, concluded that seven major ways of evaluating organizational effectiveness existed: rational goal model, systems resource model, managerial process model, organizational development model, the bargaining model.

Management control refers to the process by which an organization influences its subunits and members to behave in ways that lead to the attainment of organizational objectives.

Management control is a systematic effort to set performance standards with planning objectives, to design information feedback systems, to compare actual performance with these predetermined standards, to determine whether there are any deviations and to measure their significance, and to take any action required to assure that all corporate resources are being used in the most effective and efficient way possible in achieving corporate objectives.

Strategic implementation control provides an additional source of feed forward information.

"Implementation control is designed to assess whether the overall strategy should be changed in light of unfolding events and results associated with incremental steps and actions that implement the overall strategy."

Strategic implementation control does not replace operational control. Unlike operations control, strategic implementation control continuously questions the basic direction of the strategy.

The two basis types of implementation control are:

1. **Monitoring strategic thrusts (new or key strategic programs).** Two approaches are useful in enacting implementation controls focused on monitoring strategic thrusts: (1) one way is to agree

early in the planning process on which thrusts are critical factors in the success of the strategy or of that thrust; (2) the second approach is to use stop/go assessments linked to a series of meaningful thresholds (time, costs, research and development, success, etc.) associated with particular thrusts.

2. **Milestone reviews.** Milestones are significant points in the development of a program, such as points where large commitments of resources must be made. A milestone review usually involves a full-scale reassessment of the strategy and the advisability of continuing or refocusing the direction of the company. In order to control the current strategy, must be provided in strategic plans.

Steps in Strategy Implementation

The steps in strategy implementation do not necessarily follow the sequential order. The sequences may vary depending on the nature of the company, nature of the strategy, approach to implementation etc.

Formulation of SBU Strategy

SBU strategy concerns how to create competitive advantage in each of the products/markets it competes with. The business-unit-level strategy is determined by the three Cs (customer, competition, and company). The experience of different companies shows that, for the purposes of strategy formulation, the strategic three Cs can be articulated by placing SBUs on a two-by-two matrix with industry maturity or attractiveness as one dimension and strategic competitive position as the other. Industry attractiveness may be studied with reference to the life-cycle stage of the industry (i.e., embryonic, growth, mature, or aging). Such factors as growth rate, industry potential, breadth of product line, number of competitors, market share perspectives, purchasing patterns of customers, ease of entry and technology development determine the maturity of the industry.

For example, in the embryonic stage, the product line is generally narrow, and frequent changes to tailor the line to customer needs are common. In the growth stage, product lines undergo rapid proliferation. In the mature stage, attempts are made to orient products to specific segments. During the aging stage, the product line begins to shrink. Going through the four stages of the industry life cycle can take decades or a few years. The different stages are generally of unequal duration. To cite a few examples, personal computers and solar energy devices are in the embryonic category. Home smoke alarms and sporting goods in general fall into the growth category. Golf equipment and steel represent mature industries. Men's hats and rail cars are in the aging category. It is important to remember that industries can experience reversals in the aging processes.

The competitive position of an SBU should depend not only on market share but also on such factors as capacity utilization, current profitability, degree of integration (forward or backward), distinctive product advantages (e.g., patent protection), and management strength (e.g., willingness to take risks). These factors may be studied for classifying a given SBU in one of the following competitive positions: dominant, strong, favourable, tenable, or weak. An example of a dominant firm is IBM in the computer field; its competitors pattern their behaviour and strategies on what IBM does. In the beer industry, Anheuser-Busch exemplifies a strong firm, a firm able to make an independent move without being punished by the major competitor. Determining strategic competitive position is one of the most complex elements of business analysis and one of the least researched. With little state-of-theart guidance available, the temptation is to fall back on the single criterion of market share, but the experiences of successful companies make it clear that determining competitive position is a multifaceted problem embracing, for example, technology, breadth of product line, market share, share movement, and special market relationships. Such factors change in relative importance as industry maturity changes.

Leadership Implementation

A Fortune Magazine study suggested that 70% of 10 CEOs who fail do so not because of bad strategy, but because of bad execution. In another study of 200 companies in the Times 1000, 80% of directors said they had the right strategies but only 14% thought they were implementing them well, no doubt linked to the finding that despite 97% of directors having a 'strategic vision', only 33% reported achieving 'significant strategic success'. The message is clear - effective strategy realization is key for achieving strategic success.

The first dimension of the leadership implementation is to make sure that the right strategists are in right position for the strategy chosen for the SBU or firm.

Real leadership is required to compete effectively and deliver growth. People look to leaders to bring meaning, to make sense of the seemingly unquenchable demand for results and the need for individuals to find purpose and value. Leadership is the common thread which runs through the entire process of translating strategy into results and is the key to engaging the hearts and minds of your people. Whether you are distilling strategy to achieve clarity of intent, engaging your people to drive the strategy into action process or performance managing the resulting actions, effective leadership will make the difference.

Communicating the Strategy

The foregoing observations beg the question, "Could communication become a strategic advantage, a core competence, or a distinctive capability?" That answer most likely is, "None of the above" since it is the way that companies make use of their communications networks that can help create and maintain strategic advantages.

A communication strategy should be placed on equal footing with all of the business frameworks, fundamentals, and revolutionary strategies that have been espoused throughout the academic and professional worlds. One suggestion for such an approach to communications' strategy is as follows:

Build the Communications Strategy as a "STRATEGY"

1. **Develop a big-picture communications strategic goal-** A vision or mission statement would be useful here.

2. **Clearly define objectives-**Communications objectives will change over time periods or functional areas, so the manager must make appropriate adjustments.

3. **Identify critical tactics-**More specific, "WHAT do you want to get WHERE?" This step can provide a good metric for feedback and evaluation of the program.

4. **Incorporate the appropriate feedback loop-**Measure results versus objectives and tactics; make appropriate adjustments and improve.

Understand the Communication Channels Chosen

Recognize limitations of various channels: If your employees are checking email via a dial-up connection, it may not be a good idea to send important communications via large, slide show presentations that take a long time to open.

Match the channel to the desired level of interaction and feedback needs: Video conferencing may be appropriate for higher levels of strategic development, while a simple memo may suffice for issuing new company policy.

Multiple channels may be necessary: Different functional areas may have differing circumstances, or levels of involvement that may call for use of an alternate communications channel (i.e., in-person task force *vs.* electronic polling).

Apply the Appropriate Packaging Technique

Using the language of the end-user will aid pull-through and execution: This tactic will lend credibility to the piece since the employee will recognize that management sees that such users have a distinct point of view.

Well-constructed communications provide an opportunity to disseminate and reinforce corporate culture: The importance of this cannot be underestimated. Each and every communication adds to the employee's view of the organization; make every communication count.

Finally, avoid pandering to the "Lowest Common Denominator": Some managers fall into this trap because they feel the chain is only as strong as its weakest link. However, all such a tactic as this does is fail to challenge and enrich employees at each and every skill level. This tip is especially useful in training functions. Don't be afraid to challenge the laggards to catch up to the high performers.

This communications plan must recognize that organizations are made up of social, communicative human beings who can achieve great things together only after they recognize that it is to their benefit to come together co-operatively and communicatively.

Annual Objectives

Annual operating objectives designed to contribute to the long term objectives is a critical step in strategy implementation. Long term objectives indicate the planned long term positioning of the organization. Short term objectives like the annual objective lay down the specific time frame so that the long term objectives would be achieved.

Annual objectives should be measurable, consistent, reasonable, challenging, clear, communicated throughout the organization, characterized by appropriate time dimension and accompanied by commensurate rewards and sanctions.

Benefits provided from annual objectives are:

1. Systematic development of annual objectives provides a tangible, meaningful focus through which managers can translate long-term objectives and grand strategies into specific action.
2. Annual objectives help objective resource allocation.
3. They become basis for monitoring the progress toward achieving the long term objectives.
4. Effective objectives become the essential link between strategic intentions and operating reality.

Functional Strategy

Functional strategies which are short term game plans for the key functional areas are the means to accomplish the annual plans.

Functional strategies help in implementation of grand strategy by organizing and activating specific subunits of the company to pursue the business strategy in daily activities. In a sense, functional strategies translate thought into action designed to accomplish specific annual objectives. For every major subunit of a company, functional strategies identify and co-ordinate actions that support the grand strategy and improve the likelihood of accomplishing annual objectives.

Resource Allocation

In strategic planning, a resource allocation decision is a plan for using available resources, for example human resources, especially in the near term, to achieve goals for the future. It is the process of allocating resources among the various projects or business units.

The plan has two parts: Firstly, there is the basic allocation decision and secondly there are contingency mechanisms. The basic allocation decision is the choice of which items to fund in the plan, and what level of funding it should receive, and which to leave unfunded, the resources are allocated to some items, not to others.

There are two contingency mechanisms. There is a priority ranking of items excluded from the plan, showing which items to fund if more resources should become available; and there is a priority ranking of some items included in the plan, showing which items should be sacrificed if total funding must be reduced.

Development of Policies

The critical element, the major analytical exercise involved in policy making, is the ability to factor the grand strategy into policies that are compatible, workable. It is not enough for managers to decide to change the strategy. What comes next is at least as important. How do we get there, when and how efficiently? This a manager does by preparing policies to implement the grand strategy.

There are generally three types of policies in an organization. They are:

1. **Corporate policies** - which apply through out the organization.
2. **Divisional policies** - which apply to the division.
3. **Departmental policies** - which apply within the department.

Organizational Implementation

A key enabler for effective strategy implementation is the ability to align organizational structure with strategic goals and objectives. The structure and strategy of the organization must be complementary. This area looks at the various methods by which companies manage their organizational structures to support strategy implementation.

A seminal understanding in the area of strategy that was developed in the 1960's is that strategy and organizational structure are closely intertwined. As strategy evolves, so too does organizational structure.

Consistent with this understanding, these studies reinforce the conclusion that organizational structure is a major variable affecting the implementation of changes in strategy. Traditional thinking in the management arena has tended to view organizational structure as a constant, unchanging element of organizational design, based on principles derived from bureaucracy and contingency theory, where the contingencies are external to the organization. In these studies, organizations in both Hong Kong and the US viewed organizational structure as fluid and evolving constantly just as strategy evolves. Even at the apex of these organizations, managerial responsibilities are constantly redefined as the organizational strategy changes.

Reward system

Reward systems can be a vital aspect of any organization. They can actively engage and renew the overall sense of community and mission of an organization. A properly administered system of rewards can provide incentive for quality workmanship and staff performance. Likewise, a poorly administered reward system can lead to low morale, unproductive performance, and even lead to a high percentage of staff turnover. A reward system is successful when the staff interprets its policies as evenhanded, consistent, and relevant.

The only way employees will fulfill your dream is to share in the dream. Reward systems are the mechanisms that make this happen. "However, reward systems are much more than just bonus plans and stock options. While they often include both of these incentives, they can also include awards and other recognition, promotions, reassignment, non-monetary bonuses (e.g., vacations), or a simple thank-you." The journey is the reward, says Steve Jobs.

The greatest management principle is that the things that get rewarded get done. "You get more of the behaviour you reward. You don't get what you hope for, wish for or beg for. You get what you reward."

When your employees do hit the target and meet a stretch standard you set for them, reward them immediately. Never stall. By doing this, you help employees directly connect the reward with behaviour and higher performance they've attained. "Fail to reward the right behaviour and you will most likely get the wrong results."

Why Strategy Implementation is so Difficult?

Strategy implementation skills are not easily mastered, unfortunately. In fact, virtually all managers

find implementation the most difficult aspect of their jobs – more difficult than strategic analysis or strategy formulation. U.S. managers spend more than $10 billion annually on strategic analysis and strategy formulation. Managers themselves report that less than half the plans resulting from these efforts are ever implemented. Outside observers put the success rate even lower — less than 10%.

Strategies that are not implemented constitute little more than academic exercises. The ability to implement strategies is one of the most valuable of all managerial skills. Managers' intent on implementing strategy must:

- master systems thinking to be able to co-ordinate a broad range of interconnected efforts aimed at transforming intentions into action, and
- take care of the factors impeding strategy implementation.

Factors Impeding Strategy Implementation

1. **The Organizational Immune System.** Strategy implementation is inextricably connected with organizational change. All organizations resist change and try to maintain the status quo, sometimes even if it yields unsatisfactory results.

2. **Numerous Complex Variables.** To translate planned intervention activities into actions that bring desired organizational outcomes requires incorporating numerous variables: individual behaviour, social factors, organizational arrangements, physical settings, and technology.

3. **The Interconnectedness of Elements Affecting Change.** Changing one organizational element has a ripple effect that impacts other parts of your organization, which in turn have their own ripple effects, and so on.

4. **The Need to Change "Everything at Once".** Changing only one or two things seldom brings any significant overall organizational change. There are no "magic bullets" that would change the entire organizations. To redirect your organization, you must address many overlapping and related issues, and the resulting impression of needling to change "everything at once" can be overwhelming.

Proven *vs.* Experimental Business

- For a proven business, strategy implementation is about performing at or above known standards.
- For an experimental business, strategy implementation is about zeroing in on the best possible strategy. And in the process, discovering what standards are possible.

Successful Implementation of Strategies

It is one thing to develop clear and meaningful strategies. It is another matter, and one of very great practical importance, to implement strategies effectively. Following are 8 common recommendations that should be considered as strategies to work.

1. **Communicating strategies to all key decisions making managers.** It does little good to formulate meaningful strategies unless they are communicated to all those managers who are in a position to make decision on programs and plans designed to implement them. However, strategies should be communicated in writing, and top executive and their subordinates must make sure that everyone involved in implementing strategies understand them.

2. **Developing and communicating planning premises.** Managers must develop premises critical to plans and decisions, explain them to all those in the decision-making chain, and give instruction to develop programs and make decision in line with them.

3. **Ensuring that action plans contribute to and reflect major objective and strategies.** Action plans are tactical or operational programs and decision, major or minor that takes place in various parts of an organization. If they do not reflect desired objectives and strategies that result will be vague hopes or useless intentions. If care is not taken in their area, strategic planning is not likely to have a bottom-line impact that is to have an important effect on company profits.

4. **Reviewing strategy regularly.** Even carefully developed strategies may cease to be suitable if conditions change. Therefore, they should be reviewed from time to time. The strategy review may require scanning the external environment for new opportunities and threats and revaluating internal strength and weakness.

5. **Developing contingency strategies and programs.** If considerable change in competitive factors or other elements in the environment mat occur, strategies for such contingencies should be formulated. Even if there is considerable uncertainty and events may occur that make a given set of objectives, strategies, or programs obsolete, a manager has no choice but to proceed on the most credible set of premises he or she can come up with at a given time. But even then, one need not be totally unprepared if certain plans can provide a degree of preparation.

6. **Making the organization structure fit planning needs.** End result areas and key tasks should be identified and assigned to single position as far down the organization structure as is feasible. If this is done, the responsibility of the various positions in the organization matrix should be clearly defined. The role of staff analyst in an organization structure should be so defined as to make it clear that the job of people in a staff position is to advice.

7. **Continuing to emphasize planning and implementation strategy.** Even if organization has a workable system of objectives and strategies and their implementation, the system can easily fail unless responsible managers continue to stress the nature and importance of these elements. This process may seem tedious and unnecessarily repetitions, but it is the best way to make sure that members of an organization learn about them. Teaching does not necessarily mean conducting seminars; rather, much of the teaching can take place in the day-to-day interaction between superiors and subordinates.

8. **Creating a company climate that force planning.** People tend to allow problems and crises of today to interface with effective planning for tomorrow. The only way to ensure that planning will be done is to develop strategies carefully and to take pains to implement them.

Management of Change

As the well known saying goes the only thing permanent in the world is change. True organization need to undergo change to survive or grow. Changes may be gradual or drastic minor or substantial, partial or whole.

Drucker observes: "Very few business can prosper even five or seven year without substantial change and massive rethinking of the very concepts on which they are based. There are exceptions, to be sure, but they are rare. It is by no means sure that it is a blessing for business to enjoy long decades of continuity without challenge to its fundamental concepts and assumptions". And the fundamental questions confronting an organization include, points out Drucker, 'how can we anticipate change?'

Companies which fail to change suitably would disappear or decline to insignificance. The Fortune has for more than 40 years been publishing each year a list of the top 500 manufacturing companies in U.S. During these years, one third of the companies in the original list have disappeared from it altogether either because they have been liquidated or merged. Another third has lost position in the list, that is, has dropped from being a major to become a relatively minor business. Only one third have maintained themselves in the list, which is in their position.

Change may be needed in portfolio strategy, competitive strategy, functional strategies, organizational structure or organizational culture. Change is a necessary part of doing business and affects all companies regardless of their size, the product they offer or their geographic location. Given below are two cases regarding organizational change.

Eastman Kodak

Antonio M. Perez is the new CEO of Eastman Kodak Co. During his previous time at Hewlett-Packard, Perez was "obsessed with creating a new (product) category every two years." Creating new product categories this rapidly and frequently is a function of learning and constant change. In hiring Perez, Kodak's board of directors believed he had the skills to help Kodak introduce new digital products and gain the knowledge required to continue changing frequently and significantly.

Albertsons Inc.

Lawrence R. Johnston, a former GE executive, is now Albertsons Inc.'s CEO. In addition to traditional grocery store competitors, Albertsons (as well as other national chains such as Safeway and Kroger) faces a serious threat from Wal-Mart. In fact, estimates are that Wal-Mart will generate over $162 billion in "super-market types of sales" by the end of 2007.This projected amount exceeds the combined annual revenue of Kroger, Albertsons, and Safeway. Knowing that his firm can't compete against Wal-Mart on the basis of price and greater operational efficiencies, Johnston is relying on technology to introduce significant changes at Albertsons as a means of competition. The goal is to change shopping within Albertsons' stores, so customers will describe their experience as "quick and easy."

To do this, hand-held scanners are available to shoppers in some locations. The scanners are linked to a company database and a global-positioning-satellite system. The scanners will keep tabs of products the consumer has selected as well as direct her or him to the quickest route to take in a store to find a requested item. At the exit, the scanners charge the purchased items to a credit card, allowing the shopper to avoid waiting in a checkout line. A technology-intensive shopping experience such as this will cause major changes in established work patterns among the firm's employees.

What Can Organizations Do To Improve Their Ability To Change?

One thing to recognize is that there are no shortcuts. Helping a firm learn how to change is hard work—work requiring dedicated efforts on the parts of many.

To help firms learn how to effectively and consistently engage in change, research suggests that strategic leaders should engage in a number of actions including the following:

(1) phrasing the need for change in ways that appeal to employees' emotions as well as their cognitions,
(2) casting the need for change as providing positive outcomes,
(3) developing a story to describe the needed changes that is simple, straightforward, and appealing,
(4) Continuously developing and describing stories about the firm's success with different change efforts.

Organizational Development

Organizations evolve through various life cycles just as people progress through different stages of their lives. Without this evolution, organizations would be unable to develop and grow. This growth often means the company must undergo momentous change at various points in their development. The impact of this change can be significant on both the employees and the organization. Often this transformation can be at cross purposes between the employees and the firm such as the decision to close a segment of the business. While this decision may be in the best interest of the long term goals of the company, the consequences can be devastating to the employees who may be faced with unemployment. The effect that changes have on both the individuals working at the company and the company itself, along with alternatives to dealing with these changes will be addressed.

Organizational Change

Organization development is a process that involves planning, implementing, and controlling the results of change in an organization. The field of organizational development (OD) specializes in evaluating specific change techniques and the impact these changes will have on all of those involved in the organization. Organizational change should not be conducted just for the sake of change as the efforts should focus on improving the performance of the organization and/or the people in those organizations. Organizational change should be a planned process based on a systematic approach.

Systems Approach to Change

There are many tools available to help guide successful change in an organization. Systems theory or systems thinking is the idea that an organization is made up of many different resources. Each resource whether it is a person, a group of people, a function, a product or a service is one part of the entire system. If one element of the system is changed, the nature and makeup of the entire system is also changed. The systems or subsystems that make up an organization are integrated to accomplish the overall goals of the company. System thinking allows the individuals who are making the decisions for the company to view the effect changes will have on the company from a broad perspective. This will help ensure that the decisions that are being made consider the overall structure of the organization rather than seeing only isolated specific events. Taking a broad view of the impact of change on the organization can help the organization identify the real causes and issues and address them quickly. Approaching change in a holistic, systematic manner does not guarantee the change will be without negative consequences, but recognizing the major organizational parts and their relationships will help the organization integrate the goals of the change throughout the organization.

Forces for Change

Change in an organization is influenced by two opposing forces: One that drives for change and one that resists.

Which of the following forces affect your organization? Check the ones which apply to your group.

DRIVING FORCES	RESISTING FORCES
• Driving forces initiate change and keep it going. They may be external or internal.	• Resisting forces act against the driving forces for change. They are usually internal.
• Your source of funding is being reduced or increased.	• Your group fears new ideas and prefers to do things the way they have always been done.
• The interests and needs of the people in your community are changing.	• Your group functions the same way it did 20 years ago, out of habit.
• Government support is increased or diminished.	• Your group performs activities just for the sake of keeping busy.
• There is pressure to use modern technology.	• Your group's executive has very few changes or low turnover.
• Membership is increasing or dropping.	
• Members have different views of the group's purpose.	

Different Types of Change

Change is inevitable in an organization. Different types of change require different strategies to implement the change successfully. Different kinds of change require different strategies and plans to effectively gain employee engagement and acceptance of change. The three types of change that occur most frequently in organizations are developmental, transitional and transformational.

Change management theories effectively support how to deal with developmental and transitional change, but are less effective at dealing with successfully implementing transformational change. A critical step in determining which approach to use in overcoming resistance to implementing organization change is to determine which type of change the organization is experiencing.

Developmental Change

Developmental change occurs when a company makes an improvement to their current business. If a company decided to improve their processes, methods or performance standards, this would be considered developmental change. Companies are continually processing developmental change to some degree in order to stay competitive. This type of change should cause little stress to current employees as long as the rationale for the new process is clearly conveyed and the employees are educated on the new techniques. When major change such as the decision to close a division, if the company attempted to implement developmental change as the first step in streamlining the business, employees may be more likely to accept the change. The employees could see that the company attempted different strategies before determining that closing the division was the only option.

Transitional Change

Transitional change is more intrusive than developmental change as it replaces existing processes or procedures with something that is completely new to the company. The period when the old process is being dismantled and the new process is being implemented is called the transitional phase. A corporate reorganization, merger, acquisition, creating new products or services, and implementing new technology are examples of transitional change. Transitional change may not require a significant shift in culture or behaviour but it is more challenging to implement than developmental change. The future of the organization is unknown when the transformation begins which can add a level or discomfort to employees.

The outcome of transitional change is unknown so employees may feel that their job is unstable and their own personal insecurities may increase. Education on the new procedures should be commenced at each stage of the new process. This will allow employees to feel that they are actively involved and engaged in the change. As an employee's level of engagement in the new procedure increases, their resistance to change may decrease. Management should be cognizant of the impact and stress these changes will have on their employees. The company should continue to inform the employees of their status offer support in helping them deal with the personal adjustments they will be forced to make.

Transformational Change

Transformational change occurs after the transition period. Transformational change may involve both developmental and transitional change. It is common for transitional and transformation change to occur in tandem. When companies are faced with the emergence of radically different technologies, significant changes in supply and demand, unexpected competition, lack of revenue or other major shifts in how they do business, developmental or transitional change may not offer the company the solution they need to stay competitive. Instead of methodically implementing new processes, the company may be forced to drastically transform themselves.

Organizational change affects all employees at some point in their career. There are several tools available which help companies facilitate a positive change experience.

Impact and Resistance to Change

"It has been said that the only people who want to change are babies who have wet diapers."

Rev. Sharon Patterson, Ph.D.

"Resistance isn't an indication that something is wrong with what you are trying to change. It is an indication that something is happening."

James Hunt

A firm's decision to close down an existing plant may be viewed as a case of disinvestment or disposing of a current investment. From a company's standpoint, closing down a plant can be seen as industrial restructuring with the overall goal of increasing the efficiency and productivity of the firm. The destruction of jobs that follows this decision is considered in the company's disinvestment decision. The impact of this change affects individuals differently than the company as a whole.

While a monumental change such as a plant closing can be seen as a necessary cost of doing business by the company, the employees affected by this change are likely to resist it. Anytime change is set in motion, companies should expect resistance. It is a natural tendency for people to reject what they perceive as a threat to their livelihood. The more drastic the change, such as shutting down an entire plant, the more intense one can expect the resistance from those most affected to be. A company's financial status will likely be driving the decision to close down a plant. The company may see this as positive step in reducing the level of debt of the firm, thus allowing them to move toward improved overall health and stability of the organization. Employees may see these same financial constraints as a method of increasing the financial status of the company without any consideration of the effect this has on their individual lives.

Diagnostic Tools to Overcome Resistance to Change

There are several diagnostic tools that company's can use to identify and start to overcome resistance to change when implementing a major change. Tools such as a force field analysis which diagrams visually the forces that act for and against an impending change may help the employees understand and accept the changes being implemented. The force field analysis presents the company's current situation and the situation as it will be once the change is implemented. It shows both the pros and the cons of implementing the decision. While the end result may still be the same (i.e., the plant is closed) by depicting that the company has considered all options, the company may be able to reduce some of the opposing force. The natural tendency when change is forced on people is to become combative or unco-operative. Showing that the company has taken into consideration the impact change will have on its' employees, may help reduce some of the resistance to change.

Facilitating Support instead of Resistance

Actively involving the employees in the change process from the beginning may solicit some commitment from the employees to accept the change. The company should continually communicate and educate the employees regarding the status of the change. The company should also recognize that employees will need support and guidance and they should be prepared to offer some conciliation to the employees. The company should strive to facilitate support *versus* resistance from the employees by showing they have weighed the pros and cons of their decision, they recognize the hardship their employees will encounter and they are willing to help make the transition as smooth as possible.

Barriers to Change

1. **Lag in recognizing the need of change:** One common barrier is the lag in recognizing the need of change. The major reason for this is the failure to understand the environmental changes.

2. **Behavioural resistance:** One of the most important barriers to change. Fry and Killing classify behavioral resistance into two categories *viz*,

- **Inertial resistance:** - "It arises from the existing perceptions, beliefs, and habits of work in the organization. Inertial obstacles are critical factors whenever the strategic requirements call for changes of culture, management style, and management preferences. The impact of inertial forces is to delay or distort awareness, understanding and response to strategic requirements."
- **Conscious resistance:** - It consists of deliberate actions or inactions that are intended to delay or deny change. Conscious resistance may be covert or overt, it may range from foot dragging to outright organized challenge, and it may spring from a variety of motives.

One source of conscious resistance is the belief that the change is not good. Or it may be that the need for change is not realized.

Conscious resistance also arises from the unwillingness to accept/acknowledge the existence/ emergence of a problem or need for change even when the existence/ emergence of a problem or need for change is really recognized. This unwillingness may be due to the lack of self confidence to solve the problem. Unwillingness to acknowledge the problem often leads to attempts to cover up problems instead of taking measures to solve them.

1. **Resource constrains:** In many instances, an important barrier to change is resource constrains. For example, change strategy may involve large investment which the organization finds very difficult to mobilize. Sometimes, there may even be human resource constrain.

2. **Environmental barriers:** Environmental factors may also come in the way of change. Examples of many Govt. policies affecting strategic change are mentioned elsewhere in this book. Sometimes a company also has to face opposition from the public on account of the technology adopted, ecological issue, product mix, labour policy etc.

Change Requirements

There are several prerequisites for change. They include the following :

1. **Urgency:** An essential requirement for change is recognition of the inevitable need for change. A firm may restore to strategic change in anticipation of environmental changes or as a reaction to the emerging changes or on account of a crisis it is in.

2. **Resources:** As has already been indicated, one of the important requirements for change is resources. Many firms are not able to carry out turnaround measures or other strategic changes for want of funds. Sometimes, there may also be problems of non-financial resources.

3. **Favourable Environment:** A favourable business environment like conductive Govt. policy etc., is also a very important requirement for strategic change.

4. **Leadership:** An able and committed leadership is an essential requirement to initiate and carry forward the change.

5. **Internal factors:** Besides the right leadership, there are several other internal factors relevant to change, like the quality and support of people at different levels, organizational culture, support of share holders etc.

Strategies for Successful Change

There may be one or many driving forces initiating change in your organization. Groups will usually respond to a driving force by showing resistance. If you push, people push back.

Resistance to Change is Normal and Can be Expected

Change is more easily accepted by decreasing resisting forces rather than by increasing the driving forces. An adult may attempt to force a child to eat vegetables by threatening the child. The driving force is the fear of punishment. Force feeding is likely to result in increased resistance, or the food being spit out. Success will only come by removing the resisting force. The child may not eat vegetables because they taste bad. The change strategy might be to coat the vegetables with good tasting cheese or chocolate. The following strategies can be used to decrease the resisting forces to change in any organization.

Strategies

Communication	Provide adequate information to your members on the need for change in order to gain their support. Make the purpose of the change clear. Fear of change can be as disturbing as the change itself.
Participation	Involve everyone in planning and making the change. It is much easier to support something you have a stake in. If possible, committees using small groups of people should be set up to review and make recommendations for change. Surveys and newsletters are also tools that can be used.
Support	Be prepared to spend extra time with members who have difficulty accepting the change. Ensure that you, as the person initiating the change, are seen as trustworthy and credible.
Negotiation	Work out a win-win situation for all parties involved. Match the personal goals of the members to the objectives of the change. The change will be resisted if it blocks personal goals.

The change process is never easy. But organizational change can happen — especially if you seek feedback and foster buy-in from the people involved. Change can originate from any level of an organization. It doesn't have to come from the top. In fact, in order to be most successful, every level of an organization must take part in defining what changes are needed and how they will be achieved.

The easiest change to create is mandatory change. Laws often require changes to be made in organizational policy. For example, non-discrimination laws require employers to investigate and put a stop to harassment if it is based on age, sex, race, color, national origin, religion, or disability. If that sort of harassment is occurring, the easiest way to make the needed changes can often be to simply point out to those with the power to make changes that the law requires it. Managing changes that are not mandatory is a little more difficult. The first step in getting an organization to change practices or policies that don't absolutely have to change is getting the ear of people who are sympathetic to your concerns. This often requires creativity. There are many individuals that may be sympathetic to your concerns in different ways. You should speak to them about your concerns in ways that they care about. For example, a boss may not be interested in hearing about how hard a particular problem makes your workday, but might be interested in hearing how that problem is hurting the organization's ability to get grants. If you are going to get people to care about the issue you are concerned about, you are going to have to interest them on their terms.

The next step is to encourage people to buy-in to the plan of action. Much of this has already been done if the creation of a plan of action was a group effort - people want to see ideas they had a part in making succeed. One good way to get other people to buy-in to the plan of action is to educate them. When people understand why a plan exists and how it is supposed to work, they feel much more inclined to support it. You may even get very valuable feedback that could help refine the action plan.

Finally, as you begin putting your plan into action, set milestones to reach and celebrate when your organization achieves those milestones. The celebration doesn't need to be an expensive party - just do something to acknowledge progress. When you reach barriers, just re-group, reexamine the goals of the action plan, and work as a team to find a way to achieve those goals. If a barrier makes a particular goal absolutely unattainable, try to figure out a second-best goal to achieve. Remember that the change process is almost never easy. It requires thoughtful consideration of the people you work with, the organization's purpose, and a thorough study of the problems faced. However, with a little persistence and a lot of patience, all can be achieved.

Implementation of Strategic Tool

1. Determination of change strategy
2. Communication
3. Leadership implementation
4. Organization
5. Resource allocation
6. Tactics-
   - Participation
   - Intervention
   - Accommodation
   - Network action.

There are only two options: Change or sink. Change is inevitable for survival. However, to be able to take advantage of change, enterprises have to welcome change. They have to consider change as normal rather than as an exception to be feared and to be avoided if at all possible. They have to be Innovative, in other words. This require that the enterprise is organized systematically to abandon the outworn and obsolete; to be rid of things that do not work, no matter how attractive they looked when the enterprise first went into them; to concentrate resources, especially of competent people, on opportunities, rather than waste them on yesterday's problem and to work together on developing tomorrow rather than depending on yesterday.

Since the only thing permanent in the world is change. Organizations need to undergo change to survive or grow. Changes may be needed in portfolio strategy, competitive strategy, functional strategies organizational structure or organizational culture. Changes may be gradual or drastic, minor or substantial, partial or whole. There are four types of changes *viz.*, incremental, piecemeal, and transformational.

1. Incremental change is more frequent type of change which is gradual changes. An incremental change is a logical relatively small departure from the past, like expansion of a firm's market to a region. It is also termed as logical incrementalism and evolutionary change process.
2. Piecemeal changes when some strategies change and remain unchanged. When strategies change without any clear direction, it is regarded as a period of flux.
3. Transformational change, which is infrequent, marks a major, discontinuous change. A change is discontinuous or novel whenever it does not directly follow the historical logic of the firm's development. A discontinuous change is a significant departure from the historical growth vector.

Change Management Principles

1. At all times involve and agree support from people within system (system = environment, processes, culture, relationships, behaviours, etc., whether personal or organizational).
2. Understand where you/the organization is at the moment.
3. Understand where you want to be, when, why, and what the measures will be for having got there.
4. Plan development towards above No.3 in appropriate achievable measurable stages.
5. Communicate, involve, enable and facilitate involvement from people, as early and openly and as fully as is possible.

John P. Kotler's Eight Steps to Successful Change

Kotler has given some steps that help to understand and managing change.

1. Increase urgency - Inspire people to move, make objectives real and relevant.
2. Build the guiding team - Get the right people in place with the right emotional commitment, and the right mix of skills and levels.
3. Get the vision right - Get the team to establish a simple vision and strategy, focus on emotional and creative aspects necessary to drive service and efficiency.
4. Communicate for buy-in - Involve as many people as possible, communicate the essentials, simply, and to appeal and respond to people's needs. De-clutter communications - make technology work for you rather than against.
5. Empower action - Remove obstacles, enable constructive feedback and lots of support from leaders - reward and recognize progress and achievements.
6. Create short-term wins - Set aims that are easy to achieve - in bite-size chunks. Manageable numbers of initiatives. Finish current stages before starting new ones.
7. Don't let up - Foster and encourage determination and persistence - ongoing change - encourage ongoing progress reporting - highlight achieved and future milestones.
8. Make change stick - Reinforce the value of successful change via recruitment, promotion, and new change leaders. Weave change into culture.

In conclusion, it can be said that there are only two options: change or sink. Change is inevitable for survival. Organizations have to consider change as normal rather than as an exception to be feared and to be innovative. They have to concentrate resources especially of competent people, on opportunities rather than waste them on yesterday's problem and to work together on developing tomorrow rather than depending on yesterday.

Organizational Culture in Strategy Implementation

A recent commercial for a major company's e-business consulting company shared a CEO, in a state of high excitement, expostulating about a thick book he held in his hands. Here is, he exclaimed, it costs $2 million. The best strategy ever!. Now the question is, "is it implementable?" we then watch his face fall as, one by one, his executives consider the question and replied "NO". Before implementation of a strategy following points must be taken into consideration:

1. What kind of general, archetypal organizational cultures are there?
2. How these cultures and their central underlying assumptions do affect the implementations of strategies and approach?
3. What kind of strategy or approach would give the best result in each type of organizational culture?

Organizational Cultures

Organizational cultures as research areas have since the late 1970s and early 1980s. Concerned areas such as administrative culture, organizational symbolism, management symbolism and organizational stories and myths.

Classifying Cultures

One way of exploring cultures is to classify them into types.

1. Role Culture
2. Task Culture
3. Power Culture.

Levels of Organizational Culture

1. Fundamental Assumptions
2. Values
3. Behavioural norms
4. Patterns of Behaviour
5. Artifacts and symbols

   Category 1 - Assumption about the environment.
   Category 2- Assumption about the nature of realty.
   Category 3- Assumption about the nature of human being.
   Category 4- Nature of human activity.
   Category 5- Assumption about the nature of human relationship.

Strong *versus* weak culture:

- The degree of consistency of beliefs, values, assumptions and practice across organizational members and
- The pervasiveness (no.) consists of beliefs, values assumptions, and practices.

Cultural Assumptions and the Success of Strategy Implementation:

1. **Foster motivation, commitment identity, solidarity and sameness:** Many early proponents of organizational culture tended to assume that a strong pervasive culture was beneficial to all organizations because it fostered motivation, commitment, identity, solidarity, and sameness, which in turn facilitated internal integration and consideration.

2. **Means of enhancing internal co-ordination and integration:** Culture was initially seen as a means of enhancing internal integration and co-ordination, but the open system view of organization recognized that culture is also important in mediating adaptation to the environment. The traditional view of a strong culture could be contrary to the ability of organizations to adapt and change.

Organizational Culture and Strategies

Culture has been on the agenda of management theorists for long. Cultural change must mean changing the corporate ethics, the images and values that inform action and this way of understanding organizational life must be brought into the management process. There are a number of central aspects of culture. There is an evaluating element involving social expectations and standards; the values and believe that people hold central and that blind organizational groups.

Culture and Success

Culture is one of the most important foster in the success of strategies. According to Deal and Kennedy (1992), there are four dimension of culture:

- **Values:** The beliefs that lie at the heart of the corporate culture.
- **Heroes:** the people who embody values.
- **Rites and Rituals:** Routines of interaction that have strong symbolic qualities.
- **The Culture Network:** The informal communication systems or hidden hierarchy of power in the organization.

Peters and Waterman (1992) suggest a psychological theory of the link between organizational culture and business performance. Culture can be looked upon as a reward of work; we sacrifice much to the organization and culture is a form of return effort.

Increasing Importance of Organizational Culture

Schein (1992) suggests that organization culture is even more important today than it was in past. Increased competition, globalization, mergers, acquisitions, alliances, and various knowledge workforce developments have created a greater need for:

- Co-ordination and integration across organizational units in order to improve efficiency, quality, and speed of designing, manufacturing, and delivering products and services.
- Product innovation.
- Strategy innovation.
- Process innovation and ability to successfully introduce new technologies, such as information technology.
- Effective management of dispersed work units and increasing workforce diversity.
- Cross cultural management of global enterprises and/or multinational partnerships.
- Construction of meta-or-hybrid cultural cultures that merge aspects of cultures from what were distinct organizations prior to an acquisition or merger.
- Management of workforce diversity.
- Facilitation and support of teamwork.

In addition, a greater need to adapt to have these external and internal changes, organizational culture has become more important. Because of an increase in number of corporation, intellectuals as opposed to material assets now constitute the main source of value. Maximizing the value of employees as intellectuals' assets requires a cultural that promotes their intellectual participation and facilitates both individual and organizational learning, new knowledge creation, and application, and willingness to share knowledge with others. Culture today must play a key role.

Leadership and Strategic Implementation

Many businesses are facing a social, economic and political climate in which change is the only constant. For many, their inability to react appropriately to changing external circumstances threatens their existence. Leadership, true leadership of the kind that provides a strong sense of purpose and which harnesses the creative energies of all the people in the business, may well be the key ingredient to making strategic change effective and lasting.

A shift in market emphasis, an adaptation to competition in a way not envisaged several years ago, using advertising and promotion strategies to advantage, countering competitive behaviour, and reacting to the new paradigms of customer service and "relationship marketing", are all part of the changing environment for better business in Australia. All this, however, requires change in the organization as a whole and in the attitudes and behaviours of the people who lead it and in those who work within it.

To succeed in putting into place lasting change requires strong leadership, or at least, a quality of leadership which creates around it a momentum for strategic change. By this, I mean an acceptance of change as a way of life, as a journey, rather than a destination.

And strong leadership requires great courage, responsibility and humility.

Management is about the nuts and bolts of moving the business from one level of success to another and good skills in this area are essential: planning and budgeting, organizing, staffing and trouble shooting.

It is important that good management skills exist. On its own, however, good management leads to consistency and predictability and is often very successful in the short term; it is not conducive to the kind of strategic change which will be the hallmark of the great businesses of the future. It is essential that management skills are complimented by those of leadership for sustained success and the ready adoption of change.

Leadership involves a combination of elements:

- establishing the overall direction through vision and the awareness of the changes necessary to bring about the vision,
- behaving with congruence of action and communication which draws the people of the business into a shared commitment with that vision, and
- creating and maintaining the confidence and energy to mobilize action to ensure that all the various hurdles in the way of the change are surmounted.

Leadership creates the potential for the kind of change which is essential for pronounced business and organizational success well into the new century. Few, if any, of the skills of genuine leadership are taught at university or college. They are all, however, essential in creating a harmonious work environment, one which encourages and supports change. They are even more critical in making strategic changes in direction. **They are skills or qualities which can be learned.**

If the skills of management and leadership are not combined in the one person, care should be taken to ensure that the key people in the business combine good management and leadership skills and that they work as a cohesive team.

I find that, in many businesses, "leadership" tends to vary between "authoritarian" and "frustrated authoritarian" based as it is on the traditional hierarchical model of organization we have all experienced. Neither model is conducive to good leadership or really strong relationships within the business. They tend to be divisive and destructive of motivation generally and the ability to handle change in particular. In these circumstances, people build protective walls around themselves and their close colleagues and tend to be governed by the "what's-in-it-for-me" principle.

In my work as a consultant I have always found three common complaints among the staff to which I speak. These are a [perception of] lack of sense of overall direction or purpose, an uncertainty about their own value as part of the organization, and lack of direct personal appreciation for the work they do.

On the other hand, many owner managers of small businesses and managers of larger organizations are strongly driven by their own [material] vision and driven distracted by staff that never seems to have the same commitment as they do.

Both of these perspectives indicate a lack of attention to the leadership qualities about which I speak. The sadness is that they can be so easily addressed.

Broadening the vision beyond survival and wealth to include some social or community purpose has an immediate effect on the willingness of their people "to go the extra mile". People want to be treated as more than "things" at work; they want to be involved in what is going on and have an opportunity to develop a healthy and productive relationship with their colleagues and their leaders. Their work has to have a sense or meaning for them to want to risk the level of commitment most owners and managers expect. True leaders; seem to have developed the capacity to extend their people in this way.

Beyond this, the qualities of good leadership include:

- Being visible in a tangible way, which means taking time to know each person in the business whatever their educational or social background, understanding their values and their interests, knowing what worries them, what challenges they face, and in what particular tasks of significance they are involved. This means going out of your way to ensure that your people are valued for the contribution they make.
- Linking information about performance, marketing and image of your business with this understanding of your people to forge a sense of vision and purpose for the business to which everyone relates.
- Ensuring that your management decisions are taken on the basis of their contribution to your firm's vision, doing so consciously even ostentatiously; rewarding people for their contribution to the vision, and not rewarding people who do not.

This involves incorporating the soft skills of empathic relationships in the way you communicate with colleagues and clients.

Leadership skills are quite separate from excellence in the technical or management aspects of your business. They have to be practiced separately and time has to be put aside to develop and maintain them. This requires commitment, determination and persistence. It requires humility in admitting to any shortfall in performance, as well as an ability to ask for forbearance and forgiveness as they are slowly learned and applied.

As these "new" conditions begin to apply, the people of your business will start to contribute directly and indirectly to its overall sense of purpose. Each person will become valued for the quality of their skills in their allotted tasks. Differences will become honoured and valued for the contribution they make to the strength of the business. Change will indeed become a way of life, and be actively and creatively sought for the value it brings to the business as a whole.

Motivation and Strategic Implementation

Despite the experience of many organizations, it is possible to turn strategies and plans into individual actions, necessary to produce a great business performance. But it's not easy. Many companies repeatedly fail to truly motivate their people to work with enthusiasm, all together, towards the corporate aims. Most companies and organizations know their businesses, and the strategies required for success. However many corporations - especially large ones - struggle to translate the theory into action plans that will enable the strategy to be successfully implemented and sustained.

Essential Elements for Strategy Implementation

1. **Motivational Leadership** - concentrates on achieving sustained performance through personal growth, values-based leadership and planning that recognizes human dynamics.

2. **Turning Strategy Into Action** - entails a phased approach, linking identified performance factors with strategic initiatives and projects designed to develop and optimize departmental and individual activities.

3. **Performance Management** - involving the construction of organizational processes and capabilities necessary to achieve performance through people delivering results.

Motivation provides the opportunities for people to realize social, psychological and economic satisfaction in their work. Since 1930, increasing attention has been focused or providing an organizational environment in which people will feel motivated and will work toward continual improvement of their interpersonal skills and enhancement of the cultural ambience.

To motivate is to provide incentives, inducements or conditions that stimulate people to dedicate themselves to attaining the organizational mission, objectives and goals in such a manner that enhance competitiveness will result.

Taken together the concept of Maslow and McGregor provides the basics for enhancing an environment in which people feel motivated to do their best work. There are other conditions that need to be created and also affect how motivated people are expected to work with others in attaining organizational goal.

By having members of the team fully participate in the design of team strategies or organization strategies, a greater understanding of those strategies and their (rationale) is gained. People will support strategies that they have had a role in developing, particularly as they sense that their input into the team strategies has been recognized. The productivity increases through the use of the self directed teams members in leading and managing the team.

There should be maximum sharing of information with team members regarding the performance of the teams and the enterprise in terms of the realization of mission, objectives and goals. When the team members are kept informed regarding how well their efforts are contributing to team and enterprise success, they will feel a greater sense of motivation. By sharing such information an important message is sent concerning trust and faith in the organizational culture.

There should be on going, continuous improvement of the interpersonal skills of everyone from senior managers to the employees who are members of the teams. Training in social skills, knowledge about the theory and practice of motivator and practice in the common courtesies of professional life are important. Working at creating an environment characterized by trust, loyalty, faith, conviction and commitment on the part of everyone will help improve the interpersonal skills of everyone. Perhaps, the golden rules says it best: "Treat everyone as you would like to be treated".

It should be recognized that some of the more important characteristics of fully integrated, motivated team include satisfaction of individual needs within the shared interest of the team members. A strong sense of belonging to the team and pride enjoyment due to the team's work is important and a commitment to team members is vital. A commitment to team members and to the team's objectives yields important advantages. Minimum conflict, comfort in the interdependence ambience of team and a high degree of interaction increase motivation. A strong commitment to attaining the performance standards that have been set for the team and the enterprise is of equal importance.

❅ ❅ ❅

7 Leadership and Group Behaviour

• Leadership • Models of Leadership • Process of Leadership • Group Behaviour

There is probably no other topic generating more interest in business and non-business organizations than that of leadership. More books and articles are published on this topic than on any other management topic, not only in the United States but in nations as diverse as Poland, China, and India. There are also countless educational and training programs devoted to the topic of leadership and there are endless discussions of the factors that differentiate entrepreneurs starting their own businesses and executives rising to top-level positions in large, multinational corporations. All this frenzied activity is understandable given the obvious importance of the topic to leaders, potential leaders, and organizations of all types.

We begin this chapter by focusing on leadership across cultures. Next, we turn our attention to the related topic of motivation across cultures. Specifically, what motivates managers and employees in different cultures, and how is this topic related to leadership? In the final section of the chapter, we consider group behaviour and the manner in which the dynamics of leadership and motivation play out within this cross-cultural context.

Leadership

Leadership is a complex and controversial process that can be defined as influencing people to direct their efforts toward the achievement of some particular goal or goals. Two areas that warrant attention as a foundation for the study of leadership in an international setting are: philosophical assumptions about people in general, and leadership styles.

The philosophical foundation is heavily grounded in Douglas McGregor's Theories X and Y. Leadership styles relate to how managers treat their subordinates and incorporate authoritarian, paternalistic, and participative approaches. These styles can be summarized in terms of Likert's management systems or styles.

The attitudes of European managers toward dimensions of leadership practice, such as the capacity for leadership and initiative, sharing information and objectives, and internal control, were examined in a classic study by Haire, Ghiselli, and Porter. They found that Europeans, as a composite, had a relatively low opinion of the capabilities of the average person coupled with a relatively positive belief in the necessity for participative leadership styles. The study also found that these European managers' attitudes were affected by hierarchical level, company size, and age. Overall, however, European managers espouse a participative leadership style.

The Japanese managers in the Haire and associates study had a much greater belief in the capacity of subordinates for leadership and initiative than the managers in most other countries. The Japanese managers also expressed a more favourable attitude toward a participative leadership style. In terms of sharing information and objectives and using internal control, the Japanese responded above average but were not distinctive. In a number of ways, Japanese leadership styles differed from those of the U.S. managers. Company size and age of managers are two factors that seem to affect these differences. Other reasons include the basic philosophy of managing people, how information is processed, and the high degree of ethnocentrism by the Japanese. However, some often overlooked similarities are important, such as how effective Japanese leaders manage high-achieving and low-achieving subordinates.

Leadership research in China shows that the new generation of managers tends to have a leadership style that is different from both the current generation and the older generation. In particular, new generation managers assign greater importance to individualism as measured by such things as self-sufficiency and personal accomplishments. They also assign less importance to collectivism as measured by subordination of personal goals to those of the group and to Confucianism as measured by such things as societal harmony and virtuous interpersonal behaviour.

Leadership research in the Middle East traditionally has stressed the basic differences between Middle Eastern and Western management styles. More recent research, however, shows that many managers in multinational organizations in the Persian Gulf region operate in a Western-oriented Likert system 3 (participative) style. Such findings indicate that there may be more similarities of leadership styles between Western and Middle Eastern parts of the world than has previously been assumed,

Leadership research also has been conducted among managers in developing countries, such as India, Peru, Chile, and Argentina. These studies show that Likert's system 3 (participative) leadership styles are more evidence than traditionally has been assumed. Although, there will always be important differences in styles of leadership between various parts of the world, participative leadership styles may become more prevalent as countries develop and become more economically advanced.

In recent years, there have been research efforts that focused on the topic of universalism in the leadership process. Bass has found that there is a great deal of similarity from culture to culture and transformational leaders, regardless of culture, tend to be the most effective. At the same time, however, he has found that culture continues to be a mitigating factor. This same conclusion has been reached by research focused on the qualities that are needed in new managers. The qualities that are demanded by companies in Scandinavia, for example, are not the same as those required by firms in Italy. Similar findings have been offered by Brodbeck and his associated who have found that leadership attributes that managers feel are important for effectiveness are culturally driven. This study found that the responses from managers in the Anglo culture, for example, were quite different from those in the Germanic culture, and these differed from the responses from other cultures including Nordic, Latin, and Near East, to name but three. Trompenaars echoes these sentiments, noting that leader behaviour needs to be adapted to the culture. In summary, current research reveals that effective leadership styles and behaviours are at least partly culture-driven.

Concepts of Leadership

Good leaders are made not born. If you have the desire and willpower, you can become an effective leader. Good leaders develop through a never ending process of self-study, education, training, and experience. This guide will help you through that process.

To inspire your workers into higher levels of teamwork, there are certain things you must be, know, and, do. These do not come naturally, but are acquired through continual work and study. Good leaders are continually working and studying to improve their leadership skills; they are not resting on their laurels.

Before we get started, lets define leadership. Leadership is a process by which a person influences others to accomplish an objective and directs the organization in a way that makes it more cohesive and coherent. Leaders carry out this process by applying their leadership attributes, such as beliefs, values, ethics, character, knowledge, and skills. Although your position as a manager, supervisor, lead, etc. gives you the authority to accomplish certain tasks and objectives in the organization, this power does not make you a leader – it simply makes you the boss. Leadership differs in that it makes the followers want to achieve high goals, rather than simply bossing people around.

Bass' theory of leadership states that there are three basic ways to explain how people become leaders. The first two explain the leadership development for a small number of people.

These theories are:

- Some personality traits may lead people naturally into leadership roles. This is the Trait Theory.
- A crisis or important event may cause a person to rise to the occasion, which brings out extraordinary leadership qualities in an ordinary person. This is the Great Events Theory.
- People can choose to become leaders. People can learn leadership skills. This is the Transformational Leadership Theory. It is the most widely accepted theory today and the premise on which this guide is based.

When a person is deciding if the respects you as a leader, he does not think about your attributes, rather, he observes what you do so that he can know who you really are. He uses this observation to tell if you are a honourable and trusted leader or a self serving person who misuses authority to look good and get promoted. Self-serving leaders are not as effective because their employees only obey them, not follow them. They succeed in many areas because they present a good image to their seniors at the expense of their workers.

The basis of good leadership is honorable character and selfless service to your organization. In your employees' eyes, your leadership is everything you do that effects the organization's objectives and their well being. Respected leaders concentrate on what they are [be] (such as beliefs and character), what they know (such as job, tasks, and human nature), and what they do (such as implementing, motivating, and provide direction).

What makes a person want to follow a leader? People want to be guided by those they respect and who have a clear sense of direction. To gain respect, they must be ethical. A sense of direction is achieved by conveying a strong vision of the future.

Important Keys to Leadership

- Trust and confidence in top leadership was the single most reliable predictor of employee satisfaction in an organization.
- Effective communication by leadership in three critical areas was the key to winning organizational trust and confidence:
    1. Helping employees understand the company's overall business strategy.
    2. Helping employees understand how they contribute to achieving key business objectives.
    3. Sharing information with employees on both how the company is doing and how an employee's own division is doing - relative to strategic business objectives.

So in a nutshell — you must be trustworthy and you have to be able to communicate a vision of where the organization needs to go. The next section, "Principles of Leadership", ties in closely with this key concept.

Principles of Leadership

For help one should follow these ten principles of leadership: Know one self and seek self-improvement. In order to know oneself, one has to understand self and know what to do and understand one's attributes. Seeking self-improvement is by means of continually strengthening of one's attributes. This can be accomplished through self-study, formal classes, reflection, and interacting with others.

1. Be technically proficient - As a leader, you must know your job and have a solid familiarity with your employees' tasks.
2. Seek responsibility and take responsibility for your actions - Search for ways to guide your organization to new heights. And when things go wrong, they always do sooner or later — do not blame others. Analyze the situation, take corrective action, and move on to the next challenge.
3. Make sound and timely decisions - Use good problem solving, decision making, and planning tools.

4. Set the example - Be a good role model for your employees. They must not only hear what they are expected to do, but also see. We must become the change we want to see - Mahatma Gandhi.
5. Know your people and look out for their well-being - Know human nature and the importance of sincerely caring for your workers.
6. Keep your workers informed - Know how to communicate not only with them, but also seniors and other key people.
7. Develop a sense of responsibility in your workers - Help to develop good character traits that will help them carry out their professional responsibilities.
8. Ensure that tasks are understood, supervised, and accomplished - Communication is the key to this responsibility.
9. Train as a team - Although many so called leaders call their organization, department, section, etc., a team; they are not really teams — they are just a group of people doing their jobs.
10. Use the full capabilities of your organization - By developing a team spirit, you will be able to employ your organization, department, section, etc., to its fullest capabilities.

Factors of Leadership

There are four major factors in leadership:

Follower

Different people require different styles of leadership. For example, a new hire requires more supervision than an experienced employee. A person who lacks motivation requires a different approach than one with a high degree of motivation. You must know your people! The fundamental starting point is having a good understanding of human nature, such as needs, emotions, and motivation. You must come to know your employees' BE, KNOW, and DO attributes.

Leader

You must have a honest understanding of who you are, what you know, and what you can do. Also, note that it is the followers, not the leader who determines if a leader is successful. If they do not trust or lack confidence in their leader, then they will be uninspired. To be successful you have to convince your followers, not yourself or your superiors, that you are worthy of being followed.

Communication

You lead through two-way communication. Much of it is non-verbal. For instance, when you "set the example," that communicates to your people that you would not ask them to perform anything that you would not be willing to do. What and how you communicate either builds or harms the relationship between you and your employees.

Situation

All are different. What you do in one situation will not always work in another. You must use your judgement to decide the best course of action and the leadership style needed for each situation. For example, you may need to confront an employee for inappropriate behaviour, but if the confrontation is too late or too early, too harsh or too weak, then the results may prove ineffective.

Various forces will affect these factors. Examples of forces are your relationship with your seniors, the skill of your people, the informal leaders within your organization, and how your company is organized.

Attributes

If you are a leader who can be trusted, then those around you will grow to respect you. To be such a leader, there is a Leadership Framework to guide you: BE-KNOW- DO.

BE a professional. Examples: be loyal to the organization, perform selfless service, and take personal responsibility.

BE a professional who possess good character traits. Examples: honesty, competence, candor, commitment, integrity, courage, straightforwardness, imagination.

KNOW the four factors of leadership - follower, leader, communication, and situation.

KNOW yourself. Examples: strengths and weakness of your character, knowledge, and skills.

KNOW human nature. Examples: human needs, emotions, and how people respond to stress.

KNOW your job. Examples: be proficient and be able to train others in their tasks.

KNOW your organization. Examples: where to go for help, its climate and culture, who the unofficial leaders are.

DO provide direction. Examples: goal setting, problem solving, decision making, planning.

DO implement. Examples: communicating, co-ordinating, supervising, evaluating.

DO motivate. Examples: develop moral and spirit in the organization, train, coach, counsel.

Environment

Every organization has a particular work environment, which dictates to a considerable degree how its leaders respond to problems and opportunities. This is brought about by its heritage of past leaders and its present leaders.

Goals, Values, and Concepts

Leaders exert influence on the environment via three types of actions:

1. The goals and performance standards they establish.
2. The values they establish for the organization.
3. The business and people concepts they establish.

Successful organizations have leaders who set high standards and goals across the entire spectrum, such as strategies, market leadership, plans, meetings and presentations, productivity, quality, and reliability.

Values reflect the concern the organization has for its employees, customers, investors, vendors, and surrounding community. These values define the manner in how business will be conducted. Concepts define what products or services the organization will offer and the methods and processes for conducting business.

These goals, values, and concepts make up the organization's "personality" or how the organization is observed by both outsiders and insiders. This personality defines the roles, relationships, rewards, and rites that take place.

Roles and Relationships

Roles are the positions that are defined by a set of expectations about behavior of any job incumbent. Each role has a set of tasks and responsibilities that may or may not be spelled out. Roles have a powerful effect on behavior for several reasons, to include money being paid for the performance of the role, there is prestige attached to a role, and a sense of accomplishment or challenge.

Relationships are determined by a role's tasks. While some tasks are performed alone, most are carried out in relationship with others. The tasks will determine who the role-holder is required to interact with, how often, and towards what end. Normally the greater the interaction, the greater the liking developed. This in turn leads to more frequent interaction. In human behaviour, it's hard to like someone whom we have no contact with, and we tend to seek out those we like. People tend to do what they are rewarded for, and friendship is a powerful reward. Many tasks and behaviours that are associated with a role are brought about by these relationships. That is, new task and behaviors are expected of the present role holder because a strong relationship was developed in the past, either by that role holder or a prior role holder.

Culture and Climate

There are two distinct forces that dictate how to act within an organization: culture and climate.

Each organization has its own distinctive culture. It is a combination of the founders, past leadership, current leadership, crises, events, history, and size. This results in: the routines, rituals, and the "way we do things." These rites impact individual behavior on what it takes to be in good standing (the norm) and direct the appropriate behavior for each circumstance.

The climate is the feel of the organization, the individual and shared perceptions and attitudes of the organization's members. While the culture is the deeply rooted nature of the organization that is a result of long-held formal and informal systems, rules, traditions, and customs; climate is a short-term phenomenon created by the current leadership. Climate represents the beliefs about the "feel of the organization" by its members. This individual perception of the "feel of the organization" comes from what the people believe about the activities that occur in the organization. These activities influence both individual and team motivation and satisfaction, such as:

- How well does the leader clarify the priorities and goals of the organization? What is expected of us?
- What is the system of recognition, rewards, and punishments in the organization?
- How competent are the leaders?
- Are leaders free to make decision?
- What will happen if I make a mistake?

Organizational climate is directly related to the leadership and management style of the leader, based on the values, attributes, skills, and actions, as well as the priorities of the leader. Compare this to "ethical climate" — the "feel of the organization" about the activities that have ethical content or those aspects of the work environment that constitute ethical behaviour. The ethical climate is the feel about whether we do things right; or the feel of whether we behave the way we ought to behave. The behaviour (character) of the leader is the most important factor that impacts the climate.

On the other hand, culture is a long-term, complex phenomenon. Culture represents the shared expectations and self-image of the organization. The mature values that create "tradition" or the "way we do things here." Things are done differently in every organization. The collective vision and common folklore that define the institution are a reflection of culture. Individual leaders, cannot easily create or change culture because culture is a part of the organization. Culture influences the characteristics of the climate by its effect on the actions and thought processes of the leader. But, everything you do as a leader will effect the climate of the organization.

Leadership Models

Leadership models help us to understand what makes leaders act the way they do. The ideal is not to lock oneself in to a type of behaviour discussed in the model, but to realize that every situation calls for a different approach or behaviour to be taken. Two models will be discussed, the Four Framework Approach and the Managerial Grid.

Four Framework Approach

In the Four Framework Approach, Bolman and Deal suggest that leaders display leadership behaviors in one of four types of frameworks: Structural, Human Resource, Political, or Symbolic. The style can either be effective or ineffective, depending upon the chosen behaviour in certain situations.

Structural Framework

In an effective leadership situation, the leader is a social architect whose leadership style is analysis and design. While in an ineffective leadership situation, the leader is a petty tyrant whose leadership style is details. Structural Leaders focus on structure, strategy, environment, implementation, experimentation.

Human Resource Framework

In an effective leadership situation, the leader is a catalyst and servant whose leadership style is support, advocate, and empowerment. while in an ineffective leadership situation, the leader is a pushover, whose leadership style is abdication and fraud. Human Resource Leaders believe in people and communicate that belief; they are visible and accessible; they empower, increase participation, support, share information, and move decision making down into the organization.

Political Framework

In an effective leadership situation, the leader is an advocate, whose leadership style is coalition and building. While in an ineffective leadership situation, the leader is a hustler, whose leadership style is manipulation? Political leaders clarify what they want and what they can get; they assess the distribution of power and interests; they build linkages to other stakeholders, use persuasion first, and then use negotiation and coercion only if necessary.

Symbolic Framework

In an effective leadership situation, the leader is a prophet, whose leadership style is inspiration. While in an ineffective leadership situation, the leader is a fanatic or fool, whose leadership style is smoke and mirrors. Symbolic leaders view organizations as a stage or theatre to play certain roles and give impressions; these leaders use symbols to capture attention; they try to frame experience by providing plausible interpretations of experiences; they discover and communicate a vision.

This model suggests that leaders can be put into one of these four categories and there are times when one approach is appropriate and times when it would not be. Any one of these approaches alone would be inadequate, thus we should strive to be conscious of all four approaches, and not just rely on one or two. For example, during a major organization change, a structural leadership style may be more effective than a visionary leadership style; while during a period when strong growth is needed, the visionary approach may be better. We also need to understand ourselves as each of us tends to have a preferred approach. We need to be conscious of these at all times and be aware of the limitations of our favouring just one approach.

Types of Leaders

Authoritarian Leader (high task, low relationship): People who get this rating are very much task oriented and are hard on their workers (autocratic). There is little or no allowance for co-operation or collaboration. Heavily task oriented people display these characteristics: they are very strong on schedules; they expect people to do what they are told without question or debate; when something goes wrong they tend to focus on who is to blame rather than concentrate on exactly what is wrong and how to prevent it; they are intolerant of what they see as dissent (it may just be someone's creativity), so it is difficult for their subordinates to contribute or develop.

Team Leader (high task, high relationship): This type of person leads by positive example and endeavors to foster a team environment in which all team members can reach their highest potential, both as team members and as people. They encourage the team to reach team goals as effectively as possible, while also working tirelessly to strengthen the bonds among the various members. They normally form and lead some of the most productive teams.

Country Club Leader (low task, high relationship): This person uses predominantly reward power to maintain discipline and to encourage the team to accomplish its goals. Conversely, they are almost incapable of employing the more punitive coercive and legitimate powers. This inability results from fear that using such powers could jeopardize relationships with the other team members.

Impoverished Leader (low task, low relationship): Here the leader uses the "delegate and disappear" management style. Since they are not committed to either task accomplishment or maintenance; they essentially allow their team to do whatever it wishes and prefer to detach themselves from the team process by allowing the team to suffer from a series of power struggles.

The most desirable place for a leader to be along the two axis at most times would be a 9 on task and a 9 on people — the Team Leader. However, do not entirely dismiss the other three. Certain situations might call for one of the other three to be used at times. For example, by playing the Impoverished Leader, you allow your team to gain self-reliance. Be an Authoritarian Leader to instill a sense of discipline in an unmotivated worker. By carefully studying the situation and the forces affecting it, you will know at what points along the axis you need to be in order to achieve the desired result.

The Process of Great Leadership

The road to great leadership - that is common to successful leaders:

1. Challenge the process - First, find a process that you believe needs to be improved the most.
2. Inspire a shared vision - Next, share you vision in words that can be understood by your followers.
3. Enable others to act - Give them the tools and methods to solve the problem.
4. Model the way - When the process gets tough, get your hands dirty. A boss tells others what to do, a leader shows how it can be done.
5. Encourage the heart - Share the glory with your follower's heart, while keeping the pains within your own.

Paradox 1: Framing Leadership: Is the essence of leadership being stuck on the horns of a dilemma?

Before reading the analysis of Paradox 1, you may want to assess your own theories and definitions of leadership. Briefly, how would you describe successful leaders in terms of specific characteristics, and what differentiates them from unsuccessful leaders? Defining a metaphor as the use of one phenomenon to describe another, what is your metaphor for leadership? Many if not all of us theorize about leadership in one form or another either consciously or unconsciously, and it doesn't matter if you borrow your metaphor and theory from others or develop it yourself. But knowing your own metaphor and theory establishes a helpful baseline. You may also want to reflect on your personal views about the dynamics and models of leadership within different cultures and clusters of national cultures, in terms of both metaphors and theories.

A seemingly incalculable number of research studies of leadership have tested hypotheses derived from specific theories. Simultaneously a voluminous literature that is post hoc and circuitous in nature has developed. Leaders are frequently assumed to be effective if they occupy positions of power, even when performance is substandard.

Chester Barnard's classic book, *The Functions of the Executive* (1968), originally published in 1938, serves as an excellent initial framework for describing and defining leadership in management. Until the end of World War II, the focus was on a firm's *tangible* resources, such as plant and equipment, as they represented an effective way of creating barriers to entry against competitors in the manufacturing-based American economy. At the time, total labour costs were the largest component of total costs. Hence it was logical for managers, writers, and researchers to focus on workers and to develop methods of motivating them to become more productive. Today the more *intangible* aspects of firms — customer perceptions of service quality, brand image, tacit knowledge based on organizational learning, and organizational culture — are frequently much more important than labour costs as they provide formidable barriers to entry against potential competitors. John Kendrick (as cited in Hitt, Ireland, & Hoskisson, 2003, p. 81), an economist, has demonstrated that the ratio of intangible to tangible resources in 1929 was 30–70; by 1990 the ratio was almost the reverse. Far ahead of other writers, Barnard in 1938 swung the focus away from the worker level and toward management in ways that are still reverberating in the management field.

Influenced by his long business experience, including the presidency of Bell Telephone of New Jersey, Barnard began by defining the three essential elements of an organization: systems of communication between individuals and groups, motivation (willingness to serve), and common purpose integrating the efforts of individuals and groups. He then described the three fundamental tasks of the executive or manager: to develop systems of communication linking individuals and groups throughout the organization; to motivate subordinates; and to define the common purpose, or what the organization is attempting to accomplish. In short, the executive is the critical factor in an organization, since the three key tasks of the executive mirror exactly the three essential elements of the organization. Barnard's book, which is a long and somewhat disjointed narrative, proved to be popular with management specialists but not the general public. He is credited with many interesting ideas that are still influential beyond those discussed above. One of the most important concepts, the *zone of indifference*, which has been aptly renamed the *zone of acceptance*, arises in the area of motivation, the second of the manager's fundamental tasks. To Barnard, the manager's task is to motivate subordinates so that they expand their zones of acceptance of the strategy, vision, and goals that the leader is promoting.

Motivational theory has built on this framework in many useful ways since Barnard's time. For example, a body of research focuses on good *Organizational Citizenship Behavior* (to borrow the title of a book by Organ, Podsakoff, & MacKenzie, 2006), that is, the degree to which members of an organization are motivated to go beyond the "letter of the law" to follow the strategy, vision, and goals of an effective executive leader. Such organizational citizens might work all night to finish a project, come to work in a blizzard, and engage in similar activities that are far beyond their official job duties, in large part because of the motivational impact that a particular executive has. One such leader among many is Herb Kelleher, a founder and former CEO who imbued seemingly everyone at Southwest Airlines to work in such a fashion.

Barnard recognized that the specific activities of executives change as they move from position to position and, more particularly, as they are promoted. Organizational levels at which managers operate and the proportion of time they devote to planning are positively correlated, while face-to-face communication with subordinates declines simultaneously. Still, regardless of the organizational level, the manager must complete Barnard's three essential tasks.

Given the manager's complex roles, it is little wonder that dilemmas in fulfilling them occur. The term *dilemma* is of Greek origin and denotes two compelling, logical, and competing premises. In an influential article, Thomas Stewart (1996) summarized the results of a large, interview-based research project in Canada, which found that leaders must address the following nine dilemmas:

1. Revenue growth *versus* cost containment
2. A short-term *versus* a long-term focus on plans and results
3. Creativity *versus* organizational discipline, that is, allowing individuals to deal creatively with issues versus demanding that they complete specific and defined activities
4. The needs of people, including adequate time away from work, *versus* the demands of productivity
5. Specific capabilities of subordinates *versus* their leadership potential
6. Independence *versus* dependence of organizational members and departments (independence achieved at the expense of others, through such activities as withholding information and not sharing resources, would be unacceptable)
7. Bureaucracy busting *versus* creating economies of scale, which leads to a large, complex bureaucracy
8. Trust versus the demand for change
9. Broad-based projects *versus* only high-visibility projects.

The Canadian researchers argued that managers must emphasize two essential roles to be effective: *polarity management*, or balancing the two premises in each dilemma smoothly, and *ambiguity management*, as managers live in a world of uncertainty and ambiguity. Stewart recommends that for each dilemma, a manager should construct a simple, two-dimensional chart with a 45° angle, which will allow the manager to see the current situation in terms of what is above the line and what is below the line.

Figure 7.1

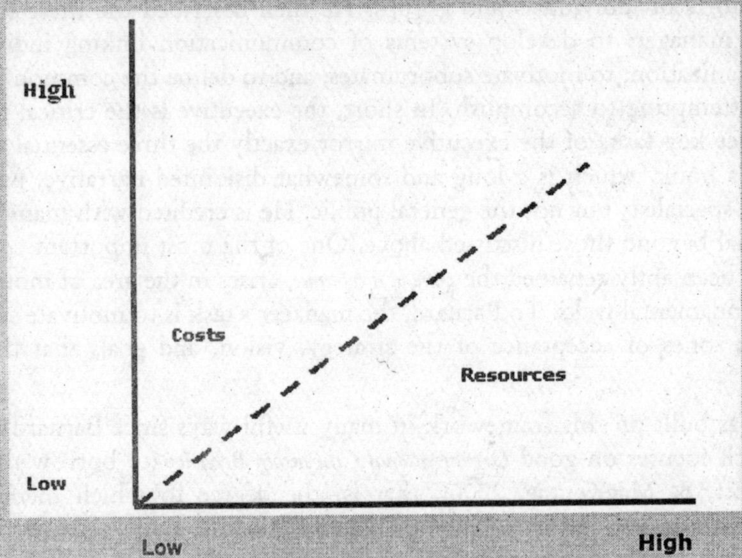

Managing the Dilemma of Balancing Cost Containment and Revenue Growth (10-point scale for emphasis on cost containment and resources devoted to revenue growth)

NOTE: As the emphasis on revenue growth increases, cost containment declines in importance. An optimal balance is achieved only along the 45° dotted line.

In this way the manager has a general guideline for deciding whether one side of the dilemma should be emphasized rather than the other at a given time. To help the leader manage such polarities, Pfeffer and Sutton (2005) have developed a set of guidelines in six key areas, including strategy, leadership, and individual *versus* group incentive systems, organizational change, and balance of work-non-work activities of organizational members, and specific financial incentives for particular purposes.

However, our review of the definitions of paradox (for example, Eisenhardt's specific definition: "the simultaneous existence of two inconsistent states such as that between innovation and efficiency"; 2000, p. 703) indicates that these polarities facing managers are in actuality that particularly important type of paradox, the dilemma. Similarly, Williams's *The Paradox of Power* (2002) revolves around the concept that a leader, in order to execute effective leadership, must give leadership away, or delegate authority to capable subordinates.

The term *dilemma* connotes two equally compelling and competing premises, and the manager must choose one of two equally attractive or unattractive premises at any given moment. This perspective finds apt expression in the aphorism "caught on the horns of a dilemma." That is, managers must manage polarities and integrate the two elements of each dilemma.

For example, Jeffrey Immelt, the current CEO of General Electric (GE), who succeeded Jack Welch in that role a few years ago, is currently stressing innovation, which was downgraded in importance during the Welch years in favour of efficiency and total revenue growth to maximize the stock market valuation of the company. Immelt's actions, and those of any manager, represent the reason managerial leadership is so complex. As expected by the GE board of directors, Immelt's long-term focus on innovation did not lead to an immediate significant increase in GE's stock market price. Many investors are much more interested in positive short-term financial results than in the predicted favourable results associated with long-term investments in innovation. Thus, the trade-off of selecting one premise over another tends to be a constant struggle.

When cross-cultural considerations enter the picture, leadership becomes even more complex. What is acceptable in one nation may be socially and even legally unacceptable in another nation, and the manager may be forced to adapt differential solutions to dilemmas in different nations. We do not yet possess a useful profile of the dilemmas that managers in various ethnic and national cultures face, but the role of the leader typically becomes more complex as the extent of global activities facing a particular firm widens.

Relatedly, research on what makes an expatriate manager successful indicates that such factors as flexibility and openness to new experiences are critical. The concept of *cultural universals*, or practices that effective leaders employ throughout the world, such as being honest, decisive, and motivational are also of significance. But they also present evidence for the existence of *cultural specifics*, that is, that some leadership practices, such as emphasizing subordinate participation in decision making and being team oriented, work well in some cultures but not in others.

Our treatment of the four types of generic cultures is consistent with the perspective of cultural specifics; what works well in an authority-ranking culture will tend to be ineffective in market-pricing and equality-matching cultures. The GLOBE researchers also indicate that some leadership practices are universally perceived as reprehensible, including being autocratic or irritable.

TABLE 7.1. Cultural Views of Leadership Effectiveness (Partial List)

Universal Facilitators of Leadership Effectiveness

- Being trustworthy, just, and honest (integrity)
- Having foresight and planning ahead
- Being positive, dynamic, motivating, and building confidence
- Being communicative, informed, a co-ordinator, and a team builder

Universal Impediments to Leadership Effectiveness

- Being a loner and asocial
- Being non-co-operative and irritable
- Being autocratic

Culturally Contingent Endorsement of Specifics That Work in Some Cultures but Not in Others

- Being individualistic
- Being status conscious
- Being a risk taker

Source: House, Hanges, Javidan, Dorfman, & Gupta, 2004; Javidan, Dorfman, Sully de Luque, & House, 2006.

Nevertheless, as Stewart has argued, polarity management and ambiguity management may be the essence of leadership. In this sense, the essence of management is being hoisted or stuck on the horns of a dilemma. Still, a manager is typically mired in day-to-day activities in which such choices are difficult to identify. As Mintzberg demonstrated in 1973, the nature of managerial work is that managers work long hours on a bewilderingly large number of activities at an unremitting pace. They must react to problems as they arise, and their work is brief in the sense that they do not have much time to devote to any one activity. The CEOs in Mintzberg's study engaged in activities extending from less than 2 minutes to approximately 2 hours.

Performing the mundane tasks of leadership daily and implementing plans successfully are critical and just as important as selecting one strategy rather than another or selecting one premise rather than another. Charon and Colvin (1999) convincingly demonstrated that the major reason CEOs fail is that they fail to implement a strategy thoroughly and successfully. Such failures include delaying the termination of a key subordinate while this individual harms the firm significantly, not being actively involved in the implementation phases of a strategy, and exercising ineffective leadership that undermines the confidence of organizational members.

In sum, it is important to select the correct premise of any dilemma, but it is equally important to implement it thoroughly. In this sense effective and thorough implementation is always required, even when the manager selects the correct premise.

Paradox 2: Who is more effective, the instrumental visionary- transformational leader or the headman?

Sports have become increasingly prominent in our world, and today sports programs are broadcast throughout the entire week and television channels are devoted specifically to promoting them. One reason often cited is that competition in sports mirrors the intense competition found in many nations, including the United States. You can reflect on what makes a successful leader on a sports team and a successful coach. Are the same characteristics that are preconditions for leadership on a sports team or for success as a coach identical to those predicting success as a manager?

The focus in this section is on the relationship between the four types of generic cultures and the appropriate pattern of leadership in each of them. You can obtain some general idea about your own leadership preferences by completing two items from the Gelfand-Holcombe (1998) survey directly below.

Suppose you had to use one word to describe yourself. Which one would you use?

(a) Unique
(b) Competitive
(c) Co-operative
(d) Dutiful

A famous photographer has offered you a very reasonable price for having a picture taken. Which picture would you choose? You with

(a) Your three best friends
(b) A very important person (a person who is bound to get into the history books)
(c) No one else
(d) Many members of the community, whom you are helping; it shows that you are sacrificing yourself for them.

After indicating your preferences, you may want to review briefly the description of the four generic types of culture.

Most of the discussion will compare leadership within authority-ranking and market-pricing cultures, the two generic types of cultures found most often throughout the world. We will also discuss briefly the GLOBE study of leadership in 62 nations, with particular attention to equality-matching, or egalitarian, national cultures.

In the developed and market-pricing nations, the focus is on visionary and transformational leadership capable of moving an organization to a new plateau of success (Collins, 2001; Collins & Porras, 1994). *Transformational leadership* represents the degree to which the leader is able to effect a change not only in the firm's culture but also in profitability. *Visionary leadership* is the degree to which the leader provides a vision of the future to which organizational members subscribe so that the transformation can occur.

Jack Welch achieved enormous success as CEO of General Electric and was a transformational and visionary leader. Overall valuation of the company increased more than 400 times during his tenure. Echoing Chester Barnard, Welch argued that it is the leader's obligation to be transformational, regardless of the number of subordinates or the organizational level at which he or she operates

(Welch, 2005). To that end, starting in 1985 he and his team developed a radical strategy focused on creating a borderless or global organization, emphasizing quality of production while minimizing costs and reducing the cycle time of production, and selling off strategic business units if they could not be No. 1 or No. 2 in their respective industries world-wide.

Welch was also the major supporter of the 20/70/10 managerial performance evaluation system, with those identified in the upper 20% in terms of performance receiving disproportionate rewards, 70% receiving adequate rewards to stimulate them to try to move into the 20% category, and 10% receiving few if any rewards. The disproportionate distribution of rewards is a cardinal feature of a market-pricing culture, whether it is an organizational culture, an ethnic culture, or a national culture. General Electric counsels members of the lowest-performing group to leave the company if their performance does not improve quickly and significantly.

As this discussion of Welch's approach implies, the visionary and transformational type of leadership must be accompanied by *instrumental leadership*, with individuals being rewarded if they achieve the goals set by the leader or leaders. This is particularly true in a market-pricing culture. Visionary and transformational leadership without adequate instrumental rewards may work in the short run in a market-pricing culture, but after a short time atleast some desired rewards must be forthcoming.

Welch and many others feel that effective visionary and transformational leaders come in all shapes and varieties (Collins, 2001; Collins & Porrass, 1994). Alfred Sloan, the legendary CEO of General Motors who is largely credited with its extraordinary success from 1920 until 1960, was known as "Silent Al." He spoke sparingly at group meetings but normally followed up with memos outlining action items. Lee Iacocca led the product team at Ford for the path-breaking Mustang and later performed spectacularly as CEO of the moribund Chrysler when it faced bankruptcy in 1980, but his personality was quite different. Iacocca is an extroverted, hard-playing, and visibly energetic presence. He is frequently cited as a classic exemplar of *charismatic leadership*, with its focus on a larger-than-life individual capable of galvanizing and motivating subordinates through his assumed special abilities.

The assumption of difficult-to-measure special abilities (*charisma*) that separates the leader from followers is the critical feature of charismatic leadership. Both Sloan and Iacocca represent visionary and transformational leadership, but Sloan was not charismatic. Most important, visionary and transformational leadership is primarily one-way and restricted to behaviour at work, with the leader developing both the vision and the transformational strategy and the followers implementing it. At the highest organizational level there may well be a high degree of subordinate involvement in the discussions of the strategic plan. Still, it is the CEO, with input from the board of directors, who decides what vision and strategy shall dominate. And, as CEOs know and at times have stated publicly, implementing the transformational plan successfully tends to require a Herculean effort. It is normally much more difficult to implement a strategic plan than to create a vision and a transformational strategy. Still, the game involving both the transformational strategy and its implementation plan is relatively simple: If subordinates do not achieve their specific and measurable goals, they are not rewarded and are usually asked to leave if more-positive results are not quickly forthcoming.

Today it is popular to talk about leadership within the context of sharing power with subordinates, although the reality may be much different in that practices do deviate from values. Even in this instance, in market-pricing cultures instrumental rewards and punishments accompany not only visionary and transformational leadership but also *shared leadership*.

There is, however, a competing type of leadership in authority-ranking cultures found in such areas as Asia, Latin America, the Middle East, and Africa and termed "the headman concept of leadership" (Westwood & Chan, 1995). In the case of *headman leadership*, a *two-way psychological* relationship based on mutual obligations exists between leader and follower and *extends beyond work to include cultural and community factors*. The leader may receive disproportionate rewards, but he also has an obligation to look out for his employees at all costs, just as the head of a family looks out for other family members and the village head is responsible for everyone in the village. In return, subordinates are expected to be committed fully to the organization's vision, strategy, and implementation plan.

For instance, Japanese automotive firms operating in the United States tend to retrain their workers and pay them their regular salaries for 6 months or more when an economic downturn occurs; American automotive firms have moved to downsize their workforces much more quickly under similar circumstances. In Japan and other authority-ranking nations governed by a sense of shame, some owners and managers will devote a year or more to ensuring that downsized employees are placed in positions elsewhere. By contrast, some Western firms provide outplacement counselling but are not as actively and directly engaged in placing downsized workers and managers.

Annually in Japan, approximately 1,000 suicides are reported among corporate executives and entrepreneurs, and many more are unreported. Many of these suicides occur because the owners and upper-level managers feel a sense of *shame* if they fail their employees in any way, and particularly in guaranteeing employment. S. Sugawara (1998) recorded a particularly incisive example of this phenomenon revolving around Nobuo Shibata, a 48-year-old president of a small sheet metal company, and his brother. These executives took their own lives and left a plaintive note apologizing to all their employees for the slump in business.

You can obtain a copy of a recent international film, *The Secret Life of the Japanese*, which mirrors such realities in modern Japan. This film vividly portrays the wrenching changes occurring in Japanese corporations as they de-emphasize the authority-ranking model. This de-emphasis encourages and even mandates the increased use of informal ways of communicating and interacting at work, faster decision making, and quicker implementation.

The new model, essentially a reflection of a market-pricing culture, also moves away from *guaranteed lifetime employment* and toward *employability* through continual educational and training programs and skill-enhancing job rotations. If a company downsizes its workforce, presumably workers and managers will be able to obtain work elsewhere because of their enhanced skills and abilities.

Downsizings in Japanese companies are now more common than in previous eras. Some of the impoverished unemployed have constructed tent cities in parks because of the situation, something unimaginable prior to 1990. In one isolated rural area, so many individuals cut off from their families and society has committed suicide that the spot is now popularly known as Suicide Mountain. Japan has moved from an authority-ranking model toward a market-pricing model largely because of the impact of globalization and a deep economic recession lasting nearly two decades.

It is very unusual for a Western CEO to commit suicide because he has failed in his obligations to his employees and subordinate managers. *Personal responsibility* is much more important than shame in market-pricing cultures, and their legal systems reinforce this emphasis. The focus is on instrumental visionary-transformational leadership that is primarily one-way in nature and restricted to the workplace. As might be expected, some companies deviate from this norm.

Costco pays its workers an average salary of approximately $40,000 per year, in comparison with $8,000 for Wal-Mart; has a no-layoff policy; and willingly accepts labor unions and works with them effectively. Other companies that are exceptional in this regard are GEICO Insurance Company, a subsidiary of Berkshire-Hathaway, and Southwest Airlines. But this small group of companies constitutes an exception rather than the rule.

And other U.S. companies guaranteeing lifetime employment just 30 years ago, including IBM and Hewlett-Packard, now emphasize employability. Guaranteed employment and employability bring into perspective the two sharply differing leadership orientations found in market-pricing and authority ranking cultures.

A reasonable justification can be made for the practice of employability in market-pricing national cultures. For instance, American-based corporations now devote more resources and money to education and training than do all the university and college business schools in the United States in combination.

Numerous companies sponsor "corporate universities" offering excellent courses tailored to specific corporate needs and required for internal promotions. Also, the United States has for decades been creating jobs far more rapidly than many other nations have, due in part to the geographical mobility of its workers and the emphasis on employability.

It is also possible to justify the practice of guaranteed employment and related practices that are more prevalent in authority-ranking national cultures than in market-pricing cultures. The relationship between top management and other organizational members is tightly entwined and tends to reflect the two-way psychological relationship based on mutual obligations.

Sharply in contrast to General Motors, Toyota is an outstanding example of this close fit. Comparing General Motors and Toyota will allow us to spotlight and contrast how leadership is actualized in market-pricing and authority ranking cultures.

During the 1980s, under the leadership of CEO Roger Smith, General Motors decided that the major problem it faced was the uneasy relationship with its workers and labor unions (Finkelstein, 2003). In short, the workers and their labor unions were the problem, and technology was the solution.

Smith advocated building technology-intensive factories requiring far fewer workers than the labor-intensive factories common in the industry at the time. This strategy was so popular that *Fortune* magazine once recognized Smith as its CEO of the Year during the 1980s. Unfortunately, the new factories experienced great difficulty, at least in part because of employee opposition and the one-way manner in which Smith attempted to implement the strategy.

Toyota, on the other hand, decided that the technology was the cause of difficulty for the workers and not vice versa. Its executives and workers rearranged the assembly line so that the worker had easy access to the necessary tools and resources and a feeling of empowerment. In the Toyota System individual workers can shut down the assembly line if they see a major problem, workers are guaranteed lifetime employment, and quality circles of workers meet regularly to address issues and problems they face on the assembly line.

General Motors was following the instrumental-visionary-transformational model of leadership befitting a market-pricing culture in which the relationship between the leader and subordinates is one-way and limited to work. Toyota, conversely, was using the headman model of the classic authority-ranking culture. Ironically, General Motors and Toyota established a joint venture in Fremont, California, in a troubled General Motors factory in the late 1980s.

General Motors wanted to learn about the Toyota system and chose the Fremont factory because it had an extremely low level of productivity and extremely high levels of employee dissatisfaction, absenteeism, and labor union hostility. Without changing the technology, management implemented both the Toyota production system and the Toyota philosophy in this factory in a spectacularly successful manner, making it one of the most successful in the General Motors system. Unfortunately, Smith and General Motors disregarded the results and failed to capitalize on this success. Today, Toyota has become the largest automotive company in the world, replacing General Motors.

Of related interest, countless Western executives have travelled to Toyota City in Japan to study the Toyota System, which consists of two parts: its philosophical assumptions and the actual production system. These executives easily comprehend how the production system works and have borrowed heavily from it in their own company operations. They have also attempted to introduce some of the philosophical assumptions in their own organizations, such as including "Respect for People" in corporate vision statements.

Thus far Western executives have implemented the Toyota Production System far more successfully than the philosophical assumptions. Jeffrey Liker (2004), a longtime observer of the world-wide automotive industry, believes that no Western company has effectively copied and implemented Toyota's philosophy, which he views as much more important than the Toyota Production System. Given that Western firms tend to emphasize market-pricing organizational cultures rather than authority-ranking organizational cultures, Liker's conclusion seems warranted.

Some Japanese companies have moved away from the authority-ranking model espoused by Toyota. Nissan, for example, was facing the possibility of bankruptcy in the 1990s. Its CEO, Carlos Ghosn, a native of Brazil, spearheaded a dramatic turnaround of the company. Some of his actions involved downsizing the workforce and relocating factories to new areas in Japan and outside the nation in order to minimize costs. In most instances, workers were given the choice of either relocating to the new factories within Japan or accepting a generous buyout offer. Nissan also reduced the number of suppliers of parts, many of whom had been working with the company for decades, to save billions of dollars. The general public in Japan saw these actions as necessary for the company's survival and hailed Ghosn as a corporate hero.

Unfortunately, there are limitations and consequences associated with both the market-pricing and the authority-ranking models as actualized in the practices of guaranteed employment and employability, as our discussion suggests. Guaranteed employment can allow employees and managers to work below their potential if they so choose. There is also a tendency to have more workers than is necessary for operating efficiently. One negative consequence of employability occurs in a downsizing, especially for workers and managers older than 40. Many of them struggle to obtain work elsewhere commensurate with their abilities and work experience. In some cases, they must accept an undesirable position; in many cases, especially those older than 50, they cannot obtain any position. Skilled workers and managers also begin to view their relationship with the firm in purely instrumental terms, are more likely to be less committed, and are more prone to leave for perceived better opportunities, taking with them valuable knowledge and contacts.

At this time it is infeasible to recommend employability as superior to guaranteed employment or vice versa. It is also infeasible to recommend an ideal system integrating aspects of both the authority-ranking and market pricing models, although Ghosn's approach at Nissan represents a successful mixture of the two approaches. Whether his successful model can be employed by other firms is questionable, given different industry and environmental conditions.

Still, in a highly competitive global environment, even the best-intentioned corporations using the market-pricing model often fail to meet their obligations, even to shareholders. A case in point is IBM Corporation from the late 1970s to 1992, even though *Fortune* magazine identified IBM as the most outstanding company in the world for 3 years in the 1980s. IBM also championed guaranteed lifetime employment during this period and was explicitly recognized in, *In Search of Excellence* (Peters & Waterman, 1982), one of the bestselling books of all time, as one of the 24 outstanding American companies.

But by 1992 the possibility of bankruptcy or being purchased by another company was realistic and threatening, largely because the capacity power of IBM's critical mainframe computers was challenged by the dramatic increase in computing efficiency of desktop computers.

When Louis Gerstner became the CEO of IBM in 1993, he created a vision around the concept of IBM's being the best company in the world offering high-tech computer-related services but one that no longer guaranteed employment. Gerstner correctly reasoned that a far-sighted strategy focusing on high-end services and a de-emphasis of mainframe computing would generate increased profits, compensation, self-confidence, and commitment in the workforce. His vision and strategy were clearly successful.

There are, then, sharply contrasting leadership orientations in authority ranking and market-pricing cultures. In some instances, as in the case of Nissan, they seem to enrich one another. Another striking illustration of enrichment involves Puter Sampoerna, who was educated in the United States and is president of the Sampoerna Company in Indonesia, the most profitable maker of Indonesian clove-based cigarettes. He employs all the modern financial, accounting, marketing, and production techniques learned at business school in the United States. But he also structures the factory in terms of the Indonesian villages in which workers were born. Each sub-division of the factory elects a headman or elder, who is responsible for hiring and disciplining workers in the "village" and handling any other matter of importance. Puter Sampoerna and other top executives do not even come onto the factory floor. They do, however, meet regularly with the headmen or elders (Blustein, 1994).

Beyond the cross-cultural comparison of authority-ranking and market pricing leadership patterns, the empirical research linking leadership to culture in the GLOBE study of 62 nations confirmed that some *universal* leadership factors are endorsed across all 62 national cultures: The portrait of a leader who is universally viewed as effective is clear: The person should possess the highest levels of integrity and engage in Charismatic/Value-Based behaviours while building effective teams. (Dorfman, Hanges, & Brodbeck, 2004, p. 678).

Such a leadership pattern represents an ideal, whether the generic culture is authority ranking, market pricing, community sharing, or equality matching. However, as indicated, actual practices frequently are far different from the ideal. It is important to note that the GLOBE study's definition of charismatic leadership is equivalent to this chapter's notion of instrumental-visionary-transformational leadership rather than to the narrow concept of charismatic leadership as defined by special abilities, or charisma, separating the leader from followers.

Briefly, the salient points of difference between the generic cultures of market pricing and authority ranking are a one-way versus a two-way psychological relationship between leader and subordinates; restriction of this relationship to the workplace versus extending it to include integration into the family, kinship group, and larger community; and radically different underlying models, one being instrumental only and the other structuring the corporation as a family.

In the GLOBE study, the researchers reduced the 62 national cultures to 10 clusters, within each of which nations expressed similar cultural values. However, there were still significant differences in values within each cluster. The researchers found that their 10 clusters and 62 national cultures differentially endorsed some distinctive leadership factors and de-emphasized others.

Of particular relevance to our discussion is the Nordic-European cluster, which includes Denmark, Finland, and Sweden, generally considered to be nations epitomizing the ideal of the equality-matching culture? That is, these nations emphasize both a high degree of individualism and a low degree of power distance as manifested in an unusual combination of highly successful corporations, entrepreneurial firms, a generous welfare system, and a legal system relating monetary fines for violations to a person's income level.

The GLOBE researchers indicate that this cluster strongly endorses the charismatic/value-based, team-based, and participative leadership dimensions. Such results are consistent with the major emphases in this generic type of culture. However, the equality-matching model is found primarily in a small number of nations with small populations, particularly Scandinavian nations, which historically have had limited multi-ethnicity. Today these nations are experiencing increasing multiethnic tensions. It is questionable whether the equality-matching model is appropriate in nations with large populations, and it is even questionable whether the Scandinavian nations will maintain their traditional egalitarian focus in a globalizing world where multiethnic tensions are increasing.

Also, as indicated earlier, Hofstede's research was not able to identify any nation employing community sharing, although it did not include the Communist nations such as Cuba and Russia, which officially endorse community sharing but in practice operate quite differently. Unless there is a resurgence of Communism or a new variation thereof throughout the world, which seems to be happening in some Latin American nations in which socialistic populism is gaining strength, it appears reasonable to conclude that globalization will play out in a world in which the authority-ranking and market-pricing models will contend with one another in many instances or integrate with one another in some fashion, as our discussion of Nissan suggests.

Paradox 3: When should a leader allow subordinates to participate in decision making?

One of the most popular topics in the area of work motivation is the degree of subordinate involvement in decision making. Participation makes eminent sense when time is not an issue, the subordinates possess knowledge that the leader does not, and participation will increase the probability of the acceptance of the leader's program. Research has consistently confirmed such findings.

However, much of the research was completed in the United States. Brockner et al. (2001) obtained survey data in several nations in a series of related studies. They demonstrated that commitment to the organization and participation were much more positively linked when respondents endorsed low power distance than when they supported high power distance. Such careful studies suggest that a leader or manager should probably consider the degree of power distance in a culture before either maximizing or minimizing the participation. These ideas are also consistent with our previous paradox emphasizing the difference between the instrumental visionary-transformational leader and the headman concept of leader.

When individuals expect that there will be a high degree of power distance in a culture, a manager who stresses the use of participation is directly challenging some core cultural values. Power distance, in short, should be taken into consideration when one is deciding whether to emphasize subordinate participation in decision making, and actions should be consistent with the extent to which it exists in a given culture.

Paradox 4: Can an effective leader be someone who publicly humiliates subordinates?

You are invited to indicate whether you would enjoy working for a superior who engaged in any or all the following: publicly humiliated and closely supervised workers, regularly pointed out supposed errors, and suggested strongly how each step of the work process should be completed.

In individualistic cultures, such a pattern of leadership would be considered not only ineffective but distasteful. Individualists would tend to favour a leader who would employ positive reinforcement, provide negative feedback in private, and allow the subordinates to work independently without close supervision. Carly Fiorina, the deposed CEO of Hewlett-Packard, was roundly criticized for publicly firing three senior executives when the company's sales did not meet the expectations that she was largely responsible for creating, atleast in part because of the public humiliation she heaped on them (Loomis, 2005).

Surprisingly, at least in some collectivistic cultures, subordinates sometimes view public humiliation in front of peers and coworkers very positively. For example, subordinates in Japan will tend to react more positively to a manager who chastises them harshly than will their U.S. counterparts because the manager's behaviour is seen as a sign of genuine care and consideration (Bond, Wan, Leung, & Giacalone, 1985). Similarly, Adler (2002) described an overbearing Filipino working in the Royal Bank of Canada who closely supervised Canadian subordinates and treated them severely.

When a superior of the Filipino discussed the matter with him, the superior learned that many Filipinos view such a managerial style as reflective of deep concern for subordinates. Also, Gausden (2003) analyzed feedback among Albanians, who tend to be collectivistic. She confirmed that the Albanians she studied viewed strictly positive feedback as having no value.

While such empirical results concerning authority-ranking cultures have been uniformly reported in the research literature, seasoned observers have pointed out that some collectivistic cultures would regard negative chastisement in public as humiliating to subordinates. For example, in macho collectivistic cultures in Africa and Latin America, such behaviour by a leader would be viewed as a personal attack and an affront. And if economic development is related to the rise of individualism, we can expect to see a more negative reaction to such leadership behaviours.

As Gary Oddou and Raj Pillai have pointed out (personal communication), the predictors of effective leadership, such as empathy, the ability to work with others, and flexibility, may be identical across cultures. However, their *surface* features, or the manner in which the leader implements these predictors, vary enormously by culture. This is consistent with the distinction between cultural universals and cultural specifics. For example, the GLOBE study concluded that individualized consideration, which is a component of transformational leadership, was manifested as concern for the employee and the person's extended family in China and Mexico; the same concern would constitute an invasion of privacy in the United States. On the other hand, behaviour such as complimenting a female job applicant or peer on her appearance is illegal in the United States but not in other nations. Hence, it is probably wise for visitors to withhold judgements and evaluations when crossing and communicating with other cultures until they are able to understand the entire situation clearly.

Conclusion

As the speed of globalization increases, as companies become flatter, and as firms engage in temporary organizations like JVs, there is a corresponding increase in the need for cross-cultural leadership. This goal of further research and publication is to explore cross-cultural leadership in the 21st century.

Is cross-cultural leadership a learned behaviors, and if it is what are its attributes and dimensions? If people are to learn this behaviour, what genetic personal characteristics should they have, if any, and what skills must they learn? In learning cross-cultural leadership skills, what metrics and techniques would be useful in training and preparing leaders to function in this new global market place?

Cross-cultural leaders must be flexible, and must be able to have an impact on followers outside of their own physical workplace, and their own firm. They will need to know how to lead, but they must also understand how to lay down the mantle of leadership and then follow when the situation requires.

Group Behaviour

Many fascinating research studies focus on small-group behavior. For example, some groups include "token minorities," whose status is questionable until the percentage of minorities increases to 20%. Automatically, it seems, such individuals are no longer perceived as tokens. Similarly, groups frequently tend to follow the *linear four-step pattern* of:

- forming, or deciding who will be a member of the group, getting to know one another, and defining precisely what the group is going to do;
- storming, or debating and fighting over specific priorities and tasks;
- norming, or creating standards and mutual expectations that group members should follow in discussions and in completing tasks;
- Performing.

In this section we discuss three key paradoxes focusing on the relationship between culture and group behaviour.

Paradox 1: Do groups contain free riders, or are all members equally responsible contributors?

At least since the time of Aristotle, writers have commented on the *free rider effect* found in groups. In small groups, this effect is evident. That is, if there is no way of assigning individual responsibility, one or more members of the small team will not do their equitable share of the work, thus forcing other members of the group to pick up the slack. It is for this reason that peer-group ratings frequently accompany group projects, both in industry and in other settings, such as colleges and universities.

Also, as the size of the group increases and assigning individual responsibility becomes increasingly difficult, the free rider effect seems to strengthen.

For example, many members of labor unions willingly contribute monthly dues but rarely attend union meetings, and many more people watch public television than contribute money to support it (Olson, 1971).

When culture is introduced into the equation, the free rider effect found in individualistic, market-pricing cultures is reversed. That is, in collectivistic, authority-ranking cultures, individuals work harder in groups than they do if they work alone (Steers & Sanchez-Runde, 2002). Karau and Williams (1993) completed a meta-analysis of 147 social loafing effects from studies completed in the United States and 15 effects obtained in collectivistic Pacific Island nations. They confirmed that on complex tasks, the results reported by Steers and Sanchez-Runde held, as expected. This pattern is consistent with our perspective on collectivism, which makes it difficult for the individual to be considered a separate entity apart from the group. Understanding the role of individualistic and collectivistic cultures, and whether individuals within each of these two cultures possess values consistent with the values of their cultures, helps us to see why the free rider effect is influenced by culture.

Such consistency predicts whether the outcome will be free riding or the active acceptance of group goals (Earley, 1993).

Paradox 2: In general and in small groups, do the personalities of individuals primarily reflect the influence of culture?

There are, however, individual personalities that deviate from the values of a specific culture. It is possible to discern individualistic personalities within collectivistic cultures and collectivistic personalities within individualistic cultures. You may want to obtain a very rough estimate of the individualism collectivism dimension of your own personality by listing 20 items, adjectives, and brief descriptions in response to the phrase "I am . . ." before reading the next paragraph.

At this individual level of analysis, collectivists tend to emphasize group oriented items, such as being a member of a family, church, or social club. Individualists, on the other hand, tend to stress person-centred items such as being achievement oriented, personally responsible, and personable. There is no magic number to be derived from the "20 items" exercise, but it does provide a rough measure of a person's tendency to favour either collectivism or individualism.

When personalities interact within either individualistic or collectivistic small groups, the results generally support the criticality of culture. A collectivistic personality strives harder in a collectivistic than in an individualistic small group, and an individualistic personality is less co-operative in an individualistic small group than in a collectivistic small group (Chatman & Barsade, 1995). It appears that individualists will adapt to collectivistic norms if they want to be accepted by the group, while collectivists begin to adopt a more individualistic orientation while in individualistic groups.

De Mooij (2005) points out that East Asians, who tend to be collectivistic, believe in the continuous shaping of personality traits by situational influences. They do not make a sharp distinction between the individual and the situation. Indeed, collectivistic cultures throughout the world tend to follow this pattern. Conversely, a Western personality assumes a norm of consistency and acting in character rather than being shaped by the situation and acting differently in different situations (see also Smith, Bond, & Kagitcibasi, 2006, Chapter 6). Such a viewpoint is consistent with the values of individualistic cultures. Similarly, Allik and McCrae (2004) have demonstrated that geographic clusters of nations exhibit sharply different personality profiles.

Paradox 13: Should multicultural small groups be managed differently from single-culture groups?

Kenwyn Smith and David Berg (1987) have developed some counterintuitive concepts about the functioning and management of multicultural small groups. In a single-culture small group, the emphasis is understandably on the similarities of group members, the open recognition of which allows the group members to establish common norms quickly and to work together very efficiently. Smith and Berg point out those similarities are frequently nonexistent in multicultural small groups, where differences predominate.

As a result, these researchers have developed a three-phase process to enhance the functioning of multicultural small groups. In the first phase, learning how to learn together, they ask group members to describe situations in which they learned something of value. An answer might describe an open sharing of information in an atmosphere encouraging and rewarding learning, for example. They then ask group members to describe situations in which learning was inhibited, which might elicit situations when time was consumed pandering to inflated egos and a climate of blame prevailed.

The second phase, discovering members' unique cultural contributions, can be addressed in many ways, such as asking group members to describe the major events in their home cultures during the past decade. Typically the descriptions vary widely, leading members to acknowledge that their knowledge of other cultures is limited. During the third phase, exploring group polarities, Smith and Berg (1987) ask each member to list 8–10 sacred, or major, rules for the way small groups should function in the member's home culture. Next, each member sits with a member from another culture to discuss their respective sacred rules, after which there is a group discussion.

As in the case of the nine dilemmas of leadership described in Paradox 1, this three-phase process appears to result in a description of dilemmas that small groups face, such as an emphasis on collectivism or individualism; autocratic *versus* participative decision making; spontaneous *versus* orchestrated decisions decided before the meeting, with the meeting serving only to legitimate them; task orientation *versus* process orientation; and quality versus quantity of actions taken. Smith and Berg (1987) argued that the group, by openly acknowledging these polarities, is now positioned to take actions that incorporate each element of each polarity.

Whether complete success in the functioning of each small multicultural group is attained is beside the point. Rather, the movement is away from a linear and non-paradoxical way of thinking to a nonlinear way of thinking that accepts paradoxes openly. Just this open acknowledgment of polarities and the need to integrate each element of the paradox should facilitate the group's dynamics, at least in many instances. Still, the paradoxes that Smith and Berg (1987) identified are of a special type, namely, dilemmas. It may simply not be possible to integrate both elements of each polarity, even when there is open acknowledgment of their existence.

This paradox, as well as the others described in this chapter, confirms that perception, leadership, motivation, and actual behavior differ significantly across cultures, particularly when we compare collectivistic, authority-ranking cultures and individualistic, market-pricing cultures.

Takeaways

1. Leadership is a dilemma, and an individual should recognize this fact before accepting any leadership position that might be uncomfortable without such understanding. From this

perspective, leaders perform two key roles: polarity management, or balancing both sides of a dilemma smoothly, and ambiguity management.

2. There are some cultural universals that characterize effective leaders across cultures, but there are also some cultural specifics of leadership behaviour that work well in some cultures but not others. There are also some leadership practices, such as lying and being ruthless, that are universally seen as reprehensible.
3. Charismatic leadership as described in this chapter is not a necessary prerequisite for effective visionary and transformational leadership.
4. While the four generic types of cultures are clearly separable from one another, it is possible to integrate at least some of them in actual situations, as in the case of Carlos Ghosn at Nissan.
5. There are strengths and weaknesses associated with each of the four types of cultures, and emphasizing one type to the complete exclusion of the other three types can be problematic in many instances.
6. Assumptions about motivation vary by culture, especially in regard to whether the critical relationship between motivation and ability is additive or multiplicative.
7. The dimension of individualism-collectivism without reference to any other dimensions is very useful for understanding many cross-cultural issues in such areas as leadership, motivation, and group behaviour.
8. Individualistic cultures display a greater tendency toward free riding in small groups than collectivistic cultures do.

Exercises

1. Class members should each identify an organization about which they are knowledgeable and draw nine charts to explore Thomas Stewart's framework for nine leadership dilemmas. The charts can be shared with another class member or the entire class. Also, this exercise can form the basis of a written assignment focusing on why the charts have been constructed in specific ways, the general profile that emerges of both leadership and the organization, and the conclusions or recommendations to management that can be derived.

2. In this chapter, several exercises were suggested, including the identification of personal metaphors for leadership and the "20 items" relating to individualism and collectivism. Each small group in the subdivided class can discuss these two exercises and the differential responses they generated, and report back to the entire class what they have learned.

3. You are a first-line supervisor in a production company. As you are observing the factory floor, you notice that one employee is working with his safety guard up. Such a practice speeds up the work and makes it easier for the worker to complete the tasks. However, having the safety guard up is a serious violation and has resulted in several accidents. As he sees you, he immediately puts the safety guard down. How would you expect the first-line supervisor, as a leader, to respond in the four types of generic cultures (community sharing, authority ranking, equality matching, and market pricing) to handle this situation? Would the leader immediately confront the worker and punish him with a 3-day layoff, as required? Would the leader take the worker aside and talk to him about the dangers but still give the layoff? Would the leader take the worker aside and discuss the matter with him, holding off on any action until he hears what the worker says? Would the leader chastise the worker in front of other workers and use him as an example? What else could the leader of each selected generic culture do that would be consistent with the values of the culture?

The instructor may choose to focus a general class discussion on this topic or to form small groups and let each of them appoint a recorder to report back to the entire class, followed by discussion.

Answers to the Two-Item Survey

For the Gelfand-Holcombe two-item survey in the chapter the corresponding answers for the first item are c, community sharing; d, authority ranking; a, equality matching; and b, market pricing.

For the second item, the answers are: a, community sharing; d, authority ranking; c, equality matching; and b, market pricing.

❄ ❄ ❄

8 Motivation

- Cultures • Theories of Motivation • Implications for Managers • Culture Effect on Motivation
- Motivation Strategies

Motivation Across Cultures

The Nature of Motivation

- Motivation
- Psychological process through which unsatisfied wants or needs lead to drives that are aimed at goals or incentives
- Universalistic assumption
- All people are motivated to pursue goals they value
- Specific content of the goals that are pursued will be influenced by culture
- Movement toward market economies may make motivation more similar in different countries.

Figure 8.1

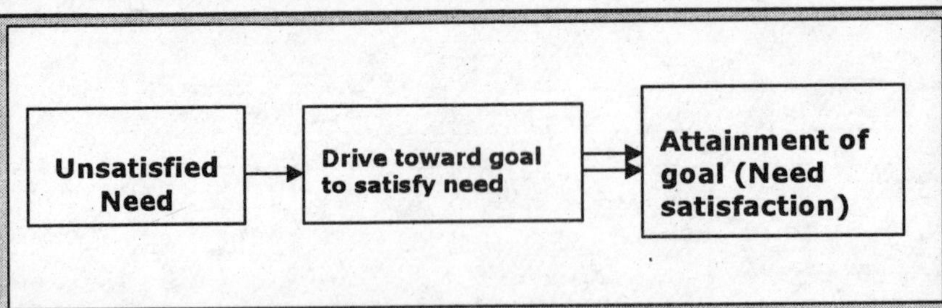

The Basic Motivation Process

Motivation is "the amount of effort that an individual puts into doing something".

Two basic types of theories explain motivation: content and process.

Content Theories focus on the "what," identifying factors that causes people to put effort into work'.

Content theories explain work motivation in terms of what arouses, energizes, or initiates employee behavior.

Content motivation theories have been given much more attention in international management research, because they provide the opportunity to create a composite picture for motivation of human resources in a particular country or region of the world. In addition, content theories apply more directly to providing ways for managers to improve the performance of their human resources.

Maslow's Hierarchy of Needs

According to Abraham Maslow every person has five basic needs:

- Physiological needs - food, clothing, shelter, and other basic physical needs
- Safety needs - desire for security, stability, and the absence of pain
- Social needs - need to interact and affiliate with others and the need to feel wanted by others

- Esteem needs - needs for power and status
- Self-actualization needs - desire to reach one's full potential by becoming everything one is capable of becoming.

Lower level needs must be satisfied before higher level needs become motivators and once satisfied; a need is no longer a motivator. Maslow's hierarchy-of-needs theory given below has been studied in a number of different countries. Researchers have found that regardless of country, managers have to be concerned with the satisfaction of these needs for their human resources.

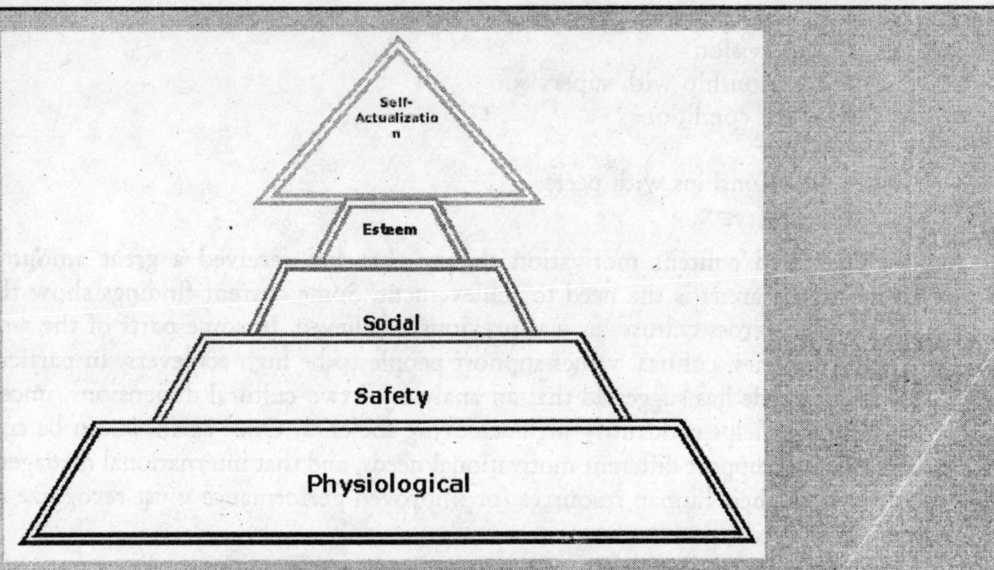

Maslow's Need Hierarchy

Figure 8.2

International Findings on Maslow's Theory

People throughout the world have needs similar to those described in the hierarchy. Each country or geographic region appears to have its own need-satisfaction profile Limitations on the theory's applicability

May have to re-rank the needs A single hierarchy may not reflect subcultures within a given culture. Theory is not sufficient alone for identifying motivational factors in international management

Some researchers have suggested that satisfaction profiles are not very useful for studying motivation in an international setting, because there are so many different subcultures within any country or even at different levels of a given organization. These researchers have suggested that job categories are more effective for examining motivation, because job level (managers versus operating employees) and the need hierarchy have an established relationship.

Like Maslow's theory, Hertzberg's two-factor theory has received considerable attention in the international arena, and his original findings from the United States have been replicated in other countries. Cross-cultural studies related to job satisfaction also have been conducted. Most of the studies reveal that job content is more important than job context to job satisfaction.

Hertzberg's Motivation -Hygiene Theory

Theory that holds there are two sets of factors-motivation and hygiene factors, which influence job satisfaction.

Motivation factors which are job content factors and include:

- Achievement
- Recognition
- Interesting work

- Responsibility
- Advancement
- Growth.

Hygiene factors which are job context variables and if absent produce dissatisfaction but not satisfaction.

Hygiene Factors which are job context variable include:

- Company policy and administration
- Supervision
- Relationship with supervisor
- Work conditions
- Salary
- Relationships with peers
- Security.

The third content motivation theory that has received a great amount of attention in the international arena is the need to achievement. Some current findings show that this need is not as widely held across cultures as was previously believed. In some parts of the world, however, such as Anglo countries, cultural values support people to be high achievers. In particular, Dutch researcher Geert Hofstede has suggested that an analysis of two cultural dimensions, uncertainty avoidance and masculinity, helps to identify high-achieving societies. Once again, it can be concluded that different cultures will support different motivational needs, and that international managers developing strategies to motivate their human resources for improved performance must recognize cultural differences.

McClelland's Needs Theory

Need for Achievement - Concern for establishing and maintaining high levels of performance quality

Need for Power - Concern for reputation, responsibility, influence, impact, and control over others

Need for Affiliation - Concern for establishing and maintaining social relationships.

Conclusions about the Content Theories

- Restrict explanations of motivation to a particular set of factors and how these motivate people
- Lack of conclusive research support
- Identify concepts useful for gaining a better understanding of motivation
- Valuable starting point for examining cultural and individual differences in motivation.

Process Theories

Process theories explain work motivation by how employee behavior is initiated, redirected, and halted.

Process theories have also contributed to the understanding of motivation in the international arena. Equity theory focuses on how motivation is affected by people's perception of how fairly they are being treated and there is considerable research to support the fundamental equity principle in Western work groups. However, when the theory is examined on an international basis the results are mixed. Perhaps, the biggest shortcoming of the theory is that it appears to be culture bound. For example, in countries like Japan and Korea, men and women typically receive different pay for doing precisely the same work and this atleast traditionally does not perceive as inequitable to women.

- Concern the "how," the steps an individual takes in putting forth effort
- Attempt to discover universal mechanisms to explain motivation
- Can incorporate specific cultural and other factors into the models to motivate individuals.

Reinforcement Theory

- Giving a reward/reinforce increases the likelihood that a behaviour will be repeated
- Ignoring behaviour increases the likelihood that it will not be repeated
- Punishment usually puts an immediate end to a behavior but does not guarantee it will stop in the long run.

Goal Setting Theory

Goal-setting theory focuses on how individuals go about setting goals and responding to them and the overall impact of this process on motivation. There is evidence showing that employees perform extremely well when they are assigned specific and challenging goals that they made a contribution in setting. On the other hand, most of the goal-setting studies have been conducted in the U.S.; few of them have been carried out in other cultures. Additionally, research results on the effects of goal-setting at the individual level are very limited and culture may well account for these outcomes.

. Higher performance can be achieved by setting goals that are specific, rather than vague.

- Difficult, but achievable, rather than easy
- Giving feedback, rather than no feedback
- Effectiveness of theory depends on commitment to goal
- Self-efficacy.

Expectancy theory postulates that motivation is largely influenced by a multiplicative combination of a person's belief that effort will lead to performance, that performance will lead to specific outcomes, and that these outcomes are valued by the individual. There is mixed support for this theory's value. Many researchers believe that the theory best explains motivation in those countries that emphasize an internal focus of control.

Expectancy Theory

Postulates that motivation is influenced by a person's belief that effort will lead to performance, performance will lead to specific outcomes, and that these outcomes are valued by the individual. Theory appears to be culture bound. Best able to explain motivation in cultures where the locus of control is high.

Job Design

A job's content, the methods that are used on the job, and the way the job relates to others in the organization.

Quality of Work Life (QWL)

All job designs tend to reflect the cultural values of the country.

Socio Technical Designs

- Designs that blend the personnel and the technology
- Attempt to integrate technology in a suitable manner from the standpoint of the workers
- Mixed results in terms of effects on efficiency
- Cultural values must support the approach to job design.

Work Centrality

- Importance of work in an individual's life relative to other areas of interest
- Countries differ in the centrality of work
- Value of Work
- Many misconceptions about the value of work in a culture
- Availability of incentives to work confounds notions about the value of work in a society.

Job Satisfaction

- Differs among samples of workers from different countries
- Reward Systems
- Managers everywhere use rewards to motivate performance
- Significant differences exist among the reward systems used in different countries.

Incentives and Culture

- Financial incentives common across cultures
- Emphases on equity and equality differs
- The effectiveness of other incentives appear to be culturally influenced
- Culture may affect the overall cost of an incentive system.

Conclusions about the Process Theories

- More effective than content theories in explaining motivational constructs that can apply globally
- Must consider cultural variations to enhance the applicability of a particular model
- Achieve a deeper level of analysis and allow for individual differences.

Culture and Rewards

- Individual *versus* group
- Masculine *versus* feminine
- Gifts *versus* rewards for performance
- Individual preferences within cultures

Organizational Reward Practices

- Appropriate rewards can be motivating
- Non-cash rewards popular in some companies
- Europe companies using more variable compensation and flexible benefits
- Companies can develop rewards that are unique to their business.

Convergence or Divergence?

- Popularity of U.S. business education leads to an emphasis on U.S. motivation theories
- Global corporations desire to develop consistent policies and practices world-wide
- Application of U.S. motivation theories not applicable across cultures
- Need to develop adaptable systems that are consistent and effective in motivating people across cultures.

Implications for Managers

- Choosing an approach to motivation is difficult
- Process theories appear more promising than content theories
- Need to understand people who work for you to select an appropriate system.

Although content and process theories provide important insights into the motivation of human resources, three additional areas that have received a great deal of recent attention in the application of motivation are job design, work centrality, and reward systems. Job design is influenced by culture as well as the specific methods that are used to bring together the people and the work. Work centrality helps to explain the importance of work in an individual's life relative to other areas of interest. In recent years work has become a relatively greater part of the average Japanese worker's life. Research also indicates that Japanese office workers are less satisfied with their jobs that are U.S., Canadian, and EU workers, suggesting that MNCs need to design motivation packages that address the specific needs of different cultures. This idea is also true in the case of rewards. Research shows that the motivational value of monetary and non-monetary rewards is influenced by culture. Countries with high individualism such as the U.S. and the U.K. tend to make wide use of individual incentives, while collectivistic countries such as Asia tend to prefer group-oriented incentives. At the same time, research shows that some motivational approaches in the U.S. have been successfully used in Russia. So while the importance of focusing on the importance of motivation in the international arena is unquestioned, the use of specific applications continues to be challenging for MNC managers.

Culture Affect on Motivation

When high-tech employees and managers from India, the US and other cultural backgrounds are thrown together in the intense environment of Silicon Valley, they often bring with them divergent expectations about workplace success factors, rewards and career development as well as differences in motivational "wiring."

Understanding these differences and adapting appropriately can be a key strategy for managers and employees alike. Failure to do so can lead to costly misunderstandings.

Five major differences in the following areas create the greatest challenges: management styles, job security and compensation structures, career development, performance evaluation, and motivational strategies.

Management Styles

American employees react well to a boss who is friendly and professional with them, treats them as equals, and expects them to be independent and self-motivated. Managers and employees do not expect the boss-subordinate relationship to be strongly hierarchical, or to be one of strongly committed personal loyalty: it is all about mutual respect. This can create a mismatch for employees from India, for whom a more quasi-paternal relationship is more the norm.

Job Security and Compensation structures

The US has been through a workplace revolution in which expectations of job security with a lifetime employer has been replaced by loyalty to one's career and the attempt to maximize one's earnings. This results in a common acceptance of modest a base salary but a high bonus-earning potential. A common complaint I have heard from Silicon Valley employers has been about the discomfort of their employees from India with such an arrangement, with a strong preference for security over higher-stake risk.

Career Development

A very common American manager's question to an employee is: "What are your career plans?" This question, which embodies the mutual expectation that employees take independent responsibility for their professional advancement, runs counter to the expectations of work cultures in many other countries, including India, where the expectation is that it is the boss's responsibility to look out for and decide on an employee's future.

Performance Evaluation

The performance evaluation process of US companies today is a major culture shock for employees and managers from elsewhere. Highly formalized, it is based on mutually agreed-upon goals, involves forthright discussion of strengths and weaknesses, and has a formal written sign-off. Elsewhere, there may be informally conducted reviews with mentoring counsel, or a pattern of reprimands. The cultural problems of adaptation on all sides are considerable: the American way seems confrontational and legalistic to others, Americans feel insecure with methods that have less clarity.

Motivational strategies

When it comes to motivation, no one strategy works for everyone — even within one culture. Across cultures, it's even more difficult. With Americans, a manager shouldn't expect much from appeals to duty, authority, company loyalty, group rewards or regular after-work socializing. Instead, he or she should emphasize opportunities for personal growth and monetary gain. With employees from India, personal loyalty, company prestige and appeal to authority can be effective, but above all, the manager should cultivate a certain "human touch" in relating to the needs of subordinates, as their guide and friend as well as their well wisher.

Regardless of whether the relationship between the leader and subordinates is one-way or two-way, leadership involves motivation. More specifically, how do leaders in different cultures motivate their subordinates?

Paradox 1: Is the relationship between motivation and ability additive or multiplicative in the prediction of individual success and performance?

One of the most fascinating paradoxes in the cross-cultural arena revolves around the issue of performance and success among individuals in both their organizations and their careers. At this point I invite you to assess the relationship between ability and motivation (sometimes thought of as effort) as either multiplicative or additive in terms of explaining the performance and success of individuals. This may seem like a trivial request, but as we will see, it is pivotal in the area of motivating across cultures.

In market-pricing generic cultures, Paradox 5 nestles in perhaps the most general theory of motivation: the expectancy theory. Simply stated, its basic postulate is that individuals must *perceive* that:

- They have the proper resources, skills, and abilities to be successful.
- If they make a given effort (motivation), they will be successful and will be rewarded.
- The rewards are ones they desire.

Collectivistic cultures, particularly authority-ranking cultures, tend to assume that the relationship between ability and motivation, or effort, is additive. Conversely, individualistic cultures, particularly market-pricing cultures, tend to assume that the relationship between ability and motivation is multiplicative (Triandis, 2002). It is difficult to overestimate the salience of this distinction.

For example, on a standard 10-point scale, receiving a 6 for both ability and motivation would give a score of only 12 for an additive relationship but 36 for a multiplicative relationship. In other words, individualistic, market-pricing cultures generally expect far more from their managers and workers than do collectivistic, authority-ranking cultures, at least in terms of putting forth maximum effort, thereby achieving a higher score for the relationship between ability and motivation. This, in turn, increases the total score or level of performance expected.

There are many programs and systems directly related to this emphasis on a multiplicative relationship between ability and motivation in individualistic market-pricing national cultures. In the United States, for instance, there is a strong belief that equality of opportunity but not equality of outcomes should prevail (Stewart & Bennett, 1991). Also, such well-known programs as "pay for performance" and "management by objectives" originated in the United States. They clearly suggest that individuals should be compensated for their levels of performance and that motivation or effort can dramatically influence performance.

Most probably, the contrasting cross-cultural leadership frameworks employed in our discussion of this paradox significantly influence whether there is a multiplicative or additive relationship between ability and motivation, or effort. As indicated previously, the authority-ranking culture sees the organization as a family in which the relationship between superior and subordinates is psychological and two-way in nature. In such cultures there is even a tendency to avoid rating and ranking managers and employees who must work with one another for 30 or more years. Statements of "average performance" or "above-average performance," at least in part because they save face for the superior and subordinates, are common. By contrast, individualistic cultures, particularly those emphasizing market pricing, are well-known for regularly and systematically rating and ranking organizational members and being far less concerned with saving face. For instance, the emphasis at GE on a 20/70/

10 performance evaluation system has been copied by many other organizations in the United States and elsewhere. As discussed previously, 20% of the managers receive disproportionate rewards, 70% adequate rewards, and 10% few if any rewards. However, an excessive emphasis on the 20/70/10 system is controversial, in both theory and practice, and organizational members have sued their companies in some instances.

In the case of leadership, numerous empirical studies have tested various theories of motivation and hypotheses derived from them. However, when culture is included in the framework, the relationship between ability and motivation is assumed to be significantly different.

Paradox 2: Can an individually based need hierarchy exist in a collectivistic culture?

It is useful to contrast two general types of motivational theories. The first focuses on the *process* of the motivational system used. Expectancy theory, discussed above, represents one of the major types of theories in this category. The second type emphasizes *internal states* such as the assumed needs and the concepts motivating individuals to behave in a particular fashion. Abraham Maslow (1970) proposed one of the best-known needs theories. He essentially posited that an individual must satisfy needs sequentially, starting with the lowest level, physiological needs. The individual then proceeds to satisfy sequentially the remaining four levels: safety and security needs; love and belongingness needs, or social needs; esteem and self-esteem needs; and self-actualization needs, or realizing one's full potential.

In several management sessions in which I have been involved over the years, the trainer asks the executives to identify the theory that they have found most helpful in their organizations and careers. Maslow's needs hierarchy ranks at or near the top of the list. Many excellent studies have focused on this theory, and one well-accepted conclusion is that Maslow's five levels can be reduced to two levels. That is, individuals must satisfy their physiological and safety needs before they can consider satisfying the remaining, higher-order needs. Hence, the hierarchy consists of only two levels. The assumption of sequencing extends to only these two levels and not to the original five levels proposed by Maslow.

As our discussion of leadership theory has indicated, however, market pricing cultures tend to focus on the following: individual responsibility, a one-way relationship extending from leaders to the subordinates they are attempting to motivate, and an emphasis on high expectations as demonstrated in the multiplicative assumption between motivation (effort) and ability.

Authority-ranking cultures emphasize a family model that is two-way between the leader and subordinates in terms of obligations and responsibilities, and an additive relationship between motivation (effort) and ability.

Such differences are important when considering the cross-cultural dimension of individualism-collectivism. In the studies scoring and ranking national cultures on this dimension, many Western nations, such as the United States, Germany, Sweden, and France, tend to rank higher on individualism than on collectivism. The opposite situation exists for many non-Western nations, whose citizens stress collectivism.

Generally speaking, collectivism emphasizes the primacy of social needs and obligations. Individuals will tend to make decisions acceptable to the larger community and kinship groups in which they reside, even when they must sacrifice their own desires and needs. They tend to see themselves as dependent on and embedded in such groups. Individualism is the exact opposite: Individuals make decisions maximizing their own self-interests, and they view themselves as distinct entities apart from the groups in which they interact.

These patterns imply that motivation in authority-ranking cultures is different from motivation in market-pricing cultures, and at least some research supports this interpretation. Iyengar (1998; see also Iyengar & Lepper, 1999) found that children of European-American backgrounds were more motivated when they had a choice and showed less motivation when the choice was made for them by either authority figures or peers. Asian-American children, however, were more motivated when trusted authority figures or peers made decisions on their behalf. Similarly Yu and Yang (1994) showed that achievement motivation in authority-ranking cultures accords primacy to group needs, even when the individual must suffer. In addition, Yu (1996) developed separate measures of individually oriented and socially oriented achievement and found them to be largely independent of one another among respondents from China. Those who possess a high degree of socially oriented achievement tend to look to others in the group to define goals.

Admittedly, motivation is a murky area, but our analysis suggests that its primary sources in collectivistic, authority-ranking cultures are social, while in individualistic, market-pricing cultures, such sources are person specific and ego centered. There are, of course, commonalities in motivation across cultures. For example, people generally want to be treated equitably and receive adequate rewards, but notions about equity and adequate rewards differ radically between market-pricing and authority-ranking cultures.

Still, the remaining paradoxes in this chapter reinforce and support this interpretation of differential motivation in market-pricing and authority-ranking cultures.

Paradox 3: Do effective executives attribute success to themselves or to others?

While leadership and motivation are closely related, it is difficult to understand them without reference to *attribution theory*. This theory essentially explores the manner in which people integrate the various perceptions and stimuli they experience, after which they make generalizations or attributions about personal responsibilities, happenings, and environmental phenomena.

Of particular interest are the *fundamental attribution error* and its derivative, the *self-serving bias*. This error is generally understood to involve attributing success or failure to one or two of three possible causes: oneself; others, including subordinates, superiors, and peers; and the environment or situation. When a person in an individualistic, market-pricing culture is successful, there is a self-serving bias, or a tendency to attribute the success to the individual's own efforts and to de-emphasize the efforts of others and the impact of the environment or situation. For example, a newly appointed CEO may take the major credit for a company's success, even when it is the result of the painstaking work of many organizational members and the strategic decisions of the previous CEO or when global demand for a company's products unexpectedly rises. Conversely, when the person is unsuccessful, there is a self-serving tendency to blame the environment or others in the situation or both.

These results are not surprising, given our previous discussion of the relationship of ability and motivation, or effort, as either multiplicative or additive.

Almost all the studies focusing on the fundamental attribution error have involved individuals from individualistic, market-pricing cultures. When someone succeeds in such a culture, it is assumed that the relationship between ability and motivation, or effort, is multiplicative, with effort dramatically altering the results. However, when culture is introduced into the equation, the results change dramatically.

Specifically, collectivistic, authority-ranking cultures also exhibit a fundamental attribution error but not a self-serving bias. In such cultures, when individuals succeed, they attribute their success largely to the work of others, such as subordinates, mentors, peers, and superiors. When they fail, however, they accept the responsibility and blame and argue that neither others nor the environment is a causative factor (Steers & Sanchez-Runde, 2002). In point of fact, the individuals may not be responsible for the failure and may have been a major causative factor for the success, but they incorrectly credit causative factors that seemingly do not serve their personal interests.

Korea stands as an exemplar of this type of perceptual framework. This nation, with its focus on a collectivistic, authority-ranking society, has deep Confucian roots. A study comparing Americans and Koreans found a self serving bias in the American sample but not in the Korean sample (Nam, 1991). Behaviour found in many Korean firms confirms the underlying model of the corporation as a family and the non-self-serving attribution error that appears to emerge because of it. For instance, in 2001 the Daewoo Motor Company was facing bankruptcy, and Lee Jon Dae, its chairman, had to authorize a downsizing of 7,000 employees. His subsequent extraordinary actions seemed to indicate that he was responsible for the unfortunate condition of the company. This was not accurate, as its founder was largely responsible and had fled the country with company funds (and is now in a Korean prison). Mr. Dae's actions included enlisting politicians in a public endorsement of buying Daewoo cars; asking each politician to buy a Daewoo car; sending a personal letter to his counterparts at 26,000 companies, begging each of them to hire at least one of his downsized employees; and abjectly bowing to a downsized employee at a job fair the company organized and profusely apologizing to him for having to lay him off. The employee was surprised at such total acceptance of responsibility and consoled Mr. Dae with the statement that the downsizing was not his fault. Such CEO behaviour is virtually unthinkable in the United States.

Gelfand et al. (2002) compared the collectivistic Japanese culture and the individualistic U.S. culture empirically in terms of their relative egotistic perceptions of fairness in negotiations within Japan and the United States. Their result strongly supported the self-serving bias found in the United States (taking credit for success but blaming others or the environment or both for failure) but much less so in Japan. Given our discussion of individualistic and collectivistic cultures, these results are expected. But the statistical support for them indicates that the self-serving bias is stronger than expected. There are, then, clear linskages between leadership, motivation, and perceptions across cultures. Such differences help explain actual behaviors, as highlighted in our final section.

❄ ❄ ❄

9 Strategic Human Resource Management

• Strategic Human Resource Management • Recent Developments • Human Capital Management (HCM) • Talent Management - The New SHRM Imperative • Benchmarking for SHRM • SHRM in Different Cultures

Organizational strategy refers to the overall positioning and competitive approach of an organization in the marketplace. Strategic management is the deliberate effort to align the organization's long-term direction with organizational strategy. Good strategic management integrates organizational functions into a strategic plan so that all organizational units operate in a co-ordinated fashion in support of the overall strategy.

Strategic Human Resource Management (SHRM), then, is the process by which an organization's management integrates its human resource plans and programs with the strategic plan of the organization. SHRM stands in contrast to traditional human resource management (HRM), which contributes to an organization at the operational level. For example, the traditional human resource (HR) concern of selecting job applicants who display skills that are predictive of good job performance may only be implicitly related to the strategic objectives of the organization.

A key feature of SHRM is the linkage formed between management and HR to align the functions of HR with the direction of the organization. SHRM links human resources vertically and horizontally as well as in present and future time-frames. Vertical linkages entail connecting HR practices with the strategic management process of the organization, while horizontal linkages involve the coordination of various practices within HR through a patterned or planned action. HR strategies are linked to organizational plans, anticipated HR needs, and to HR programs that will be implemented to meet those needs. SHRM involves multiple HR processes, such as recruiting, selection, performance management, employee and career development, succession planning, retirement, and termination. Each of these can be linked to an organization's strategic objectives.

For example, a planned business expansion into Eastern Europe could be supported by strategic employee development (e.g., providing language and cultural training to key employees to prepare them to meet business needs) or by strategic recruitment and selection (e.g., hiring Eastern European employees prior to the expansion).

Steps in SHRM

SHRM involves three steps: forecasting, strategy formulation, and implementation.

Forecasting is the attempt to predict future events that will impact the organization and its needs through the analyses of the organization's internal and external environments (e.g., mission statement, goals, labor markets, opportunities and threats).

HR strategy formulation – that is, strategic human resource planning (SHRP) – involves the development of initiatives that are aligned with the organization's, mission statement, strategic objectives, strengths and weaknesses, and opportunities and threats.

Finally, HR strategy implementation involves putting the HR plan into action with HR programs that support the organization's overall strategy.

Forecasting

Predictability and control increase the precision of forecasting. Predictability is the degree to which one can estimate the occurrence of an event, and control is the ability to orchestrate the likelihood of an event occurring. Greater control implies greater predictability, although some events over which one has little or no control are predictable. Predictability and control have important implications for how forecasting should be approached. Forecasting is more effective when forecasting techniques are compatible with levels of predictability and control. For simplicity, it is appropriate to distinguish among four levels of predictability and control. The first consists of events over which an organization has control — for example, closing outdated plants and scheduling layoffs. The second level involves events over which the organization has little control but which are nevertheless predictable. For example, in some countries organizations can predict retirements with a high degree of certainty because of government mandated retirement ages. The third level consists of events that are probabilistic. Although they can be anticipated by extrapolating from historical trends, they involve a low to moderate degree of certainty because extraneous factors often alter previous patterns and because the limits to human rationality constrain the degree to which such events can be predicted. An example would be predicting skill sets that could have strategic implications. The fourth level involves events that are unknown, unanticipated, or random. These can include, for example, the unexpected death of a CEO or the introduction of new technologies that dramatically change labour requirements.

To be most effective, forecasting techniques should be congruent with the degree of uncertainty in a system. The greater the predictability and control of events, the more specific predictions can be. Techniques that use productivity ratios (i.e., the ratio of labour to output) to forecast labour demand are appropriate for predictable situations because they are based on straightforward prediction equations and they forecast specific numbers of workers for given conditions. However, in situations with less predictability and control, it is not possible to make specific predictions, and therefore the most appropriate forecasting techniques are those that provide general information. Forecasting in less predictable situations might, for example, involve looking at historical cycles in workforce demand and supply or at trends in demand for skills sets. Finally, in situations where future events are unpredictable, planning for any particular outcome is unwise.

When forecasting is not possible, a diversity (or variation) strategy is the best approach. As financial analysts have known for years, a diverse investment portfolio is the best hedge against losing money due to the uncertainty of the stock market. Similarly, SHRM activities that focus on variation are the best insurance against uncertain futures. A diverse HR portfolio increases the probability that one of the variants may prove useful for unexpected contingencies. Examples of HR programs that foster variation include allowing employees to choose a certain proportion of their yearly training courses; randomly selecting job applicants from a generous short-list of those who meet basic qualifications; formalizing structures that encourage frequent informal interaction; instituting more lenient performance management policies that do not punish employees who work in non-traditional ways and who think unconventionally.

HR Strategy Formulation

The HR strategy formulation phase is a complex process that involves making decisions about HR activities based on forecasts, organizational strategy, and the anticipated effects of HR programs on strategic objectives. An important process in SHRP is *linking* HR functions to other processes in the organization. The goal of linking is to establish a closer relationship between management and HR, and therefore increasing the likelihood of developing HR policies that are congruent with the organization's strategic objectives. Linkage is related to the amount of contact among the organization's strategic planners, the HR department, and the managers who will be responsible for executing the plans. Linkages can range from minimal (groups working independently) to full integration (groups working interdependently), but they are typically blended. For instance, information pertaining to hiring may flow both ways, whereas information regarding funding of projects might be handed down from the top management to HR.

The appropriate degree of linkage depends on the business climate, organizational needs, and corporate strategy; however, some linkage between HR and management is generally necessary. A disconnect between planners and managers can easily derail the planning and implementation processes. The probability of successful SHRP can be enhanced by starting with a simple plan (for example, forecasting the number of anticipated hires needed the following year based on typical levels of attrition at a given site). As leaders gain experience using simple forecasting models, and as those models provide useful data that integrates with and helps guide strategic business planning, the level of sophistication of the SHRP may increase. In some cases, however, it may never progress beyond a basic attrition-based replacement model; that may be all that's required under the circumstances. In other cases, complex algorithms based on multiple data sources may generate the needed (and useful) data. The point for HR to keep in mind is to use only what works and is needed — not more, and not less.

Implementation

Strategy implementation involves the integration of the larger organizational strategy into the HR functions of the organization, and it is arguably as – or more – complex than strategy formulation. Employee recruitment and selection, training and development, performance management, and labour and employee relations may all have to be altered by HR in order to integrate with the organizational strategy.

Unlike the formulation process, implementation is an organizational intervention; and organizational interventions require assistance – at the very least, co-operation – from members of the organization. Unfortunately, resistance to the planning process and to the strategic HR plan is a common outcome of planning, and therefore it must be managed appropriately. Resistance on the part of any group can be detrimental for strategy implementation. Resistance may stem from internal organizational politics, and it may influence the accuracy of the data that managers provide in the forecasting and planning stages. For example, managers interested in protecting turf or enhancing their unit's power may inflate their estimate of the number of new employees they need. In other cases, managers may just not respond to requests from HR for planning because of heavy workloads, competing business priorities, and uncertainty about future needs. Managers may view the outcome of SHRP as being of little value — because they view it as providing insufficient information to guide policy or business decisions (e.g., number of hires is given for a region, rather than an individual location or country; the types of skills, experience or education required are not described) or because they view it as so detailed that implementing it would be too burdensome (e.g., a plan calling for Master's level chemical engineers, with at least at a 3.27 grade point average, who have worked in the USA doing polymer chemistry to be split evenly across 5 sites in south-east Asia). In these cases, calls to implement the plan will probably be resisted or simply ignored. Strong relationships with business leaders, a good understanding of the business, and a willingness to modify plans where necessary are helpful in implementing strategic HR plans. Given the possibility of pushback from business leaders and lack of utilization of SHRM processes and plans, HR must take an active role in ensuring that the SHRM process is relatively painless and provides truly useful data to assist in business planning. Understanding what information business leaders need, what is actionable, and what is realistic are keys to making SHRM work. A strategic HR plan that is not, or cannot be, implemented is of no use to the organization.

Costs and Benefits in SHRM

If the success of any type of strategic planning is measured by the accuracy with which actual plans and forecasts come to pass, then the success rate of strategic planning is rather dismal. In most situations, managers and HR professionals cannot accurately forecast how the environment will change in the future and what specific HR capabilities will be needed to perform effectively in future environments. Planning involves assumptions about the environment and about the future. As environments become more complex, uncertainty increases and assumptions are more tenuous, and most organizations typically operate in complex social, political, and economic environments.

Fortunately for practitioners, empirical studies show a positive relationship between the use of SHRM and bottom-line outcomes, such as stock share price and employee productivity. In contrast, there does not appear to be a relationship between competent performance of technical HR duties and organizational performance. This underscores the importance of strategic, rather than technical, human resource management.

These successes of strategic planning may be due to a number of factors. One is that organizations may be tailoring their planning processes to uncertainty levels — planning more generally in more uncertain environments, which in turn produces adaptive outcomes (not all of which can be predicted). In addition, the planning process may be just as important, if not more important, than the plan itself. Organizations that engage in strategic HR planning are likely to have processes that require frequent interaction among executives, managers, and HR professionals. This means that the right people are talking about the right things at the right time. Plans themselves inevitably need updating and modification as circumstances dictate. Processes that modify and update plans help to ensure that plans stay relevant and useful.

Recent Developments

Globalization, technology, and diversity are recent developments that have had a significant impact on the process and use of SHRM. Globalization has brought with it increased competition and uncertainty, making future planning critical but increasingly difficult. The movement of people between countries has increased because of free trade agreements and visa programs. No longer is an organization limited to local hiring programs. Organizations can (and often should) consider regional, or even global, talent pools. Multinational organizations must plan not only for the needs of one country, but must consider the cumulative impact of events in all countries in which they operate. Recent discussions of off-shoring highlight the need to think about a company's talent management and planning in global terms. Technology has enabled instant, electronic collection of SHRM data and development of complex models to better predict human capital needs. However, it has also given rise to new forms of work (e.g., telecommuting, globally-distributed teams, 24-hour operations) and new skills (e.g., computer literacy) that have added a layer of complexity to the SHRM process. The increasing importance of skilled human resources in information-age economies and diversity of employee populations are increasingly important issues in planning. Skilled employees are as important as capital and technology in high-tech and sophisticated service organizations. Acquiring, developing, and retaining high-talent employees cannot be done by seat-of-the-pants methods that use little or no planning and which do not integrate HR programs with strategic plans. Diversity has become important because of equal opportunity and affirmative action laws, which are no longer limited to the US but are becoming widespread internationally (e.g., Brazil, South Africa, India, Canada, Malaysia). In addition, matching employee demographics to the demographic make-up of the regions in which the company does business is now a critical ingredient of successfully competing in a global marketplace. Diversity of thought, style, and experience is also a growing consideration in the planning and implementation processes based on the premise that greater diversity leads to greater innovation, productivity, and company value.

Organizations now operate in an increasingly global, technologically sophisticated, and interdependent world, which has intensified competition among organizations. This, in turn, increases the importance of human resources and makes viable SHRM processes all the more critical to organizational survival and effectiveness. Without processes to explore organizational needs, create and modify plans to meet those needs, and align human resource management practices with the strategic objectives, organizations will increasingly be at a competitive disadvantage.

To meet business challenges today and tomorrow, organizations must maximize the potential of their workforce – the human capital that is pivotal to their success – while increasing efficiency. This requires transforming traditional HR functions into a SHRM with a comprehensive human capital management (HCM) program; that is, employee processes and knowledge must be integrated with business processes and strategies.

Forward-looking organizations no longer think in terms of HR; they think in terms of HCM. There is an important distinction between the two: HR is an administrative function. HCM is a business strategy in which people are leveraged to increase production, provide continuous improvement, and create value for the stakeholders. CFOs and other leaders need to see HR as a strategic function that is embedded in the operations of the business and influences operating and financial results. To that end, HR must morph from an administrative area to the enabler of HCM – a business strategy focused on business performance. Through HCM, every employee is viewed as a competitive asset contributing to the end goal of positive business results.

A recognized need to align business and individual performance goals, along with better tools to accomplish this, is driving HCM investments at many organizations. Another key priority, especially at large organizations, is the need to consolidate multiple HR transactional systems for efficiency and global workforce visibility. For HR executives to be viewed as trusted advisors, they must use the right processes and technology to deploy industry best practices that deliver measurable results. A broad spectrum of analytics, shared-service models, and outsourcing arrangements can enable HR departments to streamline business processes to save operating costs and focus on strategic functions such as talent management, workforce process management, and improved workforce deployment.

Human Capital Management (HCM)

In a highly competitive business environment, organizations can differentiate themselves through their employees. Employees understand the business, carry out operations, mitigate risk, and build the brand. Employees are the most important asset and should not be viewed differently from other assets on a balance sheet. Ultimately, people drive profit. Transforming traditional HR functions into a comprehensive human capital management program is therefore not only an operational directive but also a key strategic initiative that is widely adopted today. For the uninitiated, HR and HCM may appear to provide the same function within the enterprise, but really, they are distant cousins in an overriding family tree.

HR, the department, handles a vitally important administrative function. It drives applications like payroll that you can't afford to get wrong. HR also has an indispensable role to play from an administrative standpoint; it ensures that trains run on time and transactional machinery is humming the way it ought to be. HCM, however, comprises the strategy and business processes that transform every employee into a competitive asset that supports operating and financial results. Employees become a competitive element in your business's operating success or your public agency's ability to deliver on the mandate given to it by constituents or public stakeholders. Everyone knows you need people to run an enterprise, but the debated issue is – at what cost? Traditionally, HR has done a poor job of quantifying its contributions to an organization's bottom line. Since CFOs think in terms of financial metrics, such as estimated value added to the balance sheet and profit and loss (P&L) statements, they can find it difficult to understand the value of a workforce if it isn't presented in financial terms. Finance executives struggle to link technology investments that support HR to tangible results. Therefore, HR is typically perceived as providing transactional support rather than enhancing the bottom line.

With people-related costs such as salary, benefits, incentives, and training representing the largest element of operating expense on your P&L statement, HR needs to translate these costs to bottom-line benefits. Thus there is a business case, for adopting an integrated HCM program, as a part of SHRM. HCM technologies can be leveraged to improve the positive impact that people can have on the bottom line. It looks at the key areas of influence and suggests technology solutions to achieve better business results through an enterprise's greatest resources – its people

Driving the Need for Change

Payroll and benefits costs as a percentage of operating budget can vary widely depending on the industry. Yet a study conducted by Mercer Human Resource Consulting, entitled "Human Capital Management: The CFO's Perspective," explains that only about 16% of CFOs have more than a moderate understanding of the return the company is realizing from its investment in people. This gap in understanding is exactly what HR executives need to rectify. This is where human capital management strategies can be focused to make the greatest impact on the organization. Whether on a corporate, revenue, financial, productivity, or departmental level - or all of these - it's up to the HR executive to demonstrate the return your organization is achieving, or should expect to achieve, on its investments in people and that's where HCM strategies can help.

Core HR applications are now being complemented by strategic HCM solutions designed to assist organizations in their efforts to acquire, develop, manage, and then measure the performance of their workforce. HCM initiatives enable the enterprise to improve workforce potential by integrating and automating business processes that support HR functions. Improved processes such as talent management, workforce process management, and workforce deployment enable the enterprise to more effectively utilize its people while fully understanding the financial and strategic impact, and potential, of these people on the business. HR can more effectively support high-cost areas, such as compliance, and measure results to demonstrate the value HCM initiatives are delivering.

Achieving Compliance More Cost Effectively

Spiraling compliance costs are often the top priority of senior executives today. HR departments and executives bear a significant amount of responsibility for compliance with legal regulations. These include - but are not limited to - International Financial Reporting Standards (IFRS), International Accounting Standards (IAS) including Accounting Standards on Human Resource Accounting. Many of the business processes that HR manages have a direct impact on the company's financial statements. In internal control over financial reporting, HR areas that may be impacted include payroll, benefits, pensions, workers' compensation, plans, stock compensation programs, executive compensation, and employee master data change.

HR must ensure that employees read and understand the company's policy on corporate governance. The department must keep track of whether employees have submitted necessary signed forms, communicate with employees about retirement plans, and continually monitor employees to prevent inappropriate processes or behaviour. HR also must determine who is authorized to see, create, or change sensitive data; who can execute sensitive reports; and how workflow is executed. Further, HR must ensure that workflows are defined and in place to initiate approvals, such as new hire transactions that prompt managers to add appropriate authorizations for security purposes or termination events that remove users' authorization automatically and prompt managers to take back assigned assets such as phones or computers. In addition, HR needs to maintain role-based segregation of responsibilities regarding payroll. That means employees cannot change their own payroll information; time and attendance data must be appropriately captured, evaluated, and approveds and the payroll database must be maintained in a secure, tamper-proof environment with audit trail capabilities.

Regarding benefits, more and more HR departments have implemented controls to ensure that pension expense accruals and liabilities are accurate and properly disclosed and third-party administrators, such as benefits outsourcers, are managing their process and controls adequately. They are taking additional measures to review the accuracy of workers' compensation claims, to limit such claims, and to review and validate that stock options are properly calculated and disclosed.

In particular, organizations those have grown through mergers and acquisitions, and have multiple business-management software systems, are struggling with these issues and are concerned about audits. Inadequate HR compliance due to inconsistent business processes and duplicate technologies can lead to significant fines and legal exposure. HR departments are constantly implementing programs, collecting and analyzing data, and disseminating information to the workforce as well as internal and external stakeholders. Well-defined HR practices can reduce risks related to hiring, succession of key positions, employee turnover, and employee grievances as well as labour-relations issues.

The challenge for HR is to integrate these programs and prove they deliver tangible value. Meeting the challenge can be achieved by using technology to ensure the quality of internal controls. The business processes and workflows identified for compliance must be made consistent and able to be incorporated throughout the HRIS to enable employees to work more effectively and reduce the noncompliance risk through appropriate HCM strategies. The HR system must have the following embedded: application security that supports segregation of duties; capability for proper authorization of HR transactions; and workflows for automatic routing of salary administration, such as notifications for event-based actions such as performance reviews, edit and audit capabilities for data integrity, and rules-based engines particularly for payroll that can run eligibility for benefits or overtime calculations. It should also have compliance reporting capabilities.

Investing in People to Improve Performance

Talent management tops the list as a strategy for radically improving the impact that the workforce has on improved business results. But the majority of CFOs don't understand the return on investment for that significant element of spend in P&L. To establish the business case for an HCM program that can enable better talent management, HR managers need to connect the dots for the CFO. The case can be made by demonstrating that an investment in people – unlike capital expenditures on equipment and supplies – will generate value for the shareholders.

HR can accomplish this by establishing the relationship between the organization's core business and the importance of workforce management. Naturally, ensuring that HR understands the company's business model, financials, and overall strategy is a must. The business case for investing in technology should then focus on things that motivate the CFO – specifically, revenue generation or the opportunity for cost savings. HR can then align its priorities with the CFO's and demonstrate the impact the organization's people and programs will have on the P&L and balance sheet.

The CFO may think of people as a line-item expense on the balance sheet, but the HR manager's mandate is to communicate that every employee must be managed as an investment and a competitive asset. HR managers need to help CFOs change the way they think about the human aspect of the business.

Achieving Best Practices

Research indicates that investments in HCM best practices are associated with higher levels of financial return to stakeholders. A study of high-performing organizations conducted by Accenture and SAP shows the top-performing organizations studied are far more likely to be engaged in best practices around HCM than those that have a poorer performance. For example, 68% of the top performers studied have specific initiatives around career development, compared to only 13% of the poorer performers in the study. Similarly, 70% of the top performers studied have learning-management programs, compared to only 14% of the poorer performers in the study.

Improving Workforce Performance

Integrated HCM solutions can help the CFO see specific fact-based information that shows the potential savings in operating expense or the incremental revenue associated with more effective talent management. Making a case based on productivity alone is not enough. Imagine the HR manager telling the CFO that an employee will be 10 minutes more productive through the use of a self service transaction. The CFO will want to know where those 10 minutes can be reallocated. Answering that question can be difficult.

Instead, the HR manager should take a P&L approach and show the CFO that the investment will count toward recruiting, learning, and performance management. This will ultimately drive better performance through individuals, which will have a measurable impact on revenue generation.

For example, assume customer service agents participate in learning programs. The learning programs might entail new-hire or orientation training or tactics for cross-selling or up-selling to the customer. It's possible to link investment in these programs to the time it takes for agents to become productive or to an ensuing increase in the group's revenue. In addition, a reduction in recurring, variable expenses can be linked to a reduction in errors accomplished through better training. For field services employees, it's possible to associate learning and performance management with incentive management. Employees with better training are less likely to leave and join competitors when advancement opportunities are evident, whereas recruiting can be a very expensive exercise.

By increasing productivity and motivating workforce behaviour, talent management can lead to higher levels of organizational performance including the following:

- Growing revenue
- Improved service delivery
- Lower operational costs
- Higher customer satisfaction.

These prized levels of performance can change the nature of conversation between HR managers and the CFO. The goals are to identify the types of workers that have the biggest impact on revenue generation or expense control and to establish programs, processes, and technologies that enable these employees to perform better. Improved results will have a direct, measurable impact on the organization's overall profitability.

Performing Analysis to Make Better Decisions

HR departments have an opportunity to build motivated, trained, highly skilled teams that provide an organization with a powerful competitive advantage ..cross all functions. The department needs to provide insight into the root cause of business results, such as why sales are declining in one region or how training impacts the ability to convert leads to revenue. Providing a snapshot of the costs of transactions, such as cost per hire, is not enough. Too few organizations have a comprehensive view of their data and the tools necessary to extract meaningful information from it. The fact that most sub-processes such as recruiting, performance management, training, and financial management haven't been integrated presents a further obstacle. Silos of information don't lend themselves to deep insight. After much effort by HR and IT resources, many organizations still don't have much more than simple transactional history reports. Without analytics, which provide the ability to track both the "what" and the "why" of a business event, organizations are put in a reactive situation, usually waiting for a crisis to force change.

As HR has the responsibility for managing the core processes that impact the effectiveness of talent, it's uniquely situated to optimize those processes and provide business insight to the organization. By deploying an integrated talent management strategy, SHRM can provide insight into questions that have direct impact on its organization's ability to execute its strategy as follows:

- Is our recruitment program attracting people who stay in the organization more the 36 months - thereby reducing recruitment and training costs?
- How much more profit did departments A and B contribute to the region based on the investment made in their training programs?
- How did our training program impact our call center agents' ability to cross-sell additional products and services?

In other words, when we take the cost of the program and add the cost of each participant's time and travel expense, did we recoup that cost in increased sales and profitability? A workforce analytics platform that integrates HR data with data from other functional areas can directly impact operational results. By providing visibility of workforce indicators and their impact on operating and financial outcomes, organizations can adapt their workforce to optimize those desired outcomes.

For example, combining call center data (from customer relationship management), and workforce data (from talent management), and financial data (from financial management) enables an organization to do the following:

- Measure agent effectiveness in finding new customers, selling new products and services to current customers, and promoting customer satisfaction.
- Measure up-sell rate, cross-sell rate, time to resolution, customer satisfaction, and so on, of the call center team, individual analyst, and/or call center manager.
- Correlate these measures with talent programs such as training programs, performance ratings, incentive programs, skills/competencies, employee tenure, manager tenure, and source of hire.
- Adjust talent programs – training programs, incentives, recruiting, and so on – to accomplish desired results and to optimize agent and call center productivity based on findings.
- Measure changes in the above metrics that occur after the new talent initiatives are rolled out.

Talent Management - The New SHRM Imperative

- More companies are beginning to adopt processes and tools to more effectively recruit, retain, develop and deploy talent.
- Workforce planning translates business strategy into talent management activities.
- Each company needs to understand the problem it faces, estimate the gaps in its industry and determine the skills it needs to meet business objectives.
- The direction in talent management is to a fact-based understanding and prioritization of what is needed.
- It's important not to adopt individual processes and tools in isolation from others, or from the human capital management (HCM) platform.
- Talent management is a new, more holistic approach to HR. HR grew up in functional silos— recruiting, benefits, learning and training. If you believe in talent management, you destroy those silos.
- Companies need to set up governing bodies that cut across all talent initiatives and include people from business units to establish priorities and review progress continuously.

Global organizations, especially MNCs know that a talent shortage is coming, if it hasn't arrived already. Talent management, backed by strategic workforce planning, can help companies face this crisis. Hardly a week passes without a headline like this: "Baby-boomers' Farewell Likely to Slow Growth." The article, in the *Financial Times* of May 30, 2007, cites a report by the Organization for Economic Co-operation and Development in Paris that predicts the rate of U.S. economic growth is at risk because baby boomers are about to retire in droves—and there is too little talent to replace them.

Many reports, research studies and statistics suggest companies face—or soon will— a talent crunch because of demographic and other trends, not just in the United States but across the industrialized world. According to staffing services and employment provider Manpower Inc., companies in most industrial nations, including India and China, struggle to fill positions.

CHART 9.1. Global Talent Shortage

Country	*% of employers having difficulty filling jobs*
China	24
Germany	53
India	12
Japan	58
U.K	42
U.S	44
World	50

Source: Manpower Inc., 2006

Talent shortage predictions began about a decade ago and were largely ignored, but surveys now suggest that CEOs are paying attention.

"Acquiring and managing talent has become the business imperative," says Mike Ryan, an executive who leads a talent management initiative at Rio Tinto Ltd., a global mining company based in Melbourne, Australia. "It is the one thing we constantly see in our corporate board reports and presentations."

Like Rio Tinto, most companies understand the trend. Some have even begun strategic workforce planning. But Rio Tinto is among a much smaller number that has gone beyond planning to adopt processes and tools to more effectively recruit, retain, develop and deploy talent. Failure to adopt a strategy for integrated talent management could result in too few workers and a slow decline in a company's fortunes. "I've been at this for 25 years and the concern over talent has never been greater," says Jay Doherty, a principle at Mercer Human Resource Consulting LLC. "Most companies fall into the area of being concerned, asking questions and not finding easy answers."

CHART 9.2. Challenges to Growth - What fast-growth CEOs see as the issues?

Challenges/Issues	*% Of CEOs*
Finding, hiring and retaining qualified employees	48
Other factors	34
Developing a strong sales and marketing strategy	18

Source: Deloitte & Touché, 2007

How Big a Talent Shortage?

The U.S. Bureau of Labour Statistics (BLS) forecasts the civilian labor force (supply) will grow to 162.1 million and the jobs available (demand) will grow to 164.5 million by 2014. Although the BLS does not officially forecast labour shortages or surpluses, together the two curves illustrate the gap between demand and supply.

The gap may be smaller than it appears. About once a year there's an article in the *BLS Monthly Labor Review* pointing out that forecasts do not take into account workers with more than one job, the vagaries of immigration or outsourcing. And the two sets of data come from different sources, which cause technical problems. Demand is projected from the total number of payroll jobs and supply from household surveys of the number of individuals in the labour force. The forecasts do not factor in unemployment.

The BLS data also suggests a starting point to understand the problem. One example: By 2010, 40 percent of the U.S. workforce will be poised to retire, and the median age of workers is rising.

"Businesses that generate a great deal of value from an older workforce will face a lot of knowledge loss over the next five to 10 years," says Doherty, singling out aerospace and heavy manufacturing. The BLS also forecasts the growth rate of employment in various occupations. For example, from 2002 to 2012, employment in Internet services, data processing and other information services is expected to skyrocket 46 percent, scientific research and development is expected to grow 21 percent and ambulatory healthcare services (except doctor's offices) would reach 46 percent. This data suggests where shortages may hit hardest and is a good starting point for any company that wants to understand trends in its industry.

The shortage is already real for some. Utilities and government have two of the most mature workforces in America, having hired heavily in the 1960s and 1970s, when baby boomers were coming of age. Healthcare demands ever more workers to care for an aging population. Most fast growing technology companies cannot find enough workers with engineering, math or science degrees.

CHART 9.3. Global Engineering Talent Shortage

Country	*% of 24-year-olds with engineering degrees*
China	1.1
European Union	3.7
India	0.2
Japan	6.1
Taiwan	6.9
U.S	1.6
World	

Source: National Science Board, 2007

The maturing workforce is especially acute. "In some areas you see fast-rising demand," says Mary B. Young, a senior researcher at New York-based The Conference Board Inc., who studies companies that do strategic workforce planning. "The problem will be more gradual in other industries."

The issue is often quality, not quantity. "A lot of companies don't have difficulty getting workers in general, but do have trouble getting the key people in the most strategic roles they need to fill," says Jennifer Schramm, manager of workplace trends and forecasting at the Society for Human Resource Management (SHRM) in Alexandria, Va.

Rio Tinto, for example, focuses on mining engineers because there's a shortage. "If we're looking for these people, all the other mining companies are, too," Ryan says. "We expect about 10 more years of this problem."

Strategic Workforce Plans

The talent shortage will impact certain jobs, regions and industries more than others, Young concluded last year in a report entitled "Strategic Workforce Planning: Forecasting Human Capital Needs to Execute Business Strategy."

She further concluded this is a good thing: "It allows companies to be more selective where they are vulnerable but they don't understand where they are vulnerable without doing the analysis. Workforce planning translates business strategy into talent management activities."

Each company needs to understand the problem it faces, estimate the gaps in its industry and determine the skills it needs to meet business objectives. Young calls this strategic workforce planning: "The analytic, forecasting and planning process that connects and directs talent management activities to ensure an organization has the right people in the right places at the right time and at the right price to execute is business strategy."

San Diego-based Amylin Pharmaceuticals Inc, is getting ready to do that. The biopharmaceutical company develops drugs for metabolic diseases, and 31 percent of its 1,700 employees have graduate science degrees, so it must get a handle on the talent issue. "Science is one area with a projected shortage," says Deborah Rocco, chief learning officer. "Based on the demographic information, we have put in place a strategic plan. Once the full impact of the shortage hits us, you won't be able to react and recover. You have to be ahead of it."

The Conference Board's Young studied 10 companies that perform gap analysis and model scenarios to develop data-driven talent management initiatives to achieve business goals. Some partnered with universities, some developed their own tools, others used commercial tools and some used spreadsheets. The important thing is to do it, but most companies still are not carrying out this level of analysis.

"It is phenomenal to me that any HR executive could survive an executive meeting without having this analytic data in their pocket," says Jeff Summers, global lead for talent management at New York-based Deloitte Consulting LLP. "The direction in talent management is to a fact-based understanding and prioritization of what is needed." In its yearly business planning process, a North American eyeglass retailer recalibrates the number of retail store managers and field managers it will need, says the company's associate vice president of learning and talent management. But that's not enough: "We plan to start doing this for three years at a time."

Talent Management Initiatives

Most large companies have processes for recruiting, reviewing and rewarding workers. Many do succession planning and learning management. Not many companies have integrated their HR processes with a single HCM platform. Tight integration would produce a robust database of information about the competencies of individuals that is available to decision makers throughout the enterprise. But some companies are making progress to close the HCM and talent management gap.

Consider the following:

Rio Tinto can't hire mining engineers fast enough; just one of its Australian business units had 2,500 open positions last year. It began to install technology for talent management a couple of years ago. The need was to find qualified applicants, so the first thing the company did was revamp disparate recruiting processes into an integrated global system, with regional recruiting teams using the e-recruiting module from its enterprise resource planning (ERP) provider.

The company had five recruiting systems, and business units did not share information. It now has central regional teams and has reduced the systems to three, with a plan to have 80 percent of business units on one integrated system by 2008 and the entire company on that system by 2010.

Rio Tinto is using the same software, with a different look and feel, for an internal program to identify skills and make the best use of existing talent throughout global operations. This starts with a self-service application employees use to bring their profiles up to date.

Florida Power & Light Co., a Juno Beach, Fla., utility with 13,000 employees, had a paper-based performance review — a mishmash of spreadsheets and word processing documents—which was nearly useless. No one had any visibility into these evaluations. Who had what skills, where and how much of that skill the company had altogether, because that kind of analysis could not be done on paper.

Changing Workforce

By the end of this decade, another critical issue for organizations world over is the aging workforce. In 2010, there will be 52 percent more people in the 55 to 64 age bracket than there were in same age group in the 2000 workforce. As per the study of Bureau of Labour Statistics, the picture would be like this:

- Number of people in the age group of 35 to 44 would reduce by 10 %
- Number of people in the age group of 45 to 54 would increase by 21 %
- Number of people in the age group of 55 to 64 would increase by 52 %

The utility recently adopted the performance review module of its ERP vendor and now has a system for all non-bargaining unit employees, integrated with compensation planning and talent assessment modules it also adopted from its ERP vendor. It is still a work in progress, but the system includes an online appraisal process that involves the employee and the manager and gives visibility to other managers and executives.

One initial focus at **Amylin Pharmaceuticals** is succession planning. The company is working with the business school at nearby University of California at San Diego on an executive assessment program. It is also working on programs to support a culture where employees share knowledge and collaborate in generating new knowledge and to look at social-networking research for how it might be applied in its workplace. There is a "branding" element in this, as Amylin wants talent outside the company to come to know it as the place to work.

Integration of Processes and Systems

Each of these examples is an illustration of talent management. Each company began with the worst pain, but the long-term goal is integrated talent management, often using tools offered by a single ERP vendor because integration is easier to accomplish. None adopted individual processes and tools in isolation from others.

At Rio Tinto, the goal is integrated talent management that includes workforce planning, reviewing and managing performance, succession planning and remuneration. This will take several years. The first step is recruiting and increasing internal use of employees. Rio Tinto also plans to adopt the other tools offered by its ERP vendor.

At Florida Power & Light, performance review and talent assessment was one of the last stages in rolling out talent management processes, following the launch of a single HCM system in 2002 and the rollout of its ERP vendor's modules for employee self-service, compensation planning, learning management and career planning.

At Amylin, the company has begun to roll out HCM software and a suite of talent management tools from the same ERP vendor to support all talent processes. Each of these companies sees the value in adopting HCM software and a suite of tools from one provider. They all wind up using data from the same database, with relatively easy solutions to integration issues.

Companies like Rio Tinto, FP&L and Amylin are still unusual. "Historically, HR has operated as a collection of discrete processes, and too often companies still think of it that way," says Heidi Spirgi, president of Knowledge Infusion, a Minneapolis-based consulting firm. "A collection of processes does not equal talent management."

Spirgi defines talent management as the process of managing the supply and demand of talent to achieve optimal business performance in alignment with organizational goals. To do this, she adds, HR departments need to not only adopt the right tools but change their approach to business.

"Talent management is a new approach to HR, a more holistic approach," agrees the eyeglass retailer executive. "HR grew up in functional silos—recruiting, benefits, learning and training. If you believe in talent management, you destroy those silos." This retailer envisions adopting a full set of talent management processes, but its pressing need is succession planning — acquisitions used up much of its bench strength of managers and the company places a premium on developing new leaders from within. By rolling out succession planning, performance review, and learning management processes and tools, all integrated with each other, executives will gain visibility into the pipeline of next-generation store and field managers.

The systems will be integrated and connected with the retailer's single HCM platform because the competencies evaluated during performance management — and emphasized in learning management— need to be considered in succession planning.

The march to integrated talent management can be long and arduous. Deloitte's Summers urges companies to start with the three to five priorities that will have the biggest impact. "You still see HR departments that have many different programs, each lacking focus, strategic intent or the appropriate level of investment to allow them to do anything well to make a difference in managing talent shortages."

Knowledge Infusion's Spirgi urges companies to develop a strategic three-to-five year roadmap for rolling out talent management applications and to not try to do it all at one time. She encourages companies to set up governing bodies that cut across all talent initiatives and include people from business units to establish priorities and review progress continuously.

The change management issues cannot be overlooked. HR professionals comfortable with administrative roles, and even some who are comfortable with the strategic business partner role, must adapt to the intensive communication and collaboration required to achieve strategically oriented, integrated talent management. But if talent management is the new business imperative — and it is — then companies would be wise to start soon.

Studies confirm that critical talent continues to become increasingly scarce. Organizations of any size are well advised to meet this trend head on. We consistently hear from our customers—no matter what the industry—that talent is a key source of competitive advantage. To successfully manage their talent, companies need to become effective at identifying developing and retaining talent.

Without defined processes to identify high potentials and top talents and to actively manage their development, companies risk poor organizational performance, loss of key talent and disruption in business execution.

As a consequence, talent management has moved to the top of board agendas. Managing enterprise talent has become a core competency for most organizations. Yet today, most companies don't have a single view of the talent available to them. Many have islands of talent-related data — in offline documents and point solutions — that are not integrated within the overall system landscape.

Integrated Talent Management is Indispensable

Effective talent management requires a comprehensive approach to talent management processes. This requires dismantling the organizational walls between traditional HR practices, such as recruiting and succession management.

Unifying processes that cross over different areas of practice adds insight and efficiency to the processes and to the managers and employees who are involved. Companies need to implement comprehensive companywide processes for determining talent needs and then take the right actions to meet those needs in the short, medium and long term. By recruiting and retaining a motivated, innovative and productive workforce, companies can generate significant value.

Organizations cannot achieve the integration of talent management processes if their technology isn't also integrated. All of these practice areas require a common understanding of the critical competencies needed to make an organization run successfully in addition to basic information about the individuals who make up the workforce and analytical tools for driving strategy in all areas.

One example of a cross-functional process: An effective employee performance management program consists of more than just automating performance appraisals. It includes identifying individual development opportunities (such as classroom training and on-the-job training), implementing succession planning and providing performance-based compensation. These processes must be supported by accurate integrated data.

There are many talent management solutions on the market today. However, most of them are composed of discrete pillars of functionality — often inherited as a result of acquisitions. This is increasingly the case as the learning, performance management and recruiting markets undergo consolidation.

Talent Management

Many organizations worldwide, including many of the companies depend on Human Capital Management solution for managing their most important resource — their people. Importance of HCM functionality over the past 20 years has been realized, yet Talent Management is the most significant area of investment needs to be understood.

Technology can support even more comprehensive talent management strategy. One needs to see talent management as a unified set of strategic employee management processes that include recruiting, succession management, performance management, enterprise learning and compensation management, all unified by analytics. To deliver maximum value, talent management processes must be connected to one another — as well as to other business processes—with a common, broad-reaching technology platform. Further, basis of talent management functionality has to be on the master data and competency database.

This enables a single view of available talent worldwide, while allowing all talent-related practices within HR to speak a common language. The key to success with all these activities is the unified technology platform on which they run.

Organizations using talent management as part of SHRM can gain the following benefits:

- Quickly find and onboard the right external people.
- Discover hidden potential in the internal talent pool.
- Consistently achieve corporate objectives by aligning team and individual goals as well as workforce training with strategic organizational goals.
- Close skills gaps by assessing an individual's training needs and turning that assessment into a development plan.
- Identify high-potential employees and implement development plans to ensure seamless coverage for strategically important positions.
- Motivate employees through clearly defined individual objectives as well as career and development plans.
- Tie compensation to performance.

The basis for all talent processes is a common set of integrated data. When HR professionals work with the same data across the company, they can do the following:

- Evaluate the efficiency of recruiting processes.
- Measure the effectiveness of learning programs.
- Assess the value of succession programs.
- Monitor the efficiency of performance management processes.
- Analyze the cost effectiveness of employee compensation programs.

In SHRM, analytics are an essential part of talent management and can greatly improve planning and decision-making through monitoring selected processes. Analytics functions give managers the insight they need to identify talent gaps and predict shortfalls based on anticipated changes in the business. By measuring and analyzing succession programs, learning programs (including attendance, usage and links to operational data to determine program effectiveness) and so on, customers receive valuable data that lets them refine their talent management abilities and plan for the future. No point solution on the market can deliver such a comprehensive solution that helps customers not only reduce the total cost of ownership but also gain unprecedented insight into all their talent management processes. In addition, companies should not underestimate the value of organic growth. All applications and processes related to talent management should be integrated with core HR data. This cross-process integration on one common data model would deliver superior data integrity — minimizing integration costs and increasing product stability and simplicity.

Proper Talent Management Drives Performance

In an era, where service sector is booming all over the world, proper talent management as a part of SHRM would not only be a positive alone be a differentiator but would drive better performance and productivity. While manufacturing companies have invested millions in more efficient processes and technologies to optimize their supply chain, the professional services industry has been slow to apply a fully optimized supply chain management process. 80% of respondents from the survey indicated that the processes they use now for business development, resource management, and HR management were only somewhat or not at all integrated. There is sorely limited advanced planning in the professional services industry overall. Inefficient staffing decisions prevail, prompting the unnecessary use of third-party contractors. More than half of the survey respondents identified squandered revenue opportunities and a decrease in client satisfaction as the key problems associated with improperly forecasting client demand based on available skill sets.

Most firms realize that optimizing talent management is crucial. 68% of surveyed firms acknowledged that, when taken together, core talent management - including retention, recruitment, training, and knowledge management - outshine performance and compensation when it comes to staff development. These results crystallize the importance of these tasks to a firm's success. However, in a surprising disconnect, 85% rated their talent management and staff development programs as standard, rudimentary, or, even worse, non-existent. In short, services firms are not satisfied with the current processes critical to their success. There is a significant opportunity for services firms to improve these talent management areas – and reap the benefits of doing so. Professional services firms must address a wide range of operational, organizational, and planning challenges if they are going to optimize their talent and improve profit enhancing performance. These vary from offer development and supplier management to retaining the best and brightest, planning resources effectively, and increasing visibility in the sales pipeline.

To improve operations that impact profits, professional services firms must also hack through three thorny market thickets: globalization, the focus on individuals over the brand, and client sophistication. To do so requires that professional services firms think in terms of a holistic, talent supply chain management environment. To extend market reach and improve the bottom line, these firms need to look at the whole talent supply chain, ensuring that they are retaining the talent needed – and optimizing their own talent reserves – to meet ever-increasing client demands for quality, delivery, and speed.

Benchmarking for SHRM

Benchmarking is an important and powerful tool for companies to achieve a balance between cost effective efficiency and contributing value-added services to support corporate strategic goals. By accurately assessing their own performance and comparing the results achieved to those of their peers, HR organizations can achieve optimal levels of efficiency and effectiveness. Moreover, if managed well, HR becomes a dynamic part of the organization that can go beyond transaction-related activities and contribute to margin growth and the long-term success of the company. ASUG and SAP established benchmarking forum to understand the dynamics of human resources organizations and the challenges faced by their managers. The ASUG/SAP study examined the best-practices record of more than 200 companies ranging in size from less than $1 billion in annual revenues to more than $10 billion. The benchmarking study analyzed the HR performance of these companies in 17 key sub-processes in three categories: process and transactional support, expertise-based business support, and strategic decision support. The two questions on which this study was based and are of great relevance to SHRM were:

- How can companies reduce HR costs and increase HR efficiency?
- How can HR organizations create value for the business and optimize effectiveness?

This study included companies with an overall number of employees ranging from 1,000 to more than 10,000 in the following industries:

- Aerospace and defense
- Automotive
- Chemical
- Consumer products
- Engineering, construction, and operations
- Financial services
- Healthcare and life sciences
- High tech
- Industrial machinery and components
- Oil and gas
- Public sector and higher education
- Retail
- Service providers
- Telecommunications
- Utilities.

The study analyzed key performance indicators (KPIs) in a number of different areas including HR staffing levels, costs, organizational model, IT deployment, and best practices. The KPIs included were:

1. Process-independent, such as HR costs per company employee and HR full-time equivalents (FTEs) per 1,000 employees.
2. Process-specific, such as time to hire, cost to hire, and payroll error rate
3. Degree of outsourcing and centralization
4. Use of shared services
5. Information technology used by HR employees
6. Degree of IT automation and integration.

The study also covers the level of best-practice adoption across the full range of HR functions, with companies providing self-evaluation for coverage and the perceived importance of each best practice. Best practices are winning strategies, approaches, and processes that produce superior performance. Some examples of HR best practices include the following:

1. Recruiting

- Ability of internal and external applicants to place themselves in the talent pipeline according to their own interests and goals
- Automated recruiting system analysis and reporting
- Integrated applicant tracking system.

2. Payroll

- Online access to direct-deposit and payroll data
- Single point of contact established for all payroll-related questions.

3. Benefits and pensions

- Benefits and retirement planning self-service.

Ability to model and analyze the impact of benefits plan changes on the overall business model.

Case Study: Utility Company Generates HR Advantage

A major North American utility company in our study faced serious challenges including inefficiencies in compensation packages and planning, ongoing government compliance audits, and an HR department focused on highly manual, paper-based transactions. In addition to these challenges, the utility's prime goals include maintaining efficient generation plants and aligning human capital management to support its brand image of low-cost power and environmental and social responsibility.To address its HR concerns, the utility implemented an IT solution with a role based enterprise portal that has enabled the company to realize great business value – and achieve an ROI of 102% in just fewer than five years. According to a company executive, cycle-time reductions allow HR employees to spend less time on administrative tasks and more time focusing on core strategic activities. Managers and employees now handle the majority of transactional activities, allowing HR to focus on hiring employees who are dedicated to and aligned with brand image. Employees are alerted to upcoming mandatory training, completion of certification requirements are automatically updated to the employee record, and the company has up-to-date, immediate information at hand for government compliance audits.

Source: ASUG/SAP Benchmarking Study, 2007

Human resources functions and responsibilities are changing and intensifying at a faster pace, and to a greater degree, than many other areas of the corporate organization. Once relegated to the back office and concerned mainly or even exclusively with transactional processes and functions, HR organizations are taking a greater role in strategic business activities. Efficiency remains the foundation of HR. More transactions must be completed at lower costs, while processes are becoming increasingly complex to manage. A typical 10,000-employee company handles more than one million employee-related transactions annually, each of which costs anywhere from US$10 to US$50. The top 10 recruiters are placing about 35,000 to 95,000 employees annually. Managing the recruitment pipeline, the selection process, and the induction process is a complicated endeavor. At the same time, however, leading HR organizations are looking beyond the execution of HR transactions to a more value-added and strategic focus. These organizations are aligning human resources and workforce planning functions with the overall business strategy to help increase profit margins and support long-term goals. To understand the changes and momentum in human capital management (HCM), there is a need to establish an ongoing HCM Benchmarking forum to study and analyze several dimensions – staffing, cost, organizational model, IT deployment, and best-practices adoption.

Some of the studies done and their key conclusions demonstrate how companies are meeting today's human capital challenges:

- As a first step, HR managers strive to optimize the efficiency of transactional processes through standardizing, automating, and integrating business processes, based on best-practice process and technology models.
- Optimizing transactional processes frees up resources that allow HR organizations to invest in more strategic functions that facilitate business growth and increase employee productivity.
- Centralizing and consolidating HR operations in a shared-services environment helps increase the efficiency and effectiveness of HR processes.
- Outsourcing, while used frequently for transactional processes, does not always drive top performance, either in cost or service quality.
- Organizations need to carefully evaluate the value, performance, and cost trade-offs in outsourced *versus* in-house service delivery.
- Information technology continues to provide the basic foundation for efficiency and acts as the key driver for effectiveness and future innovation.
- Leading organizations recognize that IT supports the development of many best practices, and they continue to invest in IT to integrate systems, data, and processes across the enterprise.

A still common perception is that managing human resources is straightforward and transaction oriented, and can therefore best be measured in terms of efficiency: the lower transactional costs, the better. This perception of HR is changing, however, and approaches to human capital management now cover a wide spectrum. At the opposite end of the range from traditional cost-centered, back-office organizations, many HR organizations now have the principal goals of providing the best possible business support and investing in resources and sophisticated tools – while de-prioritizing or ignoring costs altogether.

Top-performing companies strike an optimal balance between the two extremes of this spectrum. These companies are transforming the way they look at HR, with human capital management taking a stronger role in contributing to the drive for higher profit margins and long term growth. Top-performing HR organizations strive to optimize both efficiency and effectiveness by minimizing transactional costs through standardization, automation, and self-service, freeing up resources that can be used to align HR with the businesses to support growth.

Key Measures for Efficiency of SHRM

Human resources management is in a state of dynamic change, under pressure to adapt to the realities of doing business in the 21st century. Efficiency, always a watchword for HR management, remains a highly important measure. The most commonly used HR efficiency metrics are as follows:

- Staffing levels – employees served per full-time HR employee, or full-time HR employees per 1,000 employees.
- Costs – HR cost per company employee.

Effectiveness is much harder to measure than efficiency, and many HR organizations rely on a combination of hard (quantitative) and soft (qualitative) metrics, such as:

- Hard metrics – cycle times (such as time to hire), error rates, and employee turnover.

- Soft metrics – employee engagement, customer satisfaction, alignment with corporate goals, impact on business results, and adoption of best practices.

Effectiveness metrics do not necessarily correlate with efficiency metrics. There are instances with strong results for effectiveness but very high costs, as well as companies with low effectiveness and low costs. The most desirable case is to achieve high effectiveness while at the same time managing costs.

Case Study: Bank Improves Services with Employee Interaction Center

Facing the daunting task of reducing staffing levels while maintaining or even improving service levels, a major bank has implemented an employee interaction center to serve more than 20,000 employees across its operations, along with enterprise-wide human capital management software. The integrated solution has enabled the bank to improve efficiency in handling large numbers of HR inquiries and orders through various channels from management and employees. As a result, the bank has increased the speed and quality of services, resulting in higher employee satisfaction and greater transparency of processes. At the same time, the implementation has enabled a significant increase in HR productivity, allowing an HR head count reduction of 20%.

Source: ASUG/SAP Benchmarking Study, 2007

Top-performing companies look for competitive advantage in HR by adding capabilities to increase the effectiveness of service delivery and bring HR more in line with business processes and strategies – while at the same time striving for the right balance with cost control. The best HR organizations follow three main imperatives:

1. Align HR closely to the business

Alignment with the business has to happen on multiple levels. Centralizing transactional and certain expertise and talent-related processes in a shared-services or centre-of-excellence environment is a crucial piece of the alignment puzzle, allowing HR as an organization to operate as a service provider to individual business units and locations.

Many larger organizations choose to establish employee service centers to align closely at the employee level, catering directly to employee needs, while at the same time preserving efficiencies. Employee service centers help increase efficiency and employee satisfaction, providing employees with a single point of contact for taking care of benefits, pensions, payroll, processing of life events, employee data entry, applicant questions, and data processing, as well as on boarding process and paperwork. Top-performing companies are looking to HR business partners for direct and strategic support.

HR business partners are responsible for developing employee relations, leading workforce planning, and supporting stakeholders on-site. Top performing companies sharply define the role of the HR business partner, while average companies allow the role to blend with that of the HR generalist who is also responsible for a variety of transactional tasks.

True HR business partners spend less than 20% of their time on administrative tasks, and make change management a key responsibility. Top-performing companies even measure HR business partners by the success of such change programs. In this role, they also work with company leadership during the business planning process to identify future competency profiles and needs.

2. Outsource wisely and with effective control

The best companies take time to analyze what to centralize in-house, what to outsource, and what to decentralize, based on the demands of their unique cultures. This study calls into question some of the conventional wisdom about outsourcing. Results are inconsistent in the sense that outsourcing does not always drive first-quartile performance. In analyzing, the cost per employee for in-house versus outsourced services, for example, one can find significant cost gaps in payroll and benefits administration between first-quartile and average companies. Even more important, best practices are not always as prevalent in outsourced functions as they are with companies that control more of their HR functions.

A possible explanation for the inconsistency of these findings is that organizations that do not outsource may already have decent scale and standardization, and are therefore already at respectable benchmark performance levels. In payroll, for example, organizations with centralized operations in a shared-services environment – with standardized and simplified processes based on a single-instance enterprise resource planning (ERP) solution – have a very good chance to achieve first-quartile performance in-house. On the other hand, companies that do outsource may have intrinsically higher cost structures to start with. Significant reductions may be made, but the impact of these results must be weighed against the higher-cost starting point. The key take-away is that, HR organizations should evaluate their outsourcing decisions carefully and establish a benefits and cost analysis up front to weigh any potential alternatives (such as an optimized in-house solution).

DM Company Supports Talent Management – Reduces Costs

A global provider of mail and document management (DM) systems has launched a shared-services initiative to meet a number of crucial targets. Overall, the company wants to support comprehensive talent management within its global workforce, reorganize HR to eliminate redundancies and duplication of effort, and leverage a new HR structure and systems to upgrade and establish quality processes that can be measured and documented. From a metrics perspective, the company's goals are to reduce the HR professional-to-employee ratio and HR service cost per employee.The foundation of the reorganized HR structure is a new global shared-services model and an integrated, enterprise-wide human capital management solution. Now, the focus on mission-critical work is enhanced, driving the hiring and retaining of top talent to contribute to strategic business goals. The company has established centers of excellence focused on strategic leadership management, talent management, workforce relations, and accelerated growth. These initiatives have enabled the company to reduce HR costs while offering a higher level of service, centralize transactional processes with an integrated database, share knowledge and processes, and leverage expertise. The company has increased transactions processed per week; shortened recruiting cycle times, and reduced its HR professional-to-employee ratio.

Source: ASUG/SAP Benchmarking Study, 2007

3. Leverage IT

IT is a critical enabler for HR efficiency and effectiveness. Companies with a single HR system are more efficient and effective – and more strategically focused – than companies with fragmented system landscapes. Companies with a single enterprise-wide IT system have lower staffing levels and enjoy higher levels of best-practice scores.

Technology Company Reduces Payroll Costs with in House HR Solution

A leading high-tech company that provides voice automation technology and services had high costs associated with outsourcing its payroll functions. Its HR software lacked flexibility and key features needed to support future growth and help the company attract top talent. The company needed to implement an IT solution that wouldn't disrupt current operations – including an important concurrent acquisition – or imperil historical employee data during the migration of HR functions to its new system.The company has implemented an enterprise-wide human capital management solution to improve HR capabilities and bring payroll operations back in house. With the new solution the company enjoys considerable operational benefits. Errors per payroll cycle are reduced from three to zero. Time to set up new hires is reduced from four to six hours to one hour. Benefits-reporting cycle times are reduced from two to three days to instantaneous. Personnel administration requests that once took from 10 to 15 hours a day are now performed almost entirely with self-service functionality. Moreover, the company enjoyed a rapid implementation time of only six months.

Source: ASUG/SAP Benchmarking Study, 2007

SHRM Matters for Profits and Growth

The top performers achieve an optimal balance between reducing costs and driving business results. Top-performing companies look beyond traditional HR activities to focus on expertise based and strategic HR functions. By optimizing and automating transaction-oriented processes, top companies can invest more in attracting and developing talent – an investment that brings returns across the entire enterprise.

Companies that wish to enact initiatives embraced by top performers need to define their goals specifically – building a road map – to achieve a balance between reducing costs and driving company growth. The best-run human capital management organizations share the following crucial practices and goals:

- Optimize process and transactional support
- Benchmark processes and performance
- Consolidate systems
- Adopt shared services
- Invest in people and talent
- Align HR with overall business strategy and goals
- Focus on value, not effort.

As an initial step, top companies optimize process and transactional support – instead of concentrating on payroll and compensation administration – to focus more on strategic workforce planning, career planning, employee development, and recruitment and retention. Since monitoring and evaluation do matter: HR organizations that establish benchmarking programs ensure that goals are mapped out and met. Standardizing, consolidating, and centralizing HR operations in a shared-services environment helps increase process efficiency and effectiveness and enables companies to raise service levels and focus on talent – not transactions. Information technology provides the necessary foundation, facilitating efficiency and driving future innovation and growth by integrating processes and data across the enterprise.

Following this road map, SHRM can contribute to long-term and immediate company goals by promoting and advancing employee productivity – optimizing the operating margin per employee. While constantly assessing and improving processes, companies can enable a shift in mind-set – to focus on value, not effort – and make HR a true business partner to the corporation.

MNCs can use four basic sources for filling overseas positions: home-country nationals (expatriates), host-country nationals, third-country nationals, and inpatriates. The most common reason for using home-country nationals, or expatriates, is to get the overseas operation under way. Once this is done, many MNCs turn the top management position over to a host-country national who is familiar with the culture and language and who often commands a lower salary than the home-country national. The primary reason for using third-country nationals is that these people have the necessary expertise for the job. The use of inpatriates (a host-country or third-country national assigned to the home office) recognizes the need for diversity at the home office. This movement builds a transnational core competency for MNCs.

Many criteria are used in selecting managers for overseas assignments. Some of these include adaptability, independence, self-reliance, physical and emotional health, age, expertise, education, knowledge of the local language, motivation, the support of spouse and children, and leadership. Those who meet selection criteria then are given some form of screening. Some firms use psychological testing, but this approach has lost popularity in recent years. More commonly, candidates are given interviews. A recent development, theoretic models that identify important anticipatory and in-country dimensions of adjustment, offers help in effective selection.

Compensating expatriates can be a difficult problem, because there are many variables to consider. However, most compensation packages are designed around four common elements: base salary, benefits, allowances, and taxes. Working within these elements, the MNC will tailor-make the package to fit the specific situation. In doing so, there are six different approaches that can be used, including the balance sheet approach, the complementary approach, localization, lump sum method, the cafeteria approach, and the regional method. Whichever one (or combination) is used, the package must both be cost-effective and fair. A manager might be willing to take an international assignment for a number of reasons, including: increased pay, promotion potential, the opportunity for greater responsibility, the chance to travel, and the ability to use his or her talents and skills. Research shows that most home countries prefer that the individual who is selected to head the affiliate or subsidiary be a local manager, even though this often does not occur.

At some time, most expatriates return home, usually when the predetermined tour is over. Sometimes, managers return because they want to leave early; other times, they return because of poor performance on their part. In any event, readjustment problems can happen back home, and the longer the managers have been gone, the bigger the problems usually are. Some firms now are developing transition strategies to help expatriates adjust to their new environments.

SHRM in Different Cultures

Training is the process of altering employee behaviour and attitudes to increase the probability of goal attainment. Many expatriates need training before (as well as during) their overseas stay. A number of factors will influence a company's approach to training. One is the basic type of MNC: ethnocentric, polycentric, regiocentric, or geocentric. Another factor is the learning style of the trainees.

There are two primary reasons for training: organizational and personal. Organizational reasons include overcoming ethnocentrism, improving communication, and validating the effectiveness of training programs. Personal reasons include improving the ability of expatriates to interact locally and increasing the effectiveness of leadership styles. There are two types of training programs: standard and tailor-made. Research shows that small firms usually rely on standard programs and larger MNCs tailor their training. The six major types of training include environmental briefings, cultural orientation, cultural assimilators, language training, sensitivity training, and field expertise. A cultural assimilator is a programmed learning approach that is designed to expose members of one culture to some of the basic concepts, attitudes, role perceptions, customs, and values of another. Assimilators have been developed for many different cultures. Their validity has resulted in the improved effectiveness and satisfaction of those being trained as compared with other training methods.

Organizational development (OD) is the deliberate and reasoned introduction, establishment, reinforcement, and spread of change for the purpose of improving an organization's effectiveness. The basic purpose of OD is to reconcile individual-group-organization differences, often accomplished through the use of OD interventions such as team building, MBO, confrontation meetings, third-party peacemaking, and survey feedback. Research shows that OD interventions often are less effective in international settings. One primary reason is that many cultures do not have low power distance or low uncertainty avoidance, which is tow key dimensions for successful OD efforts. This is why team building has not worked well and MBO has been greatly modified. On the other hand, third-party peacemaking and survey feedback have been successful, because they can be adapted to the two cultural dimensions of power distance and uncertainty avoidance. Also, proven techniques such as Organizational Behaviour Models have been shown to hold considerable potential for improving employee performance across cultures.

❄❄❄

10 Developing a Global Management Cadre

• Developing a Global Management Cadre • Women in International Management

Once a company in the emerging world has developed distinctive capabilities, it must learn to move them across markets. Becoming a powerful global player is an imperative, not a choice, for the world's largest companies - and those that aspire to join their ranks. As global companies strives for competitive advantage wherever they can find it, its not of a stretch to suggest that developing a cadre of outstanding global executives offers a sustainable advantage that meet most of the criteria. A Cadre principally refers to committed people within an organization that form, or have the capacity to form, the backbone of that organization. They are specially trained personnel able to assume leadership and train others.

A global Cadre is a group of employees, formally recognized, who are available for multiple successive international assignments.

Need for developing a global cadre

Research has shown that the best global companies - the Global Champions, the top 60 companies in the world 1 - clearly outperform market indices over long periods of time ('Global Champions Significantly Outperformed The Market') and handle global volatility very well for example the traditional Triad - the US and Canada, western Europe, and Japan. Although non-Triad countries contribute nearly 15% of the world's GDP and have a proportionate number of 'global leaders', these regions have a much lower share among Global Champions for example China, India, Korea, Russia and elsewhere storm into the Global Champions league. A few non-Triad companies have captured the benefits of global growth. One such company, HSBC Holdings, has grown from its Hong Kong base to be the world's third largest financial services institution by market capitalization, with revenues of $40 billion and close to 30 million customers worldwide. Samsung Electronics, the world's fastest growing consumer electronics brand, is another. Samsung Electronics reported revenues of about $54 billion in 2003, only a few years after beginning to expand outside Korea ('Asian Companies are Emerging Rapidly'), its market capitalization now far exceeds Sony's. these companies outside the triad however have a much lower share among Global Champions. Countries outside the Triad have found the global journey to be challenging.

The globalization efforts of many non-Triad companies have been hamstrung by three primary factors:

1. Lack of competition in their home markets: First, non-Triad companies have been severely handicapped by the lack of competitiveness in their home markets. Government policy, high tariff protections, non-tariff barriers, and small market size have all served to shield non-Triad companies from global competition. These historical barriers are responsible for the large number of uncompetitive banks, insurance companies, steel mills, utilities, retailers, healthcare companies, and so on in non-Triad countries. Consequently, few of these companies are prepared to deal with strong competition from international attackers, or to export their businesses to new markets.

2. A highly local workforce and management culture: A second major handicap facing large non-Triad companies is their highly local workforce and management culture. Compared with their counterparts in the Triad, companies tend to be much less aggressive and much more internally focused in hiring, managing, compensating, and retaining talent. Non-Triad companies typically have few executives who are comfortable operating in other countries. The single-culture nature of these organizations gives them a limited understanding of overseas markets and little experience in handling diverse workforces. Moreover, executives at these companies receive relatively low total compensation, a fact that makes it difficult and divisive to add a global perspective by bringing in highly paid international executives.

3. An organizational structure that is ill-equipped to handle a federation of far-flung operations: A final challenge facing non-Triad companies is the organizational structure and the processes required to manage complex, far-flung operations. Most executives in these companies still have the typical 'export from the factory' mindset, with almost all decision making and resources concentrated in the home market. International markets are seen as outposts best handled through a sales office staffed solely with trusted expiates. How else to explain why most senior executives of Indian IT services firms, for example, reside in India, while their entire customer base is in the US and Europe?

Overcoming the Challenges

Building capabilities, executives, and an organization that can operate across national boundaries is far more important than deciding which markets to enter and when. In fact, there is a vast difference between 'going global' and 'becoming global'. Simply stated, becoming global is about adopting a global approach and mindset across the business model. It is a long journey, fraught with peril, in which managers must constantly ask the question: "Do our actions help build a company that can beat the best in the world?" Only a few will truly be able to answer: "Yes."

Only talented people deeply versed in the new country's business culture and in the operating practices of the company can make the tradeoffs that preserve its distinctiveness while helping it adapt to local requirements. Companies must support these executives with an organizational structure that allows them to make decisions on the ground, in the new country, without unnecessary hurdles imposed by the head office.

Thus, to succeed in the wider world, a company must develop a cadre of talented international executives who carry its DNA-core skills and organizational culture _ and have experience in diverse markets. A methodical approach to building such a group is more important for aspiring global companies than any tangible asset, such as factories, property or equipment.

Global leaders realize that it is best to groom executives from within, beginning with locally recruited, entry-level executives. Such executives can be fully trained in a company's processes and operating methods while retaining the ability to customize these practices to their own cultures. One Indian IT services firm has begun recruiting from top-tier US business schools with the specific objective of grooming globally mobile executives. It has created two separate career tracks, one for the domestic market and one for international markets, with distinct recruitment, job rotation, and compensation policies. These efforts are paying off as this new crop of global executives, able to combine relationship-management skills and offshore delivery knowledge, begins selling high-end solutions to large accounts.

Global job rotation is crucial to grooming global executives. Such practices typically target the creation of an expert general manager, someone with deep functional expertise in a single area but also a CEO-type cross-functional perspective and high cultural sensitivity. HSBC, for example, puts 400 handpicked 'international managers' through a global rotation programme to expose them to various situations, training them to parachute into troubled operations and fix those problems. CEMEX's programmed assigns top-performing executives to M&A, due diligence, and post-merger management projects in foreign countries, where they are also trained to understand different cultures.

The best global corporations emphasize unique practices that their executives absorb at a visceral level. One leading business services company, for instance, creates a worldwide culture around its basic values, such as professionalism and collegiality, and the rigorous processes it uses to evaluate and develop talent. It does, however, accept significantly way in the particulars of interaction with clients in specific countries. In addition, apprenticeships and rotations help global executives to build internal networks that not only engender mutual trust and shared understandings but also promote the efficient functioning of informal processes and the transfer of knowledge within the company. These experiences also subject budding executives to the management challenges they will encounter from country to country.

HSBC, for example, puts 400 hand-picked international managers through a global-rotation programmed that trains them to respond quickly and effectively in troublesome situations. These managers learn to distinguish the non-negotiable aspects of a business model from those that can be modified as necessary.

Steps for Developing a Global Cadre

1. Get the strategy in place: develop a clear understanding of what kinds of global executives you will need. One of us was asked "we don't have a global strategy, but what should we be doing to develop global executives?" Until at least a general direction with guidelines for where to go is available, development efforts will be ineffective and misguided .one must show that development contributes to the business."

2. Translate the strategy into challenges: What work will need to get done, what capabilities will be needed, what challenges will our executives face? We know now that executives develop from the challenges they face, and the particular challenges determine the particular capabilities they are likely to develop. The development is in the challenges; they must be identified.

3. Design a process for helping executives learn the essential lessons: Companies ask, "What can we do to develop global executive talent?" The answer lies in the fact that the technology is there; put it in place. One may not know exactly how people learn and exactly how to help them learn faster, but it is known how to design processes that put talented people into the jobs that teach them the lessons they need to know.

4. Vaccinate against failures: Derailment (when an otherwise talented executive gets off-track) is a hazard that any executive risks, but our research found that the risks are far greater in global work. Global work is fraught with derailment "opportunities." Our research found that the reasons for global derailment are the same (e.g., early strengths become weaknesses) but the dynamics are more complex and the risks greater in proportion to the distance from corporate headquarters. Organizations make mistakes in managing global executives that magnify the risks. The solution: take preventative measures to make sure it doesn't happen.

5. Mind the transitions: It is the transitions in careers that offer quantum leaps in opportunities for executives to learn. Going out, coming in, getting a new boss, getting a new boss from another culture — all of these transitions are fertile development opportunities. But it is also during transitions that the executive is most at risk for missing the lessons offered, or worse, for derailing. Global work, often far from home and the home office, many times deprives us of the support we are accustomed to that which smoothes the rough places. Again, we know what to do, but few companies do it. Transition support gets lost in the business demands with sometimes devastating results for the executive and for the organization.

6. Stay the course: The very things that make global business exciting and attractive to many people and organizations — the uncertainty, the rate of change, the constantly shifting landscape— these are also the things that make global executive development so "devilishly difficult" and cause companies to abandon their efforts. All of us would like to accelerate development so that we could develop an executive in 2 years rather than 5, or 5 years rather than 10 or 20. But, it can't be done.

The rewards in this race are not necessarily to the swiftest, but to those who stay the course. Year in and year out!

Implementation: The Cadre Process

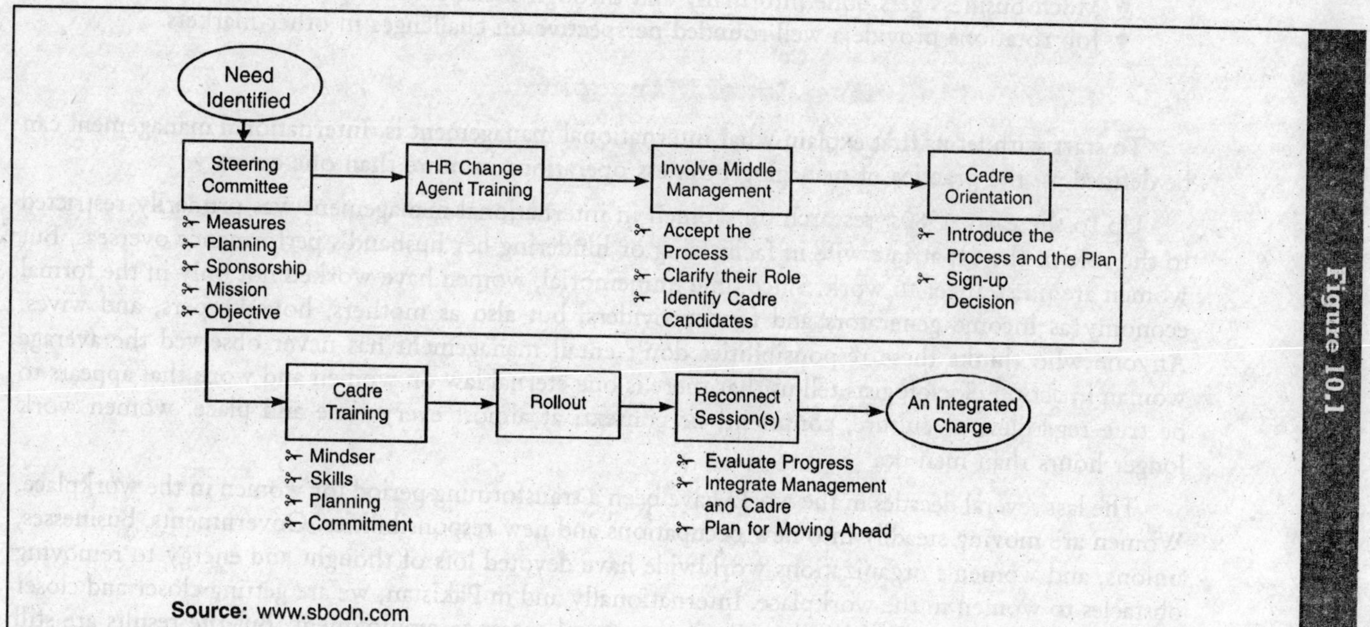

Source: www.sbodn.com

Figure 10.1

Implementation Advice

- Choose Cadre members very carefully
- Clear and compelling linkage to the strategic direction
- Spend time on the management team and cadre dynamics
- Set up a recognition process for Cadre performance
- Set a formalized communication channel for new information
- Confirm "peer referral" as a critical lever.

The Global Cadre Framework

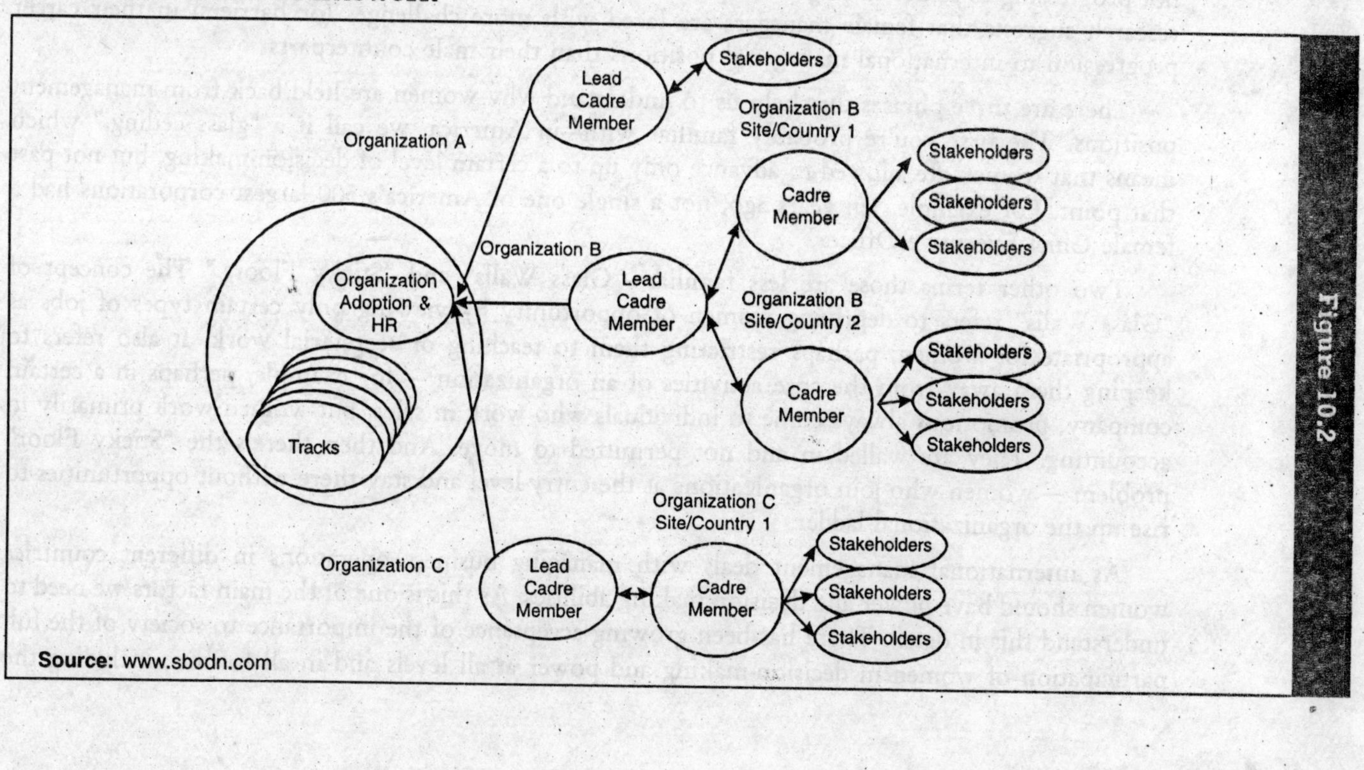

Source: www.sbodn.com

Figure 10.2

Conclusion

- A cadre of global executives makes a global organization more feasible.
- Co-ordination processes run smoothly because participants trust each other.
- Much business gets done informally and through social contacts.
- Job rotations provide a well-rounded perspective on challenges in other markets.

Role of Women in International Management

To start with let us first explain what international management is. International management can be defined as- the practice of managing business operations in more than one country.

Up to the early 1980s, research on women in international management was primarily restricted to the role of the expatriate wife in facilitating or hindering her husband's performance overseas. But women are no stranger to work. Since time immemorial, women have worked not only in the formal economy as income generators and food providers, but also as mothers, housekeepers, and wives. Anyone who thinks these responsibilities don't entail management has never observed the average woman in action. Sociologists tell us that there is one eternal law on women and work that appears to be true regardless of culture, continent, or context: at almost every time and place, women work longer hours than men do.

The last several decades in the world have been a transforming period for women in the workplace. Women are moving steadily into new occupations and new responsibilities. Governments, businesses, unions, and women's organizations worldwide have devoted lots of thought and energy to removing obstacles to women in the workplace. Internationally and in Pakistan, we are getting closer and closer to a level legal playing field in allowing women equal access to employment. But the results are still short of true equality of opportunity - particularly for advancement.

When we compare the managers based in Ireland, England, Belgium and Germany who had worked in European countries, US and Japan we find that- many of the constraints that often hinder women in attaining senior managerial positions are quite similar in most countries.

There are, for example, cultural, educational, legislative, attitudinal and corporate constraints in most countries. The relative importance of each constraint varies from society to society. Prior research in international human resource management in Europe indicates that female managers are not progressing to senior management positions at comparable rates to their male counterparts. This research suggests that female managers are faced with more challenges (or barriers) in their career progression to international managerial positions than their male counterparts.

There are three phrases that help us to understand why women are held back from management positions. The first you're probably familiar with—in America, we call it a "glass ceiling," which means that women are allowed to advance only up to a certain level of decision-making, but not past that point. For example, ten years ago, not a single one of America's 500 largest corporations had a female Chief Executive Officer.

Two other terms those are less familiar—"Glass Walls" and "Sticky Floors." The concept of "Glass Walls" refers to depriving women of opportunity by viewing only certain types of jobs as appropriate for women, perhaps restricting them to teaching or secretarial work. It also refers to keeping them away from the core activities of an organization — for example, perhaps in a certain company, promotions always come to individuals who work in sales, but women work primarily in accounting. They are walled in and not permitted to move. And then there's the "Sticky Floor" problem — women who join organizations at the entry-level and stay there without opportunities to rise up the organizational ladder.

As international management deals with managing business operations in different countries women should have power and decision making abilities. As this is one of the main factors we need to understand this in detail. There has been growing acceptance of the importance to society of the full participation of women in decision-making and power at all levels and in all forums, including the intergovernmental, governmental and non-governmental sectors. In some countries, women have also attained higher positions in these spheres.

Positive changes

1. Increase in number of women parliamentarians in those countries where awareness rising on equal participation.
2. More women entering into local politics in some countries in transition as a result of democratization, decentralization and development of civil society.
3. New opportunities for these women to gain leadership skills, experience, knowledge and networking capacity.

Obstacles and barriers

1. Persistent prejudice and cultural attitudes that exclude women from leadership especially in some political parties (party culture of masculinity) and countries.
2. Persistence of racism, discrimination and other ideologies of intolerance leading to limited access to decision-making bodies for some women because of their cultural and ethnic background.

Other obstacles

1. Bias and obstacle in the selection process for an international assignment was their gender.
2. Promotion of females to senior international management positions has proceeded at a very slow rate.
3. Mentoring relationship.

Corporate barriers

These barriers are still strong in many European countries. The managers highlighted, for example, that recruitment and selection barriers and the formal policies and informal processes of organizations often prevent many women from reaching senior managerial positions. The managers also suggested that many jobs are still seen as "men's" or "women's" jobs and this influences the initial intake of a particular gender to organizations.

Lack of monitoring

This is one of the informal barriers. There are not enough women in senior international managerial positions yet to act as mentors for other women. In the absence of family and friends, their mentors also helped in keeping them in touch with their home organizations, which in turn reduced the "out of sight, out of mind" syndrome.

In conclusion, despite these obstacles, which the interviewees reported to be overt and covert, female managers are available, suitable and motivated to partake in international management.

Presumptive and erroneous attitudes are adopted by top management about female managers' potential abilities, willingness and availability for international assignments. Women tend to be better than men at empowering staff. They encourage openness and are more accessible. Women are more tolerant of differences, so they are more skilled at managing diversity.

International Scenario

Past Scene

FORTUNE examined 1990 proxy statements of the 799 public companies on its combined lists of the 1,000 largest U.S. industrial and service companies. The cold-shower findings: Of the 4,012 people listed as the highest-paid officers and directors of their companies, we spotted 19 women — less than one-half of 1% (see chart). True, there has been progress, but it has been remarkably limited. When FORTUNE undertook a similar project in 1978, out of 6,400 officers and directors on its combined lists, which then included 1,000 industrial and 300 service companies, ten were women.

Further down the ranks, the numbers are more heartening but only slightly. To get an idea of the count — there are no authoritative studies of the number of women in upper management — FORTUNE looked through the names at the back of the annual reports of 255 major corporations. The list often goes as deep in the organization as division head and assistant vice president, and includes positions like corporate secretary that have frequently gone to women. Of the 9,293 names, 5% were women.

Present Scenario

Women still not present in fair numbers within organizations. Just when companies talk about the diversity buzz and begin tracking their gender ratio, here are a few numbers they would want to note. Only 26.1 percent of the listed companies (392 of 1,500 firms) have a woman on their boards. Out of the 278 directors on the BSE Sensex companies, there are only 10 women directors. Out of the 9,000 people on boards of the BSE-listed companies, only five are women. Indian companies seriously lack women in senior management roles, HR consultants say. Women executives in India earn 40 percent less than what men earn over their entire career, as per HR experts. Corporate India fairs very poorly *vis-à-vis* its global counterparts, the study reveals. Over 77 percent of the 200 largest companies in the world, as ranked by Fortune, had at least one women director on their board as of 2006.Even here, China outpaces India. Only 36 percent of Indian companies have women holding senior management positions as compared to 91 percent of companies in China. The global average also stands much higher at 65 percent. Almost 85 percent of the women managers are in supporting roles (like HR, PR and customer service). Women are far more stable in their jobs and their average turnover rate is far lesser than men.

Businesses with Women in Senior Management

97% of businesses in the Philippines1 have women in senior management positions, the highest in the survey, in contrast to the lowest Japan, with only 25%. Four out of the five countries with the lowest figures are in Europe: the Netherlands (27%), Luxembourg (37%), Germany (41%) and Italy (42%).In total, over half of all European businesses surveyed (52%) have women participating in senior management, while in NAFTA (North American Free Trade Agreement) countries 68% of businesses have females in senior roles. Compared with three years ago, European businesses have 4% more women in senior management, whereas NAFTA countries have 6% more.

Since 2004 the global figure for businesses with 'no women' in senior management positions has remained unchanged at 38%. Countries with businesses reporting a fall in businesses with female senior managers include Mexico (a drop of 24%), Russia (15%), Poland (9%), Italy (6%), New Zealand (6%) and the US (6%). Countries which report increased participation of women in senior levels are: Spain (16%), India (14%), Taiwan and the Philippines (13%) and Hong Kong and Sweden (both 9%).

Percentage of Women in Senior Management Roles

The percentage of women in senior managerial positions globally has grown slightly from 19% to 22% since 2004. The Philippines comes out top with 50% of managerial positions being held by females, ahead of Brazil (42%) and two other Asian countries - Thailand (39%) and Hong Kong (35%). Lowest in the table is Japan with just 7%, below three European countries Luxembourg, Germany and the Netherlands at 10%, 12% and 13% respectively.

The EU's proportion of women in senior management has remained static at 17%, while NAFTA's figure has increased from 20% to 23%.Commenting on the results, April Mackenzie, executive director of public policy for Grant Thornton International, said: "It is disappointing that the participation of women in senior business management has not increased more dramatically over the last three years. It is however encouraging to see some of the Asian economies leading the way. North American and European businesses in particular continue to disappoint.

Hopefully we will see this change in coming years as more women play increasingly prominent roles in business and public life such as Indra Nooyi, the new chief executive officer of PepsiCo,

Angela Merkel, German chancellor, Margaret Whitman, chief executive and president of eBay and Anne Lauvergeon, chief executive of France's state-owned nuclear group Areva."

26% of respondents in the Philippines did not respond to this particular question. Therefore, the results are based on a robust sample of businesses who provided a response to this question.

Note: The Global and East Asia figures exclude mainland China in order to make a like-for-like comparison with the 2004.

Barriers

Contrary to popular corporate myth, female managers often report the biggest barriers coming from within the corporation, rather than from situations actually encountered during foreign assignments.

An Australian survey has concluded that women's accomplishments are attributed to luck and external factors, including affirmative action, whereas men's are attributed to skill and ability. The latter have higher worth in the labour market.

In addition, theories of statistical discrimination hold that employers expect lower productivity returns for professional women than for equally qualified men due to probability estimates of turnover, work commitment, and skills that encompass the population at large. This thinking can lead to job assignments for women that limit their skill and knowledge gains, including those across borders. "We talk about the fact that women have to be "overripe" for promotion - they have to demonstrate they can do the next job before they get promoted to it, while men are promoted much earlier when they're hungry, not when (they're) ready." says Jennifer Allyn of Catalyst, a New York-based nonprofit research and advisory group.

Dr Nancy Adler, a professor at McGill University in Montreal and an authority on women's global leadership, has identified three key barriers to selection of women on international assignments:

- The assumption that women simply do not want to be international managers because of work/family conflicts (particularly married women and working mothers).
- The outright refusal of some companies to send women abroad, owing to fears about their competence or their physical safety.
- The belief that many foreigners are prejudiced against women expatriate managers.

Research has indicated that because men hold most upper level management positions, they do most hiring, including sending individuals on overseas assignments, and they may not be willing to offer career advancement opportunities to women subordinates.

Overcoming Barriers to Women Advancement

In South Africa, women hold only 4,3% of directorships of companies, as indicated in a survey done by Corporate Women Directors International. It can be argued that since laws have been passed to ensure gender equity, organizations have become more aware of gender discrimination and more females occupy senior positions.

The path forward: creating an equitable system.

In the increasingly diverse workplace, women and minorities make up a growing percentage of the workforce. What this implies is that managerial talent needs to be drawn from this diverse pool to deal with discrimination in the workplace. These recommendations should be seen as a beginning for breaking the glass ceiling and a way of opening up avenues to banish discrimination against women.

Succession Planning

Succession planning for women employees can be achieved by assisting women to overcome their lack of confidence. This will improve the numbers of women in various employment categories. Companies should be encouraged to introduce development career planning for both managerial and non-managerial women. These plans should include development, career planning, workplace culture and flexible working arrangements. Progress in this plan should also be linked to the performance assessment of managers.

Enskilling - Through Training And Education.

The most important issue within training and development is the fact that learning and education must be based on developing skills for the new economy in other words, thinking in the future tense. As more and more organizations must be competitive not only in their internal markets, but also globally, these economic changes impact on the content and context within which training takes place. Training and development must not only teach women how to think about business, but also how to practically manage business.

The South African government and business schools that are responsible for training women have to play an important role in changing the situation. Government should realize that it is a waste of scarce resources to train women in management subjects if their talents are not likely to be used by South African companies. Researching the role of women in modern companies and the contribution they can make at all levels of corporate management could contribute greatly in the effort to eradicate the outdated gender preconceptions prevailing in companies today. In the new South African environment, to develop women to their full potential, the following five pillars in developing leadership should always be borne in mind:

- Through emancipation, women must be set free from the illusion that they cannot be leaders.
- Especially in the new South African environment, women should be encouraged to want to become corporate leaders.
- We need to teach South African women what leadership is so that they can develop an understanding thereof through enlightenment.
- As managers in the organization, we need to ensure our future female leaders through enablement in other words, as leaders ourselves; we must give them the skills to become leaders.
- If people are not given a platform through exposure; they will never be able to become leaders.

Changing the Scene

As we know a small number of women have managed to break through the glass ceiling the boardroom or to the top levels of their organizations. Given below are some examples and reach from corporate worl.

Microsoft opens windows for woman MD - Microsoft India is among the very few top firms, and not just InfoTech entities, to have appointed a woman in the top professional slot. It is a rare occurrence even for Microsoft to have a woman leading its crucial subsidiary in a key geography. What is even more creditable is that Dhawan has served in India for last two decades. Dhawan will be in charge of the IT behemoth's sales and marketing efforts in India. She will be responsible for growing Microsoft's products and services businesses and also play a key role in driving the company's partnerships and strategic alliances.

Known to be aggressive and a go-getter, Dhawan has been in the IT hardware industry for 22 years and has risen from the ranks. Before joining Microsoft, she was serving as vice president, Customer Solutions Group, HP India, with a focus on enterprise, public sector and SMB sectors for all computing products and services. She was also responsible for strategic alliances and partner relationships. Prior to joining HP in 1999, Dhawan had served IBM and HCL.

Indra Nooyi- Chief Executive (Designate), Pepsi Co. 1st position

This Madras born woman was a straight "A" student in her school. Nooyi did her bachelors from Madras Christian College and MBA from Indian Institute of Management, Kolkata. Nooyi then went to USA and attended Yale University. From Yale, she obtained degree on management.

This brilliant corporate woman started her career in Boston Consulting Group and moved on to Motorola and Asea Brown Boveri. She joined PepsiCo. in 1994. She turned the company into a bold risk taker. In 1998, Pepsi acquired Tropicana. In 1997, Pepsi started its own fast food chain. In 2001, she became President of Pepsi Cola. Wall Street Journal included her name in their top 50 women to watch in 2007. Fortune magazine declared her 1st most powerful women in business.

Anne Mulcahy Chairman and CEO Xerox (XRX)

In May, Xerox's credit was upgraded to investment-grade status from junk, and analysts love the new focus on growth and expansion - a sign that Xerox is back to health. Recent acquisitions like Global Imaging Systems should add close to $1 billion in sales to the $16 billion company. The stock is up 10% in the past year.

A chairman of the board and chief executive officer of Xerox Corporation, Stamford, Conn. She was named CEO of Xerox on Aug. 1, 2001, and chairman on Jan. 1, 2002. In addition to the Xerox board, she is a member of the boards of directors of Catalyst, Citigroup Inc., Fuji Xerox Co. Ltd. and Target Corporation, and is a member of The Business Council.

Dr. Kiran Mazumdar-Shaw, Chairman & Managing Director, Biocon Ltd

Kiran Mazumdar Shaw is the Chairman & Managing Director of Biocon Ltd, India's biggest biotechnology company. In 2004, she became India's richest woman. Kiran Mazumdar Shaw was born on March 23, 1953 in Bangalore. She had her schooling at Bishop Cotton Girls School and Mount Carmel College at Bangalore. After doing completing her B.Sc. in Zoology from Bangalore University in 1973, she went to Ballarat University in Melbourne, Australia and qualified as a master brewer. Kiran Mazumdar Shaw started her professional career as trainee brewer in Carlton & United Beverages in 1974. In 1978, she joined as Trainee Manager with Biocon Biochemical's Limited in Ireland. In the same year, Kiran Mazumdar Shaw founded Biocon India in collaboration with Biocon Biochemical's Limited, with a capital of Rs.10, 000. She initially faced many problems regarding funds for her business. Banks were hesitant to give loan to her as biotechnology was a totally new field at that point of time and she was a woman entrepreneur, which was a rare phenomenon. Biocon's initial operation was to extract an enzyme from papaya. Under Kiran Mazumdar Shaw's stewardship Biocon transformed from an industrial enzymes company to an integrated biopharmaceutical company with strategic research initiatives.

Today, Biocon is recognized as India's pioneering biotech enterprise. In 2004, Biocon came up with an IPO and the issue was over-subscribed by over 30 times. Post-IPO, Kiran Mazumdar Shaw held close to 40% of the stock of the company and was regarded as India's richest woman with an estimated worth of Rs. 2,100 crores. Kiran Mazumdar Shaw is the recipient of several prestigious awards. These include ET Businesswoman of the Year, Best Woman Entrepreneur, Model Employer, and Ernst & Young's Entrepreneur of the Year Award for Life Sciences & Healthcare, Leading Exporter, Outstanding Citizen, Technology Pioneer, etc. Government of India also felicitated her with Padmashri (1989) and Padma Bhushan (2005).

- In the future there will be two types of companies : those who promote women in leading positions , and those who NOT
- Top management has to own the Gender Diversity Initiative; promotion of women in leading position must be a part of the development plans.
- Interlink the strengths of different leadership styles.

Women: Development of relationship and communities, consideration of different perspectives, multitasking.

Men: Orientation to hierarchy, concentration on final results.

Conclusion

A pervasive myth is that European women are not capable of assuming managerial positions in Asia, because of the ongoing exclusion of women from these positions in Asian countries. In reality, European women are often more effective than men as managers in Asia because they frequently utilize intuitive and empathetic skills that are highly valued in that region.

Research shows that women handle emotions and relationships differently than men. Women's empathy and insight is receiving boardroom attention as companies realize that in an ever-globalizing world, these skills are indispensable. Multinationals are incorporating elements of interpersonal and intercultural expertise into their workforce, but may be overlooking a key resource.

❄❄❄

11 Challenges of Global Management

• Challenges in Global Management • The World Wide Learning Challenge • Knowledge Management • Managing Across Boundaries • Transnational Corporations • Multinational Corporations • Indian Multinationals

Globalization is no longer an abstraction but a stark reality that virtually all firms, large and a small, face. Firms that want to survive in the 21st century must confront this all encompassing force that pervades every aspect of business. In a wide range of industries from automobiles to food and clothing, firms face the pressures of global competition at home as well as in international markets. Choosing not to participate in global markets is no longer an option. All firms, regardless of their size, have to craft strategies in the broader context of world markets to anticipate, respond and adapt to the changing configuration of these markets.

Navigating global waters successfully and establishing direction to guide the firm in an increasingly turbulent world environment, is a key challenge facing today's managers. To date, this has largely been perceived as the purview of large multinationals with diverse far-flung operations in all parts of the global market.

For large multinationals with experience in plying global waters, this orientation is not misplaced. However, the conclusions and implications do not apply to firms with limited experience in international markets who are just beginning to target customers in other countries and learning how to build operations in these markets. Today, an increasing number of small and medium-size firms are going global and their concerns are markedly different from those of established multi-nationals.

Firms initially entering international markets, will be more concerned with learning about international markets, selecting an appropriate arena to compete, and determining how to leverage core competencies in international markets. Once in international markets, firms have to build their position in these markets, establishing a strong local presence by developing new products and adapting to local tastes and preferences. As the firm expands internationally, it will need to move away from country-centred strategies and improve integration and coordination across national markets, leveraging its competencies and skills to develop a leadership position.

Globalization

The process of interaction and interconnection among people, companies, government of different nations, a process driven by international trade and investment and aided by development in information and communication technology and other major areas.It can be found in five different areas such as **economic, cultural, political, religious,** and **social systems.**

In the present situation the **objective of the organization** is to remain responsive to local markets, while at the same time achieving global efficiency through integrating and coordinating operations across world markets and allowing for the transfer of learning from operations in one part of the world to another.

Factors for Companies to Go Global

Greater market share: Due to the vast opportunities companies are compelled to be an effective player in the global market to boost its market share and brand image.

Economic Liberalization & Free Trade Zone: A very important factor for globalization. Due to the increase in the free trade zone such as **GATT, NAFTA, EU & WTO** & economic liberalization of global economy, trade barriers are significantly reduced which are helping companies to search for a low cost manufacturing location. This is one of the main reasons behind the globalization of Asian companies from China and India etc.

Facilities: The extent to which an enterprise can develop globally from home country base depends on the facilities available like infrastructural facilities such as Transport, location etc.

Resources: Resources are one of the important factors which often decide the ability of a firm to globalise. Resourceful companies may find it easier to thrust ahead in global market. Resources include finance, technology, R&D capabilities human resource etc.

Competitiveness: The competitive advantage of the company is a very important determinant of success in global business. It includes factors as low cost & price, product quality, product differentiation, after sales service, marketing strength etc.

Changing Global Scenario

Establishing a clearly defined competitive strategy to provide direction for their efforts was a paramount concern of managers in the '80s. As competitive pressures became more acute, management recognized that they needed to develop a strategic thrust geared to securing and sustaining a competitive advantage in their served markets. Effective strategy moves were grounded in assessment of the firm's current competitive position and identification of the skills and capabilities affording the most leverage in the light of future market developments. More recently, the validity of traditional approaches to strategy and even the value of strategic thinking have been questioned. The transformation of the competitive landscape by broad-based changes in technology, structural changes impacting industry, the emergence of new sources of competition, and increased environmental concerns, have all led to a re-evaluation of strategic thinking and strategy development. In particular, the changing competitive landscape and increasingly turbulent environment suggest the need for new approaches and a broader view of how the organization should respond to changing environmental conditions.

Technology is rapidly altering the nature of competition and strategy in many industries. The global proliferation of relatively inexpensive computing power and global linkages of computer networks through telecommunications have resulted in an information-rich, computation-rich and communication-rich organizational environment. Telecommunications and computer networks are changing the way in which managers' work and interact, providing links between country-centred organizations, and permitting technology to be rapidly shared and learning transferred throughout the organization. As a result, speed of technological diffusion and change is rapidly increasing. At the same time, the growing technological orientation of many industries and use of computers and telecommunications technology have created greater knowledge intensity and dependency. Often, technological knowledge and rapid product and process innovation is the *sine qua non* to achieving and sustaining competitive success in the global marketplace.

The telecommunications revolution has also stimulated major structural changes in industries and organizations. Vertically integrated, centralized organizational systems have given way to decentralized, highly fragmented fluid structures, linked by agreements, contracts and working relationships. This has radically changed the nature and basis of competitive advantage and the economics of doing business. At the same time, traditional industry boundaries and demarcation lines are breaking down as business and technologies fuse or converge (for example, communications and consumer electronics, entertainment and education) and new industries emerge, with as yet no clearly defined boundaries.

Competition is also intensifying, as globalization changes the boundaries of competition and new sources of competition emerge. The basis for competition is also changing, as new players are able to enter the market with an ease unknown even ten years ago. Information technology has dramatically transformed the costs of doing business and enabled firms to bypass stages in the value chain, for example, going directly to customers, or outsourcing functions and operations. Such factors have changed the nature of the value chain in many industries, enabling new and non-traditional competitors to enter the market rapidly and compete effectively.

Concern over the impact of industrial activity on the environment has also heightened, adding to the complexity of doing business in today's world. New forms of packaging, demand for recycling, more efficient use of resources, greater responsibility for protecting the environment, limiting toxic waste, as well as to educate consumers and to develop more "user friendly" products are all compounding the tasks and demands placed on the organization. Increasingly, firms are called upon not only to be environmentally and politically correct, but also to be more responsible citizens in all their activities worldwide.

Challenges Facing Global Markets

Involvement in global markets presents the firm with a number of challenges. These challenges influence competitive advantage in global markets, and in part determine how readily the firm can achieve economies of scale and scope as well as realize synergies from operation in a multi-country environment. In striving to develop a strategy that will make it more competitive.

Key Challenges for the Firms:

1. **Change:** Rapid change pervades all aspects of operations in global markets as well as the context in which they take place. Not only are the rates of technological evolution, knowledge obsolescence and the intensity of competition increasing at an alarming pace in many industries, but unforeseen events are dramatically changing the political and economic context in which markets develop and strategies are formulated.

Technological change renders product development, production processes, and experience rapidly obsolete and contributes to escalating investment costs as well as heightened competitive pressures. In the notebook segment of the personal computer industry, for example, the cycle of new model introduction has shrunk to less than three months, rendering models rapidly obsolete and requiring constant vigilance to new product development and attention to keeping ahead of the competition.

The rapid pace of change is further complicated by its increasingly discontinuous nature. Until the late 80's, change was somewhat predictable and linear in nature. Today, established models for predicting change no longer work in many instances due to the discontinuity of change. At one time, market trends and growth in a developing country could be predicted on the basis of trends in more advanced countries ten years earlier. For example, development of telecommunications networks within a country progressed slowly and required massive investment in wires and cables to connect customers. Today's cellular technology makes it possible for a country to quickly develop a modern telecommunications system and "leap frog" the wire stage. Further, cellular technology opens up the market for fax machines, personal digital assistants, modems, etc.

At the same time, as customers become more mobile and are exposed to new ideas and patterns of behaviour through the new global media, the diffusion of new products and innovation takes place more rapidly. Rather than first being adopted by opinion leaders and then trickling down to other members of society, innovations are now spreading horizontally across countries and societies. No sooner does a new trend or fashion emerge in one country than it spreads rapidly to another. Not only are global marketers agents of change in introducing new and innovative products and services to other countries, but in addition, they must respond to the rapid pace at which societies are changing and market trends evolving.

While the pace of change is accelerating, pushed by the engine of technology and global communication, it is becoming increasingly uncertain and unpredictable-occurring in unexpected ways from unexpected sources. Events such as the break-up of the Soviet Union have had far-reaching, often cataclysmic effects on world markets and the geopolitics of world trade. Subsequent political and economic events dramatically halted the rate of economic growth and foreign investment in the Soviet economy. The break up also had an impact on former trading partners such as India,

Cuba, Vietnam, and Northern Korea, forcing them to seek out new markets for their products, and sources for energy, arms, minerals, and other raw materials. It also put a sudden end to the Cold War and ushered in a new political era. Industries such as defence, which fed on the desire to maintain the geo-political balance, declined, triggering the realignment of related and tributary industries such as aerospace, electronics, and vehicles.

A new economic order thus appears to be emerging, characterized by new players and new and more diverse patterns of trade. Yet, all these changing patterns appear fraught with uncertainty, as a surge in one direction is countered by a pull in another. A new instability has crept into world markets, threatening at any moment to tilt the precarious balance of economic forces. Moves toward world economic growth, regional integration or the empowerment of Third World nations, can without warning be thwarted by pressures to retreat behind the bulwark of economic nationalism.

2. **Complexity:** Complexity in the global environment is a product of contextual factors such as technological advances, diverse social and economic change, and political upheavals. More directly, for the firm complexity is intensified by the scope of its operations in global markets, at different levels of the value chain and how they are arrayed across markets, the inter-linkages and interdependencies between markets, and the increased blurring of product market boundaries, both functionally and geographically. Challenge arises from the increasing complexity of managing international operations. Technological advances, on the one hand, enable management to direct, coordinate, and control operations on a much broader and diverse geographic scale and scope than previously possible. Yet at the same time, such advances add further complexity, as management has to master the tools and skills required to handle the burgeoning international infrastructure. As the geographic scope and scale of operations extends further and further, management is faced with the task of directing and controlling diverse and far-flung activities at various stages in the value chain, often in widely divergent environmental contexts. Additional layers of organization begin to creep into the corporate infrastructure and further complicate the global management task. With trends toward regional market integration, management systems are established to direct and coordinate market operations within a region, and to provide an intermediate link between corporate headquarters and local management. At the same time, organizational links between functions in each stage of the value chain are added at a global level to ensure the transfer of ideas, information and experience across geographic areas and to exploit potential synergies worldwide. Similarly, as customer markets become more dispersed, establishment of linkages with customers and suppliers becomes increasing critical in order to co-ordinate supplying and servicing these markets rapidly and efficiently, and to compete effectively in global markets.

Sometimes links are established with other organizations, in some cases competitors, to exploit newly emerging opportunities in specific product markets or parts of the world. Strategic alliances may be formed with firms to provide desired geographic market coverage, or skills and resources needed to implement a given strategy. In other cases, temporary networks are formed by far flung partners (suppliers, customers, and competitors) sharing costs, skills, access, and operations in global markets through electronic links, utilizing the latest information technology, to take advantage of a specific market opportunity. These networks are fluid and flexible, evolving in response to changing market conditions. Once an opportunity is met, or disappears, so the network will disband.

Spatial market patterns are also becoming increasingly complex. Configuration of markets was predominant national in character, surrounded by seemingly impenetrable boundaries. However, the gradual breaking down of such boundaries in many parts of the world, means that markets previously viewed as separated and independent are becoming linked and beginning to function as one.

3. **Competition:** Increasing intensity of competition in global markets constitutes yet another challenge facing companies at all stages of involvement in international markets. As markets open up, and become more integrated, the pace of change accelerates, technology shrinks distances between markets and reduces the scale advantages of large firms, new sources of competition emerge, and competitive pressures mount at all levels of the organization.

As more and more firms venture into global markets, competition proliferates, posing new threats and dangers to be reckoned with. In addition to facing competition from well-established multinationals and from domestic firms entrenched in their respective product or service markets, firms face growing competition from firms in newly industrializing countries and previously protected markets in the Third World, as well as emerging global networks or coalitions of organizations of diverse national origins.

Firms from newly industrializing nations such a Taiwan, Singapore, Korea and Hong Kong are increasingly taking the initiative in competing in global markets, rather than acting as low-cost suppliers to firms in the Industrial Triad. The threat of competition from companies in countries such as India, China, Malaysia, and Brazil is also on the rise, as their own domestic markets are opening up to foreign competition, stimulating greater awareness of international market opportunities and of the need to be internationally competitive. Companies which previously focused on protected domestic markets are entering into markets in other countries, creating new sources of competition, often targeted to price-sensitive market segments.

At the same time, spurred by new advances in communications technology and rapid obsolescence, the speed of competitor response is accelerating. No longer does a pioneer in global markets enjoy a substantial lead time over competitors. Nimble competitors, benefiting from lower overhead and operating costs, enter rapidly with clones or low-cost substitutes, and take advantage of the pioneer's investment in R&D and product development. Modern communications and information technology also encourage rapid competitor response to price changes, or new distribution and promotional tactics, and further heighten the pace of competition.

Not only is competition intensifying for all firms regardless of their degree of global market involvement, but the basis for competition is changing. Competition continues to be market-based and ultimately relies on delivering superior value to consumers. However, success in global markets depends on knowledge accumulation and deployment. Firms that win in the market place will be those that can use information to their advantage to guide the delivery of superior value. Further, the increased blurring of product market boundaries and interlinking of markets means that how value is perceived and by whom is less clear. Firms beginning to enter international markets are in a position to limit competitive exposure by choosing markets that are free of formidable foes. They can zero in on markets where they have a competitive advantage, such as being the low cost supplier in a price sensitive market.

4. Conscience: The fourth challenge relates to the firm's moral and social responsibilities in the global marketplace. A host of such responsibilities can be identified, covering a broader spectrum of social and corporate issues. Environmental issues, for example, have emerged as a key theme in the 90's Companies have become increasingly aware of the need to take measures to limit destruction of the environment. These include measures to limit pollution of the atmosphere through the emission of gases and other toxic substances, to conserve resources such as paper and plastic, whose production results in environmental destruction, and to produce and design products and packaging which are environmentally friendly.

Such measures need to cover all aspects of the firm's activities from R&D and production to marketing and service, as well as its operations in all parts of the world. Production should be engineered so as to conserve resources and limit toxic waste. Products should be designed to be free of environmentally harmful substances, such as phosphates and fluorocarbons. Use of recyclable packaging and refillable containers also helps reduce environmental pollution.

Another area of social responsibility of particular relevance in international markets is concern with customer education and general well-being. This is often an important issue in marketing in Third World countries, where disadvantaged or poorly educated consumers are less able to judge the merits of a product or service or understand how to use it. Attention to the potential of promotional material or product information to mislead customers is important. While customers in industrialized nations are accustomed to puffery or exaggerated product claims, and are typically highly sceptical of manufacturer-originated material, customers in developing countries are often less well-equipped or less likely to screen such material. Ability to read or understand usage instructions is another issue requiring attention. Hiring support staff to explain appropriate usage and educate consumers is often an effective approach. Product safety standards should also meet the most exacting international standards, even in countries where no such regulation exists. This is especially critical in the case of products such as pharmaceuticals, where substantial health risks are present. Firms must take the responsibility to provide accurate information to the industry and regulatory bodies, and to educate consumers and distributors to ensure appropriate usage. Intense competition, rapid change, and increased complexity in the global marketing environment make it more difficult, but all the more imperative that a firm act in a socially responsible manner.

Organizational Responses to Global Challenges

The challenges of global markets imply that managers need to radically transform the organization and rethink the ways in which they respond to the new competitive landscape. Organizational transformation involves three main components:

1. Information Systems

Information systems play a key role in shaping the response, not only in providing external linkages to the marketplace, customers, agents and suppliers and other organizations, but also in forging links within the organization and creating strong coordinating mechanisms, and enabling the emergence of new organizational forms.

Information technology and telecommunications are radically reshaping the competitive landscape, and changing the way in which individual managers and firms interact with each other around the globe. Information systems are a potent tool in shaping the firm's response to the emerging challenges. They provide the foundation that enables the firm to compete effectively in global markets.

In the initial phase of entry, information systems are critical to funnel information relating to customers, suppliers, distributors and product markets in different parts of the world to guide the firm's strategic thrust, and at the same time direct the flow of goods and services and financing to the markets targeted. At first, this information will consist primarily of secondary data relating to market and environmental conditions in different regions, and will provide input for choice of countries and markets to enter, and modes of market entry. Later, as the firm begins to enter and operate in these countries, information can be collected from personal sources such as local managers, salespeople, agents, and distribution channel members to provide richer insights into the nature of markets and operating conditions as well as the effectiveness of the firm's operations in these markets. A key function of this information is to enable management to learn about differences in market conditions, competition, and market infrastructures in other parts of the world, and to determine the need for adaptation to these markets.

In **entry phase**, information plays a key role not only in guiding marketing strategy and operational decisions, but also in reducing uncertainty and perceived risk. To the extent that management lacks familiarity with foreign markets, operations in these markets are perceived as uncertain and to be approached with caution. An effective information system helps to reduce perceived risk and uncertainty, and enables the firm to link directly with customers and markets, keeping abreast of changing market conditions, and adopting a proactive approach in entering and pursuing these markets.

In **local expansion** phase, emphasis is placed on building internal information systems within the firm, linking functional units, and providing mechanisms for coordination and control. As the firm's operations become more geographically dispersed, information systems linking operations across national boundaries become critical in order to ensure improved co-ordination of operations in different countries, and exchange of ideas and experience. Information systems thus enable firms to operate in multiple countries and contexts without loss of efficiency, and at the same time take advantage of their geographic dispersion and diversity, by linking up and facilitating the instantaneous exchange of information between any parts of the organization regardless of its geographic location.

In the **global rationalisation** stage, information systems provide both horizontal linkages to facilitate communication and co-ordination of activities across boundaries, but also vertical linkages guiding the flow of goods and services from production to point-of-sale. Establishment of direct information linkages enables the firm to respond more rapidly to fluctuations and changes in demand, and improve the efficiency of global logistics. Establishment of a global information system is also essential to monitor environmental trends, identify new product and market opportunities, track competitor moves and performance worldwide, and thus guide allocation of resources in global markets.

Information systems also provide the firm with a competitive edge in global industries, by enabling them to respond more effectively to the emergence of new industries or the restructuring of industries, by developing a more effective competitive strategy within a business, among vertical businesses, or across horizontal businesses, or thirdly by developing collaborative strategies, with suppliers, buyers or competitors.

2. Organizational Structure

Organizational structures also need to be adapted to respond to the changing dynamics of the environmental and competitive landscape. Firms organized on the basis of vertical, hierarchical structures will no longer be able to respond rapidly enough or to compete effectively, and need to be replaced by flatter co-ordination-intensive horizontal structures.

Organizational structure is another aspect where changing technology both facilitates and provides the stimulus for adaptation to the changing configuration of the market environment. In the initial phase of entry into international markets, organizational structure is unlikely to play a catalytic role in internationalization, but rather will follow the sequence/speed of management moves into international markets. Initially, responsibility for international markets is likely to remain within the domestic organization, with international operations viewed as an appendage to the domestic market. As these grow, a separate organization or manager responsible for international activities will be designated.

In **local expansion** phase as emphasis shifts to developing local markets, separate organizational entities or country subsidiaries with substantial autonomy are typically established. Links with corporate headquarters are likely to be relatively weak based primarily on financial controls. With the integration of markets, and increasing intensity of competition, pressures arise for tighter links across geographic boundaries, to improve co-ordination, eliminate duplication of effort, and allow for transfer of learning and experience from one part of the organization to another. Advances in communications technology facilitate the growth of new information-rich, co-ordination-intensive organizational structures. As a result, traditional hierarchical models of organizational structure are giving way to "heterarchies" with strong organizational links based on close working relationships rather than formal clearly defined organizational principles and responsibilities. These facilitate joint development and worldwide sharing of knowledge so that strategic capability and competitive advantage is enhanced and the firm's core competencies and expertise are leveraged worldwide across geographically dispersed operations.

In the **global rationalisation** phase of internationalization the organizational structure must not only provide strong horizontal links between operations worldwide, but also strategic flexibility to facilitate rapid deployment of resources in response to competitor moves or changing market, resource and environmental conditions. Especially in industries where technology is changing rapidly or characterized by highly volatile turbulent environments and discontinuity, development of adhocracies-organizational structures which are project based, may be most effective. This type of structure is based on the use of project teams, or highly decentralized networks of relatively autonomous individuals or groups. Intensive lateral communication is then required in order to manage interdependencies and ensure that the team or network functions effectively.

In a global organization, project teams may take the form of cross-functional teams, set up to deal with issues which cross geographic and functional boundaries, as, for example, the design or development of global or regional products or the management of global or regional brands or alternatively the management of global customer accounts. Top management's role thus shifts from that of controlling functions and activities in an organizational hierarchy to one of managing a geographically dispersed network. In a large organization, this may lead to the creation of a superstructure or basic infrastructure of assets, resources and management practices, which supports and nurtures flexible networks of individuals or groups which operate on top of this infrastructure.

New coordination intensive networks also result in a shift to greater reliance on markets and outsourcing of functions and operations rather than performing them internally. Hence organizations may participate as part of a virtual organization co-ordinating or collaborating with other organizations for a specific project or task. As a result, not only will internal organizational structures become flatter, and be characterized by stronger horizontal co-ordination, but external networks will become more crucial and communication intensive, as an increasingly number of functions are performed by loose networks of businesses collaborating together across time and space.

3. Resource Deployment

Resource deployment at different stages of the value chain needs to be orchestrated so as to stretch and tap new opportunities in different parts of the globe, while ensuring global efficiently and counterbalancing risk.

Management also needs to deploy resources to achieve the desired levels of growth in the direction targeted. As in the case of organizational structure, in the initial phase of international operations, resource allocation is relatively straightforward, and is made within the framework of domestic market operations. The primary issue is the relative allocation of resources to international markets. Often this allocation is made incrementally, as the firm gradually edges into international markets, rather than targeting a specific goal or level of international sales.

As the firm expands in international markets and moves into Phase 2 - local market expansion - resource allocation decisions are likely to be made on a country by country basis, as each local unit or country subsidiary operates autonomously. Often these results in resource deployment focused on current market potential, with limited attention to future market development and growth, or potential in areas outside the existing scope of operations, as, for example, in emerging markets. At the same time, co-ordination of resource deployment across national boundaries is typically lacking, resulting in duplication of effort.

In the phase 3 of globalization, as the firm seeks to rationalize operations worldwide, and map out a globally integrated strategy, effective resource deployment plays a greater role. Portfolio analysis provides a useful tool to assess global resource deployment and to determine which areas of the world and product businesses provide the most attractive opportunities for future growth and where operations should be harvested or divested. The interconnectedness of geographic markets and product businesses can also be assessed to determine how far expansion or retraction decisions will impact profitability in other markets or product businesses. Resources can then be deployed so as to achieve a balance between growth and mature markets, so as to ensure that the firm is well-placed for the future and that risk is diversified.

At the same time, the interconnectedness of markets has to be considered, as it affects management's ability to diversify risk by being in independent markets as opposed to achieving economies through building a strong competitive position in highly interconnected (interdependent) markets. Opportunities for achieving global efficiencies through scale economies, or improved co-ordination and integration of operations or alternatively the transfer of ideas and experience across geographic markets and product businesses can also be identified.

A global portfolio of countries, product businesses, and market segments should thus be selected which enables the firm to push forward the frontiers of global market expansion. Resource deployment should at the same time, position the firm to compete on multiple fronts, and meet diverse sources of competition, while retaining strategic flexibility to respond to a turbulent and rapidly changing market environment.

Regardless of where the firm is on the path towards globalization, it must respond to the forces shaping the global environment and the challenges they present. The precise nature of the challenges continues to change and the form they will take in the twenty-first century remains uncertain. It is however clear that to be successful; the firm must be an even more astute marketer than in the past. The necessity to respond quickly and appropriately to opportunities and challenges throughout the world places a premium on developing an effective global strategy.

An increasingly turbulent environment poses new challenges to managers that require different organizational responses depending on the degree of involvement in international markets. The firm's information system and its use of technology, facilitates initial involvement in international markets and establishes the foundation for subsequent expansion. As the firm expands its involvement in international markets, the organizational structure must evolve to coordinate operations in diverse and far-flung markets. Finally, as the firm seeks to consolidate its position in global markets, the ways in which it deploys resources through out the world takes on paramount importance. To succeed the firm must become an organic process that continually evolves, adapts, and responds to the changing realities of the global marketplace. Firms that are able to do this will prosper; firms that do not, will wither.

Challenges in Global Management

"The process of planning, organizing, leading and controlling the work of organization members and of using all available organizational recourses to reach stated organizational goals" is Management.

"The recognition by organizational that business must have a global, not local focus" is Globalization.

In this complex and dynamic environment, manages must continually adjust to changing conditions. It should come as no surprise, and then today's managers look at change as a constant in their lines. The following challenges that confront managers as they deal with a changing world on the door step of the 21st century.

The need for vision – The world is shrinking new telecommunication technologies to expand our reach and speed up our communications. In addition world is being reshaped, both by technologies, such as genetic engineering, automated manufacturing, lasers etc.

The Millennium marks a watershed. After 2000, companies will not survive long unless they join a threefold revolution - in management itself, information technology, and global markets. The three feed off each other. The radical changes in management have become inseparable from those in technology. Without either, the global revolution could never have developed such power.

The technology of information and communications did not create **the triple revolution,** but is the great enabler. Technology is expediting the onrush of organizations into brilliant new modes of management: not only global, but interactive, innovative, collaborative, anti-hierarchical, user-friendly. But the technology and its suppliers are themselves changing at critical speed, which puts further intense pressure on managements. They cannot stand still: they have to ride the revolution.

It did not spring full-born out of cyberspace. The late Twentieth Century revolution in management was accelerating well before the Internet rewrote the business books: the first Website opened as late as 1993. The revolution is being driven by irresistible forces: fragmentation of markets, anarchic technologies, more demanding customers, intensified competition and general over-capacity have all helped to undermine the old principles of business economics.

The challenges in front of organizations and its individual departments are:

- Transformations appear to produce the best results when executives mobilize organizational energy and communicate their objectives in a clear, comprehensive, and engaging way.
- The new corporate armory includes integrated database systems, 'virtuality' (in which company, customer and supplier are wired together), mass customization, and flexible organizational forms. These developments, along with many others, are changing the nature of management.

A networked company is a different kind of company, but most managers do not yet appreciate the difference.

Merely to stay in business, IT companies, in Silicon Valley and elsewhere, have been forced to take the lead in developing brand-new managerial concepts. True, management strata are fewer, product life-cycles shorter, dress and manners more casual. But that hardly adds up to a revolution. Increasingly, a winning strategy will require information about events and conditions outside the institution: non-customers, technologies other than those currently used by the company and its present competitors, markets not currently served, and so on. That information may already exist: harvesting the data and, still more, making sense of the crop has been the essence of the alleged "information overload."

Strategy in an Era of Global Giants

- The world's largest corporations are greatly increasing their scale and scope, and the resulting mega-institutions are fundamentally changing the landscape of business.
- These mega-institutions have disproportionately high profits and market values because they understand the link between their profitability and the talents of their professionals and knowledge workers.
- Mega-institutions are pioneering a new model of competitive advantage by using their huge size to develop and exploit intangible assets in novel ways.
- The corporate strategists of these companies must now develop new performance metrics and business models as well as find ways of overcoming the organizational barriers that size creates.

Next Challenges For Global Securities Firms

- The global securities industry has recently enjoyed good times—but its strong short-term performance may mask underlying vulnerabilities.
- With several traditional sources of profits under pressure, the best firms are anticipating changes in market structure.
- While too many banks continue to chase big M&A deals, more interesting profit opportunities lie in the next tier and in providing new kinds of risk-management advice. In a world dominated by sponsors and hedge funds, market participants should also rethink their strategies for generating ideas from the middle tier of companies.
- In mature financing markets, seamless product-neutral execution will be required, while new skills will be necessary to manage the expected turbulence in non investment-grade corporate and consumer credit markets.

People Problem in Talent Management

- Global executives say that talent management is one of their foremost concerns.
- Yet a majority of the business leaders and human-resources (HR) professionals interviewed by McKinsey say that a lack of time and attention from senior executives and line managers is one of the principal barriers to managing talent effectively. Insular thinking also emerged as a key issue.
- These findings reinforce the need for companies to integrate talent management into their wider business strategy, to move key people around the organization, and to make performance in this area a significant part of the annual evaluation process.

Talent Factor in Purchasing

- Executives know that talent matters when it comes to purchasing. But how important is it? A survey of global purchasing executives finds that three talent dimensions are associated with the lion's share of the differences between the financial performances of high- and low-performing companies.

- Top purchasers hire better people for sourcing roles, set clearer performance aspirations for these people, and create strong purchasing cultures that align the purchasing function with corporate strategy.
- The pay off? The overall annual savings realized by the top purchasers are nearly six times greater than those of the low performers.
- Winning the Multi-Channel Challenge - Customers, Channels and Marketing Management.

Survey covering five industries in seven European countries showed that adaptation is still far from complete in most industries, and in some industries, still in its infancy.

It was clear that the arrival of the internet as the new medium for interaction with customers would disrupt multi-channel configurations. It was less clear what form this disruption would take, how long it would last, or what new multi-channel configurations would emerge. As it turned out, the internet's impact was less dramatic in the short-term than expected. In recent years, however, the pace of change has accelerated. In travel, for example, the organization of trips and booking behavior has changed dramatically since 2000, and revenues generated online have been growing strongly.

Leadership quality, customer focus and the unremitting pace of globalization are among the top challenges facing competitive organization. The market place as well as the work place is increasingly multicultural together with colleges and customers from different countries. The organizations will need to the capacity for people to handle the challenges of working with other cultures if they are to participate successfully. Leadership must be feasible and be able to adapt to diverse workforce and global consumers.

Co-ordination and Control of Global Management

Here we will be discussing certain question pertaining to Co-ordination and control of global management. Why do we need Co-ordination and control of global management? One of the major advantages of Co-ordination and control is that we can eliminate risks and thus cut costs and maximize profits. There are various methods used to control the critical developments or unforeseen activities that may effect the growth of an organization.

However we can't generalize and say which strategy would be best in a certain situation as market is not stable. We can though estimate or forecast the problem and take steps to eliminate it.

What is Co-ordination and Control?

Co-ordination is the act of co-ordinating, making different people or things work together for a goal or effect and Control on the other hand is concerned with tracking the strategy as it is being implemented, detecting problems and making necessary adjustments.

Controlling is a very important function and needed in all the organizations, whether small or large. Though it may have a negative connotation but in reality the function is not to control but to guide.

Co-ordination is needed in many companies namely:

- Transnational companies: a company with many operations and investments in many countries around the world. It is also known as multi national companies.
- Multi domestic corporations: focused on specific domestic market.
- International companies.
- Global companies.

Types of Control

1. **Strategic control:** is concerned with tracking the strategy as it is being implemented, detecting problems or changes in underlying premise. Strategic control is concerned with controlling and guiding efforts on behalf of the strategy as action is taking place and while the end result is still several years into the future. Types of strategic control usually used are:

- Premise control: strategies are often based on premise i.e., assumptions or conditions. Changes in the premise may necessitate changes in the strategy. Examples are environmental factors like government policies and regulations, socio demographic factors, economic conditions etc.
- Implementation control: the lessons of the first phases of the implementation could be helpful in the implementation of the subsequent phases. For example, take the case of a company implementing a project involving a chain of holiday resorts in a phased manner. The experience gained from the implementing the resort in the first phase would help to make the implementation of the subsequent phases more efficient.
- Strategic surveillance: Strategic surveillance is designed to monitor a broad range of events inside and outside the company that are likely to threaten the course of a firm's strategy. This is done to eliminate risk. For example, the success of Arvind Mills' Ruf n Tuf encouraged rampant sale of furious products under the same brand name compelling the company to form vigilance squads to crack down on the unscrupulous businessman.
- Special Alert Control: sudden and unexpected developments like alliance between competitors, takeover/mergers etc could have a serious impact on firm's strategy. For example Hindustan lever taking over Tomco, Godrej Soaps felt so insecure and forged an alliance with Procter and Gamble.

2. **Operational control**: guide, monitor and evaluate progress in meeting annual objectives. In operational control top management monitors and steers the basic direction of the company should be supplemented by a control system at the operational level of strategy implementation. Types of operational control usually used are:

- Budgeting: is a statement or planned expenditure for a specific purpose for a specific period of time. Budgets themselves do not control anything but they set standards against which performance can be compared. Budgeting may be done in respect of all important activities. For example-there may be a sales budget estimating sales for a for a future period, territory wise, product-wise etc.
- Scheduling: is an important tool for allocating the use of time constrained resources or arranging the sequence of interdependent activities. Scheduling help optimum utilization of facilities.
- Key success factors: to focus on factors that contribute to success like productivity, quality, employee morale and market share.

Essential Features of Control System

- Objective based: clarity about the purpose of evaluation is essential for choosing the appropriate evaluation system. Only such an objective based system will provide adequate, useful and timely information for effective control.
- Economic: costs must be justifiable with its utility. Too much information, and too many controls can do more harm then good.
- Objectivity: it must be reality oriented. For example the standards or targets must reflect the internal and external realities.
- Simplicity: Strategy evaluations should be simple, not too cumbersome, and not too restrictive. Complex strategy systems often confuse people and accomplish little. The test of evaluation system is in its usefulness and not complexity.
- Deciding criteria & standards for evaluation: Criteria and standards for evaluation provide the base for evaluation. There are two types of criteria, namely, quantitative and qualitative. Quantitative are those that can be measured in perfect quantitative measures like ROI, profitability, market share, growth rate etc. Qualitative are subjective and not measurable like customer satisfaction, employee morale etc.
- Measuring & comparing performance: the actual performance is measured and is compared with the standards to identify the shortfalls if any.

- Performance gap analysis: is the difference between the actual performance of a given organizational unit and the planned performance of that unit. If there is any gap performances, it is necessary to identify the reasons for the gap and take corrective measures.
- Corrective measures: Performance gap analysis will reveal the reasons for the gap and will help decide the corrective measures.

Contingency Planning

A company should be well prepared to deal with contingencies, i.e., unforeseen or other critical developments that affect a company like sudden change in the Government policies, strikes, boycotts, natural calamities. Some of the examples are as follows:

1. If an important player is taken over by another important firm, what strategy should the company employ to deal with the new situation?
2. How will the company face the collective boycott of its products?

One of the advantages of contingency planning is that "when external opportunities occur contingency plans allow an organization to capitalize on them quickly. According to Linneman and Chandran, Contingency planning gives 3 major benefits. They are as follows:

1. It helps permit quick response to changes.
2. It prevents panic in crises situations.
3. It makes managers more adaptable.

Budgetary Control

A business budget may be described as "a predetermined plan of action developed and distributed as a guide to current operation and as a partial basis for subsequent evaluation of performance".

An organization may have a master budget encompassing the important functional areas and strategic plans for the whole organization. The master budget is decomposed into many functional/ unit budgets and sub-budgets, R and D budgets etc., as required.

Budgets provide standard for performance evaluation, which is needed for taking corrective measures.

Preventive Control

Weirich and Koontz advocate preventive control as an alternative to the direct control to improve the control system. The principle of preventive control is that the higher the quality of managers and their subordinates, the less will be the need for direct control. This suggest the need to develop better managers who will skillfully apply concepts, techniques and principles and who will look at managerial problems from a systems point of view ,thus eliminating undesirable results caused by poor management. According to Weirich and Koontz, Preventive Control rests on 3 principles:

1. Qualified managers make a minimum of errors.
2. Managerial performance can be measured.
3. The application of management fundamentals can be evaluated.

According to Weirich and Koontz, the Preventive Control has the following advantages:

- Greater accuracy is achieved is assigning personal responsibility.
- Preventive control should hasten corrective action and make it more effective.
- May lighten managerial burden.

There are many strategies to compare co ordination and control in an organization. However, there is no certain strategy that can be useful to measure the accuracy of a single strategy. We cannot even select one particular strategy that will prove effective. A strategy depends on various factors like the uncertain environment, government. Strategies are mostly situation based, so however methods one may develop for effective control ultimately it depends on situations and environments. Event though strategies might be situation based it is still necessary to have planned strategies that might prove effective for forecasting certain unwanted hurdles.

Organization Challenges

It really doesn't matter whether your company is old or new, the challenges remains the same; Think Global or become subsumed by the challenges, the new Global Economy is already in. This thought leadership gives some solid guidelines of how an organization must consider its Strategic planning Process.

Five of the most critical challenges in the role of management at the start of the 21st century are:

1. Establishing business ethics
2. Managing globalization
3. Dealing with downsizing
4. Valuing employee diversity
5. Exploiting new technology.

Although we can analyze each of these aspects of management separately they are interlinked like Olympic cycles. They share common causes and are affected by the convergence of economic, political, scientific, social, and competitive factor.

1. **Establishing business ethics:** Good management of the organization goes an all the time quietly unnoticed. It "is usually the cases of bad management that grab the banner headlines. On the global scene, TV images of Enron's top managers, the directors and chief executive officers being led off by the authorities to face charges of the serious mismanagement offered visual evidence of the urgent need for greater corporate responsibilities.

2. **Managing globalization:** "Think globally, act locally!" Has been the dictum for over three decades. Globalization is the ' phenomenon of the transition of industries whose competitive structure changes progressively from multinational to global examples of global companies include – Coca Cola, Pepsi , Sony , CityBank , any company that sells into the main market of the world in an integrated management and co-ordinate way. Global product development likewise, pulls together research and development units and marketing terms from across the world.

3. **Dealing with downsizing:** Downsizing, began as a short term management strategy in the mid-1980s, has become a permanent feature in the world's economic landscape. Downsizing in which large number of employee are dismissed en masse now impact all enterprises that seek competitive gain through cost advantages. The three main drivers of downsizing are:

- Global competitive pressure
- New technology
- The demand of customer requirement, including database driven marketing and other customer focused actives. The main reason for downsizing is to save money.

4. **Valuing employee diversity:** Basically, an organization is an entity managed by one or more person to achieve stated goals. The Gallup organization. One is management author , professor , and consultant Peter Drucker believes that managers have two basic tasks :"One running a business and two building an organization" to do both, manager's in charge of actives must co-ordinate what they do with each other while simultaneously accepting "the value the goal of organization". Values constitute beliefs and basic tents that are important and meaningful to those individuals and organization that hold them.

5. **Exploiting new technology:** In 1990s can be simply stated as the ability if the firm to establish and maintain a competitive advantage through the effective allocation of limited resources to capitalize on market place opportunities. The first step require to meet this challenges is the establishment of an effective strategic business plan. In second step of planning process management focuses on the creation of business forecast. The third step of planning process, management focuses on the current and long-term assets necessary the revenue plans outlined in the firm's business forecast. Finally and the last step, corporate plans are disaggregated and passed down to the firm's business unit. The goal is to ensure that strategic objectives can be realized by the existing business unit structure.

Worldwide Learning Challenges in Global Management

Globalization is no longer an abstraction but a stark reality that virtually all firms, large and a small, face. Firms that want to survive in the 21st century must confront this all encompassing force that pervades every aspect of business. In a wide range of industries from automobiles to food and clothing, firms face the pressures of global competition at home as well as in international markets. Choosing not to participate in global markets is no longer an option. All firms, regardless of their size, have to craft strategies in the broader context of world markets to anticipate, respond and adapt to the changing configuration of these markets. Involvement in global markets presents the firm with a number of challenges. These challenges influence competitive advantage in global markets, and in part determine how readily the firm can achieve economies of scale and scope as well as realize synergies from operation in a multi-country environment.

The major challenge that any organization or an individual has to face is CHANGE, learning how to tackle the change. While the pace of change is accelerating, pushed by the engine of technology and global communication, it is becoming increasingly uncertain and unpredictable-occurring in unexpected ways from unexpected sources. To cope up with this, learning was triggered in organization without waiting for a crisis. There were learning challenges due to mergers and acquisitions and even some went to unlearning process i.e., divestments.

As opportunities for global expansion increase, so does the trend toward more diversity in the workplace. Successful companies are recruiting professionals with different backgrounds, cultures, styles and motivations. Yet this great resource presents increased possibilities for misunderstanding and cultural blunders. Cultures are different in different countries be it working style, communicating style, etc. For example, Japan believes in teamwork but US is highly individualistic. If Indians say yes to something, it means there are least chances that things will get done, while in some other countries it is different.

Another challenge facing is technological advancement. The technology used in countries may vary. Like US is more advanced than India. So people might find it difficult to learn different technologies. Organizations may find it difficult to integrate the technology and at all places since technology used may differ at places. Due to this communication and working of organization or individual face problems.

Learning to leave old skills behind: Divestments is yet another problem since there may be huge amount of resistance. In organizations people may resist to change this may lead to dissatisfaction among employees, thus creating problems in organizations plans and development. To overcome such situation proper training, proper guidance, active leadership is required. In all, employee interests should be protected as far as possible.

Yet another thing that matter is countries legal, economical, political structure and society at large. There is no uniformity in world regarding law. Policies be it economical or political, it changes as boundaries are crossed. Even within a country, different places have different rules and regulations, so it becomes a great challenge to run firm in such conditions. Even society at large may cause a hindrance to organization. For an individual, new organizational structure creates again a problem for adjustment. Thus, when it comes to coping up with change all the external factors and internal factors come into play.

Leaders and executives in organizations must broaden their framework of diversity to include the cultures - both domestically and abroad - with whom they do business, (including race, religions, genders, national customs, age and generational differences). Leaders must also realize there are a variety of ways in which people work (communication styles, negotiation skills, relationship to time and status). As this century evolves, it becomes increasingly important for leaders to be open-minded and flexible, with a high degree of emotional intelligence, if they are to be effective. They must still produce results. This requires the ability to successfully manage the tension that arises when people from different cultures don't see eye-to-eye.

Organizations and their leaders are responsible for encouraging multi-cultural awareness. To facilitate this, it is necessary to enable discussion of differences through the use of *neutral descriptors* and vocabulary, so that people can address cultural differences and experiences in a way that is non-judgmental and non-threatening. It may be necessary to expand current diversity awareness training and workshops to include global perspectives. The services of coaches and consultants with international experience can help employees and leaders learn about other perspectives and culture driven differences. People must move beyond simply accepting cultural identities and differences to a place where they can be leveraged for competitive advantage, superior performance and creative growth. There is tremendous creative energy and innovation that can be harnessed when people from different perspectives work successfully together.

Global business is challenging in large part because cultural habits and attitudes blind people to other ways of doing things and make them unwilling or unable to change.

Knowledge Management

The business landscape is changing rapidly. The competitive environment is no longer linear or predictable. Survival and success of the organization entirely depends on its ability to adjust to adjust the dynamics of the business environment. Changes in information technology have generated gaps in access and control of information and knowledge. Even when these gaps are bridged, several fundamental challenges remain. How do we apply knowledge for value added and competitive advantage? How do we convert information into knowledge? How do we use technology to convert challenges into opportunities?

Knowledge Management is the solution for realigning the firms technical creates the knowledge that drives the firm forward.

There is obvious room for change in the way we work and communicate and in the relationships and processes among the people within and across organizations. To be empowered to face these challenges means not only accessing the technology, but also the ability to manage the knowledge.

Knowledge management means thinking outside the boundaries of current practices, products, services and organizations. The new and unpredictable business environment puts a premium on innovation and creativity much more so than it has in the past. We have progressed from the data processing age of 1960s to information age of 1980s to knowledge age of 1990s.

Background

Before one can talk about knowledge management, it is useful to have an understanding of "What is knowledge?"

Knowledge is defined by Peter Drucker as "Information that changes something or somebody either by becoming grounds for actions or by making an individual (or an institution) capable of different or more effective action."

"Knowledge is a fluid mix of framed experience, values, contextual information, expert insight, and intuition that provides an environment and frame work for evaluating and incorporating new experiences and information."

Why is Knowledge Management Important in Today's Business Climate?

Today's business environment is characterized by continuous, often radical change. Such a volatile climate demands a new attitude and approach within organizations—actions must be anticipatory, adaptive, and based on a faster cycle of knowledge creation.

Some of the current challenges in business are:

- A growing emphasis on creating customer value and improving customer service;
- An increasingly competitive marketplace with a rising rate of innovation;

- Reduced cycle times and shortened product development times;
- A need for organizational adaptation because of changing business rules and assumptions;
- A requirement to operate with a shrinking number of assets (people, inventory, and facilities);
- A reduction in the amount of time employees are given to acquire new knowledge; and
- Changes in strategic directions and workforce mobility that lead to knowledge loss.

New products and innovations are increasing at a faster rate than ever before, along with evolutions in customer preference and need. Managers must no longer investigate their customers superficially; they must dig more deeply than surveys and feedback forms.

As organizations have become more complex and information more readily accessible, forward thinking managers have grown concerned with how to allow knowledge to flow freely and how to control and manage this vital flow of information and technology at the same time.

What is Knowledge Management?

KM is the process through which organizations generate value from their intellectual and knowledge based assets. Most often generating value from such assets involves sharing them among employees, departments and even with other companies in an effort to devise best practices. Building knowledge assets and managing it continuously is facilitated by technology enablers.

Knowledge *vs* Information

The challenge of Knowledge Management is to determine what information within an organization qualifies as "valuable." All information is not knowledge, and all knowledge is not valuable. The key is to find the worthwhile knowledge within a vast sea of information.

Understanding Knowledge management

1. Knowledge Management is about people. It is directly linked to what people know, and how what they know can support business and organizational objectives. It draws on human competency, intuition, ideas, and motivations. It is not a technology-based concept. Although technology can support a Knowledge Management effort, it shouldn't begin there.

2. Knowledge Management is orderly and goal-directed. It is inextricably tied to the strategic objectives of the organization. It uses only the information that is the most meaningful, practical, and purposeful.

3. Knowledge Management is ever-changing. There is no such thing as an immutable law in Knowledge Management. Knowledge is constantly tested, updated, revised, and sometimes even "obsolete" when it is no longer practicable. It is a fluid, ongoing process.

4. Knowledge Management is value-added. It draws upon pooled expertise, relationships, and alliances. Organizations can further the two-way exchange of ideas by bringing in experts from the field to advise or educate managers on recent trends and developments. Forums, councils, and boards can be instrumental in creating common ground and organizational cohesiveness.

5. Knowledge Management is visionary. This vision is expressed in strategic business terms rather than technical terms, and in a manner that generates enthusiasm, buy-in, and motivates managers to work together toward reaching common goals.

6. Knowledge Management is complementary. It can be integrated with other organizational learning initiatives such as Total Quality Management (TQM). It is important for knowledge managers to show interim successes along with progress made on more protracted efforts such as multi-year systems developments infrastructure, or enterprise architecture projects.

Six Principles and Key Characteristics in Leading Organizations

1. Recognize the role of information management in creating value. An organization must recognize and accept the critical role information management plays in the success of an organization and the leadership role the CIO must assume in order to maximize the full potential of information technology.

2. Position the CIO for success. The CIO must be recognized as a full participant of the executive management team, and be given the technical and management skills to meet business needs.

3. Ensure the credibility of the CIO organization. Without credibility, the CIO organization will struggle. The CIO must have the commitment of line management; must accomplish quick, high-impact, visible successes balanced with longer-term strategies; and must learn from partnering with successful leaders in the external information management community.

4. Measure success and demonstrate results. Technical measures must be balanced with business measures, and managers must continually work to establish active feedback between performance measures and business processes.

5. Organize information resources to meet business needs. In order to execute its responsibilities reliably and efficiently, the CIO organization must have a clear understanding of its responsibilities in meeting business needs. The organization should be flexible enough to adapt to change.

6. Develop information management human capital. The CIO organization identifies the skills it needs to implement information management in line with business needs; develops innovative ways to attract and retain talent; and provides the training, tools, and methods IT professionals must have to effectively perform their duties.

Knowledge in organizations seems to manifest itself in one of two forms — explicit and tacit. The transfer of one kind to another has been explained using the Knowledge creation SECI model propounded by Nonaka *et al.* Technologies of various kinds seem to further facilitate these transformations. However, it is becoming increasingly clear that the presence of technology without a context is irrelevant and Ba, another concept defined by Nonaka provides this context. Even when knowledge transformation using various technologies is adopted and a context is provided for these processes, the essence of knowledge creation lies in a holistic approach. Knowledge harvesting, a proprietary process developed by Lerner is one such holistic approach. In a constantly changing knowledge economy, the only sustainable competitive advantage is the knowledge capital of a firm. This knowledge capital lies in the minds of the firm's employees in either explicit or tacit form, waiting to be reaped.

This analysis presents an inquiry into effective transformation of tacit knowledge into explicit knowledge within organizations. The importance of this transformation as a lever for competitive advantage is discussed. An exposition of types of knowledge and transformation processes in organizations, with emphasis on the SECI model follows. Various technologies and their utilization in the externalization of tacit knowledge are discussed for their relevance and effectiveness. The absence of an appropriate context and environment emerges as the key impediment to the working of these technologies. The concept of context is also therefore explored. A strong case emerges for a strategic, context providing knowledge transformation algorithm and knowledge harvesting, as one such available algorithm is also given.

Knowledge Creation as a Key Competitive Advantage

Major economics and business theorists have pointed to knowledge as the ultimate competitive advantage for the modern firm. It is a resource hard to imitate, difficult to co-opt, giving its possessor a unique and inherently protected commodity. Therefore, any techniques or methods that sustain knowledge growth and distribution are key to the success of today's organizations. Given the dynamics of hyper-competition and globalization, the resulting reinventions of businesses and pressure for innovation, and the related realignment of corporate activities, the efficient transfers of existing but dispersed knowledge, as well as the effective creation of new knowledge, have become two major management tasks. Changes in the variables of the business eco-system, environmental, structural and internal include the following:

- Accelerating pace of change
- Staff attrition (especially that resulting from years of downsizing and reengineering)

- Growth in organizational scope.
- Geographic dispersion associated with globalization of markets
- Global integration
- Increase in networked organizations
- Growing knowledge-intensity of goods and services
- Revolution in information technology

With this shift in organizational focus from the capital and physical assets to the capabilities, competencies, information and knowledge base of human capital, it has become increasingly important for a greater amount of the information to reside within the physical domains of organizations rather than in the minds of people. This growing realization was captured in a survey by The Delphi Group. There is a clear understanding across industries that the tacit knowledge base can account for as much as 75 percent of an organization's collective knowledge. The study also found that on average, organizations believe that 42 percent of corporate knowledge is housed exclusively in the brains of employees.

Firms do not significantly differ from one another in terms of the basic resources of capital, manpower, or raw material. What differentiates one firm from another are the additional unique and sustainable competitive advantages that it can offer to the external world. Intellectual capital or knowledge has in the recent years emerged as one such major advantage

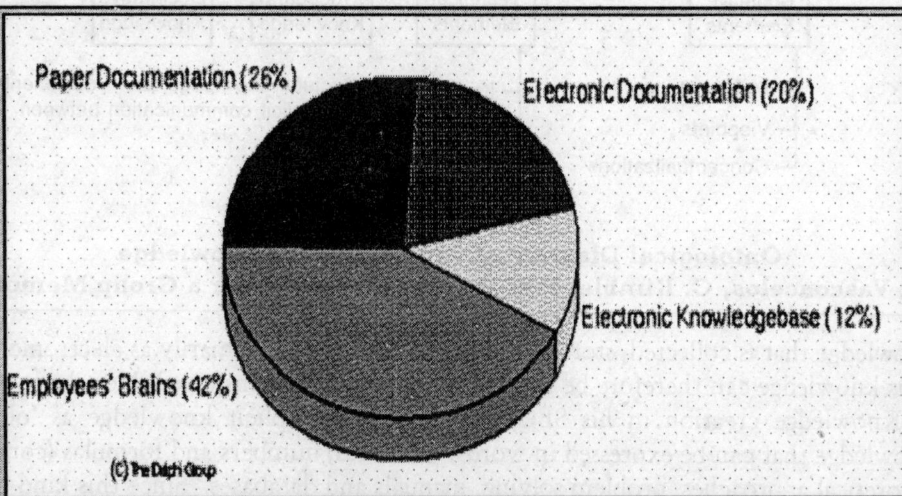

Figure 11.1

Repositories of Corporate Knowledge Sources
(*Source*: After the Gold Rush: Harvesting Corporate Knowledge Resources by Carl Frappaolo and Larry Todd Wilson, Intelligent KM website)

Definition of Knowledge in an Organizational Context

For an organization to develop knowledge as its competitive advantage, it helps to have a clear understanding of knowledge in an organization, the forms it exists in, and the nature of processes involving it.

Knowledge in an organization is commonly referred to as intellectual capital. It 'exists in two basic forms: explicit knowledge, which is easily codified and shared asynchronously and tacit knowledge, which is experiential, intuitive, and communicated most effectively in face-to-face encounter. However, pioneers in the knowledge management industry have found a middle ground. Some knowledge believed to be tacit can be transformed into explicit knowledge producing a body of knowledge known as the organization's implicit knowledge.'

The classification of knowledge in the organizational context is understood from figure, an ontological diagram of organizational knowledge. This shows the relationship of various kinds of knowledge within an organizational domain.

Explicit Knowledge

The Delphi Group's Carl Frappaolo as succinctly defines explicit knowledge in an organizational context that 'which is easily codified and shared asynchronously'. Explicit knowledge includes information and skills that are easily communicated, documented and conveyed to others. It is the

Figure 11.2

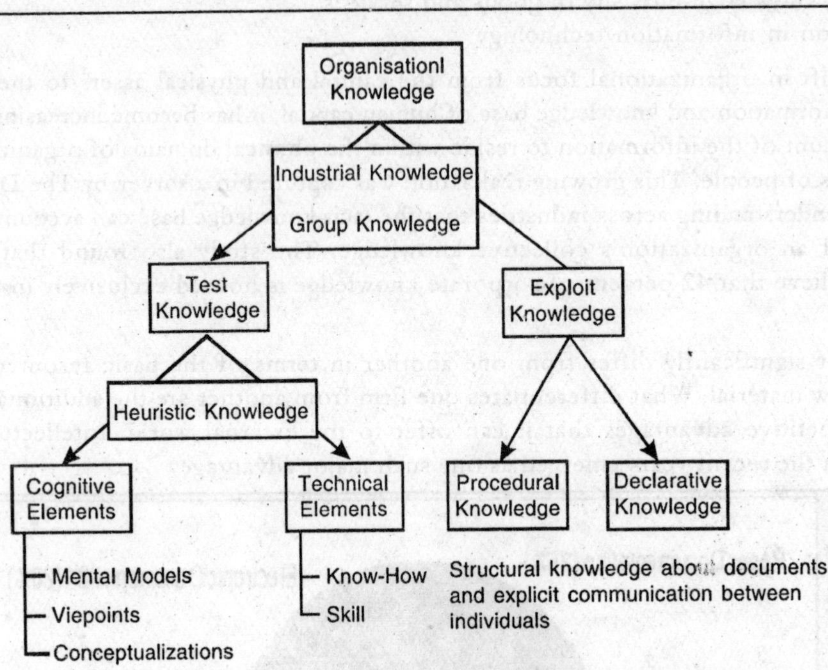

Ontological Diagram of Organizational Knowledge
(*Source*: J. Vasconcelos, C. Kimble, F.R. Gouveia- A Design for a Group Memory System)

knowledge that is collected, stored, distributed and shared primarily as electronic or paper documents. This knowledge can therefore be formally expressed and transferred. Nonaka in explaining the modes of Knowledge creation in his SECI model defines explicit knowledge as 'objective and rational knowledge that can be expressed in words, sentences, numbers and formulas (context free). It includes theoretical approaches, problem solving, manuals and databases.' Since this kind of knowledge usually appears in media such as manuals, documents, and standard forms it is often referred to as codified knowledge.

Tacit Knowledge

Tacit knowledge is that which is experiential and intuitive. It is the 'subjective and experience-based knowledge that cannot be expressed in words, sentences, "... (It) also includes cognitive skills such as beliefs, images, intuition and mental models as well as technical skills such as craft and know-how". This definition of tacit knowledge refers to the individuals within an organization. In an organization, "...tacit knowledge is made up of the collective mindsets of everyone in the organization."

Implicit Knowledge

Some theorists believe there exists a middle ground between tacit and explicit knowledge. They call it implicit knowledge. Implicit knowledge is the subset of tacit knowledge that can be transformed into explicit knowledge. Knowledge, which could be codified if subjected to some type of a mining or translation process, is another view of implicit knowledge. In this discussion, tacit and implicit knowledge will be used interchangeably.

The mapping of these kinds of knowledge with human elements of the organization, i.e. the employees is now elaborated.

The relationships between the individual, knowledge and the organization

From a legal stand point, organizations are going concerns with indefinite life and may hence be considered perpetual entities. The essential elements of any organization however are the individual employees that form them. Figure 11.3 attributed to Warnecke, Gissler and Stammwitz shows three dimensions of knowledge; along the y-axis is knowledge as possessed by the individual or by the entire group. Along the x-axis is the aforementioned classification of implicit-explicit knowledge and the third dimension represent whether the knowledge internal to this entity or external to it.

The following analysis focuses on the translation of individual implicit knowledge to common external knowledge that is internal to the entity. The traversal of knowledge along the x-axis, given that the boundary conditions on the y and z axes are group knowledge and knowledge internal to the organization. This concept shall become clear as we proceed to understand the possible modes of knowledge conversion which are elucidated by Nonaka in the SECI model.

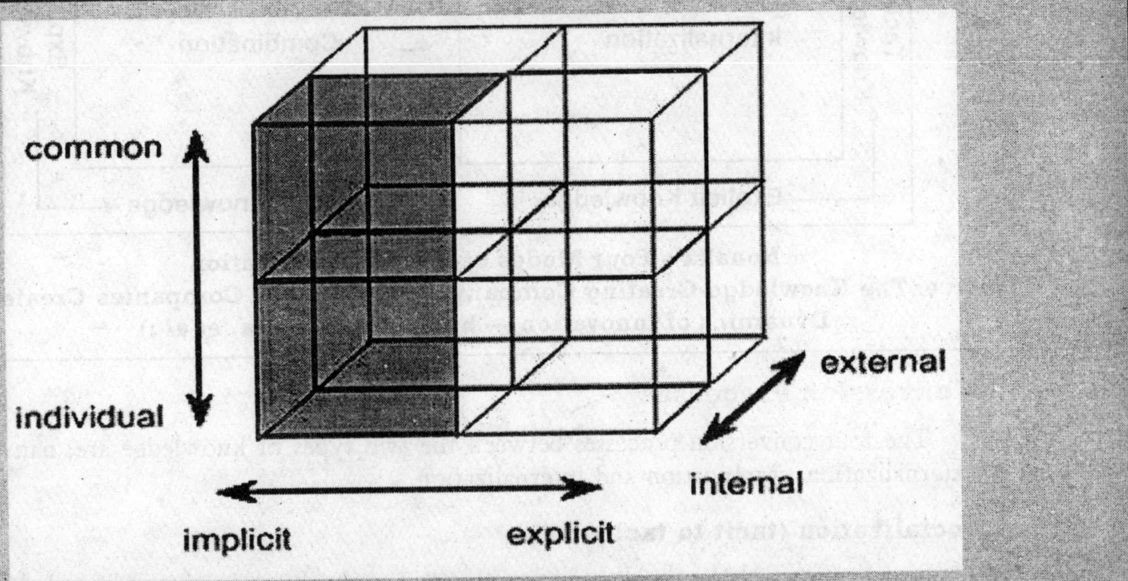

Figure 11.3

Dimensions of Knowledge
(*Source:* Warnecke, Gissler, Stammwitz, 1998. IM Information Management & Consulting 1998 - Reference Model Knowledge Management: A Beginning For The Model-Based Organization Of Knowledge-Intensive Processes.)

Modes of Knowledge Conversion - The SECI Model

Nonaka models the translation of individual implicit knowledge to common external knowledge within an entity as a spiral process. In the SECI model, tacit and explicit knowledge are deemed to be transferable into the opposite form freely, and each transfer is defined as a specific process. These conversions between the two kinds of knowledge are the essence of knowledge creation.

Nonaka and Takeuchi believe that 'tacit and explicit knowledge are mutually complementary entities, which interact with and interchange into each other in the creative activities of human beings' The SECI model is based on the fundamental assumption that knowledge is created and expanded through social interaction between tacit and explicit knowledge. This interaction is referred to as knowledge conversion.

Nonaka *et al.* argue that the transformation is interactive and spiral unlike the proponents of the ACT model who consider the transformation as mainly unidirectional. When viewed as a continuous process, the model becomes a clock-wise spiral, increasing in depth with passing iteration.

A detailed look at the four knowledge conversion processes is now in order to understand the spiral process.

Figure 11.4

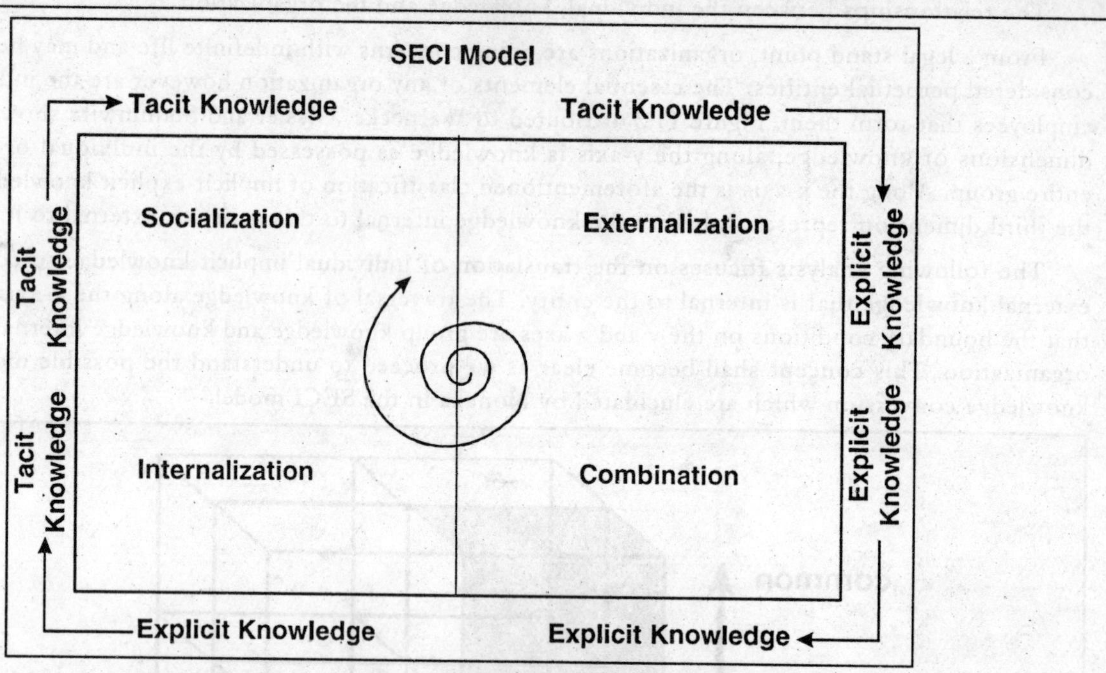

Nonaka's Four Modes of Knowledge Creation
(*Source:* The Knowledge-Creating Company: How Japanese Companies Create the Dynamics of Innovation — by Ikujiro Nonaka, *et al* ;)

Conversion Processes

The four conversion processes between the two types of knowledge are, namely, socialization, externalization, combination and internalization.

Socialization (tacit to tacit)

Socialization includes the shared formation and communication of tacit knowledge between people. Knowledge sharing is often done without ever producing explicit knowledge. This kind of tacit knowledge sharing takes place between people who have a common culture and can work together effectively. Thus tacit knowledge sharing is connected to ideas of communities and collaboration. A typical activity in which tacit knowledge sharing can take place is a team meeting during which experiences are described and discussed, with much communicated between the lines.

Externalization (tacit to explicit)

By its nature, tacit knowledge is difficult to convert into explicit knowledge. Through conceptualization, elicitation, and ultimately articulation, typically in collaboration with others, some proportion of a person's tacit knowledge may be captured in explicit form. Typical activities in which tacit knowledge is captured as the first step towards the conversion are in dialog among team members, in responding to interview questions or through the elicitation of stories.

Combination (explicit to explicit)

Explicit knowledge can be shared in meetings, via documents, e-mails, etc., or through education and training. The use of technology to manage and search collections of explicit knowledge is well established. However, there is a further opportunity to foster knowledge creation, namely to enrich the collected information in some way, such as by reconfiguring it, so that it is more usable. An example is to use text classification to assign documents automatically to a subject schema. A typical activity here might be to put a document into a shared database. In the 7 years since Nonaka *et. al* published the SECI model, many document management and knowledge management software systems have implemented a variety of approaches to automatic document classification, storage and retrieval. Several such technology solutions are discussed further in the paper.

Internalization (explicit to tacit)

In order to act on information, individuals have to understand and internalize it, which involves creating their own tacit knowledge. By reading documents, they can to some extent re-experience what others previously learned. By reading documents from many sources, they have the opportunity to create new knowledge by combining their existing tacit knowledge with the knowledge of others. However, this process is becoming more challenging because individuals have to deal with ever-larger amounts of information. A typical activity would be to read and study documents from a number of different databases by an employee who wishes to learn regarding the previous history of the task he is now given.

Technology solutions seem to play a vital role in each of these knowledge conversion processes. The discussion now veers towards a study of technology solutions in each conversion process, with emphasis on the tools available, their advantages and shortcomings.

Knowledge Harvesting: A proprietary solution to knowledge creation

Even when knowledge transformation using various technologies is adopted and a context is provided to these processes, the essence of knowledge creation lies in a holistic approach. Knowledge harvesting is one such proprietary, comprehensive approach that is gaining wide acceptance. Knowledge harvesting may be seen as a strategic solution to knowledge creation as it synthesizes the advantages of technology with the relevance of a context.

'Knowledge Harvesting is a proprietary suite of methodologies and technologies for efficiently capturing the implicit intuitive knowledge of top performers, converting that expertise into explicit knowledge, and transferring it to users.' It is predominantly an exercise of making implicit knowledge explicit. Larry T Wilson and the group at Learner First developed it.

The nine-stage knowledge harvesting process is as under:

Stage 1: Identification of knowledge - Identification involves mapping the organization's key processes and the individuals who possess the best know-how. In this step, the origin, nature, or definitive characteristics of the organization's processes are ascertained. The initiating step involves determining two things: top performing people and their critical activities.

Stage 2: Elicitation of knowledge - Experts and activities are first identified; the experts are then asked to explain the activities. Knowledge is gathered from the various departments. The activities of the top performers are deduced and logically mapped in the knowledge harvesting process. As with expert systems, knowledge engineers realized that the most difficult function of creating an expert system was the process of eliciting information from key performers (experts) about the activities they performed and the rules they used in decision-making. This stage is thus critical and it is imperative that the company communicates its intentions to the top performers and provides the culture that encourages sharing of expertise.

Stage 3: Capture of knowledge - The expertise of the top performers must be preserved to continue the success of the organization. In the elicitation process, a great deal of information is extracted from top performers. Contained therein are the key decision rules that need to be preserved. The capture phase distills these decision rules from the bulk of information and stores them. Examples of knowledge that might be organized and captured include best practices, patterns, software code, project experiences, and information on tools that have used. By capturing and storing the information, the knowledge harvesting process adds value to the future of the corporation. This process in its ideal form makes a permanent copy of the memory of the organization's top performers.

Stage 4: Organization of knowledge - The knowledge captured from top performers must be arranged in a coherent or systematic form. This procedure of structuring the knowledge into orderly and functional structures allows anyone in the organization to retrieve the necessary information quickly and efficiently.

Stage 5: Application of knowledge - The purpose of organizational knowledge is to be able to ensure that the application of expert knowledge by the top performers is replicable by all. The whole point of a knowledge management system comes down to later applications by individuals. These individuals may request or seek assistance or advice for performance of a specific task. The applications not only produce results at the moment but also advance the user's learning. This learning is aided by context-sensitive assistance embedded in the applications. Support information such as terminology, descriptions, visual aids, and examples should be available on demand. To enhance performance, each individual may be given detailed guidance about information to gather, issues to consider, decisions to make, actions to take, or resources to consult.

Stage 6: Recording of knowledge - Once an application has been created, it requires refreshing so that it can evolve with use. This sub-process records the learning that takes place with the user, causing the database of knowledge to grow. The process collects and preserves information on a particular subject, capturing the history of performance, activities, or achievement. This preserved knowledge causes learning in an organizational context. Recording means that the application will never forget what has worked in the past and why. Good documentation helps users understand how to handle similar situations in the future, and multiple instances of similar situations can be analyzed as an aggregate.

Stage 7: Sharing of knowledge - Knowledge that has been captured must be shared or its capture will be irrelevant and the effort and expense wasted. Additionally, sharing will likely lead to the seeking and capturing of other knowledge and uses of previous and new knowledge. This knowledge can be distributed throughout the organization to individuals or groups.

Stage 8: Evaluation of the knowledge creation process - Appraisal occurs during application and sharing. This completes a feedback process. In the elicitation and capture steps, inevitably some decision rules are gathered that have little value or lose relevance over time. Evaluation should be continuous so that the database can be kept up-to-date, relevant, and as small as possible. At the most basic level, learning should be evaluated by assessing the impact on individual performance. Ultimately, the evaluation must be in terms of the contribution to organizational performance.

Stage 9: Improvement of the knowledge creation process - The improvement sub-process is the continuous betterment of the entire process. By improving the process or the flow of knowledge throughout the organization, the productivity or value to individuals or groups is enhanced. The improvement should be of both — the stored knowledge and its application.

This discussion is at best a first step in analyzing the development of knowledge creation as a strategic competitive advantage. The ability to create and harvest knowledge is increasingly becoming a key factor in the competitiveness of nations, industries and firms. Organizations may be reluctant to allocate resources towards developing knowledge, since it is a non-tangible asset. Perhaps, mechanisms that measure the economic benefits of knowledge are needed in order to convince organizations that their future competitiveness depends in part on knowledge creation and harvesting.

Managing Across Boundaries

The impact of organizational restructuring on organizational boundaries has become increasingly important, especially became modernization of work practices with large organization generates increasing boundary complexity. Psychoanalytic theory offers a mean of exploring boundaries and emphasizes the importance of boundary in the emergence of an integrated sense of identity.

When organizations intend to expand their boundaries and go global (globalization) strategies play an important role and help to manage across boundaries. They are basically about the direction the company intends to peruse in order to achieving its objectives. When we say a company it could be small business involved in a single/product/market/business, or a large, multi-product, multi-location, complex and diversified conglomerate (large corporation formed by the merging of separate firms, e.g., Reliance) with several different business.

When an organization or a company decides to expands it needs to decide the right strategies to make the expansion a success. Following are few strategies which are a part of stability strategies.

Maintain Strategy: It can be described an no change strategy. Here the company will by choice, maintain it position and implement the similar strategies. But this works only when the environment is stable, existing competition is manageable and also stable.

Small Exploration Strategy: It can be described as pause/proceed with caution strategies. This is a typical strategy taken by companies in gauging new products and markets, where they will explore tentative by small tent markets, launcher to gauge the reaction of the customer. This normally would be done before an expansion strategy. It could be also to gear up the entire company in the new direction and also could help the company to learn before they go full fledged in the market.

Consolidation/Better Profit Strategies: Here the company tries to initiate a lot of internal action like cost cutting and quality improvement which will defiantly result in a positive payoff, there is practically no risk at all and the outcome will always be beneficial. This is often undertaken when the company is insecure of the external markets and waiting and watching for the right movement to undertake some other strategy. Quite often this in also an ongoing strategy adopted along with other strategy for many companies to remain competition.

Expansion Strategy: All organization look for expansion, thus expansion strategies are the most popular and common corporate strategies. The recent example can be observed of Arceller & Mittal or Tata's acquiring Rover. It was an expansion strategy. After expansion the scope of the business is broadened in terms of their respective customer groups, customer function and alternative technologies - singly or jointly in order to improve its overall performance.

Expansion strategy is implemented when environment demands increases in pace of activity, due to increase in market size and large opportunities being available. Many times after a long time barrier, companies often feel they can take advantage from their experience to go in for expansion. There may be enough resources generated from existing operations that companies feel that the best way to utilize these resources is to go is for expansion.

Expansion strategies can be undertaken in variety of ways:

Expansion through Concentration: For expansion is the first preference strategy for a company. The simple reason for this is that it would like to do more of what it is already doing. A company that is familiar with an industry would naturally like to invent more in known business rather than in unknown.

E.g.:- As reliance communications expanded their business and launched GSM mobile service in London 'Flag' a 100% subsidiary of reliance communications. It involves investment of larger resources in a product line for an identified market with the help of proven technologies.

Advantages:

- It involves fewer changes.
- It is less threatening and more comfortable staying with prevention barner.
- It enables an organization to specialize by gaining an in depth knowledge of these barriers.
- It helps a company to develop a competitive advantage.
- Decision making has a high level of predictability.
- Past experience is valuable, as it is replaceable.

Disadvantages:

- It heavily depends on the industry, so adverse condition in an industry can and do affect companies if they are intensely concentrated.
- Product obsolesce, fickleness of market and new technologies can be threat.
- It requires large cash flow which can effect the prevent barriers.

Expansion through Integration: Integration basically means combing activities on the basis of the value chain related to the present activity of a company. It results in widening of the scope of the company. There are two types of integration- Vertical and Horizontal.

Vertical Integration – It could be of two type's backward and forward integration.

Backward integration - means retreating to the source of raw material – becomes your common supplier. e.g., An automobile company going in for steel wheels backward integration.

Forward Integration - means the organization nearer to the ultimate customer –becoming your own customer. e.g., Titan going into setting their own retail outlet & Yash Raj film distributing their own movies in India is forward integration.

Horizontal Integration – When a company starts serving the same customers that is known as very well additional product that is different from earlier products. e.g. Microsoft after selling software also is planning to sell the gaming hardware which would be manufactured in India.

Expansion through Cooperation:

Mergers: For a merger to take place two organizations are needed. One is the buyer organizations and the other is the seller. Both these types of organizations have a set of reasons on the basis of the merge. Important inner in merge: Strategic - whether the company has synergies.

Transnational Corporations

Transnational corporations — those corporations which operate in more than one country or nation at a time — have become some of the most powerful economic and political entities in the world today. Transnational corporations are a powerful force for binding national economies together. Through complex corporate strategies and intricate network structures, transnational corporations engage in international production characterized by a sophisticated intra-firm division of labors for each corporate function. As a result, they create an integrated international production system which places about one third of the world's private sector productive assets under the governance of transnational corporations. Transnational corporations hold ninety percent of all technology and product patents worldwide, and are involved in 70 percent of world trade. More than thirty percent of this trade is "intra- firm"; in other words, it occurs between units of the same corporation.

The number of transnational corporations in the world has jumped from 7,000 in 1970 to 40,000 in 1995. While global in reach, these corporations' home bases are concentrated in the Northern industrialized countries, where ninety percent of all transnational are based. More than half come from just five nations: France, Germany, the Netherlands, Japan and the United States. But despite their growing numbers, power is concentrated at the top. i.e., the 300 largest corporations account for one-quarter of the world's productive assets. The United Nations has justly described these corporations as "the productive core of the globalizing world economy." Their 250,000 foreign affiliates account for most of the world's industrial capacity, technological knowledge, international financial transactions, and ultimately the power of control. In terms of energy, they mine, refine and distribute most of the world's oil, gasoline, diesel and jet fuel, as well as build most of the world's oil, coal, gas, hydroelectric and nuclear power plants. They extract most of the world's minerals from the ground. They manufacture and sell most of the world's automobiles, airplanes, communications satellites, computers, home electronics, chemicals, medicines and biotechnology products. They harvest much of the world's wood and make most of its paper. They grow many of the world's major agricultural crops, while processing and distributing much of its food. Given their dominance of politics, economics and technology, it is not surprising to find the big transnational deeply involved in most of the world's serious environmental crises.

Transnational corporations exert significant influence over the domestic and foreign policies of the Northern industrialized government that host them. Surprise! Indeed, the interests of the most powerful governments in the world are often intimately intertwined with the expanding pursuits of the transnational that they charter. At the same time, transnational corporations are moving to circumvent national governments. The borders and regulatory agencies of most governments are caving in (or being paid off) to the New World Order of globalization, allowing corporations to assume an ever more stateless quality, leaving them less and less accountable to any government anywhere.

These corporations, together with their host governments, are reorganizing the world economic structures — and thus the balance of political power — through a series of intergovernmental trade and investment accords. These treaties serve as the frameworks within which globalization is evolving — allowing international corporate investment and trade to flourish across the Earth. They include:

- The Uruguay Round of the General Agreement on Tariffs and Trade (GATT).
- The World Trade Organization, which was created to enforce the GATT's rules.
- The proposed Multilateral Agreement on Investment. (MAI)
- The North American Free Trade Agreement (NAFTA).
- The European Union (EU).

These international trade and investment agreements allow corporations to circumvent the power and authority of national governments and local communities, thus endangering workers' rights, the environment and democratic political processes.

Transnational corporations are among the world's biggest economic institutions. A rough estimate suggests that the 300 largest TNCs own or control at least one-quarter of the entire world's productive assets, worth about US$5 trillion. TNCs' total annual sales are comparable to or greater than the yearly gross domestic product (GDP) of most countries (GDP is the total output of goods and services for final use by a nation's economy).

History of Transnational Corporation

The earliest historical origins of transnational corporations can be traced to the major colonizing and imperialist ventures from Western Europe, notably England and Holland, which began in the 16th century and proceeded for the next several hundred years. During this period, firms such as the British East India Trading Company were formed to promote the trading activities or territorial acquisitions of their home countries in the Far East, Africa, and the Americas. The transnational corporation as it is known today, however, did not really appear until the 19th century, with the advent of industrial capitalism and its consequences: the development of the factory system; larger, more capital intensive manufacturing processes; better storage techniques; and faster means of transportation. During the 19th and early 20th centuries, the search for resources including minerals, petroleum, and foodstuffs as well as pressure to protect or increase markets drove transnational expansion by companies almost exclusively from the United States and a handful of Western European nations.

US TNCs heavily dominated foreign investment activity in the two decades after the Second World War, when European and Japanese corporations began to play ever greater roles. In the 1950s, banks in the US, Europe, and Japan started to invest vast sums of money in industrial stocks, encouraging corporate mergers and furthering capital concentration. Major technological advances in shipping, transport (especially by air), computerization, and communications accelerated TNCs' increasing internationalization of investment and trade; while new advertising capabilities helped TNCs expand market shares. The large number of TNCs can be somewhat misleading, however, because the wealth of transnational is concentrated among the top 100 firms which in 1992 had US$3.4 trillion in global assets, of which approximately US$1.3 trillion was held outside their home countries. The top 100 TNCs also account for about one-third of the combined outward foreign direct investment (FDI) of their countries of origin. Since the mid-1980s, a large rise of TNC-led foreign direct investment has occurred. Between 1988 and 1993, worldwide FDI stock — a measure of the productive capacity of TNCs outside their home countries — grew from US$1.1 to US$2.1 trillion in estimated book value.

There has also been a great increase in TNC investment in the less-industrialized world since the mid-1980s; such investment, along with private bank loans, has grown far more dramatically than national development aid or multilateral bank lending. Burdened by debt, low commodity prices, structural adjustment, and unemployment, governments throughout the less-industrialized world today view TNCs, in the words of the British magazine The Economist, as "the embodiment of modernity and the prospect of wealth: full of technology, rich in capital, replete with skilled jobs." As a result, The Economist notes further, these governments have been "queuing up to attract multinationals" and liberalizing investment restrictions as well as privatizing public sector industries.

Strategies of Transnational Corporations

The ability of transnational corporations to contribute to international economic integration is a result both of their attributes and of how they respond to the economic and policy environment in which they operate. The strategies of transnational corporations evolve, as firms respond to various pressures and opportunities, including improvements in information technologies, the convergence of demand patterns across countries, the intensification of competition and the opening of markets to international trade and foreign direct investment. The new strategies imply significant changes in how production is organized across borders; they have led firms to locate a wider range of their value-adding activities abroad.

Stand-alone Strategies

One common form of TNC strategy is the establishment of stand–alone affiliates-affiliates that operate largely as independent concerns within the host economy. The main link between a parent and its foreign affiliates is control through owner ship; other links include transferring technology and the supply of long term capital. The parent may exercise very little control over the affiliate, so long as the latter is profitable. In general, a stand alone affiliate is responsible for most of the value chain in its output; through it may develop substantial links with local suppliers and subcontractors. It may also hire local workers and managers, borrow and lend with local financial intermediaries and engage in international trade with other countries. Large TNCs can control many stand- alone affiliates, each serving a separate host economy.

A stand-alone affiliate can be seen as a smaller version of the parent firm .It might in manufacturing, especially where the host economy can provide resource inputs and where imports of materials and components are difficult or expensive. However, stand-alone affiliates are particularly common in services. Since many services are tradable, affiliates need to operate as self–contained units, replicating the production organization of their parents.

Figure 11.5

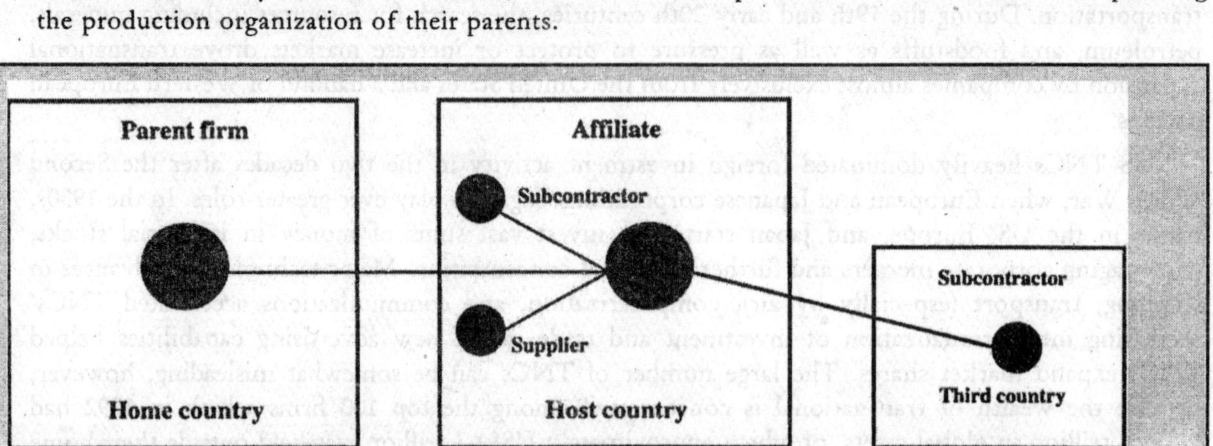

Stand-alone Strategy

Source: www.rrojasdatabank.org

Simple Integration Strategies

For some TNCs their main involvement in international production is via outsourcing some activities being performed in host countries and linked to work done elsewhere, mainly in home country. In manufacturing the clothing industry provides many examples of outsourced international production: large retail chains such as Marks and Spencer (United Kingdom), rely heavily on outsourced production from developing countries. The primary motive for outsourcing is to utilize the location advantages of a host country with respect to a portion of TNCs value chain. Outsourced production is controlled by the parent TNC either through ownership of the affiliate or through non-equity arrangements with local firms, such as subcontracting, which enables a TNC to concentrate on certain parts of the value chain, while subcontractors specialize in the production of other usually labour intensive parts. In effect, subcontracted firms are linking themselves with TNCs or their affiliates, thus becoming part of the production system of TNCs. Components, for example, may not only be produced by subcontractor; they may also be designed by it according to the specification of the TNCs.

Outsourcing is predicated on the absence, reduction or elimination of trade barriers between home and host countries, on TNCs being able to invest in host countries and on transport cost being only a small proportion of the value of outsourced output. Since policy and technology are working to bring all these conditions about, the out sourced international production is increasing considerably.

To a significant extent, outsourcing is cost driven. Nike (United States) for example, subcontracts the manufacture of its athletic shoes and clothing to 40 separate locations, mostly in South and South East Asia. Design and marketing are done by parent firm, with new designs relayed by satellite to a computer –aided design /computer aided manufacturing (CAD/CAM) facility run by subcontractor in Taiwan Province of China. Prototype are constructed and modified, and final plans are sent by facsimile to subcontractors throughout the region, where some Nike employees are present to ensure quality control. The output is world wide. Since individual subcontractors are dependent the parent for design, standards and marketing, they are not capable of standing-alone.

Figure 11.6

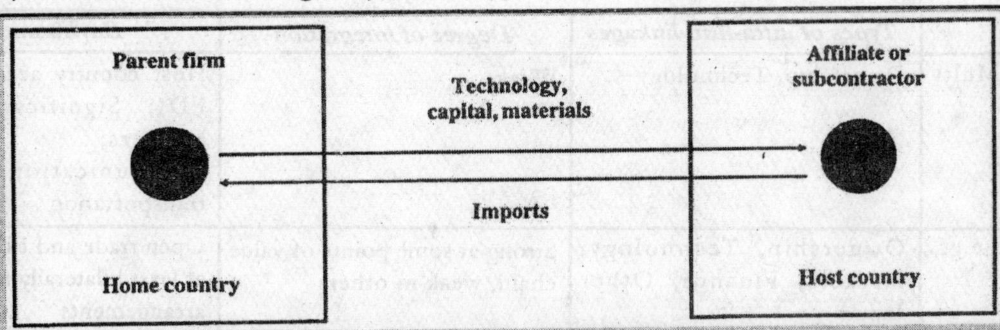

Simple Integration Strategy (Outsourcing)

Source: www.rrojasdatabank.org

Complex Integration Strategies

This new approach—"complex integration"—is made possible by huge improvements in communication and information technologies. They allow transnational Corporations to coordinate a growing number of activities in a widening array of locations. This, in turn, changes the way in which transnational corporations structure their activities. In a number of instances, indeed, information technology is leading to a "re-engineering" of relationships within firms.

Complex integration is also being driven by the tendency for markets to converge. More products are sold in the same or similar form in a growing number of national markets. In addition, competition forces firms to seek cost savings and profits from all segments of their value chains. As a result, companies are arranging certain functions-research and development, procurement, accounting, data entry and processing, as well as activities for specific products or product lines, such as component manufacturing and assembly—in a way that requires close links between parent firms and foreign affiliates, among foreign affiliates themselves and between parents and affiliates and firms linked via alliances. With that type of integration, separate activities performed in international locations are valued according to how they contribute to the objectives of the firm as a whole, rather than their profitability at the host country location.

Figure 11.7

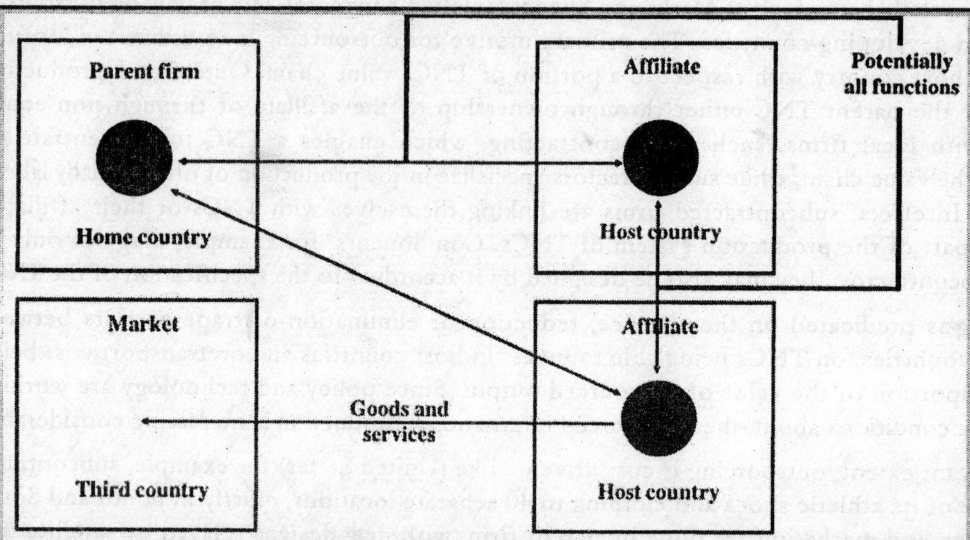

Complex Integration Strategy

Source: **www.rrojasdatabank.org**

Evolution of the Strategies and Structures of Transnational Corporations

Form	*Types of intra-firm linkages*	*Degree of integration*	*Environment*
Stand-alone- e.g., Multi domestic	Ownership, Technology	Weak	Host country accessible to FDI; Significant trade barriers; costly communications and transportation
Simple integration- e.g., Outsourcing	Ownership, Technology, Markets, Finance, Other Inputs	Strong at some points of value chain, weak in others	Open trade and FDI regime, at least bilaterally non-equity arrangements
Complex integration- e.g., Regional core networks	All Functions	Potentially strong throughout value chain	Open trade and FDI regime; information technology; convergence in tastes; heightened competition

Source: UNCTAD, Programmed on Transnational Corporations, World Investment Report 1993: Transnational Corporations and Integrated International Production.

Benefits of Transnational Corporations

- TNCs, and the FDI they bring, have the potential to "generate employment, raise productivity, transfer skills and technology, enhance exports and contribute to the long-term economic development of developing countries."
- They infuse money into an economy where it can supplement or free-up government revenues and/or development assistance funds.
- TNCs also bolster the private sectors of the countries where they operate, a process deemed important to overall economic growth and economic health.

Problems Arising from Transnational Corporations

- For both real and ideological reasons, some stakeholders distrust the impact of TNCs on vulnerable economies. It has been reported that "Twenty-nine of the world's 100 biggest economic entitles are multinational companies." That degree of economic strength wielded within a weak economy by an powerful organization required by fiduciary responsibility to give top priority to shareholder return cannot be counted on to respect the best interests of the host country.
- Specific instances of serious problems with TNC practices — frequently related to environmental despoilment — have created civil unrest and a backlash against the presence of multinational companies, especially large and politically well-connected ones. Shell Oil Company in Nigeria, Bechtel in Bolivia, Union Carbide in India, and Chevron Texaco in Ecuador are cases of major TNC presence that has generated major problems.
- While TNCs can come, bringing jobs, money and technology to areas that need them; they can also leave, possibly taking some of those benefits away with them. Sony Corporation left West Java, Indonesia due to a poor business climate. Anglo-American, a mining company, withdrew copper investments from Zambia as part of a restructuring. Emerging market Asian countries worry that China will attract investment that had been coming to them.
- TNCs, for their part, may be discouraged by obstacles facing them in host countries: opaque legal/regulatory systems, corruption, inadequate infrastructure, political uncertainty and other elements of an unfavourable investment climate. Nationalization or expropriation may also be a concern to them.
- Developing country governments sometimes fear that powerful TNCs will "crowd out" domestic industry or damage "infant industries" that they hope to nurture.

Multinational Corporations

A Multinational Corporation (MNC) is a corporation or enterprise that manages production establishments or delivers services in at least two countries. Very large multinationals have budgets that exceed those of many countries. Multinational corporations can have a powerful influence in international relations and local economies. Multinational corporations play an important role in globalization; some argue that a new form of MNC is evolving in response to globalization: the 'globally integrated enterprise'. Nearly all major multinationals are American, Japanese or Western European, such as Nike, Coca-Cola, Wal-Mart, AOL, Toshiba, Honda and BMW.

Definitions: "A corporation that owns and operates production facilities in two or more countries" or "A company with production and distribution facilities in more than one country".

Nature of Multinational Corporations

- Multinational Corporations (MNCs) are economic organizations engaged in productive activities in two or more countries.
- Typically have Headquarters (HQ) in the country of origin.
- Build or acquire affiliates or subsidiaries in other countries (the host nation).
- This kind of expansion is referred to as Foreign Direct Investment (FDI).

Foreign Direct Investment

- Foreign direct investment refers to investment in which firm in one country directly controls or owns a subsidiary in another.
- If a foreign company invests in at least 10% of the stock in a subsidiary, the two firms are typically classified as a multinational corporation.
- 10% or more of ownership in stock is deemed to be sufficient for direct control of business operations.

- In addition, international borrowing and lending sometimes occurs between a parent company and its subsidiary.

Strategies for Multinational Corporations

1. Mergers and Acquisition
2. Joint Ventures
3. Strategic Alliance
4. Licensing and Franchising.

1. Mergers and Acquisition: Mergers and acquisitions are very important market entry as well as growth strategy. Mergers and acquisition have certain advantages. It may used to acquire new technology, Mergers and acquisition would have the effect of eliminating/reducing competition. One great advantage of mergers and acquisitions in some cases is that it provides instant access to markets and distribution network.

For example: Given below is Tata Steel Company that has been merged with or has been acquired by Tata Group companies (for a year-wise listing)

Tata company	*Acquired company*	*Country*	*Stake acquired*	*Value*	*Year*
Tata steel	Millennium Steel	Thailand	67.11 per cent	USD167 million (Baht 6.5 billion)	April 2006
	Nat Steel Asia	Singapore	100 per cent (wholly-Owned)	S$468.10 million	February 2005
	Corus	UK	100 per cent		January 2007

2. Joint Ventures

- A JV is formed by two businesses that conduct business in a third country (French firm + Japanese firm jointly operate in the Central Europe - TPCA)
- Joint venture with a local firm (Copirisco [POR] + Cautor [CZ]
- Joint venture includes local government (Messerschmitt-Boelkow-Blom, Germany => Iran Oil Investment Company + National Iranian Oil Company.

3. Strategic Alliance. Strategic Alliance provides enormous scope for any country business to enter/expand the international business. This is particularly important for technology acquisition and overseas marketing. Alliance is indeed an important international marketing strategy employed by several Indian firms.

4. Licensing and Franchising. Licensing and franchising, which involve minimal commitment of resource and effort on the part of the international marketer, are easy ways of entering the international market. Many Indian firms can use licensing or franchising for the overseas market; particularly the developing countries. For example: Ranbaxy has licensing arrangement in countries like Indonesia and Jordan.

Theory of Multinational Corporations

Why are multinational corporations created and why do they undertake direct foreign investment? These questions are rephrased into those dealing with:

A. Location: Why is a good produced in two countries rather than in one country?

Internalization: Why is production in different locations done by one firm rather than by separate firms? Internalization occurs because it is more profitable to conduct transactions and production within a single organization than in separate organizations. Reasons for this include:

• Technology transfers: It transfer of knowledge or another form of technology may be easier within a single organization than through a market transaction between separate organizations.

- Patent or property rights may be weak or non-existent.
- Knowledge may not be easily packaged and sold.

B. Vertical integration: It involves consolidation of different stages of a production process.

- Vertical integration would involve consolidation of one firm that produces a good that is used as an input for another firm.
- This may be more efficient than having production operated by separate firms (avoid monopoly conflicts, coordination problems if supply/demand uncertain, risk of price fluctuations). For example, having farms and flour mills consolidate into one organization to make flour may be more efficient than having farms and flour mills as separate organizations.

C. Why production occurs in separate locations is often determined by the location of necessary factors of production:

- Mining occurs where minerals are;
- Labour intensive production occurs where relatively large pools of labour live.
- Transportation costs and other barriers to trade may also influence the location of production.
- These factors also influence the pattern of trade.

Multinational corporations undertake foreign direct investment, possibly because: locating production in foreign countries is efficient,

- Internalizing technology transfers is efficient or
- Vertical integration is efficient.

Evolution of Multinational Corporations

Normally, a firm passes through different stages of development before it becomes a truly global corporation. Typically, a domestic firm starts its international business by exporting. Later it may establish joint ventures or subsidiaries abroad. From an international firm it may then develop into a multinational firm and finally into a global one. Usually, three stages of evolution are seen:

Export stage: As the product receives positive customer response, the international demand for the product begins. The manufacturer begins exporting to increase its market share. E.g., Personal computer (PC) craze of the early 1980's. In 1980, 55,000 PCs sold in the US. By 1984 the industry experienced a 136-fold increase to 7 million PCs (Richter-Buttery, 1998).

Foreign Production Stage: As demand increases with the new global market, it becomes economically feasible to begin local production in various nations. By sharing technology on the manufacturing of the product, the company has lost an advantage. The end of this stage signifies the highest point in the International Product Life Cycle Theory. Once the firm chooses foreign production as a method of delivering goods to foreign markets, it must decide whether to establish a foreign production subsidiary or license the technology to a foreign firm.

Multinational Stage: The company becomes a multinational enterprise when it begins to plan, organize and coordinate production, marketing, R&D, financing, and staffing internationally. For each of these operations, the firm must find the best location. Thumb rule to determine whether a company is MNC or not is - A company whose foreign affiliates' sales are 25% or more of total sales.

Examples: Manufacturing Macs, 24 of top fifty firms are located in the U.S. out of which 9 are in Japan and 6 are in Germany.

Petroleum companies: 6/10 located in the U.S.

Multinational Corporate Structure

Multinational corporations can be divided into three broad groups according to the configuration of their production facilities:

1. Horizontally Integrated Multinational Corporations - It manages production establishments located in different countries to produce the same or similar products. E.g. MacDonald's

2. Vertically Integrated Multinational Corporations - It manages production establishment in certain country/countries to produce products that serve as input to its production establishments in other country/countries. E.g., Adidas ltd AG is a major German sports apparel manufacturer, part of the Adidas Group, consisting of Reebok Sportswear Company; Taylor Golf Company, Maxfli Golf Balls, and Adidas Golf and is the second largest sportswear manufacturer in the world.

3. Diversified Multinational Corporations - It manages production establishments located in different countries that are neither horizontally or vertically or straight, or non-straight integrated. E.g., Microsoft Corporation is an American multinational computer technology corporation with 79,000 employees in 102 countries and global annual revenue of US $ 51.12 billion as of 2007. It develops, manufactures, licenses and supports a wide range of software products for computing devices.

The Rise of the Multinational Corporations - Reasons to go Global There are some essential conditions to be satisfied on the part of the domestic economy as well as the firm for successful globalization of the business. They are:

1. Business freedom
2. Facilities
3. Government Support
4. Resources
5. Competitiveness.

1. Business Freedom: There should not be unnecessary Government restrictions which come in the way of globalization, like import restriction, restrictions on sourcing finance or other factors from abroad, foreign investments etc. That is why the economic liberalization is regarded as a first step towards facilitating globalization.

2. Facilities: The extent to which an enterprise can develop globally from home country base depends on the facilities available like the infrastructural facilities

3. Government Support: Although unnecessary government interference is a hindrance to globalization, government support can encourage Globalization. Government support may take the form of policy and procedural reforms, development of common facilities like infrastructural facilities, R and D support, financial market reforms and so on.

4. Resources: Resources is one of the important factors which often decide the ability of a firm to globalize. Resources include finance, technology, R and D capabilities, managerial experts, company and brand image, human resource etc. It should, however, be noted that many small firms have been very successful in international business because of one or other advantage they possess.

5. Competitiveness: The competitive advantage of the company is a very important determinant of success in global business. A firm may derive competitive advantage from any one or more of the factors such as low costs and price, product quality, product differentiation, technological superiority, after sales service, marketing strength etc. Some times small firms may have an edge over others in certain aspects or times of business.

Product Life Cycle and the MNC

1. The launch phase:

- Products are developed and marketed in developed countries.
- Multinational spread likely to be limited.

2. The growth phase:

- Increasing competition and rapid product adoption.
- Marketed primarily in developed countries.

- Product is exported to developing countries.
- MNC likely to shift production abroad in order to retain cost competitiveness.

3. Maturity phase:

- Product is adopted by most target consumers.
- Sales are levelling off.
- Profits decline due to intense competition.
- Manufacturing operations move to developing countries to take advantage of cheap labor.
- New competitors: firms from developing countries.
- MNC increasingly seeks markets abroad as growth in home market slows.

4. Late maturity and decline phase:

- Products are rapidly losing ground to new technologies and product alternatives.
- Decrease in sales and profits.
- Product lifecycle is extended through sales to consumers in developing countries.
- MNC increasingly seeks both markets and ever lower cost production abroad.

Problems Facing Multinationals

- Language barriers
- Selling and marketing
- Cultural issues
- Relations with host governments
- Relationships between subsidiaries - Possible diseconomies of scale - Easier if subsidiaries are run independently'
- Political instability
- Fluctuation currency prices
- Supply chain management
- Fast changing customer preferences.

Indian Multinationals

Economic integration across countries has created a global market for different types of products and services. It has given companies an access to the world's best resources – cheap but talented labour, largest markets in terms of size, vast capital market, most advanced technologies and lowest-cost suppliers of inputs. Global companies find their origin not only in developed countries, but also in emerging markets. Emerging markets in particular provide an invaluable springboard to companies to achieve global standards of competitiveness in their core activities at home, which are then leveraged internationally.

Globalization has given new meaning and dimension to corporate India. Many Indian firms have slowly, but surely, embarked on the global path, leading to the emergence of Indian multinational companies. Indian industry has crossed domestic frontiers and established a credible presence in markets abroad in a very short time.

Indian multinational have evolved over diverse sectors, right from pharmaceuticals to automotive to hotels to textiles to engineering goods and entertainment. With each passing day, Indian businesses are acquiring companies' abroad, becoming world-popular suppliers and are recruiting talent cutting across national boundaries.

This trend truly typifies the global aspirations of Indian companies, but more importantly, represent the ability of Indian businesses to achieve global standards of competitiveness.

It has been said that the battles of this century will be fought and won on the "power of ideas." Societies will increasingly become knowledge based and promote knowledge-based industries.

As more multinationals open development centers in India, it will become harder for the Indian companies to retain people. Multinationals can always afford to pay better, not because of their financial muscle, but because of the nature of the relationship between the parent company and its center here. For illustration purposes, let us consider a company in USA which does software development for itself. Say, it costs the company $7000/- per person month in USA. If it opens a development center in India, and spends $4000 per person month, it still saves $3000 per person month. On the other hand, an Indian software company developing software for clients, even if it charges $4000/- per person month, it cannot spend the entire amount as it must also make a profit in this $4000 rate. That is, given a rate in India, the multinational makes a profit even if it spends the entire rate amount on the Indian center. On the other hand, the Indian company can spend only about 60-70% of this on the center (assuming a profit margin of 30-40%). Clearly, if salary wars really start, Indian companies will find it hard to win against multinationals.

However, this economic logic can be inverted and used by Indian companies to increase their profitability and strength by going multinational. The idea is as follows: An Indian company starts a full fledged software development center in the USA, manned by people from USA (and India). As a US company, this company charges US rates. However, it sub-contracts parts of its work to its parent company in India, making double profits on these parts (the US company makes a profit as well as the Indian company makes a profit).

Note that the relationship between the Indian company & its subsidiary is just reverse of the relationship a typical multinational has with its subsidiary in India. With multinationals, they provide work to their center, while in the case of Indian companies; it is their overseas center that will provide work to them. Note also this concept is different from setting up centers in other Asian countries to meet the manpower needs. The driving force here is not shortage of manpower, but the desire for higher rates and profits.

There is another economic reason to support such a move. Currently, Indian companies charge between $15 to $25 per person-hour of effort from their overseas clients. The rates for comparable expertise in the US are around $50 to $70; the rates in other developed or semi-developed countries might be lower. This means, that Indian software companies are already operating at around one third to half the hourly cost in the west. As most Indian software companies deploy lesser tools, and the level of technical education of many software professionals is not always very high, the chances are that the productivity and quality of Indian software may not be as high as in the West. All this means that it is unlikely that the rates that Indian companies can charge will increase as much in future as they have in the past—after all if the rate is close to the rate of an US or an European company, why would a US or European customer come all the way to India to get its software developed, given the perceived risks and psychological barriers that exist? On the other hand, the salaries are likely to continue rising. This will create pressure on the profit margins, and alternative means will have to be devised to increase profit margins. Going multinational might be just the right alternative for this.

Focusing Further

Even if an Indian company wants to start a company in USA, how should it face the competition there and create a market for itself? Unless there is a reasonable chance of succeeding, no company will make this move as investments are likely to be high. An average SW professional in USA costs about $80,000. Hence, the cost of running a 50 person company in US is about $400,000 per year. In addition, there is also the cost of setting up the company.

First prerequisite for this model to succeed is that the subsidiary should have a strong US or European face. In other words, it should be a *bona-fide* local company, with local people, and, perhaps even local share holders. It should not be perceived as a marketing or work sourcing arm of an Indian company—in this situation, it is unlikely that any client will pay the prevailing local rates.

In addition, it will be most useful if the Indian connection of this US Company can be exploited to create a niche in the US software services market. One possibility is to exploit the time zone difference and the internet and multimedia technology to offer Rapid Application Development (RAD) services in well defined business areas. In the current times, there are many business sectors, in which time to market is one of the most important parameters. For these business segments, a rapid development service offering for their support software can create a niche for itself. An example of this is financial services where frequently the window of opportunity is small and so the software to support the services for this window has to be developed rapidly.

However, just having development teams in two time zones is not going to be sufficient to provide a true RAD. Suitable development process models will have to be developed, and technology will have to be fully exploited for this. For example, incremental development models, or the evolutionary object-oriented models might have to be used to reduce dependencies between work elements, libraries of reusable components for the market segment will have to be built before hand to reduce the cycle time, proper distributed work-flow management tools will have to be built on the internet, and multimedia workstations might have to be used to pass work products and instructions from one developer to another. In other words, a lot of work will have to be done to precisely define and make possible the service offering. However, it is technically feasible (which was not the case a few years ago).

Risks involved........

Most of the risks in this strategy revolve around opening a center in the West, where costs are very high, and market fiercely competitive. One risk is whether there is a demand for the proposed service. A market survey can be used to get actual estimates of the market size and estimate the value of the proposed service. Another risk will be in marketing this service and showing that it is different and more effective than those offered by the competitors in the west. This is where the companies will have to apply their business and marketing expertise to make such a venture successful.

Strategies Followed to Establish Global Footprints

The attitudinal change to turn global has led to the emergence of many Indian MNCs who have overcome geographic boundaries by adopting a mix of business strategies. Most commonly, companies have used the route of Greenfield investments or acquisitions overseas or a combination of both. Others have made their exports more cost competitive *vis-à-vis* global peers. A few have entered into technical tie-ups with global partners to build capabilities and then leverage them in the international markets. Several companies have ramped up their scale of operations to a level essential for a global foray.

1. Making Investments in Greenfield Venture or Acquisitions

For those companies concentrating on making investments outside India, a mix of organic and inorganic growth has been the most common route towards globalization. The industry leading on this front is the IT industry, which has put India on the global map. TCS, with 169 offices in 35 countries world-wide, is not only dominant in English speaking countries, but also has a strong presence in the Spanish and Portuguese speaking regions of the world. Its strategic acquisitions of a banking and BPO business in Chile, and a banking solutions company in Australia, have helped it to gain complementary skills and geographic presence. Wiper, which commenced operations in the vegetable oils business, today has a presence across the largest number of verticals in the IT industry. What has set Wiper apart from its peers is its aggressive acquisition strategy to grow its technology and industry capabilities. The company, which sees inorganic growth as a key to expanding its business, has made several acquisitions since 2002 and is looking for more opportunities to build scale. Old economy industries like auto-ancillaries, paints, pharmaceuticals, agro-chemicals, etc, are also part of this trend. Sundram Fasteners, the first Indian engineering company to set up a Greenfield venture in China to manufacture high tensile fasteners, has made acquisitions in Europe to establish a strong position in developed markets and gain access to blue-chip customers. Another company in the automotive space, Armtek Auto has followed a similar strategy for global growth. Driven by its vision to attain proximity to customers and reduce lead times for delivery, it has set up a ring gear unit in Detroit, the global hub of automotive manufacturing, and has made strategic acquisitions in the US, UK and Germany. Asian Paints, one of the top ten decorative paint companies in the world, has pursued a globalization strategy of entering fast growing markets with robust demand and low per capita consumption of paints. In the initial years it focused on forming joint ventures with existing players in growth markets. Later its focus shifted to acquisitions, the most important being that of Berger International, which gave it access to the growing markets in Asia, Africa and the Caribbean countries. Driven by its global vision, the company today services customers across 65 countries and has manufacturing facilities across 22 countries.

United Phosphorus has successfully transformed itself from a domestic insecticide player to a global generic agrochemicals player, through a string of acquisitions of companies and products. Crucial acquisitions of European companies have helped it to establish a strong foothold in the highly competitive developed markets that are dominated by giants like Dow Chemicals, DuPont, BASF, etc. VSNL, one of India's largest telecom companies, has acquired Teleglobe International Holdings and Tyco Global Network in its drive to offer global connectivity and confirm its position as a leading global telecom service provider. In the pharmacy space, Nicholas Piramal, which has positioned itself as a high-end contract manufacturer for bulk drugs and formulations for renowned global companies, has made a strategic acquisition of Avecia Pharmaceuticals (UK), which has given it access to new clients as well as critical technologies. Prior to this, its acquisition of Rhodia's inhalations anesthetics business, giving it access to technologies and state-of-the-art manufacturing facilities, has helped to make its contract manufacturing business stronger. Wockhardt, a large biotech products company, has established marketing subsidiaries in the large market of the US and the growing market of Brazil. Acquisition of three companies in Europe has helped it to establish a strong position in the region, especially UK. The hotel industry is not far behind in this trend. Indian Hotels, which operates the largest hotel chain in India, has nearly 16 per cent of its revenues coming from international operations. While management contracts have been the preferred route for the company to establish a global presence, it has not shied from making strategic acquisitions of hotel properties in growth markets like Australia and Zambia whenever the opportunity arose.

2. Making Exports Cost Competitive in Relation to Global Peers

For some players having global plans, lowering cost of production *vis-à-vis* key competitors has been a strategy for establishing a global footprint through exports. For instance, Tate Steel, representing India's largest, integrated steel plant in the private sector, is firmly entrenched as a low cost producer among global steel majors. It has leveraged on captive raw material resources in the form of in-house mines and collieries.

This has been augmented with rightsizing of its employees, rise in employee productivity through training and modernization and a strategy of split-location manufacturing of producing semi-finished products in proximity to raw materials and by finishing them at locations which are near to markets. Tata Motors, India's largest manufacturer of commercial vehicles and second largest manufacturer of passenger cars, began exports from India by leveraging its low-cost manufacturing base, a result of its rationalized vendor base improvements in its supply chain and developing low-cost product development capabilities. Gokaldas Exports, the largest apparel exporter from India, has leveraged the advantage of low labour costs in India to export to large retailers and brands across the world and has nearly its entire turnover coming from international markets. Its supply chain is also global, with nearly three-fourths of its raw material requirements being imported.

3. Forming Alliances with International Companies

A few companies, whether in the manufacturing sector or the services sector, have formed alliances with global companies for acquiring technology and accessing customers in global markets. Satyam Computer, which has grown from a mere domestic IT services company to becoming a global player, has nurtured strategic alliances with over 50 technology leaders, wherein Satyam uses the technology, goes to market with these technology leaders, or provides services based on their technologies. Thermax, which has grown from a small boiler company to a large, multi-divisional energy and environment solutions provider, has formed alliances with global players of the likes of Babcock & Wilcox, Honeywell and Kawasaki to access key markets and technology. Larsen & Turbo, the largest engineering and Construction Company in India, has collaborated with several international engineering companies to be able to give impetus to the solutions provided to its clients globally. Some of its prominent global partners include Chiyoda Corporation of Japan, Sargent & Lundy LLC, USA, Ramboll A/S of Denmark and Voith Paper, Germany. In the manufacturing sector, Motherson Sumi Systems Limited (MSSL), India's largest producer of integrated wiring harnesses, has built its strong engineering skills and machining capabilities through joint ventures with several international tier-1 auto component companies. MSSL acquires technology from these companies for manufacturing, as a result of which it is in a position to provide end-to-end solutions to its global customers, including its technology partners. Rico Auto, one of the largest full service suppliers of auto components and assembly in India, has grown mainly through alliances and joint ventures with global companies. Its partners include FCC Co. Japan (for clutch assemblies for two-wheelers and automobiles and flywheels for automobiles), Pierburg, Germany (for water pumps and oil pumps) and Teksid Aluminum, Italy (for aluminium engine blocks and heads).

Mahindra & Mahindra (M&M), market leader in India in multi-utility vehicles and tractors, has a strategic technical partnership with International Truck and Engine Corporation to manufacture and market vehicles in India as well as exports, besides providing components and engineering services to International's North American operations. Its joint venture with Jiangling Motor Company Group for tractors has given it access to the Chinese market and other export markets, besides giving it an opportunity to source components from China. Ashok Leyland, whose exports of commercial vehicles account for nearly 50 per cent of commercial vehicles exports from India, has a global presence across 30 countries in Asia, Africa and the Middle East. It has fostered a tradition of technological leadership achieved through a combination of robust in-house R&D and technology tie-ups with international leaders – Hino Motors (Japan) for engines, ZF (Germany) for gearboxes and Dana Corporation (USA) for axles.

4. Ramp-up in Scale of Operations

Another way in which companies have effectively competed in global markets has been by achieving scale by investing in global size capacities. This is most evident in the case of Moser Baer, the second largest optical media manufacturer in the world, which has scaled capacity over the last few years to cater to large global orders. Today it is a supplier-of-choice to all the top twelve global optical media brands and exports constitute nearly three-fourths of its total revenues. Bharat Forge, the largest exporter of auto components from India and the second largest forging company in the world, has continuously relied on creating capacities in India and abroad, with a view to cater to the quality as well as quantity requirements of its global customers. Reliance Industries, the largest private sector business house in India having activities spanning exploration and production of oil and gas, refining and marketing of petrochemicals and textiles, has created world-class capacities across its entire product portfolio. Today, it is the world's largest producer of PSF and PFY, third largest producer of paraxylene, third largest producer of MEG and sixth largest producer of PTA. Its oil refinery in Gujarat is the third largest in the world. Similarly Arvind Mills, which is today the third largest denim manufacturer in the world, has invested heavily in increasing capacity for denim fabric and has a vertically integrated denim plant that ranks amongst the most modern in the world. In the media and entertainment industry, Zee Telefilms, revolutionized the satellite television industry in India before undertaking its global initiatives. It today caters to more than one million subscribers outside India through its large scale of operations comprising its bouquet of 22 channels that are beamed across 120 countries.

5. Leveraging International Capital Markets

Several companies growing on the globalization platform have leveraged international capital markets to fund their globalization activities, a case in point being Sterlite Industries, the flagship company of the Vedanta Resources Plc. Sterlite has gained from the money raised by Vedanta through its IPO on the LSE, this being the first primary listing by an Indian company on the LSE. Its success in the later years in tapping the global financial markets has paved the way for it to position itself as a major player in the global non-ferrous metals market through acquisitions and capacity expansions targeted at exports.

Lessons from Globalization History of Indian Companies

The experiences from the growth path of companies from an emerging economy to global ones have several lessons to offer to those looking for a similar growth. This path is not an easy one and organizations need to translate their homegrown capabilities and the talent of their people to cross geographic boundaries.

One key learning from the experience of Indian MNCs is that companies need to build a core competency and possibly avenues to generate internal accruals or external finances for funding globalization plans. There are examples of several companies that have first built a robust and sustainable domestic business model by honing it through continuous experimentation in the home market and thus creating a core competency. This has provided for an ability to build difficult-to-imitate capabilities to achieve global standards of competitiveness. This has been ably supported by the willingness of their promoters and management to stay invested in their new businesses for a longer duration of time. For instance, Titan, India's largest watch manufacturer first developed a formidable distribution network and superior designing capabilities in India, which were used to compete with the designing capabilities of players in the European market.

The domestic business also helped in staying invested in the global operations for a longer time. Voltas, today enjoys the distinction of being the country's premier exporter of electromechanical projects, with a footprint in over thirty countries. This is mainly a result of its experience in India built across varied applications, which is being leveraged for several prestigious mandates as an EPC contractor across Asia. Similarly, ITC, India's largest cigarette producer and a diversified FMCG company, has anchored on its core competencies of strong distribution reach, superior brand building capabilities and effective supply chain management. Its global initiatives, ranging from exports of cigarettes to agri-products to paper and packaging, have been built on the foundation of its backward integration linkages with Indian farmers for procurement of inputs.

Marico, another well-known FMCG company, has successfully created brands in the largely commodity-oriented business of hair oils and edible oils. These brands have been leveraged to develop a significant franchise across countries, including the US, Middle East, Asia and Australia by targeting the Indian Diasporas.

In the pharmacy space, Dr Reddy's Laboratories, one of India's largest pharmaceutical companies, has built a core competency in R&D by investing heavily in research and drug discovery. It has moved from being a seller of bulk actives in India to an exporter of difficult-to-manufacture bulk actives to highly regulated developed markets. Another pharmacy company, Glenmark, has leveraged its well integrated business model in India covering activities ranging from drug discovery to development of API to marketing of formulations to an increasing number of markets, both regulated as well as unregulated.

Last, but not the least, to support its globalization activities, it is also imperative for a company to manage a team of talented executives with international experience, who are the repository of its core skills and organizational culture and are given the independence to take decisions in diverse markets. For instance, Dabur, whose international operations are handled by its subsidiary Dabur International in Dubai, has its own independent team to oversee all global activities and monitor its manufacturing subsidiaries in other countries. Tata Tea, which became the second largest branded tea company in the world, after the acquisition of Tetley, successfully created a structure that facilitated joint working of its employees in India and abroad. A well thought through process was adopted for the integration of the two companies by identifying the common beliefs between them. A Steering Committee was created with several task forces reporting to it and comprising managers of both companies. Some teams were given time bound tasks while others worked on unification of some processes. This structure was converted into a Supervisory Board, reporting to the Board of Tata Tea, and taking decisions on matters concerning both companies. It was supported by four integration teams, with people from both companies and having an agenda to drive geographical and product category growth improve operational performance and drive common business processes. For Infosys, the second largest foreign exchange earner in the software services business in India, the most important factor responsible for its success has been its ability to attract, develop and retain outstanding human capital.

Given the nature of its business, the company competes on the strength of its people and has invested heavily in recruitment and training. Some of its pioneering initiatives include a residential Global Education Centre for training, which is the largest corporate training centre in the world capable of training 4,500 people at a time, and its initiative Campus Connect, a nation-wide programme which focuses on aligning the needs of colleges, faculty and students with industry needs. Its Employee Stock Offer Plan has been an important factor to attract and retain high quality staff in India as well as in the talent competitive markets of Europe and the US. To build a strong senior management, the company's Infosys Leadership Institute facilitates the development of a cadre of global leaders with the competencies required to steer the company into the future.

Trends in Future

As India makes rapid strides in its economic growth, it is increasingly becoming an attractive destination for international companies, thus heating up the competition in the domestic market. Indian companies cannot ignore the fact that in order to face this competition, they not only have to emerge stronger in the domestic market, but also challenge these companies in their international turf. There are several instances of Indian companies who have become MNCs in their own right through sizeable investments made abroad or becoming suppliers of choice for global companies by leveraging lower costs in India. This trend will increasingly extend to the next rung of companies who are looking at aggressive growth, with overseas acquisitions being the most preferred route for this. These companies realize that it is essential for them to achieve global size and competitiveness to establish a broader market position and to sustain a strong position in the global markets. To achieve global size they need to look at growth opportunities outside the domestic borders. Whether it is manufacturing companies that are adding relationships and customers by transferring work into India, or software firms that are strengthening their domain capabilities and filling in gaps in their business portfolios, the message is very clear for all companies. In order to succeed they need to expand their global reach by developing vision, capability and management bandwidth.

Financial Performance

With an estimated $8 billion spent on overseas mergers, acquisitions and expansion, 2006 turned out to be a year of global consolidation for India Inc., and Indian multinationals became a reality.

So much so that India - which is itself seeking huge doses of foreign investment — is for the first time witnessing its companies invest more capital abroad this year than the inward flow of overseas investments, placed at around $5 billion.

Both smaller and large companies were on a buying binge, says the study, adding the average size of acquisition for pharmaceutical firms, for example, was $61 million — the largest valued at $777 million and the smallest at $1.2 million.

In the past three months alone, Indian firms sought to strike some mega deals in the overseas market - the Tata's bid a whopping $18 billion for Anglo-Dutch steel-maker Corus, Videocon bid $695 million for South Korea's Daewoo Electronics and ONGC Videsh bid $425 million for Omimex de Colombia.

The other big-ticket transactions included Tata Tea's acquisition of US food and beverage firm Energy Brands for $677-million, Aban Lloyd's buyout of Norwegian oil major Sinvest for $425-million and Suzlon Energy's acquisition of Belgium's Hanson Transmission for $565-million.

But there was unprecedented consolidation within the country as well. The value of mergers and acquisitions in India jumped to $9.5 billion this year from $5.37 billion in 2005, according to industry studies

Similar growth was witnessed in industries like telecommunications, automobiles, aviation, retail trade, hospitality and transportation.

Overall, the corporate sector continued to show buoyancy — evident from the second quarter results for this fiscal — where profits after tax grew 49.5 percent, against 25.8 percent in the previous figure, said a CII study.

Impact on the Economic Growth

- In the process, India's share in global deals also jumped to 1.30 percent from 0.72 percent.
- India ahead of two places in the Global Competitiveness Index (GCI) rankings for 2006-07 coming in 43rd place.
- Well ahead of Brazil (66), China (54) and Russia (62).
- From large business groups such as the Tata's, Reliance Industries and Ranbaxy to smaller firms with turnover as less as $1 million, an unprecedented effort was made in 2006 to expand abroad for global integration and economies of scale.

  "India recently displaced Japan as the second-largest investor in the UK," said the Duke of York, Prince Andrew. "Indian businesses investing in the UK have increased from 19 four years ago, to over 100 today."

Acquisitions made by Indian Companies

- Amtek Auto Zelter GmbH, Germany; GWK Group, UK; Lloyds, Beverly Hill, UK; Midwest Mfg. Co., USA
- Asian Paints Delmege Forsyth, Sri Lanka; Pacific Paints, Australia; Berger International, SCIB Chemical, Egypt; Taubmans Paints, Fiji
- Aurobindo Pharma Milpharm, UK
- Bharat Forge CDP Aluminiumtechnik, Germany; Federal Forge, USA; Imatra Forging Group, Sweden and Scotland
- Dr Reddy's Labs Roche's API business in Mexico; Betapharm Group, Germany
- Glenmark Pharma Laboratorios Klinger, Brazil; Servycal, S.A., Argentina and Bouwer Bartlett, South Africa
- Indian Hotels Hotels in Zambia and Australia
- M&M Jiangling Tractor Company, China
- Marico Sundari LLC, USA
- Motherson Sumi Reiner Präzision GmbH and G+S Kunststofftechnik GmbH in Germany
- Nicholas Piramal Rhodia's IA in UK and India; Avecia, UK
- Satyam Computer Citisoft, UK
- Sterlite Industries Monte Cello Corporation, Netherlands, the holding company of copper mines in Australia
- Sundram Fasteners Dana Spicer, UK; Peiner Umformtechnik GmbH, Germany
- Tata Motors Daewoo Commercial Vehicles, Korea; Hispano Carrocera, Spain
- Tata Steel NatSteel Asia
- Tata Tea Tetley, Good Earth, JEM_A, Glaceau

- TCS Comicrom, Chile; FNS, Australia
- United Phosphorus MTM Agrochem, UK; Agrodan, Denmark; Midland Fumigants, Europe; Cequisa, Spain; Shaw Wallace Agrochem,
- India; Advanta (seed business), Netherlands
- VSNL Teleglobe International Holdings, Tyco Global Network
- Wipro Spectramind, GE's healthcare software arm, global energy practice of American Management Systems, Nervewire,
- US; Ericsson's Indian R&D arm.

Indian MNCs and its CEO's

TCS	T.Ramadorai
INFOSYS	Nandan Nilekani
BIOCON	Kiran Mazumdar
BHARTI AIRTEL	Sunil Bharti Mittal
KINGFISHER AIRLINES	Vijay Mallya
SAHARA GROUP	Subrata Roy
RELIANCE INFOCOMM	Anil Ambani

Indian MNCs Listed in Fortune 500 companies

S.No	*Company*	*Rank*	*Revenues($ millions)*	*City*
1	Indian Oil	135	45,216.6	New Delhi
2	Reliance Industries	269	25,158.9	Mumbai
3	Bharat Petroleum	325	21,862.2	Mumbai
4	Hindustan Petroleum	336	20,935.6	Mumbai
5	Oil & Natural Gas	369	19,237.4	Dehradun
6	State Bank of India	495	15,119.4	Mumbai

Globalization, particularly the dismantling of trade barriers, has allowed MNC to spread widely in search of cost efficiency and to implement integrated production strategies across regions and even continents. But unquestionably, they bring resources of great potential benefit to developing countries.

Future Challenges in Global Management

To identify the future challenges in global management one needs to observe and analyze the current and future trends in globalization and business environment and hence uncover the future risks and opportunities. This in turn helps the corporation to anticipate, adapt and evolve for the future competition. According to McKinsey, the future trends and challenges in globalization and business environment which will shape the business landscape in the decade to come are as follows:

1. Management will go from art to science: Bigger more complex companies demand new tools to run and manage them. Improved technology and statistical control tools have given rise to new management approaches. Scientific management a present is a skill that creates competitive advantage for the corporation. In the coming decade, it will be a necessity for the management to adopt to remain and sustain in the business.

2. Cultural challenges: The cultural dynamics of different countries are different and can be understood by studying the respective people, their patterns of life, their traditions, social interaction, sensibilities and their faiths and fancies. The cultural dynamics also have an impact on the management style of that region. Therefore to succeed, the corporation has to communicate with the people of

that culture in their lingo and idiom. Hence, the multi-national enterprise management must function in the contrasting cultural dynamics, and manage across boundaries and cultures.

3. Free, global and instantaneous access to information is changing the economics of the knowledge: New models of knowledge production access, distribution and ownership are emerging. At present, there is a rise of open-source approaches to knowledge development and it is very likely that it will continue as communities, not individuals become responsible for innovation. Therefore, therein lies the challenge for global management to adopt to this new model and learn how to leverage this new knowledge universe.

4. Economic challenges: The centre of economic activity will shift profoundly not just globally, but also regionally. This is due to the economic liberalization, technological advances and demographic shifts which is currently leading to the massive realignment of economic activities and will continue to do so in the future. Also, a billion new consumers will enter the global market place in the next decade as economic growth in emerging markets pushing the consumers spending power from current $4 trillion to $9 trillion. Hence, the challenge will be to be in the right markets and geographies. Innovating new products and services, developing new strategies and planning for them and exploit it profitably will be vital to corporate success.

5. Social and environmental challenges: There will be a shift in the behaviour of consumers or people due to the technological connectivity which is presently transforming the way people live and interact, and will continue to do so in the coming decade. Presently, we are at the early stages of knowledge revolution. Individuals, public sector and businesses are learning how to make the best use of IT in designing the processes and in developing and accessing knowledge.

6. There will be shortage of talented workforce. This lack of talent will become a new corporate risk factor and a drag on profit. This power shift from employer to employee will change the entire idea of human capital in the coming decade, making it a strategic asset for which the companies will compete. Hence, therein lies challenge to hire the best talent, to train them and leverage their talent and skill. Retention of employees will also be a major challenge in the future.

The demand for natural resources will grow as will the strain on the environment. Therefore, to preserve the environment and for optimal use of natural resources, innovation in technology and regulation will be central to drive robust economic growth and also sustain environmental demand.

❅ ❅ ❅

12 Innovation and Global Organizations

• The Foundation For Innovation - Is Your Groundwork In Place? • Cultivating the Habit of Innovation • Managing For Innovation • The Only Sustainable Advantage • Innovation Through Global Collaboration: A New Source of Competitive Advantage

The Foundation For Innovation - Is Your Groundwork In Place?

Creativity is Not Innovation - Innovation is just "creative thinking" until those ideas begin to produce consistent results. May be your company is the master of creativity (that is, there is no lack of "bright" ideas), but you need to see consistent ROI on implementation. Perhaps, your staff isn't comfortable with the idea of being innovative; "why isn't one good trick for the pony enough"? Or, if your deliverable is a customer-centric process, thinking that you've just developed a "process for the ages" is in a word, naïve. What's stopping you — the constraint — (or, is it *restraint?*) from being innovative?

While creative ideas may come from a research fellow, from members of a "think tank," or from practically anyone, the pragmatic challenge of creativity is to then birth the resulting product or process successfully into the demanding reality of the competitive marketplace. The transformation of creativity into innovation requires a special process cmbedded within an organization's culture and environment. This process often becomes a "group think" and involves people of many and varied "stripes" all focused on a common objective; marketplace success. Again and again, to do this continuously — and as near to predictably as possible — requires an organizational "way" in which the total environment and the process protocols shepherd and pull the right ideas into market fruition.

Peter Drucker (*Innovation and Entrepreneurship*, Harper Business, 1993) said this about the need for innovation: *Innovation is the specific instrument of entrepreneurship. It is the act that endows resources with a new capacity to create wealth.* Developing the concept further, Paul Schuman, Donna Prestwood, *et al.* (Schuman, Prestwood, Tong, Vanston, *Innovate*, McGraw Hill, 1994), dropped the altitude a bit in describing why innovation is so important: *Innovation is the basis of all competitive advantage; the means by which organizations anticipate and fill customer needs and the method by which organizations utilize technology. Innovation is the organization's way of implementing new ideas, of turning the creative concepts of its members into realities.*

The quotations above reflect a common theme; innovate or fade. Once the corporate commitment to innovate is made — or perhaps innovation is the very nature of the product or process strategy — what next needs to be constructed is the one thing from which creativity is consistently turned into innovation. We can call this as the *Foundation of Innovation.*

For a successful enterprise, innovation is a key element that initiates and then sustains continued forward movement. It is not achieved, however, without careful thought, planning and execution. That is, it is purposeful and intentional. Successful, consistent innovation requires its own framework, structures, and support systems. Innovation works where it is designed into an organization's modus operandi. This chapter will address some of these "innovation by design" considerations.

The transformation of creativity into innovation requires a special process imbedded within an organization's culture and environment. An organization's technology, whatever it is, is not enough to sustain continued, profitable enterprise.

The *Foundation* is really a set of intertwined pillars or foundation elements, so closely connected and so interdependent that if even one is weak or missing, innovation will be rendered more problematic than reliable. There are five such foundation elements, all critical and each equally important: *People, Culture, Structure, Process,* and *Technology.* Further, some of the sub-elements of which these are comprised are linked into two supporting cross members, the load bearing beams that bind these elements together: overall *Corporate Strategy* and *Innovation Strategy.* This then is the *Foundation for Innovation.* The whole works because all the parts are present and work together.

Viewing the foundation elements — people, culture, structure, process, technology — it can be said that these must be correctly present in almost any successful enterprise regardless of its nature and mission. However, how these are defined, implemented and practiced in an innovatively successful organization requires a special set of definitions, linkages, and coordination.

The real issue with innovation is to be repeatedly, reliably successful. A really great idea that becomes a "one trick pony" or the current "process of the month" usually provides only temporary organization success, and yet many such organizations burgeon and fatten up around this one-time "innovation."

When the vagaries of the market rear up — and they will — and the competition begins to encroach on your previously hallowed domain — and they will - with what will you answer, how will you respond? Has your "system" provided you with a process that breeds a continuing string of innovative successes?

Assuming, for the sake of discussion, that your organization has been reasonably innovatively successful, what degree or type of innovation does your track record point to? Incremental innovations?

Distinctive innovations?

Truly breakthrough innovations?

Each and all are fine . . . but what has your competition been doing, and why?

Has your company's innovative performance been commensurate with its strategy and objectives? Consistently?

Has your revenue and profit and market share performance reflected an organization that possesses innovative know-how? If so, is it due to a solid environment and infrastructure that breeds these successes, or is it because that "research fellow" has been consistently able to come up with yet another good idea in the nick of time?

The Vital Role of Foundation Elements

Remembering that the foundation for continued innovation is comprised of the elements of people, culture, structure, process, and technology, let's see why they are necessary.

Technology, as key as it is, is not enough by itself. What is equally important is what you do with it and how you employ it. The other elements must be equally present and supportive.

Let's do a brief examination of why these "unsung" four elements are so important:

People

You of course hire people who are compatible with and can enhance your core competencies, but how do you put them together; individuals and/or teams? How are they empowered (if they are)? How are they rewarded? What role do your non-technologists play; are they a part of your innovativeness?

Highly creative people, in any field, tend to be independent thinkers . . . and doers . . . all of the time. How do you marshal their talents (and behaviour styles) within the operating norms of others whose creativity may lie in planning, managing, analysis and the like (that is, in the business of managing the business)?

Culture

If you have a clearly defined policy of product/process innovation, is it understood, how is it practiced, by all? Does everyone — individual contributors, managers, executives — participate, and "pull their weight"? Do your "good management practices" encourage and support an innovative environment? How? Do you recognize and instill the belief that innovative ideas may come from any source, even unexpected ones, and does your radar screen have a broad enough sweep to pick them all up?

Structure

Does your organizational structure facilitate open communication and cooperation within and between departments and operating units? Is this communication timely and rapid (and these are not the same)? What about ownership and accountability for the successes and the failures? Does your structure serve to enhance non-parochial innovation or does it provide a hiding place, a convenient dodge for any who may have a different view of "moving forward"?

Process

Have you ever mapped your innovation process? How does it *really* work? Are innovative opportunities market driven? Are they proactively sought out and encouraged? Do you periodically review the market status of all your products and processes; are they continuing to meet their goals? How is employee innovation encouraged and followed up? Do you systematically measure innovative performance to plan, and how do you know what success looks like? How many new products and or processes have you successfully inserted in the marketplace in the last measurably significant period . . . *versus* your competitors? Are your processes enabling or disabling? and then . . .

Technology

Does your technology (it can be any "degree" or type of technology) continuously result in product and process benefits that produce recognizable and significant customer value? How do you know if your technology is continuing to serve you and your customers well? Do you have a formal, documented new product and processes assessment system and do you follow it? Does your technology lend itself to rapid response changes in the market and competitors' strategies? Are you locked-in to "home grown" innovation or do you consider all sources as potentially viable?

Final Thoughts

Instilling (Random House Dictionary: "to infuse slowly into the mind") a process for innovation is, as the definition implies, a time consuming commitment. This commitment encompasses plans, strategy, and execution all of which ensue from a statement, an understanding, and an agreement of purpose. This purpose becomes part of the organization's foundation and begins at its creation or as the result of a subsequent, and usually massive, re-engineering of the operation.

An organization's technology, whatever it is, is not enough to sustain continued, profitable enterprise. The people you hire, the structure you build, the culture you and your employees create together, and the processes you develop, follow and continuously improve must all be energized from and bound together by your Corporate and Innovation Strategy.

Without these strategies, properly executed, you will simply wind up somewhere you had never intended to be, instead of continuing successfully on the path to where you wanted to go.

Cultivating the Habit of Innovation

To most of us, innovation is a process executed at "special" times when we need to break new ground. Ironically, at those times, we're usually too rusty to be innovative. Why should we save our best efforts for rare occasions? A rare breed of individual never gets out of practice-innovation is a habit. It's easy to find them: In all walks of life, they're the most satisfied, ingenious (regardless of natural intelligence), and high achieving. Four distinguishing traits work in tandem to set personal innovators apart: awareness, curiosity, focus, and initiative.

By developing these traits, you will cultivate what I call the habit of innovation. This will empower you to succeed-by your standards and on your terms-in your occupation, and education, as a parent, in personal relationships, and while pursuing your interests.

Awareness

Robotically reacting and thinking repels innovation. The first trait integral to the habit of innovation is awareness-of yourself and external circumstances.

To become self-aware, start noticing your thoughts-where they are and how they affect your emotions and actions. When your thoughts are not in the present, you miss life's magnificence as well as subtle signals of trouble. Don't get caught up in your thoughts, including opinions about yourself. They may not be "reality."

Also, become fully aware of yourself beyond your thoughts. How are you breathing? Moving? What do you feel and need? Don't try to make changes or pass judgement — just observe. Practice self-awareness a few times a day; soon it will come without effort.

Be warned: Self-awareness can be uncomfortable. We learn early to avoid pain by not thinking about what bothers us. Notice your tendency to pull away from where you need to look.

Once you're cultivating self-awareness, apply these skills outside yourself. Really being in the present moment-which could be all there is, after all-will show you what's working and what's not.

Here are some strategies to become more aware:

- Accept different perspectives. Each of us has a context for our views and behaviour. The more perspectives you consider, the more choices you will have about how to respond. But find a balance, neither clinging white-knuckled to your own views nor letting others define you and your behaviour.
- Be aware using all your senses.
- Look closely at processes, considering how and why things are done. Notice how obstacles are part of the process, not a negative to avoid.
- Peel back the layers, avoiding sweeping statements. Instead of "Oh no-here comes another change in the workplace," for example, consider what you fear. Forging new relationships? The loss of control? Changes to your routines? Having to be a novice again? Being specific shows ways you can have power over a situation. This skill will help you communicate with others, too.

Curiosity

Curiosity flows seamlessly from awareness. Once you open yourself to the nuances of life, it's hard not to find things that fascinate you and to begin wondering why.

To be curious, you must give yourself the freedom to risk and make mistakes. Interestingly, curiosity requires trust-trust that everyone and every situation have something to teach you. Even when there's no immediate practical application of the things you learn, you're training creative muscles that innovators keep "buff."well toned.

Curiosity jump-starts the habit of innovation by taking you to deeper levels of knowing and helping you to relate to others.

To develop curiosity:

- Routinely seek opinions from people who have no experience with the subject. These can be the most refreshing sources of new information, since they are not entrenched in assumptions and mindsets.

- Seek alternative solutions, even when all is well. This gives you fallback positions.
- Try new things. Even if they don't work out, you'll learn lessons to apply elsewhere.
- When you have a problem, work like a detective. Ask questions. Look at everything. Seek out experts for their views. Do your own research.
- Notice and eliminate assumptions. They're usually wrong, yet we accept them as "fact."
- Fire your inner judge. Give ideas time to percolate before assessing them.
- "Browse" everywhere-at the library or newsstand, at friends' homes (stick with what's in the open!), with the yellow pages. Explore new places and types of information. Take different routes.
- Ask questions of those you encounter—find out what they do and what else they do. Find out how these their activities fit into the world and how the their interest began.

Focus

Awareness and curiosity expand your options, but once you move toward a solution, you need to focus-to go beneath the surface and give full attention to what you're doing.

Regardless of the task, focus pays. In ***Finding Flow,*** Mihaly Csikszentmihalyi explains that evidence shows that people feel the worst — worse than when they are forced to do things, when they act by default and without focus.

To improve your focus:

- Fine-tune its intensity. Focus gently and guard against obsession. Allow time for ideas to simmer while you do other things.
- Direct your focus appropriately. Find a balance between physical and cerebral pursuits, easy and challenging activities, and solitude and activities with others. Let go of things that sap your energy. Prioritizing helps you to be sure you're focusing on the right things.
- Really listen to others with focus. So often, we go through the motions and miss opportunities to learn. What are the person's eyes telling you? Body language? Is it consistent with the words you're hearing?

Initiative

Awareness awakens us to what's going on, curiosity lets us gather ideas, and focus lets us nurture particular ideas. But the innovative spirit without action is like the proverbial tree falling in the forest with no one to hear it. Initiative to act gives purpose and momentum to the habit of innovation.

Imagine a Spring Training invitee who has studied baseball for decades, soaking up information, asking questions and chasing answers, and focusing on how to hit against each pitcher. But once at the plate, he never takes the bat off his shoulder. Not once. Finally, he is cut from the roster.

"But someone incapable of action would never make it to Spring Training," you might say. Exactly! But capability without initiative does not translate into results.

You no doubt know gifted people who lack initiative. They languish in jobs they hate, have ideas they never pursue, or are perpetual students, never venturing into the world. It's easy to see that they need initiative, but what about you? You have once-in-a-lifetime opportunities everyday of your life to shape the world. Are you seizing them?

Why do we avoid taking initiative? In a word, fear. We're afraid of putting ourselves out there, of failing, of risking, of looking stupid. Eventually, we must decide that our goals matter more than our fears.

To develop initiative:

- Define your goals, whether they're parenting your children to reach their full potential, making a six-figure income, or getting a starting position on a Major League Baseball team. Then do what it takes to propel yourself toward those goals.

- Make your environment motivating. Change what saps your energy. Surround yourself with natural light, energizing people, reminders of those you admire, and inspiring quotes or pictures.
- Become optimistic, looking for the positive lessons, the good in others and yourself, the win-win solutions. Visualize yourself succeeding.
- Take risks, which bring increased confidence.
- Use awareness to assess the impact of all you do. Measure actions by impact; small actions can have great results.
- Live so that you will have no regrets about paths not taken and actions undone.

Putting It Together: The Habit of Innovation

While each of these traits is worth pursuing, the power comes for those who combine them into the habit of innovation.

Consider the late Charles Schulz. The Peanuts comic strip resonates with a broad audience, thanks largely to his awareness of everything from applied psychology to the way adults sound to children. After his death, Billie Jean King described Schulz's curiosity-how he called her to ask questions about competition and other issues. "He would probe and probe and probe, ask questions all the time." Extreme focus is apparent in the unforgettable characters and stories he created. And he had the initiative to persevere when an editor decided to stop publishing his comic strip five decades ago-and to continue touching lives long after he could have retired. His daughter said it was no coincidence that he died just as his final strip was being published.

With the habit of innovation, you too will use your unique abilities to make a difference. Awareness and curiosity will illuminate your life, focus will intentionally direct those your tremendous light beams, and initiative will push you to do something with all this ingenuity.

Managing For Innovation - The Only Sustainable Advantage

Innovation is critical to the competitive success of virtually all companies. Whether you're on the leading edge, or following an imitation strategy, innovation is the only sustainable competitive advantage. Creativity and innovation are often used as synonyms terms. This is unfortunate because there is much more to true innovation than just being creative. This paper examines a proven, four-step process that allows you to have successful, repeatable innovation as part of your company's portfolio of skills.

TO ACHIEVE SUCCESS IN MANAGING FOR INNOVATION, YOU MUST ACKNOWLEDGE THAT INNOVATION IS A PROCESS.

TO BE SUCCESSFUL, A METHOD MUST BE IDENTIFIED TO MANAGE THAT PROCESS AND THE RIGHT PEOPLE INVOLVED.

Creativity Is Not Innovation

Innovation is the transformation of creative ideas into tangible, practical products, services, or business practices. Those ideas can come from inside your firm, or they can be ideas that have been successfully adapted from elsewhere. The key is to understand that even the best ideas are meaningless until and unless they are actually implemented. Unfortunately, knowledge alone doesn't necessarily or automatically lead to the actions required to result in implementation. An unimplemented idea is meaningless and useless.

Given the critical importance of innovation, it's imperative that companies find a predictable, repeatable process that can assure dependable innovation. Remember, coming up with the idea is just the beginning. It's not an innovation until it is reduced to practice.

Substantial evidence from theoretical, as well as from real world research, demonstrates that effective and efficient innovation requires the joint efforts of a team of people. Managing the interactions of these diverse people to assure a profitable result is complex. You must match the knowledge, expertise, thinking styles, action-taking methods, and risk aversion of the available pool of people to a process that can assure execution of the innovation.

Innovation Is a Process

To achieve success in managing for innovation, you must acknowledge that innovation is a process. Further, to be successful, a method must be identified to manage that process and the people involved. Integrating the right set of people skills into a proven process results in effective innovation. So what is a proven innovation process?

Four Steps to Successful Innovation

Investigation into innovation methods has evolved a technique for describing a four-step process that results in innovation. The four steps can be described as:

1. Creating;
2. Advancing;
3. Refining; and
4. Implementing.

Each step is discrete and necessary to assure innovation happens. To move an idea through each of these four steps so that an innovation results, requires matching the "right" people with each step of the process. What are the characteristics of the "right" people?

Well, clearly, they must have the knowledge and expertise required to perform the needed tasks. That's no real revelation, and is usually not the problem. The difficult piece of the puzzle involves thinking style and action-taking method. By thinking style we do not mean IQ, but rather how you process information. By action-taking method we don't mean will you or won't you take action, but again, how do you go about it.

Step 1 – Creating

Let's see how these two human characteristics are important to innovation. The first step of the process is creating. In this step, ideas and concepts are generated. Often the problem will be reframed and solutions that may be unusual, unique, or that go beyond the obvious, may be identified. Fresh and original concepts are often generated. The creating step is characterized by a lack of constraints regarding existing rules or boundaries. Success in this step requires a view of the "big picture" and a mind open to alternative solutions.

People who are successful in the creating step are usually conceptual thinkers and demonstrate an initiating action-taking method. Conceptual thinkers do not follow a predictable thinking path. Their thinking style could be accurately described as elliptical or abstract. The initiating action taking method is succinctly described as one who is more comfortable going where no one has gone before than in following the "proven" path.

A person who is likely to perform well in the creating step can be described as someone who:

- Likes to come up with new ideas
- Is good at exploring alternatives and discussing concepts
- Is capable of realizing the master plan
- Focuses on the future
- Can easily move from one subject to another
- Can focus on many things at once
- Probably is impatient
- Likes respect and influence
- Doesn't follow tradition
- Goes with "gut feeling" when making decisions.

While the creator is a wonderful source of new ideas and concepts, they often have a tendency to move quickly from idea to idea without understanding the consequences.

Step 2 – Advancing

The second step in the innovation process is the advancing step. In this step of the process the ideas and new directions conceived in the creation step are moved forward. These ideas are promoted and, using past experience and successful methods, a plan for implementation is developed.

Top performing people in this role usually prefer ideas that are familiar, but they are willing to bend rules and push beyond existing boundaries if the action can be directed forward, achieving objectives in a direct and efficient manner.

They demonstrate a linear thinking style and an initiating action-taking method. The linear thinking style is characterized by a sequential process. The linear thinker will solve the following sequence: 2, 3, 4 . . . with the number 5. The linear thinker is usually also very able to evaluate the pros and cons . . . and will do so. Additionally, people who perform well as advancers:

- Recognize ideas and directions early
- Think of how a new idea could actually be implemented
- Are usually skeptical of new ideas, but will go with their feelings
- Give the team a purpose
- Focus on the purpose of achieving objectives efficiently
- Can easily deal with more than one thing at a time
- Like the creator, need respect and influence.

Advancers can be energetic promoters of the team's objectives. Since they usually recognize the value of a new idea or concept, they will actively move it forward.

However, if the only other person on the innovation team with them is a creator, these two may move new ideas through that are "half baked" while ignoring danger signals and potential barriers to actual implementation.

Step 3 – Refining

The refining or evaluating step is the third phase in the process. Concepts are challenged in this stage. This is the "Ya but . . ." step. A methodical process of analysis is used to look for flaws or problems with the innovation ideas from the creating step.

In addition, the refiner looks at the implementation plans from the advancing step to try to "poke holes" in the approach. Sometimes the refiner will suggest new ways to solve the problem, or they may "push it back" onto the advancer or creator. The refiner is generally a conceptual thinker with an adopting action-taking method. An adopting action-taking method is the converse of the initiating method. That is, people with this tendency will always prefer to follow the "beaten path." In addition, great people in the refining role:

- Believe consequences are important and therefore plan for contingencies
- Like to find a way to create order from chaos
- Are often referred to as "the devil's advocate"
- Prefer order
- Are methodical
- Gain satisfaction from the mental exercise of debate.

While the refiner's role is critical to assure the concepts are well thought through, if they control the whole process they will usually lead the group toward low-risk ideas.

Step 4 – Implementing

The last, and certainly not the least step is the execution. This step takes the concepts and implements them according to the plan developed in the advancing step. The focus is on an orderly implementation that achieves a high quality outcome. Executors are linear thinkers who exhibit an adopting action-taking method. In addition, great executors:

- Pay attention to details
- Try to assure the plans follow an orderly process
- Are methodical
- Are cautious with new approaches
- Think things over carefully
- Finish everything they start
- Are usually uninterested in the early part of the innovation process.

Successful execution requires focused objectives and guidelines. These will be natural results of the prior three steps . . . if they are done well.

Putting It Together

Finding people with the needed combination of knowledge, expertise, thinking style and action-taking method is always a challenge. Until recently the problem was further compounded by an inability to accurately understand a person's true proclivity for each role in the process.

Recently a very low cost, self-scoring instrument has been developed that accurately and repeatable identifies the natural and best role in this process. Armed with an understanding of the process, and ability to match people to process requirements should naturally result in more successful innovation in your company.

Innovation through Global Collaboration: A New Source of Competitive Advantage

Many recent studies highlight the need to rethink the way we manage innovation. Traditional approaches, based on the assumption that the creation and pursuit of new ideas is best accomplished by a centralized and co-located R&D team, are rapidly becoming outdated. Instead, innovations are increasingly brought to the market by networks of firms, selected for their unique capabilities, and operating in a co-ordinated manner.

This new model demands that firms develop different skills, in particular, the ability to collaborate with partners to achieve superior innovation performance. Yet despite this need, there is little guidance on how to develop or deploy this ability. This part describes and tries to understand the strategies and practices used by firms that achieve greater success in their collaborative innovation efforts.

It is found that many firms mistakenly applied an "outsourcing" mindset to collaboration efforts which, in turn, led to three critical errors:

First, they focused solely on lower costs, failing to consider the broader strategic role of collaboration.

Second, they didn't organize effectively for collaboration, believing that innovation could be managed much like production and partners treated like "suppliers."

Thirdly, they didn't invest in building collaborative capabilities, assuming that their existing people and processes were already equipped for the challenge.

Successful firms, by contrast, developed an explicit strategy for collaboration and made organizational changes to aid performance in these efforts.

Ultimately, these actions allowed them to identify and exploit new business opportunities. In sum, collaboration is becoming a new and important source of competitive advantage.

There are several frameworks to help firms develop and exploit this new ability. The management of innovation is changing. No longer is the creation and pursuit of new ideas the bastion of large central R&D departments within vertically integrated organizations. Instead, innovations are increasingly brought to the market by networks of firms, selected according to their comparative advantages, and operating in a co-ordinated manner.

In this new model, organizations de-construct the innovation value chain and source pieces from partners that possess lower costs, better skills and/or access to knowledge that can provide a source of differentiation. The aim is to establish mutually beneficial relationships through which new products and services are developed. In short, firms increasingly seek superior performance in innovation through collaboration.

This new model is being driven by a series of trends forcing firms to re-think traditional approaches to innovation. First, the complexity of products is increasing, in terms of the number of technologies they include. No longer is it possible for one firm to master all these skills and locate them under one roof. Second, a supply of cheap skilled labour has emerged in developing countries, creating incentives to substitute these resources for higher-cost equivalents. Third, different regions of the world have developed unique skills and capabilities, which leading firms are now exploiting for advantage. And finally, advances in development tools and technology combined with the rise of open architectures and standards have driven down the costs of coordinating distributed work.

In sum, collaboration is no longer a "nice to have." It is a competitive necessity.

Collaboration is not "Outsourcing"

Studies reveal dramatic differences in the performance of firm's collaboration efforts, driven by contrasting approaches to their management. In particular, many firms mistakenly applied a "production outsourcing" mindset to collaboration, viewing the use of partners only as a means to achieve lower costs through "wage arbitrage" – substituting a US resource with a cheaper one of equivalent skill. These firms saw little need to change the way they organized their innovation efforts to facilitate collaboration.

By contrast, successful firms went beyond simple wage arbitrage, asking global partners to contribute knowledge and skills to projects, with a focus on improving their top-line. And they re-designed their organizations, to increase the effectiveness of these efforts.

Managing collaboration the same way a firm handles the outsourcing of production is a flawed approach. Production and innovation are fundamentally different activities – while the former seeks to replicate an existing product at low cost, the other seeks to develop something entirely new and valuable. In addition, outsourcing and collaboration have very different objectives.

Outsourcing involves procuring a commodity asset or resource at the cheapest price. Collaboration, by contrast, entails accessing globally dispersed knowledge, leveraging new capabilities and sharing risk with partners. It is a much more sophisticated skill. While "outsourcers" achieved lower R&D costs in our study, rarely was this a source of advantage. "We lowered costs, but so did our competitors," said one manager. "Our process is not differentiated at all." By contrast, "collaborators" leveraged partners to create new sources of value. As Mak Agashe, General Manager for Windows Serviceability at Microsoft remarked, "We use partners to gain access to capabilities we don't possess. They have a huge impact on our ability to innovate that goes way beyond low cost and allows us to achieve significant advantages in time to market, results that we could not realize working with just our own resources."

Firms which manage collaboration using an "outsourcing" mindset made three critical errors, as compared to more successful organizations:

- They didn't consider the *strategic* role of collaboration, but saw it only as a tactic for reducing cost. As a result, their efforts were misaligned with their business strategy.
- They didn't *organize* effectively for collaboration. Instead, they treated partners like suppliers of parts or raw materials, and managed them using a procurement function.
- They didn't make long-term investments to develop *collaborative capabilities*.

Instead, they assumed their existing staff and processes could handle the challenge. In combination, these errors meant firms systematically missed opportunities to use collaboration for competitive advantage. By contrast, successful firms found that attention to these critical areas generated new options to create value that competitors could not replicate.

Below, the principles that these latter firms employed, are described.

1. Develop a Global Collaboration Strategy

In many firms, little thought was given to strategy; these companies typically began using global partners to lower costs, and did not evolve from that goal even after executing a half dozen or more projects. The result was a *de facto,* unarticulated cost-reduction strategy, driven at a departmental or divisional level. Collaboration received little senior management attention; when it did, it was because expectations were not being met.

Leading firms, by contrast, developed an explicit strategy for collaboration, designed to support their business goals. In contrast to organizations that viewed collaboration only as a tool for reducing cost, these firms considered a variety of more strategic benefits, in particular, assessing how collaboration could improve their top line through increased product differentiation. Successful organizations achieved this in two ways: first, by leveraging a partner's superior capabilities (i.e., know-how that the firm did not possess internally); and second, by accessing a partner's contextual knowledge (i.e., knowledge that the partner possessed by virtue of its local position). In combination, these benefits comprise the "3C's" of a global collaboration strategy (see Table 12.1)

TABLE 12.1. **The Benefits from Collaboration Lower Costs**

Lower Costs	*Superior Capabilities*	*Contextual Knowledge*
Low cost labour	Rapid access to capacity	Market access
Low cost materials	Technical know-how	Supplier relationships
Low cost suppliers	Process expertise	Institutional ties
Low cost infrastructure	Domain knowledge	Government connections
Lowering R&D Costs		

Reducing R&D costs was the number one priority for firms using partners to innovate. Firms in our sample reported between 10-30% reductions in cost, as compared to their performance prior to partnering. But savings were often lower than expected, due to the added costs associated with the need for greater coordination. Firms using an outsourcing mindset sought to lower costs through "wage arbitrage," replacing US resources with cheaper ones of equivalent skill. Leading firms however, lowered cost in a different way. Rather than swap one resource for another, they "reconfigured" their operations to optimize performance at the system level. While the decisions they made, in isolation, sometimes appeared to add cost, these firms understood the need to change the way they organized to maximize the value of collaborative efforts.

Consider SemCo, a leader in the contract manufacturing industry, which designs and develops electronic components and systems for own-equipment manufacturers (OEMs). When SemCo built a semiconductor plant in China, it did not replicate the design of its US facilities. While substituting US staff with Chinese staff would yield lower costs, SemCo saw a bigger opportunity in revisiting how the facility would operate. So it recruited a huge engineering staff — an order of magnitude greater than the US - and devoted them to process and product improvement. The result: a facility with the highest productivity of any in their network, independent of wage levels. Substituting one worker for another merely yields a one-time saving that can be easily copied. SemCo, by contrast, built the capability to lower costs systematically over time.

It is often noted that the wage difference between a US engineer and an Indian or Chinese engineer is in the order of 3:1-5:1. However, rarely is this wage difference realized in its entirety, given the added costs needed to effectively run a distributed project.

Leveraging Superior Capabilities

Leading firms focused greater attention on how to leverage partner capabilities. We observed two broad types of capability in action: First, the ability to rapidly bring online large amounts of *capacity*, allowing firms to lower time to market and increase responsiveness, while avoiding the cost of full-time staff; and second, the ability to access unique *competencies*, technical know-how and/or process expertise that firms did not possess internally. Successful firms sought partners with a blend of both abilities, giving them instant access to a repertoire of skills not available in-house. As one manager recalled, "It takes us nine months to find and hire a new employee. But using our partner, we staffed up in two weeks, accessing a skill that we don't have internally." Microsoft used the capabilities of a partner to dramatically improve agility and quality in one business unit. This unit provides periodic updates to customers – billions of downloads every quarter. Testing for these updates includes operating system, hardware, chipset and 3rd party application testing. It spans 5 operating systems covering millions of lines of code. Microsoft's partner helped apply "Lean" manufacturing techniques to this process, streamlining and prioritizing tests and re-designing tasks to allow staff to work in parallel. For one of the projects, the team improved time to test by 90%, lowered costs by 70% and reduced "failure" rates to near zero.

Accessing Contextual Knowledge

An increasing focus for many firms was gaining access to the knowledge and relationships that a partner possessed by virtue of its position in a local context. In our study, examples included partners who possessed a deep knowledge of local firms with specific production skills, relationships with university faculty in a new research area, and contacts with the government officials who approved market access. These benefits, being based upon the knowledge and relationships that come from a local presence, were difficult to value. As a result, many firms tended to underestimate their impact.

Consider NewCo, a firm that designs enterprise servers sold to OEMs like HP and Sun. To complement its US staff, NewCo established an Owned Development Center (ODC) in Taiwan and teamed with a partner in India. In one recent project, the firm was having difficulty in meeting the target cost due to the high price of one particular component. So NewCo asked its ODC to leverage its knowledge of different local manufacturer's costs and capabilities to solve the problem. The organization eventually located a new supplier that could source an equivalent component at lower cost. In this case, the value of the ODC was not in providing better capability; it came from superior local knowledge.

Thinking Strategically

Viewing collaboration through this broader lens highlights how it can be used to support a firm's strategy. It forces managers to understand the competitive implications of partner selection, by assessing their merits along multiple dimensions, instead of only one. And it helps firms understand where to use collaboration, in terms of the parts of the innovation value chain where a focus on cost versus differentiation is most appropriate. To illustrate, consider the strategies of two firms – A and B – depicted in **Figure 12.1,** using the classic dimensions of strategic positioning – low cost and product differentiation – as discussed in Porter (1985).

Initially, firm B has a dominant position, with lower cost and superior differentiation. But firm A has identified opportunities to improve its position through collaboration. It can move along the horizontal to position C, achieving lower cost, or along the vertical to position D, achieving superior differentiation. Or it can move to position E, which is superior on both dimensions. Note that position E cannot match the cost of C or the differentiation of D due to trade-offs between these performance dimensions. In essence, collaboration has the potential to move firm A to the "frontier" of the space joining C, D and E. Contrast this with a firm that views collaboration only as a way to lower cost; this firm sees only one position to move to. While this may be a good choice, this firm does not see that it is not the only choice.

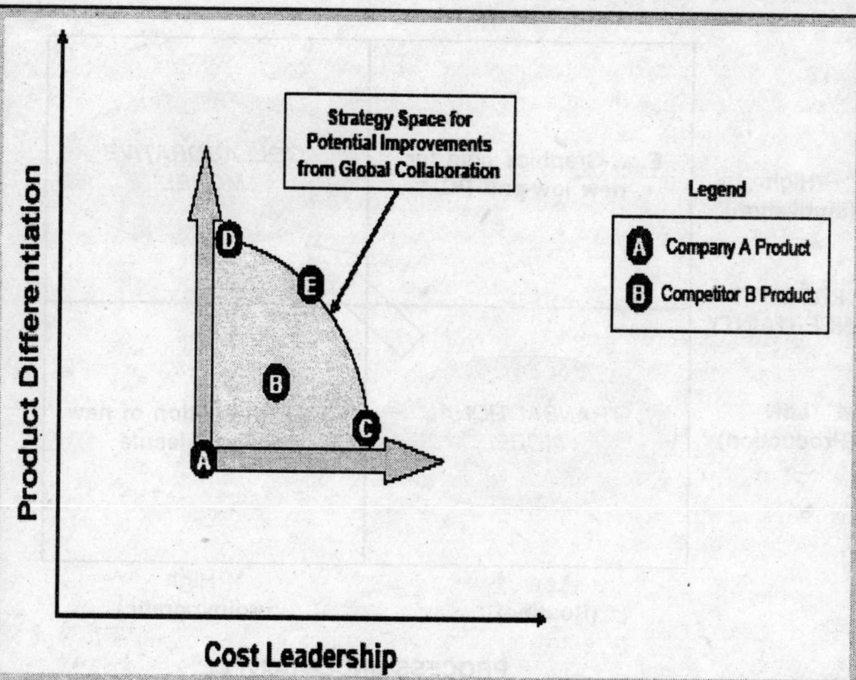

Figure 12.1

While successful firms often used different terms to those above, all had developed similar methods to align collaboration efforts to their business strategy. Collaboration received visibility at a senior level, and was an integral part of the strategic-planning process. Increasingly, the focus was not on wage arbitrage, but on using partners to increase business value. These firms grew more sophisticated in the use of collaboration over time; by contrast, poor performers remained stubbornly focused on cost.

2: Organize for Collaboration

The second area separating leading firms from others was how they organized. Firms that viewed collaboration through an outsourcing lens adopted a "transactional" model. They focused on how to break up the innovation value chain and specify in detail the deliverables required from each part. In procuring these parts, the selection of partners was driven mainly by cost. These firms treated partners like "suppliers" and adopted organizational structures, management policies and contracts reflecting this mindset. By contrast, successful firms recognized the uncertainty in their innovation efforts and sought mechanisms to overcome it. This required a more "collaborative" model. The need for a different model can be seen by considering the challenge of partnering along two dimensions: The degree of uncertainty over the product to be produced; and the degree of uncertainty over the process to produce it (see **Figure 12.2**).

Replicating an existing product (i.e., production) involves little uncertainty while developing a new one (i.e., innovation) is far more uncertain. Similarly, some processes are routine and easily specified whereas others are idiosyncratic and rely on trial and error learning. When firms face little uncertainty on both dimensions – the arena of production outsourcing – traditional models work well, given firms can specify *what* they want and *how* it should be made. As uncertainty increases however, a more collaborative approach is needed. Economic theories argue that these problems are best resolved by vertical integration, given the difficulty in writing "complete contracts" between firms (Williamson, 1980; Teece, 1986). Increasingly however, this is not a viable solution given the number of technologies in a product is steadily rising, while the particular technologies themselves vary with each new product generation.

Firms that adopted a more collaborative model made different choices in terms of team design, contract structure and intellectual property management.

Figure 12.2

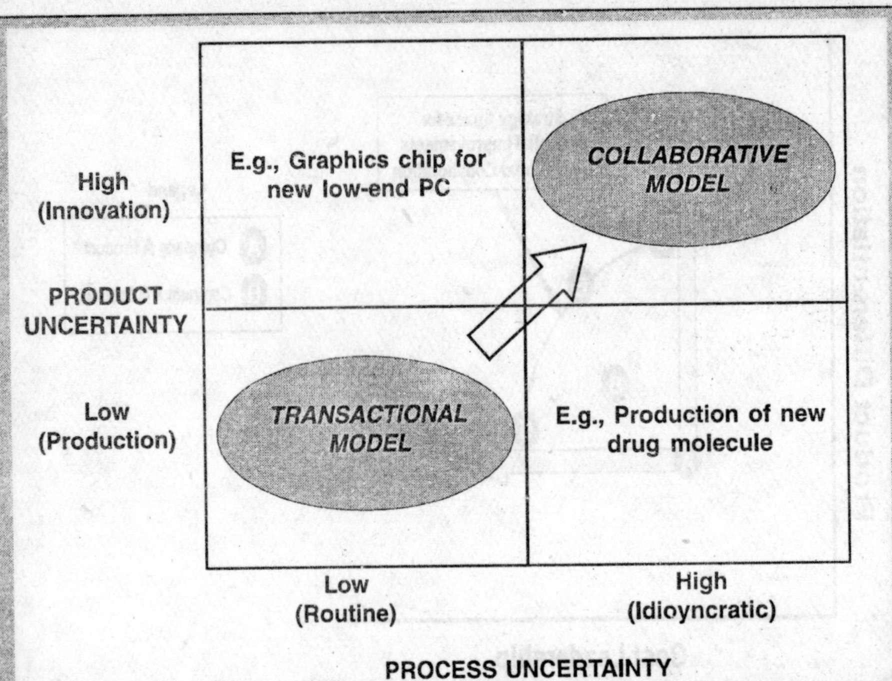

Challenges of Partnering

Leading firms viewed partners as an extension of their own development organizations, seeking their participation in meetings and including them in internal communications. As part of this philosophy, they required greater continuity in partner staff, in contrast to a transactional model, in which people move in and out of projects. This ensured the "tacit" knowledge of a project's context was retained, and improved communication between teams. As one manager explained, "It takes time to appreciate the skills of each team member and understand how to work together. When people leave, we have to go through that learning curve again. So we put a premium on ensuring staff continuity."

Successful firms focused on improving the efficiency of information transfer between teams given the need to jointly solve problems, the specifics of which cannot be predicted in advance. Having a partner liaison manager on-site, though expensive, was viewed as critical for resolving higher-level issues. For day-to-day problems however, direct contact between team members proved more effective, helping to get questions to the right place and resolved quickly. Several firms created a "buddy" system at the start of projects, linking offsite staff to onsite staff with similar responsibilities. By contrast, in projects that tried to manage communication at a single senior level, the transfer of information was often delayed, resulting in expensive rework and reduced trust.

Leading firms also made different choices in the contract terms that governed the funding of projects and payment of rewards. They aimed to align the incentives of client and partner, reducing the need to specify what was required from each in great detail. While service level agreements were common substitutes for time and material contracts, these firms went further, sharing risks with partners and rewarding them for their top-line impact. Partners often absorbed costs in return for payments tied to revenues or profits.

In some cases, they acquired stakes in the business. As one manager noted, "We ask partners for ideas, so we need to reward their ideas and not just the effort in developing them. We give them a share of the pie, but their ideas make the pie bigger."

The final area in which firms made different organizational choices was in intellectual property (IP) management. Global partners increasingly develop their own IP – new components, technologies and processes – to improve project performance. Furthermore, collaboration often requires that partners re-use and add to a firm's existing IP in the search for new solutions. Given these trends, traditional approaches to IP which assume that a firm must develop, own, protect and isolate its IP are increasingly outdated.

While successful firms in our study differed on the specifics of their IP policies, their actions reflected a common shift in values; towards a more open and flexible approach. These firms sought to leverage partner IP, focusing on the cost and speed advantages, which outweighed concerns about the need for control. They developed mechanisms for partners to access their own IP, in a way that facilitated collaboration but ensured the protection of competitive assets. And they shared newly developed IP when the firm and its partners could benefit from its application, as long as the uses were not competitive.

3. Build Collaborative Capabilities

The final area separating leading firms from others was their willingness to invest in developing "collaborative capabilities." All too often, firms assumed that their existing employees, processes and infrastructure were capable of meeting the challenge of collaboration. But successful collaboration doesn't just happen – it is a skill that must be learned. Rarely do firms get it "right first time." Leading firms recognized this reality, and made investments to enhance their performance over time. Successful firms targeted investments in four areas: people, process, platforms and programs. We call these the "Four Pillars" of collaborative capability (see **Figure 12.3**).

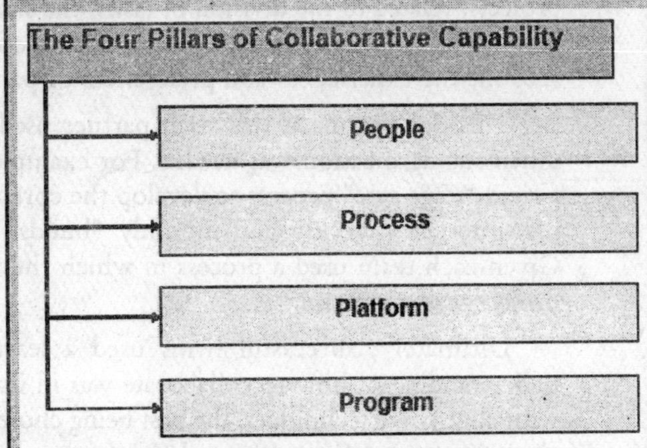

The Four Pillar's of Collaborative Capabilities

Figure 12.3

These investments were typically funded outside the budgets of individual projects, given few projects can justify the levels of infrastructure needed to perform well on their own. In essence, leading firms made a strategic decision to invest in collaborative capabilities, and sought to leverage these investments across projects and over time.

Developing People

Superior performance in collaboration requires people with different skills, given team members often lay outside the boundaries of the firm, are located in far flung countries and have vastly different cultures. The "art" of management in such projects is in finding ways to exert influence over resources not under a firm's control. Rather than a focus on

deep technical expertise, managers therefore require a much broader skill set, associated with the need to orchestrate and co-ordinate the work of distributed teams. Successful firms tackled this challenge through changes to their recruitment, training, evaluation and reward systems. For example, as well as training in technical disciplines, these firms ensured that engineering staff were educated on how to partition work into parts that can be worked on by different teams and how to manage the multiple workflows that result. The emphasis was on "softer" skills, such as communication and motivation, as opposed to discipline-based content. Increasingly, firms invited partners to these sessions, to develop a shared understanding of how best to work together.

The emphasis on developing new people skills was reinforced by a firm's evaluation and reward systems. Unfortunately, these systems were often poorly equipped for the challenge, given they focused solely on assessing the performance of internal teams. For example, while 360 degree reviews for managers were increasingly common, rarely did firms seek feedback from partners; a critical omission given partner performance is central to effective collaboration. Leading firms recognized the need to assess this aspect of performance, developed metrics to make it visible and rewarded those who excelled. They viewed collaboration as a skill to be learned and took actions to develop it in staff.

Designing Processes

Most projects we observed employed a formal product development methodology based upon a modified "stage-gate" or "waterfall" type process. A stage-gate process consists of a series of standard phases separated by ago/no go decision points called gates (Cooper, 1990).

These processes are increasingly popular ways to ensure greater control and consistency in the execution of projects. But these techniques, and others that share their roots, are often predicated on the assumption of single-site development. There is a need to re-think how they should operate when managing the distribution of work among a team of global partners.

Distributed development requires a variety of additional activities as compared to single site projects, related to the division of tasks, the sharing of artifacts, the co-ordination of handoffs, and the integration of components. Leading firms designed processes to address these activities, taking into account the experiences and preferences of partners.

This did not mean that each partner used the same process; rather the aim was to decide how much standardization was needed. For example, in one software project we observed, one team used a rigid "stage-gate" process to develop the core technology, and another used an "agile" process for the user-interface. Weekly and monthly "builds" were used to synchronize the work of both teams. Given each team used a process in which they were skilled, as well as one which fit their goals, the project was successful.

Ultimately, successful firms used a learning-driven approach to process design given their understanding of how to collaborate was in its infancy. Small pilot projects were used to experiment with alternative techniques, the best being chosen for a wider roll-out. For example, German electronics giant Siemens, recruited several university teams around the globe to contribute to a project led by staff in its Princeton R&D centre.

The firm tested different approaches to managing distributed teams, gaining insight on how contextual differences (e.g., between Indian and Irish teams) affected performance. The results are helping the firm decide what information to share with teams, how frequently, they should interact and what modes of communication are the most effective.

Building Platforms

Leading firms developed technology "platforms" to improve the coordination of work. These platforms comprised four main parts: First, development tools and technologies to improve the efficiency of distributed work; second, technical standards and interfaces to ensure the seamless integration of partner outputs; third, rules to govern the sharing of intellectual property among partners; and fourth, knowledge management systems to capture the firm's experience on how distributed work is best performed. This collaboration "infrastructure" was leveraged across multiple projects over time. The goal was to promote a long-term view of the assets needed for effective collaboration.

Consider TransCo, a leading transportation firm which undertook a multi-year project involving engineering work by over 50 global partners. The firm needed a platform that ensured the output from different partners was compatible, enabled the frequent integration of components, and facilitated testing of the entire system. Developing the platform was a multi-year undertaking, involving hundreds of staff from the firm and its partners. This effort focused on *minimizing* the constraints on each partner. As one manager noted, "We asked 'what is the minimum level of commonality in process, data and computing to allow us to work together?" The resulting capabilities were vital to success – for example, the firm could make global design changes (e.g., to the system's electrical standards) and have these "ripple through" to all affected components.

While some firms like TransCo developed customized tools for collaboration, many used off-the-shelf products. In these cases, it was common to ensure that partners used the same version of the same tool, ensuring seamless data transfer. Where this was not possible, significant up-front effort was devoted to defining how integration would be handled. Failure to do this led to major problems.

Consider the troubles at Airbus, in developing its flagship A380 aircraft. Airbus' German and French partners chose to work with different versions of Dassualt Systems' CATIA design software. But design information in the older system was not translated accurately into the new one, which held the "master" version. Without a physical mock-up, these problems remained hidden throughout the project.

The result: 300 miles of wiring, 100,000 wires and 40,000 connectors that did not fit, leading to a 2-year production delay at a cost of $6bn. Yet the cause of Airbus's problems was not in choosing different software versions; rather it lay in the lack of an effective process for dealing with the problems this created.

Managing "Programs"

Successful firms managed their collaboration efforts as a coherent "program," in contrast to organizations which ran each project on a stand-alone basis. A program view was critical given collaboration projects rarely met expectations early on, and performance often deteriorated when the scope of efforts was increased. Leading firms did not differ from others in this respect; but they did differ in the rate at which they improved. Top performers put in place mechanisms to help improve their collaboration skills over time.

A program view was cultivated by allocating responsibility for all of a firm's collaboration efforts to one senior manager. In large firms, this took the form of a formal VP or director-level position; in smaller organizations, a senior manager added this role to existing responsibilities. This "Chief Collaboration Officer," while not a direct report on each project, was tasked with developing a plan for improving the performance of all collaboration efforts. The involved the creation of a firm-wide collaboration strategy, as well as organizational changes to improve the effectiveness of execution.

The most progressive firms managed the "trajectory" through which they developed skills by carefully selecting the projects that used collaboration. Early efforts were chosen to minimize complexity, with an emphasis on "learning the basics;" more ambitious projects were tackled as skills increased. The focus was on assembling a pool of knowledge to aid future efforts, through post-mortems conducted with partners. Hence top performers set up systems to codify lessons learnt from past collaborations; and often linked partners into these systems to benefit from their broader collaboration experience.

A New Source of Competitive Advantage

Firms that devoted attention to the three areas above – strategy, organization, and capability development – were more successful in their collaboration efforts. For a few firms in our study however, these efforts not only lent support to their existing business strategies, but also led to new value creation opportunities. Their investments to build capabilities, in turn, created options to pursue strategies that could not be replicated by competitors; especially those that managed collaboration like outsourcing. For these firms, collaboration had become a source of competitive advantage (see **Figure 12.4**).

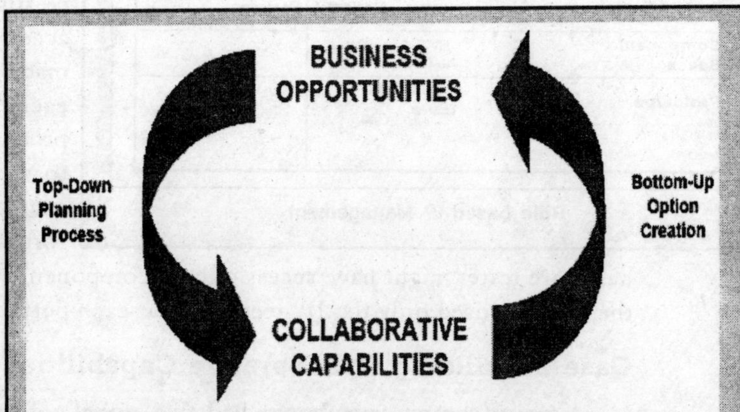

Collaborative Capabilities Create New Business Opportunities

Figure 12.4

A striking example of these dynamics was in Boeing's development of its 787 "Dreamliner" aircraft. Boeing builds the most complex commercial product in the world, each project being almost literally a "bet-the-company" experience. The levels of capital investment required and the increasing breadth of technologies that must be mastered – from digital cockpit design to new lightweight materials – have forced Boeing to look at new forms of organization, the aim being to share risk with partners while exploiting the unique technical expertise that each brings to development.

Boeing's approach to the 787 was the epitome of global collaboration. The project included over 50 partners from over 130 locations working together for more than four years. From the start, the aim was to leverage advanced capabilities from this network.

For example, in technologies like composite materials, which are being used for the first time for large sections of the airplane, smaller more focused firms had developed expertise that was unique. Rather than replicate this expertise, the firm sought to tap into it, blending it with skills from other partners developing complementary technologies. Furthermore, the relationships it established were not the traditional "build-to-print" contracts of past years. Instead, partners designed the components they were to make, ensuring a seamless integration with the outputs of other partners.

In our view, Boeing's source of competitive advantage is shifting; it is less and less related to the possession of deep individual technical skills in hundreds of diverse disciplines. While the firm still possesses such knowledge, this is no longer what differentiates it from competitors such as Airbus, who can access similar capabilities. Rather, Boeing's unique assets and skills are increasingly tied to the way the firm orchestrates, manages and coordinates its network of hundreds of global partners.

Boeing's experience is increasingly common across the industries and it can be observed that: Collaboration is becoming a new and important source of competitive advantage. Boeing spun-off its Wichita plant in 2004, its biggest internal supplier of fuselages and nose cones (*Source: Business Week*, February 19th 2007). The new owners subsequently announced plans to begin selling to Airbus. Boeing's move seems illogical if you consider these technologies "core" to Boeing's competitive position. But it makes sense if you view Boeing's competitive advantage to come from the way that it selects and manages the work of its network of partners.

Case 1: Managing Intellectual Property

Figure 12.5

Artifact Type	Product / Version				
	Product A V1	Product A V2	Product B V1	Product B V2	...
Market Forecast	Designer	Designer			
Requirements			Designer	Designer	
Project Design	Designer	Designer	Designer	Designer	
Component Specs		HW Tester			
Prototype	HW Tester	HW Tester			
....					

Role based IP Management

More than 200 people from one firm and its three partners were involved in developing software for a new system-on-a-chip design. Initially, all team members had access to the firm's entire code repository, including much code unrelated to their own work. Realizing the risk of exposing a thousand person-years of code, the firm rethought its approach, creating role-based control so each partner could only access the IP it needed. Business decisions were first made as to the IP required by each partner, and then each team member was assigned one or more products in one or more roles, each role having access to specific types of artifact (see **Figure 12.5**). For example, a "designer" might have access to market forecasts, product designs and prototypes. But a hardware tester might have access only to component specifications and prototypes. With this system, the firm exposed only the IP necessary for each partner to meet its goals.

Case 2: Building Collaborative Capabilities

A major computer company had five global collaboration projects underway, working with two partners. Executives realized that each project was experiencing similar problems in project management, partner management, staff turnover and communication.

Yet each was attempting to solve these issues on its own. With this insight, the company made strategic changes spanning all five projects.

— It created a Global Product Development Director responsible for oversight of all global projects. The Director instituted quarterly meetings where project sponsors and program managers shared their lessons learned. By establishing best practices, the company began institutionalizing its global collaboration skills.
— It developed a curriculum to train project managers on managing distributed teams and working in multi-cultural environments. It also arranged a product development methodology course to be taught to internal engineers and those of its partners.
— It implemented mechanisms to aid communication. For example, each partner placed a project manager liaison onsite. In turn, company project managers made more frequent visits to partners. The company began to emphasize staff continuity, securing engineers who had become skilled in its products for follow-on projects.
— It identified initiatives to make partner team members feel more valued. For example, it sponsored trips to the US for engineers, awarded certificates of achievement, and increased management visibility for senior technical staff. These efforts reduced partner staff turnover to 4% as compared to 20%+ on earlier projects.

Fostering an Innovative Culture - Sustaining Competitive Advantage

To sustain competitive advantage, companies must institutionalize their innovation process by creating an environment in which creative thinking is central to their values, assumptions, and actions. Constant innovation is a hallmark of successful growth companies — staying ahead of the competition requires inventiveness at the individual, group, and company levels. As companies grow, market demands and competition can force them to maintain a culture of non-stop innovation. Growth, however, also creates a need for structure and control, which can make a culture of innovation difficult to sustain.

Sustainable growth requires increased operational scale, but companies cannot scale its operations effectively without implementing formal structures, processes, and controls. Growth can strain the entrepreneurial philosophy that has driven a company's success. More importantly, it can erode corporate flexibility — as management layers increase, they create islands of data, knowledge, and intelligence that can complicate a company's decision-making processes. Developing new ideas is a risk-intensive process that requires significant resources. As companies grow, their risk profile must become more conservative as shareholders will expect them to stabilize operations and manage their business to financial expectations.

As companies grow, they require people who can guide them through each stage of their organizational development. However, companies also have to evolve to meet changing internal and external priorities. As a result, a company's corporate culture is pulled between two poles: established employees who are used to a stable and familiar environment, and newer employees who have a different mindset, a higher tolerance for risk, and place less value on organizational structure. Left unchecked, this dichotomy can cause a company's culture to be dictated by employees self-interest rather than corporate objectives.

Addressing the Challenge

Sustaining an innovative culture requires companies to create environments where creative thinking is central to corporate values, actions, and assumptions. Innovative companies require employees who seek new opportunities, accept risk, collaborate well with others, and commit themselves to the organization. Innovative companies also require leaders that will work to create those kinds of environments and will guide and promote innovative behaviour.

1. Create the Required Foundation

As companies grow, their leadership teams must manage increasingly complex organizations while maintaining a commitment to innovation. To do this, companies need to assess the state of their innovation and find means to enhance and foster it.

Assess the State of Innovation

The goal of innovation is to develop products that generate above-average returns. These returns allow companies to re-invest in activities designed to give them a competitive advantage in the marketplace. When the innovation cycle is disrupted, companies do not have this incremental capital

TABLE 12.2. Understanding the Role of Innovation in Your Company

Factors	*Key questions*	*Actions*	*Key steps*
Company goals	Does innovation play a critical role in your success?For example, does innovation drive revenue, cost savings,or both?	Analyze performance to determine what is driving revenue, growth, and cost savings.	Understand and define what role innovation can play in the company's financial performance (e.g., Will reduced time-to-market affect revenues? Will innovation increase production efficiency and lower costs?).Understand how competitors are innovating. Do they outperform your company in time-to-market, cost efficiency, customer service, and return on investment? Determine if you need to re-examine your objectives. Analyze performance to determine what is driving revenue, growth, and cost savings.
Organizational structure	Is innovation pervasive, or is it confined to specific groups?What is causing this? Who are the star performers? Why?	Create criteria to aid the measurement of achievement, degree of communi-cation,appropriate rewards, and training.	Compare the achievementof various groups within your organization.Understand what is unique about the groups that innovate. Understand why certain groups do not innovate (e.g., Are these groups facing barriers in making decisions?Do they need a champion? Do they have inappropriate members or an inappropriate structure?). If you determine that an innovative culture does not exist, understand the underlying reasons. (e.g., Do employees understand the company's goals? Is there low employee morale, corporate bureaucracy, or weak leadership?).
Employee behaviour	Do your employees recognize your company's innovative culture?Are their views consistent? Are the company's values, beliefs, and norms driving youremployees' behaviour and decision-making?	Consult employees across the organization.	If you determine that an innovative culture does not exist, understand the underlying reasons. (e.g., Do employees understand the company's goals? Is there low employee morale, corporate bureaucracy, or weak leadership?).

base and, therefore, have to fund innovation-related activities with capital initially allocated for other purposes. **"Strong culture enhances performance in two ways. First, it energizes employees by appealing to their higher ideals and values, and by rallying them around a set of meaningful, unified goals. Second, it boosts performance by shaping and coordinating employee behaviour."** Companies must understand the role innovation plays in influencing their business goals, organizational structure, and employee behaviour and use this knowledge to decide how and where improvements should be made (see **Table12.2**).

Define the Elements of Culture

"Culture consists of the values, beliefs, and norms that are exhibited in the way that people in the organization accomplish their work, relate to one another, and solve the problems that confront them on a daily basis: 'The way we do things around here.'"

Companies need to focus innovation-related activities around the three principal elements of corporate culture: core values, beliefs, and norms. Core values are principles that help employees make decisions about what is important for the company. Beliefs are the shared views of what is right and wrong. Norms are the operating rules that determine acceptable employee behavior. A single set of core values, beliefs, and norms will focus the entire work- force on a set of common goals.

> 3M's original pacing rule was that 25 percent of sales should be derived from products that were created within the last five years. 3M's culture enabled it to successfully meet this target. Its corporate values — "thou shalt not kill a new product idea," "make a little sell a little," tolerance for failure, and bias for action — are relied upon to empower innovation.

Redefine the Role of Leaders

An important role of a company's leaders is to communicate and reinforce the core values, beliefs, and norms of corporate culture. Company leaders also serve as role models to the employees who look to them to provide inspiration, support for their ideas, and the guidance required to excel.

2. Enhance Operations to Foster Innovation

A change in culture necessitates more than just a unified vision and strong leaders — it requires a structural change in a company's recruitment practices, its methods of assigning responsibilities, the way groups within the organization interact, and the way achievements in the company are rewarded.

Develop the Employee Base

Creativity is the force behind innovation (see **Figure 12.6**). Innovative achievements are the product of employees who have the right expertise, can think creatively about problems that arise, and are motivated to persevere through the discovery process.

Guiding Principles for Recruitment

- Recruit people who are willing to challenge the status quo and seek out new trends and directions.
- Attract individuals who can communicate and defend their ideas.
- Hire talented agitators, even if they make you uncomfortable.
- Complement creative optimists with pragmatists.
- Attract productive workers who have the stamina to recover should an initiative fail.

To sustain a positive and productive corporate culture, managers must be mindful of the personality and beliefs of the employees they hire. Also, companies must be aware that, while recruiting the right individuals is important, an ability to integrate new employees into the organization will ultimately determine the company's success. New employees can change the dynamics of a company, and existing employees may perceive an erosion of a familiar identity. To ease the integration of new employees, companies should involve existing employees in the hiring and integration process.

Figure 12.6.

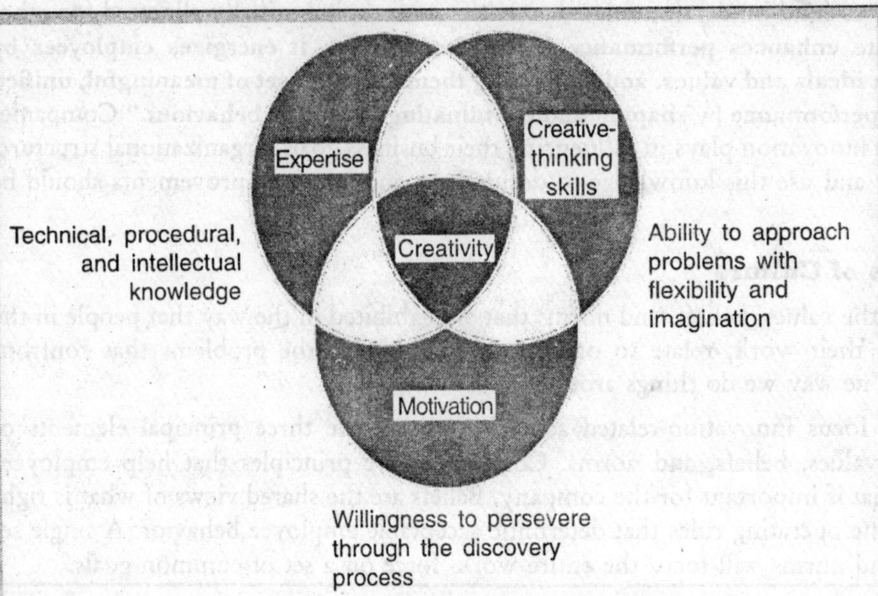

Components of Creativity

Companies must also communicate their reasons for recruiting new employees and the roles these employees will play in guiding the success of the company.

"Culture gets revealed to new employees by their immediate surroundings and the behavior of the people around them ... companies should ensure adequate interaction between new employees, the people that will carry the culture forward, and existing employees, the keepers and creators of the culture."

"It is difficult to maintain culture through periods of rapid growth. New people bring new ideas, but there is a risk that these new ideas will overwhelm the established culture of the organization. We tried to mitigate this risk by increasing corporate communications and internal marketing when we doubled in size."

In order to foster a culture of innovation, companies need to motivate their employees with rewards, recognition, and empowerment.

"Hiring from within allows us to shape the culture and succession for the organization while strengthening commitment and long-term potential. When hiring from outside, we place people at a level where they can understand the culture, be evaluated by their peers, and build respect/rapport with the members of the target team."

Empower Employees

Creating a true feeling of empowerment among employees is vital to fostering a culture of innovation. Assigning ownership of activities and giving employees the authority to make appropriate decisions are key motivational tactics. Companies can empower their employees by encouraging divergent thinking, listening to them and being open to new ideas, and ensuring that they have the information and resources they need to follow through with their ideas.

"I empower all employees by encouraging them to better understand their importance and role within Redknee and rely less on me to provide guidance. A company has to be bigger than any one employee. This is the only way to create a scaleable organization."

Empowerment does not mean simply handing over control. Freedom and authority must be complemented with accountability, management discipline, and feedback. To be effective, a corporate culture must be focused on achieving the results outlined in the business strategy. Also, a consensus on the qualitative and quantitative metrics that will govern success must also be created.

"For each department, we determined the critical success factors required to meet the company objectives. Those became the foundation of the parameters that I monitored on an ongoing basis, and thus held my managers accountable for."

Organizational structure will have a critical bearing on how decisions are made throughout a company, and it will define the network of relationships and interactions that contribute to the execution of the company's strategy. The organizational structure has to evolve to deal with changing priorities and increased business complexity. Growth inevitably leads to a buildup of management layers, which in itself creates islands of responsibility, authority, and influence. This proliferation can complicate decision-making processes and hinder innovation.

"The larger and more complex a company becomes, the more important it is for senior managers to train employees throughout the organization to make independent decisions about priorities that are consistent with the strategic direction and the business model of the company."

Foster Collaboration

Innovative ideas, by definition, rarely confine themselves to a single group, but instead require support throughout the company. Taking an idea from concept to reality requires a high degree of trust and communication, so it is important that leadership teams be at the forefront of activities that require collaboration.

"The innovative culture thrives on the free exchange of ideas. Be communicative and train managers and supervisors to allow the free flow of information among them, their subordinates, and their superiors."

"The primary engine for innovation at IDEO is its distinct approach to brainstorming — the only part of company life where strict rules do apply ... To help maintain the right spirit, IDEO's five principles of brainstorming are emblazoned on the walls: 'stay focused on the topic,' 'encourage wild ideas,' 'defer judgement,' 'build on the ideas of others, 'one conversation at a time.'"

Activities that instill a sense of collaboration are:

- Have structured brainstorming sessions that are open to all employees. During these sessions, ensure that all ideas are heard and duly evaluated.
- Allow job rotation. For example, have a research engineer spend time in the field with your sales team to experience direct customer interaction.
- Implement a mentorship program to connect senior personnel with new employees.
- Create cross-functional teams to complete tasks of strategic importance. In each team, include individuals from different groups, geographical locations, and, if possible, cultural backgrounds.
- Create a regular schedule of mini-conferences where internal groups present their ideas to one another.
- Use events, such as sporting activities, charity events, or lunch-time lectures to promote inter-departmental interaction.

"We made a decision to incorporate a policy whereby each individual is systematically rotated into different groups for a specified period of time. The initial reaction from employees was not overly positive. They realized later, however, that the interactions and knowledge from this experience have helped to solidify the foundations of open communication and trust within our company."

Encourage Employees and Create Reward Programs

A company's reward system must be designed to encourage innovation. Employees will be apprehensive of innovative activities if they perceive that they will be exposed to considerable personal risk. A truly innovative culture must make employees aware that the failure of a new idea or initiative to fulfill all expectations will not affect their position within the firm. In cases were expectations are not realized, it is important to emphasize the lessons that were learned.

"Leaders need to let employees know that they are prepared to support people who have taken up initiatives that have gone against the grain of the organization but have failed to deliver on the first or second try."

When structuring formal and informal reward schemes, it is important for companies to understand what their employees' value. Individuals that are attracted to creative activities are generally driven by the excitement of seeing their ideas transformed into something of value.

These people need to be rewarded through the use of intrinsic rewards, such as peer recognition. It is also important to publicize these rewards, as employees learn from the success of others. To further reinforce innovation, individuals' incentives should include both financial and intrinsic incentives linked to achieving agreed-upon performance targets.

To reinforce knowledge sharing and collaboration, group-based incentives should be used to reward teams when appropriate. These rewards should be based on the performance of the team in achieving its goals (see Figure 12.7).

Figure 12.7

Individual incentives		Group-based incentives	
Financial • Bonuses and rewards linked to individual and company targets	**Intrinsic** • Individual awards • Peer recognition • Increased responsibilities • Carry through projects (ownership)	**Financial** • Bonuses and rewards linked to group goals	**Intrinsic** • Group awards • Peer recognition • Senior management recognition
Base compensation packages			
Compensation		**Soft benefits**	
• Base salary • Bonus • Pensions. • Cars, computers • Healthcare and insurance • Stock options		• Work-life balance • Training • Career development • Challenging assignments • Recognition • Promotions	

"Innovation is a people process. It happens when people work together on a challenge that energizes them in an open environment of trust and respect in which mistakes are considered learning events and everyone understands what value is being created and for whom."

"In addition to being a really tough, results-oriented culture, we are also a culture of caring. I'm not talking about grand gestures. I'm talking about the day-to-day realities — being generous with acknowledgment, always making people feel important, always communicating. More than anything else, these informal methods of recognition are what stick. A private e-mail, a private telephone call — the spirit that [these] create is incredible."

"Do not wait until the completion of the innovation process to reward an employee. For example, move the employee onto the project full-time, commit additional resources to the project, or grant promotions. Such reward programs will not determine a project's fate, but your commitment to the idea will encourage your workforce to take chances."

3. Manage the Ongoing Change

Promoting a creative culture may require adjustment to a company's internal and external operations. Companies need to create a management team to oversee innovation and to communicate expectations to employees. It is also important to create a series of milestones to be used to gauge the progress toward a more innovative culture.

Create a Change Management Team

A company's leadership team has an important role in advocating the organizational changes required to sustain innovation. Employees need to understand that change is routine. Therefore, companies need to create a change management team dedicated to the change process.

"Sustaining innovation requires treating everything, including teams, organizations, procedures, and product lines, as temporary."

The change management team's primary responsibility is to obtain company-wide support for the change effort. This begins with clearly communicating the need for change. The team then needs to ensure that all projects are aligned with any changes in direction, and make sure that there are no inconsistencies in the practices expected and those performed. The change management team should also be given the authority to allocate resources to specific strategic areas and to terminate projects that are deemed unnecessary. **"You cannot sell change, or anything else, without genuine conviction, because there are so many sources of resistance to overcome. Especially, when you are pursuing a true innovation, as opposed to responding to a crisis, you've got to make a compelling case."**

Manage Employee's Anxieties

The change management team will need to manage employee's expectations and anxieties. When people are placed in an environment of change, resistance naturally occurs. Employees may be unsure of the outcome of the change, or they may be worried about the impact it may have on their positions and careers. These feelings can be mitigated by —

- Creating dissatisfaction with the status quo: Make employees understand why change is required. Highlight a credible reason for change that is simple, realistic, and is communicated frequently.
- Encouraging participation: Involve employees in the implementation process (e.g., task forces, planning committees). This increases individual ownership and excitement for the changes and decreases resistance.
- Providing time and opportunity to disengage: Help employees disengage from the status quo by using simple gatherings such as lunches and ceremonies to communicate the change and to generate excitement about the future.

Set Small Milestones

Transforming a company into an engine of innovation is a time-intensive process. By articulating clear short-term goals and measuring progress companies can communicate evidence of success to help maintain momentum behind the change effort. **"A renewal effort risks losing momentum if there are no short-term goals to meet and celebrate ... without short- term wins, too many people give up or actively join the ranks of those people who have been resisting change."**

Given the unpredictable nature of innovation, companies may find it difficult to meet their objectives (see **Figure 12.8**). Companies may have to invest more time or money than expected into activities before their full benefits can be realized. Companies must be prepared to modify their plans and communicate setbacks and adjustments as required.

Creating the required foundation, enhancing operations to foster innovation, and managing change are important steps in transforming your company into an engine of innovation. Given below is the Table which has 20 questions, which can be used as a checklist to assist any organization in ensuring that key aspects of the transformation, have been articulated and addressed.

Figure 12.8

Potential setbacks	Counter measures
Forecasts fall short: When attempting to innovate, it is difficult to predict how long something will take and how much it will cost.	• Understand and communicate reasons for any shortfall • Propose and implement new plans
Roads curve: There may be unanticipated events that change priorities.	• Be prepared to respond, troubleshoot, and adjust plans as necessary • Communicate changes and their impact to employees
Critics emerge: Critics, skeptics, and cynics will challenge the change initiatives.	• Use tangible results, supporters, and acknowledged experts to respond to criticism

Dealing With Setbacks to Change

Question	*Yes*	*Some what*	*No*
1. Create the required foundation			
1. Does innovation continually contribute to revenue generation and cost savings within your company?			
2. Is innovation pervasive across the company, or is it isolated to specific groups?			
3. Do your employees understand how innovation relates to the corporate vision and goals?			
4. Have you created a set of core values, beliefs, and norms in order to guide the development of your corporate culture?			
5. Have you redefined the roles of your company leaders to encourage and champion creative activities?			
2. Enhance operations to foster innovation			
6. Does your workforce consist of people who have the ability to approach problems in an unconventional manner?			
7. When hiring new employees, do you look for people who are willing to challenge the status quo and pursue new trends and directions?			
8. Do you involve employees in the hiring process?			
9. Do you have programs and activities that allow for meaningful interaction between new and existing employees?			
10. Do you encourage your employees to be divergent thinkers and ensure that they have the right information and resources to follow through on their ideas?			
11. Have you assessed your company's organizational structure to identify and remove decision-making bottlenecks?			

12. Is there a high degree of trust and open communication between various groups in your company?
13. Do you balance empowerment with accountability by creating a set of metrics for your employees to work toward?
14. Do your employees feel secure enough to believe that should their ideas fail to realize the desired result it will not affect their position within the company?
15. Does your company have a reward system that fosters behaviour that contributes to innovation?

3. Manage the ongoing change

16. Do you have a team of dedicated individuals, composed of representative employees, that lead and champion the changes required to sustain innovation?
17. Does this team monitor the activities of the company and ensure that there are no inconsistencies in the practices expected and performed?
18. Does this team use dialogue and consensus-building to garner support for the changes at the departmental level?
19. Do you manage the expectations and anxieties of your employees by communicating why change is important, involving employees in the implementation process, and providing the time and opportunity to disengage from the status quo?
20. Do you articulate clear short-term goals and objectives, measure progress, and communicate evidence of success to maintain the momentum and enthusiasm of your employees as changes are implemented?

Check score

1. If more than 75 percent of your answers (16 of 20) are "Yes," then your company is addressing the challenge of fostering an innovative culture.
2. If 50 to 75 percent of your answers (10 to 15) are "Yes" or "Somewhat," there is more work to be done in order to foster an innovative culture.
3. If less than 50 percent of your answers are either "Yes" or "Somewhat," your company needs to re-evaluate its approach towards fostering an innovative culture.

Scoring key

1= 75–100% means "Ready".

2= 50–75% means "Need more work".

3= 0–50% means "Re-evaluate".

❋ ❋ ❋

13 Global Strategic Management in a New World

• The Trajectory to Global Maturity • Critical Issues Blocking the Passage Ahead • Strategy Based On a New Global Perspective

The globalization of business has become so rapid that a new field called "Global Strategic Management" has now emerged. This new field is a blend of strategic management and international business that develops worldwide strategies for global corporations. Whereas, most studies in this field focus on ordinary business conditions, the revolutionary events of the past few years make it clear that the present is not ordinary. Such epoch-shattering events as the collapse of communism, the unification of Europe, the information revolution, the arrival of an environmental ethic, and other remarkable new developments signal that a new era is emerging in global affairs. This chapter describes a broader approach to global strategic management that encompasses these revolutionary changes, in a new world.

The viewpoint presented here was developed in a project sponsored by the World Future Society called "WORLD 2000." WORLD 2000 focuses on conducting a global strategic management process among business, government, education, and other sectors of society to define the emerging global system and help institutions adapt to changes. It represents a fresh examination of the forces that are integrating the earth into a coherent global order as well as those that are creating the disorder that tends to characterize our time: the unification of markets and communications, as well as the vast differences in cultures, local problems, and values erupting around the globe. By gaining new insights into the emerging world system, social institutions may better understand how they can adapt to these changes.

This seems to be an opportune time for such an examination. The transition to a new global system is likely to be made during the next decade; the year 2000 offers a highly symbolic turning point at which the emerging global order can be shaped and molded. Following is a global strategic plan, developed by synthesizing the literature and then reviewing the plan with groups of executives. It follows the logic of a typical strategic plan but carried to a global level. First, we summarize nine super trends that describe a long-term trajectory toward an advanced stage of "global maturity." Second, we note five principal obstacles that must be overcome to clear the way ahead. Third, we argue that these issues can be resolved by a newly emerging perspective that recognizes the essential unity of a global community.

The Trajectory to Global Maturity

The following trends represent the principal driving forces that are now moving the world in new directions. They could be called "super trends." Little attempt is made to offer justifications, and many other trends that capture finer details are not covered. This summarizes the major features that characterize the emerging shape of the globe as it moves along a long-term trajectory toward a new stage of global maturity.

Trend 1: A Stable Population of 10-14 Billion

The earth, which already is teeming with 5.5 billion people, is expected to double its population to reach a stable level somewhere between 10-14 billion humans by the mid-21st century. About 95 percent of this growth will occur in the less developed countries (LDCs).

Trend 2: Industrial Output Will Increase by a Factor of 5-10

The aggregate level of material consumption, or industrial output, should increase by a factor of 5-10 over the next few decades as most remaining parts of the world industrialize to reach the equivalent standard of living enjoyed by Americans, Europeans, and Japanese. Industrial throughout, however, is likely to grow less as more efficient means are found to insure a sustainable form of development.

Trend 3: The Wiring of the Globe

Information technology (IT) is a revolutionary force that will continue to overthrow governments, restructure corporations, and unify the world. This revolution will wire the earth into a single communication network, a central nervous system for a planetary society. However, the gap between information haves and have-nots is apt to persist.

Trend 4: The High-Tech Revolution

The IT revolution is accelerating technical advances to create breakthroughs in all fields: the mapping of DNA, genetic therapy, robotics, materials research, sustainable "green technology," automated transportation, and even a "technology of consciousness."

Trend 5: Global Integration

The globe is becoming integrated into a single community connected by a common communication system, a global economy, and a shared international culture. In time, this process may unify today's growing economic blocs and political federations into a universal system of open trade, a global banking system and common currency, and some form of world governance.

Trend 6: Diversity and Complexity

It is a great paradox that global integration will be accompanied by disintegration into a highly diverse system. Ethnic enclaves, such as those in the former republics of the USSR, will continue to seek autonomy; various groups within nations will form pockets of self-governing subcultures; and modern societies generally will splinter into a far more complex, differentiated social order.

Trend 7: A Universal Standard of Freedom

Freedom and the recognition of human rights should continue spreading around the globe, though this movement may ebb and flow at times. A majority of nations now have political democracy and free market systems, and the number should grow to the extent that freedom becomes the accepted norm, with authoritarian systems being the exception.

Trend 8: Continued Crime, Terrorism, and War

Traumatic upheaval is likely to produce disgruntled individuals, groups, and nations resorting to a variety of crimes, terrorism, and limited wars. However, global wars and the old fear of nuclear holocaust now seem unlikely.

Trend 9: Transcendent Values

As this transformation unfolds, most people in advanced nations should strive for quality of life, community, self-fulfillment, art, spirituality, and other higher-order values that transcend material needs. Many are cynical about such claims, but as the philosopher Andre Malraux predicted, the twenty-first century will be the century of religion.

Critical Issues Blocking the Passage Ahead

Although this evolutionary trajectory is likely to stabilize into a mature, coherent global order in the mid-twenty-first century, business and government must resolve the following five issues, which pose barriers to this forward movement. Once again, this represents a quick survey — not a detailed summary — to highlight key issues that now present major obstacles to progress.

Issue 1: Making the Leap to a Global Order

Most of the problems the world struggles with result from the fragmented economic and political systems that continue unchanged from the industrial past. Trade barriers, fluctuating currency exchange rates, and difficulties in communicating are "old" problems that should not exist in a "new" global order managed as a coherent system; they do not exist in the United States, Germany, China, or other societies governed as coherent systems. The transition to some type of world order is monumental because it requires sophisticated global systems that integrate the world into a single whole, permitting a quantum leap to a global level of governance heretofore unknown.

Issue 2: Reconciling Economic Interests

Communism may have yielded to markets, but markets do not exist only in capitalism. The strength of Japan, for instance, hinges on a market system that is based on collaborative working relations: a "Human Enterprise System" (Ozaki 1991). In contrast, the capitalism practiced in Western nations, such as the United States, is in trouble because it exacerbates conflicts between labour and management, rich and poor, business and government, domestic and foreign trade, private and public sectors, and other basic incompatibilities. A sound global economy for the future, therefore, awaits the creation of a new economic paradigm based on some form of free enterprise that can reconcile these diverse interests into a productive and harmonious community.

Issue 3: Achieving Sustainable Development

The present conflict between economic growth and environmental protection will be resolved either rationally or through some form of decline. The anticipated five or ten-fold increase in industrial output is incompatible with any reasonable forecast under existing conditions. Many solutions are being proposed to achieve sustainable development, but the task of implementation remains formidable. Ecological systems are suffering unsustainable stress even under today's far more modest load. Developed countries (DCs) show little inclination to alter their profligate lifestyles, and LDCs seem to be striving for Western affluence.

Issue 4: Managing Complexity

One of the most striking trends of the emerging future is the explosion of complexity that is almost impossible to contain within today's cumbersome institutions. Much of what passes for unsolvable disorder reflects an inability to respond effectively to the diversity of individual and community challenges. This problem, which toppled communism, is becoming severe in the West. Top-down corporations are struggling to diversify so they can serve myriad market niches; governments have not yet begun to grapple with the intricacies of education, poverty, crime, and other chronic social problems. Dramatically, different institutions are needed to manage this complex new world, which may require an upheaval similar to the one now plaguing the former communist bloc.

Issue 5: Alleviating the North-South Gap

The enormous disparity between the wealth of LDCs in the South and the DCs of the North shows little sign of improvement, fanning an explosive antagonism between these two halves of the globe. Average income in the South is now about six percent of that in the North; little progress is being made in alleviating the misery of these people, who make up three-quarters of all humanity. Unless serious efforts are made to close this gap by bringing LDCs into the modem world, the Southern hemisphere will seethe with the same potential for violent confrontation that was released in the Los Angeles riots of 1992.

These five dilemmas are exacerbated by one of the most pervasive problems of our time: a collapse of faith in the familiar old ideology that guided humans through the past epoch with good success. It could be thought of as a "meta-issue." With the USSR now defunct and the United States in crisis, the lack of superpower leadership has left a vacuum of power, ideas, and moral guidelines at a time when the world is facing Herculean new challenges. The result is political gridlock, economic stagnation, destructive personal stress, social disorders, and many other symptoms of breakdown. From all this apparent chaos, a new paradigm, model, or belief system must somehow be formed that allows people to make sense of today's different global realities.

Strategy Based On a New Global Perspective

An enormous variety of policies and remedial programs are being proposed to resolve all these problems, but their sheer number and diversity scatter attention into confusing, uncoordinated, and ineffectual directions. This section synthesizes these proposals into a "master strategy" based on a different perspective now gaining increasing attention, one that recognizes the essential unity of the emerging global system.

The key to understanding the emerging world view is to see that unprecedented new imperatives have arisen — especially the revolutionary force of IT— that are unleashing powerful new forces to integrate the globe. As communication systems encircle the earth to form a central nervous system for the planet, the fragmented parts of today's failing global order are being joined together into an interconnected, coherent system. The most recent report of the Club of Rome (King and Schneider 1991) notes that current dramatic changes represent the first global revolution because the entire earth is experiencing these events together at the same time. This shift to a new global perspective is summed up in the Table. This perspective then leads to the following elements of a master strategy required to overcome the issues defined before:

TABLE 13.1. The Transition to a New Global Perspective

Parameters	*Old Perspective*	*New Perspective*
Technological Base	Physical Technology	Information Technology
Economy	Capital-Centered	Human-Centred
Frontier of Progress	Material Growth	Sustainable Development
Institutions	Hierarchical	Decentralized
Working Relationships	Conflict	Cooperation

Strategy 1: Disseminate Advanced Technology to Unify the Globe

Although many people fear its effects, the relentless advance of modern technology — especially information technology — is the primary force driving the globe through its present transition. It was the ubiquitous presence of television, radio, facsimile, and video, for instance, that armed citizens of the former USSR and the Eastern Bloc with the knowledge required to overthrow their governments.

Information technologies should be diffused, therefore, by corporations selling sophisticated products abroad, governments fostering joint research and development projects, individuals sharing technical knowledge, and any other reasonable methods. There is a particular need to find ways of introducing these technologies into LDCs to advance their modernization and unite them with the world. All technology can be misused, so care is needed to ensure that it is applied appropriately. The emerging global order is being constructed on a technological foundation; the sooner that foundation is in place, the sooner this system can behave as a coherent global community.

Strategy 2: Integrate Economics and Society

The conflict between economic life and social life is being reconciled, as evidenced by breakthroughs that would have been unthinkable a few years ago. Japan has shown the world that a union of economic and social interests is more productive, spurring others to emulate this "human-centered" form of enterprise. Even General Motors, long regarded as the antithesis of this idea, has formed GM-Saturn as a prototype of socially responsive business, managed by a coalition of workers, customers, suppliers, distributors, and local citizens. Saturn production lines cannot keep up with demand because Saturn cars are now the best in their class, proving that social goals are compatible with economic goals.

Intense global competition should, in time, drive most economies in this direction because it is efficient. Decisions ranging from the shop floor to national macroeconomic policy may then be made collectively by all affected parties, including workers, labour, consumer advocates, governments, and citizens. If this can be done, the leaders of business and other social institutions may then act as stewards rather than managers, creating the badly needed trust, quality, mutual service, and collaborative economic relationships that can instill the essential sense of community that vitalizes society.

Strategy 3: Create a Symbiotic Society-Environment Interface

A harmonious economic-societal relationship will mean little if it is not supported by a viable ecosystem. Civilization must be carefully redesigned to form a symbiotic society-environment interface. Business firms are now competing to prove their environmental consciousness because of public pressure. Stephen Schmidheiny, Chairman of the Business Council for Sustainable Development, described the advantages (1992): "Progress toward sustainable development makes good business sense because it can create competitive advantage and new opportunities."

A wide range of difficult adjustments are under way to integrate ecological realities into economic and social life. Sustainable technologies and practices are being developed to increase economic efficiency, advance more modest but wholesome lifestyles, develop renewable energy, reforest denuded lands, convert to organic agriculture, recycle waste, and improve pollution controls. To evaluate this complex situation realistically, social indicators must be incorporated into such financial measures as GNP; social costs, such as pollution, should be internalized in the form of taxes and credits to guide balanced economic choices.

Strategy 4: Decentralize Institutions to Empower Individuals

Almost all analysts agree that social institutions need to be restructured for a knowledge-based global order, but confusion reigns over what is needed. The most useful guide can be found in a dominant imperative now sweeping through modern nations: institutions are being decentralized into networks of small, autonomous units to master complexity. This imperative is the entrepreneurial half of the new role emerging for institutions; the move toward collaborative, democratic policymaking described in Strategy 3 constitutes the other half that unifies this diversity into a harmonious whole.

For instance, large corporations are being disaggregated into small "internal enterprises" that form the equivalent of market economies inside organizations—"internal markets" (Halal *et al.* 1993). Under the pressure of limited budgets and public demands, governments are also allowing the public to choose among competing agencies. A good example is the way U.S. education is introducing market competition among schools, which are also governed democratically by teachers, parents, local citizens, and administrators.

The result of all these changes is to restructure authority relationships. Markets and democracies share the common feature of placing control in the hands of ordinary people to harness the growing diversity of thought and values into creative forces of change, with institutions providing the overarching systems that support and guide change. The decentralization of authority, then, empowers people to care for themselves more effectively, which provide a self-organizing system for managing a complex world.

Strategy 5: Foster Collaborative International Alliances

A knowledge-based society fosters pockets of collaborative problem solving in which all partners benefit, while competition drives collaborating parties together. This is why business managers and politicians are creating a flurry of strategic alliances with their competitors. Co-operation has now become the most powerful force in world affairs.

This new ethic of strategic collaboration is also being extended to forge productive alliances between business and government, economists and ecologists, and competing nations, knitting together a global community of diverse groups. Note that an ethic of co-operation implies not altruism but a reciprocity of interests that benefits all partners. It is enlightened self-interest.

The conflict between North and South, for example, could yield cooperative ventures, such as the North American Free Trade Agreement, between DCs and LDCs based on mutual advantages for both parties. LDCs gaining capital, jobs, and know-how, while DCs gain access to markets and less costly labor.

Obviously there is no assurance that the world will pursue a path of this type. And it is certainly true that difficult choices at dangerous junctures could deflect the trajectory toward maturity into other directions. However, historic breakthroughs have occurred in the past few years — the collapse of communism, a greatly reduced threat of nuclear holocaust, and worldwide concern over the environmental crisis — largely through the natural evolution of the global order. Barring unforeseen disasters, it seems reasonable to expect that the other remaining obstacles noted above could also be resolved from this same natural process, though we cannot now anticipate how or when.

This does not mean that individuals and institutions are passive observers of an immutable process of natural development: change is the sum of countless small human actions that collectively produce social transformation. A coherent new world order will emerge only if global corporations, national governments, and educational institutions are able to adopt major strategies such as those outlined above. Developing and disseminating advanced technologies, especially information technology, will be essential in forming the foundation for a mature global society. A collective model of enterprise must be defined that reconciles the interests of capital with mounting social concerns, particularly environmental sustainability. Large firms must be decentralized to empower individuals if we hope to manage a complex and diverse world. Strategic alliances must be encouraged on a global scale to avoid the conflicts that now divide the world.

Accomplishing these ambitious tasks will test us all because our individual perspectives will have to yield to a broader perspective. In our work conducting the WORLD 2000 global strategic management process for corporations, government agencies, and other management groups, we find a common theme running through all these changes: the emerging global order can be integrated into a workable whole only by accepting the legitimacy of other views, even those we feel are antithetical to our own.

The primary skill required to survive this critical transformation, therefore, is an attentive ability to reconcile the conflicting, endlessly changing, overwhelming complexity posed by today's diverse world. A crucial paradox lies at the heart of this challenge. What is involved, fundamentally, is cultivating a more transcendent mode of thought that can permit all of us to regain command over our affairs by relinquishing the illusion of self-control in favour of shared control.

14 Case Studies

WORLD WIDE CASES INDEX

1. Globalization and World Developments – India
2. The Political, Legal, and Technological Environment – Vietnam
3. Ethics and Social Responsibility - Saudi Arabia
4. The Meanings and Dimensions of Culture – Taiwan
5. Managing Across Cultures – Mexico
6. Organizational Cultures and Diversity – Japan
7. Cross-Cultural Communication and Negotiation - China
8. Strategy Formulation and Implementation – Poland
9. Entry Strategies and Organizational Structures - Australia
10. Managing Political Risk, Government Relations, and Alliances – Peru
11. Motivation Across Cultures - Singapore
12. Leadership across Cultures – Germany
13. Human Resource Selection and Development Across Cultures - Russia
14. Labour Relations and Industrial Democracy – Brazil

CORPORATE CASES

1. General Motors Ltd.
2. Microsoft Corporation
3. Toyota Corporation
4. Tata Consultancy Services Ltd.
5. Bharat Sanchar Nigam Ltd.
6. The General Electric Company Ltd.
7. Google Inc.
8. Nokia Corporation Ltd.
9. Ranbaxy Pharmaceuticals Ltd.
10. ICICI Ltd.
11. TATA Motors Ltd.
12. Wal-Mart

1. Globalization and World Developments – India

India is located in southern Asia, with the Bay of Bengal on the east and the Arabian Sea on the west. One-sixth of the world's population (approximately 1 billion people) lives within the country's 1.27 million square miles. Though Hindi is the dominant language in terms of number of speakers (it is the mother tongue to over 40 percent of Indians), India is essentially a multilingual nation with more than 10 other languages spoken by 20 million people or more. These include Telugu, Tamil, Marathi, and Bengali. Most states are divided along linguistic lines, with that language accepted as the "official" language in different states (one each). English serves as the national language among the educated Indians. Higher education in science and engineering is in English. The Indian economy derives only a quarter of its output from agriculture, with services contributing almost 55 percent. However, more than 70 percent of Indians are directly or indirectly dependent on agriculture. Three quarters of Indians live in over 600,000 villages. Many of these communities lack infrastructure such as roads, power, and telecommunications. Hence, India's rural population presents a huge untapped potential for many marketers. The country operates as a democratic republic, and for the most part, one party has dominated the government since independence in 1947. At that time, India was born of the partition of the former British Indian empire into the new countries of India and Pakistan. This division has been a source of many problems through the years. For example, much to the dismay of the world community, both countries had nuclear tests in a cold war atmosphere. Also, many millions of Indians still live at the lowest level of subsistence, and the per capita income is very low. India's misaligned central and local public finances have contributed to an overall fiscal deficit of more than 10 percent of GDP.

In the past, doing business in India has been quite difficult. For example, it took PepsiCo three years just to set up a soft drink concentrate factory, and Gillette, the U.S. razor blade company, had to wait eight years for its application to enter the market to be accepted. Additionally, many MNCs have complained that there are too many barriers to effective operations. In the mid-1970s, the country changed its rules and required that foreign partners hold no more than 40 percent ownership in any business. As a result, some MNCs left India.

In recent years, the government has been relaxing its bureaucratic rules, particularly those relating to foreign investments. From 1981 to 1991, total foreign direct investment in India increased by $250 million, and between 1991 and 1993, it jumped by an additional $2.5 billion. In 2000, foreign direct investment exceeded $3 billion and is projected to grow by 7 percent in 2004. Most of this investment has come from the United States and nonresident Indians. One reason for this change in the nation's policies toward business is that the government realizes many MNCs are making a critical choice: India or China? Any monies not invested in India may be lost to China forever. Additionally, it can be seen that foreign investments are having a very positive effect on the Indian economy. After the first big year of new investments (1991), India's annual GDP jumped to over 4 percent. In 2003, GDP increased by more than 8 percent.

With the disbandment of the "License Raj," a socialist inspired system that made government permits mandatory for almost every aspect of business, the climate for foreign investment has improved markedly. Coca-Cola was able to get permission for a 100-percent-owned unit in India in eight weeks, and Motorola received clearance in two days to add a new product line—and did all of this via fax. Other companies that have reported rapid progress include Daimler Chrysler, Procter & Gamble, and Whirlpool. At the same time, however, not everything is roses. Many MNCs are still reporting problems.

Nevertheless, the Indian government's new approach is helping a great deal. In addition, there are other attractions that entice MNCs to India. These include (1) a large number of highly educated people, especially in critically short supply areas such as medicine, engineering, and computer science; (2) widespread use of English, long accepted as the international language of business; and (3) low wages and salaries, which often are 10 to 30 percent of those in the world's economic superpowers. While these factors will continue to have a positive impact, the growing debate over jobs outsourced from the United States could dampen some of the impressive growth prospect for India. In addition, the election upset of May 2004, in which the opposition National Congress Party defeated the ruling BJP Party, suggests Indians are concerned about attention to social needs, not just economic growth.

Questions

1. What is the climate for doing business in India? Is it supportive of foreign investment?
2. How important is a highly educated human resource pool for MNCs wanting to invest in India? Is it more important for some businesses than for others?
3. Given the low per capita income of the country, why would you still argue for India to be an excellent place to do business in the coming years?

❄ ❄ ❄

2. The Political, Legal, and Technological Environment – Vietnam

Located in Southeast Asia, the Socialist Republic of Vietnam is bordered to the north by the People's Republic of China, to the west by Laos and Cambodia, and to the east and south by the South China Sea. The country is a mere 127,000 square miles but has a population of almost 80 million. The language is Vietnamese and the principal religion Buddhism, although there are a number of small minorities, including Confucian, Christian (mainly Catholic), Caodist, Daoist, and Hoa Hao. In recent years, the country's economy has been up and down, but average per capita income still is in the hundreds of dollars as the peasants remain very poor.

One of the reasons that Vietnam has lagged behind its fast-developing neighbors in Southeast Asia, such as Thailand and Malaysia, is its isolation from the industrial West, and the United States in particular, because of the Vietnam War. From the mid-1970s, the country had close relations with the U.S.S.R., but the collapse of communism there forced the still-communist Vietnamese government to work on establishing stronger economic ties with other countries. The nation recently has worked out many of its problems with China, and today, the Chinese have become a useful economic ally. Vietnam would most like to establish a vigorous trade relationship with the United States, however. Efforts toward this end began over a decade ago, but because of lack of information concerning the many U.S. soldiers still unaccounted for after the war, it was not until 1993 that the United States permitted U.S. companies to take part in ventures in Vietnam that were financed by international aid agencies. Then, in 1994, the U.S. trade embargo was lifted, and a growing number of American firms began doing business in Vietnam.

Caterpillar began supplying equipment for a $2 billion highway project. Mobil teamed with three Japanese partners to begin drilling offshore. Exxon, Amoco, Conoco, Unocal, and Arco negotiated production-sharing contracts with Petro Vietnam. General Electric opened a trade office and developed plans to use electric products throughout the country. AT&T began working to provide long-distance service both in and out of the country. Coca-Cola began bottling operations. Within the first 12 months, 70 U.S. companies obtained licenses to do business in Vietnam. Besides the United States, the largest investors have been Singapore, Taiwan, Japan, South Korea, and Hong Kong, which collectively have put over $22 billion into the country.

Over the past couple of years, Vietnamese authorities have acted swiftly to implement the structural reforms needed to modernize the national economy and to produce more competitive exports for sale in the global economy. In July 2000 the United States and Vietnam signed a bilateral trade agreement that opens up trade and foreign investment in Vietnam and gives Vietnamese exporters access to the vast U.S. market. The treaty, which entered into force near the end of 2001, is also expected to increase foreign direct investment from the United States over the next decade. This, in turn, should help stimulate direct investment from other pro-trade societies around the world. As in China, many U.S. firms have found doing business in Vietnam frustrating because of the numerous and ever-changing bureaucratic rules enacted by the communist government officials, but if relations between the two countries continue on their present course, more and more opportunities should open up for American multinationals.

Questions

1. In what way does the political environment in Vietnam pose both an opportunity and a threat for American MNCs seeking to do business there?
2. Why are U.S. multinationals so interested in going into Vietnam? How much potential does the country offer? Conversely, how much benefit can Vietnam derive from a business relationship with U.S. MNCs?
3. Will there be any opportunities in Vietnam for high-tech American firms? Why or why not?

3. Ethics and Social Responsibility - Saudi Arabia

Saudi Arabia is a large Middle Eastern country covering 865,000 square miles. Part of its east coast rests on the Persian Gulf, and much of the west coast rests along the Red Sea. One of the countries on its borders is Iraq. After Iraq's military takeover of Kuwait in August 1990, Iraq threatened to invade Saudi Arabia. This, of course, did not happen, and Saudi Arabia was not an Iraqi target during the U.S. led war in Iraq during 2003–2004. However, accusations stemming from rumours of terrorist financing activities have made Saudi Arabia a focus in the global war on terrorism, and Saudi Arabia itself was the target of terrorist attacks in 2003–2004.

There are approximately 22 million people in Saudi Arabia, and the per capita income is around $11,500. This apparent prosperity is misleading because most Saudis are poor farmers and herders who tend their camels, goats, and sheep. In recent years, however, more and more have moved to the cities and have jobs connected to the oil industry. Nearly all are Arab Muslims. The country has the two holiest cities of Islam: Mecca and Medina. The country depends almost exclusively on the sale of oil (it is the largest exporter of oil in the world) and has no public debt. The government is a monarchy, and the king makes all important decisions but is advised by ministers and other government officials. Royal and ministerial decrees account for most of the promulgated legislation. There are no political parties.

Recently, Robert Auger, the executive vice president of Skyblue, a commercial aircraft manufacturing firm based in Kansas City, had a visit with a Saudi minister. The Saudi official explained to Auger that the government planned to purchase 10 aircraft over the next two years. A number of competitive firms were bidding for the job. The minister went on to explain that despite the competitiveness of the situation, several members of the royal family were impressed with Auger's company. The firm's reputation for high-quality performance aircraft and state-of-the-art technology gave it the inside track. A number of people are involved in the decision, however, and in the minister's words, "Anything can happen when a committee decision is being made."

The Saudi official went on to explain that some people who would be involved in the decision had recently suffered large losses in some stock market speculations on the London Stock Exchange. "One relative of the King, who will be a key person in the decision regarding the purchase of the aircraft, I have heard, lost over $200,000 last week alone. Some of the competitive firms have decided to put together a pool of money to help ease his burden. Three of them have given me $100,000 each. If you were to do the same, I know that it would put you on a par with them, and I believe it would be in your best interests when the decision is made." Auger was stunned by the suggestion and told the minister that he would check with his people and get back with the minister as soon as possible.

As soon as he got back to his temporary office, Auger sent a coded message to headquarters asking management what he should do. He expects to have an answer within the next 48 hours. In the interim, he has had a call from the minister's office, but Auger's secretary told the caller that Auger had been called away from the office and would not be returning for at least two days. The individual said he would place the call again at the beginning of this coming week. In the interim, Auger has talked to a Saudi friend whom he had known back in the United States and who was currently an insider in the Saudi government. Over dinner, Auger hinted at what he had been told by the minister. The friend seemed somewhat puzzled about what Auger was saying and indicated that he had heard nothing about any stock market losses by the royal family or pool of money being put together for certain members of the decision-making committee. He asked Auger, "Are you sure you got the story straight, or as you Americans say, is someone pulling your leg?"

Questions

1. What are some current issues facing Saudi Arabia? What is the climate for doing business in Saudi Arabia today?
2. Is it legal for Auger's firm to make a payment of $100,000 to help ensure this contract?
3. Do you think other firms are making these payments, or is Auger's firm being singled out? What conclusion can you draw from your answer?
4. What would you recommend that Skyblue do?

4. The Meanings and Dimensions of Culture – Taiwan

Taiwan is an island located 100 miles off the southeast coast of the China mainland. Taiwan is only 13,900 square miles, and with a population of approximately 23 million, it has one of the highest population densities in the world. In 1949, the communists under Mao Zedong defeated the Nationalists under Chiang Kai-shek and the latter government moved to Taiwan, where it established dominance. The People's Republic of China still considers Taiwan to be a breakaway province, and tensions between the two flare up frequently.

The government of Taiwan was totally controlled by the Nationalists until 1996 when the first democratic election was held. In 2000 the Democratic Progressive Party candidate, Chen Shuibian, was elected president for a four-year term, although the Nationalist Party continued to hold over 50 percent of the seats in the country's parliament, the Legislative Yuan. He was reelected by a narrow margin in March 2004 after an apparent assassination attempt appeared to bolster his position.

The country's gross domestic product is approximately $406 billion and per capita GDP is around $18,000. In the late 1990s many Asian economies slowed down sharply, caught in a vicious economic crisis. Japan, South Korea, Indonesia, Thailand, and Malaysia, all saw their GDP growth decline, and some of them, especially Japan, are still running budget deficits as high as 10 percent of GDP. Taiwan, on the other hand, had steady GDP growth in the range of 6 percent throughout this period. In particular, the country's economy has been managed carefully through a combination of tight exchange controls, low foreign debt, conservative fiscal policies, and relatively austere and transparent banking.

Taiwan is one of the 15 largest trading powers in the world, and one of the strongest sectors of its economy is information technology. The value of computer-related products produced in Taiwan is over $35 billion annually. Taiwanese manufacturers build two-thirds of the motherboards and keyboards sold worldwide, in addition to 60 percent of the monitors and almost 40 percent of the notebook PCs. A number of major high-tech firms have set up operations on the island, including Sun Microsystems, Microsoft, and Intel. All three realized that costs here are lower than in most other places and the quality of the workforce would allow them to produce state-of-the-art products. Other firms, including locally based manufacturers, also followed this strategy. As a result, by the mid-1990s Taiwan had leapfrogged South Korea in the production of PCs. Some of this success was a result of Taiwanese firms entering into a series of private-label contracts with U.S. importers.

By the late 1990s Taiwan-based chipmakers were investing billions of dollars annually in semiconductor fabrication plants. By 2002 annual investment in research, development, and new capacity was in excess of $17 billion. The world is so dependent on Taiwan for computer-related equipment that when a devastating earthquake hit the island in September 1999, the global informational technology (IT) market shuddered and the price of PC chips immediately rose sharply. Although the IT companies emerged relatively unscathed, the incident served to underscore the importance of Taiwan's semiconductor, electronic components, and PC industry. During the first decade of the millennium Taiwan's importance in these areas is likely to grow.

Questions

1. What are some current issues facing Taiwan? What is the climate for doing business in Taiwan today?
2. In terms of cultural dimensions, is Taiwan much different from the United States? (Use Figure 4–7 in your answer.) Why or why not?
3. In what way might culture be a stumbling block for firms seeking to set up businesses in Taiwan?
4. How are the three high-tech firms in this case managing to sidestep or overcome cultural barriers?

5. Managing Across Cultures – Mexico

Located directly south of the United States, Mexico covers an area of 756,000 square miles. It is the third-largest country in Latin America and the thirteenth-largest in the world. The most recent estimates place the population at around 107 million, and this number is increasing at a rate of about 1.4 percent annually. As a result, today Mexico is one of the "youngest" countries in the world. Approximately 55 percent of the population is under the age of 20, while a mere 4 percent is 65 years of age or older.

Today, even though the economy is uncertain as in the rest of the world and has political risk, Mexico has made itself attractive for foreign investment. Trade agreements with the United States and Canada (NAFTA), the EU, Japan, and dozens of Latin American countries have begun to fully integrate the Mexican economy into the global trading system. Multinationals in a wide variety of industries, from computers to electronics and from pharmaceuticals to manufacturing, have invested billions of dollars in the country. Telefonica, the giant Spanish telecommunications firm, is putting together a wireless network across Latin America, and Mexico is one of the countries that it has targeted for investment. Meanwhile, manufacturers not only from the United States but also from Asia to Europe have helped sustain Mexico's booming maquiladora assembly industry. By the turn of the century over 1.2 million people were employed in this industry including 600,000 in the two border states of Baja California and Chihuahua.

Thomson SA, the French consumer electronics firm, has three plants in the border states that make export TVs and digital decoder boxes. And like a growing number of MNCs located in Mexico, the firm is now moving away from importing parts and materials from outside and producing everything within the country. One reason for this move is that under the terms of the North American Free Trade Agreement only parts and materials originating in one of the three NAFTA trading partners are now allowed to enter the processing zones duty-free. Anything originating outside these three countries is subject to tariffs of as much as 25 percent. So the French MNC Thomson is building a picture-tube factory in Baja California so that it will no longer have to import dutiable tubes from Italy. In many cases, imported items from the European Union, however, are allowed to enter duty-free because in 1999 Mexico signed a free-trade agreement with the EU. As a result, a host of firms, including Philips Electronics and Siemens, poured large amounts of investment into the country. At the same time Mexico also has begun negotiating another free-trade pact with the four Nordic countries, raising the likelihood that firms such as Nokia, Ericsson, and Saab-Scania will also invest heavily in the country.

While many European MNCs are now investing in Mexico, the United States still remains the largest investor. Over 60 percent of all outside investment is by U.S. firms. Asian companies, in particular Japanese MNCs, also have large holdings in the country, although these firms have been scaling back in recent years because of the import duties and the fact that Mexican labor costs are beginning to rise, thus making it more cost-effective to produce some types of goods in Asia and export them to North America. The largest investments in Mexico are in the industrial sector (around 60 percent of the total) and services (around 30 percent).

One of the major benefits of locating in Mexico is the highly skilled labor force that can be hired at fairly low wages when compared with those paid elsewhere, especially in the United States. Additionally, manufacturing firms that have located there report high productivity growth rates and quality performance. A study by the Massachusetts Institute of Technology on auto assembly plants in Canada, the United States, and Mexico reported that Mexican plants performed well. Another by J. D. Power and Associates noted that Ford Motor's Hermisillo plant was the best in all of North America. Computer and electronic firms are also finding Mexico to be an excellent choice for new expansion plants.

Questions

1. Why would multinationals be interested in setting up operations in Mexico? Give two reasons.
2. Would cultural differences be a major stumbling block for U.S. MNCs doing business in Mexico? For European firms? For Japanese firms? Explain your answer.
3. Why might MNCs be interested in studying the organizational culture in Mexican firms before deciding whether to locate there? Explain your logic.

❆ ❆ ❆

6. Organizational Cultures and Diversity – Japan

Japan is located in eastern Asia, and it comprises a curved chain of more than 3,000 islands. Four of these — Hokkaido, Honshu, Shikoku, and Kyushi—account for 89 percent of the country's land area. The population of Japan is approximately 128 million, with over 12 million people living in the nation's capital, Tokyo. According to the World Bank, the country's gross domestic product in 2003 was approximately $28,700 per capita. The country has been in the throes of an economic recession that has been going on for over 10 years. While economic conditions have been slowly improving, Japan's huge government debt, which is approaching 150 percent of GDP, and the aging of the population, are two long-run problems that must be addressed. On the positive side, Japan's economy surged in early 2004, with 5.6 percent GDP growth in the first quarter and a rise in industrial production of 3.3 percent.

An optimistic outlook is shared by two multinationals, one from the United States and the other from Germany. These two MNCs recently joined forces with a large Japanese MNC to create a new retailing chain throughout Japan. The joint venture will limit its merchandise selection to clothing and toys, which are two product areas where Japanese prices are relatively higher than those paid by consumers in other countries. The U.S. and German partners will design the clothing and toys, but they will be produced in Japan by local labor and sold there. The U.S. and German partners will contribute most of the capital needed for the venture, and they also will help design the production and distribution system as well as the retail store layout. The Japanese partner will be responsible for choosing the type of merchandise to be produced, manage or co-ordinate (for sub-contractors) the production facilities, and handle the marketing.

To provide a managerial presence in Japan, the two foreign partners will share a new headquarters building with their local partner. Located approximately 60 miles outside of Tokyo, this building will house the senior-level management from all three MNCs as well as key finance, production, and marketing personnel. The plan is to have strategy and major decisions made at this headquarters, then disseminated to the production facilities and retail stores. The joint venture hopes to have six stores operating within 24 months, and 20 more within five years.

Questions

1. What type of organizational culture is each of the three partners likely to have?
2. Which of the organizational cultures will be most different from that of the other two? Explain.
3. What types of problems might the culturally diverse top management team at headquarters create for the joint venture? Give some specific examples. How could these problems be overcome?
4. In terms of organizational culture, what is your estimate of success for this joint venture?

7. Cross-Cultural Communication and Negotiation - China

China, with more than 1.3 billion people, is the world's most populous country and has a rapidly growing economy. Economic development has proceeded unevenly. Urban coastal areas, particularly in the southeast, are experiencing more rapid economic development than other areas of the country. China has a mixed economy, with a combination of state-owned and private firms. A number of state-owned enterprises (SOEs) have undergone partial or full privatization in recent years. The Chinese government has encouraged foreign investment—in some sectors of the economy and subject to constraints—since the 1980s, defining several "special economic zones" in which foreign investors receive preferable tax, tariff, and investment treatment.

In March 2003, a long-expected transition in China's political leadership took place. Hu Jintao assumed the country's presidency as well as chairmanship of the ruling Communist Party. Wen Jinbao became the new premier. Former president Jiang Zemin retained the chairmanship of the Central Military Commission.

With China's entry into the World Trade Organization in November 2001, the Chinese government made a number of specific commitments to trade and investment liberalization that, if fully implemented, will substantially open the Chinese economy to foreign firms. In telecommunications, this will mean the lifting or sharp reduction of tariffs and foreign ownership limitations, but China will retain the right to limit foreign majority ownership of telecom firms. There are still lingering concerns about China's enforcement of intellectual property protection and its willingness to fully open access to its telecommunications market.

China's real GDP grew by 9.1 percent in 2003, an impressive performance given the SARS epidemic and the generally sluggish conditions in the global economy. This growth brought China's GDP to $1.41 trillion and, for the first time, boosted per capita GDP above $1,000. Indeed, there are concerns that China's economy may be growing too fast: The government is planning to hold economic growth to about 7 percent in 2004. Layoffs have been part of the restructuring of the SOEs, for many were severely overstaffed. The layoffs have created unemployment, which is a burden on the government budget as the government begins to provide social benefits that were previously the responsibility of the SOEs. The geographic concentration of privately owned industry in the urban centers along the coast also has created social strains. Today, China's investment laws seek to channel foreign investment into infrastructure building, industries involving advanced technologies, and high-value-added export oriented products.

In June 2003, Bruce Claflin, CEO of struggling networking company 3Com Corp., caused quite a stir by announcing a joint alliance with China's Huawei Technologies—just weeks after Huawei had been sued on a range of intellectual property rights (IPR) violations by 3Com's Silicon Valley neighbor Cisco Systems. The suit claims that Huawei's products include some of Cisco's carefully guarded source code and that Huawei infringes on copyrights related to Cisco's computer commands.

According to Claflin, 3Com's negotiations with Huawei began in mid-2002, long before Cisco filed suit. Although he admits that the deal took some by surprise, Clafin insists that it was a "no brainer." "Let's face it, people have the perception of China as a low-tech, low-cost kind of place. But my first impression was that this was truly a great technology company. It blows your mind when everyone thinks China is all about exploiting low-cost labour."

Claflin believes that Cisco's argument of IPR infringement is more complicated than it sounds: "There are two courts they care about: the court of law and the court of public opinion. I bet there's not one company out there that doesn't somehow infringe on Cisco in some way." Cisco says it respects 3Com as a rival and is hopeful that 3Com's promise that products sold by the Huawei-3Com joint venture won't infringe on Cisco's patents will come to pass. Still, it's quite possible that Cisco will file suit against the joint venture, raising questions about IPR protections in China and the United States.

Questions

1. Do you think China will continue to achieve record growth? What factors could hurt its prospects?
2. Today, because of an abundance of cheap labor, China is a hot destination for global corporate outsourcing. Do you think this will still be the case a decade from now? Why or why not?
3. What communication and negotiation challenges may have arisen in the three-way exchanges among Cisco, 3Com, and Huawei?
4. Can 3Com take any proactive measures to help limit the possibility of Cisco moving forward with litigation?

❄ ❄ ❄

8. Strategy Formulation and Implementation – Poland

Poland is the sixth-largest country in Europe. It is bordered by Germany, the Czech Republic, and Slovakia in the west and south and by the former Soviet Union republics of Ukraine in the south, Belarus in the east, and Lithuania in the northeast. The northwest section of the country is located on the Baltic Sea, named after the Polane, a Slavic tribe that lived more than a thousand years ago, Poland has beautiful countryside and rapidly growing cities. Rolling hills and rugged mountains rise in southern Poland.

There are approximately 39 million Poles, and GDP is around $227 billion. Poland's per capita GDP of $5,943 is about 40 percent of the EU average. Seventy percent of Poland's exports go to the EU. The Polish economy grew rapidly in the mid-1990s, but growth slowed considerably in recent years. Agriculture employs 26.3 percent of the workforce but contributes only 3.1 percent to GDP, reflecting relatively low productivity. Unlike the industrial sector, Poland's agricultural sector remained largely in private hands during the decades of communist rule. Most of the former state farms are now leased to farmer tenants. Lack of credit is hampering efforts to sell former state farmland. In preparation for accession into the EU, Poland began restructuring its agriculture sector. The EU is unwilling to subsidize the vast number of subsistence farms that do not produce for the market. The changes in agriculture are likely to strain Poland's social fabric, as family-based small farms are split up as the younger generation drifts toward the cities.

Throughout the 1990s the United States and other Western countries supported the growth of a free-enterprise economy by reducing Poland's foreign debt burden, providing economic aid, and lowering trade barriers. Poland graduated from USAID assistance in 2000. As a result of Poland's growth and investment-friendly climate, the country has received over $65 billion in direct foreign investment since 1990. However, the government continues to play a strong role in the economy, as seen in excessive red tape and the high level of politicization in many business decisions. Investors complain that state regulation is not transparent or predictable. The economy suffers from a lack of competition in many sectors, notably telecommunications. In early 2002, the government announced a new set of economic reforms designed in many ways to complete the process launched in 1990. The package acknowledges the need to improve Poland's investment climate, particularly the conditions for small and medium-sized enterprises, and better prepare the economy to compete as an EU member.

Despite continuing problems, the Poles have made some progress in establishing a viable economy. To take advantage of this economic situation, a medium-sized Canadian manufacturing firm has begun thinking about renovating a plant near Warsaw and building small power tools for the expanding Central and Eastern European market. The company's logic is fairly straightforward. There appears to be no competition in this niche, because there has been little demand for power tools in this area. As the post communist countries continue to struggle in their transition to a market economy, they will have to increase their productivity if they hope to compete with Western European nations. Small power tools are one of the products they will need to accomplish this goal.

A second reason for the Canadian firm's interest in setting up operations in Poland is that the price of labor is still relatively low. Other nearby countries have lower wage rates, but Warsaw, the company's specific choice, has a cadre of well-trained factory workers who could be recruited to this renovated factory. Product quality in the production of these tools is critical to success, so for this Canadian firm, Poland seems an ideal location.

In addition, Poland likely will continue receiving economic and moral support from Western Europe as well as Canada and the United States. Exporting from Poland to Western Europe or the United States therefore should be easier than from more developed countries. Moreover, the manufacturing firm is convinced that its proximity to Russia will open up that market as well. Transportation costs to Russia will be low *vis à- vis* competitors, and the Russians currently are looking for ways to increase their own worker productivity.

Finally, there likely will be little competition for the next couple of years, because small power tools do not carry a very large markup and no other manufacturer is attempting to tap what the Canadian firm views as "an emerging market for the twenty-first century." However, a final decision on this matter is going to have to wait until the company has made a thorough evaluation of the market and the competitive nature of the industry.

Questions

1. What are some current issues facing Poland? What is the climate for doing business in Poland today?
2. Is the Canadian manufacturing firm using an economic, political, or quality imperative approach to strategy?
3. How should the firm carry out the environmental scanning process? Would the process be of any practical value?
4. What are two key factors for success that will be important if this project is to succeed?

❄ ❄ ❄

9. Entry Strategies and Organizational Structures - Australia

Australia is the smallest continent but the sixth-largest country in the world. It lies between the Indian and Pacific oceans in the Southern Hemisphere and has a landmass of almost 3 million square miles (around 85 percent the size of the United States). Referred to as being "down under" because it lies entirely within the Southern Hemisphere, it is a dry, thinly populated land.

The outback is famous for its bright sunshine, enormous numbers of sheep and cattle, and unusual wildlife, such as kangaroos, koalas, platypuses, and wombats. Over 19 million people live in this former British colony, and 20 million are projected within the next couple of years. Although many British customs are retained, Australians have developed their own unique way of life. One of the world's most developed countries, Australia operates under a democratic form of government somewhat similar to that of Great Britain. Gross domestic product is over $525 billion, with the largest economic sectors being services (71 percent), trade, and manufacturing.

A large financial-service MNC in the United States has been examining the demographic and economic data of Australia. This MNC has concluded that there will be increased demand for financial services in Australia during the next few years. As a result, the company is setting up an operation in the capital, Canberra, which is slightly inland from Sydney and Melbourne, the two largest cities.

This financial-services firm began in Chicago and now has offices in seven countries. Many of these foreign operations are closely controlled by the Chicago office. The overseas personnel are charged with carefully following instructions from headquarters and implementing centralized decisions. However, the Australian operation will be run differently. Because the country is so large and the population spread along the coast and to Perth in the west, and because of the "free spirit" cultural values of the Aussies, the home office feels compelled to give the manager of Australian operations full control over decision making. This manager will have a small number of senior-level managers brought from the United States, but the rest of the personnel will be hired locally. The office will be given sales and profit goals, but specific implementation of strategy will be left to the manager and his or her key subordinates on site.

The home office believes that in addition to providing direct banking and credit card services, the Australian operation should seek to gain a strong foothold in insurance and investment services. As the country continues to grow economically, this sector of the industry should increase relatively fast. Moreover, few multinational firms are trying to tap this market in Australia, and those that are doing so are from British Commonwealth countries. The CEO believes that the experience of the people being sent to Australia (the U.S. expatriates) will be particularly helpful in developing this market. He recently noted, "We know that the needs of the Australian market are not as sophisticated or complex as those in the United States, but we also know that they are moving in the same direction as we are. So we intend to tap our experience and knowledge and use it to garner a commanding share of this expanding market."

Questions

1. What are some current issues facing Australia? What is the climate for doing business in Australia today?
2. What type of organizational structure arrangement is the MNC going to use in setting up its Australian operation?
3. Can this MNC benefit from any of the new organizational arrangements, such as a joint venture, the Japanese concept of keiretsu, or electronic networks?
4. Will this operation be basically centralized or decentralized?

10. Managing Political Risk, Government Relations, and Alliances – Peru

Peru is located on the west coast of South America. It is the third-largest nation on the continent (only Brazil and Argentina have more area), and it covers almost 500,000 square miles (about 14 percent of the size of the United States). The land has enormous contrasts: a desert drier than the Sahara, the towering snow-capped Andes Mountains, sparkling grass-covered plateaus, and thick rain forests. Peru has approximately 27 million people, of whom about 20 percent live in Lima, the capital. More Indians (one-half of the population) live in Peru than in any other country in the Western Hemisphere. The ancestors of Peru's Indians are the famous Incas, who built a great empire. The rest of the population is mixed, and a small percentage is white.

The economy depends heavily on agriculture, fishing, mining, and services. GDP is approximately $139 billion and per capita income stood at around $5,000 in 2002. In recent years the economy has gained some relative strength, with GDP growth of more than 4 percent in 2003. In addition, the U.S. government recently began trade negotiations with Peru, Colombia, and Ecuador, perhaps leading to a formal trade agreement that would make permanent trade concessions under the earlier Andean Trade Preferences Act. In response, multinationals are now beginning to again consider investing in the country. One of these potential investors is a large New York bank that is considering a $25 million loan to the owner of a Peruvian fishing fleet. The owner wants to refurbish the fleet and add one more ship.

During the 1970s, the Peruvian government nationalized a number of industries and factories and began running them for the profit of the state. In most cases, these state-run ventures became disasters. In the late 1970s, the fishing fleet owner was given back his ships and allowed to operate his business as before. Since then, he has managed to remain profitable, but his ships are getting old and he needs an influx of capital to make repairs and add new technology. As he explained to the New York banker: "Fishing is no longer just an art. There is a great deal of technology involved. And to keep costs low and be competitive on the world market, you have to have the latest equipment for both locating as well as catching and then loading and unloading the fish."

Having reviewed the fleet owner's operation, the large multinational bank believes that the loan is justified. The financial institution is concerned, however, that the Peruvian government might step in during the next couple of years and again take over the business. If this were to happen, it might take an additional decade for the loan to be repaid. If the government were to allow the fleet owner to operate the fleet the way he has over the last decade, the loan could be repaid within seven years.

Right now, the bank is deciding the specific terms of the agreement. Once these have been worked out, either a loan officer will fly down to Lima and close the deal or the owner will be asked to come to New York for the signing. Whichever approach is used, the bank realizes that final adjustments in the agreement will have to be made on the spot. Therefore, if the bank sends a representative to Lima, the individual will have to have the authority to commit the bank to specific terms. These final matters should be worked out within the next 10 days.

Questions

1. What are some current issues facing Peru? What is the climate for doing business in Peru today?
2. What type of political risks does this fishing company need to evaluate? Identify and describe them.
3. What types of integrative and protective and defensive techniques can the bank use?
4. Would the bank be better off negotiating the loan in New York or in Lima? Why?

11.Motivation Across Cultures - Singapore

Singapore is an island city-state that is located at the southern tip of the Malay Peninsula. The small country covers 239 square miles and is connected by train across the Johore Strait to West Malaysia in the north. The Strait of Malacca to the south separates Singapore from the Indonesian island of Sumatra. There are approximately 4 million people in Singapore, resulting in a population density per square mile of almost 18,000 people. About three-fourths of Singaporeans are of Chinese descent, 15 percent are Malays, and the remainders are Indian and European. The gross domestic product of this thriving country is over $112 billion, and per capita GDP is around $25,200. One of the so-called newly industrialized countries or Four Tigers (along with Korea, Taiwan, and Hong Kong), Singapore in recent years has been affected by the economic uncertainty around the world, but the currency and prices have remained relatively stable. The very clean and modern city remains the major commercial and shipping center of Southeast Asia. In May 2003, the governments of the United States and Singapore signed the U.S.–Singapore Free Trade Agreement (USSFTA), the first bilateral free-trade agreement between the United States and an Asian country.

For the last six months, the Madruga Corporation of Cleveland has been producing small electronic toys in Singapore. The small factory has been operated by local managers, but Madruga now wants to expand the Singapore facilities as well as integrate more expatriate managers into the operation. The CEO explained: "We do not want to run this plant as if it were a foreign subsidiary under the direct control of local managers. It is our plant and we want an on-site presence. Over the last year we have been staffing our Canadian and European operations with headquarters personnel, and we are now ready to turn attention to our Singapore operation." Before doing so, however, the company intends to conduct some on-site research to learn the most effective way of managing the Singapore personnel. In particular, the Madruga management team is concerned with how to motivate the Singaporeans and make them more productive. One survey has already been conducted among the Singapore personnel; this study found a great deal of similarity with the workers at the U.S. facilities. Both the Singapore and the U.S. employees expressed a preference for job-content factors such as the chance for growth, achievement, and increased responsibility, and they listed money and job security toward the bottom of the list of things they looked for in a job.

Madruga management is intrigued by these findings and believes that it might be possible to use some of the same motivation approaches in Singapore as it does in the United States. Moreover, one of the researchers sent the CEO a copy of an article showing that people in Singapore have weak uncertainty avoidance and a general cultural profile that is fairly similar to that of the United States. The CEO is not sure what all this means, but she does know that motivating workers in Singapore apparently is not as "foreign" a process as she thought it would be.

Questions

1. What are some current issues facing Singapore? What is the climate for doing business in Singapore today?
2. Based on the information in this case, determine the specific things that seem to motivate human resources in Singapore.
3. Would knowledge of the achievement motive be of any value to the expatriate managers who are assigned to the Singapore operation?

12. Leadership across Cultures – Germany

The reunification of Germany was a major event of modern times. Despite problems, Germany remains a major economic power. The unified Germany is big, though only about the size of the state of Nevada in the United States. With a population of about 84 million, Germany has about three times the population of California. Germany still is far behind the economic size of Japan and 20 percent that of the United States. Because Germany was rebuilt almost from the ground up after World War II, however, many feel that Germany, along with Japan, is an economic miracle of modern times. Unified Germany's GDP of $2.16 trillion is behind that of both the United States and Japan, but Germany exports more than Japan, its gross investment as a percentage of GDP is higher than that of the United States, and its average compensation with benefits to workers is higher than that of the United States or Japan. It is estimated that Germany has direct control of about one-fourth of Western Europe's economy, which gives it considerable power in Europe. The German people are known for being thrifty, hardworking, and obedient to authority. They love music, dancing, good food and beer, and fellowship. The government is a parliamentary democracy headed by a chancellor. Although Germany has experienced a difficult economic environment in recent years, recent governments have pushed through labour reforms designed to improve productivity and stem unemployment.

For the last 13 years, the Wiscomb Company has held a majority interest in a large retail store in Bonn. The store has been very successful and also has proved to be an excellent training ground for managers whom the company wanted to prepare for other overseas assignments. First, the managers would be posted to the Bonn store. Then, after three or four months of international seasoning, they would be sent on to other stores in Europe. Wiscomb has holdings in the Netherlands, Luxembourg, and Austria. The Bonn store has been the primary training ground because it was the first store the company had in Europe, and the training program was created with this store in mind.

A few months ago, the Wiscomb management and its German partners decided to try a new approach to selling. The plan called for some young U.S. managers to be posted to the Bonn store for a three-year tour, while some young German managers were sent stateside. Both companies hoped that this program would provide important training and experience for their people; however, things have not worked out as hoped. The U.S. managers have reported great difficulty in supervising their German subordinates. Three of their main concerns are as follows:

(1) Their subordinates do not seem to like to participate in decision making, preferring to be told what to do. (2) The German nationals in the store rely much more heavily on a Theory X approach to supervising than the Americans are accustomed to using, and they are encouraging their U.S. counterparts to follow their example. (3) Some of the German managers have suggested to the young Americans that they do not share as much information with their own subordinates. Overall, the Americans believe that the German style of management is not as effective as their own, but they feel equally ill at ease raising this issue with their hosts. They have asked if someone from headquarters could come over from the United States and help to resolve their problem. A human resources executive is scheduled to arrive next week and meet with the U.S. contingent.

Questions

1. What are some current issues facing Germany? What is the climate for doing business in Germany today?
2. Are the leadership styles used by the German managers really much different from those used by the Americans?
3. Do you think the German managers are really more Theory X–oriented than their U.S. counterparts? Why, or why not?
4. Are the German managers who have come to the United States likely to be having the same types of problems?

13. Human Resource Selection and Development Across Cultures – Russia

Russia is by far the largest of the former Soviet republics. Russia stretches from Eastern Europe across northern Asia to the Pacific Ocean. The 150 million people consist of 83 percent Russians, 4 percent Tartars, and a scattering of others. The largest city and capital is Moscow, with about 9 million people. At present, there is continuing social and economic turmoil in Russia. Although prices are no longer controlled and privatization is well under way, the value of the ruble continues to deteriorate. At the same time, however, there are many pockets of prosperity in the country and under President Vladimir Putin positive efforts are under way to bolster the economy.

By 2003, Russia's GDP had reached $1.4 trillion, and Russia's privatization and liberalization program was attracting substantial foreign investment. One MNC that has been extremely interested in the country is Earth, Inc. (EI), a farm-implement company headquartered in Birmingham, Alabama. EI recently entered into an agreement with the government of Russia to set up operations near Moscow in a factory that was operating at about one-half of capacity. The factory will produce farm implements for the newly emerging Eastern European market. EI will supply the technical know-how and product design as well as assume responsibility for marketing the products. The Russian plant will build the equipment and package it for shipping.

The management of the plant operation will be handled on a joint basis. EI will send a team of five management and technical personnel from the United States to the Russian factory site for a period of 12 to 18 months. After this time, EI hopes to send three of them home, and the two who remain would continue to provide ongoing assistance. At the same time, EI intends to hire four middle-level managers and eight first-level supervisors from Italy and Germany, because the operation will need Europeans who are more familiar with doing manufacturing in this part of the world. Very few locals have inspired EI with confidence that they can get the job done. However, over a two-year period, EI intends to replace the third-country nationals with trained local managers. "We need to staff the management ranks with knowledgeable, experienced people," the CEO explained, "at least until we get the operation up and running successfully with our own people. Then we can turn more and more of the operation over to local management, and run the plant with just a handful of headquarters people on-site." This arrangement has been agreed to by the Russian government, and EI currently is identifying and recruiting managers both in the United States and in Europe. Initially, the firm thought that this would be a fairly simple process, but screening and selecting are taking much longer than anticipated. Nevertheless, EI hopes to have the plant operating within 12 months.

Questions

1. What are some current issues facing Russia? What is the climate for doing business in Russia today?
2. What are some of the benefits of using home-country nationals in overseas operations? What are some of the benefits of using host-country nationals?
3. Why would a multinational such as EI be interested in bringing in third-country nationals?
4. What criteria should EI use in selecting personnel for the overseas assignment in Russia?

❆ ❆ ❆

14. Labour Relations and Industrial Democracy – Brazil

After three centuries under the rule of Portugal, Brazil became an independent nation in 1822. By far the largest and most populous country in South America, Brazil has overcome more than a half century of military intervention in the governance of the country to pursue industrial and agricultural growth and the development of the interior.

After crafting a fiscal adjustment program and pledging progress on structural reform, Brazil received a $41.5 billion IMF-led international support program in November 1998. In January 1999, the Brazilian Central Bank announced that the real would no longer be pegged to the U.S. dollar. The consequent devaluation helped moderate the downturn in economic growth in 1999, and the country posted moderate GDP growth in 2000. Economic growth slowed considerably in 2001–2003—to less than 2 percent—because of a slowdown in major markets and the hiking of interest rates by the Central Bank to combat inflationary pressures. President Luiz Inácio Lula da Silva, who took office on January 1, 2003, has given priority to reforming the complex tax code, trimming the overblown civil service pension system, and continuing the fight against inflation. By exploiting vast natural resources and a large labour pool, Brazil is today South America's leading economic power and a regional bellwether.

After winning a landslide victory in 2002 on a campaign to revamp the economy and battle for the poor, President Lula da Silva reassured worried investors when he continued his predecessor's plan of strict financial austerity. Instead of catching the jitters as predicted, the country's bond and stock markets enjoyed stellar returns in 2003 and are still going strong. But within a year, pressure was mounting on Lula da Silva to keep true to his populist roots. After riding a wave of popular support through his first year, Lula da Silva faced sharp criticism from within his own Workers' Party and governing coalition as well as from ordinary voters. Lula has also gained a reputation for being thin-skinned when it comes to criticism; he expelled a foreign journalist critical of his policies. Some feel betrayed by Lula da Silva's rejection of the socialist policies that the Workers' Party has always fought for. In a March 2004 opinion poll, only 28 percent of Brazilians voiced support for the government, down from 41 percent in December. Both the right and the left are frustrated with economic performance, which has grown an average of only 2 percent a year since the mid-1990s. In addition, Brazil has emerged as a leader of developing countries concerned about the imbalance in global trade rules, and Brazil led the "Group of 20" countries responsible for slowing progress in the Doha development round of global trade talks. Because of the same concerns, Brazil also dimmed prospects for a hemisphere wide free-trade agreement — to the frustration of the United States and other countries, which went ahead with bilateral and regional FTAs to fill the gap.

Brazil's policies toward energy and telecommunications firms that entered the country as part of the privatization wave have also raised concerns. BellSouth, with operations in 10 Latin America countries—Argentina, Uruguay, Colombia, Venezuela, Chile, Peru, Ecuador, Panama, Nicaragua, and Guatemala—announced recently it would sell its operation in southern Brazil. It has more than 11 million subscribers in the region, making it the largest U.S. wireless player there and the second-largest player after Mexico's América Móvil. AES Corporation also pulled out some of its electricity investments because of general instability in the region, difficult labour relations, and lawsuits over service disruptions brought on by illegal line cutting by consumers wanting free electricity.

Questions

1. In your opinion, what are the main challenges facing Brazil?
2. How would a move toward populism affect Brazil's stability, future growth prospects, and attractiveness to MNCs?
3. Do you think abandoning socialist policies is in the best interest of Brazil? Why or why not?
4. How should BellSouth, AES, and other companies address concerns about government policies and labour relations in Brazil?

❄ ❄ ❄

CORPORATE CASES

1. General Motors Ltd – Hummer

Hummer is a brand of large off-road vehicles (H1) or sport utility vehicles (SUVs) (H2, H3,) sold by General Motors, also known as GM. The H1 version is based on the military High Mobility Multipurpose Wheeled Vehicle (HMMWV, or Humvee). The Hummer is one of the larger 4x4 types, with commensurate high fuel consumption. In most countries, a hummer is considered to be a truck, rather than a regular SUV as it does not meet environmental protection standards. In some countries, including New Zealand and Australia, a truck license is needed in order to operate some of the heavier models of Hummer.

Executive Strategies:

- King of the road: driving the four-passenger open-top
- Hummer is an experience in power - Style of Life

IN THE FIELD OF SPORT utility vehicles, some stand out more than others. The newer, gargantuan size SUVs, like the Ford Excursion or the Chevrolet Suburban, have taken the SUV from a rugged vehicle to one full of creature comforts, from off-road work to soccer practice and paved highways. But one vehicle remains true to form as the most rugged people-mover on the planet: the Hummer.

In 1979, the US Army requested a troop carrier described as a "High Mobility Multipurpose Wheeled Vehicle" or HMMWV. The vehicle that emerged, nicknamed the "Humvee" by soldiers who used it, has survived rugged conditions (including combat) for 12 years. When it became available for civilian purchase, the vehicle was slightly modified - off came the roof mounted machine gun and in went the amenities such as door locks - but essentially it remained the same. As an SUV concept, there is something very different about the Hummer. Its size is the first clue: The Hummer is more than six feet tall and more than seven feet wide, even without the mirrors (with mirrors, it's nine feet wide). This makes driving the Hummer challenging.

The interior is laid out well as far as the driver is concerned, with a cockpit configuration. The instruments are plain and simple, with the radio and climate control significantly turned towards the driver. Due to the height and the size of the engine and transmission, there is significant intrusion into the interior. The whole center of the vehicle houses the transmission and exhaust system. As a result, the passengers sit five feet from each other, pushed to what seems the very outside of the vehicle. Conversation over the roar of the 6.5-litre turbo diesel engine is difficult, and holding bands on a date is almost impossible. Clearly the US military was not thinking about sex appeal.

Although the Hummer offers all of the expected conveniences, it maintains its personality as a serious performance vehicle. After literally climbing into the driver's seat and turning the ignition switch, there is an immediate sense of power. Driving the car on a daily basis, you must hold back from using it as an urban assault vehicle. If someone cuts you off, you might think about pressing the accelerator and clearing a path. Inside the 11,000-pound machine, you feel nearly unstoppable.

The performance numbers show the Hummer is capable of tackling virtually any terrain. It is able to climb at a grade of 37.5 degrees and go down at 72 degrees, with an unsurpassed 16 inches of ground clearance that lets it go through high-water obstacles. Its 72-inch track width gives it extreme stability. In addition, the Hummer's body is made of a heat-treated aluminum alloy where the panels are bonded together and then riveted.

One of the options on the Hummer is a system that enables the driver to adjust tire pressure from the control panel. By inflating or deflating the tires, one can create a bigger "footprint" that allows for better traction in snow, mud or sand. Another option is the "runflat" system that allows the vehicle to travel on flat tires at 30 mph for a distance of 20 miles. The Hummer is basically an all-terrain urban assault craft, the kind of vehicle you'd want in your driveway if the end of the world comes.

All this power does not come cheap, however. The soft-top, four-door model we tested was priced at more than US$100,000. And there are more expensive models, including the four-passenger hard-top and the wagon. The only other downside is that even with its gargantuan size, the Hummer will only seat four people. But those four will be traveling in the king of all SUVs.

Base Price	*US$83,733*
Price as Tested	US$101,375
Engine	6.5-litre, Turbo diesel V-8
Horsepower	195 hp @ 3,450 rpm
Torque	430 lb-ft @ 1,800 rpm
Fuel Capacity	25 gallons
0 to 60 mph	18 seconds
Maximum Speed	83+ mph

Background

Hummers were originally built by AM General Corporation, formerly the military and government vehicle division of American Motors, in its South Bend, Indiana assembly plant. AM General had planned to sell a civilian version of the Hummer as far back as the late 1980s. In 1990, two matching white Hummers were driven from London to Beijing over the rough roads of central Soviet Union. The Hummers made the trip with ease, for they were built to drive on off-road terrain. The highlights of this journey were broadcast in the United States on ESPN. This publicity would pale in comparison to the attention that the HMMWV received for its service in Operation: Desert Storm the following year.

In 1992, AM General began selling a civilian version of the M998 High Mobilit Multipurpose Wheeled Vehicle (HMMWV or Hum-Vee) vehicle to the public under the brand name "Hummer". According to sources, they began doing so after Arnold Schwarzenegger asked them to; apparently, he was impressed by a convoy of HMMWVs that drove by during his filming *Kindergarten Cop* in 1990.

In 1998, AM General sold the brand name to General Motors but continued to manufacture the vehicles. GM is responsible for the marketing and distribution of all Hummers produced by AM General. In the next few years, GM introduced two new homegrown models, the H2 and H3, and renamed the original vehicle H1. AM General continues to build the H1 and is contracted by GM to produce the H2. The H3 is built in Shreveport, LA alongside the Chevrolet Colorado and GMC Canyon pickups. Unlike the H1, which is a true off-road vehicle the H2, H3 and H4 are SUVs.

As of 2006, Hummer has gone international with selected importers and distributors in Europe and other markets. Since October 10, 2006, GM has been producing the Hummer H3 at its Port Elizabeth plant in South Africa for international markets. Hummers at the Port Elizabeth plant will be built both for local South African consumption and for export to Australia (for the 2008 model year), Europe, the Middle East, and Japan. As of October 2006, Hummer vehicles are marketed by about 300 dealers in 34 countries. 173 of those are in the U.S. The H2 is also assembled in Kaliningrad, Russia, by Avtotor, starting in June 2004. The plant produces a few hundred vehicles annually, and its output is limited to local consumption (five dealers in Russia initially).

On May 12, 2006, GM announced it would cease production of the original H1 Hummer. GM CEO Rick Wagoner has said the Hummer brand of trucks will run on Biofuel Powertrains in Last Year's Los Angeles International Auto Show. Schwarzenegger has subsequently had one of his Hummers converted to run on biofuel and now promotes this approach.

Hummer H1 compared with HMMWV

The Hummer H1 is basically a HMMWV built for civilian use; it has no armour or weapons fittings. However the powertrain, chassis, body, suspension, etc., are the same. The H1 differs from the HMMWV in having a civilian interior, including trim, comfortable seats, stereo radio, and air conditioning as standard options. As a result of its commercial use, features introduced in the civilian

Hummer have been incorporated into improved military versions. The H1's electrical system is 12-volt, with the two batteries wired in parallel. The HMMWV runs on a 24-volt system, where the two batteries are run in series.

Owner efforts

Since all Hummer vehicles have heavy-duty capabilities, they have been employed by owners for aid in large disaster situations. Hummer Owners Prepared for Emergencies (HOPE) was created by the efforts of The Hummer Club, INC. and the American Red Cross. Together, the two organizations train Hummer owners with CPR and First Aid skills, and basic off-highway skills so that they may assist victims during a disaster situation.

Racing

Team HUMMER stock-class H3 driven by Rod Hall. Hall finished first in class with the H3 in the 2005 Baja 1000.

Team Hummer Racing was created in 1993 and showcases the Hummer's abilities. Led by off-road racing legend Rod Hall, Team HUMMER competes in the Stock classes of both BitD and SCORE, which feature production-based vehicles with stock frames, stock suspension designs and production-based engines. Only specialized racing shock absorbers, tyres and other minor modifications are allowed, along with the required supporting components and mandatory safety equipment. Minor modifications are allowed to the powertrain, although the rules stipulate it must be based on the stock engine and transmission combination. The team's latest victories came in February 2007, with the H2 and H1 Alpha earning class wins at the Parker 425. Team HUMMER has tallied one of the most impressive records in production-class racing, earning 11 class wins at the Baja 1000.

Licensing

GM has been very active and effective in licensing the Hummer. Various companies have licensed the Hummer trademarks for use on colognes, flashlights, bicycles, shoes, coats, hats, skateboards, laptops, clothing, jewellery, CD players and other items.

Criticisms

Along with other heavy passenger vehicles Hummers have very poor fuel economy. For instance, the H2 in one engine configuration averages about 15 mpg (US) (16 L/100 km) on highways, (10 mpg or 24 L/100 km on the street), has a curb weight of over 6000 pounds (2722 kg), and has relatively high maintenance costs. Also, just like an average SUV it is not taken off the paved roads by an average consumer to justify its off-road capabilities.

What sets the Hummer H1 and H2 apart from other large SUVs and pickup trucks is that their large size, resulting in this elevated fuel consumption, has lost most of the utilitarian justification. While design of heavy pickup trucks is intended for transporting large objects in construction work, for instance, or an SUV van can be viewed as an alternative to a mini-van for transporting large groups of people, according to critics the main appeal of a Hummer H1 or H2 for those who do not use it off-road is that it looks big and dominant.

Models

There are three current and possibly two future models in the Hummer line:

Production models

- Hummer H1 (discontinued)
- Hummer H2
  - o Hummer H2 SUT

1. Hummer H3
   - o Hummer H3t

- o Hummer H3x
- o Hummer H3 Alpha
- Concept vehicles
  - o Hummer HX

Hummer's target market: According to AM General's market research, Hummer's market is divided into four categories:

1. The realist.
2. The discerner.
3. The conqueror.
4. The adventurer.

The realist considers Hummer for its practical purposes, and will therefore make use of the vehicle's off-road prowess. The discerner is a connoisseur for the finer things in life, who appreciates Hummer's status, but is unlikely to go off-roading. The conqueror is a successful person who wants people to know it, who appreciates Hummer for its exclusivity and attention grabbing looks.

The fourth type of buyer is the adventurer, who wants to take the Hummer off-road.

By analyzing the percentage of the population that has these qualities, I think that Hummer's U.S. target market segment is males between the ages of 25 and 64 who earn over $100,000 per year.

ANALYSIS Demographic Information: Hummer's target market segment cannot be very large because of the high price of the vehicle, which can be in excess of $90,000. Hummer must gear its marketing strategies towards this small group of individuals. Hummer's market segment consists of males between the ages of 25 and 44 who earn over $100,000 a year. This demographic group consists of Generation X'ers and some of the Baby Boom generation. These males are looking for specific vehicles that are geared towards luxury and status. According to 1999 census data, in the approximation of 40,698,000 males between the ages of 25 and 44, only 2,011,000 of them earn enough money to purchase a Hummer. This would give Hummer a market base of over 2 million consumers. This market segment is growing because of the change in this base from 1998 to 1999. The number of males within this age group who earned over $100,000 was 1,730,000 in 1998. That reveals a growth rate of 16% in one year. Also, you can infer that the number of people in general who can afford a Hummer is increasing due to the low unemployment rate, and the steadily growing U.S. economy.

Hummer's sales would continue to grow due to the increase of its market segment coupled with the fact that the company is preparing to release new models that may cater to a whole other marketing segment. Cultural Trends, Attitudes, Values of Target Market The outlook on the buying attitudes of Hummer's target market remains robust in the future. The demand for luxury items has been steadily growing for the past couple of years. With the existence of a bull market, and a steady increase in national prosperity, today's high-income individuals have a healthy demand for luxurious goods and services.

The SUV market in general has been steadily increasing over the past five years. According to American Demographics, forecasters estimate that 49% of the new vehicle market will be that of light trucks in 2001, and light truck sales will be greater than that of car sales in 2002. Today's consumers stress safety over other attributes when buying vehicles, which show the increase in demand for SUV's, which are proven to be safer than most cars in crashes. Also, American Demographics' study revealed that empty nest baby boomers are not moving towards sedans, but towards SUV's. Another value of today's consumers is in styling. Today's SUV's have been appealing to consumers because of their current styling blend of ruggedness and beauty. The image factor is also big in analyzing consumer trends. Consumers have a liking for SUV's because of the image that it projects. If one drives an SUV, they feel confident that they are seen as a person who is strong or who knows what he wants. These consumer values are crucial in analyzing Hummer's fit within the SUV market.

GM must market the Hummer as a vehicle that will make the driver appear to be a person of high stature and class. These trends of high image and luxury appreciation are the main values that

Hummer's market segment possesses. Hummer must tailor its marketing plan towards the idea of a luxurious alternative to a sedan that will make you look like the man! Hummer must make its vehicle appeal to the high income individuals by making it a status symbol. Competition Hummer's most important competitors are other luxury SUV's, such as Range Rover, Lincoln, and Lexus. These manufacturers all have SUV's that are all in the upper echelon of the industry. They are all considered a status symbol in the SUV market. Hummer's disadvantages to this group of manufacturers are mostly in performance and ride quality. These other SUV's all have a more car-like ride, a faster 0-60mph time, and are comparable in luxury offerings such as TV's, navigation systems etc., and also has more passenger capacity (see exhibit A). Also, they are all slightly cheaper than the Hummer.

The way in which Hummer differentiates itself is in off-road performance, in which there is no substitute. Hummer is the leader in off-road capability because of the vehicle's military background. Newsgroups You might want to regularly monitor certain newsgroups on the web that will give you insight into consumer needs and wants. The fact that consumers are expecting something new from Hummer in the near future, and that consumers have financial concerns about a large vehicle such as Hummer. GM can use the consumers' wants to tailor their marketing plan towards them.

References

1. www.hummer.com
2. www.deja.com
3. www.free-essays-free-
4. en.wikipedia.org/wiki/Hummer

❁ ❁ ❁

2. Microsoft Corporation

Microsoft Corporation (NASDAQ: MSFT) (SEHK: 4338), or often just MS, is an American multinational computer technology corporation with 79,000 employees in 102 countries and global annual revenue of US $51.12 billion as of 2007. It develops, manufactures, licenses and supports a wide range of software products for computing devices. Headquartered in Redmond, Washington, USA, its best selling products are the Microsoft Windows operating system and the Microsoft Office suite of productivity software. These products have prominent positions in the desktop computer market; with market share estimates as high as 90% or more as of 2003 for Microsoft Office and 2006 for Microsoft Windows. One of Bill Gates' key visions is "to get a workstation running our software onto every desk and eventually in every home". Founded to develop and sell BASIC interpreters for the Altair 8800, Microsoft rose to dominate the home computer operating system market with MS-DOS in the mid-1980s. The company released an initial public offering (IPO) in the stock market, which, due to the ensuing rise of the stock price, has made four billionaires and an estimated 12,000 millionaires from Microsoft employees. Throughout its history the company has been the target of criticism for various reasons, including monopolistic business practices — both the U.S. Justice Department and the European Commission, among others, brought Microsoft to court for antitrust violations and software bundling.

Microsoft has footholds in other markets besides operating systems and office suites, with assets such as the MSNBC cable television network, the MSN Internet portal, and the Microsoft Encarta multimedia encyclopedia. The company also markets both computer hardware products such as the Microsoft mouse and home entertainment products such as the Xbox, Xbox 360, Zune and MSN TV. Known for what is generally described as a developer-centric business culture, Microsoft has historically given customer support over Usenet newsgroups and the World Wide Web, and awards Microsoft MVP status to volunteers who are deemed helpful in assisting the company's customers. The company's official website is one of the most visited on the Internet, receiving more than 2.4 million unique page views per day according to Alexa.com, who ranked the site 18th amongst all websites for traffic rank on September 12, 2007.

Background

1975–1985: Founding

Following the launch of the Altair 8800, Bill Gates called the creators of the new microcomputer, Micro Instrumentation and Telemetry Systems (MITS), offering to demonstrate an implementation of the BASIC programming language for the system. After the demonstration, MITS agreed to distribute Altair BASIC. Gates left Harvard University, moved to Albuquerque, New Mexico where MITS was located, and founded Microsoft there. The company's first international office was founded on November 1, 1978, in Japan, entitled "ASCII Microsoft" (now called "Microsoft Japan"). On January 1, 1979, the company moved from Albuquerque to a new home in Bellevue, Washington. Steve Ballmer joined the company on June 11, 1980, and later succeeded Bill Gates as CEO.

DOS (Disk Operating System) was the operating system that brought the company its first real success. On August 12, 1981, after negotiations with Digital Research failed, IBM awarded a contract to Microsoft to provide a version of the CP/M operating system, which was set to be used in the upcoming IBM Personal Computer (PC). For this deal, Microsoft purchased a CP/M clone called 86-DOS from Seattle Computer Products, which IBM renamed to PC-DOS. Later, the market saw a flood of IBM PC clones after Columbia Data Products successfully cloned the IBM BIOS, and by aggressively marketing MS-DOS to manufacturers of IBM-PC clones, Microsoft rose from a small player to one of the major software vendors in the home computer industry. The company expanded into new markets with the release of the Microsoft Mouse in 1983, as well as a publishing division named Microsoft Press.

1985–1995: OS/2 and Windows

In August 1985, Microsoft and IBM partnered in the development of a different operating system called OS/2. On November 20, 1985, Microsoft released its first retail version of Microsoft Windows, originally a graphical extension for its MS-DOS operating system. On March 13, 1986 the company went public with an IPO, with a starting initial offering price of $21.00 and ending at the first day of trading as at US $28.00. In 1987, Microsoft eventually released their first version of OS/2 to OEMs.

The Redmond Microsoft campus today includes more than 8 million square feet (approx. 750,000 m^2) and over 30,000 employees.

In 1989, Microsoft introduced its flagship office suite, Microsoft Office. This was a bundle of separate office productivity applications, such as Microsoft Word and Microsoft Excel. On May 22, 1990 Microsoft launched Windows 3.0. The new version of Microsoft's operating system boasted such new features as streamlined user interface graphics and improved protected mode capability for the Intel 386 processor; it sold over 100,000 copies in two weeks. Windows at the time generated more revenue for Microsoft than OS/2, and the company decided to move more resources from OS/2 to Windows. In the ensuing years, the popularity of OS/2 declined, and Windows quickly became the favored PC platform.

During the transition from MS-DOS to Windows, the success of Microsoft's product Microsoft Office allowed the company to gain ground on application-software competitors, such as WordPerfect and Lotus 1-2-3. According to The Register, Novell, an owner of WordPerfect for a time, alleged that Microsoft used its inside knowledge of the DOS and Windows kernels and of undocumented Application Programming Interface features to make Office perform better than its competitors. Eventually, Microsoft Office became the dominant business suite, with a market share far exceeding that of its competitors.

In 1993, Microsoft released Windows NT 3.1, a business operating system with the Windows 3.1 user interface but an entirely different kernel. In 1995, Microsoft released Windows 95, a new version of the company's flagship operating system which featured a completely new user interface, including a novel start button; more than a million copies of Microsoft Windows 95 were sold in the first four days after its release. The company also released its web browser, Internet Explorer, with the Windows 95 Plus! Pack in August 1995 and subsequent Windows versions.

1995–2005: Internet and Legal issues

In the mid-90s, Microsoft began to expand its product line into computer networking and the World Wide Web. On August 24, 1995, it launched a major online service, MSN (Microsoft Network), as a direct competitor to AOL. MSN became an umbrella service for Microsoft's online services. The company continued to branch out into new markets in 1996, starting with a joint venture with NBC to create a new 24/7 cable news station, MSNBC. Microsoft entered the personal digital assistant (PDA) market in November with Windows CE 1.0, a new built-from-scratch version of their flagship operating system, specifically designed to run on low-memory, low-performance machines, such as handhelds and other small computers. Later in 1997, Internet Explorer 4.0 was released for both Mac OS and Windows, marking the beginning of the takeover of the browser market from rival Netscape. In October, the Justice Department filed a motion in the Federal District Court in which they stated that Microsoft had violated an agreement signed in 1994, and asked the court to stop the bundling of Internet Explorer with Windows.

The year 1998 was significant in Microsoft's history, with Bill Gates appointing Steve Ballmer as president of Microsoft but remaining as Chair and CEO himself. The company released Windows 98, an update to Windows 95 that incorporated a number of Internet-focused features and support for new types of devices. On April 3, 2000, a judgment was handed down in the case of United States v. Microsoft, calling the company an "abusive monopoly" and forcing the company to split into two separate units. Part of this ruling was later overturned by a federal appeals court, and eventually settled with the U.S. Department of Justice in 2001.

In 2001, Microsoft released Windows XP, the first version that encompassed the features of both its business and home product lines. XP introduced a new graphical user interface, the first such change since Windows 95. Later, with the release of the Xbox Microsoft entered the multi-billion-dollar game console market dominated by Sony and Nintendo. Microsoft encountered more turmoil in March 2004 when antitrust legal action was brought against it by the European Union for abusing its market dominance (see European Union Microsoft antitrust case), eventually resulting in a judgment to produce new versions of its Windows XP platform—called Windows XP Home Edition N and Windows XP Professional N—that did not include its Windows Media Player.

2006 – Present

In 2006, Bill Gates announced a two year transition period from his role as Chief Software Architect, which would be taken by Ray Ozzie, and planned to remain the company's chairman, head of the Board of Directors and act as an adviser on key projects. As of December 2007, Windows Vista, released in January 2007, is Microsoft's latest operating system. Microsoft Office 2007 was released at the same time; its "Ribbon" user interface is a significant departure from its predecessors. On 1st February, 2008, Microsoft made an unsolicited bid to purchase the fully diluted outstanding shares of Yahoo for up to $44.6 billion, following the company's struggle against rival search-engine company, Google.

Corporate Structure

The company is run by a Board of Directors consisting of ten people, made up of mostly company outsiders (as is customary for publicly traded companies). Current members of the board of directors are: Steve Ballmer, James Cash, Jr., Dina Dublon, Bill Gates, Raymond Gilmartin, Reed Hastings, David Marquardt, Charles Noski, Helmut Panke, and Jon Shirley. The ten board members are elected every year at the annual shareholders' meeting, and those who do not get a majority of votes must submit a resignation to the board, which will subsequently choose whether or not to accept the resignation. There are five committees within the board which oversee more specific matters. These committees include the Audit Committee, which handles accounting issues with the company including auditing and reporting; the Compensation Committee, which approves compensation for the CEO and other employees of the company; the Finance Committee, which handles financial matters such as proposing mergers and acquisitions; the Governance and Nominating Committee, which handles various corporate matters including nomination of the board; and the Antitrust Compliance Committee, which attempts to prevent company practices from violating antitrust laws.

There are several other aspects to the corporate structure of Microsoft. For worldwide matters there is the Executive Team, made up of sixteen company officers across the globe, which is charged with various duties including making sure employees understand Microsoft's culture of business. The sixteen officers of the Executive Team include the Chairman and Chief Software Architect, the CEO, the General Counsel and Secretary, the CFO, senior and group vice presidents from the business units, the CEO of the Europe, the Middle East and Africa regions; and the heads of Worldwide Sales, Marketing and Services; Human Resources; and Corporate Marketing. In addition to the Executive Team there is also the Corporate Staff Council, which handles all major staff functions of the company, including approving corporate policies. The Corporate Staff Council is made up of employees from the Law and Corporate Affairs, Finance, Human Resources, Corporate Marketing, and Advanced Strategy and Policy groups at Microsoft. Other Executive Officers include the Presidents and Vice Presidents of the various product divisions, leaders of the marketing section, and the CTO, among others.

Stock

When the company debuted its IPO in March 13, 1986, the stock price was US $21.By the close of the first trading day, the stock had closed at twenty-eight dollars, equivalent to 9.7 cents when adjusted for the company's first nine splits. The initial close and ensuing rise in subsequent years made several Microsoft employees millions. The stock price peaked in 1999 at around US $119 (US $60.928 adjusting for splits). While the company has had nine stock splits, the first of which was in

September 18, 1987, the company did not start offering a dividend until January 16, 2003. The dividend for the 2003 fiscal year was eight cents per share, followed by a dividend of sixteen cents per share the subsequent year. The company switched from yearly to quarterly dividends in 2005, for eight cents a share per quarter with a special one-time payout of three dollars per share for the second quarter of the fiscal year.

Around 2003 the stock price began a slow descent. Despite the company's ninth split on February 2, 2003 and subsequent increases in dividend payouts, the price of Microsoft's stock continued to fall for the next several years.

Diversity

In 2005, Microsoft received a 100% rating in the Corporate Equality Index from the Human Rights Campaign, a ranking of companies by how progressive the organization deems their policies concerning LGBT (lesbian, gay, bisexual and transsexual) employees. Partly through the work of the Gay and Lesbian Employees at Microsoft (GLEAM) group, Microsoft added gender expression to its anti-discrimination policies in April 2005, and the Human Rights Campaign upgraded Microsoft's Corporate Equality Index from its 86% rating in 2004 to its current 100% rating.

In April 2005, Microsoft received wide criticism for withdrawing support from Washington state's H.B. 1515 bill that would have extended the state's current anti-discrimination laws to people with alternate sexual orientations. Microsoft was accused of bowing to pressure from local evangelical pastor Ken Hutcherson who met with a senior Microsoft executive and threatened a national boycott of Microsoft's products. Microsoft also revealed they were paying evangelical conservative Ralph Reed's company Century Strategies a $20,000 monthly fee. Over 2,000 employees signed a petition asking Microsoft to reinstate support for the bill. Under harsh criticism from both outside and inside the company's walls, Microsoft decided to support the bill again in May 2005.

Microsoft hires many foreign workers as well as domestic ones, and is an outspoken opponent of the cap on H1B visas, which allow companies in the United States to employ certain foreign workers. Bill Gates claims the cap on H1B visas make it difficult to hire employees for the company, stating "I'd certainly get rid of the H1B cap."

Logos and Sogans

In 1987, Microsoft adopted its current logo, the so-called "Pacman Logo" designed by Scott Baker. According to the March 1987 Computer Reseller News Magazine, "The new logo, in Helvetica italic typeface, has a slash between the o and s to emphasize the "soft" part of the name and convey motion and speed." Dave Norris, a Microsoft employee, ran an internal joke campaign to save the old logo, which was green, in all uppercases, and featured a fanciful letter O, nicknamed the blibbet, but it was discarded.

Microsoft's logo "Your potential. Our passion." tagline below the main corporate name is based on the slogan Microsoft had as of 2008. In 2002, the company started using the logo in the United States and eventually started a TV campaign with the slogan, changed from the previous tagline of "Where do you want to go today?"

Microsoft "blibbet" logo, used until 1987.

Microsoft logo with the 1994–2002 slogans "Where do you want to go today?"

Microsoft logo as of 2008, with the slogan "Your potential. Our passion."

Microsoft Community Affairs

Microsoft Community Affairs administers all of Microsoft's community investment programs.

Founded in 1983, Microsoft Community Affairs was one of the first corporate community investment programs in the high-tech industry. Today, Microsoft is the largest contributor in the high-tech industry and one of the largest among all businesses in the United States. Microsoft employees give more per person than any other company's employees. Last year, Microsoft donated more than US$68 million in cash and $331 million in software to nonprofit organizations throughout the world. Ultimately, Microsoft believes that by providing training and tools, we can partner to create social and economic opportunities that can transform communities and help people realize their potential. Microsoft's community investment efforts are focused on increasing digital inclusion and bringing the benefits of technology and technology skills to a billion more people by 2015.

Learn about Microsoft Unlimited Potential – Community Technology Skills Program designed to help broaden digital inclusion and aid global workforce development by providing technology skills through community technology centers (CTCs). From 2003 to 2007, Unlimited Potential described a community investment program supporting community technology centers. Beginning April 19, Microsoft Unlimited Potential is used to describe Microsoft's expanded, integrated and accelerated long-term global business and citizenship commitment to bring the benefits of technology to those who currently receive little or no benefits from technology. The work that Microsoft has done together with NGOs and IGOs over the years has laid the foundation for this broader corporate commitment to bring technology to the next five billion people, with a goal of reaching the first billion by 2015. Learn more about Microsoft's other community investment programs, which focus on improving the quality of life for underserved individuals around the world through monetary grants, software, technology solutions, curriculum donations, and employee volunteer hours.

References

1. www.business-strategy
2. www.microsoft.com
3. www.en.wikipedia.org/wiki/Microsoft

❄ ❄ ❄

3. Toyota Corporation

Toyota Corporation is a Japanese automaker. Toyota is presently the world's second largest automaker and the largest Japanese automaker. In terms of name recognition, Toyota is the only car manufacturer to appear in the top 10 of the. Toyota is headquartered in Toyota and Nagoya in Aichi Prefecture and in Tokyo. It also provides financial services through its division Toyota Financial Services and also creates robots besides automobiles. The company along with the original Toyota Industries form bulk of the Toyota Group, one of the largest conglomerates in the world.

Toyota's mission has always been to provide clean and safe products. Thus, the company has positioned the environment as one of its most important issues and has been working toward creating a prosperous society and a world that is comfortable to live in. With this goal in mind, Toyota has been actively developing various new technologies from the perspective of achieving energy security and diversifying energy sources, which is necessitated by the dwindling supply of petroleum resources.

Background

In 1933, Toyoda Automatic Loom Works created a new division devoted to the production of automobiles under the direction of the founder's son, Kiichiro Toyoda. Kiichiro Toyoda had traveled to Europe and the United States in 1929 to investigate automobile production, and had begun researching gasoline-powered engines in 1930.Toyoda Automatic Loom Works was encouraged to develop Automobile production by the Japanese government, which needed domestic vehicle production partly due to the worldwide money shortage and partly due to the war with China. In 1934, the division produced its first Type A Engine, which was used in the first Model A1 passenger car in May 1935 and the G1 truck in August 1935. Production of the Model AA passenger car started in 1936. Early vehicles bear a striking resemblance to the Dodge Power Wagon and Chevrolet, with some parts actually interchanging with their American originals.

Toyota Motor Co. was established as an independent and separate company in 1937. Although the founding family's name is Toyoda, the company name was changed in order to signify the separation of the founders' work life from home life, to simplify the pronunciation, and to give the company a happy beginning.

Toyota Today

Toyota has grown to a large multinational corporation from where it started and expanded to different worldwide markets and countries by becoming the largest seller of cars in the beginning of 2007, the most profitable automaker ($11 billion in 2006) along with increasing sales in, among other countries, the United States. Its subsidiary, Toyota Financial Services sells financing and participates in other lines of business. Toyota brands include Scion and Lexus and the corporation is part of the Toyota Group. Toyota also owns majority stakes in Daihatsu, and 8.7% of Fuji Heavy Industries, which manufactures Subaru vehicles. They also acquired 5.9% of Isuzu Motors Ltd., on November 7, 2006 and will be introducing Isuzu diesel technology into their products.

Toyota has introduced new technologies including one of the first mass-produced hybrid gas-electric vehicles, of which it says it has sold 1 million globally (2007-06-07), Advanced Parking Guidance System (automatic parking), a four-speed electronically controlled automatic with buttons for power and economy shifting, and an eight-speed automatic transmission. Toyota produced Lexus and Scion automobiles, consistently ranks near the top in certain quality and reliability surveys.

In 2005, Toyota, combined with its half-owned subsidiary Daihatsu Motor Company, produced 8.54 million vehicles, about 500,000 fewer than the number produced by GM that year. Toyota has a large market share in the United States, but a small market share in Europe. It's also sells vehicles in Africa and is a market leader in Australia. Due to its Daihatsu subsidiary it has significant market shares in several fast-grc wing Southeast Asian countries.

In the first three months of 2007, Toyota together with its half-owned subsidiary Daihatsu reported number one sales of 2.348 million units. Toyota's brand sales had risen 9.2% largely on demand for Corolla and Camry sedans. The difference in performance was largely attributed to surging demand for fuel-efficient vehicles. In November 2006, Toyota Motor Manufacturing Texas added a facility in San Antonio. Toyota has experienced quality problems and was reprimanded by the government in Japan for its recall practices. Toyota currently maintains over 16% of the US market share and is listed second only to GM in terms of volume. Toyota Century is the official state car of the Japanese imperial family, namely for the Emperor of Japan Akihito.

Worldwide Presence

Toyota is largest global company in the automobile sector after GM. Toyota has factories all over the world, manufacturing or assembling vehicles for local markets. Toyota has manufacturing or assembly plants in Japan, Australia, Canada, Indonesia, Poland, South Africa, Turkey, the United Kingdom, the United States, France, Brazil, and more recently Pakistan, India, Argentina, Czech Republic, Mexico, Malaysia, Thailand, China, Vietnam, Venezuela, the Philipines, and Russia.

Toyota - Global Company

In January 2004, leading global automobile company and Japan's number one automaker, Toyota Motor Corporation (Toyota), replaced Ford Motors (Ford), as the world's second largest automobile manufacturer; Ford had been in that spot for over seven decades. In 2003, Toyota sold 6.78 million vehicles worldwide while Ford's worldwide sales amounted to 6.72 million vehicles (General Motors, the world's largest car manufacturer sold 8.60 million vehicles).

According to reports, while Toyota's market share in the US increased from 10.4% in 2002 to 11.2% in 2003, Ford's declined from 21.5% to 20.8% during the same period. Reaching the No.2 slot was a major achievement for Toyota, which had begun as a spinning and weaving company in 1918. Ford was reportedly plagued by high labor costs, quality-control problems, lack of new designs and innovations, and a weak economy during the early 21st century, which made it vulnerable to competition. Toyota, aided by its new product offerings and strong financial muscle had successfully used this scenario to surpass Ford and affect a dramatic increase in its sales figures. In November 2003, Toyota announced its financial results for the half-year ended September 30, 2003.

The company reported a 23% increase in net income (as compared to the corresponding period of the previous year) to $4.4 billion on revenues of $69.7 billion. This took Toyota way ahead of World's top three automobile makers (at that time) by sales, General Motors (GM), Ford Motors (Ford) and Daimler Chrysler. Its market capitalization of $110 billion (on November 05, 2003) was more than the combined market capitalization of these three players.

Given the fact that in 2003, these top three companies were struggling to maintain their sales and profitability targets, Toyota's performance was termed remarkable by industry observers. Toyota had emerged as a formidable player in almost all the major automobile markets in the world. Interestingly, one of its strongest markets was the US, the world's largest automobile market and the home turf of Ford and GM. Toyota had emerged as a strong foreign player in Europe as well, with a 4.4% market share. In China, which the company had identified as a strategic market for growth in the early 21st century, it had a 1.5% market share. Analysts attributed Toyota's growing sales across the world to its aggressive globalization efforts that began in the mid-1990s.

The company constantly strived to ensure that each of its market segments - Japan, North America, and Europe and other markets generated one-third of the annual sales. This goal was at the heart of Toyota's three globalization programs

- New Global Business Plan (1995-1998)
- Global Vision 2005 (1996-2005)
- Global Vision 2010 (2002-2010)

In the light of Toyota's intensifying globalization efforts, Toyota's competitors themselves stated that Toyota could not be taken lightly.

Early Globalization Efforts

In June 1995, Toyota announced the "New Global Business Plan", aimed at advancing localization (of production) and increasing imports (through collaboration with foreign automobile companies) over a three year period. A major objective of this plan was to increase Toyota's offshore production capacity to 2 million units by 1998. As part of the localization efforts, Toyota focused on increasing overseas production significantly by establishing new plants and expanding the capacity of the existing plants

Toyota also came up with a long-term global business vision in June 1996, named the "Global Vision 2005". The major components of this were, asserting a competitive edge in technology and accelerating globalization, while sustaining market leadership in Japan, by reclaiming its above 40% market share. As part of its globalization efforts, the company focused more on increasing the production of automobiles in the most demanded areas.

The company's approach is developed further in Toyota's **"Global Vision 2010"**, which was adopted in April 2002 and proposes a series of long-term policies on the theme of "Innovation into the Future". It guides management in its response to long-term social changes, combining consideration for the environment, the benefit to customers of value-added products and the encouragement of employees through shared prosperity and social involvement.

The Second Phase of Globalization

Toyota decided to focus more on localization it believed that by doing so, Toyota would be able to provide its customers with the products they needed, where they needed them. This was expected to help build mutually benefiting, long-term relationships with local suppliers and fulfill Toyota's commitments to local labor and communities. It defined globalization as 'global localization.' Therefore, besides focusing on increasing the number of manufacturing centers and expanding the sales networks worldwide, Toyota also focused on localizing design, development, purchasing in every region and country.

The Globalization Pay-Off

Toyota was present in almost all the major segments of the automobile market that included small cars, luxury sedans, full-sized pickup trucks, SUVs, small trucks and crossover vehicles. The global vehicle production increases by 3.3 times since the early 1960s, Toyota's production had increased by 38 times. As a result of its localization initiatives, Toyota had 45 manufacturing plants in 26 countries and regions by this time, and sold vehicles in 160 countries.

Toyota seemed to be well on its way to achieving its globalization goals - worldwide sales of 6.57 million units in fiscal 2004; sales of 2.12 million units in North America by 2004; a 5% market share (800,000 units sales) in Europe by 2004; a 15% market share in the global market and a 10% market share in China by 2010. Analysts felt that the following factors were helping the company in its quest to become a truly global automobile major:

- Strong financial condition
- Globally efficient production system
- Unique corporate culture, and
- Ability to develop product range that meets the unique needs and desires of customers of different regions.

Purchasing and Manufacturing Globally

T..yota development, procurement and production systems are precisely aligned to client needs ... limitations. Their systems are built around the global ...rer. They satisfy the locally. They have to develop business relations with new parts suppliers, and this requires an excellent knowledge of quality standards, pricing and productivity. It also requires the ability to conduct tough negotiations. Toyota excellent and experienced staff has what it takes. Their overseas operations harmonize with the global objectives of automotive manufacturers. This creates opportunities for them to form global links with new parts suppliers.

Technology and Expertise Transfers to Manufacturing Operations Overseas

When pursuing a global strategy, a Japanese corporation must take techniques and expertises's developed in Japan and transfer them to its operations abroad. Overseas business operations can be successful only if the company's expertise, in everything from development to production, is linked and applied locally. The global manufacture of the same car model is a new development, as Toyota Motor Corporation's Corolla and Camry, and the new Innovative International Multi-purpose Vehicle (IMV) show. To adapt to this changing situation, we have established highly efficient local overseas operations encompassing all phases from procurement and production preparation to the actual production.

Interaction

Expertise passes to the next generation of local industry leaders. It is very important that a global manufacturer understand the cultures of the countries it operates in. Toyota now has a network of more than 50 overseas bases, and an overseas staff of more than 10,000. Their Japanese staff posted overseas imparts their skills and knowledge of quality control and business management to local personnel, and this creates greater opportunities for success when developing new projects. In addition, this interaction with local staff gives the Japanese staff the international management skills and advanced engineering know-how they will need in the future.

Three-stage Development Strategy

The Japanese carmaker was a latecomer to the China market. Within its global strategies, North America is the top priority, followed by its home country Japan. China has been included in Toyota's top development strategy in recent years with its first China-made VIOS sedan produced in Tianjin in October 2002. Toyota is going for expansion in China market and planning to introduce high-end brands. Considering China is an immature auto market, the company has adopted three-stage development strategies

- Establish a local sales network.
- Launch brand promotions to build auto parts manufacturing bases.
- Establish joint ventures (JVs) with local players and produce automobiles.

Strategy of Uniqueness

Toyota's new goal is to conquer the German automobile market, which is probably the most attractive one in Europe. Unfortunately Germany is also the home of DaimlerChrysler, BMW and Volkswagen, which will make it hard for Toyota to get a stake in that market, as they have already failed to do so during the last two decades. Attempts to sell their Lexus models right in the financial district of Frankfurt have bitterly failed in the past. As the home of some of the most successful automobile manufacturers, the German people are a unique bunch and their culture is embossed by the past development of the automotive industry. So, the Toyota planning to coming up with the latest technology, the engineering power, the high quality and the attractive design especially for the German cars.

Only Business Strategy, No Technology Strategy

Toyota has only business strategy no technology strategy. It is built around continuously searching for better ways to improve its manufacturing and business processes, and ultimately achieve customer ... Information technology often plays the role of bringing those processes to life, be it using new software to shorten the cycle from accepting a customer order or monitoring equipment on the factory floor to prevent breakdowns and defects.

Internal Approach and Strategies

Quality and Comfort

It is result of Toyota's better engineering system, using simple concepts like chief engineers with real responsibility for products, concurrent and simultaneous engineering practices, and sophisticated knowledge capture methods.

Working with suppliers: Toyota is getting brilliant results and lower prices from American suppliers like Delphi while also giving suppliers adequate profit margins. This is done by relentlessly analyzing every step in their shared design and production process to take out the waste and put in the quality.

Management cultures: Toyota has a brilliant job of making one person responsible for every key business process. A free environment naturally emerges, but not because everyone has received cultural training to spur teamwork. Rather, if ordinary people are put in a great business process they become great team players.

Customer Satisfaction: Toyota's has created a new and better customer experience. Customers cheerfully pay more for the car and the service and then come back for more cars because they love the treatment.

Conclusion

Toyota as global company is becomes the largest car manufacturer in the world due to its unique business practices and strategies. Toyota mainly emphasis on the culture of the area in which they are working this leads to successful achievement of their objectives and goals. By implementation of new strategy **Global Vision 2010** and their best **Knowledge practices,** they are able to become the world's largest manufacturer of cars in all aspects. To summarize, the Toyota Way is based on two main objectives:

- Continuous Improvement (Kaizen)
- Respect for People.

These main objectives, in turn, are each reflected in the five key values that make up the Toyota Way:

- Challenge
- Kaizen (continuous improvement)
- Genchi Genbutsu (going to the source to make correct decisions)
- Respect
- Teamwork

References

1. **www.toyota.com**
2. **www.en.wikipedia.org/wiki/Toyota**
3. **www.icmrindia.org/casestudies**
4. **www.business-strategy- case.blogspot.com**

Articles

1. Vision & Strategy
2. (http://www.toyota-europe.com/images/Chapter_1.pdf)
3. Toyota Info (http://www.triple-rrr.com/pdf/toyota.pdf)

❄❄❄

4. Tata Consultancy Services Ltd.

Tata Consultancy Services Limited (TCS), is an IT services, business solutions, and outsourcing organization that deliver real results to global businesses, ensuring a level of certainty. TCS offers a consulting-led, integrated portfolio of IT and IT enabled services delivered through its unique Global Network TM Delivery Model, recognized as the benchmark of excellence in software development. While the phenomenon of the global delivery of IT services has only recently captured the world's imagination, TCS pioneered this business model in 1968 as a means to provide increased value to their customers.

As a part of the Tata Group, India's largest industrial conglomerate, TCS has over 94,000 of the world's best trained IT consultants in 47 countries. The company generated consolidated revenues of US $4.3 billion for fiscal year ended 31 March 2007 and is listed on the National Stock Exchange and Bombay Stock Exchange in India.

TCS have more than 35 years of expertise in enterprise consulting, complex applications development, and infrastructure services. TCS also brings a global perspective with local execution through its more than 150 offices in 30 countries truly, a global footprint. Being a best-in-class global company means more than just using technology.

Background

Tata Consultancy Services was established in 1968. It started off as a division of the Tata Group, Tata Computer Centre, whose main business was to provide computer services to other group companies. However, the potential of computerization and computer services was realized early on, and an electrical engineer from the Tata Electric Companies, Fakir Chand Kohli, was brought in as the first General Manager. Soon after, the company was named Tata.

TCS's first software export project was undertaken in 1974 when it converted the Hospital Information System from Burroughs Medium Systems COBOL to Burroughs Small Systems COBOL. This project was carried out entirely in TCS Mumbai on the ICL 1903 Computer. In 1980, TCS and a sister Tata firm accounted for 63% of the Indian software industry exports, $4 million shared by 21 firms. In 1984, TCS set up an office in the Santa Cruz Export Processing Zone (SEEPZ) Mumbai.

The early 1990s saw a tremendous surge in TCS's business, which also resulted in a massive recruitment drive by the company. In early and mid-1990s, TCS re-invented itself to become a software products company. In the late 1990s, to accelerate its revenue growth, TCS decided to employ a three-pronged strategy - developing new products with high revenue earning potential, tapping domestic and other fast growing markets and focusing on inorganic growth through mergers & acquisitions. In late 1998, the company decided to concentrate on new revenue opportunities including Y2K and Euro conversion. E-business was a major area of focus in the late 1990s. TCS started a project aimed at removing illiteracy in India with a pilot project in Andhra Pradesh. In 2001, Tata Consultancy Services (TCS) commissioned the latest 64-bit zSeries, eServer from IBM, there by becoming the first organization in the Asian and South Asia region to adopt the latest technology in mainframe computing. In 2004, TCS became a public listed company.

Worldwide Presence

TCS is large global company in the IT services. Toyota has branches all over the world like India, South Africa, China, Japan, Malaysia, Saudi Arabia, Singapore, South Korea, Taiwan, UAE, Australia, Europe, Canada, Mexico, USA. Thus, TCS has the vast presence all over the world.

TCS - Global Company

A unique aspect of the firm's style of functioning was that despite being an IT company, it was run along the lines of a manufacturing concern, with a factory approach. The company managed its new recruits similar to how a manufacturing concern managed the inflow of raw material. TCS looked after its work force like a manufacturing company dealt with its inventories. The company allocated its work force to its branches spread across the world, similar to a retailing company managing its stores.

Concept of Offshore Development Centers

TCS introduced the concept of Offshore Development Centers, where TCS engineers based in India worked on projects for clients abroad and saved costs for both TCS and its clients. By consistently undertaking and performing good quality jobs for clients at a fraction of the cost they would otherwise have incurred, TCS put India on the global map and became a premier IT outsourcing destination for companies in the West, particularly the US. eTCS is an effort in that direction. The aim of eTCS is to reduce cycle time, leverage and provide better employee experience.

The company is exploring places like Hungary and China to set up offshore development centers. The number of firms using offshore providers will grow offshore budgets more than double. The offshore services won't be just for upgrades and maintenance, but also for strategic IT activities like application architecture and design. TCS has a total of 25 offshore development centres across the globe.

The Growth Strategy

In the late 1990s, to accelerate its revenue growth, TCS decided to employ a three-pronged strategy. This involved developing new products with high revenue earning potential, tapping domestic & other fast growing markets and focusing on inorganic growth through mergers and acquisitions.

Growth strategies adopted by TCS are as follows:

- Assist enterprises worldwide to achieve Business Transformation by Leveraging on TCS Industry and Technology Expertise.
- **Strong Financials:** Build a robust organic top line Revenue of USD 600 million by FY10.
- **Business Links:** Develop strong business links with Global 2000 companies to generate downstream revenue opportunities.
- **TCS Integration:** Tightly integrate Think-Build-Operate services of TCS using Consulting as a front-end strong.
- Establish TCS as a Top-of-Mind Global Consulting Brand where Business and IT Meets.

Figure

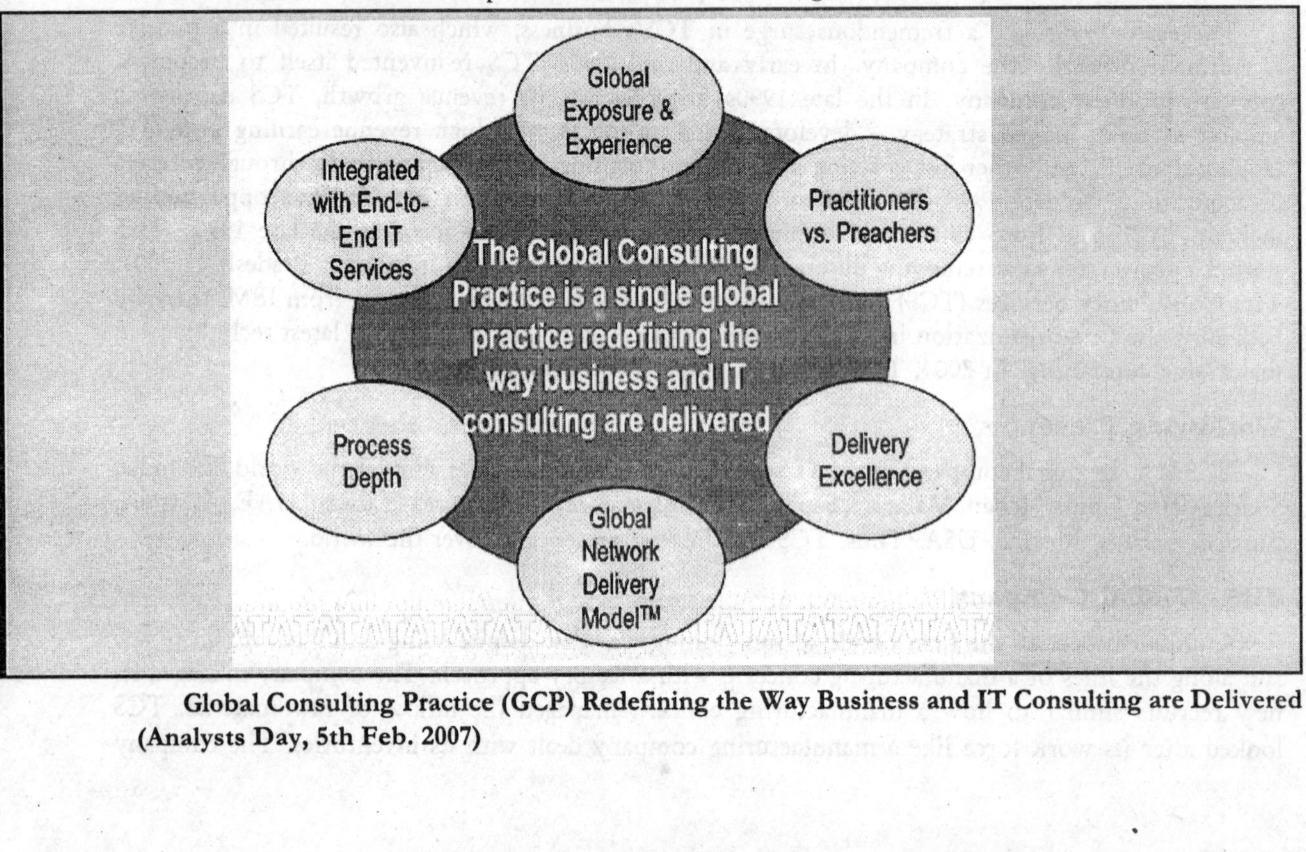

Global Consulting Practice (GCP) Redefining the Way Business and IT Consulting are Delivered (Analysts Day, 5th Feb. 2007)

• Adopting the Global Network Delivery Model to Position TCS in the Consulting Space.

Figure

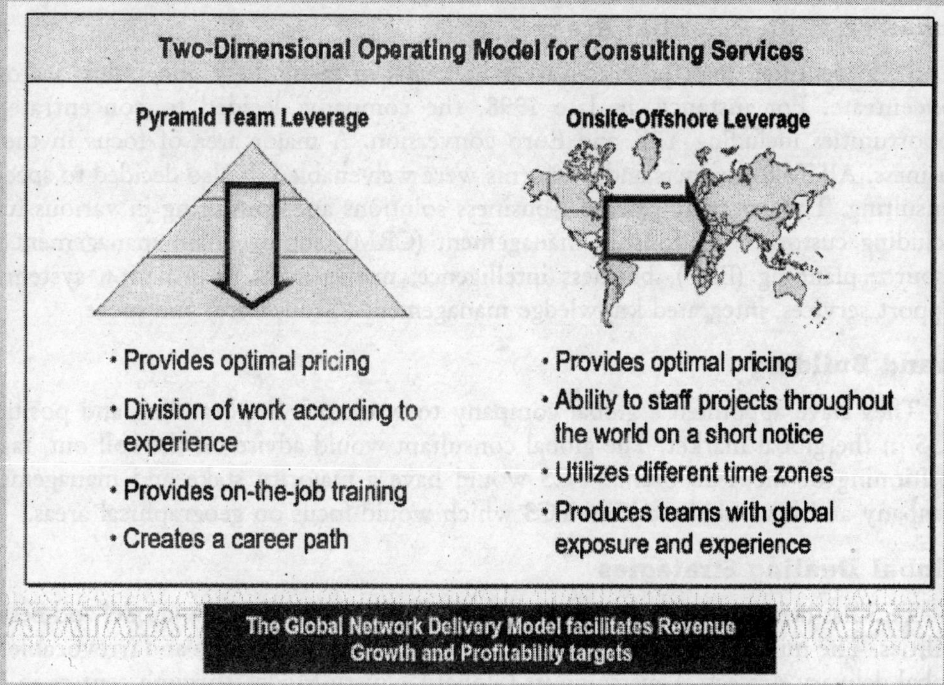

Global Consulting Practice (GCP) Redefining the Way Business and IT Consulting are Delivered (Analysts Day, 5th Feb. 2007)

• TCS is Rapidly Expanding its Consulting Capabilities across all dimensions.

Figure

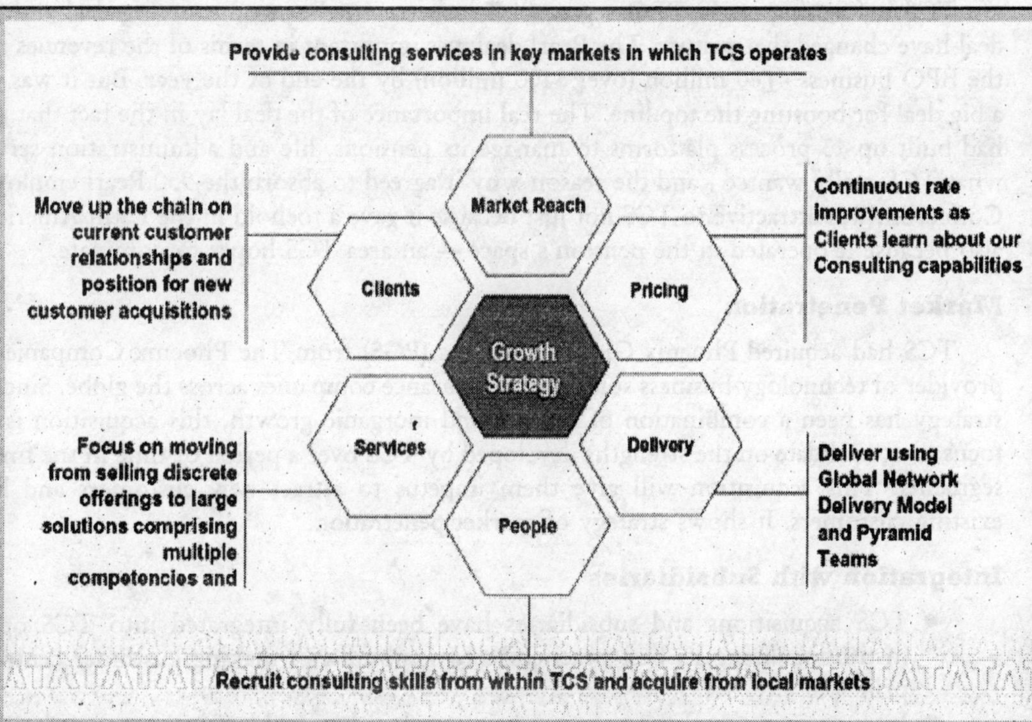

Global Consulting Practice (GCP) Redefining the Way Business and IT Consulting are Delivered (Analysts Day, 5th Feb. 2007)

TCS efforts in recent years in aggressively pursuing its growth strategy helped it script one of India's greatest success stories and earned the company worldwide recognition.

Focus on High Potential Areas

TCS identified high potential areas in terms of technology and industries on which it would concentrate. For instance, in late 1998, the company decided to concentrate on new revenue opportunities including Y2K and Euro conversion. A major area of focus in the late 1990s was e-business. All TCS products and platforms were web-enabled. It also decided to specialize in e-business consulting. The company offered e-business solutions and consulting in various functional processes including customer relationship management (CRM), supply chain management (SCM), enterprise resource planning (ERP), business intelligence, management information systems (MIS), customer support services, integrated knowledge management (Groupware) and more.

Brand Building

They have appointed a global company to work out the branding and positioning strategy for TCS in the global market. The global consultant would advise on the roll out, tagline, graphics and positioning of the TCS brand. TCS would have a majority stake and management control of the company and it would be a Mini-TCS which would focus on geographical areas.

Global Dealing Strategies

TCS has been investing continuously to build its global delivery model and best-in-class execution abilities. The milestone engagement with ABN Amro is a complete and irrevocable validation of their global delivery strategy. Leveraging its Global Delivery Model, through centers in Latin America and Hungary, TCS will manage a major part of ABN AMRO's Application Support and Enhancement services for its operations in the Netherlands, Brazil as well as its Private Client Business globally. In addition, TCS will also provide Application Development for the Dutch Bank as one of the top five preferred suppliers and deliver ABN-AMRO's Strategic Banking Platform.

TCS is focusing in the BPO segment. But the recent Pearl outsourcing deal and the Comicrom deal have changed that picture. The Pearl deal was important in terms of the revenues it would add to the BPO business - £60 million (over $100 million) by the end of the year. But it was more than just a big deal for boosting the top line. The real importance of the deal lay in the fact that the Pearl group had built up 13 process platforms to manage its pensions, life and administration services. This was what TCS really wanted - and the reason why it agreed to absorb the 950 Pearl employees. Similarly, Comicrom was attractive to TCS not just because it gave a toehold in the Latin American market but also because it operated in the pension's space — an area TCS hopes to dominate.

Market Penetration

TCS had acquired Phoenix Global Solutions (PGS) from The Phoenix Companies Inc. PGS is a provider of technology-business solutions to insurance companies across the globe. Since, their growth strategy has been a combination of organic and inorganic growth, this acquisition is in line with a focus to consolidate on the strengths developed by TCS over a period of time in the financial industry segments. This acquisition will give them impetus to attract new customers and help grow our existing customers. It shows strategy of market penetration.

Integration with Subsidiaries

- TCS acquisitions and subsidiaries have been fully integrated into TCS operations. It is institutionalizing its best practices across subsidiaries making customer centricity a guiding principle.
- Intra-organizational synergies are being explored to enable joint go to market strategies and a common face to the customer to the advantage of all concerned.
- TCS is strengthening its domain-specific offerings and end-to-end solutions that will lead to higher value contracts.

- TCS has taken steps to increase its visibility across the globe through intense marketing and branding campaigns.
- They have unexplored opportunities in Eastern Europe, Russia and China that will become potential markets or global delivery centeres.

Expanding Presence in Emerging market

- New strategy to diversify revenues and risks, expand business in emerging markets and explore new sources of talent.
- New Unit will focus on emerging markets across Eastern Europe, Middle East, Africa and Latin America.

In order to further increase their market leadership in emerging markets and build a strong franchise in these geographies, they are setting up a new strategic business unit to help leverage new opportunities in Eastern Europe

Service Level Enhancement

TCS substantially reduced policy issuance and claim management time for a large export insurer. The recommended online workflow-based policy processing system provides the sales force quicker access to customer and product information.

Risk Minimization Strategies

TCS recommended an end-to-end security solution, and implemented a systematic risk identification and remediation process to various organizations in the world.

Other Strategies of TCS

- Optimize information worker infrastructure
- Enable teams to work better together
- Improve business insight
- Support compliance and governance
- Improve business process management
- Enable enterprise information accessibility
- Accelerate business solutions and services
- Optimize core infrastructure
- Enable mobile workforce.

Challenges

- Develop profitable customer relationships.
- Improve operations.
- Reduce costs.
- Build and strengthen connections to partners and suppliers.
- Create innovative products and services.

Conclusion

In today's fast-moving business environment it is critical to identify emerging opportunities and take decisive action. TCS eliminates boundaries between their people and the information they need empowers them to anticipate and respond to change. TCS pioneered the Indian software industry and has played a seminal role in the global acceptance of the Indian software capabilities. The way forward for TCS is to become a complete solutions company and provide higher value solutions to its customers. Growth avenues through inorganic means via mergers and acquisitions also have to be explored to complement their capabilities and plug gaps in our portfolio of offerings. Being a best-in-class global company means more than just using technology. It means empowering your people. It means developing profitable customer relationships, improving operations and strengthening deep connections with partners and suppliers.

References

1. www.tcs.com
2. www.download.microsoft.com/download/Microsoft_Alliance_Brochure.pdf
3. www.abhi5hek.blogspot.com/2005/11/tcs-awake-and-hungry.html
4. www.cbronline.com/article

Articles

1. Development of a globally integrated product lifecycle management led engineering strategy - http://www.tcs.com/eis/japanese/servicelines/
2. Consulting with TCS - http://tcs.com/investors/pdf/Consulting.pdf

❀ ❀ ❀

5. Bharat Sanchar Nigam Ltd.

India's telecom market has grown rapidly in the last few years...

- Revenues - USD 19.5 billion (2006)
- CAGR (FY 2002-06) - 21%
- Have doubled in last 3 years
- Subscribers ~ 160 million (Aug 2006)
- CAGR (FY 2002-06) - 38 %
- Nearly quadrupled since FY 02
- 5-6 million being added every month
- Tele-Density 14.8 (Aug 2006)
- Has doubled in 3 years
- Target set for 2007 under NTP 1999 achieved during FY 2005.

India is the third largest market for telecommunication industry in the world after China and US, adding close to seven million subscribers every month. With a tele density below 20%, telecommunications has huge potential market in India. Gone are the days when Public Sector Undertakings (PSU) was considered to be slow moving. Bharat Sanchar Nigam Ltd. (BSNL) is the largest Public Sector Undertaking in India for providing telecom infrastructure and services. Its net worth is above US$ 10 Billion and its annual turnover is of the order of US $ 4.6 Billion. More than 85% of the market share of the telecom sector is with BSNL.

The history of BSNL is linked with the beginning of Telecom in India. In 19th century and for almost entire 20th century, the Telecom in India was operated as a Government of India wing. Earlier it was part of erstwhile Post & Telegraph Department (P&T). In 1975 the Department of Telecom (DoT) was separated from P&T. Presently, there is an intense competition in Indian Telecom sector and various Telco's are rolling out attractive schemes and are providing good customer services. However, BSNL being legacy operator and its conversion from a Government Department earns lot of criticism for its poor customer service. Although in recent past, there have been tremendous improvement in working of BSNL but still it is much below the industry's expectations.

BSNL's future plans include 100% expansion of telecom network within a few years and introduction of multi-service platform for range of new services. Bharat Sanchar Nigam Ltd. (BSNL) has added more fuel to the telecom market and accelerated the mad rush for numbers by announcing the target of 36 million subscribers per year. As of now the entire Industry is adding close to 7 millions every month, BSNL's plan to capture about half (3 millions) the total acquisition speaks the aggression. And as the punch line "Connecting India" goes, BSNL will connect rural India to the world and has accordingly bagged about 80 per cent of the Department of Telecom's Rs. 2,500 crore, rural mobile telephony projects for which bids were invited by the Universal Service Obligation Fund to build about 8,000 mobile towers.

Vision: "To become the largest telecom Service Provider in Asia".

Mission

- To provide world class State-of-art technology telecom services to its customers on demand at competitive prices.
- To provide world class telecom infrastructure in its area of operation and to contribute to the growth of the country's economy.

Contribution

- BSNL is committed to provide quality Telecom Services at affordable price to the citizens of the remotest part of the Country.
- Strive to provide a balance between the provision of universal service to all uncovered areas, including the rural areas, and the provision of high-level services capable of meeting the needs of the country's economy.

- They plan to extend broadband coverage to 1,500 cities/towns and 20,000 villages during the current year.
- An ambitious project is being taken up to deploy 1.8 million ports for providing broadband connectivity to rural areas through wire line as well as wireless techniques.
- Multiply services over broadband connections have already been launched in some cities and they plan to roll out these services in a number of important cities progressively. Through a single connection, the customers will have the freedom to talk, surf internet and watch cable TV or video simultaneously. Facilities like online gaming etc., are also available over broadband.
- BSNL has planned to expand its fixed wireless (WLL) network to provide telephone connections on demand. Expansion of WLL network would also help faster rollout of services in rural areas.
- BSNL has formulated new schemes to provide free Centrex facility to Corporate Customers/ Commercially Customers/Multi-storey complexes/Residential Housing Societies etc., where customers do not have to pay for the cost of the equipment.

Cellular Mobile Telephone Services in BSNL

Cellular mobile telephone services (CMTS) in BSNL is based on the Global System for Mobile communication (GSM) Technology. Though the erstwhile Department of Telecom Services (DTS) of the Department of Telecommunications (DoT) was given a licence in February 2000 for operation of CMTS in the country, BSNL could commence countrywide large-scale rollout of post-paid (CellOne) and prepaid (Excel) CMTS only in October 2002.

CMTS systems for 297 lakh lines at a cost of Rs. 10,759 crore were procured by BSNL under phases-I to IV of its 'India Mobile Personal Communication Services' (IMPCS) project. BSNL installed systems having equipped capacity of 194 lakh lines up to March 2006 and the capacity utilization as of March 2006 was 89 per cent. BSNL Board initially approved (January 2005) a major expansion of CMTS by 641 lakh lines under phase-V of the IMPCS project. The process of selection of suppliers had still not been completed as of September 2006, though the project was to be completed by December 2007.

Since the commencement of CMTS, a total of 72 lakh connections had been closed due to surrender by the customers or disconnections by BSNL due to non-payment of dues by the customers. 20 lakh connections were closed in just four months. As of March 2006, BSNL's share in the country's total CMTS customer base of 692 lakh customers was 25 per cent. BSNL suffered financial losses due to inadequate customer care and deficiencies in billing and collection of revenue. Besides, the deficiencies in planning, creation of infrastructure, procurement, installation and commissioning of systems and network coverage, delays in rectification of faults during AMC and warranty were also noticed. BSNL also could not achieve the quality of service benchmarks prescribed by TRAI, which had adversely affected the customer base.

In order to become the leader in providing CMTS, it not only needs to strengthen and improve its planning and procurement procedures but also the systems for customer care, billing and collection of revenue. The quality of service needs further improvement through better network coverage and customer care to achieve the benchmarks prescribed by TRAI. In pursuance of the New Telecom Policy 1999, the Government of India decided to corporatize the service provision functions of Department of Telecommunications (DoT). Accordingly, Bharat Sanchar Nigam Limited (BSNL) was incorporated on 15 September 2000 as a wholly owned Central Government Company under the Companies Act, 1956, with its registered and corporate offices located in New Delhi. The business of providing telecommunication services in the country, entrusted to the Department of Telecom Services (DTS) and the Department of Telecom Operations (DTO), was transferred to the newly formed company, BSNL, with effect from 1 October 2000. However, the functions of policy formulation, licensing, wireless spectrum management, administrative control of Public Sector Undertakings (PSUs), standardization and validation of equipment and research and development (R&D) were retained by the Government under the responsibility of the Department of Telecommunications (DoT) and the Telecom Commission.

BSNL is carrying out the duties and responsibilities relating to establishment, maintenance and working of all types of telecommunication services in the country in accordance with and under the terms and conditions of the licence granted by the Central Government under the Indian Telegraph Act, 1885 and such other directions as may be given by the Central Government from time to time.

Organizational Setup

The administrative and overall functional control is vested with the Board of Directors headed by the Chairman and Managing Director (CMD), who is assisted by five functional Directors (Finance, Commercial and Marketing, Operations, Human Resource Development and Planning and New Services). Consequent upon the retirement of the CMD with effect from 31 December 2003, the Director (Planning and New Services) held the additional charge of CMD from 1 January 2004 to 15 September 2004 and thereafter, the regular CMD was appointed by the Government.

The operations of BSNL are managed in 24 telecom circles excluding the project and maintenance circles. In addition, seven telecom factories at Mumbai, Alipore and Gopalpur in Kolkata, Wright Town and Richhai in Jabalpur, Bhilai and Kharagpur are also managed by BSNL. These factories manufacture various types of ancillary equipment such as microwave towers, modems, sockets, pay phones, cable termination boxes etc.

Investment and Returns

Against the authorized equity share capital of Rs. 10,000 crore and preference share capital of Rs. 7,500 crore, the paid-up equity share capital and preference share capital as on 31 March 2004 were Rs. 5,000 crore and Rs. 7,500 crore, respectively. In consideration of taking over the business of the erstwhile Department of Telecom Operations and Department of Telecom Services with effect from 1 October 2000 along with all the assets, liabilities and other contractual obligations, BSNL's total paid-up equity capital of Rs. 5,000 crore and preference share capital of Rs. 7,500 crore were treated as investment by the Government of India. In addition, another amount of Rs. 7,500 crore has been treated as a loan to BSNL from the Government. BSNL has been exempted from payment of dividend on preference share capital up to 31 March 2004. Besides, BSNL has also been exempted from payment of dividend on equity share capital up to 31 March 2002 and enjoyed 50 per cent and 25 per cent waiver on dividend due on equity share capital for the years 2002-03 and 2003-04, respectively. Accordingly, BSNL proposed dividend of Rs. 281.25 crore for the year ending 31 March 2004. The Government will not receive any interest or repayment of principal amount on the loan of Rs. 7,500 crore, as BSNL has a moratorium on repayment of principal and interest thereon up to 31 March 2004. Even interest will not accrue on this loan up to 31 March 2004.

DoT, while approving a package of measures in the form of financial/fiscal relief for BSNL, decided (June 2002) that BSNL would be liable to pay license fees and spectrum charges in full and BSNL would also be allowed reimbursement of losses incurred by it on rural telephony operations and other socially desirable projects. It was also decided that the amount of reimbursement to BSNL was to be decided annually by DoT in consultation with the Ministry of Finance. Accordingly, BSNL has been paying the due amounts of license fees and spectrum charges to DoT annually. In turn, DoT, in consultation with the Ministry of Finance, has been annually reimbursing the amount of losses incurred by BSNL on rural telephony operations and other socially desirable projects. During the year ending 31 March 2004, an amount of Rs. 2,300 crore was reimbursed by the Government on this account. BSNL also received Rs. 230.20 crore and Rs. 310.25 crore for the years ended 31 March 2003 and 2004, respectively, from the Universal Service Fund towards reimbursement for maintenance of village public telephones (VPTs). During the year, BSNL redeemed its bonds worth Rs. 510 crore with interest. Since the Department of Telecom Services (DTS) was corporatized as BSNL, the complete network of telecommunications of DTS came under the control of BSNL with effect from 1 October 2000.

Phases of Development

Telecom proved to be a powerful attractor of foreign investment. The cumulative FDI inflow into telecom since 1993 has exceeded Rs. 43,000 million. Within telecom, the cellular industry has attracted most of the foreign investment since 1993, accounting for almost 50% of the FDI inflow into telecom -representing amongst the biggest investments in any one sector in India.

New Telecom Policy - 99

To further strengthen the Telecom Sector, NTP 99 was announced by Govt. of India. NTP 99 is an extremely forward-looking policy. It significantly changed the dynamics of the Indian telecom industry as it not only replaced the high cost fixed licensing regime with a lower cost licensing structure through revenue sharing, but also provides for greater degree of competition and more flexibility in choice of tech.

TRAI and TDSAT

Govt. of India established Telecom Regulatory Authority in 1997 to regulate the telecom sector and safeguard consumer interests. The TRAI Act was subsequently amended in year 2000 giving more autonomy to TRAI and also Establishment of TDSAT. The amendments in the TRAI Act resulted in a considerable strengthening of the Regulator & greater clarity on its role and powers. It also put in place a separate dispute settlement mechanism in the form of the Telecom Dispute Settlement and Appellate Tribunal (TDSAT) to expeditiously deal with and resolve issues relating to the telecom sector.

BSNL and MTNL Entry in Mobile market

The year 2000 also saw the licensing of BSNL and MTNL as the third cellular operators as had been mandated in NTP 99. Further, in July 2001, cellular licenses were awarded to the 4th cellular operators in different telecom circles and cellular operators licensed to operate have gone up to 89 licensees.

Cellone–The Dawn of Mobile Revolution

BSNL came into existence on 1'st Oct 2000.

- BSNL as a corporate entity identified mobile as the thrust area of operations.
- Country-wide launch of its mobile services branded as CellOne on 19th Oct. 2002, brought about a 'tide' that caught the mobile service industry unaware.
- CellOne became a popular brand across the country and laid the foundation for mobile revolution.

Launch of CellOne unearthed vast potentials of mobile services in hinterland areas where private operators dreaded to foray into. The potential unearthed by CellOne has caught the imagination of competitors in the market and have since followed, to fuel the growth pattern.

The entry of BSNL in mobile market changed the whole dynamics of the market with the introduction of incoming free call regime and drastic reduction in tariff.

- Cellular tariffs have dropped by over 90% since May 1999 –a feet unparalleled by any other sector or industry in India.
- Peak ceiling tariffs of Rs. 16.80 per minute prior to implementation of NTP 99 took a nosedive to settle around Rs. 2 per minute by end 2002, bridging the digital divide by bringing the vast population of country in the mobile coverage map.
- CellOne has enabled practice of socialism through competition.

CellOne services have presence in over 1800 towns/cities .

- CellOne provides coverage in 561 districts out of 593 districts in the country.
- The districts uncovered shall be provided the services by Oct 2004, which are primarily in the states of J&K, NE and Assam.

- CellOne follows the national highways to ensure its subscribers remain connected and BSNL boasts of covering national highways & important trunk railway routes of around 42,000 kms.
- It has over 5.5 million satisfied customers.

Mobile Telephony –A success story

As of March 2004, the Indian cellular mobile industry had 74 GSM networks on air, serving 30 million subscribers across the country and 38 million including CDMA subscribers. The quality of the service is widely accepted to be of international standards and till date there has been no waiting period involved in availing of this service. In year 2004, Government Issued Guidelines for Unified licensing which allows Operators to provide all kind of services with a single license using GSM / CDMA / Fixed line Technology. Unified licensed operators have further contributed for the growth of mobile market.

The cellular industry has been growing at an average rate of 85% per annum, which has advanced the achievement of Tele-density of 7 in Mar. 2004 *vis-à-vis* as targeted in NTP 99 to be achieved by 2005. Morgan-Stanley has projected Indian mobile market to grow to 100 million by Mar. 2008.

- CellOne is chartered to grow from present 5 million to 25 million by Dec. 2005.
- It is expected that the mobile industry will sustain its present growth in the coming years and shall grow together to prove wrong the predictions of experts to achieve the projections of 100 million, earlier by Dec 2005.

BSNL Marketing Strategies

It is true for individuals as well as organizations. The strongest form of vision / motivation is to base vision on "What Legacy we want to leave." And to achieve it we must take a principled centered path. History is full of examples that many organizations have vanished grown and vanished overnight as their path to achieve vision was not based on principled way.

Vision of the organization can only be translated into reality, if it is shared by one and all. The best way to implement is to involve them in formulation. But even if it is conceived by higher management, then it has to be explained to each and every individual of the organization, otherwise it may remain as a showpiece.

Marketing vision of the BSNL has to be based on overall mission and vision of the organization. The mission of BSNL is

- To provide world class State-of-art technology telecom services on demand at affordable price.
- To provide world class telecom infrastructure to develop country's economy.

The ultimate objective of any marketing activity is to satisfy the customers and today even a step ahead i.e. 'delighting' the customers, for which customers are offered something beyond their expectations from the service or the product. The objective being to acquire and retain the customers, who should continually feel that they are getting more value of the money, they are departing with. Marketing is the establishment, development, maintenance and optimization of long-term mutually valuable relationships between consumers and organisation. Successful Marketing focuses on understanding the needs and desires of the customers and is achieved by placing these needs at the heart of business by integrating them with the organisation strategy, people, technology and business processes. At its most basic, Marketing involves customers, organizations and relationships and the combination creates the need for the management.

Marketing is about creating a competitive advantage by being the best at understanding, communicating, and delivering and developing existing customer relationships in addition to creating and keeping new customers. The concept of the product life cycle is giving way to customer life cycle, focusing on developing products that anticipate the future needs of existing customers and creating services that extend the existing customer relationship beyond the mere transaction. The customer life cycle will focus on lengthening the life span of the customer with the organisation rather than the endurance of a particular product. Customers have changing needs as their life styles alter- the development and provision of products and/or services that continuously seek to satisfy those needs is good Marketing. The Marketing will focus greater attention on how to deliver customer satisfaction and organisation will begin to structure itself around customer segments and not product lines. A good Marketing Strategy will take the business vision and apply it to the customer base.

According to the Dictionary of Marketing Terms, 2nd edition, published by the American Marketing Association, c1995, "Marketing is the process of planning and executing the conception, pricing, promotion, and distribution of ideas, goods, and services to create exchanges that satisfy individual and organizational objectives."

Once marketing is understood, we can define marketing management process as analyzing marketing opportunities, researching and selecting target markets, designing marketing strategies, planning marketing programs, and organizing, implementing, and controlling the marketing efforts. In simple words it implies a buyer, a seller, bonded by the mutual need, satisfying offer and a medium/process to exchange the offer.

Marketing Process

We often talk of marketing & sales and often use it interchangeably without understanding the difference in it. Marketing is everything we do to get and leverage a client relationship. Marketing process is broad and includes all of the following:

- Discovering what product, service or idea customers want.
- Producing a product with the appropriate features and quality.
- Pricing the product correctly.
- Promoting the product; spreading the word - why customers should buy it.
- Selling and delivering the product into the hands of the customer.

Selling is one activity of the entire marketing process. Selling is the act of persuading or influencing a customer to buy (actually exchange something of value for) a product or service. Marketing activities support sales efforts. The concepts surrounding both selling and marketing also differ. There is a need for both selling and marketing approaches in different situations. One approach is not always right and the other always wrong - it depends upon the particular situation. In a marketing approach, more listening to and eventual accommodation of the target market occurs. Two-way communication (sometimes between a salesperson and a customer) is emphasized in marketing so learning can take place and product offerings can be improved.

A salesperson using the sales concept, on the other hand, sometimes has the ability to individualize components of a sale, but the emphasis is ordinarily upon helping the customer determine if they want the product, or a variation on it, that is already being offered by the company. In the sales approach, not much time is spent learning what the customer's ideal product would be because the salesperson has little say in seeing that their company's product is modified. Furthermore, they aren't rewarded for spending time listening to the customer's desires unless they have a product to match their desires that will result in a sale.

Brand Equity

In simple words, it is how far people are willing to pay if we increase our prices i.e. premium for our services. We may feel happy to say there is lot of black marketing of our SIM cards. Is it a healthy sign? We reduce prices when competitors launch new schemes. Does it imply poor brand equity? Brand Equity can be built with good equity of quality of services at the affordable price. Continuous innovation in product and delivery of services with the appropriate pricing is the key strategy for developing the trust in customer so that he keeps his loyalty with BSNL. We have to be first mover in our efforts for product and price differentiation. Presently the market is in growth phase and price could be a differentiating factor, but how long? Is any scope left for further cuts? Ultimately, it is the quality, customer care, and timely availability apart from price, which will matter. Quality depends on many parameters such as tangibles (like physical facilities, appearance of personnel, tools or equipment used to provide service, physical appearance of service, other customers in the service facility), Reliability, Responsiveness, Competence, Courtesy, Credibility, Security, Access, and Communications with customer, Understanding etc. Quality definitely commands premium. Why are people willing to pay more for Raymond's or Adidas or Sony when comparable offers exist in market? One may say that customer perception of quality is not built overnight; it may require a brand and brand building investments apart from a quality product. How many brands do we have? Our investments get diluted with more number of brands. Even Airtel merged the Touchtel brand with more popular one. Can't we have just one brand i.e., BSNL? Have we ever tried to examine our revenue breakup? While majority of the revenue comes from landline (DELs plus PCOs), how many people know of Bfone? CellOne happens to be more popular.

What is USP (Unique Selling Proposition) for BSNL?

A Government company which delivers. A government company which gives service better than private could be a deadly combination, which no competitor can copy.

Social Responsibility

The most trusted telecom brand in year 2003 & 2004 and has been given Golden Peacock award for Best Corporate Social responsibility. How can it leverage these distinctions? These achievements need to be highlighted through public relation exercise like press meet. This will help us in building our marketing image. In sales and distribution front though we have over one-lakh retailers, 1000 franchisees, 3300 CSCs, 36000 exchanges why are we not visible like others? Why can't we utilize all possible space? Can't we leverage our franchisee and STD-PCO strengths? Can we make these outlets as our core strength? Why our recharge coupons, India Telephone Cards are in shortage when there is no capacity constraint? Does it imply that our planning for printing, inventory management, logistics, and supply chain and of course franchisee management is inefficient?

Do we have targets for these just like DELs & CellOne? Why can't we leverage this huge network for better customer care and improve collection efficiency? We must realize that with waiver of security deposits, no OYT schemes, no advance rentals, adjustment of landline security for CellOne, we don't get fixed deposits to meet our funds requirements. Everything has to be met from operating revenues. We need to improve collections, realize bills early, not on the last day of payment and reduce bad debts. We need to provide 24×7 culture in our organization, though we have been providing operation and maintenance on 24×7 basis in the past and we will continue to provide in future too, but what about provisioning customer care and marketing on 24×7 basis?

Customer Retention

After four and half year of corporatization of BSNL, a customer-focused approach among its employees is still not present. In this era of intense competition, it is very important for any service company to understand that merely acquiring customers is not sufficient because there is a direct link between customer retention over time and profitability & growth. Customer retention to a great extent depends on service quality and customer satisfaction. It also depends on the ability of the organization to encourage customers to complain and then recover when things go wrong. Complaints are natural part of any service activity as mistakes are an unavoidable feature of all human endeavor and thus also of service recovery. Service recovery is the process of putting things right after something goes wrong in the service delivery.

Importance of Customer Retention

Why are customers more profitable for service firms over a period of time? There are a number of reasons for this. To begin with, to acquire a customer a company incurs promotional costs like advertising, sales promotion etc. It is said that it costs five times more to attract a new customer than retaining one. The operating cost decreases when a customer stays. Services being rich in experience and credence qualities, it takes some time for customers to get accustomed to it and once they are used to the service and are satisfied with the service provider ,they tend to purchase more over a period of time. As they remain satisfied with a service provider, they spread a positive word of mouth, which is very effective in case of services for attracting new customers. Longer the customer stays with an organization, more the organization knows about him, which enables it to offer customized services which make it difficult for the customer to defect. This may even provide opportunities to the organization to charge price premium by offering individualized services which may be difficult for the competitors to offer.

Considering the importance of retaining customers in service business, Reichheld & Sasser coined a term 'Zero Defection'. They highlighted that companies can boost profits by almost 100% by retaining just 5% more of their customers. Further, it is also very important to understand the life time value of a customer. For example, if an average customer of BSNL pays Rs. 500 per month and stays with the company for 20 years., his average lifetime value will be Rs. 500x 12x 20=Rs. 1,20,000. Further, if by a positive word of mouth, he brings just one more customer to the organization, his value to the organization doubles. Therefore, it is important for all the employees in the organization to understand the life time value of their customers. Once they understand it, they will treat the customer accordingly and will focus on building relationship with the very people who keep them in business.

Customer Switching - Reasons

The reasons for customer switching can be identified as following:

1. Pricing (High price, unfair pricing, deceptive pricing)
2. Inconvenience (Wait for service, wait for appointment)
3. Core service failure (Service mistakes, Billing errors)
4. Service encounter failure (Uncaring, impolite, unresponsive behavior)
5. Response to service failure (Negative response, no response, reluctant response)
6. Competition (Found better service)
7. Ethical problem (Cheating, Unsafe)
8. Involuntary switching (customer moved, provider closed).

An important aspect of the above is that six out of the eight service switching factors are controllable from a service organization's point of view.

Strategies for Customer Retention

(A) Complaint Management System: Any worthwhile complaints management system has to have following basic features:

- **Visibility:** Customer should know where to complain.
- **Accessibility:** Customer should know how to complain. As a rule of thumb, the more formal the system for lodging complaints, the less accessible it is to customers.
- **Responsiveness:** Complaints need to be dealt quickly. The quicker the complaints are dealt with, the higher the customer satisfaction.
- **Customer-focused approach:** A service provider who adopts customer-focused approach, invites complaints and indicates commitment of resolving complaints by its words and actions in all fairness.
- **Accountability:** Someone in the organization has to take responsibility for complaint handling.
- **Continuous Improvement:** This is about looking at the root causes and fixing them.

A good complaint management system must ensure that that complainant is kept informed, the staff understands the complaint processes, complaints are taken seriously and employees are empowered to deal with situations.

(B) Service Recovery Strategies: Consider the following incident regarding airlines (British Airways). "An aircraft door was left open in a rainstorm before take off and a passenger near the door unfortunately got showered. The flight attendant not only did everything that was routine- offered to have the customer's garments cleaned and made sure that a customer relations representative contacted the customer later to demonstrate that they genuinely cared- but also made special gesture by offering the passenger a complimentary choice of certain tax free goods."

It is very important for service companies to have service recovery strategies which can be applied in case of service failure. The following steps are useful in an effective service recovery system.

- Measure the costs of effective service recovery. It should include the indirect cost also, when a customer departs unhappily.
- Break customer silence and listen closely for complaints.
- Act fast.
- Train and empower employees. The front line people must be trained and empowered by the organization.
- Close the customer feedback loop.

(C) Managing Customer Waiting: Sometimes, it is not possible to match demand & capacity, and hence waiting by customers becomes inevitable. While reducing waiting time is important for a marketer, it is equally if not more, important to reduce the customer's perceived waiting time. If a customer's perceived waiting time is less, he will be more satisfied with the service. Various ways of managing customer waiting are as follows:

- The organization should analyze its operational processes in order to identify and remove inefficiencies or bottlenecks, if any.
- In case waiting cannot be avoided, a reservation system can be used.
- Since unoccupied time feels longer than occupied time, keep customer occupied by installing distractions that entertain and physically involve them. For example, TV sets, magazines reading material can be provided in waiting area.
- Provide 'waiting duration information' i.e., information about the expected length of wait and/or 'queuing information' i.e., a customer's position in queue with continuous update.
- If unexpected delays occur, explanation should be given to the customer. This helps in reducing uncertainty and customer irritation. The key is to impress upon the customer that he has not been forgotten. Simple things like providing a glass of water or a cup of tea to the waiting customer can do wonders.
- Keep resources not serving customer out of sight. This can be done by keeping idle employees out of view and conducting activities that do not involve customer interactions out of customer's sight.
- Try to reduce pre-service waiting time by transferring some of the pre-service waiting to the service encounter phase.
- A smiling service person who knows his job well can be very helpful in overcoming many negative effects of waiting. Therefore, training and incentive/ rewards for providing good service should be made.

BSNL's Plan

Pilot Project for 200 KC IP TAX equipment, to introduce IP, in transit network is under implementation:

- Plan to add 6.4 million Class-4 Transit capacity through IP TAX by 2008-2009
- Plan to Strengthen SSTP Networks, to become the *de-facto* Signalling Network
- Replacement of Legacy switches nearing expiry/expired switches to begin from 2008-2009
- Plan to introduce SIP based services by 2008-2009
- Migration to IMS
- Introduction of new applications such as presence information, videoconferencing, multiparty gaming, community services and content sharing expected to roll out in a phased manner from 2009.
- Full migration to NGN with replacement of PSTN by 2015.

Plans to be implemented in phases are:

- IP Core to support IPv6
- The IP Core spreads over more than 100 locations with each node capable to handle 160 Gbps of traffic
- The Core network to have two layer structure
- Primary Nodes are fully mesh connected at 2.5 Gbps
- The secondary nodes connected to at least two other nodes with 1 Gbps links
- Plans to increase the interconnectivity to 10 Gbps.

Current Status of Telephone Network

India's 164 million robust telephone network, including mobile phones, is one of the largest in the world and 2nd largest among emerging economies (after China) with a wide range of services like basic, cellular, internet, paging, V-SAT etc. Further, National Internet Exchange of India (NIXI) has been set up by DIT to ensure that Internet traffic, originating and destined for India is routed within India. This will substantially bring down the cost of Internet usage. It is expected that NIXI will take appropriate steps for increasing the utilization of such facilities.

Trend in Teledensity

Teledensity in the country is steadily increasing from 5.11% as on 31.3.03 to 12.74% as on 31.3.06 and currently stand at 15.12% as on 30-09-2006. However, there is a wide gap between urban teledensity (47.58%) and rural teledensity (1.84%). The rural telephony has not kept pace with the impressive growth in urban connectivity.

BSNL's Impact on Internet

BSNL is India's no. 1 Internet service provider with more than 17 lakh subscribers, providing Internet service throughout the entire country (except in New Delhi and Mumbai) under the brand name of "Sancharnet". Sancharnet provides free all India roaming and enables it's users to access their accounts, using the same access code (172233) and user ID from any where in the Country. In order to make Internet available throughout the length and breadth of the Country Internet Dhabas are being commissioned at all the Block Headquarters. BSNL has also started DIAS and Account free internet access (CLI based) facility on few select cities recently.

BSNL has launched "SANCHARNET CARD" recently. The Sancharnet Card" is a prepaid Internet Access Card with following features for customers:

- Self-register for internet access with your choice of user id
- Renew your existing Sancharnet account
- Wide Range of Internet access packages.

Web-Hosting Service is also provided by the BSNL. It allows customers to host their static or dynamic web-sites on BSNL servers. Web-hosting service provides basic features like Web-space (Data Storage) on servers for hosting HTML pages with browser supported MIME types, Primary or Secondary Domain Name Hosting, Server Side Scripting: Perl, Java Servlets, JSP, Database Access (MySQL), Email Access and Web-email, Multiple Email IDs as per the plan, Ftp access for uploading and downloading pages as per the plan, Continuous usage billing for Web, Messaging and FTP etc. BSNL provides Internet services to the customers located in about 450 locations. Web Co-location is an easy and cost effective solution to house a company's powerful infrastructure without losing the administrative control on the equipments. Web Co-location eliminates much of the Infrastructure costs as well as the maintenance cost of such equipments apart from avoiding the last mile problems. Web Co-location enables customers' equipment/ Servers to be treated as a part and parcel of the ISP network enjoying all the facilities as the ISP servers.

SMS and BULK SMS Services: It allows you to send SMS using Sancharnet Email service. Sending SMS using Sancharnet account is very easy and cost effective. There is no need of a mobile phone to send SMS. Moreover it is easy to type a message on computer keyboard. Bharat Sanchar Nigam Ltd. formed in October, 2000, is World's 7th largest Telecommunications Company providing comprehensive range of telecom services in India: Wireline, CDMA mobile, GSM Mobile, Internet, Broadband, Carrier service, MPLS-VPN, VSAT, VoIP services, IN Services etc. Within a span of five years it has become one of the largest PSU units in India. BSNL has installed Quality Telecom Network in the country and now focusing on improving it, expanding the network, introducing new telecom services with ICT applications in villages and wining customer's confidence. Today, it has about 47.3 million line basic telephone capacity, 4 million WLL capacity, 20.1 million GSM Capacity, more than 37382 fixed exchanges, 18000 BTS, 287 Satellite Stations, 480196 Rkm of OFC Cable, 63730 Rkm of Microwave Network connecting 602 Districts, 7330 cities/towns and 5.5 lakh villages.

BSNL is the only service provider, making focused efforts and planned initiatives to bridge the Rural-Urban Digital Divide ICT sector. In fact, there is no telecom operator in the country to beat its reach with its wide network giving services in every nook & corner of country and operates across India except Delhi & Mumbai. Whether it is in inaccessible areas of Siachen glacier and North-eastern region of the country, BSNL serves its customers with its wide bouquet of telecom services. BSNL is numero uno operator of India in all services in its license area. The company offers wide ranging & most transparent tariff schemes designed to suite every customer.

BSNL cellular service, CellOne, has more than 17.8 million cellular customers, garnering 24 percent of all mobile users as its subscribers. That means that almost every fourth mobile user in the country has a BSNL connection. In basic services, BSNL is miles ahead of its rivals, with 35.1 million Basic Phone subscribers i.e. 85 per cent share of the subscriber base and 92 percent share in revenue terms. BSNL has more than 2.5 million WLL subscribers and 2.5 million Internet Customers who access Internet through various modes *viz.* Dial-up, Leased Line, DIAS, Account Less Internet (CLI). BSNL has been adjudged as the NUMBER ONE ISP in the country. BSNL has set up a world class multi-gigabit, multi-protocol convergent IP infrastructure that provides convergent services like voice, data and video through the same Backbone and Broadband Access Network. At present there are 0.6 million DataOne broadband customers. The company has vast experience in planning, installation, network integration and maintenance of switching & transmission networks and also has a world class ISO 9000 certified Telecom Training Institute.

Scaling new heights of success, the present turnover of BSNL is more than Rs.351,820 million (US $ 8 billion) with net profit to the tune of Rs.99,390 million (US $ 2.26 billion) for last financial year. The infrastructure asset on telephone alone is worth about Rs.630,000 million (US $ 14.37 billion). BSNL plans to expand its customer base from present 47 millions lines to 125 million lines by December 2007 and infrastructure investment plan to the tune of Rs. 733 crores (US$ 16.67 million) in the next three years. The turnover, nation-wide coverage, reach, comprehensive range of telecom services and the desire to excel has made BSNL the No. 1 Telecom Company of India.

References

1. **www.bsnl.co.in**
2. **www.bsnl.co.in/onlinedirectory.htm**
3. **www.oneindia.in/phonecalls/bsnl/landline.shtml**
4. **www.kerala.bsnl.co.in/images/photogallery**
5. **gigaom.com/2006/12/25/bsnl-promises-broadband**
6. **wiki.broadbandforum.in/BSNL www.physorg.com/news11133.html**
7. **www.techtree.com/techtree/jsp/user_review.jsp?**
8. **www.vccircle.com/2008/01/15/state-owned-telco-bsnl-plans-indias-largest-ipo**

6. The General Electric Company Ltd.

The General Electric Company (GE) is a multinational technology and services company. It was the largest corporation in terms of market capitalization and the number of conglomerate firms that are attached to it. Through these businesses, GE participates in a wide variety of markets including generation, transmission and distribution of electricity, lighting, industrial automation and medical imaging equipments. It has also ventured into the manufacture and distribution of motors, railways, locomotives, aircraft engines, aviation services and other materials such as plastics, silicones and abrasives (Eckes 2001).

Background

The company also owns 80% of NBC Universal and the National Broadcasting Company. Through its financial arm named GE Commercial Finance, the company established the GE Consumer Finance, GE Equipment Services and GE Insurance that offers insurance services in over 100 countries. GE is also one of the world's leading lenders (Eckes 2001). The market capitalization of the company is also bigger than that of Microsoft in a sum of almost $100 billion and in 2004; the company was named number one company for employers and employees based on the Forbes 500 Global Player List.

Since the company has enjoyed enormous amount of profits while it is constantly expanding and increasing in terms of size, profits, employees and field of business, this success can be attributed to a various factors. First would be the global and reputable name that the company offers to its costumers. The integrity and the brand name of GE present trust and reliable service for its consumers. Since the company is made of a group of interrelated industries and sub-companies, the company enjoys low production cost since it can outsource its raw materials and products from other members of the conglomerate without having to pay extra cost if these materials are bought from the outside.

The success of the company can also be attributed to its successful human resources management; it has implemented policies and regulations among its employees that enabled them to increase production and to be costumer oriented. It has implemented programs that would entice and attract potential and present employees of the company. To achieve excellence in terms of strategic human resources management, employee empowerment, commitment and development were largely implemented by the company.

SHRM

The first policy implemented by the company on its employees is a program that would seek to help and empower employees and to instill the value of commitment among the workforce.

To provide comfort and to bring out commitment for the employees, various policies and programs were initiated by the company. For example, while many competitors often place an entry-level manager, high level employee in a cubicle desk within a large office space filled with other cubicles, GE assigns a private or semiprivate closed office to every manager or pairs of employees (Levinson 1984).

Various incentives and stock options are also presented to the employee if the manager or supervisor sees that progress and improvement is being done in the workplace. In addition, key decision-makers at every level are either managers or former managers of the division or section that will be affected by the resolution. In a sense therefore, the managers and all levels of employees at GE are considered as the "stars" of the company. The company does not only emphasize work ethics and proper work conditions but it also promote a mentality of looking out for the team and the company. To promote the "we-ness" mentality of the workforce and of the whole company, GE organizes sports events, symposiums and dialogues that would tend to bring out the thoughts and perspective of the workforce (Levinson 1984).

These activities do not only bring all workers of the company together but it also promotes esprit de corp, togetherness and camaraderie. These company events are also important for the leaders and the hierarchical officials of the company because they can gauge and determine the outlook and inner thoughts of their employees, thereby aiding them in what aspect of the company must be further developed (Levinson 1984).

To further elaborate incentives such as stock option scheme, the former CEO of the company, Jake Welch implemented the rank and yank system in the company. Rank and yank system of management is derived from the vitality curve which states that certain proportions of the production is proportional to the producing population. In the rank and yank system initiated inside the GE corporation, each employee was ranked according to his/her contributions, input and involvement in the production process of the company. These three ranks therefore are the basis if the employee can be retained or fired by the company. In practice, Welch asked each manager to rank his or her employees on a forced ranking of the top 20%, the highly valued 70% and the least effective 10% in what he frequently termed "vitality curve" (Lowe 2000). He then encouraged managers to focus rewards and development efforts in top performers and urged them to counsel those who remain in the bottom 10% or move out of the organization. The class of employees then, who has satisfactory demonstrated their importance to the company retained and encouraged by giving rapid promotions, greater benefits, larger bonuses and stock options (Lowe 2000). Stock options, especially for employees based on the United States enjoy several U.S. tax benefits.

GE has also set up a learning and development program for employees with the aim of harnessing and discovering new talents from the current workforce or to further develop the skill gained by an employee before he/she entered the company. This L and D program is important not only for the employees but also for the company because this policy supports the planning process of the organization. As a result, the company invests about US$1 billion annually on L and D programs such as assembly lines management to corporate classrooms.

A senior official of the company, Steve Bertamini stated that it is important to chart out the process to ensure they have the right development for each person and that individual development needs within GE at the HR level refers in looking at issues such as skills gaps and how to best address them (Ford 1997). This approach therefore does not only emphasize the skills that will be gained by the individual but in addition, this program seeks to develop each employee individually. On this program, the organization has set-up a comprehensive business development course designed for the functional and unit business heads. The course sees each head undergoing simulations in running other business units in order to develop broader business skills. In these learning experiences, the CFO (Chief Finance Officer) might take up the role of COO (Chief Operating Officer) in the simulation, for example, while a senior HR executive could be shouldered with the position of CFO (Ford 1997).

This scheme is unique since it forces people to take on different roles and run a fairly sophisticated simulation against other teams. Skills in interacting, making important decisions and interpreting data and information quickly can be sharpened and would be beneficial if it was applied in the real world. It can also highlight the weaknesses and pitfalls of certain employees, managers and officers of the company thereby remedying them at the first opportunity.

Bertamini recounts seeing very senior people early in their careers that didn't perform well in a public forum, yet their skills were highly polished two to three years later after working on particular skill deficiencies using the simulation (Ford 1997).

GE also uses certain unique human resources tools called the "9 Block" to gauge and assess the KPI (Key Performance Indicators) of a specific employee. The 9 Block is a chart that is divided into nine squares, which are used to plot an employee's ability to meet KPIs against their individual demonstration of GE's values (Ecker 2001). Employees are assessed on how well they perform on both counts, and their position on the chart determines their annual performance rating. The same 9 Block framework is also used to plot the performance of an employee against their potential. Again, employees are rated for both factors and are slotted into one of the nine blocks to give the company a view of their growth and succession potential.

Sam Sheppard, an executive of the company, states that the values play an important role in sorting out the managerial chaff from the leadership wheat, as these values help pinpoint the behaviors needed to climb up the GE leadership ladder (Ecker 2001). He further said that values are good indicators whether the individual is a genuine leader or a simple manager who gives simply out tasks, manages deliverables and get results. Bertamini added that if a person achieves their results through autocratic management or using bullying, then that person has no place in the GE portfolio (Ford 1997). Hence, the process of the company is to really examine how individuals demonstrate values that would inspire the people that they actually work with and that the achievement of the result is equally important with the results itself.

Bertamini emphasizes that this is probably the biggest single factor in determining whether an organization is serious about culture, especially at senior levels. He also added that the "9 Blocks" is augmented by skip level meetings, reviews and employee surveys and these programs would try to identify and counsel the employees (Ford 1997). If certain employees does not quickly change or correct their behaviours and work ethics, they are exited from the organization. The company stresses that values play an essential role in the achievement of business results, hence their reason for inclusion in GE's performance management system. If employees don't meet their KPIs, but score well on values, they are given a second chance, as opposed to those who get the results but don't exhibit the values.

Aside from assessing employees and giving benefits and incentives, the company also has a policy of giving out free annual health assessment. Since the employees are working in different fields and in different conditions depending on the workplace that they are in, health assessment is a must for employees since some of them are exposed to harmful chemicals or are surrounded by dangerous situations and materials (Lowe 2000). This health services offered by the company is available to both employees and their families. These health services are composed of constant check-ups, medical examinations and work related surgeries and treatment. GE expects that by offering health services to its employees, it can help in sustaining the workforce while decreasing the frequency of absenteeism and inefficiency.

Different divisions and sub-companies of GE use a wide range of health and fitness programs that are suitable to its employees. Health seminar topics conducted inside GE in the last 4 years have included nutrition, men's health, and exercise and sleep management (Lowe 200). The latter is very important to the company from a perspective, as fatigue is a workplace safety issue especially in the aircraft engine assembly section. These health incentives make the employees feel that they are being valued by the company, moreover, there is higher health awareness in the organization and some individuals have had impressive weight loss.

GE has approached the issue on health employee through annual week-long corporate health expos held at various sites. All employees can have mini health assessments on site, attend lectures on weight control, stress management and nutrition, have skin checks and ergonomic consultations, and participate in yoga or other exercise sessions (Ecker 2001). Flu vaccinations are available to everyone each year. GE also sponsors employees who participate in touch football competitions and other sports events.

The company encourages groups of managers and employees to organize cycling races that would pit one section of a division with another section of the company. This promotes health awareness as well as harnessing intersection friendly competition. Executive health assessments are offered to all senior staff because if constant health monitoring can prevent a senior member of the organization from having a health issue, this fact will not only have a very positive individual result but it will also ensure that the organizational structure has no gaps that would bring in confusion and disorder. The company has also introduced smoke-free workplace legislation that has benefited workers.

Welch, the former CEO of the company also initiated policies that strengthened and empowered employees. He organized the "Work Out" initiative and over the past six years, in groups of 50 to 100, over 200,000 company employees met for two or three days to discuss how their particular area or work could be made more effective (Ecker 2001). The "Work Out" program encourages bottom up initiative by giving those on the front line voice. This policy made by the former CEO also signalled a shift in the mentality of the employees towards breaking down the barriers that divided each sectors of the company. Through years of initiatives such as this program, a new set of norms, values and behaviours emerged that defined as the social architecture of the company.

To monitor and to find out the insights, desires and hopes of the employees, the company in its worldwide operations conduct an annual employee survey that polled employees on issues ranging from GE's overall attractiveness as an employer to personal job satisfaction and career opportunities. Breakdown by business and region allowed the organization to identify potential trouble spots and year on year comparison that would help the top level executives of the company in making important decisions (Ford 1007). This survey is also beneficial to the company because managers can see what their employees are thinking with regards to the day-to-day operation of the company.

As GE is constantly expanding into new industries such as nuclear power, computers and plastic products, the company needed new and highly developed workforce especially composed of HR managers. To meet this demand, past CEOs of the company created the Executive Manpower Staff (EMS) which reports directly to the CEO (Lowe 2000). Welch and other past CEO challenged the business leaders of the company in identifying potential managerial talents from the engineers and professionals in their staff. The CEO would then ask the members of his/her EMS to review, compile and collect these managerial talents then track all the performances of the potential candidates in different managerial positions. Through this process of deeply involvement in the production and assembly of products and goods, the future and potential manager can have a holistic an entire understanding that would be useful if a problem in assembly line occurs.

GE also has a unique way of recruiting its employees. Its recruiting mechanism has a longstanding relationship with many U.S. schools. In 1980s, realizing that the company got better results from a particular candidate profile; GE began to reconsider the allocation of recruiting resources. The company resisted competing against recruiters from the Wall Street and consulting firms for the most hunted college and business school graduates, figuring that those interested in a management career would be available to GE later. GE hires open-minded, customer-oriented people with a propensity to learn new ideas (Levinson 1984). Skills and other strong point of the applicant are asked because the organization wanted to ensure that those coming on board had these skills rather than hiring someone only to have to train them. Not only were questions asked about computer skills, but it was a factor in the hiring decision. There are also questions during the acquisition stage of employment that seeks to identify work ethics, quality criteria, work experiences and aptitude towards quality improvement.

Employees and managers must be willing to work from the bottom act taking hard work and accept frequent relocation to learn from GE's vast operation. Employees and managers are also urged to study post graduate courses where the fees, book allowance and other incentives are paid by the company. Some common post graduate courses being paid by the company are courses and academic studies that concerns with aeronautics, engineering, chemistry, laser and nuclear technology (Levinson 1984). This step is advantageous to both, employee and the company. At first glance, the individual can enjoy post graduate education without spending his/her own money thus increasing his/her qualification in the labour market while for the company, that individual is an investment that can contribute valuable knowledge or method that can be solely used by GE.

In this program, the individual who underwent the education program developed by the company must remain working for the company in a defined and specific period of time. After this, the individual can either stay in the company or seek other employment. In most cases, the employee stays in the company.

In order to focus on people and employee development, EMS consultants moved from headquarters out into the filed to help business leaders develop their talent. In addition to it, acting as an information source and sounding board for the business leader, these HR professionals used their networks with EMS to facilitate the transfer of managers across the organization and they also helped the CEO keep tabs on the Senior Executive Band (SEB), a group of 600 managers whose development career progress are directly monitored by the president of the company.

Proper allocation and identification of human resources weaknesses and advantages are vital in the success and progress of the company. GE has been dominating in its market because of the competitive advantages that it gains in term of developing and harnessing the positive characteristics of its employee,

To attain heightened productivity, the company emphasizes employee, empowerment, training and development to effectively recruit and retain its employees. In relation to the development of its employee's skills and education, GE strives hard to identify employees and managers that would likely to succeed when they are educated and schooled in relation to their line of work in the company. In the short run, this practice is not beneficial to the company since there is no assurance that the money invested on that particular individual will be used in the future but in terms of the long term effect, this policy can improve the standing and knowledge base of the company when new industries such as microprocessors, lasers and genome projects will be popular.

In order to attract and retain employees, the company also offers benefits, medical insurances, incentives, stock options and rapid advancement of career. These steps therefore assure the company that all competent and highly skilled individuals will be drawn into the company.

Although steps mentioned above are being taken into practice by GE, these practices generates negative publicity and image that would also hurt the sales and reputation of the company. Many former employees criticize the system of firing employees based on the perceptions of the managers handling them. These people argued that perception made by an individual is always subjective and is not free from any biases and prejudices. Other groups meanwhile stated that the company is a heartless and cruel company because it removes employees without seeing the contributions that they brought to the company during the years they are employed.

To effectively implement a strategic human resources management program based on employee empowerment, training and development, the company must walk in a thin and blurry line that defines management from sympathy and its idea between simple employees from a human being. Profits and production must be equally placed and juxtaposed with the conditions, feelings and emotions of employees.

7. GOOGLE INC.

Arguably the most popular search engine available today, Google is widely known for its unparalleled search engine technology, embodied in the web page ranking algorithm, and running on an efficient distributed computer system. In fact, the verb "to Google" has ingrained itself in the vernacular as a synonym of "[performing] a web search." The key to Google's success has been its strategic use of both software and hardware information technologies. The IT infrastructure behind the search engine includes huge storage databases and numerous server farms to produce significant computational processing power. These critical IT components are distributed across multiple independent computers that provide parallel computing resources. This architecture has allowed Google's business to reach a market capital over $100 billion and become one of the most respected and admirable companies in the world.

Background

Google's mission is to organize the world's information and make it universally accessible and useful.

As a first step to fulfilling that mission, Google's founders Larry Page and Sergey Brin developed a new approach to online search that took root in a Stanford University dorm room and quickly spread to information seekers around the globe. Google is now widely recognized as the world's largest search engine — an easy-to-use free service that usually returns relevant results in a fraction of a second.

When you visit www.google.com or one of the dozens of other Google domains, you'll be able to find information in many different languages; check stock quotes, maps, and news headlines; lookup phonebook listings for every city in the United States; search billions of **images** and peruse the world's largest archive of **Usenet** messages — more than 1 billion posts dating back to 1981.

The **Google Toolbar** enables you to conduct a Google search from anywhere on the web. And for those times when you're away from your PC altogether, Google can be used from a number of wireless platforms including WAP and i-mode phones.

Google's utility and ease of use have made it one of the world's best known brands almost entirely through word of mouth from satisfied users. As a business, Google generates revenue by providing advertisers with the opportunity to deliver measurable, cost-effective online advertising that is relevant to the information displayed on any given page. This makes the advertising useful to you as well as to the advertiser placing it. We believe you should know when someone has paid to put a message in front of you, so we always distinguish ads from the search results or other content on a page. We don't sell placement in the search results themselves, or allow people to pay for a higher ranking there.

Thousands of advertisers use **Google AdWords** program to promote their products and services on the web with targeted advertising, and we believe AdWords is the largest program of its kind. In addition, thousands of web site managers take advantage of our **Google AdSense** program to deliver ads relevant to the content on their sites, improving their ability to generate revenue and enhancing the experience for their users.

What's a Google?

"Googol" is the mathematical term for a 1 followed by 100 zeros. The term was coined by Milton Sirotta, nephew of American mathematician Edward Kasner, and was popularized in the book, "Mathematics and the Imagination" by Kasner and James Newman. Google's play on the term reflects the company's mission to organize the immense amount of information available on the web.

Business Model

Since its beginning as a research project from two Computer Science doctorate students at Stanford University, Google has continued to follow its mission "to organize the world's information and make it universally accessible and useful." From Google's founding in 1997 until 2000, the company did not have a well-defined business model to generate revenues. In 2001, Google's two co-founders hired Eric Schmidt, the chairman and CEO of Novell and former CTO at Sun Microsystems, as the new CEO of Google to help drive the effort in creating a business model for Google. With new management leadership, Google created a core business in online advertising, enabled by the millions of users using its search engine everyday. Revenue generation and profit growth in online advertising came from both Google's search engine homepage and partner websites that display Google sponsored advertisements. Google created a cost-per-click pricing scheme for sponsored advertisements such that advertisers only pay a base fee, and for the number of referrals to their site.

From the metric above, Google's revenue is affected by three factors: quantity (users * queries/user * ads/query), quality (clicks/ads), and price (revenue/click). Quantity is dependent on the number of keywords, advertisers, and users. Quality is based on advertisements relevant to users and is determined by the click-through rate. Lastly, price is affected by the conversion probability between the click-through rate and the consumers actually purchasing products or services on the advertiser's site. The ability for advertisers to determine the value per click can be computed using Google's conversion tracking or internal tool to calculate online advertising retention rate. Furthermore, advertisers can bid on the maximum price they are willing to pay per click for their specific advertisements. Minimal value of the bid starts from $0.01 cost-per-click with an upper limit of $100. To control costs, advertisers can set an upper bound dollar limit they are willing to spend for online marketing. Once cost-per-click reaches the budget limit set by the advertiser, their advertisements are taken offline.

Business Strategy

Google is generally secretive about its business strategy, but it is evident that Google is building the foundation for all of its products and services under the central theme of leveraging advanced search technology and personalized advertising. For example, Google's popular web-based email service called GMail, allows users to store and search old emails rapidly using text search integrated into the email client and then placing sponsored advertisements on the side based upon email content a user is currently reading. The GMail client is also able to identify email contents in which it can link information onto Google Maps and track packages from UPS and USPS.

Existing search results are primarily textual-based. More advanced search technologies will allow users to search for other information besides textual data, such as multimedia content (e.g., audio, image, video). To maintain its reputation as a forefront technology leader and innovator, Google has been aggressively acquiring software start-up companies that can be easily integrated into its existing solutions, and can instantaneously gain visibility through Google's leverage. However, this strategy of growing through small acquisitions is also used by Yahoo, one of Google's major competitors, although the underlying methodology of the acquisitions is different.

Yahoo's acquisitions have been focused on acquiring search technology companies having specialized search functionalities. For example, Yahoo acquired Inktomi, Overture, and Stata Labs to perform web search, locating advertiser key words, and retrieval of Yahoo email client, respectively. Yahoo has a group of search technologies for different products and services, while Google has only one search technology. Over time with greater competition, an online advertising network may be commoditized and Google will need to develop new business models to entice new customers and enhance relationships with existing ones for customer lock-ins (Elgin, 2004). For existing customers, Google has Advanced Tools & Reporting to support sophisticated advertisers, and Google plans to tighten integration with other Google related products in advertising. Since Q4 of 2005, Google is offering Google Analytics as a free service. Google Analytics, formerly called Urchin, is a web-based service that provides log analysis and web statistics that lets advertisers know about their visitors and how they interact with their site. Google Analytics is integrated with AdWords and allows advertisers to optimize their keywords so they can better target resources for their marketing campaigns and deliver higher return on investment. This has served well for many small and medium size businesses using AdWords as the primary marketing tool for reaching to the customers.

Google has begun targeting its vertical sales in advertising to focus on Fortune 1,000 companies, where they have only captured one-forth of the market share.3 Fortune 500 companies have not caught on as quickly using online marketing, and have relied more on traditional marketing techniques. However, according to a study conducted by Advertising Age, "Nearly half of the chief marketing officers at Fortune 500 companies said they plan to increase their online advertising budgets by 30% in 2006."4 Out of the $250 billion dollar advertising industry in the United States alone, only $11 billion is spent online with about $5 billion attributed to search advertising where Google has 79% of the market share. To reach new markets faster, Google is expanding its advertising business beyond online marketing to other mediums, including radio and print. Google has already exhibited some efforts to diversify its advertising business by acquiring dMarc Broadcasting in January 2006, a company that develops a unique automatedradio–advertising-selling process between radio stations and advertisers (Perez, 2006). Google plans to integrate its AdWords platform with dMarc's software that automates the buying and placing of radio advertisements. Google is also experimenting with integrating its AdWords platform with print media by running classified advertisements for its AdWords customers through a limited trial in PC Magazine, Maximum PC, Budget Living, and the Chicago Sun Times (Hoover, 2006).

Google's Analytics Strategy

The online giant's decision to make its Urchin Web Analytics software free could spell disaster for search-engine optimization companies The surge in online ads has spawned hundreds of companies whose purpose is to help advertisers figure out how to get their message across via the Web. Some define their work as analytics. Others call themselves search-engine optimization companies. Whatever the name, they all aim to help businesses manage online advertising, distill what works, and determine where ad dollars are best spent.

These companies have another thing in common: At least until recently, they could thank Google (GOOG) and Yahoo! (YHOO) for a lot of their success. The Web giants are at the forefront of the online-ad spending spree (see BW Online, 10/21/05, "Google and Yahoo!: Rolling in It").

Pretty soon, they may be blaming Google for taking it away. Google became a competitor when it bought a small analytics company, called Urchin Web Analytics, back in March. It upped the ante when it slashed the price of Urchin's software to about $200 from about $400. But the final nail may have come when Google announced on Nov. 14 that the software is now free.

Rapid-Fire Launches

"When they first announced Urchin, I speculated about a couple of possible outcomes," says Eric Peterson of Jupiter Research. "The most frightening for Web analytics companies was that they would do tag-based analytics, freely available and supported by the global Google brand, and that's exactly what they've done." Google has been making new-product announcements at a rapid clip. Many have been aimed at getting the search giant into other companies' businesses.

This one is directed at protecting Google's home turf of paid search, where the company generates sales from advertisements — so-called AdWords — that run alongside search results. Some analysts saw the timing of Google's latest announcement as significant: It came on the heels of a Microsoft (MSFT) manifesto that Web and ad-subsidized services were the future (see BW Online, 11/10/05, "Microsoft: Ozzie's Online Charge"). "It's a bit of a slap of the face to Microsoft, reminding them, 'We're in this game,'" says Marc Strohlein, vice-president and lead analyst at Outsell, a market research firm.

Inevitable Casualties

It also sends a message to larger Web analytics companies like WebSideStory (WSSI), whose stock fell nearly 9%, to close at $16.42, on Nov. 14. WebSideStory Chief Executive Jeffrey Lunsford says he has little cause for concern. His company sells products tailored for big, sophisticated businesses. Its software costs about $40,000 a year — not $500. Lunsford notes that the stock also took a hit when Google bought Urchin, and when it cut the price to $200, though neither affected his business. "If cutting the price in half didn't materially impact us, I don't believe cutting it to zero will impact us," he says. Efficient Frontier also handles search ads for major clients, relying on a sophisticated algorithm that analyzes not only Web traffic but also where advertisers should spend more money. Efficient Frontier CEO Ellen Siminoff says she's similarly unfazed. "If people don't have good technology, they will get washed out," she says. "Hundreds of companies are trying to do this. Only 10 are doing it well." Of course, with such a fragmented market, it's hard to say which companies will suffer most. All of them will say they have defensible methods or technologies. But, no doubt, there will be casualties — particularly among those aimed at small and mid-size businesses.

"Another Arrow"

While Google says several members of the Fortune 500 use Urchin's products now, this is clearly a play at the middle market, which makes sense for Google. Increasingly, software vendors want to reach the mass market, but that can be a logistical challenge. No deal alone is very big, and it's difficult to call on individual companies without a large, direct sales force. But Google has a ready-made sales infrastructure: According to Nielsen/NetRatings, the site has 380 million unique users every month. And thousands of small businesses already rely on search ads to lure customers to their sites and products. According to Jupiter, some 83% of businesses advertising on the Web aren't using analytics now and don't know they need to. Many of those are likely small companies. By offering a free service — and one that's tightly integrated with AdWords — Google is almost the *de facto* standard. This approach also helps it build up a disparate base of small companies for its local search efforts — which many consider the next frontier of search, one where Google will have to compete hard with Yahoo and MSN. "This basically put another arrow in the quiver," Outsell's Strohlein says "BETTER WEB EXPERIENCE."

Google says the free-software move is not about going after former partners or competitors: It's about making the Web the best it can be. Google is betting the technology will be used not only by its advertisers but by all Web publishers, who can use the software to determine what parts of their Web sites resonate most with viewers. "Our objective is to take what are extremely powerful tools and make sure all advertisers have access to them to make a better Web experience," says Richard Holden, director of product management at Google. That may be true, but it's likely cold comfort for Google's erstwhile partners.

How Google Innovates?

Google is a technology innovator that focuses on developing revolutionary ideas as well as complementary products and services. More than two-thirds of the company's employees are engineers and scientists. The company is a powerhouse of new technology innovations driven by software, and has a division unit called Google Labs which the company termed as an "engineer's playground."[5] Google Labs was developed since the early days of the company, and there is a place on the website to showcase new experimental products developed by Google employees. The product prototypes are available for anyone to download as beta version prior to commercial release. Unlike many engineering developments that never see daylight, this gives engineers a sense of satisfaction that their ideas turn into products that people can use.

One of the most important characteristic for Google's innovative thinking is attributed to its work atmosphere. Unlike typical corporate environment, Google's headquarters in Mountain View, called the Googleplex, is reminiscent of a college campus, and operate like a graduate school atmosphere with numerous guest speakers everyday and where open mind is encouraged. Other technology companies have previously tried to mimic a similar university culture but Google goes a long way in providing flexibility, openness, and fun workplace for its employees.

To minimize management from getting into the way of the engineers, Google adopts a very flat organizational structure. Google engineer Joe Beda praised the positive atmosphere inside the Google headquarters: "The intrapersonal environment at Google is very energizing. When someone comes up with a new idea, the most common response is excitement and a brainstorming session." 6 Google implemented a 20 percent rule in which engineers spend 80% of their time at work on Google's core products, and the freedom to dedicate the remaining 20% of their working time on any "pet projects." The 20 percent rule was a way of encouraging innovation at Google. Adopting the philosophy of 20 percent rule has enabled the engineers at Google to develop a number of products including Froogle, Google News, Google Finance, Orkut, and GTalk. In 2005, the company changed this policy slightly with a 70/20/10 rule, where 70% of time is spent on search and advertising, 20% on a work-related product, and 10% on other ideas. Following the principles from management guru Peter Drucker that "knowledge workers believe they are paid to be effective," Google employees are provided with free laundry services, free gourmet food, barbers, massages, gym, commuting buses with Wi-Fi access, as well as on-site oil changes, car washes, and physician doctors.

Firm Growth: Financial Performance

Google was first funded by angel investors that include corporate executives and retired technologists. The first capital for Google occurred on August 1998 in the amount of $100,000 from Andy Bechtolsheim, a co-founder of SUN Microsystems. Shortly thereafter in September 1998, Google raised another $1 million from other private investors including David Cheriton from Netscape and Amazon executive, Ram Shriram (Rivlin, 2004). In early 1999, Google went through a round of venture capital funding, raising $25 million from Sequoia Capital, Kleiner Perkins Caufield & Byers (KPCB), and a few private investors. When news spread that Google received funding from the prestigious venture capital firms, many technologists and investors in Silicon Valley took a closer look at Google. Unlike many start-up companies that were greatly impacted by the dot-com bubble, Google grew slowly, yet steadily, with positive cash flow. Google began to generate robust advertising revenues in 2002, mainly through google.com. By 2003 and 2004, the company achieved over 100% annual growth in advertising revenues from both its Google site and partner network . Google maintained very healthy revenue growth from 2002 to 2005 with over $6 billion in revenues by the end of fiscal year 2005.

Advertising Revenues

For several years, Google enjoyed being a private company without having to disclose financial and other information to the public. However, in April 2004 Google filed with the SEC to become public later that summer to raise $2.7 billion in order to reward its employees and investors. However, the IPO process took an unconventional Dutch-auction method where normal individual investors along with financial institutions can participate in purchasing Google IPO shares online. Besides, not following the typical Wall Street IPO process, remarkably, Google sold only Class A shares while its management retained all Class B shares, in which Class B shares has ten times more voting rights. This essentially means that the Google management team retains majority control of the company and its board of directors when the company becomes public. Prior to the IPO, Google received a lot of media attention and created a website solely discussing the event.ix On August 13th, 2004, Google went public on the Nasdaq Stock Market under the symbol GOOG with a selling price set at $85 per share. At the close of the IPO, Google raised $1.67 billion from the public. As of 2006, Google's stock price was around $300 to $500 per share. Many investors have complained that Google's stock has become too expensive to purchase, at least from the number value perspective. The Google management does not believe in stock splits to lower cost of their stock price while increasing the number of shares. In fact, Brin and Page have quoted billionaire investor, Warren Buffet, as their role model and would like Google to follow the same financial methodology that was set for Berkshire Hathaway, holding company on the opposition of stock splits.

Global Expansion

The international markets are critical for many technology companies in expanding new business opportunities and generating more revenues. Similarly, this principle is reminiscent in Google's case, as the international markets contribute from 30% to 40% of the company's total revenues every quarter for the past two years.4 In order to tap into the international market, Google's search engine has been translated to allow multi-language search capabilities, while maintaining its philosophy of objective and unbiased search results (Brin, 2001). The strong international markets for Google include the United Kingdom, Western Europe, Japan, Canada, and Australia. Google has transformed from a start-up firm to a multi-national corporation; however, the majority of its employees are still based in the Mountain View headquarters. Google has international presence in all continents of the world other than Africa and Antarctica.

However, the location of its international employee base is divided into two primary groups: engineering and product development team, and a sales force team. Google offers customer interfaces in over 40 different languages and close to 50 different currency exchanges to date.

Threats and Challenges

Google is vulnerable in various aspects. Weak customer lock-in, eroding public trust, lawsuits, and too much dependence on search advertising are risks that the company faces. Google's stock price has been viewed as overvalued by many financial analysts and resulted in a recent decline. Google has almost twice as many search advertising click-through as its nearest competitor; however, they lack maturity and customer lock-in that Yahoo possesses. Yahoo has the advantage of having over 141 million customer profiles that can be integrated with their search engine to customize search results tailored for individual interests. Google only began subscribing customers via GMail and its personalized homepage for users.The competitive threat from Microsoft is foreboding. Microsoft is expected to aggressively compete head to head with Google by leveraging its Windows monopoly to win the search market. Microsoft's search engine will be embedded into the core of Microsoft's nextgeneration operating system, Windows Vista. At a technology conference in March 2006, Neil Holloway, Microsoft President for Europe, Middle East and Africa indicates, "What we're saying is that in six months' time we'll be more relevant in the U.S. market place than Google" (Reuters, 2006a). Only time will tell whether Microsoft is able to compete successfully in the search market, Microsoft certainly has scale, industry influence, and capital. They can quickly ramp up using its $7 billion plus budget in R&D annually. Steve Ballmer, CEO of Microsoft, has acknowledged that in recent years Microsoft has not been spending enough R&D in the area of search technology, and has promised to put a big emphasis on it in the future (Linn, 2004). Microsoft is known to setup a R&D center on search technology in Mountain View, California. While Yahoo and Microsoft's MSN are leading the assault as large companies in search engines, there are many new start-ups in the search industry that specialize in niche search capabilities. Larry Ellison, CEO of Oracle, has claimed that Oracle will be filling the gap in enterprise search business, a market that Google has not penetrated rigorously (Reuters, 2006b).

In order for Google to stay ahead of its competitors, it must broaden its horizons. "Google needs to make that leap into display advertising," says Charlene Li, a Forrester Research analyst. "Right now, their advertising base is really comprised of direct marketers, not traditional brand marketers, and they really don't have the expertise and credibility that Microsoft and Yahoo and AOL have in that area" (Elgin, 2004). Google is beginning to diversify its revenue stream by branching into different areas of advertising. Google Video, a pay-for-video service allows content owners to charge fees for users to watch programs on their PCs. Content include NBA basketball games, music videos, news, and CBS prime-time shows. Google's acquisition of dMarc is also evidence of its efforts to expand its customer base to attract the offline customers as well, specifically through the radio broadcast medium. Then, there are political, copyright, and privacy issues that Google constantly deals with. Google has been the subject of much debate at GMail's release, as the correlation between GMail and Google's search poses enormous privacy risks. A California state senator proposed a law to ban advertising function where Google sponsored ads is displayed based on keywords found in an email read. Privacy advocates addressed the danger of having personal email retained in Google's servers even after being deleted by the user explicitly. However, many critics are triggered by public reaction to information stored on external computers that sometimes fall into the wrong hands. Computer users should be aware of the perils they potentially face and should not expect more privacy in an email than sending a telegram or postcard. Google also faced an onslaught of lawsuits, especially over the past 18 months (LaPlante, 2006). There have been numerous occasions when Google's AdWords customers had to pay for clicks that turned out to be fraudulent or manipulated in some way. Other threats include allegations of stolen source code in their Orkut software; "Google bombing" where some users deliberately undermine the effectiveness of the PageRank algorithm by changing site linkages to web pages to gain ranking scores; and copyright law violations for digitizing books without the permission of copyright holders in the Google Book Search initiative. These issues still remain controversial and some are still being fought in court.

Current and Future Perspectives

Google has already started initiatives to target radio, print media, and other media advertising. GTalk, Google's advertisement-free instant messaging and Internet telephony application may become an appealing option as well. The company is looking to advance its VoIP services with potential for GTalk to become an advertisement-supported voice-calling product, integrating phone number and Web searches into the interface. Among new products, Google is planning to release the GDrive, an online disk storage drive for users. In addition, there is evidence that Google is moving into telecommunications business as the company has been interested in buying dark fibers nation-wide owned by various telecom service providers. Google placed a job listing seeking telecom expertise who could procure dark fiber for the company. It is rare for companies to buy sizable amounts of cable unless they have huge data demands (e.g., banks), but it may be an attempt for Google to further cut down costs in network usage in the future (Hansen, 2005). Other future product speculations include a Google web browser. Google has also expressed interest in the wireless market space and has formed partnerships with mobile phone vendors Samsung and China Mobile. At the 2006 Consumer Electronics Show in Las Vegas, Page announced Google's plans to distribute a consumer software bundle called Google Pack. Google Pack is the answer to Page's frustration that new home computers do not come with enough easy-to-use applications. It contains Google software including Google Desktop, GTalk, anti-virus, anti-spyware, FireFox browser, and Adobe Reader. Dell Computer is considering using GooglePack as part of its preinstalled software packages for selling new PCs.

In 2006, Google released the 802.11 Wi-Fi initiatives in the San Francisco area. A Wi-Fi VPN client called Google Secure Access allows all San Francisco's residents wireless Internet access. Supplying free Wi-Fi is a major step of making information more available and to get people onto the Internet more easily, a significant move to ubiquitous, affordable Internet access. Furthermore, Google invest in wireless start-up companies that are developing Wi-Fi community networks including FON and Meraki. Google is partnering with other companies to invest approximately $100 million to develop broadband Internet over power lines. Network computer maker Wyse Technology says there were speculations about a $200 Google-branded PC that would likely be marketed in China and India through local telecommunication companies. The only relevant source of information to support the claim is Google's funding support of the one laptop per child (OLPC) non-profit association dedicated to research and development of cheap laptop computer for children in developing markets. The initiatives potentially allow more users access to educational information over the Internet, benefiting society and increasing the standard of living around the world.

In only a short period of time, Google has become a dominant player in search technology and a formidable threat to many other technology firms in various industry sectors including advertising, standard software, web application development, and telecommunication networks. Behind the scenes, the use of information technology has been strategic and critical for Google's search engine success and other Google products and services. A variety of advanced concepts in computer science have been applied to many of Google's products and services ranging from topics in distributed systems, machine learning, software architecture, and communications networks. Google's vision of applying advanced computing concepts and innovative ideas has allowed the company to stay as a forefront leader. However, there are even greater challenges for Google as it matures into a multi-national corporation. How will Google be able to enter international markets where information dissemination is highly regulated and controlled by the foreign governments? Can Google continue to sustain its rapid growth while continue to hold on its unique work culture? With the massive amount of information collected on a daily basis, will Google invade privacy concerns? Will Google be able to maintain its technology leadership as competition gets even more intense? And how real is the threat from Microsoft as it claims to defend itself and compete rigorously with Google in the search market? The story behind Google is only a start. Only time will tell Google's destiny. Many futurists predict that Google may perhaps become the most important technology company this decade, similar to how Microsoft and Intel have changed the technology industry in the past.

References

1. www.google.com/corporate/index.html
2. www.google.com/press/

Articles

1. Educating Learning Technology Designers: Guiding and Inspiring Future Creators of Innovative Educational Tools, Chris DiGiano, Shelley Goldman, Mike Chorost, 2008
2. Extracting knowledge from the World Wide Web, Monika Henzinger, Steve Lawrence, *Mapping Knowledge Domains*, 2003.

❈ ❈ ❈

8. Nokia Corporation Ltd.

Nokia Corporation is a Finnish multinational communications corporation, focused on wired and wireless telecommunications, with 112,262 employees in 120 countries, sales in more than 150 countries and global annual revenue of 51.058 billion euros as of 2007.It is the world's largest manufacturer of mobile telephones: its global device market share was about 40% in Q4 of 2007. Nokia produces mobile phones for every major market segment and protocol, including GSM, CDMA, and W-CDMA. Nokia's subsidiary Nokia Siemens Networks produces telecommunications network equipments, solutions and services.

Background

Nokia's corporate headquarters are located in Espoo, a city neighbouring Finland's capital Helsinki. It has sites for research and development, manufacturing and sales in many continents throughout the world. Nokia employed 21,453 people in R&D in 2006. Nokia Research Center, founded in 1986, is Nokia's industrial research unit of about 800 researchers, engineers and scientists. It has sites in seven countries - Finland, Denmark, Germany, China, Japan, United Kingdom and United States. Production facilities are located at Espoo, Oulu and Salo, Finland; Manaus, Brazil; Beijing, Dongguan and Suzhou, China; Fleet, England; Bochum (closing planned for mid-2008), Germany; Komárom, Hungary; Chennai, India; Reynosa, Mexico; Cluj-Napoca, Romania and Masan, South Korea. Nokia's Design Department remains in Salo, Finland.

Nokia plays a very large role in the economy of Finland as it is by far the largest Finnish company, accounting for about a third of the market capitalization of the Helsinki Stock Exchange (OMX Helsinki) as of 2007; a unique situation for an industrialized country. It is an important employer in Finland and several small companies have grown into large ones as Nokia's subcontractors. Nokia increased Finland's GDP by more than 1.5% in 1999 alone. In 2004 Nokia's share of the Finland's GDP was 3.5% and accounted for almost a quarter of Finland's exports in 2003. In 2006, Nokia generated revenue that for the first time exceeded the state budget of Finland.

Finns have ranked Nokia many times as the best Finnish brand and employer. Nokia is listed as the 5th most valuable global brand in Business Week's Best Global Brands list of 2007 (1st non-US company), the 20th most admirable company worldwide in Fortune's World's Most Admired Companies list of 2007 (1st in network communications, 4th non-US company), and is the world's 119th largest company in Fortune Global 500 list of 2007, up from 131 of the previous year.

Vision

A World Where Everyone Can Be Connected - June 2007

Everyone has a need to communicate and share. Nokia helps people to fulfill this need and we help people feel close to what matters to them. We focus on providing consumers with very human technology – technology that is intuitive, a joy to use, and beautiful. We are living in an era where connectivity is becoming truly ubiquitous.

The communications industry continues to change and the internet is at the center of this transformation. Today, the internet is Nokia's quest. Nokia's strategy relies on growing, transforming, and building the Nokia business to ensure its future success. Clearly the industry is thriving. Throughout 2004, around 800,000 new subscribers have joined the mobile world every day. "As a result of fast growth in the number of new subscribers, we now expect the mobile subscription base to reach two billion in 2007, one year earlier than our previous forecast," Alahuhta added. Nokia also revised its previous first-quarter global mobile device market volume estimate to 141 million units. Nokia's first-quarter sales were 44.7 million units, representing market share of close to 32 percent.

Globally, there are now almost six million 3G WCDMA subscribers and Nokia anticipate that 2004 will be a pivotal year for 3G WCDMA. Indeed, analysts estimate that over 60 commercial 3G WCDMA networks will be in service by the end of the year. The company's aim to fulfill the promise of 3G was demonstrated by the launch of the Nokia 6630 mobile device in an attempt to bring 3G to the mass market, and the new Nokia MetroSite50 base station for 3G WCDMA deployment.

Branding Strategy

Nokia has detailed many personality characteristics for its brand, but employees do not have to remember every characteristic. They do, however, have to remember the overall impression of the list of attributes, as you would when thinking about someone you have met. As the focus is on customer relationships, the Nokia personality is like a trusted friend. Building friendship and trust is at the heart of the Nokia brand and the human dimension created by the brand personality carries over into the positioning strategy for the brand.

Positioning

When Nokia positions its brand in the crowded mobile phone marketplace, its message must clearly bring together the technology and human side of its offer in a powerful way. The specific message that is conveyed to consumers in every advertisement and market communication (though not necessarily in these words) is "Only Nokia Human Technology enables you to get more out of life". In many cases, this is represented by the tag line, "We call this human technology". This gives consumers a sense of trust and consideration by the company, as though to say that Nokia understand what they want in life, and how it can help. And it knows that technology is really only an enabler so that you-the customer-can enjoy a better life. Nokia thus uses a combination of inspirational, benefit-based, emotional features, and competition-driven positioning strategies. It owns the "human" dimension of mobile communications, leaving its competitors wondering what to own (or how to position themselves), having taken the best position for itself.

Product Design

Nokia is a great brand because it knows that the essence of the brand needs to be reflected in everything the company does, especially those that impact the consumer. Product design is clearly critical to the success of the brand, but how does Nokia manage to inject personality into product design? The answer is that it gives a great deal of thought to how the user of its phones will experience the brand, and how it can make that experience reflect its brand character. The large display screen, for example, is the "face" of the phone. Nokia designers describe it as the "eye into the soul of the product". The shape of phones is curvy and easy to hold. The faceplates and their different colours can be changed to fit the personality, lifestyle, and mood of the user. The soft key touch pads also add to the feeling of friendliness, expressing the brand personality. Product design focuses on the consumer and his needs, and is summed up in the slogan, "human technology."

Nokia now accounts for over half of the value of the Finland stock market, and has taken huge market share from its competitors. According to one brand valuation study carried out in mid-1999, it ranked 11th on the world's most valuable brand list, making it the highest-ranking non-U.S. brand.

As has been pointed out, it has unseated Motorola. Nokia achieved its brilliant feat through consistent branding, backed by first-class logistics and manufacturing, all of which revolve around what consumers what.

Reality Room

To bring Nokia's evolutionary vision alive, the Nokia Reality Room will lend a real touch and feel to various technologies by showing live EDGE and live WCDMA voice and data demonstrations on pre-commercial platforms. These access solutions will be supported by network planning, optimization and services such as charging. This will show real Nokia end-to-end solutions, underscoring Nokia's leadership in enabling operators to build the multimedia future today by maximizing their current return on investments and minimizing costs.

Nokia will bring its 3GPP standards compliant commercial WCDMA 3G system to the market in the third quarter of this year. Features will include voice and packet data, which are currently being tested by Nokia's 3G customers in more than 40 pre-commercial networks around the world. Of these customers, 26 are already rolling out their 3G networks. Nokia is focusing on compatibility with the commercial WCDMA 3G standards, which is essential for the end-to-end functionality, interoperability and backward compatibility of the equipment. The first networks will be launched during the second half of 2002, and the mass market will start in 2003.

Shown live at the Nokia Connection, MobileOne (M1) will publicly make a third-generation packet data call on its WCDMA network, which is currently being rolled-out in the country. This Nokia supplied network is compliant with the latest global 3rd Generation Partnership Project (3GPP) standard. At the Nokia Connection, Nokia will also showcase the Nokia UltraSite and MetroSite WCDMA base station solutions, the Nokia MetroHopper microwave radio for urban areas, and the Nokia Dual Masthead Amplifier, a compact package consisting of two amplifier units optimized for use with Nokia WCDMA 3G base stations.

Other solutions on show to enhance the operators' competitiveness include the Nokia Advanced Indoor Radio (AIR) for cost-efficient indoor coverage, and Nokia RealTilt, a remote antenna tilt solution for optimizing network performance in real time.

High-Capacity Base Station Controller - BSC3i

As part of Nokia's network evolution strategy, Nokia will introduce its newest high-capacity base station controller. The Nokia BSC3i offers all of Nokia's proven GSM and EDGE RAN control features, as well as GSM/EDGE/WCDMA interworking functionality, in a compact one-cabinet configuration with extremely high capacity. The Nokia BSC3i is equipped with extensive IP connectivity facilities, and it will support GSM and EDGE evolution far into the future.

All-IP Mobility System

Nokia will also demonstrate the latest architecture, functionality, applications and benefits of its All-IP solutions, including All-IP Radio-Access Network (RAN) and All-IP Core Network. The All-IP network architecture will enable mobile operators to offer rich-call experiences. Within a single session different kinds of media, including, text, pictures, music and video, can be combined with voice calls. By systematically separating network resources used for the control and user functionalities, All-IP networks will also bring significant cost efficiencies to mobile networks while delivering IP multimedia services. The Nokia All-IP Core Network demonstration exhibits IP multimedia applications and the technologies that enable them, including new protocols such as 3GPP-based SIP (Session Initiation Protocol). Based on standards, this solution will enable mass-market adoption of seamless multimedia services. The All-IP RAN experimental system demonstration presents how the packet optimized multiradio access network handles increasing amounts of packet data with fewer network elements, thus improving QoS (Quality of Services) and radio network efficiency.

To support the development of All-IP RAN, Nokia recently announced at the 3GSM World Congress, an initiative to jointly define a revolutionary Open IP Base Station Architecture, leading to modular base stations with open internal interfaces. The architecture is intended for use in next-generation All-IP Radio Access Networks supporting multiple standards. Nokia has invited other industry players to join the initiative, which will bring more innovative and cost-effective base stations to operators. A market leader in the cellular industry in Asia Pacific, Nokia provides innovative, industry-leading and market-relevant technology and products to around 20 diverse markets in the region.

Nokia is the world leader in mobile communications. Backed by its experience, innovation, user-friendliness and secure solutions, the company has become the leading supplier of mobile phones and a leading supplier of mobile, fixed broadband and IP networks. By adding mobility to the Internet Nokia creates new opportunities for companies and further enriches the daily lives of people. Nokia is one of the most broadly held companies in the world with listings on six major exchanges.

Marketing Strategy

NO DOUBT THAT the products from the Finnish company, Nokia, are some of the very best in the world, but the company still hasn't found a profitable way to market its goods. The very reason that other mobile phone companies are fast eating up Nokia's market share is their superior (yet simple) marketing practices. Motorola and Samsung must now be in the FUW (frequently used words) list in Nokia's board meetings. These companies have made Nokia pay dearly for its rudimentary approach in marketing its phones. The aggressive marketing practices followed by Motorola have hit Nokia very hard and it is losing very crucial global market share every month to its American competitor.

Nokia, quite alarmed by the dropping sales of its phones, is now putting all its weight behind the N-Series range. The N-Series is packed with multimedia features and Nokia believes that these phones might woo the costumers back to the big daddy of the mobile phone world. But Espoo, we have a problem!! (Nokia is headquartered at Espoo, Finland). While Motorola (quite intelligently) gives a dashy-flashy name to every phone it brings into the market, Nokia tends to do the exact opposite. Nokia from the very start has relied on numbers rather than names. This strategy worked very well in the past, but only because there wasn't much competition back then. But times have changed. Every month the market sees at least a dozen new handsets from an equal number of manufacturers. Consumers now have more than they can choose.

Consumers are more attracted by names because they can thus easily relate to the features of the phone. This is evident from the success of the MotoRazr, MotoSlvr, MotoRizr and MotoKrzr. These phones are not packed with heavy multimedia features like the N-Series; still they are selling like hot cakes. Just by reading the name of the handset, one gets a broad idea what the phone looks like or what its features are. Nokia advertises more than Motorola. Still its market share is dropping. Motorola does not need to spend much money for the promotion of its products and it doesn't have to worry about the marketing of these phones; it just simplifies its job by naming its products right. Take the example of Apple, it did not have to do much to promote its iPhone. Thanks to the leaked photos and technical specifications, it became the most anticipated gadget of all times.

It is high time that Nokia starts applying some common sense to its marketing strategies. It doesn't have to do anything great, other than just naming its phones. A few months ago, a highly placed Nokia official told Reuters that his company would soon go the Motorola way and start using names for its new phones. It is in Nokia's best interest that it takes to this path as early as possible, otherwise the once market leader might see its market share plummeting to even lower depths.

Promotion - Push and Pull Strategies

"Push or Pull"? Marketing theory distinguishes between two main kinds of promotional strategy - "push" and "pull".

A "push" promotional strategy makes use of a company's sales force and trade promotion activities to create consumer demand for a product. The producer promotes the product to wholesalers, the wholesalers promote it to retailers, and the retailers promote it to consumers. A good example of "push" selling is mobile phones, where the major handset manufacturers such as Nokia promote their products via retailers such as Carphone Warehouse. Personal selling and trade promotions are often the most effective promotional tools for companies such as Nokia — for example offering subsidies on the handsets to encourage retailers to sell higher volumes. A "push" strategy tries to sell directly to the consumer, bypassing other distribution channels (e.g., selling insurance or holidays directly). With this type of strategy, consumer promotions and advertising are the most likely promotional tools.

A "pull" selling strategy is one that requires high spending on advertising and consumer promotion to build up consumer demand for a product. If the strategy is successful, consumers will ask their retailers for the product, the retailers will ask the wholesalers, and the wholesalers will ask the producers. A good example of a pull is the heavy advertising and promotion of children's' toys –

mainly on television. Consider the recent BBC promotional campaign for its new pre-school programme – the Fimbles. Aimed at two to four-year-olds, 130 episodes of Fimbles have been made and are featured everyday on digital children's channel CBeebies and BBC2.

As part of the promotional campaign, the BBC has agreed a deal with toy maker Fisher-Price to market products based on the show, which it hopes will emulate the popularity of the Tweenies. Under the terms of the deal, Fisher-Price will develop, manufacture and distribute a range of Fimbles products including soft, plastic and electronic learning toys for the UK and Ireland.

In 2001, BBC Worldwide (the commercial division of the BBC) achieved sales of £90m from its children's brands and properties last year. The demand created from broadcasting of the Fimbles and a major advertising campaign is likely to "pull" demand from children and encourage retailers to stock Fimbles toys in the stores for Christmas 2002.

One Global Branding Strategy

One global strategy for Nokia, "1,001 reasons" for mankind: The Wall Street Journal reports on Nokia's strategy to move to a single global message. But is the message the right one to achieve a global identity for the Nokia brand? NOKIA CORP., the world's largest cellphone maker, is going global with its advertising, a first for the company, as it tries to create a stronger, more-unified identity in the increasingly tough cellphone-branding war.

The corporate campaign, which carries the slogan "1,001 reasons to have a Nokia imaging phone," is rolling out across Europe, Africa and Asia, showing up in television, print and online ads. Nokia also plans to bring it to the U.S., tentatively in several months. It aims to send one message in all countries where Nokia is sold, a strategy that departs from past approaches that used different images and messages in different countries.

Yet, a global strategy has some risks. A one-size-fits-all approach could translate into bad business if consumers misunderstand nuances or cross-cultural differences. For Nokia, Grey Worldwide agency SEK & Grey created the ads for Europe, the Middle East and Africa. Another agency, Bates Advertising in Singapore, part of WPP Group, is handling the Asia Pacific region. The two worked together to come up with one campaign. Effective messaging creates emotional connections with your audience. True-to-the-brand evocative messaging creates a want-to-know-more, lean forward reaction. A strategy that focuses the consumer on a single key product difference creates an industry conversation Nokia could own.

Instead of expressing one best difference in their products over those of the competition, Nokia decided an additional thousand reasons are better than one great one. Not only that, but as Pekka Rantala, senior vice president of marketing for Nokia's multimedia business teases, Nokia does not tell you what the reasons are, just that there are 1,001 of them. Mr. Rantala envisions future ads for Nokia identifying at least some of these 1,001 reasons.

As Nokia will soon discover, consumers do not waste their time with obscure advertising messaging. If the consumer must spend more than a few seconds decoding an advertising message, the advertising is doomed. And besides, who has time to filter through 1,001 reasons in making a purchase decision? According to *The Journal,* the ad uses bright, crisp photos, such as a close-up of a baby's cherubic face, to denote using the phones to store cherished pictures. How often have we seen this, the ineffective message glossed over by high-production-value creative and sold as effective brand strategy? For Nokia, a global company based in Finland, staying with this strategy will create future ads lost in the white noise of global culture, falling short of developing human connections so necessary for market traction, in any language.

Corporate Culture

Nokia's official corporate culture manifesto, The Nokia Way, emphasizes the speed and flexibility of decision-making in a flat, networked organization, although the corporation's size necessarily imposes a certain amount of bureaucracy. Equality of opportunities and openness of communication are also stressed, along with management leadership and employee participation. Nokia is a progressive and forward-thinking mobile technology group that spends a significant amount of its revenue on research and development, and prides itself on often being the first to market with new products and applications.

The official business language of Nokia is English. All documentation is written in English, and is used in official intra-company spoken communication and e-mail. Until May 2007, the Nokia Values were Customer Satisfaction, Respect, Achievement, and Renewal. In May 2007, Nokia redefined its values after initiating a series of discussions worldwide as to what the new values of the company should be. Based on the employee suggestions, the new values were defined as: Engaging You, Achieving Together, and Passion for Innovation and Very Human.

References

1. www.infonortics.com/publications/PDF
2. www.multilingualwebmaster.com/qa/google.html
3. www.wx.bsjh.tcc.edu.tw/Anatomy.pdf
4. www.google.com/webmasters/bot.html
5. www.nokia.com
6. www.companyinfo.com

9. RANBAXY PHARMACEUTICALS LTD.

Ranbaxy Laboratories Limited is an integrated, research based, international pharmaceutical company, producing a wide range of quality, affordable generic medicines. Ranbaxy is ranked amongst the top ten global generic companies and has a presence in 23 of the top 25 pharmacy markets of the world. The company is headquartered in India. It has presence in 49 countries, with manufacturing facilities in 11 and a diverse portfolio.

Background

Ranbaxy was incorporated in 1961, Bhai Mohan Singh was the founder of the company. He bought the company from his cousins Ranjit Singh and Gurbux Singh. Ranbaxy's name is a fusion of Ranjit and Gurbax's names. Ranbaxy went public in 1973.

Ranbaxy Laboratories Limited (Ranbaxy) established in 1961 is a research-based international pharmaceutical company. It is India's largest pharmaceutical company and is among the top-10 generic pharmaceutical companies in the world. The company caters to the Indian market through its seven marketing business units with each business unit providing differentiated services to the market. Ranbaxy has invested approximately 10 per cent of its revenues in R&D, among the highest in Indian pharmaceutical companies. It offers a wide range of high-quality pharmaceutical products in key therapeutic areas such as urology, inflammatory respiratory diseases, infectious diseases, metabolic disorders, cardiovascular, dermatological, and central nervous system. It has been actively participating in the development of innovative drugs for certain common as well as under-treated diseases such as malaria and AIDS. These activities are a part of its corporate social responsibility initiative. The company is fully integrated and develops and manufactures products starting with Active Pharmaceutical Ingredients (API) to the finished dosage form and ultimately markets these products under the Ranbaxy label throughout the world.

Ranbaxy Laboratories Limited, headquartered in India, is an integrated, research based, international pharmaceutical company, producing a wide range of quality, affordable generic medicines, trusted by healthcare professionals and patients across geographies. It is ranked amongst the top ten generic companies world-wide. The company serves its customers in over 125 countries and has an expanding international portfolio of affiliates, joint ventures and alliances, ground operations in 49 countries and manufacturing operations in 8 countries.

Ranbaxy's global sales for the year 2005 stood at EUR 968 million with over 75 per cent of this coming from international markets. The US continues to be its largest market contributing 28 per cent to its global sales. The company is further accelerating its pace in Europe which currently accounts for 17 per cent of its global sales. In early 2006, the company acquired Terapia the largest independent generic company in Romania. Furthermore, in Italy, the company acquired the unbranded generic business of Allen S.P.A., a division of GSK while in Belgium it acquired Ethimed N.V. Later during the year, the company also acquired Mundogen, the generic business of GSK in Spain, further consolidating its position in the region.

Background

Ranbaxy's first joint venture was set up in Lagos (Nigeria) in 1977. In 1985, Ranbaxy Research Foundation was established and Stancare, Ranbaxy's second pharmaceutical market division started functioning. In 1987, production started at Ranbaxy's Toansa Plant (Punjab) and with this Ranbaxy became India's largest manufacturer of antibiotics/antibacterial. In 1988, Ranbaxy's Toansa Plant got US FDA approval. In 1990, Ranbaxy was granted its first US patent, for Doxycyline. In 1993, Ranbaxy set up a joint venture in China. In 1994, Ranbaxy established regional headquarters in UK and USA. In the same year, its GDR was listed in Luxembourg Stock Exchange. In 1995, Ranbaxy acquired Ohm Laboratories, a manufacturing facility in the US and inaugurated state-of-the art new manufacturing wing at Ranbaxy's US subsidiary Ohm Laboratories Inc. In 1997, Ranbaxy crossed a sales turnover of Rs. 10,000 million.

In 1998, Ranbaxy entered USA, world's largest pharmaceutical market, with products under its own name. In the same year, Ranbaxy filed its first Investigational New Drug (IND) application with the Drugs Controller General of India for approvals to conduct Phase 1 Clinical trials. In 1999, Ranbaxy commenced trials for its NCE. In 2000, Ranbaxy acquired Bayer's Generic business in Germany, and entered into Brazil, the largest pharmaceutical market in South America. In 2001, Ranbaxy set up a manufacturing facility in Vietnam. In 2003, Ranbaxy launched Cefuroxime Axetil after approval from USFDA. It was the first approval granted to any generic company for this product. In 2003, Ranbaxy and Glaxosmithkline PLC entered into an alliance for drug discovery and development. In 2004, Ranbaxy acquired a wholly-owned subsidiary RPG (Aventis) SA and began operations in France as a Top 10 generic company. In 2005, Ranbaxy launched operations in Canada and acquired generic product portfolio from EFARMES of Spain. In 2006, Ranbaxy acquired Be Tabs pharmaceuticals of South Africa, unbranded generic business of GSK in Italy & Spain, and Terapia of Romania.

- 1962: Ranjit Singh and Gurbux Singh incorporate Ranbaxy to market pharmaceuticals in Amritsar, India, and borrow funding from moneylender Bhai Mohan Singh.
- 1966: Bhai Mohan Singh takes over Ranbaxy in lieu of repayment of the loan.
- 1967: Son Dr. Parvinder Singh joins the company, which begins producing generic drugs.
- 1969: Calmpose, a Valium generic, is launched, becoming the company's first success.
- 1973: Ranbaxy goes public and builds new API chemicals facility in Mohali.
- 1977: The Company begins production in Lagos, Nigeria through a joint venture.
- 1983: The company opens a dosage plant in Dewas.
- 1987: The Company builds a state-of-the-art API facility in Toansa in preparation for entry into the U.S. market.
- 1988: The Toansa facility receives FDA approval.
- 1992: The Company launches a joint marketing agreement with Eli Lilly.
- 1993: A joint venture is launched in China; a new research-driven NCE and NDDS strategy is launched.
- 1994: The Company opens a new research and development facility in Gurgaon, India.
- 1995: The Company acquires Ohm Laboratories in the United States and builds a new FDA-approved production facility.
- 1998: Ranbaxy begins marketing its own branded drugs in the United States; the company launches clinical trials on the first in-house developed molecule.
- 2000: Ranbaxy acquires Basics, Bayer's generics business in Germany; the company enters Brazil.
- 2003: Ranbaxy successfully completes the first NCE phase I clinical trial; the company acquires RPG (Aventis) in France, becoming the leading generics manufacturer for that market.
- 2005: The Company launches a new $100 million production facility in Brazil.

Development Phases

Ranbaxy Laboratories had its origins in the early 1960s when Ranjit Singh and Gurbux Singh, two employees of a Japanese pharmaceutical company operating in India, formed their own pharmaceutical preparations company in Amritsar, in Punjab state. The two merged their names to form the name for their company, Ranbaxy. Through the 1960s, India's pharmaceutical market remained dominated by foreign drug makers. The domestic pharmaceutical manufacturing industry was limited in large part to the dosage preparation, packaging, and distribution of existing formulations. Like many Indian drug companies of this period, Ranbaxy linked up with a European pharmaceutical company, and began production in 1962.

Ranbaxy's owners sought additional financing and turned to a local moneylender, Bhai Mohan Singh. By 1966, the pair had built up debts to Singh of more than the equivalent of $100,000. When Singh, a native of Pakistan who had arrived in India at the beginning of that decade, came to collect, the Ranbaxy partners offered to turn over their company to him instead. Singh agreed to the deal and launched the Ranbaxy family on the path toward building one of India's largest business empires. Under Bhai Mohan Singh, Ranbaxy initially maintained its course of preparing and packing existing branded pharmaceutical products for the Indian market. The entry of Singh's eldest son, Parvinder, into the company in 1967, however, set the company on a new course to become a fully independent pharmaceutical company.

Parvinder Singh had just graduated with a Ph.D. in chemistry from the University of Michigan. The younger Singh's background in chemistry complemented his father's business flair. Yet Parvinder Singh himself quickly displayed a talent for business and was credited, in large part, with guiding the company into the ranks of the global pharmaceutical leaders. Ranbaxy's good fortune came in 1970, when the Indian government passed legislation that effectively ended patent protection in the pharmaceutical industry. Indian pharmaceutical manufacturers were now able to produce low-cost, generic versions of popular, yet expensive drugs, revolutionizing the drug industry in India and in much of the world. The Singhs quickly took advantage of India's large, highly trained, yet inexpensive workforce, building up a strong staff of chemists and chemical engineers.

The company struck pay dirt early on, when it launched Calmpose, a generic formulation of the hugely popular Roche discovery, Valium. Released in 1969, Calmpose immediately placed Ranbaxy on India's pharmaceutical map. The company expanded quickly, and by 1973, Ranbaxy opened a new factory, in Mohali, for the production of active principal ingredients (APIs). This facility enabled the company to expand its range of generic medications and ingredients. To finance its growth, the company listed on the Indian Stock Exchange that year. Ranbaxy's ability to produce generic medications at far lower cost than its branded competitors placed the company in a strong position for international expansion, especially in less developed markets. The company began its internationalization early on, launching a joint venture in Nigeria. That operation opened a production facility in Lagos in 1977.

Ranbaxy expanded its production at home as well, opening a new state-of-the-art dosage plant in Dewas in 1983. In 1987, the company became India's leading antibiotic and antibacterial producer when it completed a new API plant in Toansa, in Punjab, that year. The Toansa facility backed up Ranbaxy's plans to enter the U.S. market, and in 1988, the Toansa plant received Food and Drug Administration (FDA) approval. Ranbaxy formulated a new strategy, that of becoming a full-fledged pharmaceutical company. The driving force behind the company's new direction was Parvinder Singh, who was named the company's managing director in 1982. Nonetheless, Bhai Mohan Singh remained in control of the company.

As part of its new strategy, Ranbaxy launched its own research and development center in 1985. The company also stepped up its marketing efforts, launching a new dedicated marketing subsidiary, Stancare, that year. By 1990, the company had a new product to sell, when Ranbaxy was granted a U.S. patent for its doxycycline antibiotic preparation. The following year, the company was granted a U.S. patent for its cephalosporin preparations, and the company built a new state-of-the-art facility for their production in Mohali. A major milestone for the company came in 1992, when it reached a marketing agreement with Eli Lilly & Co. The companies set up a joint venture in India to produce and market Lilly's branded pharmaceuticals for the domestic market. At the same time, Lilly agreed to begin marketing Ranbaxy's generic medications in the United States. In this way, Ranbaxy gained wide scale access, backed by the highly respected Lilly, into the world's single largest drugs market.

Parvinder Singh took over as head of the company—ousting his father in what was described as a family feud—in 1992. By then, Ranbaxy had grown into one of India's largest pharmaceutical companies on the basis of its generics production. Yet as pressure grew on India to begin enforcing international drug patents, the company itself appeared to have reached a crossroads—whether to remain focused on copying generic molecules, or to begin developing new drugs in-house. The company chose the latter, and in 1993 adopted a new corporate mission to announce its reformulated ambitions: "To become a research-based international company."

New Century - Global Branding

Ranbaxy made good on its mission—by the middle of the next decade, nearly 80 percent of its sales came from outside of India. As a first step, the company launched a new joint venture, in China, backing its entry into that market with a production facility in Guangzhou. The following year, the company established subsidiaries in London, England, and in Raleigh, North Carolina. In 1995, the company stepped up its U.S. presence with the purchase of Ohm Laboratories Inc., which gave the company its first manufacturing plant in that market. Ranbaxy then launched construction of a new and state-of-the-art manufacturing wing, which completed that year, gained FDA approval.

This new facility enabled Ranbaxy to step up its presence in the United States, and in 1998 the company began marketing its generic products under its own brand name. That year, in addition, the company filed an application to begin Phase I clinical testing on its first in-house developed NCE. The following year, the company's NDDS efforts paid off as well, when Bayer acquired the rights to market Ranbaxy's single daily-dosage ciprofloxacin formulation. Ranbaxy's international expansion continued as well, with the launch of marketing operations in Brazil. As the largest pharmaceuticals market in Latin America, that country was the cornerstone of the company's plans to expand throughout the region. Ranbaxy also expanded in Europe, with the agreement in 2000 to acquire Bayer's Germany-based generics business, Basics. The company also added production plants in Malaysia and Thailand.

Parvinder Singh died in 1999 and longtime right-hand man D.S. Brar took over as company leader, naming family outsider Brian Tempest as company president. The new management team continued Singh's expansion strategy, opening a new manufacturing plant in Vietnam in 2001. Ranbaxy also sought new alliances, and in 2003 the company reached a global drug discovery and development partnership with GlaxoSmithKline. That agreement called for Glaxo to handle the later-stage development process for Ranbaxy created molecules. The company's international expansion also took a major step forward at the end of 2002, when it agreed to acquire RPG (Aventis) in France, that country's leading generic drugs producer.

Ranbaxy's sales had by then topped the $1 billion mark, placing the company not only as the leader in India's pharmaceuticals industry, but also among the ranks of the world's top 100 pharmaceuticals companies. Ranbaxy also boasted a place among the world's top ten generic drugs producers. In addition, the company had advanced a growing number of its own NCE and NDDS molecules into clinical testing. The company's transition into research-based product development was seen as crucial as India announced its intention to enforce international drug patents at the beginning of 2005.

Ranbaxy appeared prepared to meet this challenge, however, and confidently set its sights on boosting its annual sales past $2 billion by 2007 and to more than $5 billion by the beginning of the next decade. International growth remained an essential part of that strategy. The company began negotiations for a major acquisition in Germany at the end of 2004, which was expected to be completed in 2005. The company also launched construction of a new $100 million production facility in Brazil. Meanwhile, Ranbaxy continued to increase its research and development budget, with the goal of generating as much as 40 percent of its revenues from its in-house innovations by the 2010s. Ranbaxy expected to remain India's drug leader into the new century.

Strategies Adopted

Ranbaxy Laboratories Ltd. (RLL) is the largest pharmaceutical company incorporated in India. It is also amongst the top league globally and is ranked 9th largest generic company worldwide. Ranbaxy is also credited with the tag of true Indian multinational. The company traces its roots to a chemist shop in Delhi. It is one of the first Indian pharmaceutical companies to start a joint venture abroad. Rapid growth of Ranbaxy is attributed mainly to its focused research and joint ventures in India and abroad. It is also innovation and market driven, with a strong distribution network. The company was able to grow successfully in highly competitive markets. In the current business scenario, Ranbaxy is focusing on innovation, alliances, mergers and globalisation to achieve its long-term vision of becoming a global pharmaceutical giant with a turnover of $ 5 billion by 2012. The fruits of such efforts are evident in the latest financial result, as a large chunk of its income comes from new products and exports of generics. The growth of Ranbaxy can be attributed to its ability to identify good windows of opportunity and its ability to grow by leveraging innovation, regulatory knowledge and alliances.

Globalization

Ranbaxy was one of the first companies to make globalization the main plank of its strategy. Starting with generics, Ranbaxy built up a global marketing network. At the same time Ranbaxy developed strengths in Research & Development (R&D). The major competitive advantage is the low cost of innovation. Thus, Ranbaxy was able to give back to the international market the same products they were used to, at much lower costs. Total vertical integration gave Ranbaxy the edge it needed to make a mark in major markets like the USA.

Innovation

The key driver behind Ranbaxy's success is innovation and this is achieved with a similar strategy that is used to market products – give people targets and motivate them. Ranbaxy has time bound targets for research. It plans to have one New Chemical Entity (NCE) by 2012 with several others in various stages of development. The Company has a mechanism to reward new ideas. The research and innovation advantage that Ranbaxy enjoys today is the outcome of the vision of Late Dr Parvinder Singh, Chairman & Managing Director, Ranbaxy. It was his dream to make Ranbaxy "A Research Based International Organization". It was his forward looking approach which ensured that Ranbaxy was way ahead of the game in the Indian pharma industry.

Planned Future

The Company has continued its focus on internationalization with marketing efforts in the USA, the UK, Brazil, China, Germany etc. The Company is now focused on changing the product mix by reducing dependence on Anti-infectives and increasing the share of lifestyle related chronic disease therapies. Ranbaxy has also focused on internationalizing its operations aiming at building privileged assets brands, distribution channels, patents, etc. To further its growth plans, Ranbaxy has not only taken the route of inorganic growth through acquisitions but it has also enhanced its R&D spend and increased the level of investments for proprietary business.

Top management leads Ranbaxy's global quality system and the philosophy is prevention, not detection. This quality culture is spread across the organization where everyone is a part of it. Key benefits from this world class quality program are customer's satisfaction, getting it right the first time and continuous improvement in products and processes. Under the leadership of Dr Brian Tempest, the Quality evolution is continuing as Ranbaxy integrates quality into the strategic planning process and begins operating at entirely new levels. Also, like in almost any endeavor, quality is taken as a core value that sets the expectations for performance across the company. It has also been recognized that Quality is a key factor for Ranbaxy to achieve its mission. Based on the above principles, Ranbaxy's Quality team has been on a journey to catapult the 'Quality Culture' globally so that it pervades the entire organization and helps us to attain sustained quality leadership.

The Strategic Planning Process - Customer Focus

The process always begins with the customers in mind: both external and internal - what they want and what trends will impact them in the future. Accordingly we regularly deliberate with internal customer departments like marketing, R&D and manufacturing to understand their perspective on how best they can serve our external customers. This has resulted in the provision of increasingly better service and products to customers delivered in the most profitable manner. This has also helped in the speedy resolution of issues and pre-empt potential ones.

Implementation

Ranbaxy's Quality management system is based on sound Quality policies and guidelines which are implemented at all manufacturing sites all over the world. In Ranbaxy, Quality is more than a regulatory requirement, rather, it is a way of life that covers the entire gamut of activities right from product development, manufacturing, transportation and complaint handling. Also, quality aspects always take precedence in our choice of business partners like contract / outsourced manufacturers, vendors and CROs. Robust selection criteria are followed while implementing and maintaining a meaningful and effective quality engagement with our partners. Our special initiative on adopting a "Risk based approach" to all time readiness for any inspection (ATR) has resulted in successful inspections of our manufacturing sites, from various regulatory agencies, across the globe.

Moving Up the Value Curve

INDIA'S pharmaceutical giants like Ranbaxy Laboratories Ltd., Reddy's Laboratories and Wockhardt, among others, are making moves to secure a bigger global presence, especially in markets like the US. Having developed a capability to reverse-engineer patented drugs, because the previous patents law in India protected only processes not products, they have trained their sights on the global generics market. The strategy is simple enough: Wait patiently for drugs to go off patent and then flood the world market with cheaper generic versions. Ranbaxy's revenues from the US generic business thus are expected to rise to $1.2 billion by 2008. In the generics business, margins are wafer-thin due to competitive conditions in the developed markets. They improve with branded generics and keep improving as one moves up the value chain to finally making patented drugs. Despite such constraints, however, Ranbaxy is moving up the value curve: from bulk drugs and intermediates to generics and conventional dosage forms. Then it moved on to value-added and branded generics and later to new drug delivery systems. Moving up such a curve improves the bottom line as margins on bulk substances and intermediates do not exceed 10 per cent but go up to 100 per cent or more for new drug discoveries. The last-mentioned is the Holy Grail for Big Pharma but Ranbaxy does not have resources to produce new drug discoveries pegged at $800 million per drug. There is no choice but to plough more resources into R&D and form strategic alliances with MNCs. Ranbaxy has had earlier alliances with Eli Lilly and its current development of an anti-malarial drug, Rbx11160, could be an exemplar for the future as the financial risk was absorbed by a Geneva-based non-profit organization, Medicines for Malaria Venture.

Business Development & Partnerships

Ranbaxy Laboratories Limited, India's largest pharmaceutical company, headquartered in India, is an integrated, research based, international pharmaceutical company, producing a wide range of quality, affordable generic medicines, trusted by healthcare professionals and patients across geographies. It is ranked amongst the top ten generic companies worldwide. The Company has manufacturing operations in 11 countries with a ground presence in 49 countries and its products are available in over 125 countries. The Company is driven by its ambition to achieve US $5 Bn Sales by 2012 and be amongst the top five generic players worldwide. To translate these objectives into reality and to optimize value creation, the Company has adopted a multi-pronged strategy. Acquisition of generic brands overseas, strong emphasis on brand marketing in the US and Europe, entering high potential new markets with value added product offerings, are the major thrust areas. Successful business development transactions form a key component of its business strategies.

Market Busting Moves

Ranbaxy Laboratories Limited has managed to lead the industry and strengthen its global presence by successfully implementing the following Market Busting moves:

- Radically improve your productivity.
- Capitalize on second-order effects of shifts in constraints
- Make a land grab.

Radically Improve Your Productivity

In the competitive and fast-paced pharmaceutical industry, Ranbaxy has actively pursued strategic alliances and acquisitions to gain access to breakthrough technologies and fast growing markets. They have managed to balance their R&D costs and work force by working with some of the leading drug development laboratories around the world, while leveraging their financial support and distribution networks in commercializing scientific discoveries. In 2003, Ranbaxy entered an agreement with Medicines for Malaria Venture, Geneva (MMV) for the development of Synthetic Peroxide anti-malarial drug. The company entered human clinical trials and got approvals to conduct clinical trials in the United Kingdom in 2004.4 As CEO and Managing Director, Dr. Brian Tempest stated, "Ranbaxy is committed to developing a drug that is not only safe and effective, but also affordable to people in India and hundreds of millions others who have to live with this terrible disease everyday." The success of the partnership has further promoted Ranbaxy's image among populations and allowed it to meet a growing and important demand in treating Malaria.

Capitalize on Second-Order Effects of Shifts In Constraints

The growth of generics grew at a faster rate than the total pharmaceutical market from 2003-04. The demand for more affordable drugs in developing countries has attracted several manufacturers to produce quality drugs at low-costs due to economies of scale and more flexible legal frameworks. Ranbaxy has aggressively followed industry trends and penetrated the generics market through alliances and heavy investments in R&D. India's low cost of innovation, production and labor allows it to market and distribute competitively in other parts of the world. Ranbaxy invests about 9% of sales into R&D as it tries to increase its share in the branded drug segments. It has discovered several chemical compounds, got US patents and FDA approval for its drugs, which it distributes in several countries abroad under its brand name. The company has managed to become the market leader in several regions with the fastest growing generics segments such as France, Spain, Russia and many others.

Make a Land Grab

After years of success, Ranbaxy has the technological expertise and strong quality culture to back it up when it entered the laboratory testing business. It has the potential to fully exploit opportunities for growth in the clinical testing areas as it happens to be the single largest source of clinical laboratory testing in South Asia offering an extensive range of diagnostic tests. With the backing of four full-fledged testing facilities in Mumbai, Delhi, Mohalli and Bangalore, the company plans to increase its presence from 215 to over 400 towns with the number of collection centres going up from the existing 500 to 2,000 across the country. The laboratory which conducted four million tests at present would have the capacity to carry out 25 million tests annually. The company would provide services of world-class tests at affordable prices in the country.

Evaluation of the Strategies

Ranbaxy positions itself as aspiring to become a research-based international pharmaceutical company. In pursuit of such an objective and in the changing environment, Ranbaxy has responded by taking three initiatives: new drug discovery, domestic strengthening, and globalization. Initially, Ranbaxy catered to the domestic market by manufacturing branded generics, pharmaceuticals, bulk actives and intermediates and spent little on R&D. In the last few years, however, the company has taken major initiatives and made investments to create infrastructure and state-of-the-art dedicated R&D facilities at its R&D centre and to enhance its capabilities in the area of New Drug Discovery Research (NDDR). According to the President of R&D, Ranbaxy's overall R&D spending of around 5% of sales continues to be the highest, in value terms, in the Indian pharmaceutical sector.

The company has decided to conduct clinical trials by itself in India, unlike Dr. Reddy's, who has opted to license out its molecules to MNCs for advanced clinical trials. The strategy is expected to save money in the short term and offer investors a large share of revenues from the new drugs, but on the other side it may also deny timely access to lucrative western markets.

Unlike NDDR, NDDS products are launched with strategic tie-ups with other leading pharmaceutical companies employing the company's proprietary technologies. Pharmaceutical research continues to strengthen the company's international presence through its focus on technology-intensive, difficult-to-make 'niche' products. In biotechnology, the current focus is to identify new biological targets (genomics, proteomics and bioinformatics) and develop DNA-based biopharmaceuticals and vaccines. In the phytomedicines (herbal drug research), the strategic focus is to develop high-quality nutraceuticals and ethical products and subsequently move into isolation and characterization of active principals, either as NCEs or as potential lead molecules for drug discovery. According to the President of R&D, Dr. Khanna, "while most of the products in these areas will be developed in-house, the company is evaluating strategic tie-ups with other partners to speed up the licensing and development process". In line with its strategy and focus, Ranbaxy is seeking licensing for NCEs at advanced preclinical stages or in early clinical phase trials from international companies for further development. Overall, this strategy reflects the company's intent in moving up the value chain and in becoming a research-based company.

Ranbaxy, the number one Indian company in the pharmaceutical market, is part of a small set of firms which are trying to create diagnostic kits through in-house R&D, (as well as through transfers from public laboratories and market transactions with foreign companies). It has developed a high class in-house R&D division which, in earlier years, had enabled the company to launch several products through reverse engineering. Ranbaxy attracted attention in the global market by developing a process for an advanced cephalosporin, and getting it patented in the USA, though Eli Lilly had patented several stages in the process of the drug. The success of Ranbaxy.s product based on quality and price had led Eli Lilly to make an agreement with Ranbaxy for joint R&D and a joint venture. Confident of its strength in traditional organic chemistry, Ranbaxy publicly made known its determination to commit funds for research in biotechnology that could lead to innovations. Ranbaxy is preparing to launch its own diagnostic kits for blood grouping, pregnancy tests, AIDS and stem cell based therapy.

Factors for Success

Ranbaxy's three distinct competitive advantages give the company an edge over the others – the first one is its strength in the Indian domestic market considered among the most competitive and aggressive marketplaces in the world. Ranbaxy carries this aggressiveness and spirit of competition to the other markets it serves. The second and the one is its manufacturing base with a strong backward integration from lab to the market. The third key advantage is the cost competitiveness and high quality of its R&D. The Company's research and innovation capabilities enable it to develop best-in-class molecules with a focus on reducing both cost and increasing efficiency.

Strong Research Focus

Ranbaxy is among the few Indian pharmaceutical companies in India to recognize the importance of Research & Development (R&D) and invest in it. The first basic research activity of the Company was initiated way back in the year 1973. Ranbaxy views its R&D capability as a vital component of its business strategy that provides the company with a sustainable, long-term competitive advantage. The focus areas for research at Ranbaxy are anti-infectives, urology, respiratory/inflammatory and metabolic diseases. Amongst the pharmaceutical companies in India, Ranbaxy has the largest R&D budget with an R&D spend of over 7 per cent of sales. Ranbaxy's continued focus on R&D has resulted in several approvals in developed markets and significant progress in New Drug Discovery Research. Presently, the company has 10 programs in the area of drug discovery. The company's foray into Novel Drug Delivery Systems has led to proprietary "platform technologies", resulting in a number of products under development.

Organic and Inorganic Routes to Growth

The company strongly believes that success in today's generic space requires size and scale. The focus is to gain critical size across key geographies such as Europe and US, this will be through internal growth and acquisitions. Ranbaxy will consider potential acquisition targets based on the value and the synergies that can be unlocked. In Europe the Company has achieved success through organic as well as inorganic means. While in the UK, the Company has grown organically, in countries such as France and Spain, significant growth has come in through the inorganic route. On a macro level, Europe is the second largest pharma market after US. The European generics market is witnessing growth on account of its ageing population, sedentary life style and rising healthcare costs. This has resulted in an increasing demand for generics in the European countries. Ranbaxy's focus is to gain a critical mass in this potential market. To accelerate its pace and gain market share in the generic business it is targeting faster regulatory filings in the EU and encouraging generic substitution. The company is also concentrating on its branded pharmaceutical portfolio in Europe alongside the acquisition of generic brands in the EU that will help in achieving its objectives.

Cost Competitiveness

The increased gentrification of the developed markets presents an opportunity for a company such as Ranbaxy which is well placed to capitalize on this changing scenario due to its inherent strengths. Ranbaxy has successfully leveraged the India advantage in terms of costs of innovation and manufacturing. The company continuously evaluates and implements newer technologies and leverages its strong scientific capabilities to squeeze costs and extract greater value and efficiencies from its manufacturing operations. Vertically integrated operations help enormously to keep costs in check through the entire process of manufacture. The company has strong chemistry and marketing skills which have helped it to attain a distinct place amongst the leading generic companies of the world. As an integrated research based company, Ranbaxy has been able to offer world class generic pharmaceuticals at affordable prices in the markets that it operates in. The company is engaged in benchmarking its operations with the best in class internationally and is taking steps to achieve operational excellence.

Future

Ranbaxy's endeavor is to be a leader in the generics space and also to build a strong proprietary prescriptions business based on the outcome of its NDDS and NCE (New Chemical Entity) research. The robust R&D environment within the company for both drug discovery & development for generics is designed to bring into sharper focus, the unique needs of both areas, equally. Ranbaxy will focus on increasing the momentum in the generics business in its key markets of US, Europe, BRICS (Brazil, Russia, India, China & S. Africa) and Japan, forging ahead to realize its aspiration of being amongst the Top 5 global generic players with USD 5 billion sales, by 2012. A fully integrated company with a rich product pipeline, strong innovation capabilities, robust marketing and distribution network, the company is poised to benefit from the opportunities emerging in Europe and in the global pharmaceutical space.

As one of the top pharmaceuticals in India and worldwide, Ranbaxy Laboratories Limited has its products sold in over 100 countries and manufactured in seven countries. The company has a strong global presence with over 78% of its sales from overseas markets. They produce a wide array of quality, generic products that are preferred by health professionals and patients world-wide. While Ranbaxy's strength lies in quality generics, it is slowly moving toward New Chemical Entities (NCE) and Novel Drug Delivery Systems (NDDS) in supporting its long-term growth focus. The company aspires to break into new markets as a research-based pharmaceutical entity. It has actively pursued strategic alliances and acquisitions to develop areas of expertise and gain access to advanced technologies. The Company's major research focus lays in Urology, Anti-infectives, and Respiratory, Anti-inflammatory and Metabolic disorders segments. Ranbaxy's vision is to achieve significant business in proprietary prescription products by 2012 with a strong presence in developed markets.

Key Lessons

Ranbaxy's manufacturing strengths have established it as a producer of world-class generics, branded generics and a major supplier of its range of Active Pharmaceutical Ingredients. Its overseas facilities are designed to cater to the needs of the local regulatory bodies of that country while the Indian facilities meet the requirements of all International Regulatory Agencies. Ranbaxy is now the 7th fastest growing pharmaceutical company in the world. It has pursued strategic alliances, leveraged its core competencies in finances, distribution network and quality processes to become one of the world leaders in the pharmaceutical marketplace. The company is growing rapidly and expanding into markets globally while investing in R&D to form its image of a research-based international pharmaceutical company.

References

1. www.ranbaxy.com
2. www.topnews.in
3. www.biopharmalink.com/
4. www.ganeshaspeaks.com
5. www.thehindubusinessline.com
6. www.outlookmoney.com
7. www.nfcgindia.org

❋ ❋ ❋

11. ICICI Ltd

ICICI Bank is a well known private sector bank in India. It is rated as the second largest bank in the country with total assets of Rs.3,44,658 crores (USD 79 billion) as on 31.03.07. It is ranked third amongst all the companies listed on the Indian stock exchanges in terms of free float market capitalization i.e. after excluding all promoter holdings, strategic investments and cross holdings among public sector entities. It has about 950 branches across the country and there are subsidiaries in United Kingdom, Canada and Russia. The bank also has branches in 17 other countries including United Sates, Singapore, Hong Kong and United Arab Emirates.

Background

- 1955: The Industrial Credit and Investment Corporation of India Limited (ICICI) incorporated at the initiative of the World Bank, the Government of India and representatives of Indian industry, with the objective of creating a development financial institution for providing medium-term and long-term project financing to Indian businesses. Mr.A.Ramaswami Mudaliar elected as the first Chairman of ICICI Limited. ICICI is a well-known name in India along with IDBI and was formed in 1955 at the initiative of the World Bank, Indian Government and Indian Industries. Both of these institutions have an exceptional brand-image and one of the highest possible ratings from CRISIL and other rating organizations. ICICI can be considered an oligopolistic corporation along with IDBI. ICICI emerges as the major source of foreign currency loans to Indian industry. Besides funding from the World Bank and other multi-lateral agencies, ICICI was also among the first Indian companies to raise funds from international markets.
- 1969: The first two regional offices in Kolkata and Chennai set up.
- 1977: ICICI sponsored the formation of Housing Development Finance Corporation. Managed its first equity public issue.
- 1993: ICICI Securities and Finance Company Limited in joint venture with J. P. Morgan set up. ICICI Asset Management Company set up.
- 1994: ICICI Bank set up.
- 1996: ICICI Ltd., became the first company in the Indian financial sector to raise GDR. : SCICI merged with ICICI Ltd. Mr. K.V. Kamath appointed the Managing Director and CEO of ICICI Ltd.

Figure 1

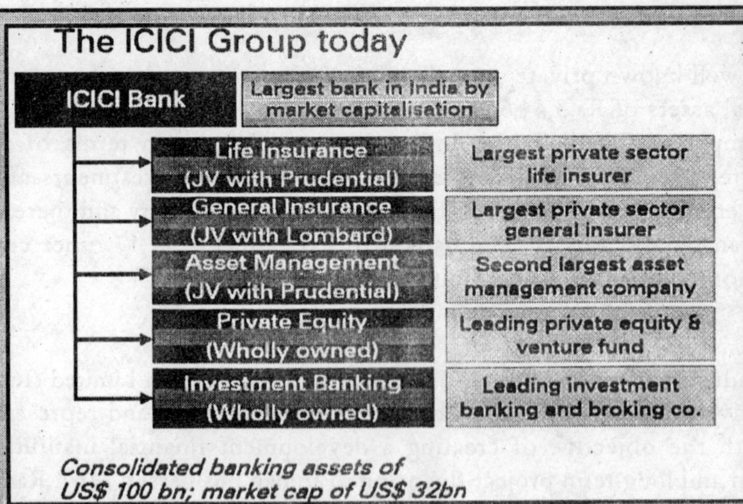

Figure 2

Figure 3

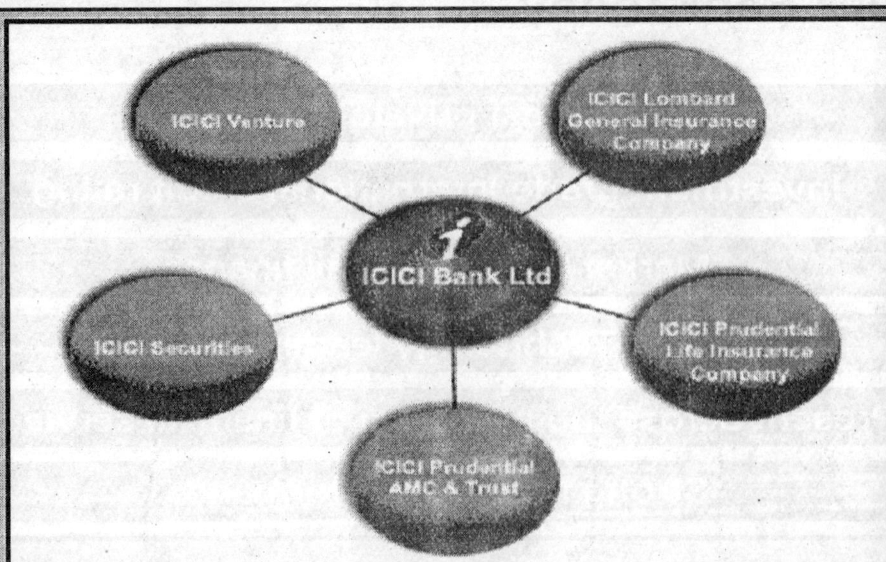

Figure 4

- 1997: ICICI Ltd., was the first intermediary to move away from single prime rate to three-tier prime rates structure and introduced yield-curve based pricing. The name The Industrial Credit and Investment Corporation of India Ltd., changed to ICICI Ltd. ICICI Ltd announced the takeover of ITC Classic Finance.
- 1999: ICICI launched retail finance - car loans, house loans and loans for consumer durables. ICICI becomes the first Indian Company to list on the NYSE through an issue of American Depository Shares.
- 2000: ICICI Bank became the first commercial bank from India to list its stock on NYSE.

Operations

Based in India, ICICI Banking Ltd., is a technology-driven virtual universal bank that delivers a wide range of corporate banking and personal finance products and services, all under one umbrella. ICICI implement an enhanced customer relationship management solution that provided front-office staff with a single view of customers and their contact history with the organization across products and channels. This solution was a key component in ICICI's overall strategy to deliver more value to its customers by deploying more customer centric communication technologies and improving online self-service. The platform supporting the e-business solution provided the highest levels of reliability, availability and scalability, along with simplified management.

When anytime, anywhere banking came to our country, ICICI Bank had to move away from the branch-centric model and make its services available nation-wide. The solution was to centralize its applications by Minu Sirsalewala.

ICICI Bank, India's second-largest bank with a network of about 540 branches and offices and over 1,000 ATMs offers banking products and financial services to corporate and retail customers through a variety of delivery channels. The legacy systems at ICICI group (now called ICICI Bank) were stand-alone systems, networked only for basic e-mail and none of the core applications were linked to the network. Around 1998 the company realized that to improve its operations and increase efficiency it needed to centralize its core banking applications. ICICI Bank is today the second largest bank in India and among the top250 in the world. In less than a decade, the bank has become a universal bank offering a well-diversified portfolio of financial services. It currently has assets of over USD 41 billion, a market capitalization of USD 9 billion and provides services to over 14 million customers through a network of about 570 branches, 2000 ATMs and a 3200-seat call center *(as of June 2005)*.

Marketing Strategies

Firstsource provides business process management to Fortune 500 and FTSE 100 companies in the Banking & Financial Services (credit cards, insurance, retail banking, collections and mortgage companies), Telecom & Media (fixed line, mobile, broadband and narrowband service providers) and Healthcare (pay or companies) industries.

First source offers customer management through a combination of call center and transaction processing capabilities for a complete range of solutions from customer acquisition, customer care, claims processing, collections and receivables management, reconciliations and investigations to customized business research and analytics.

Headquartered in Mumbai, India, the company currently has over 8000 employees across fourteen state-of-the-art centers in India, UK and the US, and in-market teams in UK and US. The company recently launched operations in South America through a centre in Buenos Aires, Argentina.

Over the years First source has earned the reputation of being an organization with the ability to rapidly scale up and manage large scale complex processes over accelerated timeframes. It has partnered with clients to create virtual extensions of their organizations so they can concentrate on their core competency. A culture of responsiveness, flexibility, operations excellence and mutual trust and transparency has led to long-standing client relationships. ICICI Group has successfully implemented

Sum Total's solution as an enterprise application for aligning the e-Learning needs of its employees. ICICI Group includes companies like - ICICI Bank Ltd., ICICI Prudential Life Insurance Co., ICICI Lombard General Insurance Company and ICICI Securities Ltd.

ICICI Group joins not only five of America's top-six commercial banks as ranked by Fortune magazine but also top-tier financial firms including Brazil's largest private-sector bank Banco Bradesco in choosing Sum Total's solutions. Sum Total Systems deployed its award-winning Sum Total Enterprise Suite™ in the bank's Learning Management System called "The Learning Matrix". "This implementation has provided ICICI an efficient and cost-effective business learning management solution making training more accessible to our employees" said Amit Sethi, Joint General Manager-IT, of ICICI Bank Ltd.

Videsh Sanchar Nigam Limited and ICICI Bank have announced a tie-up for the distribution of Tata Indicom's dial-up Internet services. The product will now be available to ICICI Bank customers through the ICICI Bank ATM network. According to a release, ICICI Bank customers will now be able to buy VSNL Internet packs (recently re-branded Tata Indicom Internet) through any of the 1675 ICICI Bank ATMs in India. "This is the first time in the country that an ISP would be using an ATM network to distribute its products," said the release.

ICICI Bank has a customer base of over 17 million accounts, and operates 610 branches and extension counters and over 2,200 ATMs across India. The bank, with assets of nearly Rs. 2,125 billion, provides a wide spectrum of financial services to individuals and companies, and to NRIs. ICICI Bank, India's second largest bank, has just tied up with Cartoon Network, the leading kids' network, and signed on their iconic cartoon stars, Tom and Jerry, as brand ambassadors for its Young Stars Account.

With 54 per cent of India's population currently under the age of 25, marketers cannot afford to ignore the young and banks are realizing the enormous size of the under-18 market in India, and are eager to sign up youngsters. The new account, Kochar believes, will inculcate the habit of saving money amongst kids, while making it a fun filled and exciting experience. The Young Stars Account allows children, up to the age of 18, to learn and manage their finances, even though it is operated and monitored completely by their parents. Children above the age of seven will get a personalized international debit card with the account. Other facilities include a special recurring deposit, free international debit card and even internet banking. But there are some facilities that only parents can access, such as online opening of fixed deposit, recurring deposit and funds transfer from parent to child's account.

ICICI Bank, India's second-largest bank with a network of about 540 branches and offices and over 1,000 ATMs offers banking products and financial services to corporate and retail customers through a variety of delivery channels. The legacy systems at ICICI group (now called ICICI Bank) were stand-alone systems, networked only for basic e-mail and none of the core applications were linked to the network. Around 1998 the company realized that to improve its operations and increase efficiency it needed to centralize its core banking applications.

Legacy Systems

The traditional systems at ICICI Bank were very centric to the branch. For example, a server at New Delhi was specific to the branch in that city; the ATMs were standalone catering only to the city branch. The banking transactions were thus limited to the respective branch offices as customer data was not available in other branches. This made banking a limited service and very branch specific. ICICI realized the importance of offering nation-wide banking but this would be possible only by having a centralized data repository.

The basic network was set up for providing the e-mail facility, but none of the applications were linked to the network. The network comprised of a mix of servers running different applications at various branches of the bank. With growing business and rapidly increasing accounts, the company found it extremely difficult to administer and manage the system. This also resulted in duplication of backend services and procedures, as the systems were not centralized for the core banking applications.

"There was a lot of additional cost being incurred due to the duplication of the backend procedures at the branch offices," said Manoj Kunkalienkar, Joint President ICICI Infotech Services Limited. The centralization procedure started around late 1999. ICICI Infotech (a company promoted by ICICI) made the first network design for the group in 1999—it was a hub and spoke architecture. Utmost care was taken to design a network with a strong backbone. According to Manoj, the key strength of a network is its back-bone. The group's various centers are connected by 2 Mbps or 4 Mbps leased lines. Manoj said the design considerations not only included high bandwidth availability but also the fact that a single point of failure should not result in lines going down.

The group realized that it had to enter into the retail space, have local regional presence, and provide alternate channels to the customer. They needed a solution whereby they could offer services across the country. "Centralizing the operations was not the solution, but centralization of data was. We had already centralized some of the operations but we still had some branch applications running independently which were not centralized and had ATMs which were stand-alones. Two major criteria considered before designing were not only the network, but also the infrastructure available in our country," said Manoj.

In the past, the infrastructure here was such that a company could not rely on leased lines completely. So ICICI needed backups on ISDN and VSATs, along with the 64 Kbps leased lines. "The leased lines were too expensive then, now the lines are better, more stable and offer good connectivity. The cost has also come down by around 15 percent." Manoj opined that what was really important was to have a world class data center and centralize everything in one place, as that's where the network can be used at the maximum. To ensure 24x7 service access and connectivity to customers one needs to have reliable backups and a robust network in place. From a business perspective, the main reason to go in for a network was centralization of data, provide all channels of communication and at the same time provide anytime, anywhere banking. "The problem we faced with our legacy systems was that they were stand-alone systems and the data from one branch was not available with another branch."

What ICICI was looking for was a robust network, which would enable it to offer services at the retail level throughout the country. The in-house ICICI Infotech was the obvious choice for consultation. The ICICI Infotech team designed the initial network topology in 1999. The team had put forward a series of designs, not radically different from each other. Eventually, a design with a mix of VSATs, leased-lines, radio-links and ISDN was selected. A mixed design was selected because of the disparate locations of the group across the country. There were different technical problems in different locations and the next best available solution had to be included.

"The basic topology has withstood over the years. What we have today is still the basic architecture with just new additions in terms of just more bandwidth," said Manoj. The advantage in a hub and spoke architecture is that multiple nodes (spokes) are connected with a hub location through a ring of single-mode fiber. Each hub-node connection can consist of single or multiple wavelengths (lambdas), each carrying a full Gigabit Ethernet channel. Protection from fiber cuts in the ring is achieved by connecting the hub and nodes through both directions of the optical ring. Service provider Gigabit Ethernet metro access rings are the main applications for this architecture. And another advantage is that nodes can be added to the network more easily.

Once the network was up, ICICI Infotech faced the challenge of ensuring smooth operation and minimum downtime. Manoj agrees glitches cannot be avoided and while one has to try and prevent these, one also has to think about the growth of the network, in line with business expansion. "No walk is very smooth. Glitches are, and will always be there," said Manoj. "What was of prime importance was to keep pace with the business and its expansions. Technical problems are not difficult to handle—there is always a solution to them but other problems like the existing infrastructure of the country, the individual business needs are very taxing."

According to Manoj, the real challenge came while designing and deploying the network, as the team had to view business processes at a very micro level. They had to identify the exact areas where the business needed to be expanded, and then find the best suitable option to connect to those locations.

The ICICI VSAT network is large, with almost a thousand nodes. Keeping it going turned out to be an even bigger challenge for the group. The entire network is monitored from one center. Any error in the network at any point is rectified in a short span of time and the system is up and running with minimum downtime.

Another challenge was to keep pace with business growth. "The only technological challenges we face are in terms of the quality of the lines, as they are not same all the time. Typically, the router and switch software is written assuming a certain quality of the line. As a result, if the quality of the line is not stable and fluctuates, the systems do not function efficiently. Ensuring the required line quality is a major challenge. An obvious solution to this is to interact and talk with the vendors and get it customized for an Indian client's requirements," explained Manoj. Manoj reiterates that it's important for the vendor and the client to have a good rapport so that they do not just provide the client with boxes but change the operating system (and other relevant software) as and when needed. The basic topology has not changed. "Initially, we had started with connecting seven locations. Today, all the centers and offices are connected making virtual banking a reality."

Benefits

With the centralization of data all applications are controlled, modified and administered from one location. The network has enabled the bank to shift from traditional banking to virtual banking thus offering modern banking services to its customers. All backend applications run from a centrally located data center. This eliminates duplication of processes like back-end operations, training of staff, administration cost, and other system related costs at branch levels. Clients can avail of anytime-anywhere banking on the Net and make use of their ATM cards at any of the ATM centers across the country. Considerable amount of cost has been saved as the backend operations of regional offices have been eliminated. The data for all the customers is centralized and processed from the centrally located data center. Information for any ICICI client will be available at any of the ICICI branches.

ICICI's KM Strategy

In the mid-1990s its business strategy shifted to take advantage of the opening up of the Indian economy. The idea was to create a diversified financial-services supplier offering a range of products, instead of concentrating purely on project finance.

ICICI Bank was, therefore, established in 1994 to provide retail banking facilities across India. The idea was well timed and proved wildly successful. Today, it is the second largest bank in India with assets of almost $40bn and can boast a network of more than 570 branches and a steadily growing international business, with branches in the UK, Russia and Canada.

First steps

ICICI Bank's knowledge management (KM) strategy was established in 2000. Back then, the company was very much smaller than it is now – just 1,200 staff compared to the 30,000 that works for ICICI Bank today.

However, the programme was started at a time when the company's growth was starting to go into overdrive. Initially, the organization developed a broad technology-linked infrastructure, including a corporate intranet, ICICI Universe, intended to provide a platform where, for instance, employees could check the human resources (HR) system for vacation entitlements, book days off or view their personal pension details.

By putting these simple, but necessary activities on the intranet, it encouraged employees to get familiar with using web-based applications, to overcome any fear of technology as well as providing them with a good reason for using the portal on a regular basis. What began more as an idea and less as a project was simply the belief that staff should have a space on the intranet where they could participate in collaborative activities, such as contribute or find documents, engage in discussions and post or answer queries. That idea, in essence, first converted the bank to KM.

Initially, the organization was motivated to act due to the upheaval caused by the tail-end of the dot-com boom, which was depriving the bank of many good staff as they left in significant numbers to join dot-com start-ups – taking their knowledge and know-how with them. We therefore developed WiseGuy, ICICI's KM intranet portal – easily accessible from the main staff portal – to provide a way of capturing and disseminating the knowledge of departing staff. To develop WiseGuy, a team was put together encompassing KM, HR, technology and research with a brief to 'just do it'. Indeed, they did and a beta version was ready within just three months.

Before the year was out, faced with the prospect of a reverse merger of ICICI Bank with its parent ICICI, which went through in 2002, the KM team had to restructure to meet the needs of the new corporate entity. Some issues articulated at the time included:

1. How to connect this vast new pool of employees with each other;
2. How to share business-related information about clients, deals and ideas;
3. How to manage staff through the change process via communication, messages, channels and so on;
4. How to overcome the problems caused by staff turnover;
5. How to ensure that every person in the company is adequately equipped with the skills and training required for their jobs and for lifelong learning and development.

The deeper question was, quite simply, how do we create a hunger among staff to acquire and share knowledge? That is to say, how do we create the culture? The aim was to ensure that employees stayed permanently aware of the external competitive challenges of the business, and to persuade them to remain constantly open to new thoughts, ideas and ways of working.

Satisfied Users

In our view, employee satisfaction drives usage and we wanted to use this as the delivery vehicle to support three major information-handling behaviours: sharing, collaboration and self-help. In essence, the workplace is no longer just a physical location. It has become a blend of physical and virtual spaces in which work is undertaken. The KM programme is now deeply embedded in the bank, but not as a result of any directive from top management. Employees work with the KM programme because they see its benefits and realize the value it brings to them on a day-to-day basis. This is what makes it vibrant and engaging. It is significant that a small project originally designed for about 1,200 employees in few locations has been flexible and scalable enough to cater for more than 30,000 employees in more than 600 locations, most of whom are customer-facing staff.

Everything they need should be at their fingertips, whether getting an answer to a problem, checking a policy or accessing standard templates and formats such as letters, agreements or guidelines. The importance of scalability cannot be underestimated. In 2005, usage increased more than six times compared to the year before and the portal marked a record one-million log-ins in November 2004 after the site was redesigned. The number of staff using the KM portal doubled in the same period. On average today, about 6,000 users visit the site daily, of which 95 per cent come from ICICI Bank's retail branches and more than 40 business divisions actively participate in the KM effort to contribute and publish content. Today, there are more than 14,000 individual items, about 1,000 daily searches for information and more than 16,000 interactive postings.

The WiseGuy KM portal also encompasses a variety of sections including: document management; news inside and outside the organisation; digital resources such as trade and news journals, research reports, maps, directories, currency and time calculators; information on the various business groups and group companies, complete employee information; and, interactive sections such as discussion forums, query boards, book reviews, online quizzes, the rewards and recognition scheme, and so on.

Corporate Learning

The ability to learn across the group and from team mates is a very powerful tool. We aim to build a learning environment by encouraging collaboration and push mechanisms, including a webzine e-mail to every employee before 9.30am. The Daily Dose, as it is called, is a summary of what is new in the outside world and on the portal. It features headlines, opinions, polls, happenings, customer appreciations, newsletters and other regular updates.

Again, one of the main benefits of the Daily Dose is the high profile it lends to our various KM initiatives. When we polled staff, almost 97 per cent said that The Daily Dose represents an important part of their working day. By delivering it direct to their mailbox, it helps the KM team to capture the 'mind space' of employees as soon as they sit down to work in the morning.

Other tools we use include Newsroom, a space on the intranet where daily news headlines are published. Here, staff can look up all the newsletters published by internal business groups, media releases, as well as tracking what our competitors are up to. Then there are 'K-mailers', which are short, one-page reviews on any one of 33 topics in six categories; internal newsletters from various domain specialists; online quizzes; 'word power' articles or glossaries; training modules; and, a whole library of online research tools.

Query Board, a central, interactive frequently asked questions repository by and for staff, is where they can post any work-related queries, such as the number of cheques that can be deposited at any one time, customer credit questions, cheque returns and so on. Indeed, anything work-related that demands authoritative responses from colleagues and in-house experts. It serves as the fastest and most reliable source for feedback on queries or doubts related to workplace rules, policies and procedures, technical know-how and much more. Remarkably, the average response time to a query ranges from five to 15 minutes, but never more than one day from the time the query was posted.

In addition to Query Board, we also offer a more general discussion forum on the intranet where staff can talk about finance, business and economy-related topics. Discussions on our forum revolve around topics highly relevant to the work in the bank, such as the automatic cheque books re-order system and solutions for detecting fake bank notes.

Challenges

The short history of KM in ICICI Bank has not been plain sailing. Having a director throw his weight behind the project certainly provided an initial thrust. It sent a positive signal across the organisation that the top brass were serious about KM, but it also ran the risk of being perceived as a pet project or flavour of the month.

While many employees actively use the portal, there are gaps in pockets among mid-level managers. 'I know best' and 'not invented here' attitudes remain a barrier. Knowledge sharing is not tightly linked to staff appraisal and neither is knowledge management activities mentioned in ICICI Bank's balanced score card index – if it were, it may be a different matter.

Certain measures can be a double-edged sword. For instance, one team started an internal initiative in which they asked team members to submit suggestions, linking their participation to performance indicators and making it a part of an employee's mandatory goals. However, it was soon observed and reported that some staff were taking ideas from WiseGuy and submitting them to their group system. Such instances undermine or detract from the overall process and can stoke internal conflict.

From a technical perspective, the KM initiatives have done a better job of capturing internal and external unstructured information, such as documents and ideas and in harnessing external structured data such as content and databases versus internal structured data, such as data warehouses, enterprise resource-planning applications and databases. Disparate systems can create fatigue and/or confusion among users about which one to use.

First-generation KM revolved around creating processes to capture, codify and organize knowledge for retrieval. In second-generation KM, knowledge flows becomes more important than the knowledge itself. The third generation of KM involves easing the creation of new knowledge, innovation and improving organizational performance. Maturity levels vary according to the applications within each team.

At ICICI Bank, the business leadership team, by sponsorship and example, has outlined principles of action that stipulate that employees must actively share knowledge and seek out colleagues' expertise to solve problems and/or improve processes. KM at ICICI Bank was started in a non-dictatorial manner and its use is voluntary, but a programme of this nature cannot be expected to continue on momentum. But to the average employee in the bank, KM now is no longer strange or a novelty, but has become the 'way we work'.

Future Challenges, Opportunities and Plans Challenges

1. Lack of product expertise
   - Traditionally focused on limited range of products
   - Primarily for corporate clients
   - Need for acquiring skills in Retail, structured finance.
2. Lack of distribution expertise
   - Relatively high unit cost of delivery given small transaction sizes.
3. Limited use of technology
   - Across both customer-facing and internal functions
   - Inefficient capital allocation.

Opportunities

The ICICI bank opportunities broadly divided in three sectors:

- Global Banking
- Corporate Banking
- Rural Banking.

Following are the opportunities for above three banking for ICICI Bank:

- The bank should go for global expansion which increases integration with global markets.
- The bank should set up its international marketing and distribution networks.
- The bank should acquire/ create production capacities overseas.
- The bank should investment in infrastructure and manufacturing.
- There is a great demand for efficient transaction banking.
- Potential for credit and liability products and transaction services for personal as well as business requirements.
- Potential for acquisition/ project financing and trade finance.

Plans

"Our aim is to ensure that no customer will be more than 3-4 km away from an ICICI point of presence." This is the statement given by the CEO of ICICI Bank which plans to open new branches for the customers. ICICI Bank plans to increase its points of presence in rural areas throughout the country from 3,500 to about 17,500. The bank hoped to tie up with around 80 more micro-finance institutions by the end of this year and with 200 more in two to three years.

The bank plans to come up with new schemes in the agricultural area by providing services such as giving working capital to farmers and selling insurance. The bank is also developing specialized products to help farmers cut their losses. These include financing against commodities, index based products, health insurance at a micro level and weather insurance. The bank plans to launch a slew of innovative products in this segment before the end of this fiscal.

Insurance penetration in India is one of the lowest among all emerging markets. Rising income levels and awareness about insurance products would lead to many years of explosive growth in this sector. So, bank is planning to come with new schemes and services which will increase their revenue at a large rate. Also, the bank is planning to set up a holding company for its investments in asset management and insurance is concerned. The bank is planning to tie up with mobile companies which allow customers to track their personal finances while on the move.

The bank plans to offer shares of its investment banking and securities arm – ICICI Securities (I-Sec) – in the stock market. The bank is planning to take initiative to achieve Six-Sigma. The ICICI bank is the first bank in India who has taken this initiative. The bank is planning to open new branches in various countries which enhance Indian companies to invest in other companies. The best example is the bank has entered into mainland Europe by opening a branch in Antwerp, Belgium. The primary reason for opening this branch is to enter into diamond financing since the Belgian branch is located in the heart of the diamond district in Antwerp, which is a hub of diamond business. The bank plans to offer corporate banking products from this branch. The bank also plans to scale up its presence in the Gulf besides exploring alliance possibilities with overseas banks to boost this business, especially in the emerging markets. Thus, for providing such new schemes and services the bank has entered into successful partnerships and alliances across segments and try to provide such value-added services to their customers.

ICICI has made profitable inroads into serving the bottom of the economic pyramid. Banking with the poor has undergone a paradigm shift. Its no longer viewed as a mere social obligation. It is financially viable as well. As part of the bank model ICICI has grown the number of SHGs from around 1500 to around 8000 within two years since their purchase of bank of Madura. Through this model, ICICI has utilized their creative thinking to create a viral growth model and utilized their financial expertise to fashion a model that is economically viable. Additionally, ICICI has created a innovative method of mobilizing rural savings that also acts as a great risk-mitigating factor when eventually providing credit. ICICI's partnership model has led to fruitful partnership with more than 10 major NGOs and MFIs who all have strong physical presence within the rural areas.

ICICI however has positioned itself as a pioneer and leader in looking at creative approaches to serving the bottom of economic pyramid. The innovation that ICICI is exhibiting towards the bottom of economic pyramid has a number of ancillary benefits. Additionally, by serving the BOP, ICICI has positioned itself as a socially conscious corporate citizen. This is looked highly upon by customers and investors in the stock market.

References

1. www.icici.com
2. www.financeindia.com
3. www.bankingnews.com

❀❀❀

11. TATA Motors Ltd.

The Tata Group comprises 98 operating companies in seven business sectors: information systems and communications; engineering; materials; services; energy; consumer products; and chemicals. The Group was founded by Jamshedji Tata in the mid 19th century, a period when India had just set out on the road to gaining independence from British rule. Consequently, Jamshedji Tata and those who followed him aligned business opportunities with the objective of nation building. This approach remains enshrined in the Group's ethos to this day.

The Tata Group is one of India's largest and most respected business conglomerates, with revenues in 2006-07 of $28.8 billion (Rs. 129,994 crore), the equivalent of about 3.2 per cent of the country's GDP. Tata companies together employ some 289,500 people. The Group's 27 publicly listed enterprises — among them stand out names such as Tata Steel, Tata Consultancy Services, Tata Motors and Tata Tea — have a combined market capitalization that is the highest among Indian business houses in the private sector, and a shareholder base of over 2.9 million. The Tata Group has operations in more than 85 countries across six continents, and its companies export products and services to 80 countries. The Tata family of companies shares a set of five core values: integrity, understanding, excellence, unity and responsibility. These values, which have been part of the Group's beliefs and convictions from its earliest days, continue to guide and drive the business decisions of Tata companies. The Group and its enterprises have been steadfast and distinctive in their adherence to business ethics and their commitment to corporate sustainability. This is a legacy that has earned the Group the trust of many millions of stakeholders in a measure few business houses anywhere in the world can match.

Tata Motors Limited is India's largest automobile company, with revenues of Rs. 32,426 crores (USD 7.2 billion) in 2006-07. It is the leader by far in commercial vehicles in each segment, and the second largest in the passenger vehicles market with winning products in the compact, midsize car and utility vehicle segments. The company is the world's fifth largest medium and heavy commercial vehicle manufacturer, and the world's second largest medium and heavy bus manufacturer.

The company's 22,000 employees are guided by the vision to be "best in the manner in which we operate best in the products we deliver and best in our value system and ethics." Tata Motors helps its employees realize their potential through innovative HR practices. The company's goal is to empower and provide employees with dynamic career paths in congruence with corporate objectives. All-round potential development and performance improvement is ensured by regular in-house and external training. The company has won several awards recognizing its training programmes. Established in 1945, Tata Motors' presence indeed cuts across the length and breadth of India. Over 4 million Tata vehicles ply on Indian roads, since the first rolled out in 1954. The company's manufacturing base is spread across India - Jamshedpur (Jharkhand) in the east, Pune (Maharashtra) in the west, and in the north in Lucknow (Uttar Pradesh) and Pantnagar (Uttarakhand). A new plant is being set up in Singur (close to Kolkata in West Bengal) to manufacture the company's small car. The nation-wide dealership, sales, services and spare parts network comprises over 2,000 touch points. The company also has a strong auto finance operation, TML Financial Services Limited, supporting customers to purchase Tata Motors vehicles.

Tata Motors, the first company from India's engineering sector to be listed in the New York Stock Exchange (September 2004), has also emerged as an international automobile company. In 2004, it acquired the Daewoo Commercial Vehicles Company, Korea's second largest truck maker. The rechristened Tata Daewoo Commercial Vehicles Company has launched several new products in the Korean market, while also exporting these products to several international markets. Today two-thirds of heavy commercial vehicle exports out of South Korea are from Tata Daewoo. In 2005, Tata Motors acquired a 21% stake in Hispano Carrocera, a reputed Spanish bus and coach manufacturer, with an option to acquire the remaining stake as well. Hispano's presence is being expanded in other markets. In 2006, it formed a joint venture with the Brazil-based Marcopolo, a global leader in body-building for buses and coaches to manufacture fully-built buses and coaches for India and select international markets. Tata Motors also entered into a joint venture in 2006 with Thonburi Automotive Assembly Plant Company of Thailand to manufacture and market the company's pickup vehicles in Thailand. In 2006, Tata Motors and Fiat Auto formed an industrial joint venture at Ranjangaon (near Pune in Maharashtra, India) to produce both Fiat and Tata cars and Fiat powertrains for the Indian and overseas markets; Tata Motors already distributes and markets Fiat branded cars in India. In 2007, Tata Motors and Fiat Auto entered into an agreement for a Tata license to build a pick-up vehicle bearing the Fiat nameplate at Fiat Group Automobiles' Plant at Córdoba, Argentina. The pick-up will be sold in South and Central America and select European markets.

These linkages will further extend Tata Motors' international footprint, established through exports since 1961. While currently about 18% of its revenues are from international business, the company's objective is to expand its international business, both through organic and inorganic growth routes. The company's commercial and passenger vehicles are already being marketed in several countries in Europe, Africa, the Middle East, Australia, South East Asia and South Asia. It has assembly operations in Malaysia, Kenya, Bangladesh, Ukraine, Russia and Senegal.

The foundation of the company's growth is a deep understanding of economic stimuli and customer needs, and the ability to translate them into customer-desired offerings through leading edge R&D. The R&D establishment includes a team of 1400 scientists and engineers. The company's Engineering Research Centre was established in 1966, and has facilities in Pune, Jamshedpur and Lucknow. The ERC has enabled pioneering technologies and products. It was Tata Motors, which developed the first indigenously developed Light Commercial Vehicle, India's first Sports Utility Vehicle and, in 1998, the Tata Indica, India's first fully indigenous passenger car. Within two years of launch, Tata Indica became India's largest selling car in its segment. The ERC in Pune, among whose facilities are India's only certified crash-test facility and hemi-anechoic chamber for testing of noise and vibration, has received several awards from the Government of India. Some of the more prominent amongst them are the National Award for Research and Development Efforts in Industry in the Mechanical Engineering Industries sector in 1999, the National Award for Successful Commercialisation of Indigenous Technology by an Industrial Concern in 2000, and the CSIR Diamond Jubilee Technology Award in 2004.

The company set up the Tata Motors European Technical Centre (TMETC) in 2005 in the UK. TMETC is engaged in design engineering and development of products, supporting Tata Motors' skill sets. Tata Daewoo Commercial Vehicle Company and Hispano Carrocera also have R&D establishments at Gunsan in South Korea and Zaragoza in Spain.

The pace of new product development has quickened through an organisation-wide structured New Product Introduction (NPI) process. The process with its formal structure for introducing new vehicles in the market, brings in greater discipline in project execution. The NPI process helped Tata Motors create a new segment, in 2005, by launching the Tata Ace, India's first indigenously developed mini-truck. The years to come will see the introduction of several other innovative vehicles, all rooted in emerging customer needs. Besides product development, R&D is also focusing on environment-friendly technologies in emissions and alternative fuels.

Through its subsidiaries, the company is engaged in engineering and automotive solutions, construction equipment manufacturing, automotive vehicle components manufacturing and supply chain activities, machine tools and factory automation solutions, high-precision tooling and plastic and electronic components for automotive and computer applications, and automotive retailing and service operations.

True to the tradition of the Tata Group, Tata Motors is committed in letter and spirit to Corporate Social Responsibility. It is a signatory to the United Nations Global Compact, and is engaged in community and social initiatives on labour and environment standards in compliance with the principles of the Global Compact. In accordance with this, it plays an active role in community development, serving rural communities adjacent to its manufacturing locations. With the foundation of its rich heritage, Tata Motors today is etching a refulgent future.

Background

The history of Telco, India's leading automobile manufacturer dates back to the early 1920s. The location of the Telco plant originally belonged to Peninsular Locomotive Company (Peninsular), which was established in Tatanagar, Jamshedpur in 1923. In 1927, Peninsular was taken over by East India Railway to manufacture passenger carriage under frames for the Indian Railways. In 1945, Tata Sons purchased the plant from the Government of India for manufacturing steam locomotive boilers and other engineering products, under the name Tata Locomotive & Engineering Company. Initially, the company manufactured broad gauge open wagons for the Indian Railways. By 1947, it started producing boilers for imported locomotives. The company also entered into collaborations with Marshal Sons (UK) to manufacture steam road roller, and with Krauss Maffei (West Germany) to manufacture steam locomotives. In 1954, the company entered into a technical collaboration with Daimler-Benz to manufacture automotive vehicles. The association with Daimler-Benz helped the company build up a strong in-house R&D center (Engineering Research Center - ERC) at Pune, Maharashtra.

In 1960, company's name was changed to Tata Engineering & Locomotive Company Ltd. By 1961, it was manufacturing construction equipments. Over the years, the company acquired technology from several collaborations and co-operation agreements with international companies.

Important Phases

The Peninsular Locomotive Co. Ltd., was formed in 1921. The plan of manufacturing 200 locomotives, being the minimum requirements of the Indian Railways, could not materialize and the Company had to shut down in 1925. The Government of India then took it over for the construction of carriage under frames and wagons. It started functioning again in 1928 and closed down in 1934 due to lack of orders. With the war emergency, the Defense Department of the Government of India resuscitated this workshop in 1940 for the manufacture of armoured vehicles. On the termination of the hostilities in 1945, the workshop had outlived its usefulness and when the Defense Department announced their intention of giving it up, the Government of India entered into an agreement with Messrs. Tata and Sons, Ltd., for the latter to take over the workshops for the manufacture of locomotive, Automobile and Foundry.

Telco for short-was incorporated in 1945 when the east Indian Railway Workshops at Tatanagar were taken over by the Company. The old workshop was completely pulled down and a new one was built up on the site. The workshop has three divisions e.g., Locomotive, Automobile and Foundry. Till now they were in trading, textile, power, steel, hotel, aviation, chemicals & consumer goods sector Just after the Independence of India, Telco Introduced steam road roller in collaboration with Marshall Sons (UK) in 1948, because this was the time for reformation of the nation building of new roads Bridges etc .Then in 1956 Joint Venture with Daimler Benz AG (West Germany) to manufacture medium commercial vehicles. Within 6 months, the first vehicle rolled out. We can say this was a forward integration for TATA group because they were already in steel business with a plant in Jamshedpur, Bihar. In 1959, Research and Development Centre was set up at Jamshedpur, Bihar itself.

Tata Motors collaborated with Germany's Daimler Benz in 1954 for 15 years to manufacture commercial vehicles. Since then, Tata Motors has grown enormously and produces several vehicles through their three main divisions – Passenger Cars, Utility Vehicles and Commercial Vehicles. In 1959, they set up their first and largest R&D center in Jamshedpur. By 1961, exports had begun and the first truck was shipped to Sri Lanka. Another R&D center was started at Pune in 1966 to support automobile research which produced the first commercial vehicle in 1977. In 1971, they introduced the DI engines, Tata Motors began the production and sale of heavy commercial vehicles by 1983 and light commercial vehicles three years later. In 1985, first hydraulic excavator was produced with Hitachi collaboration. With increasing sales and popularity, they sold their one millionth vehicles by 1991. 1991 Tata Sierra launched TAC 20 crane produce. Their interest in tapping the diesel engine market was evident through their joint venture with Cummins Engine Co. Inc. in 1993 for the production of high horsepower and emission friendly diesel engines. Their interest in tapping the diesel engine market was evident through their joint venture with Cummins Engine Co. Inc., in 1993 for the production of high horsepower and emission friendly diesel engines. Their interest in tapping the diesel engine market was evident through their joint venture with Cummins Engine Co. Inc. in 1993 for the production of high horsepower and emission friendly diesel engines. Tata Quality Management Services institutes the JRD QV Award, modelled on the Malcolm Baldrige National Quality Value Award of the United States, laying the foundation of the Tata Business Excellence Model.

For getting deep in the automobile business Tata Motors has made substantial investments in building associate and subsidiary companies that complement and support its business activities. These include:

- Tata Daewoo Commercial Vehicle Company manufactures heavy trucks ranging from 15T GVW to 45T GVW. Tata Motors acquired this company in March 2004.
- Tata Cummins, a joint venture with Cummins, USA, manufactures Cummins engines for Tata Motors.
- Telco Construction Equipment Company, a joint venture with Hitachi Machinery Company, Japan, is engaged in the manufacture and sale of earthmoving machinery and construction equipment such as hydraulic excavators, cranes and wheel-loaders.
- Tata Technologies provides IT support in the areas of engineering design, development and validation, business information systems and ERP systems.
- HV Axles manufactures axles for Tata Motors' medium and heavy commercial vehicles.
- HV Transmissions, supplies gearboxes for the company's medium and heavy commercial vehicles.
- TAL Manufacturing Solutions manufactures painting systems, welding lines, material handling systems and robotics. It also develops factory automation solutions and provides consultancy services in the field of manufacturing processes and factory layouts.
- Concorde Motors (India): Retails Tata Motors' range of passenger vehicles.
- Tata Precision Industries, Singapore and Tata Engineering Services, Singapore, are engaged in the manufacture of high precision tooling and spare parts, and warehousing, respectively.
- Nita Company, Bangladesh, is engaged in the assembly of Tata vehicles for the Bangladesh market.

Globalization

The world is becoming smaller, both metaphorically and literally. The Iron Curtain and the Berlin Wall have been disbanded, changing the fortunes of many economies. India is no exception to this change. The wave of liberalization has given Indian corporate a new dimension to 'globalization'. Tata Motors, a trendsetter in the Indian automobile industry, is setting a new direction to the globalization of the Indian auto industry. The question that has been in the minds of the senior management at Tata Motors was — will we remain exporters of vehicles or do we venture into the international automobile market as a company that can match the best in the business? The answers were obvious. The first step was to align the international business to the two business units — the Passenger Car Business Unit (PCBU) and the Commercial Vehicle Business Unit (CVBU), to bring greater focus and increased synergy between the domestic and international operations.

International business needs to be looked at from a perspective that goes beyond volumes and presence in many countries. Dr V. Sumantran, executive director, PCBU, says, "The Company has now embarked on a road where we have made exports an integral part of our business. We do not think of sales outside the country as a separate activity. It is now integrated within the mission of each of its businesses."

Ravi Kant, executive director, CVBU said; "In a cyclical business such as ours, it is important that we hedge against cyclicality. International business offers an opportunity as different countries go through peaks and troughs in demand at different points in time. Our capacity utilization is more effective and risks of downturns can be mitigated."

The Business Units have classified different markets in terms of size, growth opportunities, product segments and target volumes. Therefore, from being present as an exporter in 70 countries, the company today focuses on 15 to 20 key countries, where it will have a significant presence in terms of volumes and market shares. As Dr Sumantran says, "With this integration and focus, we have stepped out in specific areas with specific products. It will be unrealistic for us to be in all places and all product segments. We will choose regions very carefully and base our strategy on well-connected product strategies. We should be in the right regions with the right product at the right time."

The implementation of the business strategy will be in three stages; product up gradation, sales and distribution processes and penetration into new markets. The three stages could run concurrently, depending on the market and product needs.

Tata Motors has taken a number of initiatives to strengthen both product reliability and durability and marketing processes. Enhancing distribution reach and a robust sales process system have been key elements in consolidating the company's leadership position in the domestic market. The implementation of this strategy has begun in a few markets abroad and in Mr Kant's words "What we needed was an integrated approach where we invest in all the critical elements — product up gradation, sales processes, distribution and above all, people."

The company's approach has been successful in Sri Lanka and Malaysia where the installation of a sales process system and face-to-face customer meets through road shows and service workshops has started yielding results. Recently, a large contingent of dealers from South Africa was invited to visit the company's facilities in Pune and experience the new face of the international business.

The second part of the business strategy is to make an entry in new and yet uncharted markets, such as China and the CIS countries. Besides the assembly plants that Tata Motors has in Bangladesh and Malaysia, the company's recent order for 500 buses from Senegal will involve providing technical and commercial assistance to the Senegalese government for setting up a bus body building plant. Tata Motors has been short-listed for South Africa's "Taxi Project" in which the government will provide an entirely new transport system in that country. A joint venture project for bus body building in Ukraine and serious due diligence into the opportunities available in the Chinese market are other areas where Tata Motors is looking to create new opportunities.

"We have identified new segments in these regions. The business strategies will be country specific. The nature of our business will depend on the country we are working in. In addition, inorganic growth through acquisitions could also quicken the process of internationalization" says Mr. Kant; the company recently signed a MOU with Daewoo Commercial Vehicle Company in Korea to acquire its truck plant. The synergies are significant - a presence in the 250 to 400 HP range of trucks is what the Korean company brings to the table. This complements the existing product range of Tata Motors which delivers vehicles up to 210 HP. In the commercial vehicle business, says Mr. Kant, "One must understand that different markets are in different stages of evolution, depending on that country's economic development. Our competitive edge will be in our ability to offer cost-effective products and services to each market, suited to the stage of development of that market. Our capabilities in design, world-leadership, software skills, technology assimilation capabilities and labour productivity will ensure that we are not only benchmarked with world-class companies, but are ourselves benchmarks in certain areas."

On the road to globalization, Dr Sumantran points out that the Rover agreement has been an important step in helping Tata Motors to gain very quick access to a fairly large market and a large distribution network. "Working alone in this area would have taken us much longer to create a distribution network. The exposure that the company and the products have received through the agreement validates the belief that we have arrived at a significant milestone in promoting the Tata brand," elaborates Dr Sumantran. "Rover is getting a Tata product, it is a road that many automakers have treaded in the past. It will take us more than three years to arrive at our goal. But at least we have started the journey in that direction."

By remaining connected with the international markets, one's learning improves. One is able to draw on experiences in different markets and create strong synergies. In doing so, the company will have created world-class products to fight competition in the domestic market as well, with little extra investment. This assures a greater degree of stability and, going forward, will strengthen the company's ability to manage risk.

Clearly, it takes the right mix of people with the right skills to make this happen. Innovation, knowledge, commitment and pride have been Tata Motors' greatest asset. It has amply demonstrated that it can meet the challenge of change. "The company is now on a course that will need a new mindset," says Mr. Kant.

In 1998 Tata Safari and Indica launched. 2 millionth vehicles rolled out. Globalization opened the door for rest of the world so first consignment of 160 Indicas shipped to Malta. Success of diesel engine in Indica leads to 2,00,000th Indica and 5,00,000th passenger vehicle rolled out. Tata Engineering signed product agreement with MG Rover of the UK and Tata Engineering became Tata Motors Limited.

Tata Daewoo Commercial Vehicle (TDCV) is the 2nd largest heavy commercial vehicle manufacturer in Gunsan, Jeollabuk-do, South Korea, established in 2003. The company is owned by India's largest commercial vehicle manufacturer Tata Motors. In 2004, Tata Motors acquired former Daewoo Motor's truck manufacturing unit (Daewoo Commercial Vehicle). TATA is one of India's giant motor companies and now it is expanding worldwide. In 2005 Inauguration of new factory at Jamshedpur for Novus Tata TL 4×4, India's first Sports Utility Truck (SUT) is launched. Launch of Tata Novus Launch of Novus range of medium trucks in Korea, by Tata this was a totally new segment targeted by the company with high quality product.

IT initiatives at TATA Motors

1. **SAP SRM Implementation:** End to end Supply Chain integration of Tata Motors (from Purchase, Supply, production, payment etc.) by the implementation of SAP-SRM project.

Benefit: My SAP Supplier Relationship Management is a purchasing platform for sustainable savings and value generation through full-cycle supply chain management.

— Reduction in Procurement cycle time

— Improve process by e-procurement

— Real time Supplier integration with business

— Knowledge sharing.

2. **SAP WM Implementation**

SAP- Warehouse Management (WM- with mobile data entry) is combined with SAP RF console technology (through bar codes) to automate all the Warehouse operations of Tata Motors.

Benefit: Improved throughput at warehouses by RF enabled processes

— Capability enhancement to handle more parts with same team size

— Real time Inventory tracking.

3. **Knowledge based Engineering Implementation in CAD/CAM :** We have developed "KNEXT" an in house software frame work to develop Knowledge Based Engineering applications. KNEXT have several modules in the areas of body design, chassis design and vehicle performance.

Benefit: Processes defined on KBE have reduced design cycle time about 30 percent

— Designer's knowledge acquired over the years and company best practices are captured and retained.

— Process is defined with KBE, reduce cycle time and improve adherence to legislations, regulations, best practices.

ERP at TATA Motors

With the SAP ERP solution in place, Tata Motors has experienced significant benefits in productivity and cost control. The number of servers as well as the number of different applications run on them has been greatly reduced. The disaster recovery management is being done only for one entity rather than for every application. Non-value-add activities have been lowered. The implementation of a single SAP instance forced a much required change in the organization. A BPR to achieve uniform processes with business users talking the same language was the outcome. There is a significant reduction in inventories and better control over receivables and other credit control. A shared services platform has also been created for IT and shared financial services. Currently, they are exploring the possibility of a shared services platform for HR too. There has been a reduction of almost 2 weeks time in financial consolidation. The statutory compliance of quarterly closing of books and audit has been very largely facilitated by SAP. Compliance has thus now become more structured and easier to manage. The speed and granularity of cost data availability is a big improvement. The richness of analytical data using BW has provided enormous benefits. SAP® SRM has provided a seamless integration with vendors. The biggest benefit has been the large unified database for the entire enterprise. "Now anyone across the enterprise can just look in and find out what customers we have, who are our suppliers and vendors, what prices we offer, etc., very easily. It brought a synergy in purchasing by strategically sourcing critical components for the entire organization. This resulted in strategic partnering with vendors with volume discounts," says Mitra.

"With the Company being listed in the New York stock exchange, SOX compliance becomes mandatory. Without SAP, SOX compliance would have been extremely difficult with the large and fragmented spread of legacy application." adds Mitra.

SAP Solution has helped Tata Motors serve their customers better and meet all their needs. Since information is now on a real-time mode, they are able to quickly respond to their customers, vendors and suppliers demands. "Previously, we had to pick up data from four different locations and then consolidate them before you could update your customer. Now, we have up-to-date information about the customer right up to his last transaction," says Mitra.

Future Plans

Tata Motors is now a satisfied customer of SAP - they have the largest deployment of the SAP Solution in the automotive industry, considering the spread of functionalities they use. They are keeping abreast of all the new developments and ensure that the applications they run commiserates with the SAP enhancements. They would definitely choose SAP for their future plans too. "Our experience with SAP has been very good. We are consistently looking to add new functionalities to our existing suite of coverage," says Mitra.

Tata Motors has been able to achieve enterprise integration, a high productivity gain and also build a stronger, enduring relationship with its customers, thanks to the SAP ERP implementation. Thus, the company has not only retained its leadership in India but has also been able to enlarge its footprint in the global automotive industry.

CRM at TATA

In 2005, TATA Motors deployed Siebel Automotive, a customer relationship management (CRM) solution, to enhance customer service, strengthen dealer relationships, and improve operational efficiency and effectiveness. Currently in use by 500 sales and service personnel, the Siebel CRM solution is expected to be deployed to Tata Motors' entire network of 250 dealer organizations in India by the end of 2005, with more than 1,600 locations and 10,000 sales and service executives expected to use Siebel Automotive.

According to K. R. Sreenivasan, head, CRM and dealer management system, Tata Motors, "Within the first year of implementing the Siebel's solutions, we have seen improvements in customer satisfaction, revenue and operating cost reductions through productivity improvements, and these benefits are expected to increase further over time. This is helping us become truly customer-centric, since we can draw upon real-time, centralized customer and vehicle data and respond better to our customer and dealer needs. "Tata Motors, a flagship company of the Tata Group, is the world's fifth-largest medium and heavy commercial vehicle manufacturer and produces more than 150 commercial vehicle models with a range of light, medium, to heavy-duty trucks, buses, and tractor-trailers with revenues exceeding $3.5 billion (FY 2003-04) and is the second-largest player in the domestic passenger car market in India The company works through a network of dealers located across the country to sell its vehicles. In recent years, this number has expanded by 50 per cent to its current pool of 250 dealer organisations. The Siebel CRM solution will enable Tata Motors to gather feedback on products to improve design or manufacturing quality as well as measure the effectiveness of marketing campaigns and programs. The automaker selected Siebel Automotive because of its partner management capabilities to handle its large dealer network, the solution's zero-footprint web-based architecture and user-friendly interface-critical to support thousands of salespeople with various skill levels.

Tata Motors is currently in the first part of a three-phase deployment. Once the current phase is completed, the company plans to deploy marketing, call centre, business analytics, and captive finance modules. This will allow Tata Motors to better understand customer needs and requirements, improve its responsiveness to service requests and problem resolution, initiate more proactive contacts with customers, add support for new products and services, and streamline dealer financing processes.

The ease of integration between CRM solution and Tata Motors' dealer management and ERP systems was also a critical factor in the company's decision process. The company says that Tata Motors has already seen improvements in a number of areas, including:

- Improved demand forecasting, planning, logistics management, and inventory management
- Overall reduction in quality-related costs due to faster product performance feedback
- Improved workflow and escalation of customer grievances for faster resolution
- Increased revenue growth from both higher vehicle sales and a rise in the company's after-sales parts business.

Ultimately, Tata Motors intends to create an open portal for customer self-service, enabling car buyers to manage product configuration and place orders online.

"The cyclical nature of automotive demand, together with competition from new entrants in the market, has made it difficult for automotive companies to achieve their growth and globalization goals," says John Gray, general manager, Automotive, Siebel Systems. "By enabling Tata Motors to manage, synchronise, and co-ordinate interactions with its dealers and customers, Siebel Automotive provides the company with an ideal platform for getting closer to its customers while strengthening its position as a world-class automotive brand," adds.

Siebel Automotive, a comprehensive suite of business applications, provides a single, 360-degree view of the customer to all who need it; facilitates co-ordination between Tata and its dealers; and enables Tata to track each vehicle throughout its life cycle. Siebel Automotive has been closely integrated with a wide array of back-office applications, including applications for inventory management, fulfillment, and parts location. Pricing and tax calculations can be adjusted for each dealer's requirements. In addition, comprehensive sales and reporting functionality built into Siebel Automotive enables Tata to distribute sales targets to its dealers and roll up sales numbers across the country. Siebel, incidentally, pioneered the industry-specific application model and today delivers 23 industry applications and more than 100 industry-specific solution sets. These solutions, which include Siebel Automotive, enable companies to establish a single, enterprise-wide view of their customers and execute key customer-facing business processes more efficiently and effectively.

In 2006 Tata Motors unveils new long wheel base premium Indigo & X-over concept at Auto Expo 2006, Indica V2 Xeta launched ,Passenger Vehicle sales in India cross one-million mark Tata Motors and Marcopolo, Brazil, announce joint venture to manufacture fully built buses & coaches for India & markets abroad Tata Motors first plant for small car to come up in West Bengal Tata Motors extends CNG options on its hatchback and estate range TDCV develops South Korea's first LNG-

Powered Tractor- Trailer Tata Motors and Fiat Group announce three additional cooperation agreements Tata Motors introduces a new Indigo range segmenting the business people specially "Business Car". On June 11, 2007, Tata Motors, India's largest automobile manufacturer, expressed its interest to acquire the premium European car brands Jaguar and Land Rover brands owned by Ford Motor Company (Ford Motors). The deal if successful was expected to be one of India's biggest overseas takeover bids in the automotive sector. The deal was estimated at US$ 1.5 billion. It was reported that Tata Motors may finance the deal along with Fiat S.P.A (Fiat) or tie-up with an equity player.

However, some analysts indicated that Tata Motors was capable of financing the acquisition as it had a cash pile of Rs. 60 billion and free cash of over Rs. 10 billion for the financial year ended March 31, 2007.1 The Jaguar, Land Rover, Aston Martin and Volvo brands were acquired by Ford Motors' as part of its strategic move in the luxury car segment in the 1990s.

Founded in 1903, Ford Motors is the world's third largest automotive manufacturer. The company's revenues were US$ 160.1 billion in 2006. The decision to sell these luxury brands was part of the restructuring exercise called the 'Way Forward' plan initiated at Ford Motors in January 2006. Many analysts saw the deal as a step in the right direction as Ford Motors was going through a difficult period. It had reported a loss of US$ 12.7 billion for the financial year ended December 30, 2006. Earlier in March 2007, Ford Motors had sold its luxury brand, Aston Martin to a UK-based company for US$ 848 million.

At that time analysts had predicted that Ford Motors would also sell its Jaguar and Land Rover brands as they had a significant contribution to the company's losses. After failing to re-brand and integrate these luxury brands with its product portfolio, Ford Motors felt that acquisition was not the right way of penetrating into the upscale segment.

The move by Tata Motors was also seen as the Tata group's emphasis on globalization. In January 2007, Tata Steel Limited had acquired the Anglo-Dutch steel company, Corus Group PLC (Corus) for US$ 12.11 billion. The Jaguar-Land Rover deal was expected to help Tata Motors gain a foothold in the European market. In addition to Tata Motors, other companies like auto major, Mahindra & Mahindra and private equity firms like Cerebrus, and Ripplewood Holdings were also in the race to acquire the Jaguar and Land Rover brands.

John Gardiner, spokesperson, Ford Motors confirmed this and said, "Ford and its financial advisers have had contacts from third parties and they are actively evaluating those as part of Ford's strategic review. These are preliminary discussions only and no decisions have been made." Analysts opined that the strength of the Tata Group may give it an edge in this deal.

Ramnath S, auto analyst, SSKI Securities said, "They (Tata Motors) are in a better position, given their size and the backing of the group." He further added, "It makes better strategic sense for Tata, and (Chairman) Ratan Tata has an obvious passion for these marquee brands."

Some industry observers noted that Tata Motors would face a challenge if was successful in acquiring these premium brands.

Jaguar and Land Rover have high production costs and require high engineering and research capabilities as they had to compete with other well-known luxury brands like BMW and Audi. An analyst said, "Taking over the brand is easy, bringing down production costs and turning around the company successfully, will be the challenge."

Some even wondered why Tata Motors had to acquire foreign luxury brands, when it had plans to invest more than Rs. 120 billion in its own ambitious expansion programs for small cars, Sports Utility Vehicles (SUVs), and trucks.

Taking the Common Man to Nano- Sphere

Despite its low-cost focus, the Nano has character, adorable looks and a finish quality that could see buyers heading to Tata showrooms in droves. Tata Motors ultra low-cost car, or the one-lakh car as it had come to be known, had sparked interest in all of us simply because of the seemingly insurmountable challenge of making a modern automobile at that price.

The people that fed the rumour mills about how it would be an auto-rickshaw with four wheels, the critics that warned about the environmental impact that such a $3,000 car would bring upon us and the politicians who were opposed to the very concept, never really expected the end product to turn out the way it did.

Setting hearts aflutter In the end, the Nano, after it was unveiled, has set a billion hearts aflutter, not merely because of its unbelievably affordable price but because of the promise it holds for providing safe personal mobility to a huge section of the Indian two-wheeler riding population. And contrary to the vitriolic criticism that it will be an environmental disaster, the Nano will be more emission-friendly than the average motorcycle and, more surprisingly, it could well turn out to be one of the cutest looking cars in town. For the section of the population that has been able to afford a car, the Tata one-lakh car would have seemed "infra-dig" to own when it was still under wraps.

After it was unveiled, though, the awe and expressions of surprise even among the well-to-do in the audience clearly indicate that when the Nano is launched, its buyers are not going to only be the ones that are currently accommodating their family of four on two wheels.

Learning Experience

Mr Ratan Tata, the Tata Group Chairman, has said that the Nano has been a huge learning experience and the challenge, though similar in terms of the fact that intrinsically it was an entirely new product segment as was the case with the Indica when it was under development, took on a whole different dimension because of the need to contain its costs within a preset target.

The Nano price was the only certainty at the time the project was conceived. And, then, starting from a clean sheet of paper, the car was designed and developed keeping manufacturing costs, material costs and post-purchase running costs at the lowest possible level. The result is a car that will be priced at Rs. 1 lakh (for the standard version), maintaining the originally mentioned price point; as Mr Ratan Tata said "A promise is a promise".

There will be other levies like VAT, transport, road tax, insurance and registration before the car reaches the hands of its owners and as such the on-road price could be Rs. 1.3- 1.4 lakh depending on location. However, after seeing the car, the price actually doesn't seem to the only reason why there will be droves of buyers heading to Tata showrooms. Despite its low-cost focus, the Nano actually has character, adorable looks and finish quality that will make the current A-segment monopolist, the Maruti 800, seem like an archaic box on wheels. The finish quality, glowing paint job, consistent and tight gaps between the Nano metal body panels, precise integration of the bumper to the car body and the Spartan but neatly finished plastic dashboard are all good indicators that the Tata mini car overall quality will not be a compromise that the rumour mills were claiming it would be.

Company as a Whole

Tata Motors Limited is the largest automobile company in India with revenues touching to Rs. 20,483 crores (USD 4.7 billion) in the financial year 2004-05. It leads the market in commercial vehicles in each segment and is the second largest in the passenger vehicles segment. Globally, Tata Motors stands fifth in the medium and heavy commercial vehicle manufacturer category.

Established just in 1945, the company's presence cuts across the length and breadth of the country. More than 3 million its-manufactured-vehicles ply on the Indian roads since the first one rolled out in 1954. This company is the first from the country's engineering sector to be listed in the New York Stock Exchange (Sep. 2004) and has also emerged as a global automotive company.

Through its subsidiaries, Tata Motors has engaged in providing engineering and automotive solutions. With the pace of new product development, the company has launched Tata Ace, in the year 2005, India's first indigenously developed mini-truck.

Tata Motor's 22,000 employees are guided with the vision, "best in the manner in which we operate, best in the products we deliver and best in our value system and ethics."

Way Ahead for TATA Motors

The market is growing at about 25% for the last three years. In the highly price sensitive market, reduction of prices because of lower duties and taxes and progressive indigenization, and rising middle class incomes are likely to further increase industry growth rate. Penetration in rural and semi urban areas is extremely low and could provide fresh markets. New entrants will have to deal with uncertainty of demand, different and evolving customer needs, a relatively poor supplier base; a market crowded with competition and industry wide capacity shortages. However, if there is a shake out as many analysts expect, further opportunities for survivors will open up. Another implication is that India could emerge as a significant manufacturing base for exports. The supplier industry is also going through massive growth, although from a small initial base. Except for Telco, product development capabilities are very low among established indigenous assemblers and suppliers, and the industry has some way to go before it becomes world class.

Change is the only constant in life. The automotive industry, like every other sphere of business, is going through a period of significant transition. A number of changes are being worked out with respect to customer expectations, regulations governing safety and environmental protection, and continual competitiveness in terms of cost. These changes cannot be brought to pass unless the company systematically drives its processes ahead through a high level of product and process innovation.

"Tata Motors has a long history of investment in R&D," states Dr V. Sumantran, executive director, passenger car business unit and Engineering Research Centre (ERC), Tata Motors. It is a statement that has been corroborated by a very large number of business successes. Most of these innovations have been, over the years, incorporated into automobiles, ensuring driver and passenger safety and convenience while driving. "The facilities in our ERC have been repeatedly identified as benchmarks for the Indian industry," Dr Sumantran asserts. The design of the Tata Indica, India's first indigenous car, is an accomplishment that has established the country's position in an elite group of countries that have proved their capability in designing, developing and manufacturing a world-class car. Tata Motors has made significant new investments in new facilities to support its product-development needs. It has hired new talent and instituted new methods such as computer-aided design, computer-aided manufacture and computer-aided engineering to help it in its research endeavour. Today, ERC takes pride in having in its service more than 900 scientists and engineers, besides a host of unique facilities, including the only crash test facility and 'hemi-anechoic noise and vibration test chamber in Asia, outside Japan or Korea. It also has to its credit other technologies, such as the advanced emission measurement systems and a digital prototyping laboratory.

Some of the other technologies that are part of Tata Motors' arsenal are those that offer improved electronic controls for engine systems, aimed at improving emission standards, and other vehicle drive-train and chassis systems, besides fuel efficiency. The work on safety engineering also occupies a large part of the R&D focus. The company is currently working on equipping the vehicles of the future with technologies for improved communication, navigation and entertainment. The use of all these technologies will go a long way towards ensuring the quality of all the vehicles that roll out of the company's plants. Automobile companies everywhere now pride themselves on offering products that score high on criteria like quality, reliability, and availability of features and specifications. The only way in which companies can set themselves apart from the competition is by spending more time and energy on innovative products. Consistent attention to research pays high dividends to a company in the long run.

In the absence of a strong and active R&D department, an automobile company aspiring to be in the league of globally competitive companies will find itself lagging far behind. Besides, the growing number of regulations in the field of auto safety demands that a company invest highly in research.

Dr Sumantran believes that the auto industry in India, consisting of two-wheelers, passenger cars and commercial vehicles, has acquitted itself remarkably in this regard. "The two-wheeler industry showcases this focus with extremely competitive products that are gaining recognition in the economy segment around the world," he says. "At Tata Motors, too, we have ourselves gained recognition for our recent products. Many of the obstacles the company faced two decades ago in acquiring technology have been substantially reduced through tier-1 suppliers and through access to specialist consultants."

Tata Motors has achieved much progress in terms of accessing advanced systems and technologies and using them to equip their products with various conveniences and features. The resultant advances have enabled the company to meet the highly stringent performance specifications that are expected from any world-class manufacturer of cars. Dr Sumantran reveals a little-known fact, "This year Tata Motors will export to Europe Indicas equipped with sophisticated safety systems, including side-airbags and antilock braking systems. In addition, these cars will also be equipped with the latest Euro-III emission compliant petrol and diesel engines. Likewise, the Tata Safari will also incorporate these features when it is exported to Europe this year."

The design and development of so many new features and specifications requires the company to protect its intellectual property rights. Dr Sumantran says, "This year several new patent applications have been processed. More importantly, our engineers and scientists have been encouraged to think more carefully and strategically about intellectual property." He is honest enough to admit that they have made fewer patent applications than he would have liked, but the company and its people are clearly striving to achieve more. The road ahead will require Tata Motors to take some crucial decisions. The company will have to learn a number of lessons from the environment, the competition, the expectations of consumers, current and upcoming regulations, and the evolution of technology. These lessons will then have to be ploughed into research that will help design and improve the vehicle of the future.

Dr Sumantran believes a roadmap will go a long way towards making the process of research easier. "A roadmap that charts a systematic cadence of development and projects allows us to pace the development of needed skills and technologies. Admittedly, some of these projects are intended to serve long-term objectives and, through their stages of development, may lead to results that prove that technology to be unfeasible or uneconomical. Modern management of R&D uses measures such as harvest ratio to evaluate the efficacy of their R&D investment and with this we are able to prioritize work in the needed areas and encourage innovation." Whatever the outcome, the company has shown its willingness to take risks and to drive it aggressively ahead. There is no doubt that Tata Motors will be at the forefront of the changes that will be evident in the automobile industry of the future.

References

1. www.tatamotors.com
2. www.tata.com/0_about_us/history/milestones.htm
3. www.tata.com
4. www.domain-b.com/people/index.html
5. www.money.cnn.com/

❄ ❄ ❄

12. Wal-Mart

Wal-Mart rose from a small chain in the Ozark Mountains to become the largest retailer in the world. But the strategies that fuelled more than four decades of growth — squeezing inefficiencies out of its supply chain, saturating the U.S. with its Supercenters, and driving down costs to uphold its "Always low prices" mantra — have now caused the retailer to stagnate. But today - Sales are flat. Expansion is stalled. Image problems abound.

So, what the world's biggest retailer is doing to tackle its strategic problems and more important is to examine its situation, understand how it got there and look at how the retailer is trying to fix its problems. But are the fixes good enough?

The world's most successful retailer needs help. Although Wal-Mart generated gross profits of $84 billion on $349 billion in revenue in 2006, its share price has stayed virtually flat since 2000. Domestic same-store sales crept up by just 1.9 percentage points in 2006 — the worst showing in Wal-Mart's history. International growth has been beset by humiliating failures. Public relations gaffes continue to dog the company, and there are little inefficiency left to squeeze from Wal-Mart's hyper-efficient distribution system. The worst part is, all of these problems are interrelated, and they're coming to a head just as competition from rivals like Target and Costco is heating up.

Issues that are dragging Wal-Mart down are:

1. Domestic Saturation

After years of U.S. expansion, Wal-Mart is running out of real estate and the challenge is opening new markets by overcoming opposition in U.S. urban centers.

Half of all Americans already live within a 10-minute drive of a Wal-Mart store. Most retailers will tell you, "If you have the opportunity to grow, you take it." That's just what Wal-Mart did, opening 2,200 Supercenters — its largest and most profitable store format — since 1988. Now, however, the company is confronting the realities of domestic saturation as it becomes harder and harder to find spots to erect new stores. "It's a huge issue for them," says Philip C. Bonanno, a management consultant with Management Ventures Inc.

Typically, when a business dominates a market, it searches for other locations where it can expand. Unfortunately for Wal-Mart, its untapped markets tend to be in densely populated cities where the company's big-box format is an awkward fit. Exacerbating the problem, cities have stricter zoning laws and property is more expensive. Once a site is selected, the company often faces stiff opposition from neighbourhood associations concerned about traffic congestion and negative impacts on local merchants, as well as labour groups who turn out against Wal-Mart's union-free policy.

"It's pretty easy to plop a store down on a highway in a small and mid-size rural community or a suburb," says Doug Fleener, a retail consultant with Dynamic Experiences Group. "But the majority of the market opportunities are in more challenging urban areas." Elsewhere, many Wal-Mart stores are so close together that they now compete with one other.

"It's the main reason why same-store sales have been flat," says David Abella, a fund manager and analyst with Rochdale Investment Management, which owns Wal-Mart stock. Analysts and shareholders are nervous — they don't see any easy ways to open up new markets within the U.S.

2. Sluggish Sales

Sales within existing stores have slowed and the challenge is luring more affluent shoppers.

In 2006, same-store sales rose by just 1.9 percent, Wal-Mart's worst showing ever. When domestic saturation becomes a problem, retailers often try to wring more sales from the stores they already have. But Wal-Mart's price-conscious customer base makes that difficult to do. Many Wal-Mart shoppers have moderate to low incomes. When gas prices rise or the job market tightens, these customers are among the first to scale back their retail spending. Appealing to more affluent shoppers

— as Target and Costco have done — would reduce sales volatility while also increasing sales of bigger-ticket items. Trouble is, the Wal-Mart brand is a turn-off to many up market consumers.

Consider Wal-Mart's recent foray into fashion. During Christmas 2006, Wal-Mart went upscale and heavily promoted its Metro 7 clothing line. The effort went nowhere, because "the Wal-Mart customer is not fashion-driven," says Eric Beder, a retail analyst with Brean Murray, Carret & Co. Indeed, Wal-Mart's traditional shoppers shunned the new apparel, and upscale customers never walked through the door. Capping off the debacle, Claire Watts, Wal-Mart's top apparel executive, left the company in July 2007 "to pursue other career interests," according to a Wal-Mart spokesperson.

Wal-Mart is "great at the science of retailing, but they aren't great at the art of retailing," says Patricia Edwards, managing director and portfolio manager at Seattle-based Wentworth, Hauser and Violich. During the 2006 Christmas season, Edwards, whose firm owns Wal-Mart stock, walked into a Wal-Mart to check out its higher-end apparel? The clothes on display were mismatched, she says, and the presentation looked awful.

Wal-Mart's "stay lean" philosophy makes the company reluctant to hire more sales staff. But departments that require lots of hands-on service to succeed — like fashion and jewellery — suffer as a result, and suffer they did. During the 2006 holiday season, fashion was one of Wal-Mart's poorest performing departments.

3. Mixed International Results

Wal-Mart has been unable to steamroll its global competition and the challenge is succeeding in competitive international markets that are already home to incumbent retailers.

In 2006, Wal-Mart shuttered its failing operations in Germany and South Korea. Another way to offset domestic saturation is by expanding internationally. In 1991 Wal-Mart launched its first international stores in Mexico. By 2005, it operated 6,200 facilities in 15 different countries. The numbers look impressive on paper, but in fact Wal-Mart hasn't been able to gain the upper hand against its international competition. The company has a foothold in Britain, Mexico, and Canada, but in the rest of the world, Wal-Mart has seen mixed results at best.— and failure at worst.

The international effort has exposed Wal-Mart's weak spots. "The challenge when expanding internationally is properly assessing the strength of your competitors," says Cynthia Cohen, president of Strategic Mindshare, a retail-consulting firm. "Where there are strong competitors, they're often the home town favourite because they do a really good job." In Germany, after Wal-Mart acquired the well-respected 21-store Wertkauf chain of hypermarkets (supermarkets combined with a department store), it also bought out Interspar, another German hypermarket chain. Unfortunately, some of "the stores that Wal-Mart bought and the locations that they were in were not 'winning sites,'" says Bonanno of Management Ventures. Many of the Interspar stores, in particular, were dingy and in need of renovation.

More importantly, Wal-Mart never developed a feel for the German retail market. "Their culture is in many ways the antithesis of the U.S.," Edwards says. In the U.S., Wal-Mart's friendly greeters and helpful staff were highlighted in ad campaigns. Bargain-hunting Germans, however, prefer to shop unassisted and regard such effusive customer service with suspicion. Even Wal-Mart's "Always low prices" approach failed to resonate in a country where roughly 30 percent of the retail market is dominated by local discount stores. Wal-Mart couldn't differentiate itself against German discounters like Aldi and Lidle, which offer low-price store-brand products considered as good as or better than national brands. In 2006, Wal-Mart gave up and pulled out of Germany.

After years of disappointment, the same thing happened in South Korea, where Wal-Mart also bailed out in 2006. Wal-Mart's Japanese subsidiary continues to lose money and after a dozen years of doing business in Argentina, the company operates only 13 stores there. Meanwhile, big retailers like Britain's Tesco and France's Carrefour are proving more adept at international expansion because they've been more willing to adapt to local conditions and develop deep relationships with local distributors.

4. Image Problems

Many Americans think Wal-Mart is evil and the challenge is rebuilding credibility as a good corporate citizen.

A 2006 document prepared by Wal-Mart's longtime ad agency deemed the company's sagging reputation as its biggest business challenge. No other company in the United States comes close to receiving the public relations beating that Wal-Mart endures on nearly a weekly basis. Labor activists complain the company underpays its workers. Local activists point to boarded-up Main Street storefronts in hundreds of American towns and complain that Wal-Mart stores kill off mom-and-pop retailers. In 2006, it was revealed that an upbeat blog called "Wal-Marting across America" was funded by Wal-Mart's PR firm. Fired marketing executive Julie Roehm, accused of violating Wal-Mart's strict ethics' policies by accepting gifts from vendors, recently sued the company, accusing CEO H. Lee Scott of doing the same thing.

Things have gotten so bad that fund manager Patricia Edwards says Wal-Mart has become the Phillip Morris of retailers — many of her clients won't touch the stock because of the company's reputation. The pounding has taken a toll. A leaked copy of an October 2006 report prepared by ad agency GSD&M, which worked with Wal-Mart on its branding and other campaigns from 1987 until early 2007, noted that Wal-Mart's consumer ratings as a "company I trust and respect" had declined steadily during the previous two years. The report asserted that Wal-Mart's tarnished reputation has become its biggest business challenge. Indeed, the bad PR fuels opposition in cities and urban areas where Wal-Mart would like to expand and create even more resistance to the brand for more affluent shoppers.

Wal-Mart felt that responding to its opponents granted them credence they didn't deserve, but "it's the wrong strategy," says David Splivalo, president of Freestyle Public Relations. "These are people who influence customers and people on Wall Street, now Wal-Mart is playing defense and catch up." "When Sam Walton was running Wal-Mart, he just kept his head down and kept doing what he was doing. He had his critics, but he thought he was doing the right thing," Fleener says. "But now the executives over there will tell you, 'We blew it. We should have fought back, and we didn't.'"

It's hard to say how many customers stay away from Wal-Mart because of the bad press. But one thing's for sure: Many of those people have no qualms about supporting other big-box stores, like Target and Costco.

5. Operational Efficiency

There's not much fat left to squeeze from Wal-Mart's ultra-lean supply chain and the challenge is finding new opportunities for cost reductions.

Wal-Mart missed its goal of installing RFID technology in 12 of its 137 distribution centers by the end of 2006. As part of its commitment to everyday low prices, Wal-Mart has developed a reputation for logistics perfectionism. That zeal extends to Wal-Mart's suppliers, who are constantly prodded to eliminate inefficiencies from their own operations. If suppliers can't drop their prices enough, Wal-Mart will simply take its business elsewhere. "They will crush you," says Bob Bartlett of Bartlett Joseph Associates, a retail consulting firm.

For the most part, when Wal-Mart spurs suppliers to eliminate supply-chain inefficiencies, the efforts are mutually beneficial. But after years of effort, Wal-Mart has the most efficient supply-chain in the business, so there's little room left for improvement. Worse, the most recent initiative that Wal-Mart promoted to kick-off a new round of efficiency gains has become a nonstarter. In 2003 Wal-Mart announced plans to embrace Radio Frequency Identification, or RFID, technology. Like high-tech bar codes, RFID chips are tiny electronic transponders that can be scanned from several yards away to provide detailed information about the contents of a box carton. Instead of scanning bar codes on each pallet of product passing through its warehouses, RFID would enable the process to be automated. Yet implementing the new technology has proven more difficult than expected. Wal-Mart had planned to install RFID technology in 12 of its 137 distribution centers by the end of 2006, but because of continuing technical snags and high costs associated with implementing the system, the goal was never met. Instead, in late 2006, the company announced it was shifting the focus of its RFID push from distribution centers to stores. Today, Wal-Mart has installed RFID systems in 1,000 of its 6,500 domestic stores.

"Wal-Mart is going slower with RFID, and I suspect that shows they recognize its weaknesses," says Russell Jones, a retail consultant with Alix Partners. The go-slow approach may be wise in the long run. In the meantime, however, the RFID failure has been a humbling experience for Wal-Mart, underscoring the need to find new ways to wring more efficiency from the company's operations.

References

1. www.walmart.com
2. www.retailowner.com/Resources
3. www.retail-vision.co.uk

❁ ❁ ❁

Key Questions

1. How does NAFTA have an impact on the economies of North America? What importance does this economic pact have for international managers in Europe and Asia?
2. How has the formation of the EU created new opportunities for member countries? Of what importance are these opportunities to international managers in other geographic regions such as North America or Asia?
3. Why are Russia and Eastern Europe of interest to international managers? Identify and describe some reasons for such interest.
4. Many MNCs have secured a foothold in Asia, and many more are looking to develop business relations there. Why does this region of the world hold such interest for international management? Identify and describe some reasons for such interest.
5. Why would MNCs be interested in South America, India, the Middle East, and Central Asia, Africa, the LDCs of the world? Would MNCs be better off focusing their efforts on more industrialized regions? Explain.
6. In what way does the political environment around the world create challenges for MNCs? Would these challenges be less for those operating in the EU that for those in Russia or China? Why or why not?
7. How do the following legal principles impact on MNC operations: the principle of sovereignty, the nationality principle, the territoriality principle, the protective principle, and principle of comity?
8. How could the national and local government bureaucracy in Japan impede the operations of a U.S. MNC doing business there? What are some Japanese laws or regulations that reduce the MNC's effectiveness?
9. Why are developing countries interested in privatizing their telecommunications industries? What opportunities does this privatization have for telecommunication MNCs?
10. Some researchers have found that when Germans work for a U.S. MNC, they become even more German, and when Americans work for a German MNC, they become even more American. Why would this knowledge be important to these MNCs?
11. When comparing the negotiating styles and strategies of French versus Spanish negotiators, a number of sharp contrasts are evident. What are three of these, and what could MNCs do to improve their position when negotiating with either group?
12. In which of the four types of organizational cultures-family, Eiffel Tower, guided missile, incubator-would most people in the United States feel comfortable? In which would most Japanese feel comfortable? Based on your answers, what conclusions could you draw regarding the importance of understanding organizational culture for international management?
13. Most MNCs need not enter foreign markets to face the challenge of dealing with multiculturalism. Do you agree or disagree with this statement? Explain your answer.

14. What are some potential problems that must be overcome when using multicultural, diverse teams in today's organizations? What are some recognized advantages? Identify and discuss two of each.
15. A number of guidelines can be valuable in helping MNCs to make diverse teams more effective. What are five of these? Additionally, what underlying principles guided NUMMI in its effective use of multicultural teams? Were the principles used by NUMMI similar to the general guidelines identified in this chapter, or were they significantly different? Explain your answer.
16. Do you think China will continue to achieve record growth? What factors could hurt its prospects?
17. Today, because of an abundance of cheap labor, China is a hot destination for global corporate outsourcing. Do you think this will still be the case a decade from now? Why or why not?
18. What communication and negotiation challenges may have arisen in the three-way exchanges among Cisco, 3Com, and Huawei?
19. Can 3Com take any proactive measures to help limit the possibility of Cisco moving forward with litigation?
20. What types of political risk would a company entering Russia face? Identify and describe three. What types of political risk would a company entering France face? Identify and describe three. How are these risks similar? How are they different?
21. Most firms attempt to quantify their political risk, although they do not assign specific weights to the respective criteria. Why is this approach so popular? Would the companies be better off assigning weights to each of the risks being assumed? Defend your answer.
22. If a high-tech firm wanted to set up operations in Iran, what steps might it take ensure that the subsidiary would not be expropriated? Identify and describe three strategies that would be particularly helpful.
23. If a company new to the international arena was negotiating an agreement with a potential partner in an overseas country, what basic steps should it be prepared to implement? Identify and describe them.
24. Wilsten, Inc. has been approached by Japanese firm that wants exclusive production and selling rights for one of Wilsten's new, high-tech products. What does Wilsten need to know about Japanese bargaining behaviors to strike the best possible deal with this company? Identify and describe five.
25. Of the four imperatives discussed in this chapter-economic, political, quality, and administration-which would be most important to IBM in its efforts to make inroads in the Pacific Rim market? Would this emphasis be the same as that in the United States, or would IBM be giving primary attention to one of the other imperatives? Explain.
26. If a locally based manufacturing firm with sales of $350 million decided to enter the EU market by setting up operations in France, which orientation would be the most effective: ethnocentric, polycentric, regiocentric, or geocentric? Why? Explain your choice.
27. When a large MNC such as Ford Motor sets strategic goals, what areas are targeted for consideration? Would this list of strategic goals be in any way very different from that formulated by the manufacturing firm in question? Why or why not?
28. One of the most common entry strategies for MNCs is the joint venture. Why are so many companies opting for this strategy? Would a fully owned subsidiary be a better choice?
29. In recent years McDonald's has found that its international franchise operation has been producing more revenue per unit than its domestic operations. What might account for this? Is it likely that the firm will continue its international expansion? Why?
30. Mercedes changed its U.S. strategy by announcing that it is developing cars for the $30, 000 to $45,00- price range (as well as its typical upper-end cars). What might have accounted for this change in strategy? In your answer, include a discussion of the implications from the standpoints of marketing, production, and finance

31. A small manufacturing firm believes there is a market for handheld tools that are carefully crafted for local markets. After spending 2 months in Europe, the president of this firm believes that his company can create popular line of these tools. What type of organization structure would be of the most value to this firm in its initial efforts to go international?
32. If the company in the above question finds a major market for its product in Europe and decides to expand into Asia, would you recommend any change in its organization structure? If yes, what would you suggest? If no, why not?
33. If this same company finds after 3 years of international effort it is selling 50 percent of its output overseas, what type of organizational structure would you suggest for the future?
34. Why are keiretsus becoming so popular? What benefits do they offer? How can small international firms profit from this development? Give an example.
35. A New York-based MNC is in the process of staffing a subsidiary in New Delhi, India. Why would it consider using expatriate managers in the unit? Local managers? Third-country managers?
36. What selection criteria are most important in choosing people for an overseas assignment? Identify and describe the four that you judge to be of most universal importance, and defend your answer.
37. Building on your answer to the question above, discuss some theoretical dimensions that may affect anticipatory and in-country adjustment of expats. Hoe can these be turned into selection criteria?
38. What are the major common elements in an expat's compensation package? Besides base pay, which would be most important to you? Why?
39. Why are individuals motivated to accept international assignments? Which of these motivations would you rank as positive reasons? Which would you regard as negative reasons?
40. Why do expatriated return early? What can MNCs do to prevent this from happening? Identify and discuss three steps they can take.
41. What kind of problems do expatriates face when returning home? Identify and describe four of the most important. What can MNCs do to deal with these repatriation problems effectively?

    In what way do formulization, specialization, and centralization have an impact on MNC organization structures? In your answers, use a well-known firm such as IBM or Ford to illustrate the effects of these three characteristics.

Glossary

Achievement culture — A culture in which people are accorded status based on how well they perform their functions.

Achievement motivation theory — A theory which holds that individuals can have a need to get ahead to attain success and to reach objectives.

Act of state doctrine — A jurisdictional principle of international law which holds that all acts of other governments are considered to be valid by U.S. courts, even if such acts are illegal or inappropriate under U.S. law.

Adaptability screening — The process of evaluating how well a family is likely to stand up to the stress of overseas life.

Adaptive organizations — Organizations that are characterized by reaction to required changes but failure to anticipate them and stay on or ahead of the cutting edge.

Administrative coordination — Strategic formulation and implementation in which the MNC makes strategic decisions based on the merits of the individual situation rather than using a predetermined economically or politically driven strategy.

Analytical manager — A manager who is systematic and logical and carefully weighs alternatives to problems.

Arbitrator — An individual who provides a solution to a grievance that both sides (union and management representatives) have been unable to resolve themselves and that both sides agree to accept.

Ascription culture — A culture in which status is attributed based on who or what a person is.

Assessment center — An evaluation tool used to identify individuals with potential to be selected or promoted to higher-level positions.

Authoritarian leadership — The use of work-centered behavior designed to ensure task accomplishment.

Balance sheet approach — An approach to developing an expatriate compensation package that is based on ensuring the expat is "made whole" and does not lose money by taking the assignment.

Benchmarking — The process of identifying what leading-edge competitors are doing and then using this information to produce improved products or services.

Bicultural group — A group in which two or more members represent each of two distinct cultures, such as four Mexicans and four Taiwanese who have formed a team to investigate the possibility of investing in a venture.

Cafeteria approach — An approach to developing an expatriate compensation package that entails giving the individual a series of options and letting the person decide how to spend the available funds.

Centralization — A management system under which important decision are made at the top.

Chaebols — In South Korea, very large, family-held conglomerates, including internationally known firms, in which many key managers have attended school in the West and use this education to help formulate successful international strategies for their firms. Chaebols have considerable political and economic power in Korea.

Chromatics — The use of color to communicate messages.

Chronemics — The way in which time is used in a culture.

Civil or code law — Law that is derived from Roman law and is found in the non-Islamic and non-socialist countries.

Codetermination — A legal system that requires workers and their managers to discuss major decisions.

Collective bargaining — The process whereby formal labor agreements are reached by union and management representatives; it involves the negotiation of wages, hours, and conditions of employment and the administration of the labor contract.

Collectivism — A culture in which people tend to belong to groups or collectives and to look after each other in exchange for loyalty.

Common law — Law that derives from English law and is the foundation of legislation in the United States, Canada, and England, among other nations.

Communication — The process of transferring meanings from sender to receiver.

Communitarianism — Refers to people regarding themselves as part of a group.

Confrontation meetings — The gathering and analysis of information related to intra- and intergroup conflict followed by the formulation of a plan of action by the participants for the purpose of resolving these problems.

Conglomerate investment — A type of high-risk investment in which goods or services produced are not similar to those produced at home.

Content theories — Theories that explain work motivation in terms of what arouses, energizes, or initiates employee behavior.

Context — Information that surrounds a communication and helps to convey the message.

Controlling — The process of evaluating results in relation to plans or objectives and deciding what action, if any, to take.

Cross-cultural school of management thought — An approach to international management holding that effective managerial behavior is a function of the specific culture: A successful manager in one location may not be effective in another location around the world.

Cultural assimilator — A programmed learning technique designed to expose members of one culture to some of the basic concepts, attitudes, role perceptions, customs, and values of another culture.

Culture — The acquired knowledge that people use to interpret experience and to generate social behavior. This knowledge forms values, creates attitudes, and influences behavior.

Decentralization — Pushing decision making down the line and getting the lower-level personnel involved.

Decision making — The process of choosing a course of action among alternatives.

Delayed differentiation — A manufacturing strategy in which all products are manufactured in the same way for all countries or regions until as late in the assembly process as possible, with differentiation of features or components introduced in the final stages of production.

Diffuse culture — A culture in which both public and private space are similar in size and individuals guard their public space carefully, because entry into public space also affords entry into private space as well.

Direct controls — The use of face-to-face or personal meetings for the purpose of monitoring operations.

Doctrine of comity — A jurisdictional principle of international law which holds that there must be mutual respect for the laws, institutions, and government of other countries in the matter of jurisdiction over their own citizens.

Downward communication — The transmission of information from superior to subordinate.

Economic imperative — A worldwide strategy based on cost leadership, differentiation, and segmentation.

Eiffel Tower cultures — A culture that is characterized by a strong emphasis on hierarchy and orientation to the task.

Emotional culture — A culture in which emotions are expressed openly and naturally.

Empowerment — The process of giving individuals and teams the resources, information, and authority they need to develop ideas and effectively implement them.

Enterprise unions — Unions that represent both the hourly and salaried employees of a particular company.

Environmental scanning — The process of providing management with accurate forecasts of trends related to external changes in geographic areas where the firm currently is doing business and/or is considering setting up operations.

Equity theory — A theory which holds that people's motivation is determined by how fairly they feel they are being treated.

Esteem needs — The needs for power and status.

Ethics — The study of morality and standards of conduct.

Ethnocentric MNC — An MNC that stresses nationalism and often puts home office people in charge of key international management positions.

Ethnocentric predisposition — A nationalistic philosophy of management whereby the values and interests of the parent company guide the strategic decisions.

Ethnocentrism — The belief that one's own way of doing things is superior to that of others.

European Research Cooperation Agency (Eureka) — An agency that funds projects in the fields of energy, medical technology, biotechnology, communications, and the like, with the objective of making Europe more productive and competitive in the world market.

Expatriates — Those who live and work away from their home country. They are citizens of the country where the multinational corporation is headquartered.

Expectancy/valence theory — A theory which postulates that motivation is influenced by a person's belief that effort will lead to performance, that performance will lead to specific outcomes, and that these outcomes are valued by the individual.

Expropriation — The seizure of businesses by a host country with little, if any, compensation to the owners.

Factual manager — A manager who looks at the available information and makes decisions based on that data.

Family culture — A culture that is characterized by a strong emphasis on hierarchy and orientation to the person.

Femininity — A situation in which the dominant values in society are caring for others and quality of life.

Formalization — The use of defined structures and systems in decision making, communicating, and controlling.

Franchise — A business arrangement under which one party (the franchisor) allows another (the franchisee) to operate an enterprise using its trademark, logo, product line, and methods of operation in return for a fee.

Geocentric MNC — An MNC that seeks to integrate diverse regions of the world through a global approach to decision making.

Geocentric predisposition — A philosophy of management whereby the company tries to integrate a global systems approach to decision making.

Global area division — A structure under which global operations are organized on a geographic rather than a product basis.

Global functional division — A structure which organizes worldwide operations primarily based on function and secondarily on product.

Global international trade union affiliations — Trade union relationships that cut across regional and industrial groups and are heavily concerned with political activities.

Globalization — The production and distribution of products and services of a homogeneous type and quality on a worldwide basis.

Globalization imperative — A belief that one worldwide approach to doing business is the key to both efficiency and effectiveness.

Global product division — A structural arrangement in which domestic divisions are given worldwide responsibility for product groups.

Global sourcing — The use of worldwide suppliers, regardless of where they are located geographically, who are best able to provide the needed output.

Goal-setting theory — A theory that focuses on how individuals set goals and the impact of this process on their motivation.

Grievance — A complaint brought by an employee who feels that he or she has been treated improperly under the terms of the labor agreement.

Groupthink — Social conformity and pressures on individual members of a group to conform and reach consensus.

Guanxi — In China means good connections.

Guided missile culture — A culture that is characterized by a strong emphasis on equality in the workplace and orientation to the task.

Haptics — Communicating through the use of bodily contact.

Home-country nationals — Expatriate managers who are citizens of the country where the multinational corporation is headquartered.

Homogeneous group — A group that is characterized by members who share similar backgrounds and generally perceive, interpret, and evaluate events in similar ways.

Honne — A Japanese term which means "what one really wants to do."

Horizontal investment — An MNC investment in foreign operations to produce the same goods or services as those produced at home.

Horizontal specialization — The assignment of jobs so that individuals are given a particular function to perform and tend to stay within the confines of this area.

Host-country nationals — Local managers who are hired by the MNC.

Hygiene factors — In the two-factor motivation theory, job context variables that include salary, interpersonal relations, technical supervision, working conditions, and company policies and administration.

Incubator culture — A culture that is characterized by a strong emphasis on equality and orientation to the person.

Indigenization laws — Laws that require that nationals hold a majority interest in the operation.

Indirect controls — The use of reports and other written forms of communication to control operations.

Individualism — A culture in which people tend to look after themselves and their immediate family only.

Industrial democracy — The rights that employees have to participate in significant management decisions.

Industrial internationals — Affiliates of the global international union groups that focus on a particular industry.

Inpatriate — An individual from a host country or a third-country national who is assigned to work in the home country.

Integrative techniques — Techniques that help the overseas operation become a part of the host country's infrastructure.

International Confederation of Free Trade Unions (ICFTU) — The most important global international union confederation.

International division structure — A structural arrangement that handles all international operations out of a division created for this purpose.

International joint ventures (IJVs) — Formal arrangements with foreign partners who typically, although not always, are located in the country where the business will be conducted.

International Labour Office (ILO) — A United Nations affiliate, consisting of government, industry, and union representatives, that works to promote fair labor standards regarding health and safety, working conditions, and freedom of association for workers.

International management — The process of applying management concepts and techniques in a multinational, multicultural environment.

International selection criteria — Factors used to choose personnel for international assignments.

Intimate distance — Distance between people that is used for very confidential communications.

Intuitive manager — A manager who is imaginative, innovative, and able to jump from one idea to another.

Islamic law — Law that is derived from interpretation of the Qur'an and the teachings of the Prophet Mohammed and is found in most Islamic countries.

Job content factors — In work motivation, those factors internally controlled, such as responsibility, achievement, and the work itself.

Job context factors — In work motivation, those factors controlled by the organization, such as conditions, hours, earnings, security, benefits, and promotions.

Job design — A job's content, the methods that are used on the job, and the way the job relates to others in the organization.

Joint venture — An agreement in which two or more partners own and control an overseas business.

Kaizen — A Japanese term that means continuous improvement.

Karoshi — Overwork or job burnout, in Japanese.

Keiretsu — In Japan, a newly emerging organizational arrangement in which a large, often vertically integrated group of companies cooperate and work closely with each other to provide goods and services to end users; core members may be bound together by cross-ownership, long-term business dealings, interlocking directorates, and social ties.

Key factor for success (KFS) — A factor necessary for a firm to effectively compete in a market niche.

Kinesics — The study of communication through body movement and facial expressions.

Labor relations — The process through which management and workers identify and determine the job relations that will be in effect at the workplace.

Leadership — The process of influencing people to direct their efforts toward the achievement of some particular goal or goals.

Learning — The acquisition of skills, knowledge, and abilities that results in a relatively permanent change in behavior.

Learning organizations — Organization that are able to transform themselves by anticipating change and discovering new ways of creating products and services; they have learned how to learn.

License — An agreement that allows one party to use an industrial property right in exchange for payment to the other party.

Localization — An approach to developing an expatriate compensation package that involves paying the expat a salary comparable to that of local nationals.

Lockout — A company's refusal to allow workers to enter the facility during a labor dispute.

Lump sum method — An approach to developing an expatriate compensation package that involves giving the expat a predetermined amount of money and letting the individual make his or her own decisions regarding how to spend it.

Macro political risk analysis — Analysis that reviews major political decisions likely to affect all enterprises in the country.

Management by objectives (MBO) — A management system for the joint setting of subordinate goals, coaching and counseling personnel, and providing feedback on their performance.

Maquiladora industry — An arrangement created by the Mexican government that permits foreign manufacturers to send materials to their Mexican-based plants, process or assemble products, and ship them back out of Mexico with only the value added being taxed.

Masculinity — A culture in which the dominant values are success, money, and things.

Mass customization — Tailor-making mass-production products to meet the expectations of the customers.

Mediator — A person who brings both sides (union and management representatives) together and helps them to reach a settlement that is mutually acceptable.

Micro political risk analysis — Analysis directed toward government policies and actions that influence selected sectors of the economy or specific foreign businesses in the country.

Ministry of International Trade and Industry (MITI) — A governmental agency in Japan that identifies and ranks national commercial pursuits and guides the distribution of national resources to meet these goals.

Mixed organization structure — A structure that is a combination of a global product, area, or functional arrangement.

Monochronic time schedule — A time schedule in which things are done in a linear fashion.

Motivation — A psychological process through which unsatisfied wants or needs lead to drives that are aimed at goals or incentives.

Motivators — In the two-factor motivation theory, the job content factors which include achievement, recognition, responsibility, advancement, and the work itself.

Multicultural group — A group in which there are individuals from three or more different ethnic backgrounds, such as three U.S., three German, three Uruguayan, and three Chinese managers who are looking into mining operations in South Africa.

Multidomestic — A firm that operates production plants in different countries but makes no attempt to integrate overall operations.

Nationality principle — A jurisdictional principle of international law which holds that every country has jurisdiction over its citizens no matter where they are located.

National responsiveness — The need to understand the different consumer tastes in segmented regional markets and respond to different national standards and regulations imposed by autonomous governments and agencies.

Negotiation — The process of bargaining with one or more parties for the purpose of arriving at a solution that is acceptable to all.

Neutral culture — A culture in which emotions are held in check.

Nonreciprocal trade partners — Nations that sell (export) goods to other countries but do not buy (import) from them.

Nonverbal communication — The transfer of meaning through means such as body language and the use of physical space.

Normative manager — A manager who is idealistic and concerned with how things should be done.

North American Free Trade Agreement (NAFTA) — A free trade agreement, including the United States, Canada, and Mexico, that will effectively eliminate trade barriers between the three countries.

Oculesics — The areas of communication that deal with conveying messages through the use of eye contact and gaze.

OD intervention — The structured activity in which targeted individuals, groups, or units engage in accomplishing task goals that are related to organization development.

Operational risks — Government policies and procedures that directly constrain management and performance of local operations.

Organizational culture — A pattern of basic assumptions that are developed by a group as it learns to cope with problems of external adaptation and internal integration and that are taught to new members as the correct way to perceive, think, and feel in relation to these problems.

Organization development (OD) — The deliberate and reasoned introduction, establishment, reinforcement, and spread of change for the purpose of improving an organization's effectiveness.

Organization for Economic Cooperation and Development (OECD) — A government, industry, and union group founded in 1976 that has established a voluntary set of guidelines for MNCs.

Ownership-control risks — Government policies or actions that inhibit ownership or control of local operations.

Paradox — A statement that appears to be contradictory but is not, such as "increases in product quality often result in a decline of the cost of producing the goods."

Parochialism – The tendency to view the world through one's own eyes and perspectives.

Participative leadership — The use of both a work- or task-centered and people-centered approach to leading subordinates.

Particularism — The belief that circumstances dictate how ideas and practices should be applied and something cannot be done the same everywhere.

Paternalistic leadership — The use of work-centered behavior coupled with a protective employee-centered concern.

Perception — A person's view of reality.

Personal distance — In communicating, the physical distance used for talking with family and close friends.

Physiologic needs — Food, clothing, shelter, and other basic, physical needs.

Political imperative — Strategic formulation and implementation utilizing strategies that are country responsive and designed to protect local market niches.

Political risk — The likelihood that a business's foreign investment will be constrained by a host government's policies.

Polycentric MNC — An MNC that places local nationals in key positions and allows these managers to appoint and develop their own people.

Polycentric predisposition — A philosophy of management whereby strategic decisions are tailored to suit the cultures of the countries where the MNC operations.

Polychronic time schedule — A time schedule in which people tend to do several things at the same time and place higher value on personal involvement than on getting things done on time.

Power distance — The extent to which less powerful members of institutions and organizations accept that power is distributed unequally.

Practical school of management thought — A traditional approach to international management, which holds that effective managerial behavior is universal: a successful manager in one location will be effective in any other location around the world.

Principle of sovereignty — An international principle of law which holds that governments have the right to rule themselves as they see fit.

Problem-solving teams — Employee groups that discuss ways of improving quality, efficiency, and the overall work environment.

Process theories — Theories that explain work motivation by how employee behavior is initiated, redirected, and halted.

Product proliferation — The creation of a wide array of products that the competition cannot copy quickly enough.

Profit — The amount remaining after all expenses are deducted from total revenues.

Protective and defensive techniques — Techniques that discourage the host government from interfering in operations.

Protective principle — A jurisdictional principle of international law which holds that every country has jurisdiction over behavior that adversely affects its national security, even if the conduct occurred outside that country.

Proxemics — The study of the way people use physical space to convey messages.

Public distance — In communicating, the distance used when calling across the room or giving a talk to a group.

Quality control circle (QCC) — A group of workers who meet on a regular basis to discuss ways of improving the quality of work.

Quality imperative — Strategic formulation and implementation utilizing strategies of total quality management to meet or exceed customers' expectations and continuously improve products and/or services.

Regiocentric MNC — An MNC that relies on local managers from a particular geographic region to handle operations in and around that area.

Regiocentric predisposition — A philosophy of management whereby the firm tries to blend its own interests with those of its subsidiaries on a regional basis.

Regional internationals — Sub-divisions of the global affiliation; regional applications of the global's activities.

Regional system — An approach to developing an expatriate compensation package that involves setting a compensation system for all expats who are assigned to a particular region and paying everyone in accord with that system.

Repatriation — The return to one's home country from an overseas management assignment.

Repatriation agreements — Agreements whereby the firm tells the individual how long she or he will be posted overseas and promises to give the individual, on return, a job that is mutually acceptable.

Return on investment — Return measured by dividing profit by assets.

Ringisei — Decision making by consensus in Japan.

Safety needs — In Maslow's hierarchy of needs, the desire for security, stability, and the absence of pain.

Self-actualization needs — In Maslow's hierarchy of needs, the desire to reach one's full potential by becoming everything one is capable of becoming.

Self-efficacy — A person's belief or confidence in his or her abilities to marshal the motivation, resources, and courses of action needed to successfully accomplish a specific task.

Self-management teams — Employee groups that take over supervisory duties and manage themselves; teams consist of individuals who learn all the tasks of all the group members, allowing team members to rotate jobs.

Simplification — The process of exhibiting the same orientation toward different culture groups.

Smallest space analysis (SSA) — A nonparametric multivariate analysis. This mathematic tool maps the relationship among the countries by showing the distance between each. By looking at this two-dimensional map, it is possible to see those countries that are similar to each other and those that are not.

Social distance — In communicating, the distance used to handle most business transactions.

Socialist law — Law that comes from the Marxist socialist system and continues to influence regulations in countries formerly associated with the Soviet Union as well as China.

Social needs — The need to interact and affiliate with others and the need to feel wanted by others.

Sociotechnical designs — Job designs that blend the personnel and the technology.

Specialization — An organizational characteristic that assigns individuals to specific, well-defined tasks.

Specialized internationals — Trade union associations that function as components of intergovernmental agencies and lobby within these agencies.

Special purpose teams — Employee groups that design and introduce work reforms and new technology.

Specific culture — A culture in which individuals have a large public space they readily share with others and a small private space they guard and share only with close friends and associates.

Strategic fit — An approach to strategically managing an organization that involves aligning resources in such a way as to mesh with the environment.

Strategic planning — The process of determining an organization's basic mission and long-term objectives, then implementing a plan of action for attaining these goals.

Strategic stretch — The creative use of resources to achieve ever more challenging goals.

Strategy implementation — The process of providing goods and services in accord with a plan of action.

Strike — A collective refusal to work to pressure management to grant union demands.

Subsidiary board of directors — A board that overseas and monitors the operations of a foreign subsidiary.

Survey feedback — An OD intervention that involves the gathering and analysis of information related to group behavior and problems and the feeding back of this information to develop effective action plans.

Tatemae — A Japanese term which means "doing the right thing" according to normal models of decision making.

Team building — An extension of classic T-groups (training groups) and sensitivity training that is geared to enhancing organizational effectiveness through cooperation and a "team" effort of key personnel.

Technology paradox — (Also see Paradox) That high-tech businesses can thrive at the very moment that their prices are falling the fastest.

Territoriality principle — A jurisdictional principle of international law which holds that every nation has the right of jurisdiction within its legal territory.

Theory X manager — A manager who believes that people are basically lazy and that coercion and threats of punishment often are necessary to get them to work.

Theory Y manager — A manager who believes that under the right conditions people not only will work hard but will seek increased responsibility and challenge.

Third-country nationals — Managers who are citizens of countries other than the one in which the MNC is headquartered or the one in which the managers are assigned to work by the MNC.

Third-party peacemaking — The diagnosis of group conflict followed by the use of an outside party (usually the OD change agent) to facilitate a constructive resolution of a problem.

Token group — A group in which all members but one have the same background, such as a group of Japanese retailers and a British attorney.

Total quality management (TQM) — An organizational strategy and the accompanying techniques that result in the delivery of high-quality products and/or services to customers.

Training — The process of altering employee behavior and attitudes in a way that increases the probability of goal attainment.

Transactional leaders — Individuals who exchange rewards for effort and performance and work on a "something for something" basis.

Transfer risks — Government policies that limit the transfer of capital, payments, production, people, and technology in and out of the country.

Transformational leaders — Leaders who are visionary agents with a sense of mission and who are capable of motivating their followers to accept new goals and new ways of doing things.

Transition strategies — Strategies used to help smooth the adjustment from an overseas to a stateside assignment.

Transnational corporations (TNCs) — Multinational corporations that view the world as one giant market.

Transnational network structure — A multinational structural arrangement that combines elements of function, product, and geographic designs, while relying on a network arrangement to link worldwide subsidiaries.

Two-factor theory of motivation — A theory that holds there are two sets of factors that influence job satisfaction: hygiene factors and motivators.

Uncertainty avoidance — The extent to which people feel threatened by ambiguous situations and have created beliefs and institutions that try to avoid these.

Union — An organization that represents the workers and in collective bargaining has the legal authority to negotiate with the employer and administer the labour contract.

Universalism — The belief that ideas and practices can be applied everywhere in the world without modification.

Upward communication — The transfer of meaning from subordinate to superior.

Validity — The quality of being effective, of producing the desired results. A valid test or selection technique measures what it is intended to measure.

Values — Basic convictions that people have regarding what is right and wrong, good and bad, and important or unimportant.

Variety amplification — The creation of uncertainty and the analysis of many alternatives regarding future action.

Variety reduction — The limiting of uncertainty and the focusing of action on a limited number of alternatives.

Vertical investment — The production of raw materials or intermediate goods that are to be processed into final products.

Vertical specialization — The assignment of work to groups or departments where individuals are collectively responsible for performance.

Virtual corporation — A network of companies that come together to exploit fast-changing opportunities and share costs, skills, and access to global markets.

Virtual organization — An organization that is able to conduct business as if it were a very large enterprise when, in fact, it is much smaller, made up of core business competencies and the rest outsourced.

Wholly owned subsidiary — An overseas operation that is totally owned and controlled by an MNC.

Work centrality — The importance of work in an individual's life relative to other areas of interest.

World-class organization (WCOs) — Enterprises that are able to compete with anybody, anywhere, anytime.

World Trade Organization (WTO) — Started in 1995 to replace GATT, the WTO has power to enforce rulings in trade disputes and monitor trade policies.

●●●

Further Readings

1. Strategic Management in the Knowledge Economy: New Approaches and Business ... by Marius Leibold, Gilbert J. B. Probst, Michael Gibbert - 2005.
2. Global Human Resource Management: Managing People in Developing and ... by Willy McCourt, Derek Eldridge – 2003.
3. Strategic Decision Making in Modern Manufacturing - by Harinder S. Jagdev, Attracta Brennan, Jimmie Browne – 2004.
4. Entry and Cooperative Strategies in International Business Expansion - by Yadong Luo – 1999.
5. Cooperative Strategies in International Business: Joint Ventures and ... - by Farok J. Contractor, Peter Lorange – 2002.
6. Managing the Global Network Corporation - by Bruce McKern – 2003.
7. Strategic Management for Tourism Communities: Bridging the Gaps - by Peter E. Murphy, Ann E. Murphy – 2004.
8. The Regional Multinationals: MNEs and "Global" Strategic Management by Alan M. Rugman – 2005.
9. Mobile Media: Content and Services for Wireless Communications - by Jo Groebel, Eli M. Noam, Valerie Feldmann – 2005.
10. International Strategic Management: Challenges and Opportunities - by Franklin R. Root, Kanoknart Visudtibhan – 1992.
11. The United Nations Library on Transnational Corporations - by John H. Dunning, Theodore H. Moran – 1994.
12. Sustainable Strategic Management by W. Edward Stead, Jean Garner Stead – 2003.
13. Strategic Global Marketing: Issues and Trends - by Erdener Kaynak – 2002.
14. The Role of Resources in Global Competition - by John Fahy – 2001.
15. Strategic Management: Concepts and Cases - by Peter L. Wright, Mark J. Kroll, John Alan Parnell – 1996.
16. Contemporary Strategy Analysis - by Robert M. Grant - 2005.
17. Operations Management in a Global Context - by Marc J. Schniederjans – 1998.
18. Selling to Major Accounts: Tools, Techniques, and Practical Solutions for ... - by Terry R. Bacon – 1999.
19. Multinational Strategic Management: An Integrative Entrepreneurial Context ... by Robert J. Mockler – 2002.
20. Transnational Corporations and Business Strategy - edited by Donald J. Lecraw, Allen J. Morrison, John H. Dunning – 1993.

21. International Business: Critical Perspectives on Business and Management by Alan M. Rugman – 2002.
22. Chinese Capitalism in a Global Era: Towards Hybrid Capitalism - by Henry Wai-Chung Yeung – 2004.
23. Global Capitalism at Bay? - by John H. Dunning – 2001.
24. Global Logistics and Distribution Planning: Strategies for Management by Donald Waters – 1999.
25. Handbook of Research in International Marketing - by Subhash C. Jain – 2003.
26. Globalization and Entrepreneurship: Policy and Strategy Perspectives - by Hamid Etemad, Richard W. Wright – 2003.
27. International Human Resource Management: Policy and Practice for the Global ... by Dennis R. Briscoe, Randall S. Schuler – 2004.
28. Canadian Banks and Global Competitiveness - by James L. Darroch – 1994.
29. Global Strategic Management: The Essentials by Heidi Vernon-Wortzel, Lawrence H. Wortzel – 1990.
30. Handbook of Strategic Management. New York: Warren, Gorham, and Lament, 1984.
31. Global Corporate Intelligence: Opportunities, Technologies, and Threats in ... - by George S. Roukis, Hugh Conway, Bruce H. Charnov – 1990.
32. Strategic Management: Formulation, Implementation, and Control in a Dynamic ... by Abbass F. Alkhafaji – 2003.
33. The Global Public Relations Handbook: Theory, Research, and Practice - by Krishnamurthy Sriramesh, Dejan Veri – 2003.
34. Global Business Strategy - by Robin John – 1997.
35. Strategies in Global Industries: How U.S. Businesses Compete - by Allen J. Morrison – 1990.
36. Who's Who in the Management Sciences? - by Cary L. Cooper – 2000.
37. International Business: Environments and Operations - by John D. Daniels, Lee H. Radebaugh, Daniel P. Sullivan – 2004.
38. Readings in International Business: A Decision Approach - by Robert Z. Aliber, Reid W. Click – 1993.
39. Malaysian Business in the New Era - by Chris Nyland – 2001.
40. Successful Strategies in Supply Chain Management - by Chi-Kin Chan, Heung Win J. Lee – 2005.
41. Global Management - by Mark E. Mendenhall, Betty Jane Punnett, David A. Ricks – 1995.
42. Managing the Global Corporations: Case Studies in Strategy and Management. New York: McGraw-Hill. Doz, Y. 1980.
43. Electronic Commerce: Opportunity and Challenges - by Syed Mahbubur Rahman, Mahesh S. Raisinghani – 2000.
44. The Strategic Management of Intellectual Capital and Organizational Knowledge - by Chun Wei Choo, Nick Bontis – 2002.
45. Technology Transfer in International Business - by Tamir Agmon – 1991.
46. Global Political Economy: Understanding the International Economic Order - by Robert Gilpin, Jean M. Gilpin – 2003.
47. Global Political Economy: Contemporary Theories - by Ronen Palan - 2000.
48. Information Technology Diffusion in the Asia Pacific: Perspectives on Policy by Felix B. Tan, P. Scott Corbett, Yuk-Yong Wong - Computers – 1999.

49. The Global System: Economics, Politics, and Culture by Barrie Axford – 1995.
50. Corporate Communications: Theory and Practice - by Joep Cornelissen – 2004.
51. Current Trends in Data Management Technology by Asuman Dogac, M. Tamer Özsu, Ozgur Ulusoy - Computers – 1999.
52. Ecosystems and Human Well-being - by Millennium Ecosystem Assessment – 2005.
53. Strategic Supply Chain Management: The Five Disciplines for Top Performance - by Shoshanah Cohen, Joseph Roussel – 2005.
54. Strategic Management of Technology and Innovation - by Robert A. Burgelman, Clayton M. Christensen, Steven C. Wheelwright - Technology – 2004.
55. Managing Across Borders: The Transnational Solution - by Christopher A. Bartlett, Sumantra Ghoshal - 2002.
56. Intellectual Property and Global Markets: An East-West Dialogue - by Ali Akhunov, George Bugliarello, Eugenio Corti – 1999.
57. Extending the Eclectic Paradigm in International Business: Essays in Honor ... by John H. Dunning, H. Peter Gray – 2003.
58. Managing Information Technology in a Global Economy: 2001 Information ... by Mehdi Khosrowpour – 2001.
59. Strategy and Human Resources: A General Managerial Perspective - by Charles R. Greer – 1995.
60. Intercultural Management - by Nina Jacob – 2003.
61. Management and Organization Paradoxes - by Stewart Clegg – 2002.
62. Routledge International Encyclopedia of Women: Global Women's Issues and ... by Cheris Kramarae, Dale Spender – 2000.
63. Strategic Information Management: Challenges and Strategies in Managing ... by Robert Galliers, Dorothy E. Leidner – 2003.
64. Euromarketing: Effective Strategies for International Trade and Export - Page 264 by Erdener Kaynak, Pervez N. Ghauri - Business & Economics - 1994 - 361 pages
65. Human Resource Management: An International Comparison - Page 235 by Rüdiger Pieper - Business & Economics - 1990
66. Strategic Alliances: An Entrepreneurial Approach to Globalization - by Michael Y. Yoshino, U. Srinivasa Rangan – 1995.
67. Entrepreneurship in a Global Context - by Sue Birley, Ian C. MacMillan – 1997.
68. Sustaining Competitiveness in the New Global Economy: The Experience of ... - by Ramkishen S. Rajan – 2003.
69. Cooperative Strategy: Managing Alliances, Networks, and Joint Ventures - by John Child, David Faulkner, Stephen B. Tallman – 2005.
70. International Management: Culture, Strategy, and Behavior 5/e - by Richard Hodgetts – 2007.
71. Global Strategic Management- by Kamel Mellahi, Jedrzej George Frynas, Paul Finlay – 2006.
72. No Best Way: An Evolutionary Perspective On Human Resource Management – by Colarelli, Praeger. Gratton, L., Hailey, V. H., Stiles, P. & Truss - 1999.
73. Strategy and Human Resources: A General Managerial Perspective - by Greer C. R. 1995.
74. Aligning Human Resources And Business Strategy – by Holbeche, L. - 1999.

Websites:

www.growth-insights.com

www.growth-insights.com
www.thinksmart.com
www.wsj.com
www.nytimes.com
www.dallasnews.com
www.worldcultures.org
www.oecd.org
www.worldbank.org
www.ideas4development.org
www.sweden.gov.se
www.gtz.de
www.diva- portal.org
www.estateagentsinwarwickshire.co.uk
www.giftsociety.org
www.geert-hofstede.com
www.kwintessential.co.uk
www.sagepub.com/journals
www. fons_trompenaars
www.hinduonnet.com
hbswk.hbs.edu
www.fastcompany.com
www.searchcio.com
www.apioutsourcing.com
www.standardandpoors.com

Journals

Academy of Management Journal
Strategic Management Journal
Technology Review
Harvard Business Review
California Management Review
MIT Sloan Management Review
Deloitte Analysis.
Business Horizons
SMR
Encyclopedia of World Problems and Potential (Munich, Germany
Business in the Contemporary World
Research in Global Strategic Management
The Futurist
Columbia Journal of World Business